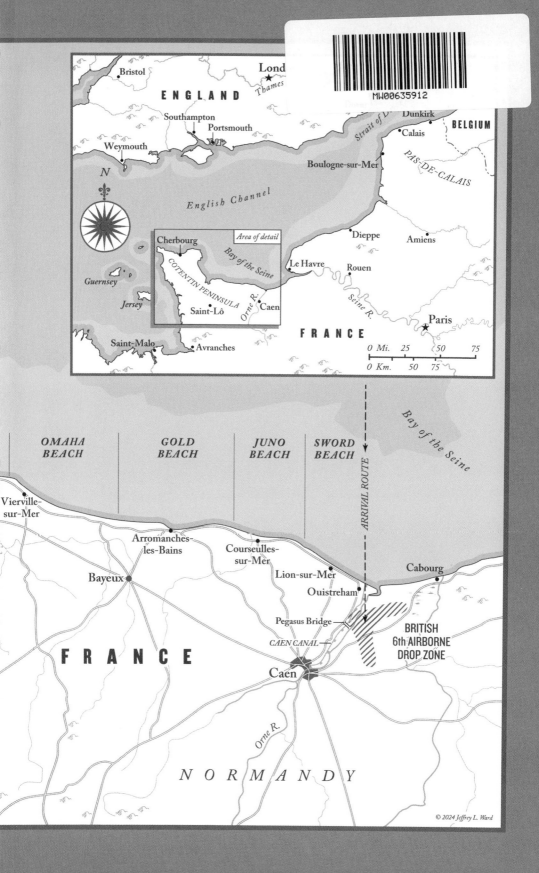

AVID

READER

PRESS

**ALSO BY GARRETT M. GRAFF**

*UFO: The Inside Story of the U.S. Government's
Search for Alien Life Here—and Out There*

*Watergate: A New History*

*The Only Plane in the Sky: An Oral History of 9/11*

*Raven Rock: The Story of the U.S. Government's Secret
Plan to Save Itself—While the Rest of Us Die*

*The Threat Matrix: The FBI at War in the Age of Global Terror*

*The First Campaign: Globalization, the Web,
and the Race for the White House*

*Dawn of the Code War: America's Battle Against
Russia, China, and the Rising Global Cyber Threat*
(with John P. Carlin)

# WHEN THE SEA CAME ALIVE

# AN ORAL HISTORY OF D-DAY

## GARRETT M. GRAFF

AVID READER PRESS

New York   London   Toronto   Sydney   New Delhi

Avid Reader Press
An Imprint of Simon & Schuster, LLC
1230 Avenue of the Americas
New York, NY 10020

First Avid Reader Press hardcover edition June 2024

AVID READER PRESS and colophon are trademarks of Simon & Schuster, LLC

Simon & Schuster: Celebrating 100 Years of Publishing in 2024

For information about special discounts for bulk purchases,
please contact Simon & Schuster Special Sales at 1-866-506-1949
or business@simonandschuster.com.

The Simon & Schuster Speakers Bureau can bring authors to
your live event. For more information or to book an event,
contact the Simon & Schuster Speakers Bureau at 1-866-248-3049
or visit our website at www.simonspeakers.com.

Interior design by Kyle Kabel

Manufactured in the United States of America

1   3   5   7   9   10   8   6   4   2

Library of Congress Cataloging-in-Publication Data has been applied for.

ISBN 978-1-6680-2781-3
ISBN 978-1-6680-2783-7 (ebook)

*To history teachers everywhere—there's nothing more important
to understanding today and anticipating tomorrow than understanding
what's come before—and, especially, to those history teachers who
encouraged my own early curiosity, from Mrs. Stocek, Mr. B, and Mr. Aja
to Profs. William Gienapp, Stephen Shoemaker, and Brian Delay*

# Contents

Author's Note . . . . . . . . . . . . . . . . . . . . . . . . . . . . .xiii

Foreword . . . . . . . . . . . . . . . . . . . . . . . . . . . . . . . .xxi

## PART I — A WORLD AT WAR

War Begins . . . . . . . . . . . . . . . . . . . . . . . . . . . . . . .3

War Comes to America . . . . . . . . . . . . . . . . . . . . . . 19

1943 . . . . . . . . . . . . . . . . . . . . . . . . . . . . . . . . . . 24

The Start of SHAEF . . . . . . . . . . . . . . . . . . . . . . . . 34

Crossing the Pond . . . . . . . . . . . . . . . . . . . . . . . . . 42

The American Invasion . . . . . . . . . . . . . . . . . . . . . . 50

Building the Atlantic Wall . . . . . . . . . . . . . . . . . . . . 61

Keeping Secrets . . . . . . . . . . . . . . . . . . . . . . . . . . . 75

Operation FORTITUDE . . . . . . . . . . . . . . . . . . . . . . 83

The Mulberry Plan . . . . . . . . . . . . . . . . . . . . . . . . . 89

At Slapton Sands . . . . . . . . . . . . . . . . . . . . . . . . . . 94

Exercise TIGER . . . . . . . . . . . . . . . . . . . . . . . . . . .106

The Transportation Plan . . . . . . . . . . . . . . . . . . . . .118

Picking the Date . . . . . . . . . . . . . . . . . . . . . . . . . . . . .126

Into the Sausages. . . . . . . . . . . . . . . . . . . . . . . . . . . . .137

Keep Calm and Carry On . . . . . . . . . . . . . . . . . . . . . . .145

Learning the Details . . . . . . . . . . . . . . . . . . . . . . . . . . .149

Spring in Normandy with the Germans . . . . . . . . . . . . . . .158

The D-Day Weather Forecast . . . . . . . . . . . . . . . . . . . .165

## PART II — THE LANDING

A Note on Chronology and Military Terminology . . . . . . . . . .183

Gen. Dwight D. Eisenhower's Order of the Day . . . . . . . . . .187

Paratroopers Take Off . . . . . . . . . . . . . . . . . . . . . . . . .190

Operation COUP DE MAIN . . . . . . . . . . . . . . . . . . . . .197

The 6th Airborne Arrives in Normandy . . . . . . . . . . . . . . 209

The Paratrooper Skytrain. . . . . . . . . . . . . . . . . . . . . . .223

Night in the Hedgerows . . . . . . . . . . . . . . . . . . . . . . . .229

Liberation Comes to Sainte-Mère-Église . . . . . . . . . . . . . 240

NEPTUNE Rises . . . . . . . . . . . . . . . . . . . . . . . . . . .250

Confusing the Enemy . . . . . . . . . . . . . . . . . . . . . . . . 266

Ashore in Normandy. . . . . . . . . . . . . . . . . . . . . . . . .273

In the Air Over the Beaches . . . . . . . . . . . . . . . . . . . . .281

Heading Ashore at Utah . . . . . . . . . . . . . . . . . . . . . . .288

Naval Forces at Utah . . . . . . . . . . . . . . . . . . . . . . . . .298

The Second Wave at Utah . . . . . . . . . . . . . . . . . . . . . .305

The Rangers at Pointe du Hoc . . . . . . . . . . . . . . . . . . . .316

Omaha Beach . . . . . . . . . . . . . . . . . . . . . . . . . 331

Into the Devil's Garden . . . . . . . . . . . . . . . . . . . .338

Ashore at Omaha . . . . . . . . . . . . . . . . . . . . . . .351

Getting Off Omaha Beach. . . . . . . . . . . . . . . . . . .363

Afloat Off Omaha Beach . . . . . . . . . . . . . . . . . . . 375

Jig Sector, Gold Beach . . . . . . . . . . . . . . . . . . . .382

The Green Howards Take King Sector. . . . . . . . . . . . . .392

Ashore at Juno . . . . . . . . . . . . . . . . . . . . . . . . 400

Sword Beach . . . . . . . . . . . . . . . . . . . . . . . . . 413

The News Spreads . . . . . . . . . . . . . . . . . . . . . . .430

**PART III — THE END OF D-DAY**

Holding the Eastern Flank. . . . . . . . . . . . . . . . . . . 449

The Walking Wounded. . . . . . . . . . . . . . . . . . . . .457

The Battle of La Fière Bridge . . . . . . . . . . . . . . . . .464

Afternoon for the Germans . . . . . . . . . . . . . . . . . . 474

End of D-Day . . . . . . . . . . . . . . . . . . . . . . . . .479

Epilogue . . . . . . . . . . . . . . . . . . . . . . . . . . . .489

Sources, Methods, and Acknowledgments . . . . . . . . . . . . . . .501

Source Listings . . . . . . . . . . . . . . . . . . . . . . . . .511

Source Notes . . . . . . . . . . . . . . . . . . . . . . . . .521

Index . . . . . . . . . . . . . . . . . . . . . . . . . . . . . 545

Image Credits . . . . . . . . . . . . . . . . . . . . . . . . .573

# Author's Note

In US military terminology, "D-Day" is the start of any major operation or invasion—a purposefully vague expression, as planning for such complex maneuvers must begin long before a specific date and time are chosen. Its first recorded use, as best as anyone can determine, is found in a September 1918 field order—the singular "D" standing for the word "Day" (just as its cousin, H-Hour, is really just a shortening of "Hour-Hour"). Across the years since World War I, in World War II and beyond, there have been many D-Days: Sicily, Tarawa, Saipan, Okinawa, Leyte, Inchon during the Korean War, the 1983 invasion of Grenada (Operation Urgent Fury), and the 1989 invasion of Panama (Operation Just Cause), among others.

But history remembers only one.

June 6, 1944, is one of the most famous single days in all of human history. The official launch of Operation OVERLORD, the long-anticipated invasion of western Europe, it marks a feat of unprecedented human audacity, a mission more ambitious and complex than anything ever seen, before or since, and a key turning point in the fight for a cause among the most noble humans have ever fought. Though there have been other days over the course of the last century that have re-routed our collective historical trajectory, one could argue that none has had more of an impact than the day 160,000 troops stormed the beaches of Normandy. When we say "D-Day," there's no doubt what day we mean.

At a strategic level, the mission of the Allied forces on June 6 was to establish a beachhead and begin the liberation of France and Europe from Nazi occupation, which had been in effect since 1939. The full plan, which took years to assemble and execute—bringing together men, planes, tanks, and ships from every corner of the world—involved the largest air and sea armadas ever assembled, spread across a battlefront more than sixty miles long, over five different beaches—their code names forever immortalized in history, Utah, Omaha, Gold, Juno, and Sword—and affected nearly a million combatants, not counting the French and British civilian populations in the war zones, let alone the families across six continents who waited anxiously for word of their loved ones' fates. Somewhere between 10,000 to 20,000 Allied and Axis combatants and civilians wouldn't live to see the end of the day.

Military victory was only one part of the overarching goal. Five years earlier, the Nazi shadow had startlingly, steadily, and powerfully begun to overtake much of the Western world, occupying various territories and major cities, and inspiring a coalition of fascist leadership known as the Axis Powers—Germany, Italy, and Japan—that threatened the very existence of global democracy. If OVERLORD failed, it might be years before the Big Three Allies—the United States, Great Britain, and the Soviet Union—could reattempt an invasion, leaving them little choice but to sue for peace with Adolf Hitler, consigning the continent to an era of authoritarian darkness and further untold horrors upon its citizens.

Precisely because it is a day of such drama and such high stakes, there is no shortage of existing material on D-Day. From the immediate aftermath to decades-later reflections, there have been plenty of excellent books written and published on the subject by the likes of Forrest Pogue, Samuel Eliot Morison, Cornelius Ryan, Stephen Ambrose, Rick Atkinson, Douglas Brinkley—and many, many, many more—that provide down-to-the-minute details about the day, as well as blockbuster films and television series that have immortalized the actions and sacrifices of servicemen—*Band of Brothers, The Longest Day, Saving Private Ryan*. Some histories have zeroed in on specific beaches, units, and aspects of the invasion that the French refer to as *Le Débarquement* (the landing), while others have centered largely on the personal stories of those involved at various levels. Ernest Hemingway, who rode in with a wave of infantry headed to Omaha Beach's Fox Green (though he did not make the landing), said it best: "You could write for a week and not give everyone credit for what he did on a front of 1,135 yards."

But among and across so many histories, there turns out to be a fuller, richer story still waiting to be told.

*          *          *

The story of D-Day writ large is not as simple as the one we usually tell ourselves. The reality of D-Day and Operation OVERLORD has, across 80 years, been almost entirely swallowed by mythology, lore, and Hollywood. In telling the story anew here, for a generation born long after the fortieth- and fiftieth-anniversary festivities popularized and celebrated the "Greatest Generation," I hope to broaden the understanding of D-Day itself, and to acknowledge the full scope of the event's complexities and nuances, as well as its high points.

That begins with the question of who was there. The story of D-Day is overwhelmingly white and male, and the experiences of the myriad women and people of color who participated in aspects of OVERLORD have historically been forgotten or relegated to side-histories. (Correspondent Martha Gellhorn, who stowed away in a ship's toilet overnight to become one of the first women to arrive at the landing site, for example, is still largely shorthanded as Ernest Hemingway's third wife; similarly, eight decades later, the heroism on Omaha Beach of Black medic Staff Sgt. Waverly B. Woodson, Jr., has still never been properly acknowledged by the U.S. government.) All told, about 2,000 Black soldiers took part in the invasion, mostly drivers and stevedores, but across the entire operation, the Allied force included just a single unit of Black troops, and their story was not told in depth until 2010, when Linda Hervieux resurrected with great effort their memories and contributions in her book *Forgotten*.* In and across northern France, liberation came at a terrible cost—the destruction of whole towns and the deaths of thousands of civilians—and a full, true accounting of D-Day's bloody cost begins long before June 1944. More Allied soldiers were killed preparing and practicing for D-Day than in the invasion itself, as historian Patrick Caddick-Adams has recently calculated. D-Day was also as international a day of combat as any in human history. There were 15 nationalities formally represented in the naval forces off the Normandy shore, including

* Not a single Black soldier, sailor, airman, Marine, or Coast Guard personnel was originally awarded the Medal of Honor in World War II, and only in 1994 did President Bill Clinton award seven such distinctions to troops recommended by a panel brought together to rectify that slight.

600 Danish sailors, and the defenses onshore were a mix of Germans with conscripts and prisoners from Poland, Kazakhstan, Mongolia, and a host of other countries. The British unit known as 10 Commando included French, Belgian, Dutch, Norwegian, and Polish troops, as well as a unit that consisted almost entirely of Jewish refugees from across Nazi-occupied Europe.

More broadly, there are four particular myths that have emerged around D-Day, each of which I try to take on and reframe in this book. One, that it was tenuous and almost failed; two, that the Atlantic Wall was impenetrable; three, that Omaha Beach was a disastrous killing zone; and four, that the British and Canadian beaches were a cakewalk. While all of these have kernels of truth, none are exactly true in the way that popular history and mythology remembers. Understanding the nuance and reality of that day does not in any way decrease or subtract from the heroism of the participants, but instead enriches our understanding of the human experience of that incredible day of days.

To find the true story of D-Day and assemble this book, I collected somewhere north of 5,000 personal stories, memoirs, and oral histories from combatants and participants from books, documents, newspapers, magazines, official reports, videos, and audio recordings. They range from hand-scrawled letters written aboard ships bound for France on the night of June 5 to local historical society pamphlets and doorstop-sized official military histories to Winston Churchill's Nobel Prize–winning six-volume memoir and retelling of the Second World War to in-the-field interviews by wartime correspondents with *Stars and Stripes* and *Yank* magazine, as well as those with surviving veterans assembled for the fiftieth anniversary in 1994 by *Time* and *Newsweek*—even the archives of the Pennsylvania newspaper *The Morning Call*, which in 2015 launched an ambitious oral history project of local veterans. A handful of books provided uniquely valuable resources, particularly George Koskimaki's *D-Day with the Screaming Eagles* and Russell Miller's *Nothing Less than Victory*. The first rough draft of this manuscript contained nearly 1.4 million words of personal testimony and oral history, snippets, quotations, and stories compiled from more than 100 published sources, as well as archival materials from more than a dozen major and minor archives from multiple countries and continents, from the Library of Congress's Veterans History Project to the Portsmouth D-Day Story Museum. At the Imperial War Museum in London, I sifted through boxes filled with hundreds of postcards, sent in as part of a contest by the *Sunday Express* newspaper for the thirtieth anniversary of D-Day of British remembrances of that day; through the National World War II Museum in New Orleans, which started as a museum focused on D-Day, I paged through hundreds of oral histories from the unparalleled archives of the Eisenhower Center, where Stephen Ambrose and Ronald Drez collected the memories of thousands of D-Day veterans in the 1980s and 1990s. Ohio University, meanwhile, has done the incredible work of digitizing the voluminous veteran questionnaires Cornelius Ryan used to write his World War II classics, *The Longest Day*, *A Bridge Too Far*, and *The Last Battle*, and which, collectively, are some of the most contemporaneous memories gathered.

Across these multitudes, some memories were recorded within days of June 6, 1944, others years or decades afterward. Some represent full-length memoirs, stretching to scores and even hundreds of pages, while others amounted to just a single sentence, observation, or paragraph—a brief snippet delivered to a passing war correspondent in the combat zone or a local reporter years later. Some benefited from reliance on documentary contemporaneous evidence, others unfurled from memory alone. History has mostly taught us about D-Day in black-and-white (the blurry news images of Robert Capa and other brave military combat photographers fill our mental images and textbooks), but those who lived June 6, 1944, felt and remembered it as an overwhelming sensual experience, one filled with explosive color—orange flames, green water, khaki uniforms, and seething red blood—vivid smells, from cordite to apple blossoms, and unforgettable sound, from the tiny clicks of the metal crickets given to paratroopers to recognize one another in the dark and the donging church bells of Sainte-Mère-Église to the overwhelming crescendo of the naval beach bombardment and the shells of the USS *Texas* at dawn. And, then of course, there was what was perhaps the defining sensory perception of D-Day: The chilling and all-consuming cold that came as thousands of troops plunged (willingly and unwillingly) into the choppy seawater of the English Channel and then spent the day of the invasion wearing waterlogged, uncomfortable uniforms.

In the end, after much editing, whittling, and carving, the story ahead features 700 individual voices from all sides of the conflict that day. Those memories captured in these pages, regardless of when they were put to paper or audio recording, were surely fallible, as all are. Traumatic memories even more so. I have tried to rely on the most trusted resources possible and cross-checked what details are available to ensure that the memories herein are as accurate as they can be. Throughout, I have lightly edited quotes for clarity, striving to balance the speaker's original words with the precision of recorded history. I have for historical accuracy corrected some dates, names, or other obviously incorrect technical details—such as when someone refers to a ship's "sixteen-inch guns" when the ship actually had fifteen-inch guns. At the same time, I have chosen to keep out-of-date references, like those of negroes and Indians, that reflected natural speech at the time.

Wartime promotions and assignment changes happened frequently—personnel were particularly shifted around and units reshuffled in the weeks leading up to the invasion itself—and so to avoid confusion, speakers are usually identified only by the title, rank, or position they held on D-Day itself, June 6, 1944. In the case of certain speakers, like Winston Churchill, Bernard Montgomery, or Fred Morgan, the lead D-Day planner in 1943, where their own professional evolution is an important part of the narrative, I have identified them by their contemporaneous title or position. For each speaker, I have included as much biographical and descriptive information as history recorded; sometimes, particularly in contemporaneous articles, there was only a rank, last name, or general description of a speaker.

Collectively, the oral histories that make up this book and the archives I drew upon are an invaluable and irreplaceable national and international treasure, a collection of stories from a generation who famously didn't like to share them. I've now spent better part of a decade immersed in oral history, and normally I talk about how the goal is to find the *ordinary* and the *extraordinary*—the people who have the most average, and thus representative experiences, and also those who have the most atypical experiences. But what is so remarkable about D-Day is how ordinary the extraordinary was that day—the tens of thousands of people who had that June Tuesday the most remarkable of human experiences, at the height of combat and at the limits of human survival.

It's here—at the human level—where we find the greatest and most true story of D-Day. D-Day stands as not just one of the greatest stories of courage of our time, but also perhaps the greatest story ever told about leadership—leadership at the top and leadership at the bottom. The first third of this book, which concerns the planning and mobilization of Operation

OVERLORD, is a story dominated by big, historic figures—Winston Churchill, Dwight Eisenhower, George Marshall, Bernard Montgomery, Omar Bradley, Bertram Ramsay—and the big, world-shaping decisions they make and plans they forge. Then, in essence, the big leaders disappear from the action itself. The remainder of the book is the story of ordinary men who found themselves thrust into almost unimaginable drama, fighting, and combat, and how, in turn, they rose to the moment and how their small moments of leadership, sprinkled across sixty miles of landings, were enough to win the day. D-Day would not have succeeded without the young Coast Guard coxswains piloting landing craft in the hairy surf, the barely-out-of-their-teens paratrooper sergeants in thick Norman hedgerows confronting German soldiers younger still, or the lieutenants who rallied forward on the beaches a stricken soldier here and an injured comrade there. And, conversely, it would not have been the success it was for the Allies without the equally important counter-lesson of the German reaction—as a divided, top-down, hierarchal, and confused chain of command failed to act and its battlefield leaders failed to lead at the moment it most mattered.

D-Day would not be the triumph we honor and remember without the most ordinary of men, figures like Dick Winters, Stanley Hollis, John Ahearn, John Howard, Marcus Heim, Len Lomell, Waverly Woodson, Jr., and countless other names—men plucked from civilian life, sometimes just weeks or months before—whom you will come to read about as Operation OVERLORD unfolds.

The greatest names in the pages ahead, as it turns out, are the ones you don't know.

*"A day unlike any other"*

# Foreword

An LCVP carrying troops, including 2nd Lt. Gardner Botsford
(*right, in profile*), nears Omaha Beach as D-Day begins.

**Capt. Henry Seitzler, Army Air Forces, 6th Engineer Special Beach Brigade:** Pardon me if I stop every once in a while. These things are so very real. Even after all these years I can see it again in my mind, just like it was happening right now.

**Andy Rooney, correspondent, *Stars and Stripes*:** There have only been a handful of days since the beginning of time on which the direction the world was taking has been changed for the better in one 24-hour period by an act of man. June 6th, 1944, was one of them.

**Ernest Hemingway, correspondent, *Collier's Weekly*:** No one remembers the date of the Battle of Shiloh. But the day we took Fox Green beach was the sixth of June.

**Oberleutnant Gustav Pflocksch, deputy commander, Widerstandsnest 28 (Juno Beach), Grenadier-Regiment 736, 716 Infanterie-Division:** This battle was the beginning of the end of the war.

**W. B. Courtney, correspondent, *Collier's Weekly*:** Not only as a military event but in the grave political economic and social fates it held, there has been nothing ever before to equal it. Beyond comparison, this is the most stupendous enterprise to which modern free men ever dedicated their fortunes and lives.

**Ronald Reagan, 40th president of the United States:** Here in Normandy the rescue began. Here the Allies stood and fought against tyranny in a giant undertaking unparalleled in human history.

**Gen. Dwight Eisenhower, Supreme Allied Commander, Allied Expeditionary Force:** These men came here—British, and our other allies, Americans—to storm these beaches for one purpose only, not to gain anything for ourselves, not to fulfill any ambitions that America had for conquest, but just to preserve freedom.

**Andy Rooney:** No one can tell the whole story of D-Day because no one knows it. Each of the 60,000 men who waded ashore that day know a little part of the story too well.

**Ernest Hemingway:** You could write for a week and not give everyone credit for what he did on a front of 1,135 yards.

**1st Sgt. Leonard G. Lomell, platoon leader, Company D, 2nd Ranger Battalion:** I've kept a low profile for fifty years, as have most of my men. We didn't write articles, books, make speeches or publicize the performance of our duties. We knew what each other did and we did our duty like professionals. We weren't heroes, we were just good Rangers.

**Sgt. Schuyler W. "Sky" Jackson, 502nd Parachute Infantry Regiment, 101st Airborne:** How do you describe the greatest military operation the world has ever seen when you yourself saw only one tiny piece of the vast and deadly jigsaw puzzle?

**Trooper Joe Minogue, gunner, B Squadron, Westminster Dragoons:** That summer day, June 6, 1944, D-Day, is etched indelibly on the windows of my mind. I can hear it, smell it, feel it, as though it happened only 24 hours ago.

**Seaman Exum Pike, USS *PC-565*:** The battle scene was the most awesome terrible thing a human being could ever witness. Looking back on that day, after these many years, I have two grown sons and as I have often told them boys I have no fear of hell because I have already been there.

**Pvt. Buddy Mazzara, Company C, 16th Infantry Regiment, 1st Infantry Division:** D-Day was an experience you would never want to live through again. But I am glad I was there.

**2nd Lt. Gardner Botsford, intelligence officer, Division Headquarters, 1st Division:** Nobody on that beach was aware of anything that wasn't right in front of his nose—and, Lord knows, that was enough. The human mind, when under great tension, closes its doors, shutters its windows, and focuses on the insignificant. When I waded ashore onto that Normandy beach, I was entering the stage set of a truly stupendous world event. All I recorded was snapshots of tiny fragments, snapshots with no anchor in time or meaning.

**S.Sgt. John B. Ellery, Company B, 16th Infantry Regiment, 1st Division:** With D-Day in Normandy as a ten, I haven't had an adventure that rated more than a two since I landed on the Easy Red Sector of Omaha Beach on June 6, 1944.

**2nd Lt. Gardner Botsford:** Sample snapshot: the hundreds of cumbersome life-preserver belts littering the water's edge, jettisoned by the troops as they reached shore. Snapshot: a makeshift aid station sheltered behind some rocks, where a medic was injecting morphine into the arm of a wounded soldier who wasn't going to make it. Snapshot: five or six German prisoners—all of them in their teens—sitting in a declivity on the beach with their hands on their heads and looking just as terrified as the nervous private guarding them.

**Andy Rooney:** We all have days of our lives that stand out from the blur of days that have gone by, and the day I came ashore on Utah Beach—four days after the initial invasion—is one of mine.

**Pvt. J. Robert Patterson, 474th Antiaircraft Artillery Automatic Weapons Battalion:** I've been married. I have six kids. I own my own business. I think the thing I'm proudest of, if I really had to remember anything—family, sure, kids, sure—but I am proud I was there on June the 6th.

**Pvt. John Hooper, Headquarters Company, 115th Infantry Regiment, 29th Division:** I doubt that any single event in my life equaled that day's event. My marriage in 1951, and later, two fine sons, has never had such an impact as did that first day's action on the Normandy coast in a sector known as "Easy Green."

**Andy Rooney:** There were heroes here no one will ever know because they're dead. The heroism of others is known only to themselves.

**Sgt. Donald L. Scribner, Company C, 2nd Ranger Battalion:** A lot of good men gave their lives that day, and I hope that no one ever forgets it. I know I won't.

**Andy Rooney:** It was one of the most monumentally unselfish things one group of people ever did for another.

**Lt. John J. Reville, Company F, 5th Ranger Battalion:** When I landed D-Day morning, I had 35 men in my platoon and in my boat. The battalion lasted in action seven days. At the end of seven days, there was myself and four men left.

**Sgt. Schuyler W. "Sky" Jackson:** When my daughter Lynne asked me the other evening, "Daddy, what was D-Day?," I found myself stumped. How do you explain to an 8-year-old that D-Day was courage and compassion, fear and confusion?

**Andy Rooney:** If you are young and not really clear what D-Day was, let me tell you: It was a day unlike any other.

**Emil "Moe" Vestuti, fire controlman, 3rd Class, USS *Corry* (DD-463):** I get tied up talking about it to my family even today because those feelings are still inside.

**S.Sgt. Myron "Mike" Ranney, Company E, 506th Parachute Infantry Regiment, 101st Airborne:** A grandson asked, "Grandpa, were you a hero in the war?" "No," I answered, "but I served in a company of heroes."

**Robert Capa, photographer, *Life* magazine:** Once a year, usually sometime in April, every self-respecting Jewish family celebrates Passover, the Jewish Thanksgiving. When dinner is irrevocably over, father loosens his belt and lights a five-cent cigar. At this crucial moment the youngest of the sons—I have been doing it for years—steps up and addresses his father in solemn Hebrew. He asks, "What makes this day different from all other days?" Then father, with great relish and gusto, tells the story of how, many thousands of years ago in Egypt, the angel of destruction passed over the firstborn sons of the Chosen People, and how, afterwards, General Moses led them across the Red Sea without getting their feet wet.

The Gentiles and Jews who crossed the English Channel on the sixth of June in the year 1944 ought to have—once a year, on that date—a Crossover day. Their children, after finishing a couple of cans of C-rations, would ask their father, "What makes this day different from all other days?" The story that I would tell might sound like this.

**Pfc. Felix Branham, Company K, 116th Infantry Regiment, 29th Division:** I never want to spend another day like that, but thank God—and only thank God—that I'm here to say that I can tell someone else the story of my experiences.

**Andy Rooney:** If you think the world is selfish and rotten, go to the cemetery at Colleville-sur-Mer overlooking Omaha Beach—see what one group of men did for another on D-Day, June 6th, 1944.

# PART I

# A WORLD AT WAR

# War Begins

The Allied evacuation from Dunkirk marked the
emotional low of the start of World War II.

**Pvt. John Barnes, Company A, 116th Infantry Regiment, 29th Division:** It's hard
to know where to begin. I could start at Omaha Beach, Dog Green Sector,
D-Day, June 6, H-Hour, 6:25 in the morning. It went on for 11 months up to
the Elbe River in May 1945, with A Company, 116th Infantry, 29th Division.
I was a rifleman, assistant flame thrower, platoon runner, company runner,
and, in the end, battalion runner. Of course, it started earlier.

3

**Capt. R. J. Lindo, naval artillery liaison, 2nd Battalion, 18th Infantry Regiment, 1st Division:** It's been very difficult for me to get started and to know where to begin and end.

**Pvt. J. Robert Patterson, 474th Antiaircraft Artillery Automatic Weapons Battalion:** As *Alice in Wonderland* said, "You have to begin at the beginning."

***Time* magazine, September 11, 1939:** World War II began at 5:20 a.m. (Polish time) Friday, September 1, when a German bombing plane dropped a projectile on Puck, fishing village and air base in the armpit of the Hel Peninsula. At 5:45 a.m. the German training ship *Schleswig-Holstein* lying off Danzig fired what was believed to be the first shell: a direct hit on the Polish underground ammunition dump at Westerplatte. It was a grey day, with gentle rain.

**Ens. George McKee Elsey, Map Room watch officer, the White House:** Nazi Germany and the Soviet Union quickly overran Poland, bringing declarations of war from England and France.

*The invasion of Poland by Adolf Hitler's Germany upended the foreign policy of British prime minister Neville Chamberlain, who for years had tried a strategy of "appeasement" amid Hitler's increasingly bellicose rhetoric and actions in Europe. Chamberlain had hoped to avoid war and only cautiously rearmed Britain amid Germany's rising threat, and as late as January 1939 believed that he and Hitler had a path for a "long peace" in Europe. Following the invasion, though, he was quick to issue an immediate ultimatum, with France, announcing they would declare war if Germany didn't withdraw.*

**Acting Lt. Gen. Bernard L. Montgomery, British Army:** I had taken over command of the 3rd Division on the 28th August. Partial mobilisation was then in process and full mobilisation was ordered on the 1st September, the day on which the Germans invaded Poland and an ultimatum was sent to Germany. In September 1939 the British Army was totally unfit to fight a first-class war on the continent of Europe.

**Pauline Edmondson, schoolchild, Sidcup, Kent, England:** I was twelve and Peter, my brother, was seven. All through the summer [of 1939] preparations for war were being made. The summer went by until September 2nd, which sticks in my mind, because it was such a hot day. It was a Saturday, and we were all up early, for we all knew that this was the weekend—short of a miracle—that war would be declared. Sand and sandbags had been delivered to all the houses, and we spent all that day filling the bags. They were then stacked all round the front of the house, so the windows were barricaded about halfway up.

**Barbara Clare (Fauks), schoolchild, East Acton, United Kingdom:** In 1939 we went down to visit my uncle in the country. We could see men practicing with guns, so we knew that the war was coming. When we got back to London, we didn't stay long, because most of the schoolchildren were shipped out of the city for their own protection.

**Grace Bradbeer, driver, Women's Voluntary Service, United Kingdom:** Another very early problem which rural areas had to deal with was the surge of evacuees who arrived in numbers both great and small. Every part of the British Isles was affected by this as those from the big towns and cities and from exposed positions on the coasts tried—indeed were encouraged—to get away as quickly as possible.

**Barbara Clare (Fauks):** There was a concern about the threat of air raids against the city. It was terrible to be separated from our parents. In fact, Mum and Dad didn't even know where we were going. The authorities took us first to our school and then marched us to the train station. I was crying, Mum was crying, and my sister Evelyn was crying. My cousin, who was a little older and later served in the war, went to the movie house not long after our evacuation. He saw me in the newsreel because there had been a cameraman present as our group of children was going away from home.

**Grace Bradbeer:** People came not only as families or individuals but also in parties—schools, nursing homes, colleges and so on; in fact one school from Acton, London, turned up in a small South Devon town three days before war was declared and was welcomed by locally organised billeting officers who found room for all. The official number of government-sponsored evacuees was 1,200,000 by the end of the war.

*On September 3, with no withdrawal in sight by Germany, Britain moved to declare war, followed by France, Canada, Australia, New Zealand, and South Africa. The Soviet Union, under Joseph Stalin, had signed a nonaggression pact, and after Germany had annexed the western portion of Poland, it invaded and annexed eastern Poland in September as well.*

**Pauline Edmondson:** We all gathered round the wireless to listen to Mr. Chamberlain's speech. I sat on the back steps to listen to the broadcast. Big Ben's chimes came over the air at 11 am, and Mr. Chamberlain announced that Britain was now at war with Germany.

**Neville Chamberlain, Prime Minister of the United Kingdom, radio address, September 3, 1939:** I am speaking to you from the Cabinet Room at 10 Downing Street. This morning the British Ambassador in Berlin handed the German Government a final note stating that unless we heard from them by 11 O'clock that they were prepared at once to withdraw their troops from Poland a state of war would exist between us. I have to tell you now that no such undertaking has been received, and that consequently this country is at war with Germany.

**William Shirer, correspondent, CBS News, broadcasting from Berlin, September 3, 1939:** The world war is on.

**Mollie Panter-Downes, London correspondent, *The New Yorker*, writing September 3, 1939:** Now that there is a war, the English, slow to start, have already in spirit started and are comfortably two laps ahead of the official war machine, which had to await the drop of somebody's handkerchief. In the general opinion, Hitler has got it coming to him.

*Britain spent the winter of 1939 and the beginning of 1940 racing a quarter million troops to Europe to support France and its allies in the Low Countries, Belgium and the Netherlands. Though the United States had been allied with the United Kingdom and France during the First World War, the nation had gone through a period of isolationism in the 1930s, and President Franklin Delano Roosevelt, now in his second term and about to be elected to a third, announced that it would remain neutral in the conflict.*

*In April 1940, Germany invaded Denmark and, after it surrendered in six hours, then Norway. That fresh crisis caused Chamberlain, under pressure, to resign as prime minister, to be replaced by Winston Churchill on May 10, 1940. That same day, Hitler's forces charged across the borders of the Low Countries, overrunning Luxembourg, the Netherlands, and Belgium, and advancing into France. By late May, the mostly British and French Allied armies were in full retreat, pinned down near the coastal city of Dunkirk. There, in the space of about a week, some 335,000 troops were evacuated from Europe to England—saving the British Expeditionary Force and the Allied Belgian and French armies, but forcing it to leave much of its equipment on the beach to fall into Nazi hands. In less than a year, continental Europe had been largely lost to the Axis Powers, and the newly installed Churchill feared Britain would be the next target.*

**John Gunther, correspondent, NBC News, May 9, 1940:** Bulletin from Berlin: Adolf Hitler in an order of the day to his troops declared that the fight that begins today will decide the fate of the German nation for the next 1,000 years. "Do your duty."

**Winston Churchill, Prime Minister of the United Kingdom:** Now at last the slowly gathered, long-pent-up fury of the storm broke upon us. Four or five million men met each other in the first shock of the most merciless of all the wars of which record has been kept.

**Lt. Gen. Omar Bradley, commander, First Army:** To trace the strategy of our cross-channel invasion to the beginning, we must go back to the midnight of June 2, 1940, and to the beach off Dunkirk where a British major general made his way in a small boat through the wreckage of an armada offshore. In the light of fires set by German bombers he searched the harbor and beaches for Allied troops awaiting debarkation. Satisfied that none had been left behind, Major General Harold Alexander, commander of the 1st Division, ordered his skipper to steer for England. He was the last of more than 335,000 Allied soldiers to quit the continent at Dunkirk for the withdrawal to Britain.

**Winston Churchill:** After Dunkirk, and still more when three weeks later the French Government capitulated, the questions whether Hitler would, or secondly could, invade and conquer our island rose, as we have seen, in all British minds.

**Lt. Gen. Omar Bradley:** The war seemed all but lost only nine months after it had started.

**Winston Churchill, speaking to the House of Commons, June 4, 1940:** The British Empire and the French Republic, linked together in their cause and in their need, will defend to the death their native soil, aiding each other like good comrades to the utmost of their strength. Even though large tracts of Europe and many old and famous States have fallen or may fall into the grip of the Gestapo and all the odious apparatus of Nazi rule, we shall not flag or fail.

**Brig. Gen. Charles de Gaulle, chairman, French National Committee, appeal of June 18, 1940, aired on the BBC, upon reaching the shores of England:** But has the last word been said? Must hope disappear? Is defeat final? No! Believe me, I speak to you with full knowledge of the facts and tell you that nothing is lost for France. The same means that overcame us can bring us to a day of victory. For France is not alone! She has a vast Empire behind her. She can align with the British Empire that holds the sea and continues the fight. She can, like England, use without limit the immense industry of the United States. This war is not finished by the battle of France. This war is a world war. Whatever happens, the flame of the French resistance must not be extinguished and will not be extinguished.

**Winston Churchill, speaking to the House of Commons, June 4, 1940:** We shall go on to the end, we shall fight in France, we shall fight on the seas and oceans, we shall fight with growing confidence and growing strength in the air, we shall defend our Island—whatever the cost may be—we shall fight on the beaches, we shall fight on the landing grounds, we shall fight in the fields and in the streets, we shall fight in the hills; we shall never surrender, and even if, which I do not for a moment believe, this Island or a large part of it were subjugated and starving, then our Empire beyond the seas, armed and guarded by the British Fleet, would carry on the struggle, until, in God's good time, the New World, with all its power and might, steps forth to the rescue and the liberation of the old.

*Britain, still largely alone on the world stage standing against Hitler's war machine, rallied to its own defense—beginning what amounted to a last-minute no-holds-barred effort to preserve its freedom against the looming German invasion, known as Operation Sealion. But as days turned to weeks, and weeks turned to months, Hitler realized he was ill equipped to carry out a cross-Channel invasion and settled, instead, on a terror-bombing campaign from the sky to weaken and force Great Britain to capitulate.*

**Maj. John Dalgleish, Planning Staff, Royal Army Service Corps:** Within one week of that great fighting speech, the first Commandos were formed from independent infantry companies of the British Army. They took up their stations along the South East Coast. They blacked their faces, replaced their heavy ammunition boots with rubber-soled soft shoes, collected a motley assortment of small craft, and prepared themselves for their initial task of raiding operations against the continental coastline.

**Winston Churchill:** Our armies at home were known to be almost unarmed except for rifles. There were in fact hardly five hundred field guns of any sort and hardly two hundred medium or heavy tanks in the whole country. Months must pass before our factories could make good even the munitions lost at Dunkirk. Can one wonder that the world at large was convinced that our hour of doom had struck? Deep alarm spread through the United States, and indeed through all the surviving free countries.

**Mollie Panter-Downes:** London was as quiet as a village. At places where normally there is a noisy bustle of comings and goings, such as the big railway stations, there was the same extraordinary preoccupied silence. People stood about reading the papers; when a man finished one, he would hand it over to anybody who hadn't been lucky enough to get a copy, and walk soberly away.

One morning, this week, postmen slipped official pamphlets in with the mail, telling householders just what to do if Britain is invaded. Official advice is to stay at home unless told by the proper authorities to leave, "because, if you run away, you will be machine-gunned from the air, as were civilians in Holland and Belgium."

**Lt. Gen. Omar Bradley:** Reluctant to risk a makeshift assault against the British navy, the Wehrmacht settled down on the coast until the Luftwaffe softened England.

**Winston Churchill, speaking to the House of Commons, June 18, 1940:** What General [Maxime] Weygand called the Battle of France is over. I expect that the Battle of Britain is about to begin. Upon this battle depends the survival of Christian civilization. Upon it depends our own British life, and the long continuity of our institutions and our Empire. The whole fury and might of the enemy must very soon be turned on us. Hitler knows that he will have to break us in this Island or lose the war. If we can stand up to him, all Europe may be free and the life of the world may move forward into broad, sunlit uplands. But if we fail, then the whole world, including the United States, including all that we have known and cared for, will sink into the abyss of a new Dark Age made more sinister, and perhaps more protracted, by the lights of perverted science. Let us therefore brace ourselves to our duties, and so bear ourselves that, if the British Empire and its Commonwealth last for a thousand years, men will still say, "This was their finest hour."

*Over the summer of 1940, the Luftwaffe battled the roughly 3,000 pilots of the Royal Air Force in the skies over Britain in an attempt to gain air superiority. Thanks to the Herculean efforts of the RAF and an astounding industrial production effort, known as the "Harrogate program," which saw England churn out 500 fighters a month through that summer, as well as an extensive ground-spotting network, and the British military's early development of a radar-type system that could detect incoming German flights and guide fighters toward them, the British were able to hold. Meanwhile, the war expanded into the Mediterranean, as Italian forces targeted British-held Malta, Somaliland, and Egypt in North Africa.*

**Maj. Ralph Ingersoll, intelligence officer, Planning Staff, Allied Expeditionary Force:** In the fall of 1940, the Empire had had the narrowest squeak in its entire history. It had survived against seemingly impossible odds—and miraculously. In surviving, it had found its soul. It was really united under Churchill's personal leadership.

**Mollie Panter-Downes:** The skill and audacity of the RAF youngsters have so captured the public imagination that the fliers are spoken of with almost poetic admiration, as though they were knights on wings.

**Winston Churchill, speaking August 20, 1940:** The gratitude of every home in our Island, in our Empire, and indeed throughout the world, except in the abodes of the guilty, goes out to the British airmen who, undaunted by odds, unwearied in their constant challenge and mortal danger, are turning the tide of the World War by their prowess and by their devotion. Never in the field of human conflict was so much owed by so many to so few.

**Harold Bird-Wilson, 17 Squadron, No. 11 Group, RAF:** You read many stories nowadays of pilots saying they weren't worried and weren't frightened when they saw little dots in the sky, which gradually increased in numbers and grew in size as they came from the French coast towards the English, over Kent and towards London. I maintain that if anybody says that they weren't frightened or apprehensive at such an occasion then I think he's a very bad liar, because you cannot help but get worried. I openly admit that I was worried and I was frightened at times.

*In September, British leaders were able to breathe a temporary sigh of relief: Hitler began dismantling the facilities at Dutch airfields where German para-troopers had been expected to embark for England. The invasion was off, for now. On September 7, 1940, the Luftwaffe, recognizing that it would not win air superiority over Britain, adjusted its strategy and began an intense bombing campaign against England, which came to be known as the Blitz, in the hope of breaking the British spirit and forcing its capitulation. At the start, London was attacked on 56 out of 57 straight days; the air campaign would continue for eight months, into the spring of 1941, killing more than 40,000 civilians.*

**Edward R. Murrow, correspondent, CBS, reporting September 8, 1940, from London:** An air-raid siren called Weeping Willy began its uneven screams. Down on the coast the white puff balls of anti-aircraft fire began to appear against the steel blue sky. The first flight of German bombers were coming up the river to start the 12 hour attack against London.

**Pauline Edmondson:** My mum and dad and everyone else who lived around us began to fix up their shelters. My father built two bunks in ours—one for Peter and one for my mother—and hung a hammock for me in the gangway. It took me ages to learn to stay in it, I was always falling out. My father never slept in the shelter; he had a chair in there which he sometimes sat on, but most of the time he was outside doing his duty as a warden. When the raids were really bad, bombs would be whizzing down, guns banging away, and shrapnel all over the place, but my dad didn't get so much as a scratch.

**Ronald Allen, Leytonstone, London (age 10):** I was visiting my grandparents who lived in Plumstead near the Woolwich Arsenal. Up until then, most of the raids had been on air fields. We'd had lots of warnings, but no actual raids so we just thought it was another scare.

**Edward R. Murrow:** They were high and not very numerous. The Hurricanes and Spitfires were already in the air climbing for altitude above the nearby aerodrome. The fight moved inland and out of sight.

Up toward London we could see billows of smoke fanning out above the river. It went on for over two hours and then the all-clear. Before 8 p.m., the sirens sounded again.

**Ronald Allen:** We went down into the Anderson shelter in the back garden and then the ack-ack guns started firing so we knew this time it was different. The drone of the aircraft could be heard and then the first bombs started falling. I hadn't heard a bomb before so when I heard this rushing whooshing sound I thought it was a crowd cheering like in a football match, not the whistling sound depicted in films. The noise of the guns and falling bombs was deafening—the ground shook and we all hung on to each other for courage.

**Edward R. Murrow:** The fires up the river had turned the moon blood red; the smoke had drifted down until it formed a canopy over the Thames. The guns were working all around us. The bursts looking like fireflies in a southern summer night.

The Germans were sending in two or three planes at a time, in relays. They would pass overhead, the guns and lights would follow them, and in about five minutes we could hear the hollow drop of the bomb. Huge pear-shaped bursts of flame would rise up into the smoke and disappear. The world was upside down.

**Ronald Allen:** My mother, sister and I tried to get home, but had to get off the tram at New Cross Gate because only dock workers were allowed to cross the river. I'll never forget the sight of the Surrey docks all ablaze as we tried to get back on that tram. We had to spend the night in a public shelter in New Cross Gate as the night bombing started. It was Sunday morning before we got home to Leytonstone and my dad was waiting outside the house. I'll never forget the sight of him standing there. He had probably been there for hours, wondering whether we were alive or dead.

**Raymond Hickey, chaplain, North Shore Regiment:** Night after night, just as darkness was falling, up would go the awful wail of the sirens. In all directions people would run to cold cement air raid shelters; on would go the search-lights that swept the sky like giant northern lights; from a distance would come the unmistakable *ou, ou, ou* of German planes; with a deafening roar, our anti-aircraft guns would open up—you huddled as small as you could, covered your head, held your breath, and waited for bombs that came with a terrifying whistle, and shook the earth with an awful blast and covered the place with death and destruction.

**Hazel Roberts, schoolchild, Essex (age seven):** As we all looked skywards we watched as wave after wave of German Heinkel and Dornier bomb-ers headed over our houses towards London. Suddenly I shouted to my brother, "Here come our boys!" as I saw our Spitfires emerging from behind the clouds. The Spitfires roared in—there were only a small number of our planes against all the might of the German Luftwaffe. We saw planes blown to pieces, both German and British, and wreckage was strewn all over a large area.

**Edward R. Murrow:** There are no words to describe the thing that is happening. A row of automobiles, with stretchers racked on the roofs like skis, standing outside of bombed buildings. A man pinned under wreckage where a broken gas main sears his arms and face. The courage of the people, the flash and roar of the guns rolling down streets, the stench of air-raid shelters in the poor districts.

**Grace Bradbeer:** Soon, rationing of food began to be proposed, though it was not finally brought in until early in 1940. All over the country, farmers were encouraged to use every scrap of available land for the growing of food crops and for grazing but at the same time they were hampered by the call-up which took away so much agricultural labour. Only a few younger men were allowed to remain in order to help cope with the extra strain put upon the farms, and the Women's Land Army stepped into the breach almost at once.

*After its stunning and overwhelming victories across Europe in 1939 and 1940, Hitler turned Germany's attention to the Soviet Union. Ignoring the nonaggression pact his government had signed with Stalin and following Germany's new combined-arms strategy—uniting armor, infantry, and airborne forces in rapid advances that overwhelmed an enemy's defenses—Hitler launched a massive invasion of the Soviet Union. In June 1941, hundreds of thousands of troops poured across the Soviet border as part of Operation Barbarossa. Joseph Stalin, who trusted in the nonaggression pact for too long, failed to prepare until it was too late. Even at great cost in men and weapons, Germany made significant advances into the Soviet Union, which quickly found a new alliance with Great Britain. The cascading developments greatly distressed President Roosevelt, who understood the impact of Germany's growing power on both the Western and Eastern Fronts. He offered support to the Soviets, but continued to struggle over the domestic politics of whether to further involve the United States in the conflict.*

**Averell Harriman, US presidential envoy to the UK:** Roosevelt was very much affected by World War I, which he had, of course, seen at close range. He had a horror of American troops landing again on the continent and becoming involved in the kind of warfare he had seen before—trench warfare with all its appalling losses. I believe he had in mind that if the great armies of

Russia could stand up to the Germans, this might well make it possible for us to limit our participation largely to naval and air power.

**Franklin Roosevelt, President of the United States, message, August 30:** I deem it of paramount importance for the safety and security of America that all reasonable munitions help be provided for Russia, not only immediately but as long as she continues to fight the Axis powers effectively.

**Averell Harriman:** The overriding motivation of President Roosevelt in giving every bit of help that was possible was that he wanted to keep the Russians in the war. He wanted to err on the side of generosity, rather than skimping the aid we sent.

*By December 1941, the United States had begun to tiptoe toward war. Its Lend-Lease program of "lending" weapons, ships, airplanes, and other supplies to Great Britain and the Soviet Union had helped both militaries survive the worst of the German offensives. Understanding the stakes of whether Western democracy would survive the encounter with the authoritarian Nazi regime, Roosevelt and Churchill had outlined that summer what was known as the Atlantic Charter, a vision for a secure peace at the end of the war. In the Pacific, the Imperial Japanese forces were on their own offensive and Roosevelt had been trying to negotiate a path to avoid conflict there too. In the end, though, he found the decision for war wasn't his to make.*

**Ens. George McKee Elsey:** On Saturday evening, December 6, 1941, some former Harvard graduate students and I had dinner. We speculated about how soon we would be at war with Germany, eager as Hitler was to wage all-out submarine war against us and end our support of England. I guessed about six weeks, the time it would take for the Germans to regain the initiative in Russia and capture Moscow. We had an answer the next day—but it was not war with Germany.

**Franklin Roosevelt:** December 7, 1941—a date which will live in infamy.

**Live NBC News Bulletin, 4 p.m. ET, Sunday, December 7, 1941:** Hello, NBC. Hello, NBC. This is KGU in Honolulu, Hawaii. I am speaking from the roof of the Advertiser Publishing Company Building. We have witnessed this morning the distant view of the severe bombing of Pearl Harbor by enemy planes, undoubtedly Japanese.

**Franklin Roosevelt:** The United States of America was suddenly and deliberately attacked by naval and air forces of the Empire of Japan.

**Live NBC News Bulletin, 4 p.m. ET, Sunday, December 7, 1941:** The city of Honolulu has also been attacked and considerable damage done. This battle has been going on for nearly three hours. One of the bombs dropped within fifty feet of KGU tower. It is no joke. It is a real war.

**Eleanor Roosevelt, First Lady of the United States:** I was going out in the hall to say goodbye to our cousins, Mr. and Mrs. Frederick Adams, and their children, after luncheon, and, as I stepped out of my room, I knew something had happened. All the secretaries were there, two telephones were in use, the senior military aides were on their way with messages. I said nothing because the words I heard over the telephone were quite sufficient to tell me that, finally, the blow had fallen, and we had been attacked.

**Pvt. Edward J. Jeziorski, 507th Parachute Infantry Regiment, 82nd Airborne:** I enlisted in the New Jersey National Guard in April 1940. I participated in maneuvers in South Carolina in 1941. On the evening of December 7, 1941, as we arrived in Culpeper, Virginia for bivouac, many civilians came up to talk to us about the Japanese attack on Pearl Harbor. We were thunderstruck. We couldn't figure out where in the world Pearl Harbor was located.

**Winston Churchill:** It was Sunday evening, December 7, 1941. [US ambassador John Gilbert] Winant and Averell Harriman were with me at the table at Chequers.

**Averell Harriman:** The Prime Minister seemed tired and depressed. He didn't have much to say throughout dinner and was immersed in his thoughts, with his head in his hands for part of the time.

**Pamela Churchill, daughter-in-law to the Prime Minister:** The Battle of Britain was over, but the outcome of the war still hung in the balance.

**Winston Churchill:** I turned on my small wireless set shortly after the nine o'clock news had started. There were a number of items about the fighting on the Russian front and on the British front in Libya, at the end of which some few sentences were spoken regarding an attack by the Japanese on American shipping at Hawaii, and also Japanese attacks on British vessels in the Dutch East Indies.

**Averell Harriman:** I was thoroughly startled, and I repeated the words, "The Japanese have raided Pearl Harbor."

**Winston Churchill:** We all sat up. By now the butler, Sawyers, who had heard what had passed, came into the room, saying, "It's quite true. We heard it ourselves outside. The Japanese have attacked the Americans."

**Averell Harriman:** The Prime Minister, recovering from his lethargy, slammed the top of the radio down and got up from his chair.

**Winston Churchill:** At the Mansion House luncheon on November 11 I had said that if Japan attacked the United States a British declaration of war would follow "within the hour." I got up from the table and walked through the hall to the office, which was always at work. I asked for a call to the President. In two or three minutes Mr. Roosevelt came through. "Mr. President, what's this about Japan?" "It's quite true," he replied. "They have attacked us at Pearl Harbor. We are all in the same boat now."

**Averell Harriman:** The inevitable had finally arrived.

**Winston Churchill:** No American will think it wrong of me if I proclaim that to have the United States at our side was to me the greatest joy. I could not foretell the course of events. I do not pretend to have measured accurately the martial might of Japan, but now at this very moment I knew the United States was in the war, up to the neck and in to the death. England would live; Britain would live; the Commonwealth of Nations and the Empire would live. How long the war would last or in what fashion it would end, no man could tell, nor did I at this moment care. Hitler's fate was sealed. Mussolini's fate was sealed. As for the Japanese, they would be ground to powder.

**Eleanor Roosevelt:** It was a little while before I was free to go and talk to my husband—until really late in the afternoon or early evening, and when I did go in, I thought him looking very strained and tired, but he was completely calm. His reaction to any great event was always to be calm—if it was something that was bad, he became like an iceberg. There was never the slightest emotion that was allowed to show.

He was on a whole almost most relieved to know the worst that had to be faced, and that this country could eventually meet it. This feeling was something one always expected of him. I have never known him not to be ready to face the worst that could happen, but always to be hopeful about the solution that could be found.

**Winston Churchill:** All the rest was merely the proper application of overwhelming force. No doubt it would take a long time. I thought of a remark which Edward Grey had made to me more than thirty years before—that the United States is like "a gigantic boiler. Once the fire is lighted under it there is no limit to the power it can generate." Being saturated and satiated with emotion and sensation, I went to bed and slept the sleep of the saved and thankful.

*"They were not going to have a war without me"*

# War Comes to America

The Japanese attack on Pearl Harbor, including the burning
USS *Nevada*, shocked America. Three years later, it would be the
only ship from Pearl Harbor also at D-Day.

*Americans woke up on Monday, December 8, to a new reality, one that would
remake almost every area of life in the weeks and months ahead as the country's
government, industry, and people turned to war. Detroit automakers who
had made and sold some three million cars in 1941 stopped manufacturing cars
almost entirely and retooled to churn out tanks, airplanes, and other wartime
necessities. (The US would manufacture just 139 cars, total, during the rest
of the war.) Meanwhile, the generation that had defended Europe against
German aggression three decades earlier now watched the country prepare*

*again to send its boys overseas to perform the same mission. Within a year, the military was inducting every month a drafted force roughly equal to the entire size of the prewar army. Altogether, about 10 million of the 16 million people who would serve in the armed forces during the war were draftees. Millions of women flowed into US factories to work the wartime assembly lines as men left for fighting overseas.*

**Brig. Gen. James M. Gavin, assistant division commander, 82nd Airborne:** The impact of Pearl Harbor was immediate and dramatic.

**Maj. John Dalgleish, Planning Staff, Royal Army Service Corps:** Britain and the United States became allies overnight. The massive manpower resources of a nation of 120,000,000 people were showered on this tiny country, which had set a ceiling of some 3,000,000 men as the maximum strength of her armed forces.

**Lucille Hoback, 12-year-old sister of two brothers serving in the 29th Division, Bedford, VA:** Everybody was very worried because we thought it meant the boys would be sent off to war. That day, my father never left the radio. In the coming days, there was a rush of local men eager to sign up.

**Cpl. Elisha Ray Nance, Company A, 116th Infantry Regiment, 29th Division:** We kept our feelings to ourselves. There wasn't much to say. The president had laid it on the line. We were going to war.

**Lt. Charles Mohrle, P-47 pilot, 510th Squadron, 405th Fighter-Bomber Group:** I was residing in Dallas when the Japanese attacked Pearl Harbor. I volunteered for service with the Army Air Corps the following day.

**S.Sgt. Harry Bare, Company F, 116th Infantry Regiment, 29th Division:** I was young, in good shape, and they were not going to have a war without me.

*As preparations began stateside to activate America's industrial might, government leaders overnight shifted their focus and planning from passive support, like Lend-Lease, to an active military strategy across both the Pacific and European Theaters. Night and day, Roosevelt met with his cabinet and advisers to discuss how best to take on and fight back against the main Axis Powers of Italy, Japan, and Germany.*

**Fleet Adm. William D. Leahy, Chief of Staff to the President:** Roosevelt, early in the war, had marked out a broad strategy of a two-ocean war against the Axis in Europe and the Japanese in Asia.

**Ens. George McKee Elsey, Map Room watch officer, the White House:** The United States and Great Britain were in agreement that the enemy to defeat first was Germany. American planners assumed this would mean a return in force to the Continent and that the attack should be directly across the English Channel. The British, remembering Dunkirk, were not so sure.

**Maj. Ralph Ingersoll, intelligence officer, Planning Staff, Allied Expeditionary Force:** In the month of August, in 1942, a Commando-type force, largely of Canadians, under the command of Admiral Lord Louis Mountbatten, crossed the English Channel and forced the heavily fortified harbor of Dieppe. They landed tanks, fought their way some miles inland and stayed on the Continent of Europe for approximately twenty-four hours. Presently, what was left of the raiders fought their way back to their boats and returned to England. They suffered extremely heavy casualties—and began a military controversy which raged with varying intensity from that date until the successful invasion of Normandy in June of 1944. Was Dieppe a success or a failure? The British were proud of the heroism displayed at Dieppe, but often, during the planning of the later invasion, took the position that Dieppe had demonstrated how difficult it was to establish a beachhead on the far shore of the Channel. When the Americans became too optimistic, wounded veterans from Dieppe were frequently introduced into conferences to remind us of the hazards we talked so glibly of overcoming.

**Brig. Gen. James M. Gavin:** By the summer of 1942 the German empire extended from the Pyrenees to the outskirts of Moscow and, with the exception of Switzerland and Sweden, from the Mediterranean to the Arctic. It had been an impressive diplomatic and military performance, and there was good reason for many Americans to doubt that we, with the British, could successfully engage and destroy the German colossus.

*The Axis Powers, strained by battlefield losses and complicated logistics, found themselves reaching the limits of their offensive capabilities and land gains, and the US and Britain began planning for their own counterattacks—debating whether it was better to strike continental Europe first, or tackle the Axis stronghold in the Mediterranean by invading North Africa. Ultimately, the Allies realized they were nowhere close in either manpower or equipment to mounting an operation as extensive as a cross-Channel invasion and instead opted for a smaller first foray, a landing in North Africa, where the Allies began to roll back the Axis gains amid heavy fighting against German forces led by Field Marshal Erwin Rommel. But they knew, at the same time, that the only way to someday bring Germany and Hitler to defeat was to bring the battle to the European continent.*

**Fleet Adm. William D. Leahy:** The first meeting of the Combined Chiefs of Staff over which I presided occurred on July 30, 1942. The war situation in general was reviewed, but most of the discussion concerned details of a projected operation in North Africa which had the code name of "Torch."

**Lt. Gen. Sir Frederick Morgan, Chief of Staff to the Supreme Allied Commander (COSSAC):** The study of history didn't bring much comfort. Julius Caesar and William of Normandy had done the job in the reverse direction. Napoleon had funked it; so had Hitler. Also in the reverse direction. There was no real precedent, even of failure, going what was now our way.

**Fleet Adm. William D. Leahy:** The Russians could not have been more disappointed than our own Army people that plans for a 1942 cross-Channel invasion had to be abandoned. There was much grumbling about the British and considerable criticism of Churchill. The Prime Minister was convinced that England was not ready to undertake such a major effort, and I did not think that we were either. I personally was interested in the safety of the United States. A cross-Channel operation could have failed and we still would have been safe, but England would have been lost.

**Lt. Gen. Omar Bradley, commander, First Army:** They would have to calculate every move, weigh every ton, in terms of its ultimate effect upon that Channel invasion. Every move throughout the world must be subordinated to it.

**Brig. Gen. Charles de Gaulle, chairman, French National Committee:** No other operation would bring matters to a head.

**Lt. Gen. Omar Bradley:** The Battle for Germany [would] start with the conquest of that Channel. From the moment Alexander cast off from the beach at Dunkirk, a Channel crossing became the inevitable forerunner to Allied victory in the West.

# 1943

The Allied commanders gathered throughout 1943
to plan the start of the second front in Europe.

*The groundwork for the Allied invasion of the European continent began in 1943,
as Roosevelt, Churchill, and Stalin, the leaders of the United States, the United
Kingdom, and the Soviet Union, respectively, discussed and debated how to defeat
Hitler's Germany in a series of high-level conferences that spanned the globe. The
first took place in Casablanca, in mid-January. Stalin was unable to attend due
to the military situation in Moscow, but Roosevelt and Churchill moved forward
with their plans to meet, and ultimately decided at that conference that the natural
next step was to launch an effort to invade France in 1944.*

*The invasion would be led by a Supreme Allied Commander, and while
the government leaders weren't ready to name that person, they knew that*

*planning needed to commence immediately for an invasion. Their solution was
to appoint a planning staff, headed by the awkwardly named "Chief of Staff
to the Supreme Allied Commander." Allied commanders charged the new office,
which would be based in government offices in London known as Norfolk House,
with developing not just plans for a major cross–Channel invasion, originally
code-named ROUNDUP, but also a plan for a rapid, unexpected cross–Channel
movement, code-named SLEDGEHAMMER, that would be used if the Third
Reich collapsed unexpectedly.\**

**Lt. Gen. Walter Bedell "Beetle" Smith, Chief of Staff, SHAEF:** At the Casablanca
Conference in January, 1943, General Morgan was appointed Chief of Staff
to the Supreme Allied Commander, though it was eleven months before a
supreme commander was selected. The initials of the new designation spelled
out COSSAC, and COSSAC became the code name of the headquarters
in London.

**Lt. Gen. Sir Frederick Morgan, COSSAC:** It is the simple fact that until the
beginning of April 1943 what became later Operation OVERLORD, the great
invasion of Europe, consisted almost exclusively of myself. However, from
the first week in April onwards things began to change very fast.

**Maj. Goronwy Rees, 21 Army Group Planning Staff:** As far as the planning was
concerned, it was an essentially British operation. Of course we had American officers with us and they worked very closely with us but the original
conception of the plan was a British one and the detailed planning of it
was also, I would say, about ninety percent British.

---

\* These code names were a source of confusion early on, until standardized. On July 6,
1942, Churchill wrote to FDR, "Our code-words need clarification. By 'Bolero' we British
mean the vast arrangements necessary both in 1942 and 1943 for the operation against the
Continent. The Joint Anglo-American Staffs committees are all working on this basis.
They are not operational, but purely administrative. What you in conversation have called
'Operation Bolero' we have hitherto been calling 'Sledgehammer.' The name 'Round-up'
has been given to the 1943 operation. I do not much like this name, as it might be thought
over-confident or over-gloomy, but it has come into considerable use. Please let me know
whether you have any wishes about this. The 'Gymnast' you and I have in view is, I think,
the variant called by your Staffs 'SeraiGymnast.' I also use the word 'Jupiter' to describe an
operation in the Far North." That certainly clears it up, doesn't it?

**Lt. Gen. Sir Frederick Morgan:** Admiral Andrew B. Cunningham wanted to give me a few words before he went off to the southward. Our interview was measurable almost in seconds, for all he wanted to say to me was this: "Now look here, General, get this quite clear. During this present war I have already evacuated two British armies, and I don't intend to evacuate a third. Good luck to you."

**Ginger Thomas, Wren, COSSAC:** I joined the Wrens [WRNS, Women's Royal Naval Service] in March 1943, when I was 22 years old. Until then I had been working as a shorthand typist in the Town Clerk's Office in Swansea. The first time I met General Morgan was in a huge room with maps covering the walls. He was sitting behind a desk, and said, "Sit down sailor." I was the only Wren working on his staff, and I suspect it was his way of putting me at ease. He called me "sailor" until the day he died.

**Maj. John Dalgleish, Planning Staff, Royal Army Service Corps:** By the end of May plans were sufficiently developed to establish a Q Planning Branch. This branch was completely segregated from the other staffs, and a 24-hour guard of military policemen was mounted at the approaches to the offices being used for planning. No one not directly connected with planning was allowed in these offices.

**Lt. Gen. Sir Frederick Morgan:** One lived at this time in an atmosphere of code-names. Conversation consisted largely of a list of code-names with suitable conjunctions. There were times when we sincerely hoped that we were confusing the enemy as effectively as we seemed to be confusing ourselves.

**Maj. Ralph Ingersoll, intelligence officer, planning staff, Allied Expeditionary Force:** In May the original plan for the invasion of northwest Europe was being written by COSSAC and it had already been given the name of OVERLORD.

**Lt. Gen. Sir Frederick Morgan:** The name OVERLORD was personally approved by the Prime Minister.

**Maj. Ralph Ingersoll:** Throughout the war the Prime Minister took a very personal interest in the selection of code words describing future operations. You could almost always read his attitude in the word he chose.

**Lt. Gen. Sir Frederick Morgan:** It was confirmed that the target date for the operation was to be May 1, 1944, and that the outline plans were to be in the hands of the Combined Chiefs of Staff by the 1st August, 1943. Five infantry divisions were to be simultaneously loaded in the landing craft and shipping to be made available, with two more divisions to follow up immediately. We were also to count on two airborne divisions so that there would be a total of nine divisions in the assault and immediate follow-up.

*           *           *

*Settled on their new mission's name—OVERLORD—the Allied leaders studied and debated three big questions: Where, and when, would an invasion happen, and who would lead it? They turned their attention first to the question of location, examining maps and studying geographical features to determine the best strategic choice. Calls went out to the British public to send in vacation photographs, postcards, and guidebooks for the European coast—and millions of such offerings filled the walls of planners' offices as they studied one beach versus another. Options were limited, but all were considered, from Norway in the north to Brittany in the south. None presented outstanding benefits, and so the group kept searching until they settled upon a strip of beaches in the south of France that would pose the least logistical and strategic issues.*

**Winston Churchill, Prime Minister of the United Kingdom:** The first question was where a landing in force could best be made.

**Lt. Gen. Sir Frederick Morgan:** Past projects had considered raids or assaults on almost every section of the coast between Brittany and Belgium.

**Lt. Gen. Omar Bradley, commander, First Army:** COSSAC's planners broke the coast line down into six prospective areas of attack. Those areas included the North Sea coast of Holland and Belgium; the Pas de Calais shore within artillery range of Dover; the mouth of the Seine near Le Havre; the Caen coast and the Cotentin Peninsula with its promising port of Cherbourg; the Brittany peninsula with its girdle of ports including the enemy submarine base at Brest; and lastly the Biscay coast as far south as Bordeaux. The North Sea coasts of Germany and Denmark had been rejected from the start, for both were well beyond the range of Allied fighter aircraft.

**Winston Churchill:** Each of these had its own advantages and disadvantages, which had to be weighed up under a whole set of different headings and varying, sometimes uncertain, factors. Of these the principal were beaches; weather and tides; sites for constructing airfields; length of voyage; near-by ports that could be captured; the nature of the hinterland for subsequent operations; provision of cover by home-based aircraft; enemy dispositions, their minefields and defences.

**Lt. Gen. Omar Bradley:** In the initial examination, four of those six zones were discarded as prohibitive risks. The coasts of Holland and Belgium were thought too distant from the airfields of Britain. Few passable exits ran from those beaches, and the soft sand dunes there threatened to slow down the movement of supply. If we were to assault the mouth of the Seine near Le Havre, our forces would be perilously split on both sides of that river and as a consequence each might be defeated in detail. Those beaches under the nose of Le Havre could be brought under fire from the harbor defenses. And the ones north of the Seine could be counterattacked by troops from the Pas de Calais.

**Lt. Gen. Sir Frederick Morgan:** It was easily seen from the start that there were not a great number of alternatives to be considered for the making of the main effort. These seemed to whittle themselves down to only two.

**Lt. Gen. Omar Bradley:** The first was the Pas de Calais, across the narrowest point of the Channel where 20 miles of choppy water separate Calais from the cliffs of Dover. As the German marshaled his troops and poured concrete into his Atlantic Wall, it became evident that he had bet on the Pas de Calais as the point of Allied attack. The remaining area comprised the 60-mile sector that ran from Caen on the east across the Carentan estuary and the Cotentin east shore to within easy reach of Cherbourg. From the enemy's point of view this remote provincial beach, 200 miles from Paris and 400 from the Siegfried Line, seemed to offer fewer inducements for attack than the Pas de Calais. As a result it was left largely unfortified until shortly before the invasion when Hitler intuitively sized it up as a prospective target for Allied attack.

**Lt. Gen. Sir Frederick Morgan:** There was no alternative if we were to keep to our timetable and attack within the year.

**Winston Churchill:** Normandy gave us the greatest hope.

**Lt. Gen. Sir Frederick Morgan:** The landing beaches were just one x in an algebraic expression that contained half the alphabet.

**Lt. Gen. Omar Bradley:** Our troubles were only beginning. To turn that outline into a blueprint would take nine more months of tactical planning.

**Maj. John Dalgleish:** What a plan! To weld together, in knowledge, experience, and ability, a million men!

**Lt. Gen. Sir Frederick Morgan, writing in his final report, July 15, 1943:** An operation of the magnitude of Operation OVERLORD has never previously been attempted in history. It is fraught with hazards, both in nature and magnitude, which do not obtain in any other theatre of the present world war. Unless these hazards are squarely faced and adequately overcome, the operation cannot succeed.

\*       \*       \*

*With the location and scope of the operation largely settled, it had advanced about as far as it could without a clear commander. Time, everyone knew, was of the essence. The war was rapidly progressing, and Roosevelt and Churchill were not only trying to monitor the progress of OVERLORD, but were also in the midst of navigating pressures from Stalin, the other member of the "Big Three," to launch a cross-Channel invasion in order to aid the Soviet Union forces fighting brutal and costly battles in the east against Nazi forces, and the still-dangerous conflict on the Atlantic with German U-boats. Still, progress was being made—Operation TORCH had succeeded in North Africa and the initial forays into southern Europe appeared promising.*

**Gen. Lord Hastings Ismay, chief military adviser to Winston Churchill:** Things were moving fast. The landings in Sicily on 10 July had been successful, in spite of rough seas and a serious mishap to our airborne troops. The enemy were putting up a stout resistance but were being pressed steadily back, and it looked as though the island would be ours in a matter of weeks.

**Lt. Gen. Sir Frederick Morgan:** There was good news coming from the Pacific, where General MacArthur was beginning to climb up the map again. India seemed safe from the Japanese. Rommel had been chased out of Africa, and we had made a spectacular bag of prisoners. The Russians were still in the war and coming along well too. There were few bombs dropping in England now. On the other hand, Germany was at last getting a proper foretaste of what was coming to her in this line.

**Gen. Dwight Eisenhower, Supreme Allied Commander, SHAEF:** In July the Germans opened their last great offensive on the Eastern Front, but made little progress, with bitter loss. At the end of July came the fall of Mussolini.

**Maj. Ralph Ingersoll:** The comeback from the awful days that followed Dunkirk had been spectacular.

**Lt. Gen. Sir Frederick Morgan:** In the matter of troops and their equipment and of air strength, things looked good. The United States was getting things rolling in fine style. The figures were so big as to be hard to grasp. The estimate in August 1943 was that men imported into the United Kingdom from the United States would total not far short of a million by the end of the year and one million and two hundred and fifty thousand by March 1944. That was one worry disposed of. But the craft and shipping situation seemed to be getting worse instead of better. It seemed almost that it would have been possible to make an immense saving in clerical labour in government offices by having actually printed on all stationery, as well as the usual letterheads, the opening gambit "Owing to the acute shortage of shipping of all kinds . . ." This had become the unvarying alibi to cover refusal of demands for everything from a new pencil to an additional staff officer.

*The natural names to command the operation were the respective highest-ranking officers in the two Allied militaries, namely Chief of the Imperial General Staff (CIGS) Alan Brooke on the British side and Army Chief of Staff Gen. George C. Marshall in Washington, but the leaders of both nations understood they needed to look elsewhere for* OVERLORD's *commander.*

**Gen. Lord Hastings Ismay:** The Prime Minister had originally thought that General Brooke should have the supreme command, and had so informed him. But when he realised that after the initial landings the Americans would have a large and ever increasing preponderance of the forces engaged, he felt bound to tell Roosevelt that the Americans were entitled to the appointment. Those of us who knew what was afoot felt sure that General Marshall would be selected; and this was undoubtedly Roosevelt's original idea.

**Lt. Gen. Omar Bradley:** If ever a man deserved the appointment, that man was General Marshall. Yet in the army hierarchy of command the appointment of General Marshall as Supreme Commander would have entailed a stepdown from his post as Army Chief of Staff. But stepdown or no, had General Marshall left Washington to go to Europe, no one could have taken his place.

**Fleet Adm. William D. Leahy, Chief of Staff to the President:** George Marshall possessed self-discipline to a remarkable degree. I believe Roosevelt wanted to give him the job. From a professional soldier's viewpoint, it would have been considered a fitting reward for the thankless, back-breaking task of moulding a citizens' army into a splendid fighting force that had consumed all of Marshall's energies for three years.

**Lt. Gen. Omar Bradley:** No one but General Marshall could have allocated manpower and resources between the European and Pacific wars as resolutely as he did. Among the Western Allies three of these giants towered above all others during this last World War—Roosevelt, Churchill, and

Marshall. Together they probably influenced the lives of more men than any other triumvirate in the history of mankind.

*Unable to spare Marshall, Roosevelt named a new, and somewhat unexpected candidate: Dwight D. "Ike" Eisenhower, a career military man who had served in World War I and spent time in the Philippines between the wars. As the Second World War began, he was promoted rapidly and experienced one of the fastest climbs of any officer in history—a lieutenant colonel in March 1941, he was a four-star general just 35 months later in February 1943. Since Pearl Harbor, he had held a number of key strategic roles in the armed forces, and in November 1942 had been named Supreme Commander of the Allied Expeditionary Force of the North African Theater of Operations and overseen the invasion of Sicily.*

**Fleet Adm. William Leahy:** The President selected General Dwight D. Eisenhower as Supreme Commander of "Operation OVERLORD." He told me about his decision as we were flying from Cairo to Tunis on December 7. His selection was something of a surprise.

**Gen. Lord Hastings Ismay:** Whatever arguments there may be about the motives which influenced the President, there is no doubt that his decision yielded the happiest results.

**Lt. Gen. Omar Bradley:** In terms of experience, tact, and perspective, Ike was admirably equipped for the job.

**Lt. Gen. Walter Bedell "Beetle" Smith:** When General Eisenhower was appointed Supreme Commander of the Allied Expeditionary Force to cross the Channel and destroy the German armies in western Europe, we were still at our headquarters in North Africa.

**Lt. Gen. Omar Bradley:** As his chief of staff, Eisenhower named the brilliant, hard-working Bedell Smith. Since 1942, the two had become inseparable partners. Their relationship had been fused into so much an entity of command that it was difficult to tell where Ike left off and where Bedell Smith began. In contrast to the suave and amiable Eisenhower, Smith could be blunt and curt. Yet like his chief, he was articulate and expressive, sophisticated, and discreet during those diplomatic crises that occasionally erupted at SHAEF. "Bedell, tell them to go to hell," Eisenhower once said in referring to a mission to SHAEF, "but put it so they won't be offended."

**Gen. Dwight Eisenhower:** Prior to leaving my Headquarters in North Africa I was able early in December 1943 to see a copy of the Outline Plan of OVER-LORD and to discuss it with Field Marshal—then General—Sir Bernard L. Montgomery, who was to command 21 Army Group, and with my Chief of Staff Lieut. Gen. (then Maj. Gen.) Walter B. Smith. I instructed them to consider the plan in detail upon their arrival in England because, while agreeing with the broad scope of the operation and the selection of the assault area, I nevertheless felt that the initial assaulting force were being planned in insufficient strength and committed on too narrow a front.

**Lt. Gen. Walter Bedell "Beetle" Smith:** It was not until Christmas Eve, 1943, that President Roosevelt announced in the course of a radio fireside talk that General Eisenhower was to be Supreme Commander, Allied Expeditionary Force, when we struck at Fortress Europa. It followed that the designation of his headquarters would be Supreme Headquarters, Allied Expeditionary Force, and from the initials of these words the accepted abbreviation of SHAEF came into existence.

**Lt. Gen. Sir Frederick Morgan:** On January 17, 1944, General Eisenhower took command.

*"A majestic, inevitable, but terrible task"*

# The Start of SHAEF

SHAEF's leadership in early 1944: *Front row (left to right)*: Sir Arthur W. Tedder;
Gen. Dwight Eisenhower; Lt. Gen. Bernard Montgomery.
*Back row (left to right)*: Lt. Gen. Omar Bradley; Adm. Sir Bertram H. Ramsay;
Air Chief Marshal Sir Trafford Leigh-Mallory; and Lt. Gen. Walter Bedell Smith

*With a Supreme Commander chosen, the rest of the invasion leadership fell into place. Sir Arthur Tedder would serve as deputy commander under Eisenhower, and then all three of the main service commanders were to be British as well: Gen. Bernard L. Montgomery would oversee the armies involved, which would be known as 21 Army Group; Adm. Bertram Ramsay would lead the naval side, known as the Allied Naval Expeditionary Force, and Air Chief Marshal Trafford Leigh–Mallory would lead the air forces.*

*Under them would serve four primary combat commanders: Lt. Gen. Omar Bradley led the US First Army, and Lt. Gen. Miles Dempsey headed the British Second Army, including the Canadian 3rd Division; the American naval forces, known as the Western Task Force, would be commanded by Rear Adm. Alan Kirk, while the British Eastern Task Force would be led by Adm. Philip Vian. As 1944 began, the Allies found themselves just months away from the target invasion date even as they formed their leadership team. In their first meetings, they began to debate and digest the outline of the plan for Operation OVERLORD and were dismayed by what they found.*

**Gen. Lord Hastings Ismay, chief military adviser to Winston Churchill:** 1944 will always live in my memory as the year of destiny. Our fate, nay the fate of the whole free world, depended upon the outcome of OVERLORD, and for the first six months of the year, thoughts of that supreme adventure dominated all our minds. Momentous events, such as the landing at Anzio, the prolonged and bitter fighting for Cassino, and the stupendous, and at times immensely costly, bombing of Germany, were dwarfed by comparison.

**Gen. Bernard L. Montgomery, commander, Allied ground forces (21 Army Group):** I had been appointed to act as Land C-in-C for a combined operation of greater magnitude than had ever been attempted in the whole history of warfare. The greater portion of the troops and of the subordinate headquarters, though well trained, lacked battle experience. It was vital to inject new blood, and to bring in more senior staff officers with battle experience.

**Winston Churchill, Prime Minister of the United Kingdom:** I was gratified and also relieved to find that Montgomery was delighted and eager for what I had always regarded as a majestic, inevitable, but terrible task.

**Lt. Gen. Omar Bradley, commander, First Army:** Psychologically the choice of Montgomery as British commander for the OVERLORD assault came as a stimulant to us all. For the thin, bony, ascetic face that stared from an unmilitary turtle-neck sweater had, in little over a year, become a symbol of victory in the eyes of the Allied world. Nothing becomes a general more than success in battle, and Montgomery wore success with such chipper faith in the arms of Britain that he was cherished by a British people wearied of valorous setbacks.

**Gen. Bernard L. Montgomery:** General Eisenhower had placed me in command of all the land forces for the assault. For this we had two armies—the Second British Army under [Miles] Dempsey and the First American Army under Bradley.

**Lt. Gen. Omar Bradley:** The news that I was to command this Army Group came to me suddenly and indirectly: I read it in a morning paper. On January 18 as I turned through the lobby of the Dorchester Hotel bound for breakfast at the mess across the street, I stopped to pick up a copy of the four-page Daily Express. The clerk at the counter grinned. "This won't be news to you, sir," he said—and pointed to a story in which Eisenhower had announced that "51-year-old Lieut.-General Omar Nelson Bradley, who led the U.S. Second Corps in Tunisia and the invasion of Sicily, is to be the American Army's 'General Montgomery' in the western invasion of Europe"—but it was.

*Settling into their new SHAEF headquarters in London, the invasion's newly appointed generals, field marshals, and admirals took charge, debating whether the original plans laid out by General Morgan's COSSAC, much of which were already under way logistically, would actually lead to a victory in Europe.*

**Lt. Gen. Walter Bedell "Beetle" Smith, Chief of Staff, SHAEF:** I flew to England in early January. General Morgan showed me the OVERLORD preparations and my first reaction was one of absolute astonishment.

**Gen. Dwight Eisenhower, Supreme Allied Commander, SHAEF:** The directive from the Combined Chiefs of Staff was very simple, merely instructing us to land on the coast of France and thereafter to destroy the German ground forces. Its significant paragraph read, "You will enter the continent of Europe and, in conjunction with the other Allied Nations, undertake operations aimed at the heart of Germany and the destruction of her Armed Forces."

**Lt. Gen. Omar Bradley:** COSSAC had proposed that we embark on a shoestring in the most decisive assault of the war.

**Brig. Gen. James M. Gavin, assistant division commander, 82nd Airborne:** It was a grossly inadequate force for the task and undoubtedly would have been an oversize Dieppe.

**Gen. Bernard L. Montgomery:** The more I examined the proposed tactical plan, based on Morgan's outline plan, the more I disliked it. The front of the assault was too narrow; only one Corps HQ was being used to control the whole front, and the area of the landing would soon become very congested.

**Gen. Dwight Eisenhower:** I felt that a three-division assault was in insufficient strength, and that to attain success in this critical operation, a minimum of five divisions should assault in the initial wave. Field Marshal Montgomery was in emphatic agreement with me on this matter, as were also Admiral Ramsay and Air Chief Marshal Leigh-Mallory, even though a larger assault force raised great new problems from both the naval and air points of view.

**Gen. Lord Hastings Ismay:** General Montgomery arrived in England early in January. He at once insisted that a bridge-head of adequate depth and strength could not be built up sufficiently quickly, unless the frontage of the attack was doubled from twenty-five to fifty miles.

**Lt. Gen. Omar Bradley:** By the time Eisenhower arrived in England, Montgomery was waiting with his recommendations that the OVERLORD plan be strengthened and widened to include the Cotentin coast.

**Lt. Gen. Walter Bedell "Beetle" Smith:** We set up a conference for January 21.

**Lt. Gen. Omar Bradley:** In addition to Tedder, Montgomery, Smith, and myself, the commanders included Leigh-Mallory for the Allied Air Forces and Ramsay for the navy. Tooey Spaatz also attended, although as chief of the Strategic Air Forces he did not yet come under Ike's SHAEF command.

**Rear Adm. Alan G. Kirk, commander, Western Naval Task Force:** At this stage it was not contemplated that the American navy should do very much in the invasion of Normandy. The plan called for three British landings on the west of the Seine River—actually the Orne that flows into the sea at Ouistreham. Then we would have just one landing, what later became Omaha Beach.

**Maj. John Dalgleish, Planning Staff, Royal Army Service Corps:** The first limiting factor was the availability of shipping. In fact, shipping was the predominant factor from the inception of the outline plan to D-Day and after.

**Lt. Gen. Omar Bradley:** As had happened in every other amphibious operation of the war, Morgan was hamstrung from the outset by a shortage in landing craft. Lift for five divisions was all that could be spared from world-wide allocations of landing craft. As late as 1944 landing-craft production lagged far behind our needs.

**Maj. Gen. Francis "Freddie" de Guingand, Chief of Staff, General Montgomery:** I put it this way in defense of the COSSAC planners—who would also have liked these modifications—but they were having to plan on certain given assets, and such changes would mean an additional allotment of landing craft, ships and aircraft. It required the appointment of a Commander who could bang the table and say what he wanted.

**Lt. Gen. Walter Bedell "Beetle" Smith:** Eisenhower was resigned to the fact that the shortage of landing craft, which had plagued him so gravely during the Salerno landings, would never permit an assault with twelve divisions. "But I must have at least five," he insisted. "Five divisions in the first assault and two to follow up."

**Gen. Dwight Eisenhower:** In addition to increasing the assault force from three to five divisions, I felt that the beach area to be attacked should be on a wider front than that originally envisaged. Particularly, it was considered that an attack directly against the Cotentin Peninsula should be included in the plan, with a view to the speedy conquest of Cherbourg. In the event that our troops were able to attain a high degree of surprise in the attack, they would be in a better position to overwhelm the strung-out defenses before the enemy could regroup or mass for a counterattack. Conversely, in the event of strong resistance, we would be more advantageously situated, on a wider front and in greater force, to find "soft spots" in the defense.

**Lt. Gen. Omar Bradley:** In COSSAC's plan, the nearest port of Cherbourg lay dangerously distant from the beachhead. The tentative point for attack had been located on a 25-mile stretch of the shingled Normandy beach, almost midway between Le Havre and Cherbourg.

**Gen. Dwight Eisenhower:** We decided to extend this area eastward to include the Ouistreham beaches, feeling that this would facilitate the seizure of the important focal point of Caen and the vital airfields in the vicinity. Westward, we decided that the assault front should be widened to include the Varreville beaches on the eastern side of the Cotentin Peninsula itself. A strong foothold on the peninsula and a rapid operation to cut its neck would greatly speed up the capture of the port of Cherbourg.

**Lt. Gen. Walter Bedell "Beetle" Smith:** The Normandy beaches had just enough capacity to allow an increase in the assaulting force to five divisions, provided we were prepared to accept some added difficulties.

**Gen. Dwight Eisenhower:** The only available beach on the Cotentin Peninsula [what would come to be known as Utah Beach] was a miserable one. Just back of it was a wide lagoon, passable only on a few narrow causeways that led from the beaches to the interior of the peninsula. If the exits of these causeways should be held by the enemy our landing troops would be caught in a trap and eventually slaughtered by artillery and other fire to which they would be able to make little reply. To prevent this, we planned to drop two divisions of American paratroopers inland from this beach, with their primary mission to seize and hold the exits of the vital causeways.

**Lt. Gen. Omar Bradley:** I had emphasized both to Montgomery and Smith the necessity for an airborne drop behind that beach. For while Utah was broad and flat and therefore suitable for seaborne assault, its exits were limited to several narrow causeways traversing a flooded marshland. As long as the enemy held those causeways he could pin us to Utah Beach.

**Gen. Dwight Eisenhower:** It was [Air Chief Marshal Leigh-Mallory's] feeling, both then and subsequently, that the employment of airborne divisions against the South Cotentin would result in landing losses to aircraft and personnel as high as 75 percent to 80 percent. In the face of this estimate, however, I was still convinced of the absolute necessity of quickly overrunning the peninsula and attaining the port of Cherbourg, vital to the support and maintenance of our land forces.*

**Gen. Lord Hastings Ismay:** Eisenhower estimated that the revised plan required at least another thousand landing-craft, over and above the three thousand odd originally contemplated—double the number of mine-sweepers, and an increase of almost fifty per cent in the number of ships of war which would be necessary for escorts and bombardment. He proposed that these requirements should be met by postponing OVERLORD from early May to early June, reducing the landing in the South of France (ANVIL) to a threat, and drawing upon the United States Navy for the additional ships of war.

**Gen. Dwight Eisenhower:** My planners had advised me that a month's additional production of assault craft in both Great Britain and the United States would go far toward supplying the deficiency foreseen for the earlier date.

**Maj. Gen. Francis "Freddie" de Guingand:** Eventually on February 1st it was agreed by the Combined Chiefs of Staffs and the British and American Governments, that D-Day should be put back until June 1st or thereabouts.

---

* Not everyone was impressed with Eisenhower in these initial meetings: The head of the British military, Field Marshal Lord Alan Brooke, spent much of the spring writing caustic notes about Ike in his private diary—but then again, as a typical entry, this from January 24, 1944, shows, Brooke didn't seem to be impressed by most people: "Left home 8 am. Had a long [meeting] at which Eisenhower turned up to discuss his paper proposing increase of cross Channel operation at expense of Southern France operation. I entirely agree with the proposal but it is certainly not his idea, and is one of Monty's. Eisenhower has got absolutely no strategical outlook and is really totally unfit for the post he holds from an operational point of view. He makes up, however, by the way he works for good cooperation between allies. After lunch Monty came to see me and I had to tell him off for falling foul of both the King and the S of S in a very short time. He took it well, as usual.

Long Cabinet from 6 to 8.15 pm with Winston in great form. He was discussing Stalin's latest iniquities in allowing Pravda to publish the bogus information that England was negotiating with Germany about a peace. He said: 'Trying to maintain good relations with a communist is like wooing a crocodile, you do not know whether to tickle it under the chin or to beat it on the head. When it opens its mouth you cannot tell whether it is trying to smile, or preparing to eat you up.' After dinner another meeting from 10 to 12 midnight, to discuss artificial harbours for the invasion. Here again he was in very good form."

**Gen. Dwight Eisenhower:** We indicated that the exact date of the assault should be left open and subject to weather conditions prevailing during the first week of June.

**Maj. Gen. Francis "Freddie" de Guingand:** There was, of course, a lot of detail work still to be done, but from that moment all the staffs knew what was wanted and could get to work in earnest.

*"Zig-zagging all over the place"*

# Crossing the Pond

By the start of 1944, US troops were arriving in
England at the rate of 5,000 per day, crossing the Atlantic
in fast ocean liners or large, slow convoys.

*The buildup of US military personnel in Great Britain was called Operation*
*BOLERO and began, officially, in May 1942—even before there was a plan for an*
*invasion of the continent. The buildup accelerated, though, as the huge logistical*
*needs of COSSAC and SHAEF's plans materialized over the course of 1943 and*
*early 1944. The ever-growing stream of personnel and matériel, the vast majority*

*of which would come on fast-moving troopships or large, slow convoys, grew, as Winston Churchill called it, "in the first year to a trickle, in the second to a river, in the third to a flood." Eventually, millions of men and women would be brought to the UK in the name of the war effort.*

*Shipping literal armies across the ocean required dodging and, ultimately, defeating the fleets of German U-boats who hoped to starve England of necessary resources through a naval blockade. The titanic fight known as the Battle of the Atlantic—the longest fight of World War II—took the lives of more than 72,000 sailors and resulted in thousands of Allied merchant ships and warships being sunk. As technology and tactics advanced—most notably, the Allies succeeded in breaking the German military's Enigma code system, allowing them to eavesdrop on U-boat deployments, and early iterations of radar allowed for better targeting at sea—the Allies broke the stranglehold on Europe imposed by marauding U-boats and devastated nearly three-quarters of the German submarine fleet, sinking nearly 800.*

*In the face of the danger, a trio of Cunard Line ships,* Queen Mary, Queen Elizabeth, *and* Aquitania, *were reactivated for transport. The* Queen Mary, *designed to carry 2,000 passengers in the height of 1930s luxury, would regularly ferry as many as 15,000 troops at a time—racing across the Atlantic at speeds of 30 knots to outrun any U-boats, as did the* Queen Elizabeth. *The* Aquitania *carried about 8,000 men per crossing.*

*Among the first wave of US troops to cross to England was the 29th Infantry Division, which would end up spending nearly two years waiting in England for the invasion. Their trip across the Atlantic in September 1942, at the height of the Battle of the Atlantic, would end up being one of the most dramatic—and tragic—of any US troop crossing.*

**Lt. Alister Satchell, cipher officer, RMS *Aquitania*, Royal Australian Navy Volunteer Reserve:** The Port of New York, which embarked over three and a quarter million troops between 1942 and 1945, moved almost double the numbers handled by the second busiest port, San Francisco. The Army established holding camps known as "Port Staging Areas" near the major ports of embarkation, and New York was served principally by Camp Shanks in the state of New York and Camp Kilmer in New Jersey. Each of these staging areas had a holding capacity of between 25,000 and 30,000 men, and from mid-1943 until 1945, they operated at or close to these limits.

**Sgt. Warner "Buster" Hamlett, Company F, 116th Infantry Regiment, 29th Division:** In September of 1942, the 29th Division set sail from Camp Kilmer, New Jersey, on the *Queen Mary*, headed for England. The *Queen Elizabeth* also carried members of the 29th Division.

**Pfc. Felix Branham, Company K, 116th Infantry Regiment, 29th Division:** We had to remain below deck, and everybody was in turmoil. First of all, it was pouring down raining when we got aboard the ship, and the fellows were already homesick—knowing that we were bound for a foreign shore, how long we would be gone, or if we would ever come back, I'm sure was going through some of their minds. But we were all eager, adventurous. We were young fellows. We wanted to see the world at any cost.

**Seaman Alfred Johnson, crewman, RMS *Queen Mary*, Merchant Navy:** The *Queen Mary* was carrying about 15,000 American troops to join the Allied Forces. She was known as a "hornets nest" in the war as there were lots of nationalities on the ship.

**Pfc. Felix Branham:** I had never seen the ocean until I went aboard the *Queen Mary*, like a lot of us had. I was a small town boy.

**Sgt. Roy Stevens, Company A, 116th Infantry Regiment, 29th Division:** We were berthed close to the privates so we could keep an eye on them. You knew where they were and they knew where you were. For most of those boys, it must have been almost like being on a trip with Mom and Dad.

**Pfc. Felix Branham:** We were fed two meals a day, which consisted of corned beef, some powdered eggs occasionally. We would have pickles and mustard and mackerel, and golly, we were so hungry, because the food was just terrible. Later at night, we were down below in our hammocks, in our quarters, hardly room to turn around in, or anything like that. These British soldiers would come around and sell us sandwiches or corned beef, or whatever, for about 35 or 40 cents—35 and 40 cents back in 1942 was a lot of money.

**Pvt. John Barnes, Company A, 116th Infantry Regiment, 29th Division:** Somewhere in the middle of the Atlantic Ocean, I celebrated my nineteenth birthday. Maybe "celebrated" is not the correct word—"passed" is more like it. It was a gray day, and we made an uneventful crossing.

*As the* Queen Mary *entered the Irish Sea on October 2, 1942, five British destroyers and a cruiser, the HMS* Curacoa, *met the troop liner to provide an escort and protection as it approached the English coast, where U-boats sallied from their Brittany port of Brest often lurked, waiting for convoys to attack. The* Queen Mary, *however, was still traveling at 26.5 knots, 1.5 knots faster than its new escorts.*

**Signal message from HMS *Curacoa* to *Queen Mary*, 12:30 p.m.:** I AM DOING MY BEST SPEED 25 KNOTS ON COURSE 108. WHEN YOU ARE AHEAD I WILL EDGE ASTERN OF YOU.

**Seaman Alfred Johnson:** A cruiser called HMS *Curacoa* met us 200 miles off the coast to escort us into Greenock. I could see her clearly as I was on the aft [deck].

**Lt. Patrick Holmes, air defense officer, HMS *Curacoa*:** It was thrilling to watch the "grey ghost," as the *Queen Mary* was nicknamed because of her wartime camouflage. She gained on us slowly, sometimes over a mile-and-a-half away on our port quarter, and at other times more or less dead astern on the starboard leg of her zigzag. There is no finer sight in the world than a great passenger ship at full speed in a heavy sea, if the passengers were close-packed American troops—over ten thousand of them.

**Seaman Alfred Johnson:** We could see our escort zig-zagging in front of us—it was common for the ships and cruisers to zig-zag to confuse the U-boats. In this particular case however the escort was very, very close to us.

**Lt. Patrick Holmes:** By 2 p.m. [the *Queen Mary*] was nearly level with us about a mile away on our port side and steaming parallel with us. Then she turned slowly towards us and that turn of 25 degrees was at first misinterpreted on our bridge as merely a yaw to starboard. We got a magnificent view of her as she approached—her bow wave gleaming in a slant of sunlight, her decks crowded with GIs, wisps of smoke streaming from her three funnels.

**Seaman Alfred Johnson:** I said to my mate, "You know she's zig-zagging all over the place in front of us, I'm sure we're going to hit her."

**Telegraphist Allin Martin, radio operator, HMS *Curacoa*:** The upper bridge speaking tube clanged and my "oppo" [opposite number-partner] indicated that if any camera was to hand a particularly good view of the *Queen Mary* was available. Unclipping the bulkhead door, I stepped outside, where, to my horror, I saw the enormous bulk of the *Queen Mary* bearing down on our port quarter at about fifty yards range.

**Lt. Patrick Holmes:** Suddenly my admiration turned to fear, and looking over my right shoulder down to our bridge I saw the captain take over the conning of the ship. I saw him speak down the voicepipe to the helmsman below, look back at the *Queen Mary* and speak again. By now the sharp bows of the *Queen* were heading directly at us.

**Telegraphist Allin Martin:** Her huge white bow wave seemed as tall as a house and it seemed inevitable that we were within seconds of being torn apart. I dived for my lifebelt.

**Lt. Patrick Holmes:** Two of the lookouts disappeared over our starboard side as we were knocked over 70 degrees or more. The noise of escaping steam from severed steam pipes was deafening.

**Seaman Alfred Johnson:** The *Queen Mary* sliced the cruiser in two like a piece of butter, straight through the six-inch armoured plating.

**Sgt. Roy Stevens:** The boat jarred. It was very quick. Soon, everybody was running upstairs to see what had happened.

**Sgt. Philip Levin:** I was in the office on the main deck at the time and felt only the slightest rattle and vibration. Actually it seemed quite normal. But word of the collision spread quickly like wildfire through the ship. I raced to the open upper decks and looked aft to see the two halves of the *Curacoa* drifting in our wake and then rather quickly sinking.

**A. W. Masson, crewman, *Queen Mary*, writing in his diary:** We rushed out on deck, and I was just in time to see the cruiser's quarterdeck and after turret passing down our starboard side. It was covered in oil and there was no one to be seen. I rushed aft and saw both parts of the cruiser, her stern sticking up, looking for all the world like the *Indefatigable* at Jutland! The forepart of the ship was at a distance to the right. The cruiser had been rammed just aft of the after funnel. It was covered in a heavy pall of smoke and steam, then slowly it sank by the bows, then it reared its bow perpendicular—and with a little water foaming round her, she quickly sank.

**Sgt. Philip Levin:** The *Mary* simply continued, uninterrupted and at relatively high speed.

**Sgt. John Robert "Bob" Slaughter, Company D, 116th Infantry Regiment, 29th Division:** My first thought was that we had been torpedoed, I saw the *Curacoa's* stern going down one side of the *Mary*, and the bow down the other—cut right in two. The *Curacoa's* crow's nest was parallel to the water, and there was a sailor in there still doing semaphore signals. His eyes looked enormous—he was so frightened. All we could do was throw life-jackets. I remember thinking: "God, here we are, haven't even got overseas, and we've killed all these British sailors."

**Staff Capt. Harry Grattidge, crewman, *Queen Mary*:** I was sick at what we had done, yet I marveled, too, at the strange and terrible impregnability of the *Queen Mary*.

**Teletype to Admiralty, from the *Queen Mary*, 2:20 p.m.:** HMS Curacoa RAMMED AND SUNK BY Queen Mary IN POSITION 55.50N 08.38W Queen Mary DAMAGED FORWARD. SPEED TEN KNOTS.

*The British cruiser sank in just 12 minutes, disappearing into the North Atlantic at 2:24 p.m.; just about a hundred of the crew survived, while 337 officers and crew were killed in the accident, which was kept secret until the end of the war.*

\*                    \*                    \*

*In the months and years that followed, hundreds of thousands of American and Canadian servicemen and -women, from all branches of the military, followed to the British Isles in the wake of the 29th Division, many on the Cunard liners. From September 1943 through June 1944, an average of 5,000 US troops would arrive every single day for eight months—as did about three and a half tons of supplies for every one of those invasion troops. But preparing to ferry those massive invasion forces from England to France also required assembling an equally massive 7,000-ship armada in the ports of England, Wales, Scotland, and Northern Ireland. Landing craft of all sizes were constructed by US shipyards up and down the East Coast—and even in river ports far inland. These craft, built to support not just the fight in the Mediterranean and the looming cross-Channel invasion but also the US Marines' fight in the Pacific, consumed vast quantities of steel and manufacturing capability; from August 1943 to May 1944, US factories churned out more than 1,500 landing craft per month, so rapid and in such large numbers that they were given only numbers, not names. Many of these craft were built by the women now populating US factories; at the Richmond Shipyards in California, about a third of its 90,000-strong workforce were women.*

*The craft were then turned over to equally hurriedly assembled Navy and Coast Guard personnel, many of whom had minimal training before embarking on their first journeys. The largest landing craft, known as Landing Ship Tanks, had crews of 9 officers and 110 enlisted sailors.*

**Ens. Walter Trombold, executive officer, USS *LST-55*:** My own particular ship, the *LST-55*—she didn't even have a name—can serve as an example of how the navy geared up to fight that war. She was built inland—in Pittsburgh, Pennsylvania, of all places. Her crewmen, few of whom had been in the service before the war started, came from the cities, towns, and farms of America. They went back to those places when their service was done. The entire commissioned life of the ship encompassed less than two years.

**Seaman James T. Fudge, USS *LST-54*:** I was sent to a sonar school in Key West, Florida, but I was only there a short length of time when they realized that they had to fill these ships that were going to Europe for the invasion. We were all placed in the amphibious navy, most of us on LSTs. I had never been on a ship before, and I immediately got a feeling of claustrophobia—taken below and being shown my bunk—but I soon discovered that I adapted to it.

**Lt. Anthony Drexel Duke, commander, USS *LST-530*:** We were trained in the Chesapeake Bay area and went on to the Great Lakes Naval Training Station on Lake Michigan for anti-aircraft instruction and training. From there we all got on the train and went down to Jeffersonville, Indiana. We arrived on a rainy day to find USS *LST 530* about 98 percent finished. Within [a few] more days, we found ourselves cruising down the Mississippi on the way to New Orleans. In New Orleans, after getting all our guns put aboard and generally straightening out our mess on the ship and getting her ready for inspection, a four-striper [Navy captain] came aboard with a band, and we were commissioned and sent to sea the next day. I will never forget going out the mouth of the Mississippi River into the Gulf and heading for Florida, around Florida and going north.

**Howard Buhl, motor machinist's mate, USS *LST-494*:** Most of the crew had never seen a ship or the ocean until put on the LST. The officers had college degrees or credits but knew little of ships. Our first executive officer was a schoolteacher who knew nothing. We had no one on the ship who knew how to operate a sextant, and almost never found Panama City, Florida. We just ran up and down the coast of Florida until it was sighted. We were as green as grass and so were the other ships.

**Seaman James T. Fudge:** We went over on the North Atlantic and that was an experience never to be forgotten. It was a convoy of perhaps 30. We did have a fairly good escort. We had destroyer escorts, mostly American destroyer escorts. It was a slow convoy, certainly no more than 8 or 9 knots. Our whole flotilla, 11 ships, were U.S. Navy LSTs, the rest were merchant [ships]. The North Atlantic, anyone who goes over in February as we did, it is just rougher than the dickens. The LSTs would go up in the air and would come back with their flat bottom, dig the nose of the ship in the sea and come up at the same time the screws would come out of the water kicking.

**Lt. Anthony Drexel Duke:** I will never forget the feeling I had when the ocean swells got under that ship and looked around and realized that the only other person who had ever been on anything bigger than a rowboat than myself was my engineering officer.

*"As inexhaustible as England's supply of Brussels sprouts"*

# The American Invasion

The presence of so many US troops, including 130,000
Black soldiers, transformed life in England.

*After their Atlantic crossings, sea-worn soldiers arrived in British ports, ready
to begin their training and contributions to the Allied cause. The sudden population growth stretched Great Britain's resources and space to the limits, as troops
occupied over 100,000 buildings across the country in what totaled more than
1,100 new military outposts, bases, depots, and training grounds, and clogged the
roads with more than 100,000 vehicles. By the time of the invasion in June 1944,
US troop levels in the UK peaked at some 20 Army divisions totaling roughly
1,650,000 personnel—about 40 percent combat troops, 30 percent services and
support personnel, and about a quarter air forces. In the spring of 1944, roughly*

*10 percent of the British adult male population, between the ages of 18 and 40, were Americans—a number that included about 130,000 Black troops, a notable fascination in the UK, a country that had fewer than 8,000 Black residents among its population of 47 million. Housing, training, feeding, and otherwise taking care of such a giant force stretched the UK to its limits, and included the construction of temporary camps across tens of thousands of acres. Another 100,000 US troops were billeted in private English homes.*

*The demographic impact, however, was nothing compared to the mental and emotional exhaustion that Great Britain faced through the war, and for many of the arriving American personnel, their first sights and experiences in the United Kingdom were startling, as they confronted up close a battle-weary country and population.*

**A Short Guide to Great Britain, booklet, published by the War and Navy Departments:** At home in America you were in a country at war. Since your ship left port, however, you have been in a war zone. You will find that all Britain is a war zone and has been since September 1939. All this has meant great changes in the British way of life.

**Edward T. Duffy, fire controlman, 2nd class, USS *Shubrick* (DD-639):** They were badly bombed out. As you looked down a street, everything looked normal but only the front facade of the rows of buildings were standing. As we walked down a street and looked at each building there was nothing there but the front walls. Through each opening which was once a window or a door we could see only daylight and a pile of rubble. It was very saddening to see how much the destruction of war had been visited upon these people.

**Seaman First Class Martin Fred Gutekunst, signalman, 2nd Beach Battalion, Naval Construction Battalions (SeaBees):** We reached Liverpool, England, January 17. We boarded a train and traveled to Salcombe, England. We arrived January 19 late at night, thereby getting indoctrinated into the complete blackouts.

**S.Sgt. Robert Arbib, Jr., 820th Engineer Aviation Battalion, 926th Engineer Aviation Regiment:** We could see nothing, not even a single light. This was our first experience with the blackout. We marveled at its completeness.

**Pvt. Norman Longmate, Company F, 3rd Sussex Battalion, Home Guard, United Kingdom:** It is hard for anyone who did not experience the total darkness of these wartime nights to comprehend the sense of isolation, verging on panic, that could so easily descend if one missed one's way. One could often hear solitary male figures swearing aloud in the darkness as they groped for some clue of their whereabouts, while many women admit to being reduced to tears. The black-out became the classic excuse for any minor injury.

**Sgt. John Robert "Bob" Slaughter, Company D, 116th Infantry Regiment, 29th Division:** It seemed to me the first few months in England the sun seemed to be rationed. Thick fog, a biting wind and cold drizzle were typical weather during November and December. We accepted bland, scanty food; little sleep and rest; and not enough warm clothing.

**Sgt. Allen Huddleston, Company A, 116th Infantry Regiment, 29th Division:** You couldn't stay dry. Water would always seep into everything. You'd lie down on your bed sheet and before long the water would come through. It was horrible.

**Pvt. Maynard Marquis, Company H, 115th Infantry Regiment, 29th Division:** The food was terrible. Black bread with marmalade and coffee every breakfast, cabbage and brussels sprouts once a day.

**Pfc. Felix Branham, Company K, 116th Infantry Regiment, 29th Division:** You'd get half an orange, half a slice of bread. You would get maybe a small ladle of powdered eggs—horrible. If someone has never tasted powdered eggs, you can't imagine how they tasted or what they looked like. We had powdered onions and powdered potatoes. In this day and time we would call them instant onions, instant potatoes, instant eggs, but we called it powdered. It came out of cans, big five-, six-, seven-gallon cans full of powder in granulated form like washing powder or cornmeal. That's the way it looked, only it was colored.

**Edward T. Duffy:** Occasionally we would stop at a neighborhood pub for a glass of beer with the local inhabitants who were warm and friendly. The beer was too. We visited one restaurant for a bite to eat. They only had beans, kidney beans, string beans, etc. which were served cold. Probably straight out of the can.

**S.Sgt. John A. Beck, Sr., Company A, 87th Chemical Mortar Battalion, 4th Division:** The English people were reduced to eating fish and potatoes and we proved to be their benefactors, especially to the children—handing out candy, cookies, and lots of other things to them.

**Lt. Lambton Burn, RNVR, Navy editor, *Parade* magazine:** It was in the long queues of tired housewives that I soon located the real heroines of the war. They looked underfed, overworked, and listless. The housewives, denying themselves for their children, were the only people who were really giving of their unrecompensed all in the national cause.

**Martha Gellhorn, correspondent, writing in *Collier's Weekly*, "English Sunday":** Mrs. Thomas managed very well, because her husband believed she ate a hot meal every noon while he was at the factory. Actually she ate some bread and tea and perhaps a bit of cheese, and that way she could save her rations for the week end when he would be home. Mrs. Johnson only bought cigarettes and bouillon cubes and a jar of jam, and all the women advised about the jam, since it cost coupons. Everyone spoke to Mrs. Johnson's daughter Betty, who was going to have her fourth birthday next week.

After this week, would come another, and then another month, and the long years of war seemed slowly to be ending. The war must be won. No one really thinks of anything else. The war must be won, and then there will again be the lovely, remembered summers with regattas on their river and sun and picnics and visitors come from London to admire their flowers and their enchanting cottages and their beautiful church. The war would be won and then at last the young people would be safe and home again.

*As American, British, Canadian, and other troops filtered into British towns and cities, civilians and servicemembers had no choice but to inevitably interact, either socially or just in passing. In some smaller towns and villages, troops were placed with local families to live, or had to construct their own dwellings, and attended social events.*

**British Army Bureau of Current Affairs Bulletin, No. 22, July 18, 1942, *Meet the Americans*:** The Americans and the British will find plenty to make fun of in each other, plenty to feel superior about. That doesn't matter so long as we also find how much there is to respect in each other. At the moment the soldiers of the two nations are in the position of two people who have just been introduced. It's good enough for a beginning. There's a bit of prejudice on both sides, a colossal ignorance of each other's attitudes and characteristics—but there's also a willingness to get together.

**Barbara Clare (Fauks), civilian, East Acton, United Kingdom:** I remember when the American servicemen showed up. There were also a lot of servicemen from the Allies: Canadians, Australians, New Zealanders, Free French, Polish, Norwegians. It was interesting to get to meet some of them. In fact, there were so many that it's a wonder England didn't sink from the added people.

**Lt. John Mason Brown, aide to Rear Adm. Alan Kirk, USS *Augusta* (CA-31):** Americans in or out of uniform, on every kind of mission, and in every branch of the service must have appeared as inexhaustible to Londoners as England's supply of Brussels sprouts did to Americans.

**Pvt. John Chalk, 1st Battalion, Hampshire Regiment, 231st Infantry Brigade, 50th Northumbrian Division:** The acute shortage of beer was one of the main bugbears. The influx of thousands of servicemen into the south of England was draining the pubs dry and the breweries couldn't cope with the extra demand. Local pubs would only have enough beer for two or three nights a week, and then they would be sold out in one and a half to two hours.

**Lt. John Mason Brown:** We moved into requisitioned buildings in every bruised village, town, or city where our forces were stationed. Where there were no towns, we built them. We built them in the rubble left by air raids or in woods and meadows hitherto unscarred. We built them in the coast towns and in parks far inland. Hut camps mushroomed over England. Our relentless bulldozers broke the ground for them, plowing up dark mud where green turf had flowered for centuries, and overturning old oaks to make way for macadam roads over which our jeeps raced.

**S.Sgt. Robert A. Wilkins, 149th Engineer Combat Battalion, 6th Engineer Special Brigade:** We were taken into the town of Paignton. The authorities would go down the street, and the truck would stop and they'd say, "All right, three of you out here." They'd march you into a house and say to the owner, "These are your American troops. They are going to be staying with you." The home that I went into, the people were named Glover. He was a retired piano dealer from New Zealand and Australia. Our boots were muddy and everything about us, I suspect, was offensive—certainly to Mrs. Glover. She made us remove our boots outside before she would even let us come in the house. We immediately thought that this was going to be a very difficult situation, and we certainly weren't happy with it at all; but after we became acquainted with the Glovers, they treated us like we were their own sons.

**Ens. Edward J. Kelly, commander, USS LCT-200:** Mr. and Mrs. George Odgers, who lived in a little two-room cottage in Polruan, across the harbor from Fowey, Cornwall—as the saying goes, they were as poor as church mice, but they had hearts as big as all outdoors. I first met George when he was working in the little shipyard where our LCT was undergoing some modifications. On behalf of his wife, George invited me to have Sunday dinner with him. I gladly accepted and had a glorious afternoon. Before dinner they had gone out and purchased some Devonshire cream and a "tin" of peaches. Together what a delightful dessert they made! It was only later that I learned that those peaches comprised a six-month ration of can fruit.

**Maj. Ralph Ingersoll, intelligence officer, planning staff, SHAEF:** The real combination was between our young soldiers and the young English girls, particularly among farm and factory workers. This was almost a case of spontaneous social combustion, so satisfactory did each seem to the other.

**Cpl. Peter Masters, No. 3 Troop, 10 Commando, 1st Special Service Brigade:** Once we passed two Yanks in conversation with a little girl, perhaps 2 years old, at a bus stop, and probably that talk went along the lines of "Any gum, chum?" which British children had learned to say to get a reward of chewing gum. But as we marched past, a disgusted voice at the back of our lot growled at the Americans, "At least you could let them grow up!"

**Winnifred Pine, Wren, Royal Navy:** Our Wrenney was on a hill overlooking the River Dart, and each morning we would wake up to the sound of Glenn Miller or the Andrews Sisters coming through their loudhailer system. They were always curious to meet us, as we were probably the first Englishwomen they had met.

**T/4 Dwayne Burns, radioman, 508th Parachute Infantry Regiment, 82nd Airborne:** We never got tired of riding the top of the double decker busses. The townspeople were very friendly and receptive to the Americans, especially the girls. Although we didn't speak exactly the same English, we did make out extremely well. Some of those cute little accents would drive you nuts. Some made friendships that would last a lifetime. Others would find the girl of their dreams and marry.

**Barbara Clare (Fauks):** Some of the English—particularly the servicemen—didn't like the Americans because we British girls were so interested in being with them. You know, you'd walk down the street, and the Americans would say, "Hi, Honey." They were really friendly, really nice guys, and the Englishmen were much more reserved. And, the Americans certainly had more money to spend than the British soldiers.

**Signalman Paul S. Fauks, Company B, 7th Beach Battalion, Navy:** On February 18 I caught a train and went up to London. All over London the British had their ack-ack guns, so we heard an awful lot of gunfire. At one point a group of us got really frightened, so we went into a pub. That was the only place we could really get into. While we were in there, we heard knocking sounds, so we got under tables. And we thought, "Well, they'll let these people in. There's somebody knocking to get in here." Some guy said, "No, that's not it. That's shrapnel hitting up against the building." When we left there we got down into the subway system, which was the most secure bomb shelter. That's where everybody went if he could.

**Forrest Pogue, combat historian, V Corps:** Although the great raids by planes had come to an end, a few aircraft still came each evening to keep alive the threat of death, and some frightened souls still sought the refuge of the friendly Tube. Beds were still set up, in tiers along the platforms, and individuals were allowed to register for the same place each night.

**Signalman Paul S. Fauks:** While I was passing the time down there, I struck up a conversation with a British girl named Barbara Clare, who was then sixteen years old.

**Barbara Clare (Fauks):** That's where I met Paul. He had on his little sailor hat and his peacoat. He was with a friend, and I was with a girlfriend. The four of us started talking. I remember that Paul was really awfully nice—he still is. We went to Covent Garden together that night, and then he came out to our house to see me the next day.

**Signalman Paul S. Fauks:** We talked that night, and I said, "Well, I'd like to come out to your home and visit you and your family tomorrow." So she gave me directions on how to get there on the subways. It was another several weeks between then and when we went over to France, so I saw her one more time. We went out to lunch, probably went to a dance that night.

**Barbara Clare (Fauks):** Then he had to go back to his camp at Salcombe, and I didn't see him for a while. After all the worries about our family members being hit by bombs, now I was concerned about his safety as well when he went off for the invasion of France. I kept a close watch on the news reports during that period. As it happened, Paul and I were together only three times that year before he went back to the United States.

**Signalman Paul S. Fauks:** I met my future wife during an air raid by German bombers.

*Despite the general positivity of the American-English relationship, there was one cultural difference that became uncomfortably clear: the treatment of people of color. While racism and prejudice were commonplace in the United States— and in the United States armed forces, in particular—there was less perceived inequity from the English, who largely interacted with Black soldiers as they would anyone else. This was shocking to the Americans, both Black and white, who had been living under Jim Crow laws for decades and had been largely segregated within military ranks. (Until 1940, "Black soldiers had been largely purged from the military during the mass downsizing that followed the end of the Great War," writes historian Linda Hervieux, and in 1940 there were just five Black officers in the entire military.) Over the years ahead, though, more than a million Black personnel would serve across and throughout the military—from December 1942 through D-Day, the number of nonwhite GIs in Britain grew from 7,000 to 130,000.*

**Pfc. Timuel D. Black, 308th Quartermaster Battalion, 1st Division:** Because the people had never seen any Blacks, they thought that we had just stayed out in the sun. Some of them had been informed by the white soldiers that we were like dogs and had tails—that we were not quite human—and they were curious about that.

**Gen. Dwight Eisenhower, letter, September 1942:** Here we have a very thickly populated country that is devoid of racial consciousness. They know nothing at all about the conventions and habits of polite society that have been developed in the US in order to preserve a segregation in social activity without making the matter one of official or public notice. To most English people, including the village girls—even those of perfectly fine character—the negro soldier is just another man, rather fascinating because he is unique in their experience, a jolly good fellow and with money to spend.

**Ollie Stewart, correspondent, *Afro-American* newspaper:** The English people show our lads every possible courtesy and some of them, accustomed to ill will, harsh words, and artificial barriers, seem slightly bewildered. They never had a chance to leave their Southern homes before, and therefore never realized there was a part of the world which was willing to forget a man's color and welcome him as brother.

**Bill Coughlan, British evacuee, Cornwall:** I had the opportunity to hear all the Black choirs from their segregated units. The Cornishmen sang in a stately, serious, hymn-like way but, in complete contrast, the Black Americans had all the rhythms of Scott Joplin, George Gershwin, and the Jazz age. The movements of their bodies in time with their voices turned the Methodist chapels where they performed from sedate places of nonconformity into places of Swing. Cornwall being a musical place, the Black GIs were not only praised for their performances but were offered the food special to Cornwall. We noticed their good manners, and I know now that the surprise on their faces confirmed that they did not expect white people to treat them as equals and brothers.

**Capt. Charles A. Leslie:** We were told by the chaplain that there was no distinction made as to color in the UK and that we would see some negroes with beautiful white girls, and they always get the best, and that he personally did not like it.

**Gen. Dwight Eisenhower:** The small-town British girl would go to a movie or a dance with a negro quite as readily as she would with anyone else, a practice that our white soldiers could not understand.

**S.Sgt. Waverly B. Woodson, Jr., combat medic, 320th Barrage Balloon Battalion:** As I danced with the postmistress, she asked me why our officers were saying such bad things about us. She couldn't understand it.

**Seaman First Class Martin Fred Gutekunst:** Entertainment was provided on a few occasions by the USO. The Navy provided dances also. At that time, there was no integration, so to avoid a lot of confrontation, the Navy declared Black nights and white nights. Neither color could attend the other's functions.

**Letter from the UK Home Office to all Chief Constables, September 4, 1942:** It is not the policy of His Majesty's Government that any discrimination as regards the treatment of coloured troops should be made by the British authorities. The Secretary of State, therefore, would be glad if you would be good enough to take steps to ensure that the police do not make any approach to the proprietors of public houses, restaurants, cinemas or other places of entertainment with a view to discriminating against coloured troops.

**Gen. Dwight Eisenhower:** Brawls often resulted and our white soldiers were further bewildered when they found that the British press took a firm stand on the side of the negro.

**S.Sgt. Waverly B. Woodson, Jr.:** Whites would come into a pub where we were sitting and they would ask the landlord, "Why do you let these people in?"

**Pvt. John Barnes, Company A, 116th Infantry Regiment, 29th Division:** The nearby village of Ivy Bridge was "off limits" to us for passes since there had been too many fights in the pubs with locals or Black American troops and the white boys.

**Pvt. Maynard Marquis, Company H, 115th Infantry Regiment, 29th Division:** There was a Black quartermaster corps stationed on the other side of town. Fights at night in town was common. A white soldier was shot by a Black one night. The infantrymen immediately went to camp and set up mortars to bomb the other camp. They were discovered and prevented from carrying out these plans. From then on, we had certain nights in town and the quartermaster had the other nights. This was not an uncommon arrangement in many towns.

**Anonymous serviceman, survey response, September 1942:** The negro problem has been very poorly handled here by our officers. What is taking place in our army together is nothing more disgraceful than what Hitler is doing to minorities in Germany. I joined the American Army to fight against the persecution of minorities. I resent that our Army actually practices the same type of persecution.

**Brendan Bracken, Minister of Information, His Majesty's Government:** The Americans have exported to us a local problem which is not of our own making.

**Pfc. Timuel D. Black:** When I was asked how can you be fighting and so loyal to a country that mistreats you by someone else, you know, French or German or whatever. I would quickly respond, "That is none of your business. I am an American. We will straighten that out, but that is none of your business."

**Anonymous Black soldier, survey response, November 1943:** I am an American negro, doing my part for the American government to make the world safe for a democracy I have never known.

# Building the Atlantic Wall

The inspection of the Atlantic Wall by Rommel (*left*)—with OB West commander
Gerd von Rundstedt (*center*)—found it not as formidable as expected.

*While soldiers waited in English towns for further instructions and Allied com-*
*manders finalized their plans and strategies for a cross-Channel invasion, the*
*Germans raced to build up their defenses against an amphibious assault. France*
*had been occupied since 1940, but life in Normandy had settled into a much*
*lighter occupation after the Germans had eased back on plans to use the coast as*
*a launching pad for its invasion of Britain. By 1943 and 1944, though, General-*
*feldmarschall Gerd von Rundstedt, the* Oberbefehlshaber West, *the Supreme*
*Commander of the West (abbreviated "OB West"), reenergized the military pres-*
*ence in the area and began preparations for battle.*

*Rundstedt, an aging Prussian commander, oversaw about 800,000 troops*
*spread across France, Belgium, and the Netherlands who served as both an*

*occupying force for civilian populations and the primary defense against poten-*
*tial amphibious incursions. His armies also included large percentages of foreign*
*conscripts—ranging from Poles to Russians to Mongolians—and forces injured*
*or worn down in the fighting on the Russian Front.*

*By 1944, the German army looked quite different from the one that had*
*overrun France and the Low Countries four years prior. Short of fuel and vehicles*
*by 1944, many of the German forces under OB West relied on horses—115,000 of*
*them by one count—wooden wagons, or bicycles for supplies and mobility. Much*
*of the military's vehicle fleet was composed of civilian vehicles seized from other*
*occupied countries—like Italian Fiats, French Renaults, and Czech Skodas—and*
*many of the gun emplacements contained captured machine guns or reengineered*
*tank turrets from other conquered countries, a collective hodgepodge that made*
*keeping adequate stockpiles of ammunition or spare parts almost impossible.*
*(Neighboring machine gun nests, for instance, often used different ammunition*
*and couldn't resupply each other in battle.) Hobbled by huge battlefield and*
*resource losses, and with key supply chains under pressure from Allied advances*
*and bombers, the mighty, technologically advanced Wehrmacht was largely a*
*figment of memory.*

**Obergefreiter Josef Brass, Pionier-Bataillon 352, 352 Infanterie-Division:** For
the most part, the French people were amiable toward us. Some hated us
and were probably in the Maquis [the French Resistance], others supported
us—the collaborators—but most were just concerned with getting on with
everyday life.

**Pvt. Aloysius Damski, Polish conscript, Artillerie-Regiment 352, 352 Infan-
terie-Division:** I was billeted with an old French lady who was very sympa-
thetic and kind because I was a Pole.

**Gren. Franz Gockel, 3 Kompanie, Grenadier-Regiment 726, 716 Infanterie-
Division:** We enjoyed contact with the French in Colleville and St Laurent,
mostly with the families whom we paid to do our laundry or the farms where
we bought milk, butter and eggs. In Colleville we would hang around this
farm where we bought butter and milk because the farmer had a very cute
daughter. She spoke German very well and was much courted.

**Lt. Gen. Max-Josef Pemsel, Chief of Staff, Seventh Army:** The Fall of 1943 went by without a large-scale attack against the Continent, and then it was important to make full use of the Winter and Spring.

**Adolf Hitler, Directive No. 51 (Top Secret), November 3, 1943:** In the East, the vastness of the space will, as a last resort, permit a loss of territory even on a major scale, without suffering a mortal blow to Germany's chance for survival. Not so in the West! If the enemy here succeeds in penetrating our defenses on a wide front, consequences of staggering proportions will follow within a short time. All signs point to an offensive against the Western Front of Europe no later than spring, and perhaps earlier. For that reason, I can no longer justify the further weakening of the West in favor of other theaters of war. I have therefore decided to strengthen the defenses in the West, particularly at places from which we shall launch our long-range war against England. For those are the very points at which the enemy must and will attack; there—unless all indications are misleading—will be fought the decisive invasion battle.

**Lt. Gen. Hans Speidel, Chief of Staff to Erwin Rommel:** Hitler had decided in 1941 that the main battle was to be on the beaches. But this front was so long that there could only be a system of strong points; a continuous line of fortifications was out of the question. The Pas-de-Calais and the Channel Islands of Guernsey, Jersey and Sark were to be made "the mightiest fortresses" in an eight-year plan. The whole development of coastal defence, that is to say, the design and lay-out of the fortifications, had been entrusted to an engineer of the Todt Organisation, who was neither tactically nor strategically proficient, had no knowledge of the general war situation and no experience of co-operation with the armed forces.

**Vice Adm. Friedrich Ruge, naval adviser to Erwin Rommel, Kriegsmarine:** To analyze this situation, the OKW, Oberkommando der Wehrmacht [High Command of the Armed Forces], in early November 1943 assigned [Field Marshal Erwin] Rommel to check the defenses of the threatened coasts.

**Field Marshal Erwin Rommel, letter to his wife, December 15, 1943:** Arrived safely yesterday. I've found myself a lovely billet in a chateau [at Fontainebleau] which once belonged to Madame de Pompadour. But I won't be here long. I'm already off on a trip tomorrow, as today's news announced. It seems that they can't tell the British and Americans soon enough that I'm here. I lunched with R. [Rundstedt] to-day. He seems very pleased and I think it's all going well, but I must first get a picture of the situation and see how things are. The old chateau is a lovely place. The French built very generously and spaciously for their upper classes two centuries ago. We're absolutely provincial in comparison.

**Lt. Gen. Max-Josef Pemsel:** From his extensive experience with landing operations in Africa and Italy, Rommel had formulated the opinion that an enemy, once landed and protected by covering fire from naval artillery and from the air, was extremely difficult to throw back into the sea. It was therefore a proposition of making the coastal defenses so strong in manpower and equipment that the enemy could never gain a foothold on the shore.

**Field Marshal Erwin Rommel:** The West is the place that matters. If we once manage to throw the British and Americans back into the sea, it will be a long time before they return.

*　　　　*　　　　*

*Field Marshal Erwin Rommel, the great hero of the German North African campaign, was still in 1943 and 1944 among the brightest stars in the German military, and his dispatch by Hitler to inspect defenses along the Atlantic coast marked a turning point in the German strategy. For years, the German propaganda machine had touted the invincibility of the Atlantic Wall, but the dashing, celebrated commander was less than impressed with what he found in his weeks of inspections up and down the coast of Europe—an ill-conceived, poorly and inconsistently executed ring of coastal defenses and a fighting force that was not only shockingly ill equipped, but, just as troublingly, variously equipped. The Seventh Army, Rommel wrote, "possessed over thirty-two different weapons systems with 252 different types of ammunition, of which forty-seven types were no longer produced." Many of the defending units were "static divisions," units expressly designed to defend fixed bunker positions and* Widerstandsnesten *(resistance nests), and* Stützpunkten *(larger strongpoints of artillery and machine guns). The Atlantic Wall, as it turned out, was anything but.*

**General der Infanterie Günther Blumentritt, Chief of Staff, OB West:** The Atlantic Wall was propagandists' bluff; it was not as strong as was believed abroad.

**Joseph Goebbels, Propaganda Minister, Third Reich:** We have fortified the coast of Europe from northern Norway to the Mediterranean and it is armed with the most implacable weapons the 20th century has to offer. This is why an enemy attack, however powerful and furious it may be, is doomed to failure. At Dieppe they only lasted nine hours and that was before the wall was built. If they last nine hours next time, they will be doing well.

**Vice Adm. Friedrich Ruge:** The Atlantic Wall, so highly praised by the propaganda, existed in harsh reality only in a few places. The newsreel pictures of the wall, repeatedly shown to the German public in all possible variations, originated almost exclusively from the Calais-Boulogne area, a remnant from the preparations for "Operation Sealion" [the aborted German invasion of England].

**Field Marshal Gerd von Rundstedt, Commander in Chief, OB West:** It used to make me angry to read the stories about its impregnable defenses. It was nonsense to describe it as a "wall." Hitler himself never came to visit it and see what it really was.

**General der Infanterie Günther Blumentritt:** Anyone who traces the German fronts of 1944 on a map of Europe can see at a glance that there was no "defense" from a military standpoint. The fronts were occupied at the most by security forces and, on long fronts, by observation posts. The fronts were northern Norway–Norway–Denmark–North Sea–English Channel–Bay of Biscay–French Mediterranean coast–the Italian "boot"– Adriatic–Dalmatian coast–Greece–Rumania–Black Sea–a long Eastern Front to Leningrad–Finland–Arctic Sea.

**Field Marshal Gerd von Rundstedt:** I had over 3,000 miles of coastline to cover from the Italian frontier in the south to the German frontier in the north, and only 60 divisions with which to defend it. Most of them were low-grade divisions, and some of them were skeletons.

**Lt. Gen. Hans Speidel:** They consisted of personnel from old-age classes, frequently without combat experience. Their training by outdated leaders of all grades was not on the level of the task ahead. Materially they were quite inadequately equipped, similar to the type of infantry division at the end of World War I! Almost immobile and poorly horse-drawn, they could never be a match for a motorized, maneuverable foe.

**Lt. Gen. Max-Josef Pemsel:** Only a few of the units of these divisions had any transport whatsoever, and their artillery was only partially mobile. The average age of the men was approximately 35 years, and, as a result of the repeated combing out of replacements for the Eastern front, there was eventually not a man left fit for duty in the East. Eight percent *Volksdeutsche* [racial Germans from foreign countries]—many of whom did not understand the German language—were assigned to the *Bodenständig* [static] divisions.

**Pvt. Aloysius Damski:** We had considerable shortages of minefield equipment. We planted scraps of metal to confuse the detectors, wired off the areas, and strung up signs reading *Achtung Minen!* Many of the real mines we used were British, captured at Dunkirk, but most of the minefields in our area were false. We had signs to remind ourselves which were genuine. If the writing sloped to the left, it was a dummy. To the right meant an anti-personnel field. Upright meant an anti-tank one.

**Lt. Gen. Max-Josef Pemsel:** Fuel was more and more strictly rationed. Thus, regimental commanders were able to use their cars only once a week. Otherwise they were dependent upon the use of horses or bicycles in the more distant areas. We had to improvise continually, and this made the situation truly difficult.

**Lt. Gen. Hans Speidel:** The Allies had all the advantages in reconnaissance during the year of preparation for the invasion. The monitoring and deciphering services were almost the only effective German source of information, whereas the Allies used their air supremacy to the full. They combined bombing with reconnaissance missions far behind the German front.

**General der Infanterie Günther Blumentritt:** Invasion was expected first in Norway, then in Denmark and the North Sea, in the OB West area, in Spain and Portugal, in Genoa and upper Italy, in the Adriatic, and in Greece and Turkey. Expectations changed continually. Moreover, there was uncertainty as to when and where the Russians would begin their offensive. We were on the strategic defensive, with all its well-known disadvantages of uncertainty. *

**Field Marshal Erwin Rommel, report to Adolf Hitler, December 31, 1943:** With difficult sea conditions, it is likely that the enemy's main concern will be to get the quickest possible possession of a port or ports capable of handling large ships. Furthermore, he will probably endeavour to capture the area from which our long-range attack is coming as quickly as possible.

**General der Infanterie Günther Blumentritt:** Therefore, invasion was expected between May and September 1944. It was assumed that there were two army groups in England with about 60 divisions and eight airborne divisions. The Americans were in western England, the British in eastern England; the boundary was Southampton. The commanders were known. Where would they come?

\* \* \*

*Rommel realized—and argued to Hitler—that if the German military had any hope of repelling an Allied invasion, it needed to completely rethink its plans and invest, quickly, in a large-scale building effort. Following his excoriating report on the state of the wall, Rommel angled to assume control of the coastal forces and embark on an ambitious construction effort to defend the French coast. While he was given command, his efforts were ultimately stymied and slowed by the very person whose power and life depended upon his success. Hitler, growing paranoid and desperate, had become distrustful of his frontline generals, often*

---

\* An initial invasion in Norway was hardly as far-fetched in 1944 as one might believe now, decades later, when the arc of World War II is clear. In fact, as late as April 1944—just weeks before D-Day—the head of the Allied air effort, Lt. Gen. Carl "Tooey" Spaatz, argued, "If I were directing the overall strategic operations, I would go into Norway where we have a much greater chance of ground forces success and where I believe Sweden would come in with us. Why undertake a highly dubious operation in a hurry when there is a surer way to do it? It is better to win the war surely than undertake an operation which has really great risks."

*playing them off one another in internal politics, and implemented a nonsensical chain of command, splitting control of the German forces across Normandy among various services.*

**Lt. Gen. Hans Speidel:** The directive that Hitler gave to the Western Command may be summarised as follows: Fight the decisive action on the Atlantic Wall itself. The defence must adhere to the coast as main line of battle, and this line must be held at all costs. The landing attempts of the enemy are to be broken up before and during beaching, and local lodgements of enemy forces are to be destroyed by instantaneous counter-attacks. There was to be no freedom to operate on the Western Front; the order was to hold every inch of ground; it was forbidden for the Staff in its operational planning to envisage the interior of France as a battlefield or to study the probable movements of the enemy after a hypothetical break-through.

**Vice Adm. Friedrich Ruge:** Effective January 15, 1944, the chain of command regulations changed Rommel's status from that of inspector back to commander in chief. It was characteristic that the first order he issued decreed the erection of offshore obstacles.

**Lt. Gen. Hans Speidel:** Rommel was bitterly disappointed over the state of construction and tried to make up for what had been neglected by the work of the troops committed. He gave fundamental instructions for the construction of "foreshore obstacles" which he had thought out—iron beams built out into the sea, with wire entanglements and mines—for a resistance zone of field-type construction, and for construction of air-landing obstacles.

**Lt. Gen. Max-Josef Pemsel:** By making a barrier of partially mined tree trunks, concrete blocks, etc., which were submerged at high tide and above water at low tide, the landing of enemy craft was to be made difficult, if not impossible. A major commitment of airborne troops was to be prevented by the emplacement of obstacles in endangered areas.

**Vice Adm. Friedrich Ruge:** He urged increased mining, also by the infantry, and stressed the necessity of moving the artillery of the reserve divisions far enough forward that it could fire on the beaches.

**Gren. Franz Gockel:** In February, 1944, during his inspection of the defenses of the Normandy coast, Field Marshall Rommel had visited our position. He had sharply criticized not only the lack of defenses constructed at our position but also those along the entire coastline from Colleville-sur-Mer to Vierville-sur-Mer. He compared the bay in our sector with the bay at Salerno in Italy and urgently ordered further defenses to be constructed.

**Lt. Gen. Max-Josef Pemsel:** Rommel had the right ideas, but they were feasible only in a smaller sector which could be defended accordingly. From an operational and strategic point of view, especially with Germany's situation at the turn of 1943–44, the basis for a defense of the West, as carried out by Rommel, was no longer present. At that time, Germany no longer had the forces and matériel available to utilize a cordon defense in a 4,000-kilometer front.

**Lt. Gen. Hans Speidel:** The "fortress construction" suffered from a shortage of material, but most of all from jurisdiction difficulties—the result of a confused chain of command.

**General der Infanterie Günther Blumentritt:** The chain of command was very complicated and muddled; there was no absolute responsibility as was given to Field Marshal Montgomery or General Eisenhower. A dictator does not favor putting too much power in the hands of one man. *"Divide et impera!"* Let this example be a warning of how *not* to organize the high-level commands.

**Lt. Gen. Karl-Wilhelm von Schlieben, Commander, 709th Infantry Division:** "Who was the actual leader in the West?" That was the question asked by many of us.

**General der Panzertruppen Leo Freiherr Geyr von Schweppenburg, Commander, Fifth Panzer Army:** On paper, Genfldm von Rundstedt was the Supreme Commander in the West. In reality, he had no decisive influence with the Luftwaffe and the Navy during the preparation of the defense. Hitler or the *Wehrmachtführungsstab* interfered in both major and minor issues. Unity of command, which had been familiar and self-evident to the experienced old general from his early military career, was further jeopardized by the assignment of Genfldm Rommel at the end of 1943 to an ambiguously outlined special mission. Rommel was an able and experienced tactician, although entirely lacking in strategic conceptions.

**Lt. Gen. Karl Wilhelm von Schlieben:** Written orders were issued by Rommel, who also gave verbal orders on the spot, which were contradictory to the former orders.

**General der Infanterie Günther Blumentritt:** Von Rundstedt and Rommel belonged to two different generations; they were so dissimilar in origin, education, and outlook that they seemed members of different worlds. Von Rundstedt—for 50 years an old-Prussian solider, a member of an old-Prussian family, a former Prussian cadet, 68 years old, he lived in his memories of 1914–1918 and before.

**Lt. Col. Fritz Ziegelmann, Chief of Staff, 352 Infanterie-Division:** Rommel's authority was not enough. Luftwaffe workers, Kriegsmarine, Organization Todt, and our own fortress engineers worked side-by-side, often duplicating work.

**Lt. Gen. Hans Speidel:** Rommel demanded in writing and verbally that all three services and the Todt Organisation in his area should be put under his command. His request was sharply refused after he had pressed it repeatedly. Hitler wanted to keep the command fluid; he did not want too much power in one hand, and particularly not in the hand of Rommel. The need of the hour was sacrificed to the suspicion of our political leaders.

*Despite being hobbled both by his limited authority and supply shortages, Rommel made impressive progress in the early months of 1944 building the Atlantic Wall into a coherent stretch of defenses—an effort driven almost more by his personal force of nature than by concrete, mines, and timber. He hoped that his vision for a series of beach obstacles and fortifications, as well as defenses against airborne landings, would devastate and paralyze Allied invaders and allow German forces time to counterattack with more mobile panzer units and push the Allies back into the sea.*

**Vice Adm. Friedrich Ruge:** The first three weeks after Rommel had assumed command had shown how disparate and weak the defenses against a landing still were, especially in western Normandy. The immense amount of work still to be done in order to execute these measures had grown more apparent with time.

**Maj. Hans von Luck, commander, Panzer-Grenadier-Regiment 125, 21 Panzer-Division:** To make up for the inadequate fortifications on the coast, Rommel ordered stake-obstacles to be erected on the shore and in the hinterland, what was known as "Rommel's asparagus." In addition, mine fields were laid wherever airborne landings might be expected.

**Field Marshal Erwin Rommel:** The important thing is to ensure that all territory which might conceivably be used for landing airborne troops is treated in such a manner that enemy aircraft and gliders will break up while landing, and the enemy as a result suffer severe losses in men and material—in addition to those caused by the quick opening of our defensive fire. All divisions will take the necessary steps, as early as possible, to have the area between the land and sea fronts thoroughly staked out.

**Maj. Gen. Fritz Bayerlein, commander, Panzer Lehr Division:** The obstacles which Rommel planned consisted of stakes approximately 10 feet high driven into the ground at 100 feet spacing. He realised, of course, that the stakes alone would present no lethal obstacle to troops landing with gliders and consequently gave orders for a high proportion of them to be fitted with captured shells at the top and for them all to be inter-connected by wire. The shells were to be so arranged that they would be detonated by a pull on the wire. Experiment showed that a glider landing in territory treated in this manner could not fail to suffer heavy losses, and would, in fact, have little hope of success.

**Lt. Gen. Hans Speidel:** Most of these defence works had to be done with local labour. Rommel gave orders that no French citizen was to be forced to work but that volunteers should be well paid. The French labourers were to be treated exactly the same as the Germans. He told the inhabitants that they had an interest in placing obstacles, as, if such obstacles stood in their fields, they would probably be spared the ravages of battle.

**Gren. Franz Gockel:** The construction of the [obstacles] was done with the help of the Bayeux Fire Brigade. One day they showed up with their equipment and with an amazingly simple method we sunk the tree trunks into the sand. The trunks were supported by a tripod and sunk in to the required depth by a fire hose pump. At the beginning we experienced problems because the pump would clog with sand. A soldier suggested that we place someone on the pump to regulate the amount of sand flowing through it. The entire project was completed in very little time.

**Pvt. Werner Beibst, infantry, 15th Army:** It was our job to fell these trees and knock off the branches, and then horses were used to drag the trunks out of the woods, back to the coast. Then we had to wait for the tide to go out to plant the trees really far out on the sand. All this we did more or less without any kind of mechanical help. It was terribly difficult work and required huge numbers of people. Once the trees had been erected, mines were planted on the seaward side of the trees. This was all intended to catch the landing craft that we expected to land in that area. We spent April doing this work.

**Capt. Curt Fromm, commander, 6 Kompanie, Panzer-Regiment 22, 21 Panzer-Division:** There were no forests in the neighborhood at all, and the tree trunks had to be brought in from some distance away. I gave a speech to the French peasants and told them that we needed their help to set these things up, in order to prevent parachutists or gliders landing. I told them that after the war, they could then have the wood and use it for heating. I also made the point that if they helped us now, planting these stakes, then we would help them with the next harvest. I enlisted the help of the local priest to persuade them, had a glass of wine with him, and the farmers helped us. My unit was the first to finish its section and even received a commendation from Rommel himself.

**Alexandre Renaud, Mayor, Sainte-Mère-Église:** "It's incredible," we commented to each other that evening. "The Germans seem to think the attack will take place in Normandy." Everyone thought this was very funny.

**Brig. Gen. James M. Gavin, assistant division commander, 82nd Airborne:** We studied intently the use of "asparagus" for a long time as a possible indication of the Germans' evaluation of each sector from the defensive viewpoint. We believed that there must be a reason for their being especially thorough in the preparation of one area and not of another. But, as one always finds, in the final analysis, human nature is still the most important factor to be dealt with in war. From interrogation of captured German commanders and French civilians, we soon found that the amount of asparagus in any one locality was more an indication of the efficiency and enthusiasm of the local German commander than anything else. Good landing areas were in some instances left untouched because the defense commander was just plain lazy. In other areas every square yard was covered because the defender had much enthusiasm for doing his job.

**Lt. Gen. Max-Josef Pemsel:** The armed forces worked with extreme devotion and ingenuity in reinforcing the defensive fronts, especially in emplacing and mining beach obstacles.

**Lt. Gen. Hans Speidel:** To make an enemy landing more difficult, under-water obstacles were laid in the form of an artificial reef. The shallow water approaches to beaches were to be mined and harbours prepared with demolition charges to make them unusable.

**Field Marshal Erwin Rommel:** If the enemy should ever set foot on land, an attack through the minefields against the defence works sited within them will present him with a task of immense difficulty. He will have to fight his way through the zone of death in the defensive fire of the whole of our artillery. And not only on the coast, for numerous and extensive minefields will also exist round our positions in the rear areas. Any airborne troops who attempt to penetrate to the coast from the rear will make the acquaintance of this mined zone.

**Lt. Gen. Hans Speidel:** The high-water mark along the beaches was mined as a continuous defence line all along the coast. The concentration of artillery fire—there was only one battery to every fourteen miles or so—could not be increased, partly because fire-control instruments were in short supply.

**Vice Adm. Friedrich Ruge:** Two months after Rommel's arrival in France, the work was proceeding generally according to his suggestions and in the intended direction. With all his energy and great tenacity, he had devoted himself to his task and developed a novel defense system. In order to impress his ideas personally upon troops and staffs and to familiarize himself with local conditions and situations, he had become an indefatigable traveller.

**Field Marshal Erwin Rommel, commander, Army Group B, Atlantic Wall Inspection Report, April 22, 1944:** From day-to-day, week-to-week, the Atlantic Wall will be stronger, and the equipment of our troops will be better. Considering the strength of our defenses, and the courage, ability, and the willingness of our soldiers to fight, we can look forward with utmost confidence to the day when the enemy will attack the Atlantic Wall. It will and must lead to the destruction of the attackers, and that will be our contribution to the revenge we owe the English and Americans for the inhuman warfare they are raging against our homeland.

# Keeping Secrets

Allied intelligence efforts sought to learn everything they could
about the evolving beach defenses across Normandy.

*While the German defenses sprouted new obstacles and minefields, and Rommel's
asparagus spread like a weed through Normandy fields, the German military
remained in the dark about the fundamental secret at the heart of Operation
OVERLORD—precisely where and when the looming invasion would take place.*

*The knowledge of OVERLORD details and the specific plan for the cross-
Channel invasion, known as Operation NEPTUNE, was granted through a special
limited, need-to-know security clearance, known as the BIGOT list. The term
came from the 1942 invasion of North Africa, during which officers and personnel
bound for North Africa had "TO GIB" (meaning, "to Gibraltar"), stamped on
their orders to hide their true destination. The designation, reversed, became the
code name for access to the most restrictive D-Day information.*

**Rear Adm. Alan Kirk, commander, Western Naval Task Force, letter to a friend, spring 1944:** I don't have to tell you what a big show this is or how important. If this is successful the war is won, if this fails it may go on for years. Perhaps too it will settle whether we or Russia dominate the world for a while.

**Winston Churchill, Prime Minister of the United Kingdom:** The enemy was bound to know that a great invasion was being prepared; we had to conceal the place and time of attack and make him think we were landing somewhere else and at a different moment.

**Maj. John Dalgleish, planning staff, Royal Army Service Corps:** This became the guiding principle of all security regulations.

**Field Marshal Lord Alan Brooke, Chief of the Imperial General Staff:** The possibility of Hitler's gaining a victory in France cannot be excluded. The hazards of battle are very great.

**Forrest Pogue, combat historian, V Corps:** The general code name for the invasion plan was OVERLORD. However, since this name had been used for some months, the decision was made to call the initial assault phase of the invasion NEPTUNE and to give all plans and papers concerning this phase the special BIGOT classification.

**Ens. George McKee Elsey, Map Room watch officer, the White House:** Only if one were designated a BIGOT—the awkward code name for a person who had the proper security clearance and had a "need to know"—was he entitled to be told the date and the hour and the place. We were so security minded that when King George VI visited [HMS] *Ancon*, and asked what lay behind closely drawn curtains in our Intelligence Center, the junior officer standing with me answered "Very secret information, Sire," and remained motionless before the curtains. The King took the hint and moved on. An angry captain demanded of my companion some minutes later why he had been so rude to the King. He received the entirely correct answer: "Sir, nobody told me he was a Bigot!"

**Pfc. Carl Howard Cartledge, Jr., Intelligence and Reconnaissance Section, 50Ist Parachute Infantry Regiment, 10Ist Airborne:** My team of six men were to guard the sand tables. There were two sand tables, one in each of two small wooden buildings—barbed wire fences surrounded the buildings with one gate in each. On the sand tables were the 501st area of Normandy, and the 2nd was of all the beaches, every road, every house, every hedgerow was in place. They looked like one would see the landscape from about 5,000 feet. There were two of us outside the barbed wire 24 hours a day for about five days. One at the gate, and one at the back, each armed with a submachine gun.

Our orders were to stop anyone approaching, ask them to produce their BIGOT card. They were to place it in their right hand, next to their cheek, then advance. Their picture was on it. Any deviation from this, we were to capture them—or kill them.

No one came night or day, until about the fourth night, when a command car drove in with black half lights on, and stopped about 50 yards away. I was at the gate, and I flashed my light on them. There were six people in the car. The driver stayed seated. General Eisenhower and his aide got out, along with Air Marshall Tedder and two aides. I halted them, asked for their BIGOT cards, and then advanced them forward. General Ike came up first, put the BIGOT card by his cheek, and gave his famous smile. So did his aide. Neither Air Marshall Tedder nor his aides produced their cards. It was a breach of orders. But I recognized him and opened the gate. General Ike was the last to go in, and as he passed me, he clapped his hand on my shoulder, and said, "How is it going, Soldier?" "Just fine, sir." I answered. He knew that the Air Marshall had breached the orders and that I hadn't made a big deal out of it.

*The OVERLORD planners also went to great lengths to protect against German spies learning the truth about the invasion and, as the date neared, imposed an ever-increasing number of restrictions on international communications to prevent the leakage of any invasion details, intended or not. A key part of these OVERLORD security efforts relied on British intelligence running an extensive "double-cross" system; early in the war, they had successfully identified, captured, and turned all the major German spies in the British Isles into double agents. Overseen by a team known as the "Twenty Committee," British intelligence officers then spent the rest of the war feeding false and misleading information back to Berlin while protecting against new spies from Ireland and elsewhere.*

**Lt. Col. Roger Hesketh, staff member, Ops (B), COSSAC:** At the beginning of 1943, [MI5] controlled 15 agents. The most notable feature was the introduction of imaginary sub-agents. By February 1944 [one of our double agents, code-named] GARBO had no fewer than twenty-four fictitious sub-agents, each clothed with a character and a story of his own. Apart from GARBO himself every one of the characters was imaginary.

**Gen. Lord Hastings Ismay, chief military adviser to Winston Churchill:** From February onwards, all civilian traffic between the United Kingdom and Eire was forbidden. In March, the whole coast from the Wash to Land's End, to a depth of ten miles, was declared a prohibited area. Shortly afterwards all embassies in London were forbidden to communicate in cypher, and their diplomatic bags were deliberately delayed. These high-handed and unprecedented restrictions may have aroused resentment at the time, but a man who is fighting for his life cannot afford to be squeamish.

**Capt. Kay Summersby, British Mechanised Transport Corps, aide and secretary to General Eisenhower, SHAEF:** The most unusual step of all came when the British Government bottled up all diplomats and couriers in the British Isles and even did away with traditional immunity of diplomatic communications.

**Winston Churchill:** Coastal areas were banned to visitors; censorship was tightened; letters after a certain date were held back from delivery; foreign embassies were forbidden to send cipher telegrams and even their diplomatic bags were delayed.

**Gen. Dwight Eisenhower, Supreme Allied Commander, SHAEF:** This was embarrassing to their government, but they were sturdy. They stuck right by it. We did everything to keep any information going out.

*All the while, as intelligence and counterintelligence did their best to keep secret the OVERLORD plans, the Allies were busy—largely at night—gathering as much information as they could about the invasion targets in Normandy.*

**Winston Churchill:** Our plans had to be altered and kept up to date as fresh information came in about the enemy. We knew the general layout of his troops and his principal defences, the gun positions, the strong points and entrenchments along the coast, but after Rommel took command in late January, great additions and refinements began to appear. In particular we had to discover any new types of obstacle that might be installed, and contrive the antidote. Constant air reconnaissance kept us informed of what was going on across the Channel. And of course there were other ways of finding out. Many trips were made by parties in small craft to resolve some doubtful point, to take soundings inshore, to examine new obstacles, or to test the slope and nature of a beach. All this had to be done in darkness, with silent approach, stealthy reconnaissance, and timely withdrawal.

**André Heintz, student, French Resistance, Caen (age 24):** We had to keep the Allies informed on the progress of "Rommel's asparagus"—those stakes that were planted in open fields around Caen—and about minefields. Quite often, for their own safety, the Germans marked them with little yellow flags with crossbones drawn on them.

**Lt. Gen. Walter Bedell "Beetle" Smith, Chief of Staff, SHAEF:** Landing parties, sent over almost nightly to some section of the Channel coast, brought back intelligence on the gun positions.

**Lt. George Lane, X Troop, 10 Commando, 1st Special Service Brigade:** Almost everyone in X Troop was a foreigner. I am a Hungarian; my real name is Lanyi Gyorgy. Mountbatten had come up with an idea to make better use of foreigners serving in the British Army. He thought that with their specialist knowledge and languages they could form a secret troop to undertake hazardous operations. Asked if I would like to be a part of it, I said, "You bet I would."

**Cpl. Peter Masters, No. 3 Troop, 10 Commando, 1st Special Service Brigade:** I was born in Vienna, Austria. When the Nazis came to Austria, things became so bad that my family, being Jewish, tried to get out. I lived under the Nazis for 6 months, which was quite sufficient to turn me from a kid that had been brought up as a pacifist to a carte blanche volunteer wanting to get part of the action against the Nazis. [In England], they lowered the age limit for the army, and I immediately enlisted. Eventually I got an interview by a visiting officer who was wearing no rank insignia, a raincoat and dark glasses. It turned out to be the skipper of a commando troop that was being formed from people just like me: refugees from Germany, Austria, Hungary, and some from Czechoslovakia and so forth. On joining the commandos, all of us were given British names. I, according to my new papers, had volunteered to join the commandos from the Queen's Own Royal West Kent Regiment, and my regimental number on my dog tags, indeed was 6387025, which is a Royal West Kent number.

**Lt. George Lane:** We were doing small-scale raiding across the Channel from Newhaven, crossing on moonless nights in an MTB [motor torpedo boat], then going ashore in a small boat called a dory. We had many different jobs to do—take samples from the beaches, photograph the obstacles, check on the disposition and strength of the coastal defenses, things like that. Sometimes we had to try and snatch a prisoner to bring him back for interrogation.

**Lt. William A. Bostick, Naval Cartographic Section, SHAEF:** Frogmen had also made forays to determine the depth soundings and beach floor, which had a very irregular surface. Our photo interpreters used this data and the aerial photos to pinpoint such defense installations as hedgehogs, curved rails, wire barriers, pillboxes, minefields, etc.

**Maj. Logan Scott-Bowden, Combined Operation Pilotage Party I (Naval Party 755), Royal Engineers:** My job was beach reconnaissance, to swim ashore at night from a midget submarine or some other vessel and to carry out a reconnaissance of the beaches where we would be landing on D-Day. There was great concern about the bearing capacity of the beaches on the Normandy coast.

**Lt. Cdr. Nigel Clogstoun-Willmott, officer in charge, Combined Operation Pilotage Party I (Naval Party 755), Royal Navy:** The thing they were most worried about [at one point] was dark areas on some of the beaches, which were said to be peat. They had gone right back into pre-Norman and even Roman history and apparently the Romans had dug up peat from these very places. If these dark areas were peat, it would be too bad and they would have to think up some means of getting vehicles and tanks over it. That really was the number one priority that we had to discover on our first operation.

**Maj. Logan Scott-Bowden:** We went over on an MTB. It was not a very pleasant night; the wind was rising, blowing up the Channel. From the MTB, we transferred to a small, shallow-bottomed reconnaissance craft. We went in on this craft some two miles, and then, well outside the breakers, my sergeant, Bruce Ogden-Smith, and I went into the water to swim ashore. We crawled back along the beach, making sure we kept below the high-water mark so that our tracks would be obscured by the rising tide. We started taking samples from the beach. When we had each filled about eight tubes, I reckoned we had got enough, and so I said, "Let's go." We went out into the water as far as we could and watched the rhythm of the breakers, hoping that we could time the moment to get out. Bogged down as we were and out of our depth, it was quite a feat to get through a breaker, but on the third attempt, having timed it right, we managed it and swam like hell.

**Lt. Cdr. Nigel Clogstoun-Willmott:** Scott-Bowden and Ogden-Smith were both pretty puffed and very seasick when we pulled them in, and I don't think they could tell me very much other than "OK, we got most of what we wanted to get. Let's go, for God's sake!" We were crashing into high seas, there was water everywhere.

**Lt. Gen. Omar Bradley, commander, First Army:** Characteristic of the enterprise the British applied to this intelligence task was the answer they brought in reply to our inquiry on the subsoil of Omaha Beach. In examining one of the prospective beach exits, we feared that a stream running through the draw might have left a deposit of silt under the sand and shingle. If so, our trucks might easily bog down at that unloading point. "How much dope can you get on the subsoil there?" I asked. Several days later a lean and reticent British naval lieutenant came to our briefing at Bryanston Square. From his pocket he pulled a thick glass tube. He walked over to the map on the wall. "The night before last," he explained dryly, "we visited Omaha Beach to drill a core in the shingle at this point near the draw. You can see there is no evidence of silt. The shingle is firmly upon rock. There is little danger of your trucks bogging down."

**Lt. William A. Bostick:** My cartographic team had been carefully chosen from enlisted men who possessed drafting or artistic skills. The chart/maps involved considerable drafting detail. Two were prepared for Utah Beach and two for the two different sections of Omaha Beach. The chart/map was on one side and on the other side were charts with the following data: sunlight and moonlight tables, beach gradients, estimated inshore currents and tidal stages. The water depth changed 20 feet between low and high tide. Our charts covered the dates in Normandy from May 25 through June 21 since we didn't know the exact date of the landing.

**Pvt. Werner Beibst, infantry, 15th Army:** From time to time, there were small commando raids on the coast. The English came at night in their rubber dinghies or small speedboats, landed, and overpowered the occupants of some of the bunkers, whom they duly took back to England. This was naturally a tremendous shock for those people—the commandos arrived silently, all dressed in black, no one saw them at all. They overpowered the guards and carried them off in their boats. It was only discovered the next day, when the bunker was found to be empty.

*"A gift of priceless value"*

# Operation FORTITUDE

Numerous deception efforts, including inflatable tanks, tried to convince German leaders that the real invasion would come in Pas-de-Calais.

*Beyond the cloak of secrecy and communication restrictions that descended over the British Isles in the spring of 1944, the Allies also mounted an extensive, multifaceted deception plan, code-named* FORTITUDE, *to deceive German intelligence about the true target of the invasion. The two core operations were known as* FORTITUDE NORTH, *which aimed to mislead the Germany military into believing that an Allied invasion was headed to Norway—a belief that would keep the Germans from pulling troops out of Scandinavia to reinforce the European continent—and* FORTITUDE SOUTH, *which tried to convince the German military what it was already inclined to believe: That the main Allied invasion across the Channel would target France's Pas-de-Calais.*

**Winston Churchill, Prime Minister of the United Kingdom:** In wartime, truth is so precious that she should always be attended by a bodyguard of lies.

**Lt. Gen. Omar Bradley, commander, First Army:** Unable to anticipate where we might strike, the enemy had been forced to spread his strength across 860 miles of European coast line. As he continued to plant more German dead on his long line of retreat from Russia, it became increasingly difficult for him to man that Atlantic Wall. To smash our way ashore we had only to concentrate a force against some single point in his line. With the fire power at our disposal we could break a hole in that line and pour our follow-up forces through it.

**Winston Churchill, reviewing the state of the war in an address to the nation, March 26, 1944:** We shall require from our own people here, from Parliament, from the press, from all classes, the same cool strong nerves, the same toughness of fiber which stood us in good stead in those days when we were all alone under the German blitz. And here I must warn you, that in order to exercise our forces, there will be many false alarms, many feints and many dress rehearsals.

**Lt. Col. Roger Hesketh, staff member, Ops (B), COSSAC:** When General [Sir Frederick] Morgan's planning staff was set up in April 1943, a section known as Ops (B) was formed to deal with deception. At the time of its formation, I was posted to it with the task of dealing with any parts of a deception operation which it was felt could best be promoted by controlled leakage, or as we usually called it "Special Means." In January 1944, when General Eisenhower took over, Ops (B) was enlarged.

**Brig. David Belcham, head of Operations and Planning Staff, British Army:** The first part of the plan was intended to indicate that the Allied campaign would begin with an attack on Norway. Camps were set up near several Scottish ports and in Northern Ireland, in which skeleton detachments maintained signs of activity for the benefit of any German air photographic sorties in those areas.

**Lt. Col. Roger Hesketh:** A team was made up from the 2nd British Corps and the 9th British Armored Division, both formations being then in the process of disbandment, to which were added personnel from Scottish Command and from certain miscellaneous small units. This unofficial group, which became active in March 1944, received the name of "Fourth Army," the imaginary force which it represented.

**Brig. David Belcham:** A fictitious "Fourth Army HQ" was simulated in Scotland by considerable wireless traffic, and training exercises were also indicated by wireless messages that included carefully prepared indiscretions pointing to preparations for operations in Norway. This activity continued until July, in the hope of discouraging any German withdrawals from Scandinavia.

**Capt. Harry C. Butcher, naval aide to Dwight Eisenhower, SHAEF:** The fact that the Germans have shifted aircraft for glider bombs to Norway may indicate their belief that our newspaper talk of a cross-Channel invasion is just talk and attack in Norway is the actual plan. I hope we have this good luck.

*Beyond the Norway feint of FORTITUDE NORTH, the even larger effort of FORTITUDE SOUTH invented a whole army out of the ether to convince Germany that the Allies' main invasion would cross at the Strait of Dover, the narrowest portion of the English Channel, near Pas-de-Calais, where the Channel is just 20 miles wide. The goal was for German High Command to believe that the Normandy landings, when they happened, were just a feint or a distraction from the main event, which would soon follow at Pas-de-Calais.*

**Brig. David Belcham:** The main effort was put into convincing German intelligence that the principal Allied thrust would be made in the Pas de Calais, sometime in the second half of July—about 45 days later than the real D-Day.

**Brig. Gen. James M. Gavin, assistant division commander, 82nd Airborne:** [We] needed the Germans to believe that the actual landings were to take place at Calais, thus tying up their major armored reserves in the Calais area long enough to permit the actual landing to establish itself successfully ashore.

**Lt. Col. Roger Hesketh:** The decision to invade west of the Seine placed in the hands of the deceivers a gift of priceless value: A cover objective which possessed all the more obvious attractions for an assault landing. Pas de Calais had most things in its favour: A short sea passage, excellent air cover, and possibilities of strategic development.

**Gen. Lord Hastings Ismay, chief military adviser to Winston Churchill:** To lend colour to this story, and lead to the belief that the Pas de Calais was our true objective, a "notional" army was created in South-East England. It was "notionally" to consist of the Canadian First Army and American Third Army.

**Brig. David Belcham:** By planned wireless deceptions, the Germans were given to understand that an American Army Group HQ, comprising two assault armies, under General George Patton, was located in Kent.

**Lt. Col. Roger Hesketh:** [Wireless] traffic was recorded in advance. A mechanism was devised which made it possible for one wireless transmitter to simulate six. Thus the wireless traffic of a divisional headquarters with its brigades might be represented by sounds emanating from a single wireless truck. To satisfy United States requirements, a complete wireless deception unit, 3101 Signals Service Battalion, arrived from the United States in the early spring of 1944 fully equipped and trained. The official claim for this unit was a capacity to represent a corps of one armored and two infantry divisions. The wireless trucks mov[ed] through the country just as the formations which they represented would have done.

**Lt. Gen. Walter Bedell "Beetle" Smith, Chief of Staff, SHAEF:** There were camps which might have bivouacked thousands of troops. Actually they were deserted tent cities, given semblance of life by enough men to keep the fires burning for German reconnaissance pilots to photograph.

**Lt. Col. Roger Hesketh:** The need for vast and complicated physical preparations followed. All the normal invasion preparations which would be visible from the air—landing craft, camps, hard standings for vehicles and so on—must be physically represented in those places where we wished the enemy to believe that we were concentrating and embarking our invasion forces.

**Winston Churchill:** Simulated concentrations of troops in Kent and Sussex, fleets of dummy ships collected in the Cinque Ports, landing exercises on the nearby beaches, increased wireless activity were all used. More reconnaissances were made at or over the places we were not going to than at the places we were.

**Lt. Gen. Walter Bedell "Beetle" Smith:** Every effort was made to convince the Germans that the 1st Army Group still existed as a formidable fighting force, and they were allowed to learn that it was commanded by General Patton.

**Brig. David Belcham:** The General himself was persuaded to be seen in the area, with his conspicuous white dog!

**Gen. Lord Hastings Ismay:** The "cover-planners" thought out a ruse which was put into operation when D-Day was imminent. Their object was to induce the Germans to believe that Montgomery, who was known by them to be the commander of the initial assault, had left the country, and to assume that the invasion could not take place until his return.

**Lt. Col. Roger Hesketh:** An actor called Clifton James, then serving in the Royal Pay Corps, was found who bore a close personal resemblance to Field-Marshal Montgomery. He was dressed in the Field-Marshal's clothes and, having accompanied him in the guise of a newspaper reporter for some weeks in order that he could study his characteristics, he set off on May 27th in a York airplane accompanied by a sham brigadier for North Africa.

**Gen. Lord Hastings Ismay:** He was to be dressed in a suit of his uniform—the well-known beret and all—and despatched to Gibraltar, as though he were on his way to Algiers. On the appointed day, Clifton James arrived at Gibraltar in the Prime Minister's aeroplane, and was met with due deference by the Governor's ADC. Meanwhile the Governor had arranged that a Spaniard, who was known to be a "double agent," should be asked on some trumped-up pretext to be in the vicinity when "Monty's" car drew up at The Convent. The timing was perfect. Our double-crossing friend spotted what he was meant to spot, returned to Spanish territory at top speed and telephoned to Madrid that he had just seen Montgomery with his own eyes. The information was passed to Berlin at once.

Clifton James was given breakfast, and taken back to the airfield. Good-byes were said in full view of spy-infested [neighboring Spanish town of] La Linea; the air marshal gave the subaltern an exaggeratedly smart salute, and the great four-engined plane soared off to Algiers. The play was over, and Clifton James reverted to his own humble status.

**Brig. David Belcham:** The overall contribution of the Deception Plan cannot be precisely quantified, but there is no doubt at all that it achieved a remarkable degree of success.

**Lt. Gen. Walter Bedell "Beetle" Smith:** It seems incredible, considering the hazards, how successful we were in keeping the enemy from learning where we intended to strike.

**Lt. Gen. Sir Frederick Morgan, Deputy Chief of Staff, SHAEF:** We were successful beyond our wildest hopes.

# The Mulberry Plan

The giant caissons of the "Mulberry" harbors proved
one of the most audacious projects of OVERLORD.

*The final major secret at the core of Operation OVERLORD was that the Allies
didn't plan to capture or target a key harbor in the opening of the invasion.
German officials believed that places like Pas-de-Calais or Cherbourg would be
vital early targets of the Allies in order to secure the port facilities necessary to
resupply their armies in Europe. Indeed, moving hundreds of thousands of military
personnel across the English Channel to a hostile, occupied Europe—as well as
all of the myriad requisite supplies and vehicles—would be the largest logistics
operations in human history, but the Allies had come up with a novel solution:
They'd bring their own portable harbor to France.*

**Adm. Ernest King, Commander in Chief, United States Fleet, and Chief of Naval Operations:** The success of our amphibious operations in North Africa, Sicily, and Italy had demonstrated that, given air and sea superiority, there would be small doubt of our initial success, even against so strongly fortified a coast as northern France. The critical factor was whether, having seized a beachhead, we would be able to supply and reinforce it sufficiently fast to build an army larger than that which the enemy was certain to concentrate against ours.

**Lt. Col. Roger Hesketh, staff member, Ops (B), COSSAC:** The success of a seaborne assault depends on the ability of the attacker to sustain a more rapid rate of reinforcements by sea than the defender is able to do by land.

**Gen. Dwight Eisenhower, Supreme Allied Commander, SHAEF:** We knew that even after we captured Cherbourg its port capacity and the lines of communication leading out of it could not meet all our needs. To solve this apparently unsolvable problem we undertook a project so unique as to be classed by many scoffers as completely fantastic. It was a plan to construct artificial harbors on the coast of Normandy.

**Lt. Gen. Sir Frederick Morgan, Deputy Chief of Staff, SHAEF:** Credit for the entire concept belongs to the then senior naval representative at COSSAC of the commander-in-chief, Portsmouth, Commodore John Hughes-Hallett, Royal Navy. It all began at one of our principal staff officers' meetings in Norfolk House. There had come revolt from the supply and movement people, who could find no way of compensating for the proposed delay in capturing Cherbourg. The commodore gave vent to a famous bon mot of the type for which he was celebrated: "Well, all I can say is, if we can't capture a port we must take one with us." We slept on that and next morning asked the commodore if he had merely meant to be funny. On thinking it all over during the night there had come an idea that there might be something in this apparently preposterous idea.

**Gen. Lord Hastings Ismay, chief military adviser to Winston Churchill:** General Morgan gives Commodore Hughes-Hallett the credit for originating the idea, but there can be no doubt that Churchill's own contribution was significant. He had proposed, as far back as 1917, the construction of flat-bottomed caissons made of concrete, which could be towed to a selected site and there sunk. It was he who, in 1942, had given directions to Admiral Mountbatten that floating piers, which would go up and down with the tide, should be designed.

**Brig. David Belcham, head of Operations and Planning Staff, British Army:** In a note to Admiral Mountbatten dated 30 May, 1942, Churchill stressed the need to develop the concept of breakwaters and floating piers—ending his note with the now-famous words, "Do not argue the matter. The difficulties will argue for themselves."

**Brig. Bruce White, Director of Ports and Inland Water Transport, War Office:** I've often been asked why the word Mulberry was used in connection with the Mulberry harbours. The simple answer is that I found on my table at the War Office a letter which had no security and was headed "Artificial Harbours." I felt this was a possibility where security might be broken and therefore approached the head of the security branch at the War Office and requested utilisation of a code word. Turning to the junior officer behind him, he asked what was the next name from the code book and the officer replied, "Mulberry."

**Lt. Gen. Sir Frederick Morgan:** The final method adopted was to construct huge reinforced concrete "caissons" designed so as to have a reasonable towing performance afloat and to be rapidly sinkable at precise stations. These "caissons" were in fact specially built blockships, each resembling the traditional aspect of Noah's Ark.

**Winston Churchill, Prime Minister of the United Kingdom:** These synthetic harbours were called "Mulberries," a code name which certainly did not reveal their character or purpose.

**Lt. Gen. Walter Bedell "Beetle" Smith, Chief of Staff, SHAEF:** The mulberries were complete harbors in themselves, built in Great Britain, towed by tugs to the Norman coast and sunk in place. Their individual elements were enormous hollow structures of reinforced concrete, which reminded me, when I first saw them, of nothing so much as a six-story building lying on its side.

**Lt. Lambton Burn, RNVR, Navy editor, *Parade* magazine:** At docks in the big ports, and in improvised basins dug into the mud of the Thames riverside, dust-covered workmen in thousands were hammering at wooden Noah's Arks which served as moulds for tons of steel reinforcing and concrete. By night the unfinished monsters, with steel reinforcing rods projecting like wireless-poles above suburban flats, were ferried to finishing and assembly points in the south until the protected waters resembled green-blue plains studded with anti-tank blocks.

**Lt. Gen. Sir Frederick Morgan:** Half of England seemed to be working on it and a lot of Ireland as well. Yet I wonder how many knew what they were really at. I was taken one day over the Surrey and East India docks, where these "phoenix" units, as the concrete caissons were called, were being built. I asked a foreman if he knew what all this was about. Of course he did. He had been called on to this job from constructing concrete grain elevators somewhere in the north. These things they were now rushing up were obviously floating grain elevators to be filled when the time came with wheat and towed over to feed starving Europe. All the chaps knew it. But it was all right; they weren't talking.

**Brig. David Belcham:** In all, some two million tons of preformed steel and concrete had to be towed or carried by sea to form the two Mulberries, including more than 200 caissons, some of them the size of five-storey buildings, and 70 block-ships. All available tugs in Britain, and even some from America, were requisitioned for the massive towing operation.

**Brig. A. E. M. Walter, Commander, British Mulberry B Port Construction Force:** My memories of those three months leading up to D-Day are of eternal conferences, eternal planning, and everlasting sailing schedules, because each piece of the jigsaw had to sail from England at an exact time to reach the other side and be fitted in according to a tight program, always hoping that the sea and the Germans would not interfere; chasing around the country trying to meet units; plans changing; an ever growing sense of bewilderment at the sheer size of the enterprise.

**Brig. David Belcham:** Each beach was to be protected by an offshore break-water, or "Gooseberry," formed by a number of old ships ("Corncobs") steamed into position and then sunk in line parallel to the shore.

**Capt. Harry C. Butcher, naval aide to Dwight Eisenhower, SHAEF:** Seventy-one 300-foot vessels would be required.

**Lt. Gen. Walter Bedell "Beetle" Smith:** The service [the Mulberries] performed was priceless during the early days before we had taken Cherbourg and could begin to repair and use that great port.

**Brig. A. E. M. Walter:** The research, designing, building, towing across the Channel and planting of the artificial harbors, code-named Mulberries, on the beaches of Normandy was probably the greatest wartime engineering feat of all time.

**Winston Churchill:** The whole project was majestic.

*"We'd circle around and invade England"*

# At Slapton Sands

Posters notified villagers of Slapton Sands that they had to
evacuate their homes to enable US invasion training.

*While generals, field marshals, and admirals plotted and planned, the soldiers,
sailors, paratroopers, marines, commandos, and coast guardsmen who would make
up the million-strong invasion force were busy learning the ropes of amphibious
warfare. Preparing for such an unprecedented invasion required equally unprecedented training—and a place to do it, as real as SHAEF planners could create.
In the summer and fall of 1943, the British government and Allied military
officials zeroed in on a quiet, rural portion of South Hams on the Devon coast in
southwest England with sandy beaches that resembled those the ground troops
would be expected to cross in Normandy. In a brusque, secret effort, the British*

*government evacuated the entire civilian population from South Hams over just six weeks and turned the town, called Slapton Sands, over to the war effort.*

**Winston Churchill, Prime Minister of the United Kingdom:** Once the size of the expedition had been determined, it was possible to go ahead with intensive training. Not the least of our difficulties was to find enough room. A broad partition was arranged between British and American forces, whereby the British occupied the southeastern and the Americans the southwestern parts of England. The inhabitants of coastal areas accepted all the inconveniences in good part.

**Maj. Gen. C. H. Miller, War Office Southern Command, letter to affected residents, November 17, 1943:** In order to give our troops the fullest opportunity to perfect their training in the use of modern weapons of war, the Army must have an area of land particularly suited to their special needs and in which they can use live shells. For this reason you will realise the chosen area must be cleared of all civilians. The most careful search has been made to find an area suitable for the army's purpose and which, at the same time, will involve the smallest number of persons and property. It is regretted that, in the National Interest, it is necessary to move you from your homes, and everything possible will be done to help you, both by payment of compensation, and by finding other accommodation for you if you are unable to do so yourself.

**Grace Bradbeer, driver, Women's Voluntary Service:** A total evacuation of 30,000 acres was to take place at once, involving parts of 6 parishes, 3,000 people, 180 farms, village shops, and other dwellings, concerning 750 families in all. The area involved consisted of a triangle from Torcross to Blackpool Sands and stretching uphill to Blackawton at its apex. It included the villages of Torcross, Slapton, Strete, Blackawton, East Allington, Sherford, Stokenham and Chillington. The clergy were also informed that the government promised to pay every expense in connection with the evacuation, would give all help in finding temporary accommodation, would pay rents, grant free storage during the period of absence, and that everything would be brought back under the same guarantee, while any damage would be repaired and paid for.

**Lt. John Mason Brown, aide to Rear Adm. Alan Kirk, USS *Augusta* (CA-31):** In British eyes, this was a necessary part of having the invasion succeed.

**Grace Bradbeer:** So began a period of the greatest upheaval, the biggest disturbance that this part of the South Hams had ever known.

*Nancy Hare and Grace Bradbeer were two of a few dozen Women's Voluntary Service members dispatched by the government to the area to help with the mass evacuation.*

**Grace Bradbeer:** The date fixed for the evacuation to be complete was 20 December.

**Nancy Hare, member, Women's Voluntary Service:** We drove through a maze of narrow lanes to reach Blackawton's school, a stone's throw from a lovely old Norman church, with a glorious view of Slapton valley to the sea. It seemed almost impossible to believe that within a few weeks the land would be barren and not a living soul, man or beast, would exist there. The Admiralty Lands' Officer had fixed his big map on the wall at the far end of the room. Representatives of the Ministries of Food and Power, Health, Labor and Transport soon arrived.

**Grace Bradbeer:** Many were at a loss to understand why such valuable land should be especially commandeered.

**Nancy Hare:** A parish meeting was arranged. The biggest congregation it had ever contained filled the old church to capacity. Seated with their backs to the magnificent screen were the Bishop of Exeter, the Regional Commissioner, an American general, the chairman of the Devon County Council, a high-ranking Royal Navy officer, the WVS county organizer, and many others. The Bishop opened the meeting with a prayer, and the Regional Commissioner spoke sympathetically of what was going to happen, of the greatness of the sacrifice and the amount of help to be given to everyone. The general and the Admiralty explained their need.

**Lt. John Mason Brown:** People, old and young, whose families had lived for generations in the same houses, were asked, for a weekly compensation and as part of the war effort, to gather up their possessions; their pictures, their china, their furniture, their clothes, their dogs, even their goats, in cars supplied by the WVS.

**Godfrey Will, farmer:** We just took things as they came then. There was a war on and we expected anything to happen. Everyone just got down to it and tried to put their own house in order. We didn't know about any plans for the evacuation until they told us. It was a surprise. It was difficult leaving because we had to get somewhere to live. And the trouble was that everyone was looking for a place.

**Grace Bradbeer:** By now so much of the South West was filled with evacuees from the more densely populated towns and cities that the villages could take no more. So, although the nearby countryside did its best, especially with regard to the farmers, private people in the area often had to go far away to find a new home.

**Nancy Hare:** They were so brave and cheerful. By the second week we had got into our stride. Gradually the smoke from the chimneys grew less and less and driving through the villages was an eerie experience. Furniture vans loaded to capacity and farm lorries stacked with hay filled the lanes and these added to the American traffic which was beginning to filter into the area made driving a dangerous business.

**Grace Bradbeer:** Those with the greatest problems were the farmers with their stock and crops, fodder and all kinds of agricultural machinery. Many had to sell whole herds, and if a man had spent nearly a lifetime in building up a particular strain it was a heart-breaking business.

**Godfrey Will:** We were one of the last to leave because we had so much stuff to get rid of. It was pretty grim. There was no one about. Everything was deathly quiet. We had to use boxes to sit on because the furniture had gone.

**Col. Ralph Rayner, member of Parliament, South Devon:** It is hard enough to be hunted from one's farm by the enemy or blasted from one's home by his bombs, but it is a great deal harder to have to cut the ties of a lifetime in order to provide Allied Arms with a stage for the dress rehearsal.

**Grace Bradbeer:** Volunteers were sent at the last to inspect every village, to make sure that everyone had gone, that each house or cottage was properly secured and that all was in readiness to be officially handed over to the American authorities.

**Nancy Hare:** We left Blackawton to the Americans on December 24. Someone suddenly remembered, "Tomorrow is Christmas Day!"

**Grace Bradbeer:** On each church's principal gate was now fastened the following notice: *To our Allies of the U.S.A.—This church has stood here for several hundred years. Around it has grown a community, which has lived in these houses and tilled these fields ever since there was a church. This church, this churchyard in which their loved ones lie at rest, these homes, these fields are as dear to those who have left them as are the homes and graves and fields which you, our Allies, have left behind you. They hope to return one day, as you hope to return to yours, to find them waiting to welcome them home. They entrust them to your care meanwhile, and pray that God's blessing may rest upon us all. Charles, Bishop of Exeter.*

\*         \*         \*

*With the South Hams region emptied of British residents, Allied forces moved in, beginning five months of intense invasion preparation and training, which would grow continuously through early May in size and complexity, despite the forces participating still not knowing when or where the invasion itself would take place. Through the exercises and other training across the British Isles, troops became familiar with loading and offloading landing craft and even got to know the very boats and crew that would ferry them to occupied Europe.*

**Pvt. John Barnes, Company A, 116th Infantry Regiment, 29th Division:** I was in boat team #2 under Lt. John Clements. Out on the moors we would practice landings from an imaginary boat. Men would line up in three columns, ten men each. The first three out the boat were riflemen. They would fan out when the ramp went down and take up protective fire positions. Next came two men who carried bangalore torpedoes, long lengths of pipe containing dynamite. These were shoved under barbed wire to blow a pathway. The next men were designated as wire cutters to help clear the further gap. Then machine gunners to cover us, and next 30 millimeter mortar gunners and ammo carriers. Lastly, a flame thrower team and a dynamite team to get close to the pillbox and blow it up.

The pillbox, we were told, was the way the Germans built their defensive setup. Huge concrete structures, 2 to 3 feet thick, round like an old fashioned pillbox, with a small hole from which they could fire their guns. It was this small hole to which we were to direct our attack. The last members of the assault team scrambled up to the target running the last steps, setting the charge, and then hurling it inside the hole and running back shouting "fire in the hole!" A few seconds later, the dynamite would go off, and our team would charge forward firing and shouting success. We practiced this routine every day, over and over. Each man knew his job. We worked together. It was different than the basic training in the United States. We took it very seriously, and the officers made it more serious when they began to set up groups of sharp shooters to freely fire at us in our dry run.

**George Robert Hamilton, anti-aircraft gunner, 320th Barrage Balloon Battalion:** We learned how to handle ourselves. Learned how to fight. We'd been taught how to wrestle with another man, how to get the best of each other, how to take a gun away.

**Celia Andrews, housewife, Signet Hill, Burford, Oxfordshire:** I remember the planes and gliders practicing, dropping large baskets, several of which fell almost in our garden. The Americans from up the road used to practice marching and hiding at the same time; I used to see them crouching and I wondered then what their future would be.

**Brig. The Lord Lovat, commander, 1st Special Service Brigade:** Even the seasoned troops back from Italy and North Africa found they were out of practice and had to work as hard as newcomers; every commando soldier struggled to keep his place in the team. They knew sound training would save lives. In war, I kept repeating, the worst casualties are caused through incompetence, and not by the enemy.

**Pfc. Felix Branham, Company K, 116th Infantry Regiment, 29th Division:** We didn't talk of dying, unless it was a joke. We used to kid a guy who had this beautiful ring and carry a big wad of money, seven or eight hundred dollars. His name was Gino Ferrari. I used to say to him, "Ferrari, when you hit that beach and you fall, man, I'm going to get your wallet out." And another guy would say, "Yep, and I'm going to have that ring." We sat around and thought about that, but never thinking that that would really happen. What else did we have to talk about?

**Seaman William T. O'Neill, USS *LCT-544*:** Most of the time up until the invasion of France was spent in making endless practice runs.

**Lt. John Mason Brown:** The maneuvers off the South Coast—each one of these was a full, grim dress rehearsal of what was to come. Each one of these involved thousands and thousands of men and countless craft. Each one of these ran the risks of enemy attack from the air or sea. As the spring flowered, these maneuvers increased as surely as the heat does before a violent summer storm.

**S.Sgt. Harry Bare, Company F, 116th Infantry Regiment, 29th Division:** With borrowed old landing boats from the British, we set out from the Royal Naval College on the Dart River, went out to sea, and then swerved back to assault the beach at Slapton Sands. This at least taught the men and myself how to work in water.

**Pvt. John H. MacPhee, Company E, 16th Infantry Regiment, 1st Division:** I went through so many amphibious landings and maneuvers, and I spent so much time in the water, I thought I was in the Navy—and I am no sailor.

**Sgt. Valentine M. Miele, Company H, 16th Infantry Regiment, 1st Division:** Boy, was it cold; in those flat-bottomed boats the spray would come over; your field jacket would get icy; that was a rough few weeks. We used to call them "dry runs" but there was nothing dry about them.

**Pvt. Harold "Hal" Baumgarten, Company B, 116th Infantry Regiment, 29th Division:** We also went on two complete landings on Slapton Sands Beach in southwest England. Each time we boarded the same ship as we would for the real invasion, the HMS *Empire Javelin*.

**Sgt. Valentine M. Miele:** We'd pull out into the bay, circle around, and we'd invade England.

**William C. Smith, Company F, 115th Infantry Regiment, 29th Division:** They used live ammunition, which was fired over your head. Occasionally they fired a live artillery shell over your head so you could get used to the sound of artillery, and as you crossed the beach they would detonate dynamite that had been buried in the sand beforehand.

**Pvt. Allen McMath, 112th Engineer Combat Battalion:** The higher brass made it seem as near like the real thing as possible with the least possible men getting wounded or killed. Of course, there were a few who got hurt, as that couldn't be helped in the Army.

**Pvt. Harold "Hal" Baumgarten:** Before each of our landings, the area was saturated with 80 mm mortar shells. On one occasion, the bombardment was not lifted in time, and [Pfc.] Ascy Peacock was wounded in his upper lip. With the lip severely scarred, he returned to the outfit in time for the invasion. He was killed in action on D-Day.

*      *      *

*Beyond learning how to board and exit landing craft, storm pillboxes, and seize beach fortifications, a key part of the training exercises ahead of Operation OVER-LORD was learning to operate some of the special armored equipment that was being prepared for the amphibious assault. These included propeller-driven Sherman tanks, known as Dual-Drive (DD) tanks, that could swim to shore ringed by an inflated waterproof canvas shroud, as well as a broader array of specialized armor known as "Hobart's Funnies," after the innovative British general who had imagined and driven their creation. These also included tanks and armored vehicles equipped with, variously, flamethrowers, special heavy bunker-busting guns, or "flails," giant spinning wheels covered in iron chains that slapped the ground and set off buried mines that could be used to rapidly clear paths through minefields.*

**Chief Yeoman W. Garwood Bacon, Jr., 7th Naval Beach Battalion:** On one of the live ammunition practice landings at Slapton Sands, we saw what was to be one of the surprise weapons of the war.

**Lt. Bill Little, commander, 5th Troop (Sherman DD tanks), C Squadron, Fort Garry Horse, 3rd Canadian Division:** This little barge turned and headed towards us, and as it rolled you could see it touch the bottom of the lake and started to roll up. This was a tremendous surprise. Then as it rolled forward the tracks kept coming higher; and then as it got to the edge of the water, down came the screen and there was the gun. This was a surprise and a shock.

**Chief Yeoman W. Garwood Bacon, Jr.:** These tanks, our secret weapons, were able to swim in to the beach like assault boats, drop their rubberized canvas boatlike sides, and quickly target their 75 mm cannons directly at the pillboxes.

**Cpl. Harvey "Willie" Williamson, commander, Sherman DD tank, Fort Garry Horse, 3rd Canadian Division:** They were one of the best-kept secrets of the war. We could only practice under cover of darkness.

**Trooper Laurie Burn, 13th/18th Royal Hussars (Queen Mary's Own):** My brother Pete and I were members of the same Sherman tank crew. Pete was the co-driver and I was the gunner. I had nicknamed our tank *Icanhopit*, and by the end of the war, we were in *Icanhopit Four*. [We] underwent weeks of practice at the submarine station in Gosport, sitting in an improvised tank turret in a twenty-foot-deep concrete bath and having two thousand gallons of water pour in, which was a strain on the nervous system to say the least.

**Trooper Joe Minogue, gunner, B Squadron, Westminster Dragoons:** I really think we were more terrified of being drowned in that damned tank than anything else.

**Lt. Ian Hammerton, commander, Sherman Crab flail tank, 22nd Dragoons, 30th Armoured Brigade, 79th Armoured Division:** We had a visit from General [Sir Percy] Hobart, who was the 79th Armoured Division's general in charge. He gathered everybody round him and said, "You're going in front, to clear up the mess. You are going to be mine-clearers: flails." Nobody had ever heard of them. The bottom dropped out of their world. They were stunned, absolutely stunned. To find out how these things worked, I was sent back to my old battalion in Suffolk, who were experimenting with flails, Snakes and Scorpions and all the other strange menagerie of things, in the Orford training area, a part of Suffolk that was sealed off, highly secret.

**Lance Cpl. Stuart Stear, 619 Independent Field Park Company, 103 Beach Group, Royal Engineers:** We built a replica of the Atlantic Wall. It took us a month to pour the concrete and complete the building work and not nearly so long for Hobart's Funnies of 79th Armoured Division to literally smash it up. It gave us a lot of confidence to see how quickly their great big demolition guns destroyed it and to watch the infantry and DD tanks practicing coming ashore.

**Lt. Ian Hammerton:** We were known as the "Funnies" because of all the secret assault equipment we had: flail tanks for clearing the mines; "snakes," which were fire hoses filled with nitroglycerin; some "Crocodile" flame throwers; "Buffaloes," armored swimming vehicles; DD tanks, which were boat-shaped Sherman tanks that provided fire support for the infantry. Anything that could blow things up—you name it, we had it.

**Trooper Joe Minogue:** Sir Percy Hobart, we were all convinced, might be a Major General, but he was "one of us," a tankman's tankman. We felt, in spite of his high rank, that he would have been happy sitting on an upturned petrol tin chewing the fat with the crew, enjoying our corny jokes and sharing a mug of tea with us.

\*     \*     \*

*Certainly not all the vehicles assigned to* OVERLORD *could swim, and thus one of the biggest logistical challenges that* OVERLORD *faced was how to ready thousands of vehicles for an amphibious landing—ensuring that they would be both safe to land in the surf and yet also ready to do battle as soon as possible when they arrived on the shore of France. Planners designed and trained crews on an extensive waterproofing process that sealed critical engine components—a process, though, that would have to happen as late as possible before boarding the transports since, once sealed, the vehicle engines could only run for a short period.*

**Maj. John Dalgleish, Planning Staff, Royal Army Service Corps:** Waterproofing was necessary to permit vehicles and tanks to "wade" ashore from landing craft, through some considerable depth of water, and then to carry on their normal tasks on land. The first requirement was that vehicles should be waterproofed to "wade" through eighteen inches of water. The requirement was [later] raised to three feet of water, and finally to four-feet six-inches of water. Each new requirement brought a host of attendant problems, as more and more parts of the vehicle were submerged.

**Lt. Gen. Sir Frederick Morgan, Deputy Chief of Staff, SHAEF:** The problem of waterproofing vehicles was not made easier by the fact that the British Army, having been caught—as usual—unprepared on the outbreak of war, had never been able to catch up with itself in the matter, among others, of standardisation of motor equipment. It possessed well over a hundred different types of vehicles and engines, each one of which presented a different problem when it came to waterproofing.

**Lance Cpl. Stuart Stear:** We were taught how to fit extensions to exhausts and engine breathing pipes to enable vehicles to drive from the landing craft onto the beach. Our final exam was to drive the vehicles down a ramp into a tank full of water, to test the sealing of the plugs in the vehicle hull. If you drove through successfully, you passed but if your vehicle stopped in the tank, you were sent back to keep practising!

**Pvt. Ray Howell, 3466th Ordnance Medium Automotive Maintenance Company, 5th Engineer Special Brigade:** I've seen them run underwater where the only thing sticking up is the driver's head and a few hoses sticking up—air intakes. The rest of that truck or jeep is underwater.

**Capt. Paul F. Hillman, 4th Armored Division, 126th Ordnance Maintenance Battalion:** We were checking them over, making sure they were doing it right, because you'd be surprised that without waterproofing, the most stupid little thing will stop your engine—shorting any exposed electricals right out—and that'd be it, you'd be a sitting duck.

**Lt. Gen. Sir Frederick Morgan:** Experiment, coupled with a study of availabilities, gave the answer as a compound of heavy grease and asbestos, but to get the proper mix that would stay put baffled all comers until Col. Norman Lack, United States Army, of COSSAC's small scientific and experimental section brought his brain to bear. He discovered that the trouble lay in the minute fraction of moisture normally held by asbestos. This was removed, by baking, and we had the answer. A little thing, maybe, but much depended on it. Once it had been a horseshoe nail that lost a kingdom. Here it was a drop of moisture in a shred of asbestos that was holding up victory.

**Maj. John Dalgleish:** Waterproofing imposes distance limits on vehicles, and had to be done in stages. Stage 1 took some two days to effect, and afterwards limited a vehicle to running 200 miles. Stage 2 took sixteen hours to effect, and limited a vehicle to running only a few miles thereafter. Stage 3 took half an hour to complete, and limited the vehicle to running only a very short distance. The vital consideration seemed to be the Stage 2 task, for this meant a sixteen-hour wait at some place not more than a certain number of miles from the point of embarkation.

**Maj. Gen. Francis "Freddie" de Guingand, Chief of Staff, General Montgomery:** Once waterproofed, vehicles could only travel a certain distance.

**Pvt. Ray Howell:** Our job [during the invasion] was to de-waterproof these vehicles and keep them from overheating, because the drivers themselves, in the process of doing what they had to do, often would neglect some of these things, and sooner or later they would have a vehicle that overheated and wouldn't run.

**Maj. John Dalgleish:** Waterproofing was a problem-child, right to the very last. Very near to D-Day waterproofing caused the abandonment of several invasion camps—on which considerable sums of money and much labour had been expended—because these camps were just outside the new radius allowed for waterproofed vehicles to travel to the ports of embarkation.

# Exercise TIGER

*LST-289* limps back into the harbor after surviving the surprise attack amid Exercise TIGER. Two other LSTs weren't as lucky.

*At the end of April, the Allied military embarked on what was supposed to be the most realistic and extensive exercise at Slapton Sands yet. Code-named* TIGER, *the exercise focused on units attached to what was known as Task Force U, the force under United States Admiral Don P. Moon that would land at Utah Beach—although that specific target and destination was still a mystery to all but the tiny slice of BIGOT-cleared personnel.*

*In Exercise* TIGER, *some 25,000 personnel, including paratroopers and amphibious assault troops, and some 337 ships and landing craft, were scheduled to land in and around Slapton Sands, overcoming beach obstacles resembling those the invading forces would face in France, and dodging live gunfire. As it turned out, though, the greatest danger to the Utah-bound troops would come before they ever touched the shore.*

**Dr. Eugene E. Eckstam, medical officer, US Naval Reservist, USS *LST-507*:** On April 25 the ship loaded army troops, trucks, Jeeps, and other equipment aboard at Brixham Harbor. All told, as we prepared for the exercise, we had on board the *LST-507* 125 navy men as ship's company, the 42-man medical detachment, and about 300 soldiers. We rode at anchor for about two days while other ships loaded for the practice landing. The ship's main deck and the enclosed tank deck below it were completely filled with vehicles and army personnel. The soldiers slept anywhere they could find a space and paraded around in a circle on the main deck in order to get the C rations that constituted their meals.

**Ens. Douglas Harlander, navigation officer, USS *LST-531*:** On the morning of April 27, 1944, as the convoy left naval headquarters at Plymouth and headed through the English Channel, the destroyer which had been assigned to protect the convoy was commanded into port for repairs. It never joined the convoy and no replacement was sent. Instead the ships were led by a small, British trawler.

**Ens. Tom Clark, USS *LST-507*:** There was a bright moon out.

**Arthur Victor, Navy corpsman, USS *LST-507*:** The heavens were blanketed with stars.

**Dr. Eugene E. Eckstam:** The convoy proceeded onward, and I turned in early to get some sleep in anticipation of the next morning's practice invasion. I was jarred awake around 1:30 in the morning by the sound of the ship's general alarm.

**Capt. Gunther Rabe, commander, E-boat *S-130*, Kriegsmarine:** We knew that during April 1944 there was constant traffic on the route off the south coast of Great Britain as we met with increasing resistance from a rapidly growing number of gun-boats, launches and other escorts. We happened to get visual contact with a convoy of LSTs, lined up in a rather long line and from our position we did not see any escorts.

**Seaman James T. Fudge, USS *LST-54*:** The E-boat—torpedo boat—was made of wood. They were light and therefore very fast. They would hit and run. You can't find them in the dark.

**USS *LST-511*, "Report of Action 28 April 1944," May 3, 1944:** First heard were the [E-Boat] motors, which were initially reported to be an airplane, as it sounded much like one. The boat approached at about 40 knots on a course heading from port to starboard, passing directly in front of the ship by no more than 15 yards. At this point none of our guns were able to depress sufficiently to fire on it. The boat then disappeared from view. No description of the craft can be given due to the darkness of the night and its coloring. Only the wake and its gunfire were seen.

**Capt. Gunther Rabe:** The shadows were clearly to be seen in a south-easterly direction. We approached in good distance at comparatively high speed in order to come in a favourable position for torpedo attack. My boat fired two torpedoes at about 2:05 a.m. As there were many more ships in the area we could not attempt to close in to look for survivors.

*Around 2 a.m.,* LST-499 *noticed the next sign that something amid the exercise was going awry—a torpedo coming toward it out of the night. It began to take evasive action.*

**Vincent Dunn, stern gunner, USS *LST-499*:** We had a fish coming at our ship at about 265 degrees. I told our gun captain. He informed the bridge. We made a slight turn and the fish went by us.

**Seaman 2nd Class Steve Sadlon, radioman, USS *LST-507*:** I was asleep in my sack when I was awakened by a scraping noise along the side of our LST. It was a torpedo that didn't explode. General Quarters sounded a moment later and I ran for the radio shack.

**Ens. Tom Clark:** I was a little nervous. We were the last ship in the formation and we were traveling very slowly at the time. Soon the radar reports became a little more ominous. Three more ships were picked up off our starboard quarter. By now we were pretty sure something was amiss. I turned my glasses [binoculars] off our starboard quarter. I had my glasses to my eyes when the torpedo hit us.

**Dr. Eugene E. Eckstam:** Just after two in the morning, I heard the sound of a tremendous explosion. In quick sequence came the sound of crunching metal, a painful landing on the steel deck with both knees, falling dust and rust. In the ensuing darkness and silence, distracted by aching knees, I wondered, "My God, what happened?"

**Seaman Steve Sadlon:** I was starting to get the radio going when a second torpedo hit right below where I was in the auxiliary engine room. I was thrown out of my chair by the concussion from the exploding torpedo. My head hit the overhead bulkhead and knocked me out.

**Arthur Victor:** I was lifted from my feet and hurled back against a bulkhead. Although my head hit so hard I almost passed out, my helmet absorbed most of the shock and I was only dazed, with nothing worse than a split upper lip. I staggered to my feet.

**Seaman Steve Sadlon:** All hell was breaking loose aboard ship.

**Lt. (jg) James F. Murdoch, executive officer, USS *LST-507*:** All of the army vehicles naturally were loaded with gasoline, and it was the gasoline which caught fire first. As the gasoline spread on the deck and poured into the fuel oil which was seeping out of the side of the ship, it caused fire on the water around the ship.

**Dr. Eugene E. Eckstam:** As I moved about below decks, I approached a hatch leading into the tank deck, a large open area filled with vehicles and men. As I looked in, I saw only fire—a huge, roaring blast furnace. I tried to enter and to call out to the men inside, but it was futile. Trucks were burning; gasoline was burning; and small-arms ammunition was exploding. Worst of all were the agonizing screams for help from the men trapped inside that blazing inferno. I knew there was no way I—or anyone else—could help them.

**Ens. Tom Clark:** At this time the ship gave a pronounced lurch and we felt sure she did not have much longer. Fred Beattie looked at me and said,

"C'mon Tom, it's time we got out of here." We looked about the stern and threw over anything which would float. All you could hear was the wail and moan of men in the water.

**Seaman Steve Sadlon:** We had nothing—we were a floating, burning hull of a ship. Finally the skipper gave the order to abandon ship.

**Raymond Bartholomay, aboard *LST-507*:** We have rehearsed this many times in boot camp, but there were a few new wrinkles here. In boot camp we were always sure to be "rescued" in a hurry as our "ocean" was a 75' x 100' swimming pool.

**Ens. Tom Clark:** Fred jumped first, and caught a board. I asked him how the water was and he said fine. I jumped and what a terrible moment. I never felt water so cold in my life. The jacket was good and it held me up. I had shoes on but I had them fixed so that I could kick them off if they got too heavy.

**Arthur Victor:** There were about fifty to seventy-five of us now as we drifted on.

*Moments later, another torpedo struck* USS *LST-531, followed quickly by a second. The mortally wounded landing ship sank in just six minutes.*

**Ens. Douglas Harlander, navigation officer, USS *LST-531*:** I went out to take a look and was standing on the starboard wing when the first torpedo hit. It felt like a sledgehammer on my feet. It threw me back eight or nine feet. We were dead in the water.

**Emanuel "Manny" Rubin, signalman, USS *LST-496*:** A gigantic orange ball explosion, like something from the movies, a flame like it had come from hell.

**Pvt. Veldon Downing, 3206th Quartermaster Service Company, aboard USS *LST-531*:** I was in my bunk asleep when it blew and all the lights went out. I got my pants on and made a beeline for the door and somehow managed to get topside. The last thing I heard in the darkness was Ivan Brown yelling to Alvin Richardson. Ivan said: "For God's sake, hurry up!" I never saw them again.

**Ens. Douglas Harlander:** The ship was sinking and fast turning over and I was the last man over the port side. As I was walking on the outside of the ship's hull, it sank beneath me. I dove off and got away as fast as I could to avoid being dragged under by the suction of the ship's descent.

**William Holland, motor machinist's mate, 2nd class, engine room crew, *LST-531*:** I jumped overboard and went down until I stopped, then—much to my relief—compressed my life belt and it brought me to the surface of burning water. I was able to get a hand on a life raft. There were so few around at the time. What there was in the area were overcrowded, and I was not too welcome.

**Ens. Douglas Harlander:** The chill of the water was almost paralyzing. Despite my heavy clothing, I swam away as fast as possible, knowing there would be suction. I realized I had lost a shoe. I untied and kicked off my other shoe after negotiating around some surface burning oil. Diesel oil covered my entire body, slowing my progress toward a small life raft. To this day I have a fearful feeling when I smell burning oil.

While swimming away I saw in the glare of the flames a life-beltless soldier hanging onto a wooden board. He shouted to a nearby sailor, "Do you want to trade my board for your life jacket?" The sailor immediately replied "Yes" and made the swap. I have often recalled this bargaining under such adverse conditions.

**Ens. Tom Clark:** Cries, screams, and moans filled the night.

*The E-boats managed to sink two LSTs before any Allied vessel even spotted them in the darkness. Over the next half hour, further torpedoes crisscrossed the flotilla, forcing other LSTs into evasive action. LST-289 was hit, wounding 21 and killing 13, but ultimately the craft survived. LST-511, meanwhile, was apparently hit near its bow by a torpedo that failed to explode and then sank harmlessly.*

**Nathan Resnick, motor machinist's mate, 2nd class, USS *LST-511*:** When I arrived on deck, *LST 507* had already been hit and was in flames. I saw *LST 531* get hit by two torpedoes, followed by a thunderous noise, an explosion, and a huge fireball. The rest of the convoy began zigzagging, and *LST 511* began firing their guns in the direction of the German E-Boats, but I could hardly see them. Friendly fire from *LST 496* and enemy fire from the E-Boats injured 15 men on the top deck of my ship. I witnessed a torpedo making contact with the hull, but it didn't explode. The Army men in the tank deck remember hearing the sound of the impact.

**Paul Gerolstein, gunner's mate, 2nd class, USS *LST-515*:** The convoy was given orders to scatter and the battle was over before we knew it.

**Dr. Eugene E. Eckstam:** As I got away from the *LST-507* I looked back and saw that the flames from the ship were shooting high in the sky and lighting up the whole area. I found a life raft about three hundred yards from the ship; on it was one of our very responsible pharmacist's mates. At first I was hanging on to other men circling the raft; I was in about the fifth or sixth ring myself. As those in front of me lost consciousness, I had to leave them to drift off. There was nothing to hold them to the raft so we could stay together. As I got closer, I was eventually able to reach in between two men and twist my hand around a piece of line that circled the perimeter of the raft; that kept me from drifting away. But I could feel myself becoming very sleepy and no longer cold; I knew that I would be unconscious soon.

*For the survivors in the cold water from* LST-507 *and -531, hours passed without rescue. Many began to die, particularly those around Arthur Victor, who, like him, were just holding on to the edges of the few life rafts.*

**Arthur Victor:** I had become almost unbearably cold. I had also been swallowing oily tasting salt water that made me nauseous, and I started puking. I pissed my pants to feel the warm. I remember how good it felt pouring over my thighs.

**Raymond Bartholomay:** I was beginning to get drowsy, a bad sign in cold water, and praying supplied some hope.

**Ens. Fred Beattie:** I remember the cold, the wet, and it seemed to be growing ever more quiet. I looked up and saw a black sky, brilliant with stars.

**Arthur Victor:** Across the raft from me my good buddy Scotty [Kenneth Scott] had been having a hard time hanging in. From the start he was in a state of frenzy and kept begging and pleading to get on the raft, asking me over and over again to help him. Star and I kept up a steady chatter to try and calm him down. But it did no good. He didn't seem to hear. He kept pleading and even tried to get on but we had to keep him off. I kept yelling at him to hold on. Then someone hollered over that he thought he was dead. He was bobbing, his belt head down. The corpsman next to him said he wasn't breathing. We had seen enough dead already. I said there was no choice but to let him drift away. Someone else moved into his spot. His death haunts me.

**Ens. Tom Clark:** It was as if I were looking down from the sky and seeing myself in the water—I was a spectator watching myself. When I awoke I would realize I was not kicking my legs. Gradually my legs froze. It didn't seem long until the cries of the stricken were no more. I awakened from one of these "sleeps" to a dead quiet, then the sounds of voices.

**Arthur Victor:** Several times, we heard the drone of an LCVP [Landing Craft Vehicle/Personnel] nearby. We shouted hoarsely to it and signaled with our flashlight, but it never came.

**Ens. Tom Clark:** It is a very distinct possibility that many lives would have been saved if rescue efforts had been made one hour earlier.

*Finally, around 4 a.m., rescue ships, including the escort destroyer HMS* Saladin *and* LST-515, *arrived at the scene.*

**Medical Officer J. B. Wilson, probationary surgeon, HMS *Saladin*:** As we neared the disaster area, we passed through a sea of hundreds of corpses, clad in life jackets but face down in the water.

**Floyd Hicks, gunner's mate, 2nd class, USS *LST-515*:** We came to a dead stop and could hear them begging to be picked up. I could see a life raft with a few people in it and many in the water, some holding on and others bobbing nearby. We immediately threw a rope ladder over the side and I climbed down into the raft. One real young fellow, wearing only underclothes, was dead. But I was able to help the others, secured with lines, up the ladder to the deck.

**Dr. Eugene E. Eckstam:** What happened after that I do not know, because the next thing I remember clearly was climbing up the side of a ship. It was daylight, and I was halfway up; I have no memory of beginning the climb. In recent years I have had the vague remembrance of hearing the engines of landing craft, of putting a knee on the lowered ramp of a landing craft, and sitting along the side once inside. None of these recollections is more than fuzzy; none presents a continuous picture.

**Joseph "Eddie" McCann, LCVP coxswain, USS *LST-515*:** My boat crew stayed busy. We did not have time to keep track of how many men we picked out of the water.*

**Cpl. Eugene Carney, quartermaster, 4th Division:** A lot of men died that night and piled up on us. I asked some soldiers to move them onto litters so we would take them below. We were hampered by the railing on the stairs and removed it with a hacksaw. Most of the younger men had never handled a corpse and hesitated to take hold of the dead. We did this detail all night, over and over until we were exhausted.

**Joseph "Eddie" McCann:** By now the sun was coming up very bright. We observed three British motor torpedo boats moving very fast from the north to the south. I felt sure they would move out and around all of the bodies and debris in the water, but they did not. Instead they cut right through and were churning up bodies in their screws. I said, "My God, they are going to go right through about a hundred or more bodies that I haven't checked for life."

---

* McCann had run away from home at age thirteen and, using false papers and permission from a pretend "father," had joined the Navy. On the night of Exercise TIGER, he was just fifteen years old and already a veteran of the invasions of Sicily and North Africa. The Navy wouldn't discover his subterfuge until 1945.

**Warrant Officer Candidate Julian Perkin, crew, HMS *Obedient* destroyer (G48):**
We arrived in the area at daybreak and the sight was appalling. There were
hundreds of bodies of American servicemen, in full battle gear, floating in
the sea. Many had their limbs and even their heads blown off. We took
aboard all those we could find still living and applied first aid and resus-
citation. One American I was attending in the wardroom collapsed and
died obviously through the terrible shock of the ordeal. They were all such
young men—it was tragic. Of all those we took on board there were only
nine survivors. Small American landing craft with their ramps down were
literally scooping up bodies. It was a ghastly sight.

**Charles E. Modeste, USS *Tide* (AM-125):** Parts of bodies, legs torn from tor-
sos, one body without a head. There were too many of them, so we finally
allowed the bow wave to push them aside.

**Sgt. Barnett Hoffner, 6th Engineer Special Brigade:** I was on the beach at the
time with my squad. We were practicing taking up mines when we saw the
bodies come floating in. I had heard the gunfire but there was always blasting
and we felt there was nothing unusual this time. We started down the water's
edge to get the bodies which were clad in fatigues when I heard a voice
yell. "Sergeant! Get your men out of there! Haven't you ever seen dead men
before?" I looked up and saw three stars on the shoulders and recognized
that it was Major General [Clarence] Huebner of the 1st Infantry Division.
I got my squad out of there fast. You don't question anything a general says.

*Ashore, the surviving casualties were raced to nearby medical facilities and the
US military began to throw a protective blanket of secrecy around the entire
fiasco—isolating participants, invoking secrecy oaths, and tamping down any
speculation about the true human cost of the incident.*

**Capt. Harry C. Butcher, naval aide to Dwight Eisenhower, SHAEF:** As the day
closed, I was in Ike's office when Beetle phoned on the intercommunication
system to say that by E-boat action last night, we had two LSTs sunk and
one damaged in the exercise. Casualties are estimated at 300 to 400. Beetle
said this reduces our reserve of LSTs for the big show to zero.

**Rear Adm. Don P. Moon, commander, Naval Task Force U:** This was a costly egg in our omelet.

**Capt. Ralph C. Greene, medical staff, 228th Station Hospital:** [We were told] in less than an hour, we will receive hundreds of emergency cases of shock due to immersion, compounded by explosion wounds. "You will ask no questions and take no histories. There will be no discussion. Follow standard procedures. Anyone who talks about these casualties, regardless of their severity, will be subject to court martial. No one will be allowed to leave our perimeter until further orders."

**Seaman Daniel Folsom, rhino barge coxswain, 111th Naval Construction Battalion (SeaBees):** They put the clamp on us so nobody could tell anybody about it.

**Capt. Ralph C. Greene:** A stream of ambulances and trucks were pouring through the gate, filled with wet, shivering, blue-skinned, blanketed and bandaged young Army and Navy men, many in great pain.

**Arthur Victor:** The next day we were taken to an army base and counted in. Then the army boys went one way and we went the other. We were taken to another area and housed in a dilapidated barracks, under guard, for three days, and ordered, under threat of court martial, not to discuss the incident with anyone outside of our immediate group.

**Cpl. Eugene Carney:** We were told to keep our mouths shut and taken to a camp where we were quarantined. When we went through the mess line we weren't even allowed to talk to the cooks. If, for example, we wanted two potatoes, we were told to hold up two fingers. If three, three fingers. We could have all we wanted but could say nothing.

**Ens. Tom Clark:** Like all men who live through something like that, I wonder why my life was spared. My roommate, fresh out of navy school, Smithy the engineer, the man with the mustache, Jim Clark, who loaned me a hundred dollars to bring Pottsie [Tom Clark's nickname for his wife] down to New Orleans. Hoffman and Sucier, veterans of three invasions, and the army officers—nine out of eleven lost their lives that night. There were twenty-three officers aboard and eight were saved. An experience like that leaves funny impressions.

**Maj. Ralph Ingersoll, intelligence officer, planning staff, SHAEF:** We asked ourselves why the Germans had chosen this moment to make their raid and the answer was obvious: It was to take prisoners who could tell them how we planned to attack. The $64 thousand question: *Had the E-Boats taken any prisoners and, if so, what did these prisoners know?* Amongst the officers and men who took part in the exercises there were a score or more—I forget the exact figure now—of Bigoted officers who knew the exact beaches on which we were to land, and, at what moon and what tide of what month. By one of those amazing miracles which characterize war, although the bodies of hundreds who went down were never recovered, the remains of every single one of the Bigoted officers were found. Each was recovered, its corpse floated by its Mae West [life preserver], and properly identified.

**Pvt. Veldon Downing:** They told us to keep our mouths shut, and we did. After the war, the parents of one of the kids I served with and who'd been lost drove all the way out here from New York just to ask me what happened. I told them I couldn't talk about it.*

**Dr. Eugene E. Eckstam:** Many years have passed since that terrible night in the English Channel in the spring of 1944, but there is some pain that the lengthening span of time has been unable to deaden. To this day I can still hear the screams of those burning men, my former shipmates in the tank deck of the *LST-507*. The agony of their final few minutes of life is embedded so deeply into my memory that I still have nightmares about them.

---

* It took decades for the US military to admit what happened off Slapton Sands; the final official death toll from that one night attack is 749 servicemen, but even that number remains heavily disputed due to the secrecy of the time and poor recordkeeping—some estimates hold that the total death toll may have even reached 1,000 or more, but even the official total is far higher than the number of infantry personnel killed at Utah Beach on D-Day itself (197).

*"Shoot up anything that moved"*

# The Transportation Plan

Allied airpower devastated train facilities across France
in the weeks leading up to D-Day.

*Though the amphibious side of the OVERLORD invasion plan still needed to be developed, one part of the Allied military effort was already well under way—and had been for some time. Since 1942, the Allied air forces had been actively attacking the heart of the German occupation from above, with British bombers taking the skies by day, and US bombers filling them by night.*

*The air effort against Germany and occupied Europe was massive: The US air fleet was divided between the Eighth Air Force, whose four-engine bombers primarily focused on larger strategic bombing runs against German industrial targets and cities, and the Ninth Air Force, which primarily oversaw more close-in tactical bombing missions. Together, they had nearly 400,000 personnel in the UK and operated from nearly 150 airfields around the countryside; the Eighth Air Force could generate more than 2,000 four-engine bombers and 1,000 fighter planes for a single large-scale bombing mission. The Royal Air Force, for its part, had nearly a million personnel of its own, including about 180,000 WAAFs— Women's Auxiliary Air Force—who filled key noncombat positions, and its Bomber Command could also launch 1,000 bombers for large missions.*

*How, when, and where to use these bombers was one of the big debates inside the Supreme Allied Command through the spring of 1944. Two different camps emerged: One wanted to continue to focus on long-range bombing of German industrial targets and its oil infrastructure, hoping to paralyze and downgrade the ability of its forces to fight. The other wanted to focus more tactically on the front lines, destroying the transportation infrastructure of Western Europe that would allow the Germans to speed reinforcements to the front. There was no room for error: Air support would be critical to the success of D-Day.*

**Capt. Harry C. Butcher, naval aide to Dwight Eisenhower, SHAEF:** The Supreme Commander's view of the problem was that the first five or six weeks of OVERLORD would be a most critical period for the Allied armies. It was essential that we should take every possible step to ensure that our forces get ashore and stay ashore.

**Gen. Dwight Eisenhower, Supreme Allied Commander, SHAEF:** Until January 1944, the view had been held that the heavy bombers of the Strategic Air Forces could make sufficient direct contribution to the assault in a period of about a fortnight before D-Day. Further consideration, however, indicated the need to employ them for a much longer period—about three months.

**Gen. Lord Hastings Ismay, chief military adviser to Winston Churchill:** Eisenhower, supported by Tedder and Leigh-Mallory, insisted that they should concentrate on the destruction of the railway system of France, the Low Countries, and Western Germany, in order to isolate Normandy and prevent the Germans opposing our landings from being rapidly reinforced. Harris and Spaatz protested. The former said that his crews were trained to bombard industrial areas and could not, at short notice, achieve the pin-point accuracy which would be necessary to destroy targets such as bridges and key points on railways. Spaatz claimed that more decisive results on the German war effort as a whole would be obtained if he were permitted to pursue his plans of destroying the synthetic oil plants, and postpone switching to railway communication until just before D-Day.

**Maj. Ralph Ingersoll, intelligence officer, planning staff, SHAEF:** At the beginning of January, the weight of the American strategic bombers in Italy—the Fifteenth Air Force—was added to the Eighth and welded into one striking force against the Continent, under General Spaatz. February saw the climax.

**Winston Churchill, Prime Minister of the United Kingdom:** All this time the Americans were intent on bringing their Fortress bombers into action by day as soon as they could be protected by fighters of sufficiently long range to seek out and destroy the enemy fighters in the air or come down and attack them on their airfields. After long delay this vital need was met. First the Thunderbolt, then the Lightning, and finally the Mustang gave them day fighters which had auxiliary fuel tanks and a radius of action which was increased from 475 miles to 850. On February 23, 1944, there began a week of concentrated bomber attacks by day on the German aircraft industry.

**Gen. George C. Marshall, Chief of Staff, US Army:** The battle raged for a week. It was fought over Regensburg, Merseburg, Schweinfurt, and other critical industrial centers. The German fighter force was severely crippled, and our attacks continued with unabated fury.

**Gen. Lord Hastings Ismay:** The part to be played in the pre-OVERLORD period by Bomber Command under Air Chief Marshal Harris and the US Strategic Air Force, under General Spaatz, was the subject of prolonged and anxious argument.

**Lt. Gen. Walter Bedell "Beetle" Smith, Chief of Staff, SHAEF:** We discussed, not once but many times, the decision General Eisenhower had reached to bomb French rail centers to isolate the battle area in Normandy and hinder the enemy's efforts to bring up men and supplies.

**Sir Arthur Travers Harris, Air Chief Marshal, RAF Bomber Command:** Railways are extraordinarily difficult and unrewarding targets for air attack. Main lines can be repaired in a few hours and through lines in wrecked marshalling yards in a few days, provided that there is an efficient organization to do the work; in this, as in everything of the kind, the Germans were extremely efficient and had unlimited slave labour. But what if the repair organization should itself be attacked? That, in effect, was what it was decided to do.

**Capt. Harry C. Butcher:** The transportation plan for bombing has won out over the oil plan largely because the oil plan will not seriously affect German military operation for six months, too long for immediate benefit to OVERLORD.

**Gen. Dwight Eisenhower:** The fate of a continent depended upon the ability of our forces to seize a foothold and to maintain that foothold against everything we expected the enemy to throw against us.

**Lt. Gen. Walter Bedell "Beetle" Smith:** To bomb French rail centers would cause the death of many French civilians.

**Gen. Lord Hastings Ismay:** It was estimated that French civilian casualties would amount to not less than eighty thousand, and Churchill and the War Cabinet were aghast at the prospect of inflicting such grievous losses on our allies.

**Lt. Gen. Walter Bedell "Beetle" Smith:** I shall not soon forget the expression on the face of General [Marie-Pierre] Koenig [commander of the Free French Forces] when I talked with him about these bombings. As a Frenchman, he was torn by the additional suffering they would cause his people. But as a soldier, he recognized the vital military part they would play in the liberation of France. I doubt if the expression "C'est la guerre" was ever used with deeper feeling. The bombings began two months before the invasion, and with leaflets and other warnings we managed to get French civilians away from the targets.

**Sir Arthur Travers Harris:** Seventy-nine railway centres were accordingly picked out, in each of which there were important repair shops, with depots containing the necessary materials for the work. Nearly all such shops and depots are situated in or beside railway marshalling yards, and the plan was to select one or more aiming points in the marshalling yards in such a way that a heavy and effective concentration of bombing round these aiming points would destroy or severely damage the repair centres.

**Gen. Dwight Eisenhower:** Blows against the railroad centers were to be started about D-60 [60 days before D-Day] and were to cover a wide area so as to give the enemy no clue to our proposed assault beaches. Shortly before D-Day, however, the attacks would be intensified and focused on key points more directly related to the assault area but still so controlled as not to indicate to the enemy the area itself.

**Sir Arthur Travers Harris:** The first attack of the campaign was on the night of March 6th–7th, when the railway yards at Trappes were bombed.

**Lt. Gen. Walter Bedell "Beetle" Smith:** Casualties were far lower than had been feared.

**Sir Arthur Travers Harris:** Most of the railway centers in France were defended by few anti-aircraft guns, and as a result we were often able to bomb from much below the usual operational height, and sometimes from well below the cloud level. This, of course, made for increased accuracy of attack.

**Lt. Edward Giller, 55th Fighter Group, 8th Air Force:** We flew almost every day the weather was favorable, and my memory is that 90 percent of that was spent in close strafing and bombing of the supply lines, communications, railroad in France, bridge bombing, and things of that nature.

**Sir Arthur Travers Harris:** After the long-term campaign against railway centers, Bomber Command, while simultaneously attacking a number of railway targets near the battlefield, had to concentrate on silencing the coastal fortifications. Here the main problem was how to give no indication to the enemy of where the actual landing was to be made. The only way of doing this was by the wildly extravagant method of bombing at least two coastal batteries or defences elsewhere for every one that was attacked on the invasion coast of Normandy. The guns were, of course, extremely small objectives, and the only chance of putting them out of action was by covering a quite considerable area round them with bomb craters.

**John McLean, 453rd Bomb Squadron, 323rd Bomb Group:** I arrived in May, and from the time I got to the squadron, we hit bridges and ammunition dumps. Our missions had suddenly become bridges all over northern France, and I don't think we hit anything else for two weeks.

**Lt. Jack Barensfeld, P-47 pilot, 377th Squadron, 362nd Fighter Group:** In mid-May Dutch and Holland trains and trucks were taken off the "no-no" list. They were fair game in preparation for D-Day. We started to block off the transportation system that would be leading to the beaches in Normandy.

**Lt. Charles Mohrle, P-47 pilot, 510th Squadron, 405th Fighter-Bomber Group:** For two or three weeks prior to the invasion, we were sent into Northern France with orders to shoot up anything that moved or even looked suspicious. Daily, we prowled the rail lines and roads, crippling or destroying every piece of rolling equipment we could find. Occasionally, during this period we worked with the FFI—the French Underground—who would have informed SHAEF of a worthwhile target. Through the FFI intelligence, we dive-bombed buildings such as houses or barns which proved to be ammunition dumps or similar storage of military equipment.

**1st Lt. William J. Moriarty, B-26 Marauder pilot, 556th Squadron, 387th Bomb Group:** I flew my first and second missions the same day, May 27. Both targets were railroad bridges on the Seine River. My third and fourth missions were on May 28, and were also railroad bridges on the Seine River. My fifth and sixth missions were on May 29. The early mission was, again, a railroad bridge, and the second was a locomotive shed on the outskirts of Antwerp.

**Carlos Pegues, B-26 Marauder turret gunner and flight engineer, 323rd Bomb Group, Ninth Air Force:** Sometimes it was one mission a day, some days two. By the time I returned home, I had flown sixty-seven missions. To say I was lucky is an understatement. When we initially landed in England, the 323rd Bomb Group had thirty-six crews which would total 216 men. I determined that of those original 216, only thirty-six of us returned home.

**Martha Gellhorn, correspondent, writing in *Collier's Weekly*, "The Bomber Boys,"
spring 1944:** It is a long night when you are waiting for the planes from
Europe to come back and it is cold, but it has to end. At four o'clock or
around then you go to the control tower. The waiting gets to be a thing you
can touch. Then the first plane calls in to the control tower switchboard.
Two WAAFs who have been up all night begin to direct the planes in.
The girls' voices—so poised and so neat—begin, "Hello, George! Pancake!
Over!" In the glassed-in room, you hear the pilots answer. Then the girls
again, "Hello, Queen Airdrome, one thousand. Over."

The planes come in slowly at first, and then there will be four of them
circling and landing. The more planes that come in and are marked up on
the blackboard, the worse the waiting gets. None of this shows. No voice
changes, no one makes a movement that is in any way unusual. The routine
proceeds as normally as if people were waiting in line to buy theater tickets.
Finally, all the planes were in except P for Peter and J for Jig. They were late.
The Job was a piece of cake. They should be in. They would, of course, be
in . . . obviously . . . any minute now. No one mentioned the delay.

We started to go down to the Interrogation Room, and the group captain
remarked without emphasis that he would just stay up here for a bit until
the chaps got in.

The Lancasters looked like enormous, deadly black birds going off
into the night; and somehow they looked different when they came back.
The planes carried from this field thousands of pounds of high explosives,
and the crews flew all night to drop the load as ordered. Now the trains
would not run between France and Italy for a while, not through that
place anyhow. It is all over. Here they are, the men who did it, with mussed
hair and weary faces, dirty sweaters under their flying suits, sleep-bright
eyes, making humble comradely little jokes and eating their saved-up
chocolate bars.

**Birdie Schmidt, American Red Cross, serving the 392nd Bomb Group:** In serving
a returning mission, we always covered the tables with white sheets because
we thought it added a homely touch. We could always tell what kind of day
it had been by the way the boys came in. If they were kidding around and
talking, it had been an easy mission. If they looked like ghosts and said "Just
give me something hot," we knew it had been a rough one.

**Lt. John Mason Brown, aide to Rear Adm. Alan Kirk, USS *Augusta* (CA-31):** In the spring, not long before the invasion, I was at the bar in the Dorchester with Ernie Pyle. Two American pilots recognized him at once, and were properly excited at seeing him, because no man in the Armed Forces is more deeply loved than he is. "It's a funny war," said one of the young pilots to Ernie Pyle. "Here I am this afternoon in London, having a drink in a super-civilized place like this and going to the theatre tonight. And this morning I was out on a short mission across the Channel, dropping bombs to beat hell and killing everyone in sight. I can't figure it out."

*All told, the execution of the spring "Transportation Plan" saw 21,949 Allied sorties, as US and Royal Air Force bombers dropped 66,517 tons of bombs across 79 specific targets—with the targets and missions carefully chosen, as always, to obfuscate the exact whereabouts of the coming invasion. The mission would be so successful that Allied planners budgeted to bring more than 1,300 bridging sets and pontoon bridges across the Channel as part of Operation* OVERLORD *to help undo the devastating effects of their own bombers and allow the Allied columns to advance across France and the Low Countries.*

# Picking the Date

Harbors across the British Isles were packed
with landing craft by the end of May.

*By May, it was impossible almost anywhere across the British Isles to ignore
that an invasion was imminent. Supplies and troops crowded open fields, and
landing ships of all sizes clogged the ports. The coalition forces included not just
US, British, and Canadian units, but also roughly 32,500 Free French Forces,
25,000 Polish, and thousands of Czech, Dutch, Belgian, and Norwegian forces,
among other Allied and occupied nations, who manned everything from fighter
planes to naval vessels that had escaped ahead of German occupation. The supplies
involved everything from drinking water and ammunition to 800,000 pints of
blood plasma—segregated, as was mandated, between white and Black donors.*

*And yet, even as the final waves of troops and matériel arrived in England, Dwight Eisenhower had yet to make one monumental decision: When, exactly, to aim to launch the invasion.*

**Robert Capa, photographer, *Life* magazine:** In May 1944, London had invasion fever. The town was jammed with uniforms of the United Nations, and whisky was scarce in the pubs.

**Capt. Kay Summersby, British Mechanised Transport Corps, aide and secretary to General Eisenhower, SHAEF:** I knew what "Allies" meant when I walked into the cleaning shop and saw as many as a dozen different nationalities' uniforms on the rack, when I saw British and American officers gabbing at the mess, when I saw RAF men with tired eyes and Polish or Czech patches on the shoulder.

**Sgt. Gordon Carson, Company E, 506th Parachute Infantry Regiment, 101st Airborne:** London to me was a magic carpet. Walk down any of its streets and every uniform of the Free World was to be seen. To Piccadilly, Hyde Park, Leicester Square, Trafalgar Square, Victoria they came. The uniform of the Canadians, South Africans, Australians, New Zealanders, the Free French, Polish, Belgium, Holland, and of course the English and Americans were everywhere. These days were not lost on me because even at twenty years of age, I knew I was seeing something that was never to be again. Wartime London was its own world.

**Mollie Panter-Downes, London correspondent, *The New Yorker*:** Living on this little island just now uncomfortably resembles living on a vast combination of an aircraft carrier, a floating dock jammed with men, and a warehouse stacked to the ceiling with material labeled "Europe." The fight everybody is waiting for hasn't started yet, but all over England, from the big cities to the tiniest hamlet, the people, at least in spirit, seem already to have begun it.

**Winston Churchill, Prime Minister of the United Kingdom:** All Southern England thus became a vast military camp, filled with men trained, instructed, and eager to come to grips with the Germans across the water.

**Pvt. Albert Mominee, Company I, 16th Infantry Regiment, 1st Division:** In May, 1944, I was back in England to train and get ready for another invasion of a foreign country. This would be my third.

**Pvt. John Chalk, 1st Battalion, Hampshire Regiment, 231st Infantry Brigade, 50th Northumbrian Division:** There was no need for us to be told officially that the "Big Do" was coming off, we all knew that. What we didn't know was where or when.

**Frank Gillard, correspondent, BBC:** In every wood and copse, in leafy dead-end-lanes and side roads, often in private gardens, under quarries and embankments, there it all was—trucks, ambulances, tanks, armored cars, carriers, jeeps, bulldozers, ducks, vehicles of all kinds, vast, really vast numbers of them. And great mountains of stores, weapons and ammunition, rations, bridging equipment, tires, timber, millions of tons.

**Lt. Gen. Walter Bedell "Beetle" Smith, Chief of Staff, SHAEF:** Portsmouth filled with vessels, of every description—battleships, destroyers, minesweepers, transports, and hundreds of landing craft. Nosed rail to rail, they opened their jaws to receive cargoes of men and vehicles and guns. Then the khaki flood began. Troops streamed off the roads and fanned out along the macadamed hards which stretched down to the water as far as the eye could reach. Gradually, bits and pieces of the gigantic assault mechanism slipped into place.

**Gen. Dwight Eisenhower, Supreme Allied Commander, SHAEF:** [In] July 1943, some 750,000 tons of supplies were pouring through English ports each month, and this amount was steadily increased until in June 1944, 1,900,000 tons were received from the United States. Much of this material was used to supply the troops already arrived in England and other amounts were stored for use as OVERLORD progressed, but the stockpile earmarked for the American forces, over and above basic loads and equipment, was a full 2,500,000 tons for the invasion alone. By 1 June also, the number of U.S. Army troops in the United Kingdom had risen from 241,839 at the end of 1942 to 1,562,000.

**Forrest Pogue, combat historian, V Corps:** Wags said that but for the barrage balloons, which could be seen straining at their cables throughout the country, the island would sink beneath the waves.

**Lt. Gen. Omar Bradley, commander, First Army:** The equipment we were to carry varied from 120-foot steel span bridges to sulpha pills. It even included fresh drinking water: 300,500 gallons of it for the first three days ashore.

**Maj. Ralph Ingersoll, intelligence officer, planning staff, SHAEF:** OVERLORD's momentum was too great to be stopped. The show was really on and everybody knew it. Escape clauses or no escape clauses, high policies and pious hopes notwithstanding, the invasion of Europe was coming off.

**Capt. Harry C. Butcher, naval aide to Dwight Eisenhower, SHAEF:** On May 8 Ike sent to the Combined Chiefs a recommendation originated by the Psychological Warfare Division as to the wording of the initial communique for OVERLORD [whenever the invasion itself launched]. The recommendation read: "Allied naval forces supported by strong air forces began landing Allied armies this morning on the northern coast of France." The Combined Chiefs approved the general wording, with one amendment; they said it should begin "under the command of General Eisenhower."

*     *     *

**Gen. Dwight Eisenhower:** The timing of the operation was a difficult matter to decide.

**Gen. Lord Hastings Ismay, chief military adviser to Winston Churchill:** At a very late hour one night the question of timing was being discussed by the Defence Committee, and I regret to admit that I was half-asleep when I heard the Prime Minister ask when William the Conqueror had landed. Hitherto I had made no contribution to the debate. Here was my chance, "1066," I exclaimed. To my surprise this was greeted with a roar of laughter, and the Prime Minister said pityingly: "Pug, you should have been in your basket ages ago."

**Lt. Gen. Walter Bedell "Beetle" Smith:** From the beginning it had been clear that the choice of D-Day depended on the weather.

**Gen. Dwight Eisenhower:** Some soldier once said, "The weather is always neutral." Nothing could be more untrue. Bad weather is obviously the enemy of the side that seeks to launch projects requiring good weather, or of the side possessing great assets, such as strong air forces, which depend upon good weather for effective operations. If really bad weather should endure permanently, the Nazi would need nothing else to defend the Normandy coast.

**Capt. J. M. Stagg, chief meteorologist, SHAEF:** The paramount requirements were in the hands of the navy.

**Sverre Petterssen, meteorologist, Norwegian Air Force, UK Meteorological Office:** What was good enough for the navy would certainly be satisfactory for the army. The air force was always, and rightly so, demanding. Although their requirements were highly varied, none of them, nor their sum, would be comparable with the do-or-die question of the navy: *Can we, or can we not, land the force in fighting shape on the coast of France?*

**Rear Adm. Alan G. Kirk, commander, Western Naval Task Force:** The night before D-Day had to be reasonably light so that convoys could keep station with ships darkened. Airborne operations also required this.

**Lt. Gen. Walter Bedell "Beetle" Smith:** For the airborne landings behind Utah Beach and at road centers around Caen, timed for 0200 hours on D-Day, we needed a late-rising full moon so the pilots could approach their objectives in darkness but have moonlight to pick out the drop zones. For the naval craft and transports, we must have a reasonable sea and good visibility to reduce the perils of navigation in crowded waters and to keep troops from arriving at the point of assault so seasick they could not leave their ships.

**Capt. Harry C. Butcher:** An adequate period after morning twilight must be available for aerial bombing of coast-defense and field batteries and strong points. Similarly, an adequate period after morning twilight must be available for naval bombardment.

**Sverre Petterssen:** To achieve surprise, the tide had to occur at dawn, which in early June is about 5:15 A.M. and varies insignificantly from one day to the next. The time of low tide, however, varies by some thirty-odd minutes during the daily cycle.

**Lt. Gen. Walter Bedell "Beetle" Smith:** We wanted low tide so that the underwater and half-hidden beach obstacles could be seen and destroyed by our demolition crews. The low tide must be late enough in the morning for an hour's good daylight to permit the saturation bombing of defenses which would precede the landings themselves. But it must come early enough in the morning so that a second low tide would occur before darkness set in. Without the second low tide we could not land the follow-up divisions.

**Winston Churchill:** Only on three days in each lunar month were all the desired conditions fulfilled. The first three-day period after May 31, General Eisenhower's target date, was June 5, 6, and 7.

**Gen. Lord Hastings Ismay:** So far as D-Day was concerned there were only three days in the month of June on which all the necessary conditions were likely to occur.

**Lt. Gen. Omar Bradley:** By scheduling H hour after dawn, we reaped double the tonnage from air in softening up the beaches. During the predawn darkness RAF nighttime bombers would saturate the shore defenses. Before that shock wore off, U.S. heavies and mediums would strike at dawn in a daylight attack. By the same token, the navy could use daylight observation to pinpoint the fire of its big guns. This in itself had become a major factor, for naval gunfire was to be our mainstay support.

**Capt. J. M. Stagg:** The naval stipulations were that throughout D-Day and for as many days as possible immediately thereafter on-shore wind should not exceed 10–12 m.p.h.—for off-shore winds a few more m.p.h. could be accepted. To allow the multitude of surface craft to keep their proper stations and also to let the naval bombarding forces sight on their shore targets not less than 3 miles visibility was essential and this would also be a minimum for the spotter aircraft operating with bombarding ships.

**Sverre Petterssen:** On these and related military considerations alone, the invasion could be attempted only from late spring to some time after midsummer. Two windows of opportunity—each of three or four days' duration—would present themselves in each lunar cycle, making a total of six or seven in a calendar year.

**Capt. J. M. Stagg:** If every one of the requirements was insisted on, OVERLORD might not get under way for another hundred years or more.

**Sverre Petterssen:** The meteorological problem was not to choose an ideal weather situation but to decide, some days in advance, whether the conditions would be above minimum requirements on the occasions when the combination of tides and twilight was close to ideal.

**Lt. Cdr. Lawrence Hogben, meteorologist, Royal New Zealand Navy, Admiralty Headquarters, Portsmouth:** Meteorologically, D-Day was bound to be a gamble against the odds.

**Sverre Petterssen:** Stagg set out to compile his own list of realistic requirements. He found that the odds against the occurrence of weather favorable to OVERLORD in early summer might be as low as 25-to-one and were unlikely to exceed 60-to-one.

**Capt. J. M. Stagg:** So the question had to be rephrased to "What are the least favourable conditions in which your forces can operate successfully?"

**Lt. Gen. Walter Bedell "Beetle" Smith:** During April, the first of the meetings was set up to drill the Supreme Commander in the weather factors that would govern his invasion decision.

**Capt. Harry C. Butcher:** At each Monday meeting, he picked a hypothetical D-Day, and the weathermen made trial predictions.

**Capt. J. M. Stagg:** Thursday of each week was to be regarded as a dummy D-day—and, as our forecast was for the whole week till Saturday, we were attempting a prognosis, though in fairly broad terms, it is true—from D minus 2 or 3 to D plus 2 inclusive.

**Gen. Dwight Eisenhower:** The big question mark always before us was the weather that would prevail during the only period of early June that we could use, the fifth, sixth, and seventh.

**Winston Churchill:** If the weather were not propitious on any of those three days, the whole operation would have to be postponed at least a fortnight—indeed, a whole month if we waited for the moon.

*     *     *

*On Monday, May 15, the commanders and leaders assembled at St. Paul's School for a final run-through of Operation* OVERLORD, *a high-level event almost more in common with a state dinner than a military planning session. Attendees had been summoned through 146 individual gilt-edged invitations, but inside it was so cold that many kept on their winter overcoats or huddled under shared blankets. Every principal member of the British Chiefs of Staff was in attendance, as were members of the War Cabinet, assorted Allied generals, Prime Minister Churchill, and the king of England.*

**Gen. Dwight Eisenhower:** During the whole war I attended no other conference so packed with rank as this one.

**Winston Churchill:** On the stage was a map of the Normandy beaches and the immediate hinterland, set at a slope so that the audience could see it clearly, and so constructed that the high officers explaining the plan of operations could walk about and point out the landmarks.

**Brig. David Belcham, head of Operations and Planning Staff, British Army:** I, acting as Montgomery's assistant, could walk on it in skid-proof socks and point out the various locations and assault lines as they were mentioned.

**Gen. Dwight Eisenhower:** This meeting gave us an opportunity to hear a word from both the King and the Prime Minister. The latter made one of his typical fighting speeches, in the course of which he used an expression that struck many of us, particularly the Americans, with peculiar force. He said, "Gentlemen, I am hardening toward this enterprise," meaning to us that, though he had long doubted its feasibility and had previously advocated its further postponement in favor of operations elsewhere, he had finally, at this late date, come to believe with the rest of us that this was the true course of action in order to achieve the victory.

**Winston Churchill:** Montgomery made an impressive speech. He was followed by several Naval, Army, and Air Commanders, and also by the Principal Administrative Officer, who dwelt upon the elaborate preparations that had been made for the administration of the force when it got ashore. The amount of paraphernalia sounded staggering. Twenty days after the landing—D+20—there would be one vehicle ashore for every 4.77 men. Each vehicle required a driver and its share of maintenance staff.

**Capt. Harry C. Butcher:** When the King departed, Ike thanked him for his attendance and reminded him that the air people said they would have 11,000 planes overhead on D-Day and that the Navy had said that, to put the Army ashore, it had marshaled the greatest armada of transports, landing craft, and warships the world had ever seen.

**Maj. Gen. Francis "Freddie" de Guingand, Chief of Staff, General Montgomery:** It had been a most satisfactory day, and at the end of it there was a confident feeling that we would not fail.*

---

* The spring and ensuing months had not changed Field Marshal Lord Alan Brooke's low opinion of Ike—nor his general sense he was surrounded by fools. Writing in his diary, May 15, he recorded, "Went straight from home to St Paul's School to attend Eisenhower's final run over plans for cross-Channel offensive. . . . The main impression I gathered was that Eisenhower was a swinger and no real director of thought, plans, energy or direction! Just a coordinator—a good mixer, a champion of inter-allied cooperation, and in those respects few can hold a candle to him. But is that enough? Or can we not find all qualities of a commander in one man? Maybe I am getting too hard to please, but I doubt it. Monty made excellent speech. Bertie Ramsay indifferent, and overwhelmed by all his own difficulties. Spaatz [US Eighth Army Air Force] read every word of a poor statement. Bert Harris

**Gen. Dwight Eisenhower:** On 17 May, I set 5 June as the "final" date for the assault, subject, of course, to last-minute revision if the weather should prove unfavorable. The selection of this date was based primarily on tidal and light conditions. The dates of 5, 6, and 7 June were all acceptable, but any postponement beyond these dates would have necessitated waiting until 19 June for a similar favorable tidal period.

**Capt. J. M. Stagg:** As the long fine days of May went by, we knew we were moving towards the climax.

**Lt. Gen. Walter Bedell "Beetle" Smith:** Except for the single worry of the weather, we were never concerned about our ability to penetrate the Atlantic Wall. Measures had been designed to overcome every hazard we could foresee.

**Capt. Harry C. Butcher, writing in his personal diary, Tuesday, May 23, 1944:** At yesterday's meeting of Ike's Commanders-in-Chief, as it has been for weeks, weather was the principal topic and arrangements were concluded for the "agreed" report from the various weather experts to be received on Sunday, May 28, and daily for consideration at meetings at the Portsmouth headquarters starting Monday, the twenty-ninth. Starting with June 1, the Commanders-in-Chief will meet daily with Ike to consider the weather report and final decision will have to be made in the morning of June 3, if the present D-Day is to be kept.

**Gen. Dwight Eisenhower:** Strategically, the postponement of the target date proved to be a sound measure. By 1 May, the original date, our forces in Italy were still encountering heavy resistance south of Rome along the Gustav

---

[Bomber Command] told us how well he might have won this war if it had not been for the handicap imposed by the existence of the two other services!! Sholto Douglas [Fighter Command] seemed disappointed at the smallness of his task, and so was I. Then Humfrey Gale and Graham on Administration, followed by Grasett on civil control of France.

"A useful run through. [The] King made a few well-chosen remarks. After lunch he presented the CB to Bradley and two other decorations. Back to WO and finished up with Monty dining quietly with me. He was in very good form and bearing his responsibilities well."

Line, while Russian forces were occupied in the Crimea and still forming for a western attack. By the first week in June, however, Rome had fallen, Kesselring's forces were in retreat, the Crimea had been cleared, and Germany was nervously predicting an all-out Russian offensive. Furthermore, the enemy had been keyed up to a 1 May Allied offensive from the United Kingdom, to judge from his "invasion any day now" feelers. The month's delay served perhaps to lull him into believing that we would now not attack until some time in July. The month's postponement also guaranteed, as events proved, the availability of assault craft and shipping to move the staggering number of men and vehicles required for the D-day assault.

**Field Marshal Lord Alan Brooke, Chief of the Imperial General Staff, writing in his diary, 27 May:** The hardest part of bearing such responsibility is pretending that you are absolutely confident of success when you are really torn to shreds with doubts and misgivings! But when once decisions are taken the time for doubts is gone, and what is required is to breathe the confidence of success into all those around. I never want again to go through a time like the present one. The cross Channel operation is just eating into my heart. I wish to God we could start and have done with it!!

*"Good Luck Boys!"*

# Into the Sausages

In late May, the invasion force was sequestered behind
barbed wire fences, in camps known as "sausages."

*With the troops' months of training and exercises complete, England filled to the
brim with supplies, and the ports clogged with the thousands of ships that had
made their way from US shipyards, the invasion was ready to move forward.
Over middle and late May, the Allied forces that would make up the initial
waves of Operation* OVERLORD *moved from their established base camps to a
series of temporary marshaling areas near ports or airfields where they would
embark ships or planes for France. Once the troops were inside, the camps were
sealed up from contact with outsiders and, for the first time, units began to learn
their specific roles in the coming invasion.*

**Maj. John Dalgleish, Planning Staff, Royal Army Service Corps:** Picture the Movement Control task. Upwards of one million men, with all their accompanying stores and equipment, had to be moved from remote parts of the country, by road and rail, and guided through some twenty points of embarkation. Each unit had a serial number, and once those units began to move Movement Control had to keep a finger on them all the time until they could be embarked and struck off the roll.

**Gen. Dwight Eisenhower, Supreme Allied Commander, SHAEF:** Every separate encampment, barrack, vehicle park, and every unit was carefully charted on our master maps. The scheduled movement of each unit had been so worked out that it would reach the embarkation point at the exact time the vessels would be ready to receive it.

**Maj. John Dalgleish:** Somewhere along the movement routes units would have to lose their unit identity and be converted into craft-loads. Immediately when a unit was broken up, it lost its power to look after itself. For instance, the cooks and cooks' vehicles might easily be the first part of a unit called forward to embark. A unit could not be left without the means of subsistence, and some organisation would have to be set up to feed and accommodate the units.

**Lt. Gen. Omar Bradley, commander, First Army:** An entire armored division had been cannibalized to help provide the 54,000 men required for housekeeping in these final marshaling areas. Among them were 4,500 brand-new cooks especially trained for this task.

**Lt. Gen. Lewis H. Brereton, commander, 9th Air Force:** It is almost beyond comprehension how much work went into the planning for the invasion. Ninth Air Force's plan for Operation NEPTUNE alone—that part of OVERLORD that has to do with the landing on the Continent—consisted of 847,500 words covering 1,376 pages of legal-size paper using both sides. It was 4 ½ inches thick and weighed ten pounds, three ounces.

**Lt. Anthony Drexel Duke, commander, USS LST-530:** On one of my liberty trips up to London, I went to see an uncle of mine, Tony Biddle. He had been the ambassador to a whole bunch of countries occupied by the Germans, France, Norway, Belgium, Poland, and so forth. And he had resigned from the diplomatic service and gone to work for General Eisenhower as one of his aides. During lunch he said, "I've got a friend who wants to meet you, and you will really enjoy meeting him." We got in a taxi afterwards and went over to his office on Grosvenor Square. He knocked on a door right next to his office and ushered me in, and who but General Eisenhower turned out to be that friend of his. I was awestruck. I stood in front of his deck and he said, "We've been waiting for you, Captain Duke." He rang a bell and called for someone and said, "Now that Duke is here, we are going to get on with the invasion plans." I was very embarrassed but thrilled at the same time. It was a moment in my life that I'll never forget.

**Pvt. Herbert Zafft, 115th Infantry Regiment, 29th Division:** We had a party at Launceston, England, for all of the G.I.s in the 29th, and they brought busloads of gals into us, and they had a dance, and then we were to take off for the marshaling areas.

**Pvt. Robert Healey, 149th Engineer Combat Battalion, 6th Engineer Special Brigade:** We marched down the main street to the railroad station. As we marched the sidewalks on both sides were lined with people, all cheering their boys on. Some of the men had been all over town in different homes, and usually the women and the children from those houses went down to see us off.

**Chief Yeoman W. Garwood Bacon, Jr., 7th Naval Beach Battalion:** Everywhere the British people gave us the V for victory sign and they too saw that something was up. They had been waiting for a long time for this occasion since 1939.

**Lt. Robert Woollcombe, 6th Battalion, King's Own Scottish Borderers:** Everywhere through London it was the same greeting; on walls and the backs of great high tenements overlooking the railway, painted in large bold white lettering: *Good Luck Boys!*

**Pfc. Joseph S. Blaylock, Sr., Baker Battery, 20th Field Artillery, 4th Division:** The whole town turned out to say good-bye to us, because they had a feeling—and we had a feeling—that this was the real thing.

\*          \*          \*

**Pvt. Harold "Hal" Baumgarten, Company B, 116th Infantry Regiment, 29th Division:** Around May 15, we were transported by truck to secret camp D-1, about ten miles north of Dorchester, England. These camps were called "sausages" because of their shape.

**Maj. Ralph Ingersoll, intelligence officer, planning staff, SHAEF:** Each sausage enclosed four or five miles of road and field. In the fields were camps. The sausages hung, not end to end but in a row, parallel to each other. They hung down from the hills to just back of the beaches, all along the south coast of England.

**Pvt. Robert Healey:** The longer we were there, the tighter the security became.

**Pvt. Len Griffing, 501st Parachute Infantry Regiment, 101st Airborne:** One day there were no more passes and security around the base kept us in and everybody else out.

**2nd Lt. Cyril Rand, platoon commander, Company C, 2nd Battalion, Royal Ulster Rifles:** When the time came for the camp to be sealed, all communication with the outside world ceased, apart from the sending of letters which all had to be censored. To avoid embarrassment no officer censored the letters written by his own platoon, nor were the contents discussed or disclosed to anyone else. The things we particularly looked for were remarks about things "hotting up," briefings taking place, live ammunition being issued, and anything else that might give any indication preparations were well under way. Many envelopes addressed to wives and girlfriends bore the popular acronyms so loved by romantic soldiers: SWALK . . . Sealed with a loving kiss: ITALY . . . I trust and love you: HOLLAND . . . Hope our love lasts and never dies, and the rather more intimate one—explained to me by my batman—NORWICH . . . Knickers off ready when I come home!

**Pvt. Tom Tateson, Company A, 7th Battalion, Green Howards, 50th Northumbrian Infantry Division:** I was very conscious of the fact that there was a real possibility of my being killed—leaving Olive widowed with a child not yet a year old and another on the way. I took the course of writing a letter which I left with Olive, to be opened only in the event of my death. Apart from an expression of the happiness which our lives together had brought me, I wanted to convey that if she should ever want to re-marry she should know that this would have my full blessing. Even in writing I felt I had to say this in coded language: *If at any time in the future you should be faced with a decision affecting your future, and you are concerned as to what I would have thought, I want you to know that whatever would ensure your happiness and the security of you and the children would be what I would want you to do.*

**Maj. John Dalgleish:** One million men disappeared from human ken under the non-committal address "Army Post Office, England."

**Leading Telegraphist Alan Winstanley, Combined Operations Bombardment Unit, Royal Navy:** The order went out for all camps in the UK to be sealed. There were a number of civilians in the camp who just got caught in it because they were either delivering supplies or doing something else. That was their hard luck. Once the camp was sealed, that was it for them as well. The only people allowed out of the camp were dispatch riders. No one else was allowed out.

**L. Cpl. C. Morris, No. 3 Troop, 6 Commando:** No chances whatever were being taken. On several occasions the Yankee guards, who were armed with .22 rifles, opened fire on civvies loitering near the wire.

**Pvt. Dennis Bowen, 5th Battalion, East Yorkshire Regiment:** The cry in the camp was "Let me out!" If there were three or four of you and you saw a sentry walking on the other side of the wire, someone would always shout, soldier to soldier, "Let me out, let me out!" It was funny, because on the day when we were leaving the camp to march to the boats, somebody in the line called back at the camp, "Let me in!"

**Sgt. W. E. Wills, 2nd Battalion, Devonshire Regiment:** All ranks were confined to camp for security reasons, but many were able to use their West Country knowledge of fieldcraft to find ways of getting through the perimeter barbed wire to slink off for a drink in various pubs. The locals knew we were there, of course, and they could guess why, but not where we were going or when. In these circumstances security was maintained—for we didn't know where or when, either.

**T/4 Dwayne Burns, radioman, 508th Parachute Infantry Regiment, 82nd Airborne Division:** One day, my good buddy John and I got the bright idea of slipping out of camp and going to town. We very nonchalantly walked away from the hangar and over to the wire fence. We slowly and calmly walked along until we found a place in the fence where we could get out. It was no feat at all to get out. We walked along the road. We were just getting into town. A jeep pulled up beside us and an officer sitting in the back asked what we were doing off base. We gave him a wild story, but I don't think he bought it. He asked, "What company are you from?" "F-company, sir." "Will you do me a favor?" "Yes, sir." "You go back to the field and tell Captain Flanders that no one is to be off base for any reason." "Sure will, sir." We saluted and watched as he drove away. John asked, "Burns, do you know who that was?" "No, I couldn't see him." "That was Jumping Jim Gavin, commanding general of the 82nd Airborne."

**Pvt. Allen McMath, 112th Engineer Combat Battalion:** We lived in tents for ten men and did nothing but eat and sleep, the two things a soldier knows how to do best.

**Sgt. John Robert "Bob" Slaughter, Company D, 116th Infantry Regiment, 29th Division:** We ate the best food. [It was] easy living: go to the range and fire all the ammunition you wanted to, play football, cards, movies—good times. The Red Cross women were there, too. For breakfast you could tell them how you wanted your bacon, and of course they had powdered eggs, and flapjacks or whatever. They gave us lemon meringue pie. We hadn't seen that since the States.

**Pvt. Albert Mominee, Company I, 16th Infantry Regiment, 1st Division:** Each meal seemed like a banquet. I wondered were they fattening us for the kill or was it just to build up our morale or did they do it to make up for the first few days after the landing, when we would have to rely on C rations to suppress our hunger, until the kitchen caught up to us?

*Final preparations for the invasion included issuing millions of pieces of equipment, from new uniforms meant to protect soldiers from a World War I–style poison gas attack on the beaches to newly printed invasion currency.*

**Pvt. Dennis Bowen:** They counted out these peculiar blue-and-white square notes, which were called "invasion money." Then, of course, we knew we were going to France.

**2nd Lt. Walter Sidlowski, platoon commander, Company C, 348th Combat Battalion, 5th Engineer Special Brigade:** Existing currency was exchanged for French francs and introductory booklets to France, a pocket French/English dictionary guide was issued.

**Pocket Guide to France, Army Information Branch:** The richest farms in France are in Normandy, the butter, egg, cheese and grazing country. You've probably sung "When It's Apple Blossom Time in Normandy." The apple orchards there are a big produce market item. Rouen is the largest inland Norman port on the River Seine. Normandy looks rather like Ohio.

**Pvt. Dennis Bowen:** As soon as we got the French money, we were told to put it in a secure place and keep it. But of course everybody immediately started playing cards for it. We didn't understand what the value of French francs was—they were meaningless bits of paper to us. I played cards for it, win some, lose some; I know when I got on the boat, I didn't have the same amount that I had started with.

**Rifleman Patrick Devlin, Company C, 1st Battalion, Royal Ulster Rifles:** I was also asked to take three condoms. We had never been given these before. I was [Roman Catholic] and refused them. I said to the major, "I thought we were going to France to fight, sir." I could see he was embarrassed and did not say anything. The color sergeant saved the day by telling me it was orders from high up. He said, "Take them."

**Pvt. John Mather, 112th Engineer Combat Battalion:** Around the first of June, we were issued clothing, which we were told was impregnated against gas. Socks, long johns, and a set of fatigues. These items felt sticky to the touch.

**Pvt. Ray Howell, 3466th Ordnance Medium Automotive Maintenance Company, 5th Engineer Special Brigade:** They were new fatigues, but they had been treated with some sort of chemical which made them kind of stiff, like starch in them. That made them hot. As soon as you started to move very much, the heat from the body would be trapped underneath. It was murder.

**Pvt. Edward J. Jeziorski, 507th Parachute Infantry Regiment, 82nd Airborne:** They were the lousiest, the coldest, the clammiest, the stiffest, the stinkiest articles of clothing that were ever dreamed up to be worn by individuals. Surely the guy that was responsible for the idea on this screw-up received a Distinguished Service Medal from the devil himself.

**2nd. Lt. Cyril Rand:** In our camp alongside us was a regiment of Canadian infantry; it seemed to be the intention of every soldier to have a Davy Crockett–type bushy-tail fastened to the rear of his cap, and in order to satisfy this demand every squirrel went in peril of its life. They were hunted with stone, catapult, knife, sten gun and—much to our concern—.303 rifle. From time to time the whine of a bullet could be heard as it passed over our heads, and it was perhaps fortunate that the poor creatures stayed in the high branches of the fir trees, as our Allies might have done for us what our enemies would be trying to do in a few days' time.

# Keep Calm and Carry On

Gen. Montgomery and other Allied leaders spent the final weeks
crisscrossing the country to meet as much of the invasion force as they could.

*With the troops assembling in the marshaling areas and sausages, the military
commanders and planners who had long labored hard for years to bring the
might of the Allied war machine to bear against the Third Reich found themselves
moving to a new role: spectators. The fate of OVERLORD and NEPTUNE lay
in the minutiae and a tightly choreographed plan to deliver each component of
the invasion to the right place at the right time. Hoping to convey their respect,*

*admiration, and hope for their men's success, Gens. Eisenhower and Montgomery, Prime Minister Churchill, and other leaders of the military effort fanned out across camps, airfields, and harbors to offer whatever inspiration they could, as well as a reminder of the importance of the task ahead.*

**Gen. Dwight Eisenhower, Supreme Allied Commander, SHAEF:** Senior commanders used every possible moment in visiting and inspecting troops. Records left by a staff officer show that in four months, from February 1 to June 1, I visited twenty-six divisions, twenty-four airfields, five ships of war, and numerous depots, shops, hospitals, and other important installations. Bradley, Montgomery, Spaatz, and Tedder maintained similar schedules.

**Gen. Bernard L. Montgomery, commander, Allied ground forces (21 Army Group):** My method of inspect was characterized by informality. When the appraisal was over, I stood on the bonnet of a jeep and spoke to officers and men, quietly and very simply, using a loudspeaker or not, according to the conditions. I explained how necessary it was that we should know each other, what lay ahead and how, together, we would handle the job. I told them what the German soldier was like in battle and how he could be defeated; that if we all had confidence in the plan and in each other, the job could be done.

**Capt. Kay Summersby, British Mechanised Transport Corps, aide and secretary to General Eisenhower, SHAEF:** General Eisenhower got a little lift of spirits when I drove him to an inspection of a British unit and the assault troops yelled, over and over again, "Good old Ike!"

**Gen. Dwight Eisenhower:** It pays big dividends in terms of morale, and morale—given rough equality in other things—is supreme on the battlefield.

**Alan Moorehead, correspondent, *The Daily Express* of London:** [Montgomery] believed that morale was everything at this stage. I traveled with him one week. He walked between the ranks, often it was a matter of half a mile. He walked slowly, peering sharply at the men, face to face. At the end of the inspection Montgomery would get on to a jeep in front of a loudspeaker and tell the soldiers to break ranks and gather round him. This was always an astonishing moment. Five thousand men in heavy boots would charge together towards the jeep like stampeding buffaloes. It caused a heavy rumbling in the earth, and often the jeep would be nearly overwhelmed.

**Brig. David Belcham, head of Operations and Planning Staff, British Army:** In addition, Montgomery was invited to visit armament factories where he was able to talk to those working on equipment for the armies. He addressed meetings of railway workers, dockers and workers in other industries directly involved in supplying and transporting the weapons and stores which were a vital back-up to the soldiers in the field.

**Gen. Bernard L. Montgomery:** I used to tell them we were all one great army, whether soldier on the battle front or worker on the home front; their work was just as important as ours. Our combined task was to weld the workers and soldiers into one team, determined to destroy German domination of Europe and of the world.

**Lt. Cdr. John D. Bulkeley, commander, Patrol Torpedo Boat Squadron 102, U.S. Navy:** King George VI and Prime Minister Winston Churchill came down to visit. Admiral Kirk had alerted me that they wanted to see a PT boat. So we went through meticulous preparations to get the *PT-504* ready for them. It was polished to a fare-thee-well. When the king came aboard, there were a number of admirals there, both British and American. Kirk told me to entertain the king for about half an hour with some sea stories. With all that had happened up to that point in the war, I had plenty to talk about. We got along fine. While all this was going on, one of my quartermasters was supposed to go around and record the names of all the visitors for the deck log. For example, he'd say: "What's your name, Admiral?"

"Kirk."

"What's your first name?"

"Alan."

Then the quartermaster would write down "Rear Admiral Alan Kirk, U.S. Navy," and so forth.

When the quartermaster got around to the king, he looked at his blue uniform and saw the big broad stripe and four smaller ones. He said, "What's your name, Admiral?"

The king smiled and said, "My name is Windsor." All the rest of the people, including Churchill, were so amused they could hardly contain themselves.

Then the quartermaster asked, "What's your first name, Admiral?"

"George."

So the quartermaster dutifully made his log entry: "Admiral of the Fleet George Windsor, Royal Navy." The king handled it beautifully, reminding those of us present that he really was a naval officer. He had been a midshipman in the Battle of Jutland in 1916.

**Sgt. Alan Anderson, 467th Anti Aircraft Artillery Automatic Weapons Battalion:** [In] the first days in June, we were all called into a tent and some colonel from public relations got up and made an impassioned and a patriotic speech about what a privilege it was for us to be in this eventful invasion, which would change the history of the world. Then at the end of his speech he made the remarkable announcement that he couldn't go with us. My buddy, Arkie Markum, poked me and said, "Well, he can have my place if he really wants to go!"

**Sgt. Debs H. Peters, 121st Engineer Battalion, 29th Division:** A few days before the invasion, we were taken, in trucks, out to the field a few miles from there, out into a formation, and waited until a British command car came around. General Montgomery asked us to gather around him, take off our helmets so that he could see our faces and started to tell us what would be in the future.

**Gen. Bernard L. Montgomery:** You have been selected to lead the assault into Europe, and this may be a surprise to you, I hope it is, because it has been very closely kept. We will be attempting an operation that has not been successful since the Battle of Hastings in 1066. In order to be sure of our success, we must choose the very best that we have, and we think that you are the best that we've got. You will have every gun, every ship, every plane—everything that we have at our command to support you—but the rest is up to you. Go along lads, I'll see you on the other side.

# Learning the Details

Sealed off from the public, units—like the
6th Airborne Division here—finally learned the precise
details of their role in the upcoming invasion.

*As June 5 approached, most participants in* OVERLORD *only learned in the final hours before they launched for France what specific role their unit would play and where, ultimately, they were headed. Group by group, unit by unit, troop by troop, they were brought into specially designed briefing rooms in each separate marshaling area where highly detailed maps of Normandy and the invasion beaches had been built. These briefings, complete often with up-to-date reconnaissance photographs, told down to the most minute detail the objectives, targets, and timelines for the coming D-Day operation.*

**Pvt. Herbert Zafft, II5th Infantry Regiment, 29th Division:** They took us down to the big tent, and let us in on the secret that we were going to be invading Normandy, France.

**Seaman James T. Fudge, USS *LST-54*:** We knew it was going to be the French coast, but we didn't know exactly where. Most of us did not know the geography of France, it wouldn't have mattered anyway.

**Sgt. John Robert "Bob" Slaughter, Company D, II6th Infantry Regiment, 29th Division:** We were told we would land on Dog Green Sector of Omaha Beach, in front of the Vierville draw. We were shown a sand-table mock-up of what the landing area would look like. They even had the steeple of the Vierville church that we were to be guided on, and electric lights simulated shell bursts to enhance the realism.

**Pvt. Ray Howell, 3466th Ordnance Medium Automotive Maintenance Company, 5th Engineer Special Brigade:** It showed the machine gun emplacements, the pillboxes, the rows of houses, everything on the beach. It was made out of material like plaster of Paris—probably 50 or 60 feet long and described the features that you would expect to see.

**Sgt. John Robert "Bob" Slaughter:** They told us we would have twenty-one pillboxes in our areas but that only one or two would actually be manned, that the troops guarding the area were old or were Russian or Polish nationals conscripted into the German Army and that they would not fight very forcefully, and that we shouldn't have any trouble just going in and marching across the beach, so we weren't worried too much about the beach.

**Pfc. Joseph S. Blaylock, Sr., Baker Battery, 20th Field Artillery, 4th Division:** They explained to us where Omaha Beach would be and then where the French and the English and the Canadians would be—and they told us about Normandy. They showed us even as far as the pear tree, or apple tree, where we would put our gun positions. That's how precise it was.

**Pvt. Robert Healey, 149th Engineer Combat Battalion, 6th Engineer Special Brigade:** It was explained fully what we would do. We were, for example, the security sections which were to move inland, set up a line about a thousand yards inland near the village of St. Laurent Sur Mer. They explained it would be no problem at all, because the Air Force was coming over in great numbers and would bomb the beach. There would be a great number of bombardments by Navy ships. There were rocket ships that would fire thousands of rockets on the beach so they created the impression that it was going to be a walkover, nothing to worry about. They did tell us we would have a problem on the night of D+1. We could expect to be counter attacked by the Panzers, which they felt would be in the battle by that time. They felt this was going to be the crucial time, D+1, when the Panzers would attack us.

**Chief Yeoman W. Garwood Bacon, Jr., 7th Naval Beach Battalion:** We were taken under guard into a BIGOT room which contained air photographs taken as recently as May 25, 1944 by low flying P-38's. And a huge rubber map approximately 20 ft x 10 ft which showed us in minute detail the exact beaches we were to hit. The types of obstacles and their positions in the water with respect to our particular beaches. The two roads leading back from our beaches to Le Moulin and Vierville Sur Mer, the sea wall along a portion of the beaches, and a ridge we could expect to sight on approaching a beach from the water. The gun emplacements, the proposed locations for army and navy evacuation centers, ammunition dumps, water and supply depots and the areas to be taken by the rangers.

**Pvt. John Barnes, Company A, 116th Infantry Regiment, 29th Division:** We came to know every house, pillbox, trench, crossroad, like it was our own home neighborhood.

**Brig. David Belcham, head of Operations and Planning Staff, British Army:** The coxswain of each landing craft was provided with a photograph of his allotted beaching point, taken 1,500 yards from the shore by an aircraft virtually skimming the sea, while each infantry platoon commander also had an oblique photograph of the terrain inland from his landing area. This degree of support by air reconnaissance was unique. Never before in war had military commanders landed on a foreign shore equipped with so much detailed information about the defensive units and minefields facing them, or about the battlefield terrain lying beyond the landing beaches.

**Pvt. John Barnes:** All this, the exact date and place, were hidden behind code names like D-Day, H-Hour, Omaha, Dog Green. The 1st Battalion was to land in a line of companies. A-Company, of course, was to be first, followed by B-Company, and C-Company to follow. Each unit had a landing time something like a train schedule: "A-Company arriving at track 1 in 5 minutes!" It seemed so organized that nothing could go wrong, nothing could stop it. It rolled along on schedule. We were almost just like passengers.

**Pvt. Len Griffing, 50Ist Parachute Infantry Regiment, I0Ist Airborne:** In the serenity of England, in our own camp, invading France seemed to be a lot easier than it turned out to be.

**Flight (Warrant) Officer Charles E. "Chuck" Skidmore, Jr., glider pilot, 9Ist Troop Carrier Squadron, 439th Troop Carrier Wing:** The briefings for the aerial invasion of Utah Beach, our particular designation, were serious matters, but not without a little pressure-relieving levity upon occasion. Our 439th Troop Carrier Chaplain, Father Whalen, had probably heard about all the profanity known to mankind because he was a prison chaplain at Joliet, Illinois prior to volunteering for the service. So he wasn't shocked at one of the briefings to hear some profanity which included the Lord's name. Upon looking around his listeners, the briefer stopped to apologize to the good Father. "Don't worry about what I think," said Father, "worry about what the Lord thinks."

**S.Sgt. Harry Bare, Company F, II6th Infantry Regiment, 29th Division:** These last few days of May seemed to have somewhat of a sobering effect on the men. Sure, some put on a big front—nothing to it, just like Slapton Sands—but I wonder really what they were thinking. The 29th men were usually very loud, friendly, and outgoing, but now, they seemed quiet. A lot were busy writing letters to be delivered later.

**Sgt. Alan Anderson, 467th Anti Aircraft Artillery Automatic Weapons Battalion:** The army was prepared to accept 100% casualties for the first 24 hours. It was interesting that we all turned around and looked at each other and said, "Well, it's tough that you have to go." It's really strange that the human mind doesn't seem to be able to comprehend that an assignment like that might not apply to you and you could very well be lost in a suicide mission, which was possible as far as the contemplated invasion of the French Coast.

**2nd Lt. Cyril Rand, platoon commander, Company C, 2nd Battalion, Royal Ulster Rifles:** It was only now that we began to realize the immensity of the forth-coming operation, and the part that we as an Assault Battalion, were to play in it. Until this time all the exercises the Platoon had carried out over the past two years had been accepted as training—something that had to be done—with no great thought as to what would happen when the training was over. Now we were all suddenly faced with the reality of the situation: that very shortly we would be face to face not with fellow soldiers firing blanks and throwing thunderflashes to simulate exploding bombs, but with a determined and aggressive enemy using live ammunition whose objectives were either to kill us or push us back into the sea.

**Archibald "Doon" Campbell, correspondent, Reuters:** In this commando camp, I felt utterly ill-equipped and unprepared to join them. They were so abso-lutely honed to perfection for this assault, this job they were going to be doing on D-Day, and there I was, with no particular training or preparation for it.

On the Sunday before embarking, there was a church service. This padre got up and preached the most appalling sermon in which he said something like "We're shortly going into the big fight and it will be a very messy affair. You're going to see your mates without their arms, no legs, but it is God's cause and if it wasn't God's cause, I wouldn't touch it with a bargepole." That was the expression he used, "I wouldn't touch it with a bargepole."

The effect was tremendously dampening; it somehow affected our morale terribly, to an extent that Lovat [commander, 1st Special Service Brigade] saw the situation and went up into the pulpit unrehearsed, and in French and English did a sort of Agincourt speech: "Gentlemen, you've been given a proud task. Sure you will acquit yourselves in a way that your children and your children's children will say they were men, they were giants in those days." He completely restored the situation and got everybody buoyant again. Lovat had sent for the padre after the service and told him he would not be going in on the first wave because of the damage his sermon had done to the men's morale.

I went off to the mess for lunch, feeling very uncomfortable. As I was walking back to the tent I was a few paces away when I heard a rifle crack. I saw the canvas move, went in, and there was the padre. He'd shot himself.

**Brig. The Lord Lovat, commander, 1st Special Service Brigade:** The new padre preached a rotten sermon about death and destruction which caused surprise. It was mistaken zeal from a man, lacking combat experience, who did not know his congregation. On the last day in camp the unfortunate man took his own life. The padre was put down as a "battle casualty."

\*          \*          \*

*A key component of the Allied invasion plan was the drop of nearly 20,000 British, Canadian, and US paratroopers along the two flanks of the invasion—the American 82nd and 101st Airborne Divisions would drop behind Utah Beach and the British 6th Airborne would secure the eastern flank. Paratroopers represented one of the major military advances of World War II, first employed by Germany in its Blitzkrieg invasions. Recognizing the benefits of such a force, the US and British had rushed to build their own airborne capability, creating regiments who ahead of D-Day had trained to secure beach exits and disrupt German counterattacks. These paratroops were all volunteers and represented some of the most elite forces in the Allied military, relentlessly trained and carefully honed; the training for the 506th Parachute Infantry Regiment began, for instance, with 500 officer candidates and 5,300 enlisted personnel, and just 148 officers and 1,800 enlisted completed the training course. The paratroop plan, though, remained controversial among the Allied leadership right up until the very end.*

**Brig. Gen. James M. Gavin, assistant division commander, 82nd Airborne:** Airborne combat in Sicily and Italy had been invaluable in preparation for the Normandy operation. We learned what could be done by parachute troops and troop-carrier pilots, but, more important, we learned what they could not do. The airborne troops had more than held their own against German infantry, but meeting German armor in good tank country could be disastrous.

**Maj. Gen. Matthew Ridgway, commander, 82nd Airborne:** We trained hard in Ireland, using every hour of the all too short winter days.

**Pvt. James O. Eads, 508th Parachute Infantry Regiment, 82nd Airborne:** Only 3 out of each 10 men passed all phases of the [paratrooper] training.

**Capt. Legrand "Legs" Johnson, commander, Company F, 502nd Parachute Infantry Regiment, 101st Airborne:** We did everything, of course, to prepare for D-Day.

**1st Lt. Jack R. Isaacs, platoon commander, 505th Parachute Infantry Regiment, 82nd Airborne:** We made two combat drops in the Mediterranean, one in Sicily on July 9, 1943, and in Italy in September of 1943. In November, the division moved from Naples, Italy to Belfast, North Ireland.

**Lt. Gen. Walter Bedell "Beetle" Smith, Chief of Staff, SHAEF:** A few days before the invasion itself, Leigh-Mallory reiterated his honest conviction of heavy losses. He felt they might run as high as 75 per cent or even higher. In the opinion of General Eisenhower and his principal ground commanders, the airborne landing was so vital to the outcome of our assault that to cancel it would endanger the whole success of our offensive.

**Maj. Gen. Matthew Ridgway:** Both General Bradley and I argued strongly that these were risks that we would have to take, and we were willing to take them. The drop was a great gamble, we admitted. The whole great operation was a desperate gamble.

**Pvt. Len Griffing, 501st Parachute Infantry Regiment, 101st Airborne:** Each man was issued a cricket, one of those children's toys, when you put it between your thumb and fore finger and squeezed the fingers together it clicked, and it clicked again when you released the pressure on the fingers.

**1st Lt. Jack R. Isaacs:** A click or two clicks was an identifying sign that it was a friendly person in the dark.

**Pvt. Donald R. Burgett, 506th Parachute Infantry Regiment, 101st Airborne:** The verbal challenge for all airborne was "Flash," the password "Thunder," and if a man wasn't sure of who challenged him, he could ask for the countersign "Welcome." The way to challenge a man is to draw a bead on him, wait until he is not more than fifteen or twenty feet away, then whisper, just loud enough for him to hear, the challenge word, "Flash."

**Pvt. Len Griffing:** Anyone who fired a gun had to be a German, and we were to do him in with grenades or whatever way we could.

**Pfc. Carl Howard Cartledge, Jr., Intelligence and Reconnaissance Section, 501st Parachute Infantry Regiment, 101st Airborne:** We would seek and destroy with knives and grenades only.

*       *       *

*While hundreds of thousands of soldiers, sailors, paratroopers, and flight crews finally learned their mission, one specific member of the Allied leadership found that he didn't want to be left out of the invasion force.*

**Gen. Lord Hastings Ismay, chief military adviser to Winston Churchill:** The Prime Minister confided in me that he had decided to accompany the invasion. I was horrified, not so much at the risk involved, but at the prospect of the Prime Minister being cut off from communication with the outside world at a time when critical and immediate decisions might have to be taken.

**Winston Churchill, Prime Minister of the United Kingdom:** I thought it would not be wrong for me to watch the preliminary bombardment in this historic battle from one of our cruiser squadrons, and I asked Admiral Ramsay to make a plan. He arranged for me to embark in *H.M.S. Belfast*, in the late afternoon of the day before D-Day. Admiral Ramsay felt it his duty however to tell the Supreme Commander of what was in the air. Eisenhower protested against my running such risks.

**Gen. Dwight Eisenhower, Supreme Allied Commander, SHAEF:** His request was undoubtedly inspired as much by his natural instincts as a warrior as by his impatience at the prospect of sitting quietly back in London to await reports. I argued, however, that the chance of his becoming an accidental casualty was too important from the standpoint of the whole war effort and I refused his request.

**Capt. Harry C. Butcher, naval aide to Dwight Eisenhower, SHAEF:** Ike said he had already told the PM that if the Prime Minister were on a ship which happened to get hit, at least four or five other war vessels would be required to come to its assistance, whereas if he were not aboard, the battle would go on and the ship would look after itself the best it could. The PM was an added burden in battle.

**Gen. Dwight Eisenhower:** He was worth too much to the Allied cause. He said, "Well, I can sign on as a member of the crew of one of His Majesty's ships and there's nothing that you can do." And I said, "That's correct. But Winston, you will make my burden a lot heavier by doing it."

**Gen. Lord Hastings Ismay:** Fortunately the King himself took a hand.

**Gen. Dwight Eisenhower:** "Well, as long as the prime minister feels that it's desirable to go along on this operation," he said, "I think that it'd be my duty now to go along with you."

**Winston Churchill:** His Majesty immediately said he would like to come too. He had not been under fire except in air raids since the Battle of Jutland, and eagerly welcomed the prospect of renewing the experiences of his youth.

**Gen. Dwight Eisenhower:** Well, of course, the Prime Minister didn't want to take a chance with the king, so he didn't go. That's the way it's done.

*"Hold each foxhole to the last cartridge"*

# Spring in Normandy with the Germans

The German forces manning the Atlantic Wall comprised soldiers and conscripts from numerous countries, including the "Free Indian Legion."

*The imminent preparations in the British Isles were hardly a secret to the Germans, despite limited reconnaissance capabilities. Instead, the German High Command, from Hitler to Rommel to OB West, wondered only where and when the invasion would come. The intense Allied bombing and the Transportation Plan, meanwhile, took an ever-greater toll on the defenders' readiness, logistics, and supply chains.*

**Lt. Gen. Hans Speidel, Chief of Staff to Erwin Rommel:** The Allies seemed to have their three-dimensional invasion forces assembled in readiness in the British Isles by the end of April. There were restrictions upon travel in the United Kingdom, the Home Guard was called up, and British industry complained of the dislocation that this produced. The sign that was most ominous was the intensifying of air attacks against the mainland, which indicated an attack to be imminent, though its exact timing would depend upon weather conditions.

**General der Artillerie Walter Warlimont, deputy chief of the Operations Staff, Armed Forces High Command:** Hitler was the first one who decided for himself that this was the most probable spot for landing. On 2 May 1944, he ordered that antiaircraft and antitank weapons were to be reinforced all through Normandy and Brittany, counting mainly on an invasion in Normandy. Hitler's view was based on intelligence received as to troop movements in the British Isles. Two main troop concentrations had been noticed there: one in the southeast with mainly British troops, and one in the southwest, in Wales and on both sides of Wales, consisting mainly of US troops. We were not quite convinced that Hitler was right in expecting that attack, but he kept harping on it and demanded more and more reinforcements for that sector.

**Vice Adm. Friedrich Ruge, naval adviser to Erwin Rommel, Army Group B:** Unfortunately our reconnaissance did not often penetrate to the enemy's concentration areas, and thus we were never safe from surprises.

**General der Infanterie Günther Blumentritt, Chief of Staff, OB West:** For us, the English southern coast was an impenetrable sphinx. Rumors and scattered reports did not give us specific information on the time and place of the landing.

**Lt. Gen. Hans Speidel:** Bomber squadrons destroyed railway junctions and cross-roads as well as buildings of all sorts so thoroughly that the supply difficulties during the invasion were insurmountable. Destruction of railways west of a line Brussels-Paris-Orleans made it impossible to organise a regular supply and replacement system by rail after the middle of May. There was not a big enough lift in motor transport to take over the burden, and not enough petrol to have moved it.

**Lt. Gen. Max-Josef Pemsel, Chief of Staff, Seventh Army:** Repair of railroad installations fell further and further behind, causing a great hold-up of trains. The construction of many defense works along the coast had to be halted because of the shortage of materials. Attacks by the Allied air force were aimed at the entire front, without any perceptible point of main effort.

**Lt. Gen. Hans Speidel:** The High Command of the Wehrmacht was advised by the German Navy that indications pointed to 18th May and named this day as "the certain date" for the beginning of invasion. This "zero-day" came and went, and the Naval Command in the West then expected the attack to be delayed until August.

**Lt. Col. Fritz Ziegelmann, Chief of Staff, 352nd Infantry Division:** In May, Hitler gave orders to hold each foxhole to the last cartridge.

*Knowing that every day mattered, Rommel continued to push hard for further construction: more obstacles, more mines, and more reinforcements. By May 1944, German forces had laid some 6.5 million mines, a seemingly huge number but still far short of his estimate that 50 million were needed to adequately secure the coastline. There were some 517,000 obstacles too dotting the Atlantic Wall, as well as some 5,000 bunkers. Altogether, from 1942 to 1944, the construction effort had consumed some 1.3 million tons of steel, and 17.3 million cubic yards of concrete, but had been compromised along the way by the shortages that plagued the Reich by 1944. Amid wood and labor shortages, much of the concrete construction in 1944 was done in blocks, not smooth casts, which made the 1944 bunkers comparatively much weaker than those constructed in 1942.*

**Lt. Gen. Hans Speidel:** The working days of Field-Marshal Rommel in the "quiet times" before the invasion were full of restless endeavour.

**Field Marshal Erwin Rommel, letter to his wife, May 15, 1944:** The middle of May already and still nothing doing, although a pincer attack seems to have started in Italy, which may well be the prelude for the great events of the spring or summer. I've been away for a couple of days, talking to the officers and men. It's quite amazing what has been achieved in the last few weeks. I'm convinced that the enemy will have a rough time of it when he attacks, and ultimately achieve no success.

**Lt. Gen. Hans Speidel:** He visited the troops daily without much entourage, accompanied usually by his adjutant only and sometimes Vice Admiral Ruge, whose refined and generous nature he particularly liked.

**Maj. Hans von Luck, commander, Panzer-Grenadier-Regiment 125, 21 Panzer-Division:** In the course of May, Rommel appeared at the division several times, to acquaint himself with its state of training and the morale of the men. On one of his visits, he expressed himself almost prophetically. "I know the British from France in 1940 and from North Africa. They will land at the very place where we least expect them. It might be here."

**Lt. Gen. Hans Speidel:** The operational Headquarters of Army Group B was near to the front in the Chateau La Roche Guyon. The chateau stood on the western fringe of the fair Ile de France in a great northward bend of the Seine and on its north bank. About forty miles downstream from Paris, between Mantes and Vernon, it was the seat of the Dukes de la Roche-foucauld. Built against the steep and worn chalk cliffs above the Seine, it had been a Norman stronghold and the ruins of the old castle with its prominent keep still dominated the hill. Rommel did not move out the ducal family, and only brought the most important members of his staff to the chateau itself.

**Vice Adm. Friedrich Ruge:** The castle, built between the twelfth and the seventeenth centuries, stood at the foot of the riverbank's slope; the oldest part, a tower built around the year 1000, capped the hill above. Over the years, the inhabitants had tunnelled several passages and caves into the soft limestone, which our engineers now had transformed into communication centers, briefing rooms, and alert quarters. The castle itself, while historically and artistically valuable, was neither especially large nor grandiose. Only part of the staff found shelter in the castle; the rest were lodged in the village. In keeping with the old customs of chivalry in war, the inhabitants were not forced to leave their property.

**Maj. Gen. Fritz Bayerlein, commander, Panzer Lehr Division:** I had a long talk with Rommel at La Roche Guyon on the differences which existed between

162 **WHEN THE SEA CAME ALIVE**

the East front generals and the men with African experience. As we strolled in the park, Rommel spoke in roughly the following terms: "We are facing an enemy who applies all his native intelligence to the use of his many technical resources, who spares no expenditure of material, and whose every operation goes its course as though it had been the subject of repeated rehearsal. Dash and doggedness alone no longer make a soldier, Bayerlein, he must have sufficient intelligence to enable him to get the most out of his fighting machine. That's something these people can do, we found that out in Africa."

**Gren. Franz Gockel, 3 Kompanie, Grenadier-Regiment 726, 716 Infanterie-Division, posted to Widerstandsnest 62 at Colleville-sur-Mer (Omaha Beach):** During May and the beginning of June, the aircraft activity increased over us, passing our positions and dropping their deadly load on the key railway junctions and road crossings in the rear. Only once or twice a week would two German aircraft be seen flying along the coastline. We named them Max and Moritz.

**Maj. Hans von Luck:** On 30 May, Rommel came to our division for the last time. Becker demonstrated his new rocket-launcher on the Normandy coast with live ammunition, which filled Rommel with enthusiasm. At the closing conference, with all the commanders of our division, Rommel exhorted us again to be extremely vigilant. It was put even more precisely by General [Erich] Marcks, commander of the 84th Army Corps, to which we were attached, "From my knowledge of the British, they will go to church again on Sunday, 4 June, and come on the Monday." The navy and our meteorologists calculated that the most favorable time for a landing would be 5 June, then not again until 28 June 1944.

**Generalfeldmarschall Gerd von Rundstedt, Commander in Chief, OB West, to Adolf Hitler, May 30, 1944:** It is true that the hour of invasion draws nearer, but the scale of enemy air attacks does not indicate that it is immediately imminent.

*The residents and troops assigned to Normandy spent those final weeks of May and the beginning of June wondering, like everyone else, where and when the invasion would take place. The troops and units assigned to the coastal defenses, though, had a sinking feeling that the war was slipping from Germany—that the momentum was now with the Allies and that they were ill equipped to handle an invasion if it hit their sector.*

**Alexandre Renaud, Mayor, Sainte-Mère-Église:** One night, little pamphlets were dropped over the Manor garden. They repeated the orders already given, but also, they described how the American and English paratroopers would be dressed, what the jeeps and light tanks would look like, as well as the bigger Churchill and Sherman tanks. There were even drawings. "Aw," someone scoffed, "those pamphlets are printed in big series, and the fact that they fell here proves nothing. They're probably sending the same ones over the North and as far south as Saint-Nazaire." I agreed.

**Gren. Franz Gockel:** These were the many hours in which no one thought of war. As the sun set on the horizon, its reflection on the surface of the water would let one forget. But there were the messages from home about brutal experiences, which showed us that the front was not just here. We waited every day for mail. Many men lived in the big cities and some had already lost their homes in air raids. There had not been any electricity for weeks, only the flickering light of candles, and the weak light from oil lamps that smelled bad.

**Lt. Heinz Fuehr, 8th Kompanie, Grenadier Regiment 916, 352nd Infantry Division:** Two days before the invasion, I was on an inspection tour with a major from the staff of LXXXIV Armeekorps. He was the officer in charge of our munitions supplies. We went from strongpoint to strongpoint. He looked in them and asked questions of the men, mostly getting the correct if uninspired answers. At one strongpoint a veteran Feldwebel stepped forward and spoke to him. He said, "Herr Major, we have enough ammunition to stop the first, second, third, fourth, and maybe even the fifth wave of Tommies. But after that they're going to kick the door in on top of us and then all is lost." The bewildered officer stepped back and stated he would ensure that enough ammunition was available. We didn't know that within 48 hours his words would ring true. Again and again in the days that would come I would hear those words. I can still hear him to this day.

**Cpl. Werner Kortenhaus, Panzer-Regiment 22, 21 Panzer-Division:** We thought, let them get here, we'll throw them out again. We genuinely believed—and we were always being told—that we were so strong we would throw them out in no time. We had rehearsed and practiced things for so long that we wanted to see some real action at last. We were simply too naive to grasp what war actually meant. We had no idea.

**Capt. Eberhard Wagemann, staff officer, Panzer-Regiment 22, 21 Panzer-Division:** It wasn't in our interests to think too much about our feelings. We were conscious that neither our men nor our tanks were good enough.

**2nd Lt. Heinrich Fuerst, medical officer, 706/8th Festungsdivision:** The situation was like you were sitting on a tropical beach, well protected, but expecting a huge hurricane to hit in the next forty-eight hours. We couldn't run and hide, we had to stay—what else was there to do? It was not a very pleasant prospect, knowing you had a good chance to get killed.

**Field Marshal Erwin Rommel:** The war will be won or lost on the beaches. We'll have only one chance to stop the enemy and that's while he's in the water. Believe me, the first twenty-hours of the invasion will be decisive. The fate of Germany depends on the outcome. For the allies, as well as Germany, it will be the longest day.

*"Face to face with a crisis"*

# The D-Day Weather Forecast

As Ike weighed the advice of Captain Stagg's meteorologists,
invasion ships were already sailing for the French coast.

*Dwight Eisenhower for months had confronted the least-worst choices in preparing for Operation OVERLORD and its initial invasion phase, known as Operation NEPTUNE. The five-division, five-beach plan wasn't as large as he wanted, but it was the largest the Allies could move across the Channel. The Normandy beaches weren't the best or the easiest to attack, but they were the best compromise among the myriad logistical and military considerations the planners confronted. Finally, in the first days of June, he confronted the most consequential least-worst choice of all: Would the weather during the one brief window in June where the moons and the tides aligned be decent enough for the whole invasion to proceed? Years of effort, millions of lives, and billions of dollars and pounds came down to the question of whether the notoriously uncooperative English Channel would cooperate. Even as a million personnel began to move from the sealed-up marshaling areas onto the ships that would carry them to France and even as those ships began to put to sea, SHAEF wasn't sure it would happen at all. Over twice-daily meetings at Southwick House, the British naval headquarters in the south of England, the Allied leadership met to consider their options—all of which seemed bad.*

**Maj. John Dalgleish, Planning Staff, Royal Army Service Corps:** June arrived. The blossoms were full. The birds trilled their songs in the woodland around the offices.

**Lt. Gen. Walter Bedell "Beetle" Smith, Chief of Staff, SHAEF:** Then it was June, and we were with General Eisenhower at the forward command post he had established near Portsmouth.

**Gen. Dwight Eisenhower, Supreme Allied Commander, SHAEF:** We came down here hoping and praying that the weather would be sufficiently good we could go on the June 5th.

**Capt. J. M. Stagg, chief meteorologist, SHAEF:** Southwick House is a spacious mansion set in extensive wooded grounds, surrounded by gardens, lawns and avenues. It lies just north of Portsmouth in the shadow of Ports Down ridge from which there is a panoramic view of the city and its harbours and anchorages. The whole water surface was so crowded with craft of every size and description—battleships, destroyers, transport-vessels and hundreds of landing craft, all lying rail to rail—that it seemed it would be impossible to get them out quickly in an orderly fashion. It was a most impressive sight.

**Lt. Gen. Walter Bedell "Beetle" Smith:** We found a good site in the patches of wood which crowned the bluff overlooking Portsmouth Harbor, not far from Southwick House where Admiral Ramsay had his headquarters. Here we set up tents and trailers and went into bivouac with the advance echelon of the staff which would move to France as soon as we had elbow room.

**Capt. Kay Summersby, British Mechanised Transport Corps, aide and secretary to General Eisenhower, SHAEF:** Nerve-ends were so exposed, security so exacting, that even the Supreme Allied Commander had to carry a pass. Everyone topside was jumpy over our Other Enemy: the weather. The area was alive with weather experts, meteorologists, and plain second-guessers—all studying, figuring, worrying about the weather, key to the whole invasion.

**Gen. Dwight Eisenhower:** If none of the days should prove satisfactory from the standpoint of weather, consequences would ensue that were almost terrifying to contemplate. Secrecy would be lost. Assault troops would be unloaded and crowded back into assembly areas enclosed in barbed wire, where their original places would already have been taken by those to follow in subsequent waves. A wait of at least fourteen days, possibly twenty-eight, would be necessary—a sort of suspended animation involving more than 2,000,000 men!

**Lt. Gen. Walter Bedell "Beetle" Smith:** June dawned dark and stormy with a gale over the Channel. Up at SHIPMATE—code name of the Advanced Command Post on the bluff—we shivered in our tents and trailers.

**Gen. Dwight Eisenhower:** We met with the Meteorologic Committee twice daily, once at nine-thirty in the evening and once at four in the morning.

**Lt. Gen. Walter Bedell "Beetle" Smith:** We knew the Channel could be an implacable enemy, capable of delivering us as disastrous a blow afloat as we should encounter from the German guns when we rushed the beaches.

*To help predict and understand the weather they'd face in the invasion, the Allies relied on a trio of two-men meteorological teams based at three weather centers—the UK Meteorological Office in Dunstable, the US Army Air Force's Eighth Air Force's headquarters, known as Widewing, and the Royal Navy's headquarters in Portsmouth on the English Channel, which was referred to as the Admiralty. Drawing upon hundreds of reports from across the British Isles, the US, North Atlantic, and Europe, each team—with its own education, theories of weather, and specialties—approached the forecasts differently, and they agreed only rarely.*

**Capt. J. M. Stagg:** After the morning consultations that day [June 1] I had reaffirmed to General [Harold] Bull for transmission to General Eisenhower and his staff that in my view the prospects for Sunday and Monday, and probably Tuesday, were poor. "There will probably be a good deal of cloud throughout those days. The situation is complex and difficult." In accepting this Bull's only comment was, "For heaven's sake, Stagg, get it sorted out by tomorrow morning before you come to the Supreme Commander's conference. General Eisenhower is a very worried man."

**Lt. Cdr. Lawrence Hogben, meteorologist, Royal New Zealand Navy, Admiralty Headquarters, Portsmouth:** We used data garnered from special weather recce [reconnaissance] flights, ship observations, UK weather sites and pinched what we could from the Germans—once we broke their weather codes—and redrew our charts every few hours.

**Sverre Petterssen, meteorologist, Norwegian Air Force, UK Meteorological Office:** Each would contribute to the forecasting for the operation. At the supreme commander's headquarters was a senior meteorological officer to serve as the chairman of telephone conferences between the participating centers. He would smooth out differences of opinion (should such occur) and formulate the advice to be given to the supreme commander.

**Capt. J. M. Stagg:** Telephone machinery had been installed in our room at SHAEF. This allowed us to speak simultaneously to the representatives of the three centres in their own rooms. When functioning well, and it mostly did, the facility never ceased to impress me with the sense that we were all sitting round an invisible table.

**Capt. Harry C. Butcher, naval aide to Dwight Eisenhower, SHAEF:** I lunched with Brigadier General Arthur S. Nevins, and we joked about the term "agreed weather report," which comes from the variety of air, naval, and ground weathermen. He said that Group Captain Stagg, who is chairman of the committee of experts, has telephone conferences via scrambler with all the prophets each morning. He said at the outset of the conversation it would seem that all are talking about a different subject, but eventually the weathermen agree on the weather, at least as to what they will predict.

**Lt. Cdr. Lawrence Hogben:** We six never agreed about anything except that Stagg was not a good meteorologist and that he was a bit of a glory hog.

**Sverre Petterssen:** Stagg was a meteorologist mainly in the sense that he was employed by the Meteorological Office. His scientific field was terrestrial magnetism and he had done some work in radiation, but none in or anywhere near subjects related to forecasting.

**Lt. Cdr. Lawrence Hogben:** None of us were operating with any of the technology and equipment that our successors today take for granted, such as satellites, weather radar, computer modeling, and instant communications, and predicting conditions more than a day or two in advance was hazardous.

**Sverre Petterssen:** From the very beginning of weather forecasting—about 1855—until about 1965, when versatile electronic computers began to make their influence felt, simple extrapolation of the movement and rate of development of weather systems remained an important technique. However, the usefulness of this method is limited largely to forecasts for short periods, say, up to thirty-six or, at most, forty-eight hours.

*Preliminary forecasts for the invasion period appeared ominous—potentially, in fact, even historically bad, with the Channel filled by a storm that almost surely would devastate the invasion fleet long before it arrived in France.*

**Capt. J. M. Stagg:** The whole north Atlantic Ocean area appeared to be filled with a succession of depressions, any one of which could blow into violence. In all the charts for the 40 or 50 years I had examined I could not recall one which at this time of year remotely resembled this chart in the number and intensity of depressions it portrayed at one time.

**Lt. Cdr. Lawrence Hogben:** All we knew was there were several storms blowing across the Atlantic towards us, any one of which would have whipped up the waters where the fleet was gathering.

**Capt. J. M. Stagg:** I do recall the earlier part of that day as the nadir of strain and despondency. When I took leave of General [Freddie] Morgan before coming away from the main headquarters to join the advance party at Portsmouth he had said, "Good luck, Stagg; may all your depressions be nice little ones: but remember, we'll string you up from the nearest lamp post if you don't read the omens aright." Though I could not foresee that happening whatever I did, the image haunted me, quite irrationally, that Saturday—and to this day still does when under strain.

**Sverre Petterssen:** I felt we stood face to face with a crisis.

**Capt. J. M. Stagg:** Those days I was sometimes all but physically nauseated at the thought of a weather chart.

**Lt. Gen. Walter Bedell "Beetle" Smith:** By 1000 hours on June 3, it was evident that the weather was worsening, not improving.

**Winston Churchill, Prime Minister of the United Kingdom:** That afternoon I drove down to Portsmouth with Mr. Bevin and Field-Marshal Smuts and saw a large number of troops embarking for Normandy. We visited the Headquarters ship of the 50th Division, and then cruised down the Solent in a launch, boarding one ship after another. On the way back, we stopped at General Eisenhower's camp and wished him luck.

**Gen. Lord Hastings Ismay, chief military adviser to Winston Churchill:** Everything seemed to be going according to plan, and the bearing of the troops was most impressive. I had never before seen British soldiers in that mood. There was no joking about the "picnic" on which they were starting, and no singing about hanging up their washing on the Siegfried Line. They seemed to have no illusions about the hazards of the enterprise to which they were committed, but to be relieved that the long suspense had ended and that the time for action had come. Above all, they appeared to have absolute confidence in themselves and their leaders. [Sir Bernard] Paget had forged a magnificent weapon, and Montgomery had imparted the final polish. The men cheered the Prime Minister with gusto, and [Minister of Labour and National Service Ernest] Bevin's eyes filled with tears when several of them called to him, "You'll look after the missus and kids, won't you, Ernie?"

*Even as the invasion troops boarded their ships that Saturday, the hours of the 3rd ticked by with little evidence of improvement in the forecast, and the Allied commanders realized that they were going to have to make a big decision on Sunday about whether to postpone the invasion.*

**Capt. J. M. Stagg:** I said, "Gentlemen, the fears my colleagues and I had yesterday about the weather for the next three or four days have been confirmed. The whole weather set-up over the British Isles and, even more so, to the west over the north-east Atlantic is very disturbed and complex."

**Gen. Bernard L. Montgomery, Commander, Allied ground forces (21 Army Group):** We decided to make no changes. But we knew that a final decision regarding postponement must be taken early on the 4th June, and even then some of the convoys would have sailed.

**Capt. J. M. Stagg:** Throughout this recital General Eisenhower sat motionless, with his head slightly to one side resting on his hand, staring steadily towards me. All in the room seemed to be temporarily stunned: the gloom attributed to me last night had now fallen on everyone. Admiral Ramsay broke the grave silence: "Are the force 5 winds along the Channel to continue on Monday and Tuesday?" "Yes, Sir." "And the cloud on those days?" "As the situation is at this moment I could not attempt to differentiate one day from another in regard to cloudiness through the whole period from tomorrow [Sunday, June 4] till Wednesday when we expect the clearing front to pass through." When he came out, General Bull told us, "The Supreme Commander has made a provisional decision to hold up the operation on a day-to-day basis. Some of the forces will still sail tonight, but General Eisenhower and his commanders will meet again at 4:15 a.m. tomorrow [Sunday] morning to hear what you have to say. They will then decide definitely whether the first assaults will be postponed from Monday to

Tuesday." As I came out of Southwick House about midnight, Air Chief Marshal Tedder passed, lighting his pipe. He turned to me and, smiling, said, "Pleasant dreams, Stagg." He knew that there could not even be sleep. Through the trees we could see that the sky was almost clear and everything around was still and quiet.

*      *      *

**Capt. Kay Summersby, British Mechanised Transport Corps, aide and secretary to General Eisenhower, SHAEF:** June 4—supposed to be D-Day—undoubtedly was the longest day of 1944.

**Maj. Gen. Francis "Freddie" de Guingand, Chief of Staff, General Montgomery:** At 4.30 a.m., June 4th, the same scene again. The same room. The coffee. The men feeling grey and a little unsteady.

**Capt. J. M. Stagg:** The tension in the room was palpable. On a nod from the Supreme Commander, serious and unsmiling, I immediately confirmed that in the interval since the last meeting no development had occurred which allowed any substantial change in the forecast I had then presented.

**Maj. Gen. Francis "Freddie" de Guingand:** The meteorologists came in, and it was seen at once that they had no better news.

**Capt. J. M. Stagg:** General Eisenhower said, "In that case, gentlemen, it looks to me as if we must confirm the provisional decision we took at the last meeting. Compared with the enemy's forces ours are not overwhelmingly strong: we need every help our air superiority can give us. If the air cannot operate we must postpone. Are there any dissentient voices?" There were none. "We must call off the sailing of the last forces and take steps to recall the forces that have already sailed." General Eisenhower instructed his Chief of Staff to inform the Combined Chiefs of Staff that the assault had been postponed by one day.

**Maj. Gen. Francis "Freddie" de Guingand:** It was an immense undertaking to postpone D-Day. The troops and tanks and guns were embarked and waiting at scores of secret ports around the coast of England. The bombers were waiting on the airfields. The whole elaborate machine was poised to move on this day [June 4th], and to upset it now, to let some ships put to sea and then bring them back, to retard the immense and exact programme of the build-up, to alter the schedule of the trains and the convoys and the loading, to keep the waiting million of men strung at high tension—all this was a fearfully dangerous prospect. Worse still, the meteorologists warned the meeting that if these next few days were lost in inaction then a week or a fortnight might go by before the channel tides would again be suitable for the landing.

**Gen. Lord Hastings Ismay:** We returned to London in an agony of uncertainty. If the bad weather persisted for another two days, OVERLORD would have to be postponed for at least a fortnight. The troops had already been briefed. What was to be done with them?

**Maj. Gen. Francis "Freddie" de Guingand:** Officers ran to send the signals to the ports and the airfields. All over England the machine sighed down into a standstill. There was nothing now to do except wait.

**Lt. Dean L. Rockwell, flotilla commander, *LCT-535*:** Should the weather make the landing unsafe, we were to be notified by a simple message called "Post Mike One." And sure enough, early in the afternoon of June 4, a picket boat came along side the *LCT-535*, from which I was commanding the 16 landing craft and handed me a telegram, which I still have, which simply says, "Post Mike One."

**Winston Churchill:** All convoys at sea turned about and small craft sought shelter in convenient anchorages. Only one large convoy, comprising a hundred and thirty-eight small vessels, failed to receive the message, but this too was overtaken and turned round without arousing the suspicions of the enemy. It was a hard day for the thousands of men cooped up in landing craft all round the coast.

**1st Sgt. Charles Malley, 502nd Parachute Infantry Regiment, 101st Airborne:** On June 4, a plane came wheeling into the Air Base, and a warrant officer was admitted to the compound. A small valise was attached to the officer's right wrist. Captain Lillyman's face became quite pale. Lillyman read General [Maxwell] Taylor's message which was inside the container. He turned to me, saying, "Sergeant, tell the troops to relax—we have one more day." The letter was burned there on the spot. The valise was returned to the warrant officer who had no realization of its contents. The officer departed.

**Capt. J. M. Stagg:** There was in fact only one day left for D-day at that time, namely Tuesday, June 6th. But at the time of the postponement there was no indication, and certainly no reason for believing, that the weather on June 6th would be more favorable than on June 5th.

**Gen. Bernard L. Montgomery:** D–Day would now be on the 6th June.

*And then, the unexpected happened. A young Irishwoman, Maureen Sweeney, a postal clerk who worked with her husband, the keeper of the Blacksod Lighthouse, on the northwestern coast of Ireland, one of the first places that could detect looming Atlantic weather approaching the British Isles, posted data on the night of June 4 that caught the attention of Stagg's team.*

**Maureen Flavin Sweeney, postal clerk, Blacksod, Ireland:** Our reports were the first to show any change coming in for good weather or bad weather. There was a query [from London] at around 11 o'clock. And then there was a second query. A lady with a distinct English accent requested me to "Please Check. Please Repeat!" We began to look at the figures again. We checked and rechecked and the figures were the same both times so we were happy enough then.

**Lt. Robert Dale, flying officer, weather reconnaissance unit, RAF Station Wyton, Royal Canadian Air Force:** There were probably four or five reconnaissances [that we flew] to keep plotting where the front was. The weather was really bad. The flights were 3 ½ hours—in a Mosquito you would cover a lot of territory in 3 ½ hours. I got the feeling they already had the picture of things in their minds. I think we just confirmed their thoughts about what conditions would be like in the next twenty-four hours over the Channel.

**Sverre Petterssen:** In the early hours of June 4 a sudden and major reorganization of the atmosphere over the Atlantic sector threw the forecasters into confusion.

**Capt. J. M. Stagg:** Between the passage of the cold front and the approach of the depression, there could be an interlude of improved weather, and this interlude—if long enough and if it occurred at the right time—might just allow the first two critical sets of assault landings to be launched, at dawn and at dusk, on the same day and that day could be Tuesday.

**Sverre Petterssen:** Much effort was expended in trying to find out what had happened and what was going on. Nevertheless, toward the end of the day, the three teams—the Admiralty, Widewing, and Dunstable—reached a state of harmony that had hardly ever been attained since February when conference discussions began. Though the conditions were deemed to be marginal, all agreed that the crossing of the Channel, with landing at dawn on June 6, would be possible.

**Capt. J. M. Stagg:** No one could have imagined weather charts less propitious for the greatest military operation in history than those we had before us that evening. Two depressions over the north Atlantic Ocean, one almost on north-west Scotland, the other south of Greenland had central pressures at or around 980 millibars: each by itself was a mid-winter phenomenon. Everything now hinged on how we believed they would behave in the next 36 hours and, in consequence, what would transpire in the ridge space between them.

**Maj. Gen. Francis "Freddie" de Guingand:** From the meteorologists this time there was a definite flicker of hope. Most unexpectedly the weather had not worsened. It was dark, it was far from favorable, but it was no worse. And there was a hope that it would continue evenly like this for a few days.

**Capt. J. M. Stagg:** As on preceding occasions in the last four days—to me on that Sunday evening (June 4th) it seemed more like four months—the Cs-in-C and their senior staff officers were assembling in the Library as

Yates and I entered the hall of Southwick House at 9.30 p.m. We waited till they had all arrived and immediately we were called in.

**Gen. Dwight Eisenhower:** He told us we might have a little bit of improvement in this weather next day. He said, "I'll give you some good news."

**Capt. J. M. Stagg:** I said, "Gentlemen, since I presented the forecast last evening some rapid and unexpected developments have occurred over the north Atlantic. In particular a vigorous front—a cold front—from one of the depressions has been pushed more quickly and much farther south than could have been foreseen. This front is approaching Portsmouth now and will pass through all Channel areas tonight or early tomorrow. After the strong winds and low cloud associated with that front have moved through there will be a brief period of improved weather from Monday afternoon."

**Gen. Dwight Eisenhower:** He predicted this good weather would last between 24 and 36 hours. It was still a chancy thing.

**Maj. Gen. Francis "Freddie" de Guingand:** Admiral Ramsay was not enthusiastic. He was still worried about the build-up. And yet the chance was there. It could be done. Things could easily go wrong on the beaches, but still the landing was possible. Leigh-Mallory, too, thought that he could manage to put up his bombers and fighters. But they would have to go in on a modified plan. Montgomery again was all for sailing. The men sat round the table going through the possibilities over again, trying desperately to bring the facts to the point where they would produce a hard inevitable decision. But that was not possible. The element of luck remained.

**Capt. J. M. Stagg:** General Eisenhower put the question directly to General Montgomery: "Do you see any reason why we should not go on Tuesday?" Montgomery's reply was immediate and emphatic: "No. I would say—Go."

After some further discussion of the possible difficulties for the allied bombers and the countervailing advantages to the night air forces of the enemy if conditions turned out poor for our interceptor aircraft, the Supreme Commander started his summing up. "After hearing all your views I'm quite certain we must give the order for Tuesday morning. Are there any dissentient voices?" At this stage General Bull conveyed to me by a nod that we were not likely to be further required. So we withdrew.

In the hall just outside the conference room groups of senior staff officers of all three services were standing about in little knots, waiting to hear what had been decided. General Eisenhower came out almost immediately. As he made for the main door he came over and said, "Well, Stagg, we're putting it on again: for heaven's sake hold the weather to what you told us and don't bring any more bad news." He smiled broadly and went out. Shortly afterwards all his company came into the hall. General Bull told me they would meet again at 4.15 a.m. [Monday, June 5] to confirm the decision.

*Just hours later, the same group gathered again at Southwick House in the midst of the howling gale that had been, it turned out, accurately forecast by Stagg's team.*

**Gen. Dwight Eisenhower:** At three-thirty the next morning our little camp was shaking and shuddering under a wind of almost hurricane proportions and the accompanying rain seemed to be traveling in horizontal streaks.

**Gen. Bernard L. Montgomery:** It was clear that if we had persisted with the original D-Day of the 5th June, we might have had a disaster.

**Gen. Dwight Eisenhower:** It certainly increased my confidence in Captain Stagg, because 24 hours earlier, when it looked so nice, they said, "This is what you're going to have," and we had it. It was really storming.

**Capt. Kay Summersby:** Everyone went to that meeting with the full knowledge that a decision had to be made this time.

**Lt. Cdr. Lawrence Hogben:** I was scared—I think we all were—of getting it wrong; we knew we were making history.

**Lt. Gen. Walter Bedell "Beetle" Smith:** There was coffee ready. I took a cup from a young flag lieutenant and moved toward the pleasant fire. All the commanders were there when General Eisenhower arrived, trim in his tailored battle jacket, his face tense with the gravity of the decision before him.

**Gen. Dwight Eisenhower:** Stagg came in, a little grin on his face.

**Capt. J. M. Stagg:** All were in battle-dress uniform except General Montgomery. Conspicuous in his customary front seat he was dressed in a high-necked fawn-coloured pullover and light corduroy trousers. Facing them General Eisenhower seemed as spruce and immaculate as ever. At the earlier meetings the Cs-in-C and their staff chiefs exchanged pleasantries among themselves as they settled into their easy chairs and sofas: but at this meeting, as at the last, the atmosphere was sombre. Faces were grave and the room was quiet.

**Lt. Gen. Walter Bedell "Beetle" Smith:** There was the ghost of a smile on the tired face of Group Captain Stagg, the tall Scot. "I think we have found a gleam of hope for you, sir," he said to General Eisenhower, and we all listened expectantly. "The mass of weather fronts coming in from the Atlantic is moving faster than we anticipated," the chief meteorologist continued.

**Gen. Dwight Eisenhower:** The forecast for the following day contained a gleam of hope.

**Lt. Gen. Walter Bedell "Beetle" Smith:** They were giving us about twenty-four hours of reasonable weather. That was all.

**Maj. Gen. Francis "Freddie" de Guingand:** Eisenhower came forward. "This is a decision which I must take alone," he said. "After all, that is what I am here for."

**Lt. Gen. Walter Bedell "Beetle" Smith:** When I was a young officer, I once heard it said that the loneliest post in the world was that of a commander of a fleet about to go into battle. Yet I have never known a lonelier decision than General Eisenhower was forced to make when he ordered the invasion to proceed. The drama of the unique responsibility which he carried that early morning makes a scene which will never leave my memory.

**Capt. Kay Summersby:** Not another person on the face of the earth could make that decision at that time and place.

**Lt. Gen. Walter Bedell "Beetle" Smith:** The silence lasted for five full minutes while General Eisenhower sat on a sofa before the bookcase which filled the end of the room.

**Gen. Dwight Eisenhower:** I sat silently just reviewing these things I'd say 35 or 45 seconds. My own chief of staff says five minutes—I know that—but five minutes under such conditions sounds like a year. I think after 30, 45 seconds, I just got up and said, "Okay, we'll go."

**Lt. Gen. Walter Bedell "Beetle" Smith:** Finally he looked up, and the tension was gone from his face. He said briskly, "we'll go!"

**Capt. J. M. Stagg:** The relief that statement brought into the room was a joy to behold. Immediately after I had finished the tension seemed to evaporate and the Supreme Commander and his colleagues became as new men. General Eisenhower had sat, turned sideways, facing me, taut and tense. Now a broad smile broke over his face as he said, "Well, Stagg, if this forecast comes off, I promise you we'll have a celebration when the time comes."

**Gen. Dwight Eisenhower:** There was a definite brightening of faces as, without a further word, each went off to his respective post of duty to flash out to his command the messages that would set the whole host in motion.

**Winston Churchill:** The die was irrevocably cast: the invasion would be launched on June 6.

# PART II

# THE LANDING

Looking out at the Atlantic Wall from a German bunker.

# A Note on Chronology
# and Military Terminology

For organizational and comprehensibility purposes, the second part of the narrative here follows the action of June 6, 1944, from west to east, which roughly coincides with how the morning unfolded chronologically.

The day generally began with the paratroop drops of the 82nd and 101st Airborne Divisions behind Utah Beach, which along with Omaha Beach saw the earliest two H-Hours that Tuesday morning. The three British and Canadian beaches, meanwhile, both had their H-Hour set about an hour later to accommodate beach-specific tidal variables.

There's one morning exception to the west-to-east morning-onward chronology: the first action of the day actually was the British airborne units dropped in to secure the eastern flank of the invasion, and I include their famous actions against Pegasus Bridge and the Merville Battery in the early sections alongside the story of the US paratroopers.

Then, in the final portion of the book primarily focused on the events of the afternoon of June 6, I reverse direction, starting on the eastern flank with the British 6th Airborne and working back west to what was effectively the westernmost battle on D-Day, the brutal fight for La Fière Bridge, which lasted all day but appears chronologically here late as the primary tank battle for the bridge took place around 4 p.m.

Also, in the pages, stories, and recollections ahead, there are numerous references to the alphabet soup of landing craft that made up the bulk of the 7,000 ships in the Allied armada. There were literally dozens of different such craft on D-Day of varying sizes and roles—one World War II tally came up with forty-six distinct types of landing craft—but for clarity's sake, the reader really need only remember a few broad distinctions.

Most troops at all five beaches headed to shore in small craft. The primary US version of this size were known as LCVPs—Landing Craft Vehicle/Personnel—or, more colloquially, "Higgins Boats," for their New Orleans manufacturer. They were flat-bottom plywood barges about 36 feet long and 11 feet wide that could carry roughly 36 troops, a platoon-sized contingent. The equivalent British workhorse was known as a Landing Craft Assault (LCA) and similarly carried roughly a platoon. These small, plodding vessels were carried aboard larger transport ships and lowered over the side far offshore, where the troops disembarked from the seagoing transport ship, often by cargo net, into the smaller LCVPs or LCAs for the final run into the beaches.

The next craft size up were known as LCTs—Landing Craft Tank—and could carry three to six tanks or equivalent vehicles, and LCIs—Landing Craft Infantry—which could carry closer to 200 troops at a time. Operation NEPTUNE included 768 LCTs, as well as 233 LSTs—Landing Ship Tank—a much larger craft that had large double doors that could open directly on the beach and carry much larger contingents, as many as 25 tanks or 33 three-ton trucks. (Two LSTs sitting side by side today would fill an American football field.) Despite their bulk and cargo capacity, the front of an LST drew just four feet of water, allowing it to beach directly on the shore.

Remembering the precise terminology isn't necessarily crucial to understanding what follows, but it's helpful in terms of imagining crew, personnel, and matériel to think of LCVPs and LCAs as "small," LCTs and LCIs as "medium," and LSTs as "large."

Similarly, the geography of the invasion beaches may seem confusing at first glance, but follows a clear logic. While history short-hands D-Day as five "beaches," the code names Utah, Omaha, Gold, Juno, and Sword technically referred to distinct operational "areas." These areas were then subdivided into sectors running alphabetically from west to east, beginning at Omaha—which had Charlie, Dog, Easy, and Fox Sectors—through Sword's Peter, Queen, and Roger Sectors. (The sectors had already been designated by COSSAC before the addition in January of the westernmost Utah Beach, so its landing sectors were known as Uncle and Tare.) Then, and lastly, each of these sectors was further subdivided into smaller "beaches," variously designated as Green (for west), White (for center), or Red (for east). Thus, technically, Green "Beach" in Dog "Sector" was in the Omaha "Area," and, as such, there were not five but dozens of distinct D-Day "Beaches." I have chosen, though, to stick with the common understanding and usage in referring to the five primary beaches.

Again, recalling the precise geography of each of the five beaches isn't necessary to follow the story, but will aid in a better understanding of the sectors that found themselves in particularly fierce battles, like Omaha's Dog Green and Juno's Nan White, elsewhere.

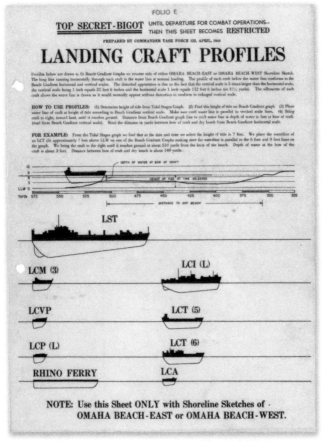

This page from the NEPTUNE operation plan, showing the size and draft of various landing craft, would have helped navy personnel determine where they could land at the beaches.

# Gen. Dwight D. Eisenhower's Order of the Day

The troops crossing to France listened to music
and recorded speeches from Ike and others.

**SUPREME HEADQUARTERS, Allied Expeditionary Force**

Soldiers, Sailors, and Airmen of the Allied Expeditionary Force!

You are about to embark upon the Great Crusade, toward which we have striven these many months. The eyes of the world are upon you. The hope and prayers of liberty-loving people everywhere march with you. In company with our brave Allies and brothers-in-arms on other Fronts, you will bring about the destruction of the German war machine, the elimination of Nazi tyranny over the oppressed peoples of Europe, and security for ourselves in a free world.

Your task will not be an easy one. Your enemy is well trained, well equipped and battle-hardened. He will fight savagely.

But this is the year 1944! Much has happened since the Nazi triumphs of 1940–41. The United Nations have inflicted upon the Germans great defeats, in open battle, man-to-man. Our air offensive has seriously reduced their strength in the air and their capacity to wage war on the ground. Our Home Fronts have given us an overwhelming superiority in weapons and munitions of war, and placed at our disposal great reserves of trained fighting men. The tide has turned! The free men of the world are marching together to Victory!

I have full confidence in your courage, devotion to duty and skill in battle. We will accept nothing less than full Victory!

Good luck! And let us beseech the blessing of Almighty God upon this great and noble undertaking.

# SUPREME HEADQUARTERS
## ALLIED EXPEDITIONARY FORCE

Soldiers, Sailors and Airmen of the Allied Expeditionary Force!

You are about to embark upon the Great Crusade, toward which we have striven these many months. The eyes of the world are upon you. The hopes and prayers of liberty-loving people everywhere march with you. In company with our brave Allies and brothers-in-arms on other Fronts, you will bring about the destruction of the German war machine, the elimination of Nazi tyranny over the oppressed peoples of Europe, and security for ourselves in a free world.

Your task will not be an easy one. Your enemy is well trained, well equipped and battle-hardened. He will fight savagely.

But this is the year 1944! Much has happened since the Nazi triumphs of 1940-41. The United Nations have inflicted upon the Germans great defeats, in open battle, man-to-man. Our air offensive has seriously reduced their strength in the air and their capacity to wage war on the ground. Our Home Fronts have given us an overwhelming superiority in weapons and munitions of war, and placed at our disposal great reserves of trained fighting men. The tide has turned! The free men of the world are marching together to Victory!

I have full confidence in your courage, devotion to duty and skill in battle. We will accept nothing less than full Victory!

Good Luck! And let us all beseech the blessing of Almighty God upon this great and noble undertaking.

Dwight D Eisenhower

*"We move tonight"*

# Paratroopers Take Off

Gliders and tow planes await the launch order.

*With the weather turned and the invasion force finally at sea, D-Day began in dozens of airfields across England. Thousands of C-47 Dakota plane engines cranked to life, ready to carry 13,348 paratroopers of the 82nd and 101st Airborne Divisions, who would drop into the western side of Normandy shortly after midnight. On the western side, the plan was for the US troops to protect the Utah beachhead from an organized German counterattack and to secure the causeways leading from the shore to the inland villages. Similarly, from the Harwell airfield in Oxfordshire, 60 pathfinders from the 22nd Independent Parachute Company took off in Albemarle transports, ready to guide the British 6th Airborne Division*

*toward the invasion's eastern flank, where paratroopers had the mighty task of*
*disabling the German battery at Merville and seizing key river crossings in the*
*darkness.*

**Pvt. William M. Sawyer, 508th Parachute Infantry Regiment, 82nd Airborne:** The
night of the 5th, we were all standing around and talking, and I said, "Uh-oh,
there's the Red Cross," and sure enough, they had coffee and doughnuts,
and I told the guys, I said, "We move tonight. When the Red Cross shows
up, we always move." And we did.

**T/5 George Koskimaki, 101st Signal Company, 101st Airborne:** As the sun was
sinking in the west, all eyes seemed to turn in one direction due to excitement
further down the line of silent, waiting planes. As the cause of the excitement approached our group, it was noted with pleasure that the supreme
commander of the invasion, General Eisenhower, had come to wish the
vanguard of the invasion Godspeed and good landings.

*As Ike and the other commanders said goodbye to the invasion forces, no one*
*knew what the coming hours would bring. All told, planners had projected rough*
*estimates that 20,000 men might be killed in the initial invasion, with perhaps*
*as many as 5,000 drowning in the Channel surf.*

**Gen. Dwight Eisenhower, Supreme Allied Commander, SHAEF:** That's the most
terrible time for the senior commander. He's done all that he can do, all
the planning. Matter of fact, there's very little more that any commander
above division command can do once you have started. So the first thing
I did, I went over and fortified myself with a lot of coffee and breakfast.
Then I began to go up and down the wharves and some of the ships were
still starting out. I saw people that had sent them off and so on. And I came
up here during the middle of the day to see if any news was coming out. I
kept pretty close to my communication center.

Finally, along about six in the evening, I went over to a field from which
the American Airborne started out. Now, I couldn't go to all these fields—
there were many of them—but I did go into the 101st Division, and it was
a very fine experience.

**Brig. Gen. Maxwell D. Taylor, commander, 101st Airborne:** I toured the airfields with General Eisenhower and answered many of his questions about the plans for the landing the following morning.

**Pvt. Clayton E. Storeby, 326th Airborne Engineer Battalion, 101st Airborne:** General Eisenhower gathered us all around him, and he talked to our pathfinders. This is a very well-known picture today. It's been in *Yank Magazine*, and on the cover of *Life Magazine*, and he told us that this was for real, and there was no excuses; we had to win—it was victory or nothing, and he would see us on the continent. He talked to the pathfinders, the ones that went in to set up the beacons for the airborne drop.

**T/4 Tom Walsh, Headquarters Company, 502nd Parachute Infantry Regiment, 101st Airborne:** I remember the visit very well. One of his motorcycle MP escorts wished he was going along with us. We were standing within earshot, on the inside of the fence, and several of us volunteered to trade places.

**T/5 George Koskimaki:** He approached with General Taylor, who had accompanied him on visits to the airfields. Major Legere, our jumpmaster, called us to attention. "At ease men," was Eisenhower's reply.

**Gen. Dwight Eisenhower:** I found the men in fine fettle, many of them joshingly admonishing me that I had no cause for worry, since the 101st was on the job and everything would be taken care of in fine shape.

**Capt. Harry C. Butcher, naval aide to Dwight Eisenhower, SHAEF:** We saw hundreds of paratroopers, with blackened and grotesque faces, packing up for the big hop and jump. Ike wandered through them, stepping over packs, guns, and a variety of equipment such as only paratroop people can devise, chinning with this and that one.

**T/4 Dwayne Burns, radioman, 508th Parachute Infantry Regiment, 82nd Airborne Division:** We blacked out faces with burnt cork. Some of the guys cut their hair mohawk style. Some shaved it all off. Each trooper was going into combat in whatever style that suited him best. I left mine in a crew cut. They said we'd be back in a month, so I wanted to come back looking like myself.

**Capt. Kay Summersby, British Mechanised Transport Corps, aide and secretary to General Eisenhower, SHAEF:** Ike had to look these troops straight in the eye, knowing that he, only he, was responsible if they and the men of the 82nd Airborne encountered sheer disaster.

**Sgt. Sidney L. "Mickey" McCallum, 506th Parachute Infantry Regiment, 101st Airborne:** General Maxwell D. Taylor, commander of the 101st Airborne Division, made a talk in which he stated: "I am always getting calls about the men of the 101st fighting and brawling with the MPs or anyone else who will stand up to them, so now I am giving you permission to do just that to the Germans in France, and I would be proud to pin a medal on your chest whether you have hair on it or not."

**2nd Lt. Parker A. Alford, Headquarters Battery, 26th Field Artillery, 9th Infantry Division:** A lump came into my throat both of fear, pride, and a dreadful hope that I wouldn't let these young men nor my country down. This was my third D-Day invasion and their first. Col. Johnson, our regimental commander came to see us—he had pearl handled .45s on each hip and a knife in his teeth, knives in his belt, and many hand grenades on his person—he came roaring into the hangar with his jeep and gave a short pep talk.

**1st Lt. Bill Sefton, 501st Parachute Infantry Regiment, 101st Airborne:** In dramatic conclusion, he whipped out his throwing knife, held it aloft, and proclaimed, "By this time tomorrow, this knife will be plunged deep in the back of the blackest Nazi in Fra-a-a-a-nce!" While the cheers were still resounding, he started shaking hands with everyone in turn. I was perhaps 150th or so in line, but even by then he was wincing from the unrestrained grips of his hyped-up troopers. And he still had well over 1,000 to meet!

**2nd Lt. Parker A. Alford:** We got in formation and walked to the air terminal.

**Cpl. Kermit R. Latta, 377th Field Artillery Regiment, 101st Airborne:** As we stood in formation waiting to board our planes, I was surprised to see General Eisenhower coming down the line of men talking to each one. While he spoke to the man beside me, I was struck by the terrific burden of decision and responsibility on his face.

**Pvt. Walter M. Turk, 501st Parachute Infantry Regiment, 101st Airborne:** Ike stuck his head in the door of our plane as we waited to taxi out onto the runway. He wished us luck.

**Capt. Harry C. Butcher:** We concluded the tour with C-47s growling off the runway, carrying the jumpers and their Major General, Maxwell Taylor, to their uncertain mission—one that Leigh-Mallory went on record against as being too dangerous and costly, and to which Ike also went on record, ordering the deed to be done, as it was necessary to help the foot soldiers get ashore.

**Brig. Gen. James M. Gavin, assistant division commander, 82nd Airborne:** Shortly after dark on the night of June 5, the pathfinder aircraft of the IX Troop Carrier Command roared down the runways of the airfield at North Witham, England.

**Maj. Gen. Matthew Ridgway, commander, 82nd Airborne:** I looked at my watch. It was 10 P.M., June 5, 1944. D-day minus 1. For men of the 82nd Airborne Division, twelve hours before H-hour, the battle for Normandy had begun.

**Pvt. John W. Richards, 508th Parachute Infantry Regiment, 82nd Airborne:** Before getting onto the plane, I looked up at the nose of our C-47. It was a picture of a devil holding a girl in a bathing suit sitting on a tray. Under the picture was the inscription saying, "Heaven can wait." I thought to myself, "Let's hope so."

**Pfc. James L. Evans, wireman, Division Artillery, 101st Airborne:** Just before the take-off General [Anthony] McAuliffe had each man on the plane sign a 100-franc note and pass it on to the others so each would have a souvenir short snorter with all the names of the stick members.*

**T/5 George Koskimaki:** The men mounted into the plane with jumper number 16 moving up the steps first followed by 15 and on down the line. A colonel from Eisenhower's party gave me a helpful boost into the plane. I moved into the darkened interior and took my seat in the fifth jump position.

---

* These signed invasion currencies, known as "short snorters," were a popular memento of the invasion and long remained prized possessions for many survivors and veterans.

**Pvt. John W. Richards, 508th Parachute Infantry Regiment, 82nd Airborne:**
Getting into the plane was something to see. It took 2 men to shove and
push to get you in the plane. The C-47 had a 4-man crew consisting of a
pilot, co-pilot, crew chief, and radio operator. There were 15 men in the stick.
I was number 11 in the stick.

**T/5 George Koskimaki:** General Eisenhower stepped back as the pilot gunned
the engines and then taxied slowly down the runway to a position facing
into the wind. The other planes fell into single file much like soldiers
assembling, and followed the lead craft. As each plane passed his position,
General Eisenhower saluted.

**1st Lt. Bill Sefton:** As our plane was taking off I could look back down at
the stream of lanes to follow, barreling along the runway. A roaring river
of black and white stripes! I had the impression someone had thrown the
"On" switch of a monstrous machine, and there was no way of stopping it.

**Pfc. Carl Howard Cartledge, Jr., Intelligence and Reconnaissance Section, 501st
Parachute Infantry Regiment, 101st Airborne:** I was in plane number 44 on the
5th row. There would be 20 serials, fifteen miles apart. The first ten would
be the 101st Airborne Division, the second would be the 82nd Airborne,
13,400 paratroopers in all, and on an armada of 300 miles long, nine planes
wide, flying in 3Vs and at altitudes from 7,000 to 500 feet. We would be
parachuting down into France from 12:30 a.m. to 2:30 a.m. on six drop zones,
each one mile long and a half mile wide. The Welford Serial would land on
DZC along the numbers one and two causeways, leading to Utah Beach.
As we took off and circled into our rows of Vs, I saw for the first time a
C-47 aircraft painted solid white out in front of us. It was the mother ship
that was to lead us in.

**Gen. Dwight Eisenhower:** I stayed with them until the last of them were in
the air, somewhere about midnight.

**Capt. Kay Summersby:** General Eisenhower turned, shoulders sagging, the
loneliest man in the world. Without a word, he walked slowly toward the
car. I hurried; we had to make the Southwick headquarters before 1 A.M.,

D-Day. "Well," Ike said quietly. "It's on." He looked up at the sky and added: "No one can stop it now."

**Capt. Harry C. Butcher:** We returned to camp about 1:15, sat around the nickel-plated office caravan in courteous silence, each with his own thoughts and trying to borrow by psychological osmosis those of the Supreme Commander, until I became the first to say to hell with it and excused myself to bed.

**Capt. Kay Summersby:** The rest of the day is history.

*Across England, the noise of the mass of airplanes assembling and moving toward Europe attracted attention. Those who watched the vast fleet fill the night sky on the evening of June 5 and morning of June 6 figured out for themselves that the grand invasion was under way long before the official pronouncements.*

**Hazel Key, special duty clerk, WAAF, RAF Headquarters, Middlesex:** At 11:45 p.m., our watch came on duty. It appeared to be another routine night duty. Suddenly, in the early morning hours, the whole atmosphere changed. Unbelievably plots from all the coastal radar stations were coming through thick and fast. The operations table was littered with identified and unidentified objects.

**Mrs. M. Harbott, factory worker, Coventry:** During the war, I worked on the outskirts of Coventry at the Rootes No. 2 aircraft factory. For three long years, we had been helping to make Wellington bombers from 7 o'clock at night till 7 o'clock in the morning. The war seemed to be going on forever.

About 4 a.m., as it was breaking light, we heard a faint humming overhead which gradually turned into a loud drone which we heard above the noise of the machines. The big double doors at the side of the machine shop were wide open, and a small group of us stood there in the half-light watching plane after plane going over. It seemed like thousands of giant birds were whizzing by. I shall never forget the impression it left on me, nor the feeling of exhilaration when we learned that D-Day had arrived at last.

*"Ham and Jam"*

# Operation COUP DE MAIN

Pegasus Bridge was D-Day's first target; in the background, the crashed gliders are visible, making clear just how close they landed to the target.

*The first mission of D-Day belonged to the British—and some might say, one Brit in particular. In fact, no Allied corps commander had a larger task on June 6 than Gen. John Tredinnick Crocker, who as head of the British Second Army's I Corps oversaw not just two beaches, Juno and Sword, but also the airdrop of the British 6th Airborne, which, much like the US paratroopers on the western edge, was tasked with securing the ground behind and along the invasion's eastern flank.*

*The British airborne invasion portion of Operation NEPTUNE included two glider missions on D-Day. The first, code-named TONGA, was meant to deliver 98 gliders; later in the day, a second landing, code-named MALLARD, would deliver 256 gliders, including heavier artillery. The flamboyant and inspiring Maj. Gen. Richard Gale led the 5,300 Canadian and British paratroopers who would be delivered to the eastern flank of the Allied invasion over the course of the day. There was also an effort to seize a series of bridges along the Caen Canal, Orne River, and Dives River, and to disable a powerful and well-fortified German gun battery at Merville that, left unchecked, could rain devastation on the landing beaches. The first two "COUP DE MAIN" (surprise) operations, against what would be called Pegasus Bridge and the neighboring Horsa Bridge would come to be known as Operation DEADSTICK.\* It involved 181 men from the 2nd Battalion of the Oxfordshire and Buckinghamshire Light Infantry, known as the "Oxs and Bucks," commanded by Maj. John Howard, who would land silently in gliders adjacent to the bridge in the hope of surprising the German guards before they could blow them up. Then, the hope was that British commandos of the 1st Special Service Brigade, under Lord Lovat, would race inland from the neighboring Sword Beach and reinforce the airborne positions.*

**Maj. John Howard, commander, Company D, 2nd Battalion, Oxfordshire and Buckinghamshire Light Infantry, 6th Airborne Division:** Our battalion was gliderborne. We were all trained up to the absolutely nth degree. Myself and my officers and NCOs thought we were absolutely the best company in the regiment. We ran this seven-mile course against every company in the brigade, and virtually the first fifteen men to finish were from D Company, and the brigadier was so cock-a-hoop about it. One day, Col. Roberts sat me down and said, "Now this is top secret, John," and that pulled me up straight away because he very rarely used the words top secret. He went on to explain that D Company plus two other platoons of another company and a platoon of Royal Engineers would be capturing two bridges on D-Day.

---

\* Some historians have come to believe that "Deadstick" was applied as a code name to the operation only after World War II and that in 1944 the British raid was known simply as "Operation COUP DE MAIN."

**Gen. Richard "Windy" Gale, commander, 6th Airborne Division:** I was convinced that once the Germans realized that airborne landings had taken place they would be prepared everywhere. They would certainly be prepared on the bridges which we knew were manned; and they would be ready, immediately, [when] they looked like being attacked, to blow these. We knew that virtually all the enemy would have to do would be to press a button or move a switch and up would go these bridges. There is always—or nearly always—a slip between the cup and the lip; orders are vague; there is uncertainty. *Has the moment arrived or should one wait? Who is the individual actually responsible both for working the switch and for ordering the bridges to be blown?* These questions are age-old and on the doubts that might exist in some German mind or minds at the critical moment I based the plan. But a moment or two was all that I knew we would get. The assault on the bridges must, therefore, come like a bolt from the blue.

**Maj. John Howard:** About two days before we took off, I heard one of the glider pilots saying that he had to go up and see "the film." I was a bit puzzled about this, so I buttonholed this one and found out that it was a film that had been made especially for the glider pilots. I said that I hadn't seen it. He said, "Oh, no sir. It's very top secret. We almost have to sign in and sign out when we go to see it and have been ever since it was made a couple of months ago." I went over to Admin and after twisting his arm, he admitted that they had a film that they showed the pilots that helped them with their landing and that they had seen it almost every day for two or three months.

**Sgt. Bill Shannon, Glider 123, D Squadron, Glider Pilot Regiment, 6th Airborne Division:** The main briefing was at 9 p.m. in the Operations Room [on June 5]. After briefing we walked down to the Towpath to see the first six gliders take-off to strike the first blows for the liberation of Europe. These were the "Deadstick" boys who were to land on the bridges over the River Orne and the Caen Canal and keep the German garrison from blowing the demolition charges.

**Gen. Richard "Windy" Gale:** That night the moon shone. The sky was clear as one by one the great aircraft, boosting up their engines, roared down the runways. Next to go were the two parachute brigades and the engineers accompanying them. Then our turn came. My glider number was 70. In the glider also were my jeep with wireless set and two motor cycles. There were twelve of us in all. Before us lay an hour-and-a-half's flight.

**Chester Wilmot, correspondent, BBC:** The hopes of every man in the division rose into the sky with them. The drone of the engines faded away, but another and greater sound welled up in its place. The throb of aircraft soon filled the night as eleven hundred transports took off from a score of airfields, carrying British and American paratroops. The planes climbed and circled above the sleeping, unsuspecting countryside, their red and green navigation lights twinkling like fireflies. Soon after 11:30 the swarm of lights moved in formation over our heads and faded into the southern distance.

**Sgt. Bill Shannon:** It was a thrilling sight to see the six "first" take-off and a large crowd stood on the perimeter track and watched them until they had disappeared altogether.

**Oliver Boland, pilot, No. 2 Glider, 6th Airborne Division:** As we crossed the coast of England, I found it to be enormously emotional to know that a very small number of us—there were just three gliders for the primary target—were setting off on an adventure as the spearhead of the most colossal army assembled in mankind. I found it very difficult to believe it was true. I felt so insignificant.

**Capt. Gerald Ritchie, 12th (Yorkshire) Parachute Battalion, 5th Parachute Brigade, 6th Airborne Division:** It was difficult to imagine that by dawn on the next day, we should have been tipped out of our aeroplane over France and should have landed in the place where there were quite a number of evil-minded Bosch, whose one object would be to liquidate us before we could do the same to them.

**Jim Wallwork, pilot, No. 1 Glider, 6th Airborne Division:** We had just hit the coast of France, and the tug pilot said, "Weather's good, the clouds are at six hundred feet, a couple of minutes before we cast off. And we all wish you the best of luck." Alter course, air speed right, John Ainsworth with the stopwatch, I'm checking the compass, he's checking the air speed. We cruise along, and then 5-4-3-2-1-bingo, right turn to starboard onto course. Halfway down the crosswind leg, I could see it—I could see the river and the canal like strips of silver and I could see the bridges. Visibility was awfully good.

**Maj. John Howard:** When we cut loose, we were on our way down and made our final turn, and you are supposed to come in at anything up to ninety miles an hour when you first touch down. As I could see old Jim holding that bloody great machine and driving it in at the last minute. I couldn't see his face, but I could see those damn great footballs of sweat across his forehead and all over his face, and I felt for him.

**Jim Wallwork:** I knew my height; I knew how far away I was, so it was a case of by guess, and I bowled down and landed rather quickly.

**Maj. John Howard:** I was surprised after the first tremendous crash, when I knew that the wheels were coming off and we were going to get onto skids, that we became airborne again. The next crash was a much more noisy affair because of the fact that we were on skids, and one saw all these sparks and everything else. I thought the sparks were tracers from the enemy, and that made me feel all the worse because I thought we were being fired on by enemy machine guns and the enemy was ready for us and there would be no surprise. And then another crash, and then the strange silence. There was silence and everybody was extremely quiet because that is what we had practiced.

**Pvt. Denis Edwards, No. I Glider, 25 Platoon, Company D, 2nd Battalion, Oxfordshire and Buckinghamshire Light Infantry, 6th Airborne Division:** The noise ceased and was replaced with an ominous silence. Nothing and no one moved. *God help me we must be all dead*, I thought.

**Jim Wallwork:** We got right into the corner of the field, the nose wheel had gone, the cockpit collapsed, and Ainsworth and I went right through the cockpit. I went over headfirst and landed flat on my stomach. I was stunned, as was Ainsworth.

**Oliver Boland:** I stretched the glide as far as I could as the bridges came into view, and I was now quite low. Suddenly there was gunfire right in front of my nose, and we then, literally, crash-landed. I had to keep to Wallwork's right, otherwise I'd have run up his bum, and I used the spoilers and dropped the last foot or so and, Bash. Then I see another bloke coming in from my right, which was the third glider. I dropped on the ground with an almighty crash, and we crashed along and managed to stop. We got down in one piece, and I said, "You're here, piss off and do what you're paid to," or something to that effect. And off they went.

**Pvt. Denis Edwards:** The pilots had done a fantastic job, bringing the glider to a halt with its nose buried into a canal bank within about seventy-five yards of the bridge. I glanced back at the glider and saw that the whole front had been smashed inwards, almost back to the wings.

**Lt. Sandy Smith, No. I Glider, Company D, 2nd Battalion, Oxfordshire and Buckinghamshire Light Infantry, 6th Airborne Division:** I was watching with these two pilots, and I saw the bridge as we passed over it and came around in a great big sweep, and then as we started to come close to the ground the pilot said, "You'd better sit down." Then we hit this, what I call a slop swamp, and there was a very large bounce as we hit the ground, and I knew we were in trouble. There were several seconds between that first bounce and then the most amazing, appalling crash. I went shooting straight past these two pilots; I shot out like a bullet and landed in front of the glider. The glider's undercarriage, had all been destroyed.

**Maj. John Howard:** The front was telescoped and the door disappeared, but that didn't stop that automatic drill of getting out as fast as you damn well can. My watch had stopped at 0016.

**Pvt. Denis Edwards:** As I hit the ground I glanced quickly around from beneath the glider's tilted wing and immediately saw the canal swing bridge structure towering above me.

**Lt. David Wood, platoon commander, No. 2 Glider, Company D, 2nd Battalion, Oxfordshire and Buckinghamshire Light Infantry, 6th Airborne Division:** I was thrown out through the side of the glider, and I found myself on the ground complete with my bucket of grenades. I still had my Sten, and I pulled myself together in the dark.

**Lt. Sandy Smith:** This is where the training comes in.

**Cpl. Jack Bailey, No. I Glider, Company D, 2nd Battalion, Oxfordshire and Buckinghamshire Light Infantry, 6th Airborne Division:** When we got out of the glider, Den Brotheridge whispered to me, "Corporal Bailey, get those chaps moving." And we moved, and we streamed across the road. The task of our section was to neutralize the pillbox. We scrambled across, and the ironwork of the bridge stood out like a great black silhouette. We went straight to the pillbox and used two 36 grenades, Wally Parr and myself, which we put through the apertures, and there was a terrific explosion. This was the first sound. The second sound was Wally Parr saying, "Pick the bones out of that, you bastards."

**Pvt. Francis Bourlet, No. I Glider, Company D, 2nd Battalion, Oxfordshire and Buckinghamshire Light Infantry, 6th Airborne Division:** We immediately ran round the back of the pillbox, which we knew contained troops. There was a large dugout, I went down one end of the dugout and O'Donnell went down the other and, lo and behold, we caught them in bed. There was approximately eight workers—these, I understand, were digging the anti-glider poles—and three Germans. We rounded them up and put them into the pillbox.

**Maj. John Howard:** I dashed up the little track that led up to the bridge where I intended to have my command post, there was the smoke bomb out in front of me, and Den [Brotheridge] passed me as I got to it, leading the rest of his platoon. It was completely as per drill. The firing didn't start until the smoke bomb. First there were shots from the Gondrée Cafe across the bridge as Den led his platoon gallantly across the bridge. Firing also started in the trenches, obviously sentries on duty, wondering what had happened, and of course the fire was the signal for us to shout our identifications and you got "Dog, Dog, Dog," and "Sapper, Sapper, Sapper!"

**Lt. David Wood:** I knew exactly what my job was—to get across the road, into the trenches on the other side, and clear them of enemy troops. Most of the enemy seemed to have run away. I found an MG-34 intact which nobody had fired.

**Lt. Sandy Smith:** The poor buggers in the bunkers didn't have much of a chance and we were not taking any prisoners or messing around, we just threw phosphorous grenades down and high-explosive grenades into the dugouts there and anything that moved we shot.

**Sgt. Heinrich Heinz Hickman, German 6th (Independent) Parachute Regiment:** They even frightened me, the way they charged, the way they fired, the way they ran across the bridge. I'm not a coward, but at that moment I got frightened. If you see a para in full pack, they frighten the daylights out of you. And at nighttime when you see a para running with a Bren gun, and the next with a Sten, and no cover round my back, just me and four youngsters who had never been in action, so I could not rely on them—in those circumstances, you get scared.

**Cpl. Wally Parr, 1st Platoon, 6th Airborne Division:** Having cleared the dug-outs, I was to meet up with Denny Brotheridge, who would be on the other side of the cafe. I went around the cafe to where he should have been and ran past a bloke lying in the road opposite the side of the cafe, looked at him, ran on, and stopped dead. I came back and knelt down, and it was Denny Brotheridge. His eyes were open and his lips moving, and I put my hand under his head to lift him up and his eyes rolled back and just choked, and that's it. All the years of training we put in to do this job, it lasted only seconds, and he lay there. I thought, *My God, what a waste.*

**Lt. Sandy Smith:** I headed for the bridge and eventually hobbled down the bridge in front of Gondrée's Cafe. There was a lot of noise, and I was in this square, and that was where I met my first German, who threw a stick grenade at me which hit me in the wrist, and I shot him. Then I heard this noise above me. Gondrée got out of bed and peered over the window ledge, and I brought my Sten up and fired and it went over his head, hit the stone roof, and ricocheted down onto the wooden posters of the bed. Seconds later someone came up to me and said, "Mr. Brotheridge is dead, sir."

**Maj. John Jacob Vaughn, medical officer, No. 3. Glider, Company D, 2nd Battalion, Oxfordshire and Buckinghamshire Light Infantry, 6th Airborne Division:** He was the first Allied soldier to be killed by enemy fire on D-Day.

*While John Howard's three teams of gliders seized the canal river bridge—what would come to be called Pegasus Bridge—other teams raced toward the Oxs and Bucks' second objective of the night, the nearby bridge over the Orne River.*

**S.Sgt. Roy Howard, No. 6 Glider, B Squadron, Glider Pilot Regiment, 6th Airborne Division:** I first saw the bridge at 800 feet and was able to land in the correct place without damaging the glider, or the troops inside it. We had been fitted with an emergency parachute brake, but I had no need to use this. I was surprised, just before touch-down, to see a herd of cows in the field. I think the cows were more surprised than I was and they quickly ran away. I shouted back into the glider, "You're in the right place," and Mr. Fox quickly led his men out.

**Lt. Dennis Fox, platoon commander, No. 6 Glider, Company D, 2nd Battalion, Oxfordshire and Buckinghamshire Light Infantry, 6th Airborne Division:** We jumped out. We saw the bridge and I sent my medium section commander forward, and he came to a standstill for apparently no reason, and I went up and asked what was the hold-up, and he said he could see someone with a machine gun, and I said, "The hell with it, let's get cracking." But he would not move, so at that stage I led, not through any sense of heroics, but just to get on, and this machine gun opened up. It was a Schmeisser, and dear old Thornton, from way back, had gotten a mortar going from his position, and he put a mortar slap down on that gun—a fabulous shot. So we rushed the bridge, and I had assumed that Tod Sweeney was already there, and I would be just further backup, but no one was around. We went across yelling, "Fox, Fox, Fox." We got to the other side and there was no opposition, and Shaugnessey, a section commander, went around to make sure and dropped hand grenades on them. Claire got through to Howard.

**Maj. John Howard:** I wondered what the devil was happening over on the river bridge. Just then [radio operator] Corporal Tappenden picked up a message from number six—Dennis Fox. His message was that they'd captured the bridge without firing a shot. Well, that was tremendous news to get. We were able immediately to start sending out our "ham and jam" radio call.

**Lt. Tod Sweeney, platoon commander, No. 5 Glider, Company D, 2nd Battalion, Oxfordshire and Buckinghamshire Light Infantry, 6th Airborne Division:** You could see the moon shining on the river as we went down. Suddenly the pilot said with an oath, "Oh, dammit, we've dropped!" He'd hit an air pocket and dropped, and the glider bounced along the field. He said, "I'm sorry, we've landed two or three hundred yards short!" We jumped out of the glider and went forward, and the first thing that we came to was a ditch, and I was up to my waist in water.

**Lt. Dennis Fox:** The next thing I saw was Tod coming charging across, shouting his signal.

**Lt. Tod Sweeney:** I went racing over with these chaps all thumping along beside me, and when we got to the far side there were clearly British figures. We came to a halt, and I must say rather disappointedly—we'd been all worked up—and there was the unmistakable figure of Dennis Fox.

**Maj. John Howard:** Sweeney arrived on the river bridge and asked Dennis Fox, "Is everything all right, Dennis?" At that time Dennis was standing in the middle of the bridge surveying the countryside, and his wonderful reply was, "I think so, Tod, but I can't see any bloody umpires anywhere," referring to the fact that as far as he was concerned, he was on an exercise back in the U.K.

**Lt. David Wood:** The whole thing was over quickly. I heard the magic words "Ham and Jam" on my 38 radio set.

**Maj. John Howard:** "Ham" for the canal bridge and "Jam" for the river bridge captured intact. There were other code words, which meant they weren't captured or they were captured but blown up, but "Ham" and "Jam" were the important words as far as we were concerned. And that's the situation some fifteen or so minutes after landing.

**Lt. David Wood:** John sent a message that he wanted to see me back on the road, and I went back toward the road. I had gone about fifty to one hundred yards, and as I went back with my platoon sergeant, Sergeant Lither, and Chapfield, my batman, all three of us were hit from a burst of Schmeisser machine pistol. I was hit in the left leg and fell to the ground and couldn't move. I was taken back to a ditch and looked after by Corporal Lawson, RMC. I was out of battle.

**Maj. John Howard:** Monsieur Gondrée was very much on the ball—not missing a trick, very anxious to help, very glad we arrived. [He] made the whole cafe at our disposal, and went into the garden and with the help of a couple of soldiers dug up a hundred bottles of champagne that he'd hidden away from the Germans for most of the war. There was a hell of a lot of cork popping that went on, which was heard the other side of the canal, and by the time I got back there, I was told that everybody wanted to report sick.

**Gen. Richard "Windy" Gale:** Meanwhile the sappers had been examining both bridges for demolition charges. It was found that, although the bridges had been prepared for demolition, the charges had not been placed. We later found out that these charges were kept in a house near the canal bridge. We had, it would seem, overestimated the German preparedness.

**Maj. John Howard:** Right on the dot at 0050 we heard the roar of many bombers coming in low, and we had a first-class view of troopers dropping from about five hundred feet, and the air absolutely full of parachutes, with searchlights going up, catching the planes and the parachutes as they dropped. It seemed that the whole of the countryside, every village, had a searchlight at the time. There was a bit of firing as they came down. It was an inspiring sight and above all it meant that we were not alone. That was the signal for me to blow the whistle in the prearranged victory V. So the whistle was blown out over that night air, and for years later, paras told me what a wonderful thing it was—those whistle blasts. It not only meant that the bridges had been captured intact to them, but it also gave them an orientation.

**Brig. Nigel Poett, commander, 5th Parachute Brigade, 6th Airborne Division:** I dropped with the Pathfinders at 0020 at the same time as John Howard should have been landing at the bridge. When I landed I had no idea where I was because I could not see the unusual church steeple at Ranville, and I started looking for my next chap, but before I had time to get out of my harness, the [whistle] blew up on the bridge, and then I knew exactly where I was.

# The 6th Airborne Arrives in Normandy

Gliders and parachutes filled the French countryside
in the early-morning hours of June 6.

*In the hour after John Howard and his men made their* COUP DE MAIN *landing,
thousands more paratroopers and dozens more gliders landed up and down the
Orne River and around the town of Ranville, with the goal of seizing or destroying
other key bridges that would lead to Sword Beach and the remainder of the British
and Canadian sector. Their night in the unknown territory would see much of the*

*same destruction and confusion that marked the American paratroopers on the other side of Normandy.*

**Lt. Col. Iain Murray, commander, No. I Wing, A Squadron, Glider Pilot Regiment, 6th Airborne Division:** My own glider carried a full complement, including Brigadier the Hon. Hugh Kindersley, Commanding 6th Airlanding Brigade, some of his staff and the war correspondent Chester Wilmot, who was doing a running commentary into a recording machine.

**Chester Wilmot, correspondent, BBC:** Does the enemy know we are coming? What will the flak be like? Are there mines and booby-traps as well as obstructions on the landing zone? Will the paratroops have had time to clear it? Will a battle be raging there already as we come in to land? Will the pilots ever find it in this weather? If these thoughts are also running through the minds of the other 26 officers and men sitting in the dark fuselage of the glider, they show no sign of it. Above the steady roar of the wind beating on the glider's wooden surface, you can hear a snatch of song or a gust of laughter.

**Sgt. Jack Harries, 9th (Eastern and Home Counties) Parachute Battalion, 3rd Parachute Brigade, 6th Airborne Division:** I wondered about my wife and little five-year-old daughter, who had no idea where I was at that moment. Our second baby was expected in about six or seven weeks. When would I see the new baby? I told my wife I was volunteering for parachuting and asked her if she minded. Her reply must have been typical of many wives: "If that's what you really want to do and it helps finish the war quicker, then I don't mind."

**Lt. Col. Iain Murray:** Turning in from the coast, the visibility became very poor. A combination of cloud, and the dust and smoke caused by bombing, obscured the ground completely. This may have been a godsend as the A.A. fire, although considerable, seemed very inaccurate. Nearing our objective the visibility improved and soon the flares, put out by the Independent Parachute Company, could be seen and gliders cast off from their tugs.

**Chester Wilmot:** As the ground rises up to meet us, the pilots catch a glimpse of the pathfinders' lights and the white dusty road and the square Norman church-tower beside the landing-zone. The soil of France rushes past beneath us and we touch-down with a jolt on a ploughed field.

**Lt. Col. Iain Murray:** In the last few yards one post [a Rommel's asparagus] tore a wing tip and one collapsed when hit head-on by the cockpit. I always think that this one must have been loosely placed by some patriotic Frenchman employed by the Germans.

**Chester Wilmot:** There is an ominous sound of splitting wood and rending fabric and we brace ourselves for the shock as the glider goes lurching and bumping until with a violent swerve to starboard it finally comes to rest scarred but intact, within a hundred yards of its intended landing place.

It is 3.32 a.m. We are two minutes late. Shouts and cheers echo down the glider.

The wreckage seems to signify the failure of the daring plan to land the gliders by night, but in fact, though we don't yet know it, 49 of the 72 destined for this field have landed accurately and, despite the chaos and the damage, the casualties to men and weapons are comparatively few. Indeed as we move off towards the rendezvous near Ranville church, men are climbing out of the broken wrecks, dragging their equipment and slashing away the splintered fuselages to set free jeeps and guns. Ten of the eighteen anti-tank guns have survived and soon they are moving to their appointed positions.

**Lt. Col. Iain Murray:** Soon after landing I found that Chester Wilmot's recorder had been smashed by a piece of shell from an A.A. gun, which was most unfortunate.

**Pvt. Frank Ockenden, Pathfinder, 8th (Midlands) Parachute Battalion, 6th Airborne Division:** Just as we made our way to the woods we saw a glider come straight down nose first and hit the ground about 80mph. It just scattered all over the place—never saw anyone left alive.

**Sgt. John Wilson, A Squadron, Glider Pilot Regiment:** When we landed, we did what we called a "kangaroo." We bounced, because we were not at the right altitude, and then hit a house. I never saw the house until we were about twenty-five yards from it. There was one hell of a bloody noise and I got this terrible pain from the waist down, virtually paralyzed. My copilot was killed outright. Somebody came to try and drag us out. He stood me up on my legs but both legs were smashed and the pain was intense. I never felt a pain like it. I lost consciousness then. I just remember saying, "Leave me, leave me. I'll be all right when it's daylight." When I came round two and a half days later I was still in the glider. They'd come round to bury the dead and found that I was still alive. But I lost one leg.

**Gen. Richard "Windy" Gale:** In a few moments [the pilot] said, "We are over the landing zone now and will be cast off at any moment." Almost as soon as he had said this we were. The whistling sound and the roar of the engines suddenly died down: no longer were we bumping about, but gliding along on a gloriously steady course. Away went the tug aircraft back to England. Round we turned, circling lower and lower; soon the pilot turned round to tell us to link up as we were just about to land. We all linked up by putting our arms round the man next to us.

**Lt. Richard Hilborn, Headquarters Company, 1st Canadian Parachute Battalion:** The plane took violent evasive action—five of us ended up in the lavatory at the back of the plane, in a heap.

**Flying Officer Graeme Metcalf, Glider Pilot Regiment:** My orders were that I had to land [the] men somewhere in France. I think the "somewhere in France" applied to a lot of people. A lot of people were literally somewhere in France not knowing quite where they were. One plane in my platoon ended up dropping their people over the Le Havre area, about 40 miles away.

**Pvt. Jan de Vries, Company C, 1st Canadian Parachute Battalion:** Then *jump!*

**Cpl. Frank Swann, 5th Parachute Brigade, 6th Airborne Division:** I still had the same thrill as whenever I jumped—that whack of the parachute opening.

**Pvt. Jan de Vries:** It's black, just total black. The chute opened with a jerk. It was just seconds and, bang, I'm on the ground.

**Cpl. Frank Swann:** I came down nicely and my kit bag hit the road, and there I landed with my chute in a tree. The first person I saw was no other than Brigadier Poett, all six-foot-three in his stocking feet, red beret on, with his side arms and his briefcase. He had dropped with the advance party to get the lay of the land, but he had lost his radio operator and he said, "Corporal, I want you to come with me now and to be my escort the remainder of the night." So just in a flash, everything I trained for, where to go, what to do, had just been canceled by the brigade commander. I had been commandeered.

**Gen. Richard "Windy" Gale:** I shall never forget the sound as we rushed down in our final steep dive, then we suddenly flattened out, and soon with a *bump, bump, bump*, we landed on an extremely rough stubble field. Over the field we sped and then with a bang we hit a low embankment. The forward undercarriage wheel stove up through the floor, the glider spun round on its nose in a small circle and, as one wing hit one of those infernal stakes, we drew up to a standstill.

We opened the door. Outside all was quiet.

**Pvt. Jan de Vries:** Out of 120 of our company, only 35 landed on the drop zone. The rest were scattered all over. I didn't know where I was, I didn't recognize anything. I was hoping to hear another footstep or bit of noise—never saw or heard a thing.

**Capt. John Madden, Company C, 1st Canadian Parachute Battalion:** I landed in soft pastureland, crouched low against a hedge, and signaled with my tiny colored light for the others. Within a few minutes I was joined by two of the men; there had been ten men in my stick, but of the remainder there was no sign. We could hear German soldiers shouting and tramping in the next field. I had orders to avoid all trouble. Never in the history of warfare were orders so implicitly obeyed.

**Lt. Richard Hilborn:** I picked up three others of my stick. It took us three hours and the assistance of a local French farmer to find where we were. We saw a crack of light under the front door [of a nearby farmhouse]. A French family was all there, all loyal and friendly. I produced my map, and using my limited vocabulary of French asked where we were. He took us to the nearest road and he sent us off in the proper direction.

**Chester Wilmot:** It seems unreal to be walking about behind the Atlantic Wall unhindered.

*         *         *

*Two of the most audacious efforts of the night fell to the 3rd Parachute Squadron, managed by Brig. James Hill. They were tasked with both attacking a coastal battery at Merville as well as blowing up four bridges over the Dives River, including the deepest inland penetration of the night, an old stone bridge in the village of Troarn, almost ten miles inland, and more than four miles from their drop zone.*

**Major John "Rosie" Rosevere, commander, 3rd Parachute Squadron, Royal Engineers:** I was delighted when I was told what our job would be—delighted. It was the best job, blowing up bridges. My unit was to be split in two. One troop went with the Canadians to blow the bridge at Varaville, and my headquarters and the rest of my squadron, which was two troops, were with the 8th Parachute Battalion. We had to blow the bridge at Troarn, on the main Caen road, and two lattice-girder bridges nearby at Bures.

**Sgt. Bill Irving, 3rd Parachute Squadron, Royal Engineers:** I found myself with a group of a dozen and a half sappers, and Major Rosevere turned up, and don't ask me how, but somehow or other in a place which was two to three miles from where we were supposed to be, people started to assemble. Foremost in our minds was, there was a bridge at Troarn that had to be blown. It probably was an hour from when we landed before we got a party of sappers together. We were on our own, and we set off under Major Rosevere's control.

**Maj. John "Rosie" Rosevere:** All we could do was jump aboard the jeep and make the best pace we could. I suppose we had about half a ton of explosives in the trailer and there were seven of us on the jeep, with me driving, so we couldn't make very high speed. As we came into the center of the town, the firing started from various windows and from the ground as well; there seemed to be a Boche in every doorway firing like mad. Our chaps were firing back. One German rushed out with an MG-34 and put it down in the road, but we were too quick for him and he had to whip it out of the way or we would have run him over. But he was terribly quick getting it out again and a stream of tracer went over our heads. The only thing that saved us was that there was a steep downward hill leading out of Troarn and he couldn't depress his gun far enough.

**Sgt. Bill Irving:** We were all so excited that there was no real feeling of being frightened. It was just sheer luck that got us through the town, and some crazy, mad driving by Rosevere.

We got safely to the bridge, and I found myself with Corporal Tellers—us being in charge of the demolition party. It was going to be my job to lay these charges while Rosevere stood at the end of the bridge and watched what was going on and gave instructions.

**Maj. John "Rosie" Rosevere:** The beauty of the charges was all you had to do was lay a solid line of them, right across the center of the biggest arch. You line up the igniters, sort of had all these primers at the top of each of these things, and you run a detonating cord to the end to where a chap can put his igniter on. I mean, less than five minutes was all that was required. Down, down, down she goes!

**Gen. Richard "Windy" Gale:** It was just before it was getting light that we heard sounds from the side of the road, difficult at first to interpret. We stopped and we listened. *Was it a party of Germans?* We kept still and waited. I don't know whether we were relieved, disappointed, or merely amused when we discovered it was only a horse grazing as unconcerned with the great adventure being enacted around it as it could be. I took the toggle rope from around my waist and, using it as a halter, took the horse along with me. I wasn't quite sure what I was going to do with it, but it made the men laugh and it amused me.

**Chester Wilmot:** In the faint half-light we can now make out a halted column of jeeps and guns close by on a side-road with Gale himself urging them on. And, walking a little fractiously beside the column, shepherded by the General's aide-de-camp, is a handsome chestnut horse which had been grazing on the landing-zone. "Take care of that animal, Tommy!" says Gale. "It's a fine morning for a ride."

**Gen. Richard "Windy" Gale:** The next day the poor brute was killed by a German mortar bomb, and we buried it in the grounds of the chateau.

**S.Sgt. Ernie Stocker, A Squadron, Glider Pilot Regiment:** [My copilot] Stan and I moved towards Ranville and en route, bumped into a major with some POWs. "Take care of this bunch" he said, which of course we did. We found a safe place down the road embankment with our six prisoners and one suspect Frenchman. They didn't seem aggressive in any way—they appeared afraid. After all, they had been turfed out of bed in the small hours! We were then joined by another glider pilot, who had misplaced his first pilot, so our guard duties were eased.

Some time later in the day, walking along the road which was some ten feet elevated and right on the skyline, came this six-foot, four-inch tall man, with no helmet on and a shock of white hair. Walking with him was his corporal bodyguard with a Sten and that's all! It was General Gale. He looked fearless while we were cringing! He said "Where's the enemy?" to me. It should be remembered that the whole situation was fluid and firing was taking place in all different directions, so I said "I don't know, Sir." He said "Come on, Corporal. Let's find somebody who does know something about this bloody war!"

*About a half hour behind John Howard's Oxs and Bucks were 32 C-47s carrying 650 troops under the command of Terence Otway, commander of the 9th Parachute Battalion. Their goal was to destroy a four-gun German battery at Merville that threatened the shore landings. The nighttime attack on the Merville battery, about five miles away from the triumph at Pegasus Bridge, would end up a much more mixed affair. While initially Allied planners weren't sure what guns were inside the giant concrete casements at Merville, it turned out they held Czech 100mm artillery.*

*Merville, in particular, showed the limits of the Allied airpower. A large-scale May raid by 56 Lancasters had failed to have any impact on the site, and a follow-on*

*raid on the battery just before midnight on the night of the invasion not only missed
the targets entirely but killed 24 paratroopers beginning to assemble for the raid.*

*Meanwhile, just one of the eight gliders designated for the attack managed to
land close to the battery, and only about 150 troops managed to assemble in time
for the attack—leaving Otway to launch his attack at 0430, two hours late, and
just an hour before the Royal Navy was set to open fire on the battery as a last
resort. One of the missing gliders crash-landed back on the English coast and the
troops, unaware they'd landed in the wrong country, charged out of the glider
and accidentally stormed a nearby Royal Air Force base.*

**Lt. Col. Terence Otway, Commander, 9th (Eastern and Home Counties) Para-
chute Battalion, 3rd Parachute Brigade, 6th Airborne Division:** The Battery
contained four guns which were thought to be 155 mm, and each gun was
in an emplacement made of concrete six-foot thick, on top of which was
another six-foot of earth. There were steel doors in front and rear. The
garrison was believed to consist of 150–200 men, with two 20 mm dual
purpose guns and up to a dozen machine guns. There was an underground
control room and odd concrete pillboxes dotted about. The position was
circular, about 400 yards in diameter, and surrounded by barbed wire and
mines. There was a village a few hundred yards away which might have held
more German troops.

**Gen. Richard "Windy" Gale:** Our task was to seize and silence this battery
before the assault craft came within its range. The sea assault was to be at
dawn, and nothing could have been more awful to contemplate than the
havoc this battery might wreak on the assault craft as they slowly forged
their way to the shore.

It was of course hoped that bombing alone could achieve this [but] the
actual guns were in enormous reinforced concrete casements and nothing
but a direct hit from one of the heaviest bombs would knock them out.

**Lt. Col. Terence Otway:** I had a battalion of 600, and then if you added in the
specialists, support teams, support troops, I had roughly 700–750. I briefed
them all in the dining hall or the barracks. I decided that I had to have a
mock-up battery resembling as near as possible the real objective. I told
the intelligence people I wanted a patch of ground, as near as exactly the

same as the drop area, the approach from the drop area to the outside of
the wire, from the wire into the battery. I flew over the area with a brigade
major, picked out the ground near Newbury. The engineers built the mock
ups out of netting, and we actually put in the ground mock mines, which
went off with firecracker noise. We rehearsed nine times—five by day and
four by night, crawling through this damn stuff. Every single man knew
exactly what he had to do and where he had to go.

**Gen. Richard "Windy" Gale:** James Hill's instructions ran as follows: "Your
primary task is to ensure that the battery at Merville is silenced by P-30
minutes (half an hour before first light). No other commitment must jeop-
ardize success in this enterprise."

**Lt. Alan Jefferson, 9th (Eastern and Home Counties) Parachute Battalion, 3rd
Parachute Brigade, 6th Airborne Division:** Nobody had moved about very
much [on the flight to Merville]. There were three containers for circulation
among us: a box of sandwiches, bread and jam only; a bucket in which to
pee; and the sick-bucket. As it was almost impossible to get one's hand
inside one's trousers with the parachute harness clasped tightly between
the legs, the first bucket was not in use. But Private Dunk seemed to need
the sick-bucket before very long in the air. After he had made frantic
signals for it, the bucket was passed down the line only to arrive too late.
I looked away.

**Royal Air Force report on "Operation Tonga," Air Publications 3231 (1951):**
[The] 11 gliders scheduled to land carrying heavy equipment for the
Merville raid were mostly unsuccessful. The weather was unfavourable
with low cloud and bumpy conditions and several pilots reported that the
Lancaster bombing raid on the Merville Battery had caused considerable
dust and smoke which obscured the landing zone. The outcome was that
four gliders landed in a semicircle ¾ miles from the landing zone while,
of the remainder, three were compelled to cast off owing to cloud over the
French coast; two landed on zone "N" and two others nearby, consequently
most of the equipment was not available for the attack on the battery.
Close behind the gliders came the main bodies of the two parachute
brigade groups. The bog-like nature of the ground in this zone made the

landings by the main body extremely hazardous; it impeded movement and rendered the task of mustering the troops at their rendezvous points all the harder.

**Lt. Col. Terence Otway:** I landed in the last place I wanted to be, pretty well on top of the German headquarters. Wilson, my batman, actually went slap through the glass roof of a greenhouse in the garden. We decided to make a hurried exit. When eventually I got to the rendezvous, almost the first man I recognized was my second in command. "Thank God you've arrived," he said. "The drop's a bloody chaos; there's hardly anyone here." He wasn't exaggerating. By this time it was nearly two o'clock. Suddenly Wilson appeared and offered me a small flask as if it were a decanter on a silver salver. "Shall we take our brandy now, sir?" he said.

**Lt. Alan Jefferson:** When I reached the [rendezvous point] beside a clump of trees, I saw Lt.-Col. Otway standing there, tense and white. I saluted and reported myself to him. He replied in an expressionless tone: "You're commanding 'C' Company." I stood in astonishment. I, the most junior subaltern of the Company in command? Impossible! Where was Ian Dyer, where was "Robbie" our second-in-command? Where indeed were "Jock" and "Dizzie," the two other platoon commanders? Why, it's ridiculous. "Well, don't stand there, go and take over your Company." I went. And there they were in a ditch, all eight of them.

**Lt. Col. Terence Otway:** Time went by and more men arrived, but only a few at a time. By 0230, 150 officers and men had turned up. Five hundred were missing. We had one machine gun. Everything else—mortars, antitank guns, mine detectors, wireless sets—was missing. An attack didn't seem to stand much chance of success, but that coastal battery had to be knocked out by 5:30 A.M. I decided to advance, come what may.

**Lt. Alan Jefferson:** I don't suppose, though, that anybody fortunate enough to be there had any doubt at all as to what we were going to do. I went back to my troops and told them that we were going ahead with the operation as planned, but because of a very dispersed drop, there were not going to be many of us to polish off those guns.

**Lt. Col. Terence Otway:** I had to reorganize. Instead of having four companies, I made it into four platoons and left at the proper time and crossed my fingers and hoped it would work, literally. I thought that when they realized what was going to happen, they'd say, "Oh god," and get the shivers and everything else. Not a bit of it. There wasn't one man who displayed any excitement or worry about it at all. They just accepted it. They just knew we had the job to do and they accepted the reorganization. I was astonished.

**Lt. Alan Jefferson:** Time was getting short. The CO had waited at the [rendezvous point] for as long as possible, to try and grasp more men from the drop. But now it was almost time for the GB Force gliders to arrive, and once they landed we had to be on the way in ourselves. There was no time for proper orders, though I knew that my task was, as always, No 1 Casemate, No 1 Gun.

**Maj. Allen Parry, Company A, 9th (Eastern and Home Counties) Parachute Battalion, 3rd Parachute Brigade, 6th Airborne Division:** The CO [Otway] decided that I must lead the assault. The signal for the assault to begin would be the blowing of the [Bangalore] torpedoes. There was no time for anything more than cursory orders. I explained that there would be no communications, as we had no wireless and that each party would have to go independently. We deployed along the line of the cattle fence which marked the perimeter of the minefield.

**Lt. Alan Jefferson:** We were going to be able to make only two gaps in the wire because of the shortage of Bangalores, two parties through each gap, one party to each gun. It was marvellous to see that rugged old soldier, Mike Dowling, preparing to blow our gap in the wire, right in front of me, grinning hugely and thoroughly enjoying himself.

**Lt. Col. Terence Otway:** The fight was short and terrible and very bloody. Like many men, I suppose, I had no great fear of being killed, but the horror of being mutilated swept over me when the moment came to go through the wire into the enemy fire. I shouted, "Come on!" and ran for it. In the circumstances, it was the only thing to do. My adjutant was hit by a burst of machine-gun fire beside me.

**Maj. Allen Parry:** I was conscious of something striking my left thigh, my leg collapsed under me and I fell into a huge bomb crater. I saw my batman, who was just alongside me, looking at me as if to say, "Bad luck mate," and off he went.

**Lt. Alan Jefferson:** We ran on, shouting blue murder. I seemed to feel something nick me between the shoulder-blades and was aware of Morgan falling down, just behind me. On, on! No looking back. Our number was dwindling. Then I felt a lash across my left thigh. I stumbled and fell. There was no pain, but I couldn't get up again. I dragged myself towards a stack of wooden poles and propped myself up beside it so that I had some cover and could also see what was going on. Exasperated by my misfortune—so far and yet no further—I saw my soldiers charging straight for the Casemate. *Good for them!* They were the brave ones. Now, instead of sharp cracks of firearms in the open air, I heard muffled detonations coming from inside the Casemates, from both 1 and 2. There were yells, agonised cries and clouds of smoke coming out. But those soldiers of mine. How proud of them I felt.

**Capt. Albert Richards, war artist, 6th Airborne Division:** Inside the battery terrific hand-to-hand fighting developed. Stens barked, grenades were lobbed into galleries, and within 15 minutes it was all over. Gun crews had been winkled out of their emplacements; 50 prisoners, some startlingly young and others equally old, were shepherded out.

**Lt. Col. Terence Otway:** The battle was over and the Merville battery had fallen. The Very light success signal was fired, but for us there was no feeling of elation. In just thirty minutes of furious hand-to-hand fighting, I had lost exactly half the remnants of my force. Inside the German battery, seventy-five British paratroopers, officers, and other ranks were lying dead or wounded.

**Maj. Allen Parry:** There were quite a few soldiers still in there and, as best I could, I shouted to them to make their way out. I felt very weary and was not as mobile as I would have wished. Slowly, and with some difficulty, I made my way to the point of exit, where I saw what can only be described as an urchin's soap box on wheels. This seemed to me a godsend and I decided to mount it and begin my withdrawal. By lying on my back on the trolley, and propelling myself with the heel of my right foot, I was able to make very slow progress. A sergeant of my company came into view, took off his toggle rope, attached it to my chariot, and proceeded to drag me along the dusty track to the rallying point. During this journey, while shells were still landing nearby, I drank several mouthfuls of whiskey from the flask which, attached to my belt, I regarded as an important part of my battle accoutrements.

**Lt. Col. Terence Otway:** I wasn't pleased, I was bloody angry. I was being unreasonably angry. My attitude is, *Why the hell does this happen to us? We knew we were going to be dispersed, but why, out of 750 men, have I only now got 100?* I'm an Irishman, so I get angry. I wasn't angry at anybody in particular—angry at circumstances, angry at God if you like. I do remember being angry.

*"We'll give the bastards hell"*

# The Paratrooper Skytrain

Crammed into the seats of the C-47 Dakota that will
carry them across the Channel, paratroopers await takeoff.

*While the British airborne descended in gliders and parachutes on the eastern
flank, the thousands of planes ferrying the US paratroopers to Normandy were
winding their way across the English Channel. For the D-Day assault by US
troops, the IX Troop Carrier Command, under Brig. Gen. Paul Williams,
readied 1,207 aircraft, as well as an additional 1,118 CG-4 Waco gliders and
301 British-made Horsa gliders. Their aircrews faced a uniquely complex flying
challenge: Crossing the Channel at night in tight formation and then, with
precision, delivering each of the six participating paratroop regiments to their
own specific drop zone.*

*Operation ALBANY was set to commence at 0020 on the morning of June 6, dropping 6,928 paratroopers from the 501st, 502nd, and 506th Parachute Regiments of the US's 101st Airborne Division, under the command of Gen. Maxwell D. aylor. Operation BOSTON would follow, one hour later, at 0120, and drop 6,420 paratroopers from the 505th, 507th, and 508th Parachute Regiments of the US's 82nd Airborne, under the command of Gen. Matthew Ridgway. Additional glider missions would follow as the morning progressed.*

*The main body of American paratroopers were preceded, by about 30 minutes, by 200 "pathfinders," two-man teams flying in specially radar-equipped planes who were to drop precisely on the designated landing zones and set up signals on the ground to indicate the right location for the following troop carriers. Altogether, the paratroopers would be on the ground in Normandy, alone, for about six hours before the invasion began at the beaches.*

**Sgt. Richard Wright, pathfinder, 506th Parachute Infantry Regiment, 101st Airborne:** The Pathfinders, we were a unique group. We had no table of organization, it was experimental. The British had used it and were very successful in North Africa, and when we formed this thing, it essentially was to define a general DZ [drop zone].

**Pvt. Fred Wilhelm, pathfinder, 502nd Parachute Infantry Regiment, 101st Airborne:** Our mission was to use radar and lights to bring in the rest of the Airborne. We were to form a "T." At a given time we were to turn our lights on; the [transport planes] were to come up the leg of the "T" and then give the green light [to jump] to the men at the crossbar.

**Col. Charles H. Young, commander, 439th Troop Carrier Group:** Serials of aircraft, made up almost entirely of thirty-six or forty-five C-47s flew as nine-ship Vs. The leader of each nine-airplane V-flight kept one thousand feet behind the rear of the preceding V-flight. This was a tight formation for night flying, with only one hundred feet between wing tips.

**Col. Joseph Harkiewicz, commander, 29th Troop Carrier Squadron, 313th Troop Carrier Group:** Intervals between aircraft were twenty seconds, and it was a wonderful sight to watch a single aircraft become one of three, then nine, to make the standard formation of a V of Vs. This sight—the throb of engines, and the knowledge that this was it, the invasion—affected everyone emotionally, leaving goose bumps.

**Sgt. Schuyler W. "Sky" Jackson, 502nd Parachute Infantry Regiment, 101st Airborne Division:** While the planes were droning on, I kept wondering how I—a Washington real estate clerk—had wound up in this situation. In all my years growing up, my wildest dreams never included flying into France at night to blow up some enemy gun emplacements.

**Pvt. John E. Fitzgerald, 502nd Parachute Infantry Regiment, 101st Airborne:** I fingered my rosary beads as I looked down the row of black faces opposite me. We had covered our faces with boot polish and streaks of white paint. Teams of men had competed to see who could become the most gruesome looking. The results in the half-light of the plane were frightening. I thought, *if we don't kill any Germans tonight, we'll sure as hell scare a lot of them.* My mouth was dry, but I did not want to drink from the small amount of water in my canteen.

**Pvt. John W. Richards, 508th Parachute Infantry Regiment, 82nd Airborne:** This jump was different. This one was for real.

**Pfc. George Alex, 82nd Airborne:** Yes, I was afraid. I was nineteen years old and I was afraid.

**Sgt. William Ashbrook, Division Headquarters, 101st Airborne:** The moon was shining real bright as we started across the Channel. Sitting beside me was Col. Gerald Higgins, at that time our division chief-of-staff. I had fallen asleep and he punched me to wake up and look at the sight below. There were so many boats in the Channel that it seemed as if you could step out of the plane and walk to France on top of the boats.

**Pvt. Donald R. Burgett, 506th Parachute Infantry Regiment, 101st Airborne:** The night air was filled with thousands of strings of fiery tracers winding their follow-the-leader, snakelike pattern up through the skies. There are four armor-piercing bullets between each two tracers. I thought, *how the hell can anything get through here in one piece?* A quick ticking sounded as a string of machine-gun bullets walked a fast line of holes across our left wing.

**Pvt. John E. Fitzgerald:** The C-47 began to bounce up and down as the pilot fought to avoid the increasing anti-aircraft fire.

**Pfc. Ray Aebischer, 506th Parachute Infantry Regiment, 101st Airborne:** Pilots began to swerve dive, and take evasive action.

**Sgt. Robert "Rook" Rader, Company E, 506th Parachute Infantry Regiment, 101st Airborne:** The order to "Stand up" and "Hook up" saved my life. After getting up, a shell passed through the metal bucket seat where I had been seated. The jump light was shot off from its position over the door.

**Pfc. John Taylor, 508th Parachute Infantry Regiment, 82nd Airborne:** We came in low. I remember looking out the plane and seeing the tops of trees—the trees in Normandy were not very large—and I thought, "We don't need a parachute for this; all you need is a step ladder."

**Pvt. Waylen "Pete" Lamb, Headquarters Company, 501st Parachute Infantry Regiment, 101st Airborne:** As we approached our drop zone I remember talking with Sergeant Stan Butkovich, another demolitions man. A few seconds later he was hit by some 20mm stuff that came through the deck of the plane. He was hit in the legs. Our stick leader, Lt. Ted Fuller, unhooked Buck from his place in the stick and we moved him to the first position in the door, sitting in the door with his feet outside. When the green light came on, Lt. Fuller gave ole Buck a shove and out he went.

**Cpl. Ray Taylor, 506th Parachute Infantry Regiment, 101st Airborne:** We were lined up in the first positions in the doorway. As first man, I was knocked backward into the plane by the force of a neighboring plane exploding in midair. One of its high explosive bundles, which were suspended underneath the plane, blew up as a result of a direct hit.

*The plane that Taylor witnessed explode was the Headquarters plane for Easy Company of the 506th Regiment; the explosion of that Douglas C-47, #42-93095, killed all five crew and 17 paratroopers, including pilot 1st Lt. Harold A. Capelluto, as well as the commanding officer Easy Company, 1st Lt. Thomas Meehan.*

*Just a couple hours earlier, Meehan had written a final note to his wife, Anne, that he had handed out the door of the plane on the tarmac in England to a friend: "Dearest Anne, in a few hours, I'm going to take the best company of men in the world into France. We'll give the bastards hell. Strangely, I'm not particularly scared, but in my heart is a terrific longing to hold you in my arms. I love you sweetheart—forever, your Tom."*

**Pvt. John W. Richards, 508th Parachute Infantry Regiment, 82nd Airborne:** The green light went on and Lt. Moran yelled "Out! Let's go!" In a matter of 8 to 10 seconds, everybody was out the door. That was the last I had seen Lt. Moran.

**Capt. Sidney M. Ulan, pilot, 441st Troop Carrier Group, 50th Troop Carrier Wing:** The sky was filled with red and green tracers, and search lights beamed up at the planes just ahead of me. I could also feel the vibration of flak coming up and shaking the plane. I remember chewing gum, and the saliva in my mouth completely dried up from the fright. After dropping our paratroopers, I hit the deck to avoid the flak and groundfire, and flying it treetop level finally ended up just above the Channel, skimming the water, then pulling up to re-form our formation. The baptism of fire was over, and I breathed a sigh of relief.

**Pfc. Carl Howard Cartledge, Jr., Intelligence and Reconnaissance Section, 501st Parachute Infantry Regiment, 101st Airborne:** The green light popped on. "Go, geronimo!" And we all jumped out. I was never so glad to jump out of an airplane in my life. The parachute slammed open, the planes were gone, taking the tracers with them. The sudden silence around me was startling.

**T/5 J. Frank Brumbaugh, 508th Parachute Infantry Regiment, 82nd Airborne:** At the airport before we got on the aircraft, the Red Cross—for probably the first time in its life and certainly the first and only time in my life—actually gave us something that we didn't have to pay for. They gave me two cartons of Pall Mall cigarettes. The only place I had to put these things was inside my pants on the inside of each leg, and that's where they were while I'm hanging in my parachute coming down over France. I watched all these tracers and shell bursts and everything in the air around me, and I watched one—obviously a machine gun—stream of tracers which looked like it was going to come directly at me. In an obviously futile but normal gesture, I spread my legs widely and grabbed with both hands at my groin, as if to protect myself. Those machine gun bullets traced up the inside of one leg, missed my groin, traced down the inside of the other leg, splitting my pants on the insides of both legs, dropping both free cartons of Pall Mall cigarettes to the soil of France.

**Ist. Lt. Richard Winters, Company E, 506th Parachute Infantry Regiment, IOIst Airborne:** OK—*let's go, Bill Lee, God damn*—there goes my knee pack, and every bit of my equipment. *Watch it, boy, watch it! Jesus Christ, they're trying to pick me up with that machine gun!* Slip, slip, try to keep close to that leg pack. There—it landed beside that hedge. There's a road, trees—*I hope I don't hit them. Thump*—well, that wasn't too bad. Now to get out of this chute.

# Night in the Hedgerows

Paratroopers, like these from the 82nd Airborne, fought alongside
whomever they could find that first day.

*Despite much confusion, cloud banks, and antiaircraft fire, about 70 to 80 percent
of the American paratroopers landed within a mile or two of where they were
supposed to, though not all were so fortunate—some landed much further afield and
others drowned immediately, trapped in the unexpectedly high waters of flooded
fields or falling into the region's rivers. It remains hotly debated still whether the
drowning toll equaled "mere" scores or reached higher, but dozens, if not hundreds,
were injured to varying degrees or killed in the landings themselves.*

*Even for those who landed with relative safety, assembling and fighting
in the Normandy darkness would prove a challenge. The high, thick hedgerows
confounded soldiers, flooded fields swallowed needed equipment, and command*

*structures were all but nonexistent; through the night many paratroopers found themselves pairing up with strangers from other units. Night, though, is short in Normandy in June—its high latitude makes it roughly equal in North America to Newfoundland, Michigan's far northern Isle Royale in Lake Superior, or Washington State's Whidbey Island, and by dawn the paratroopers were organizing themselves into capable fighting units. The good news for the men of the 82nd and 101st Airborne, though, was that as disoriented as they were, the Germans seemed even more confused.*

**Maj. Gen. Matthew Ridgway, Commander, 82nd Airborne:** I was lucky. There was no wind and I came down straight, into a nice, soft, grassy field. I rolled, spilled the air from my chute, slid out of my harness, and looked around. In the tussle to free myself from the harness I had dropped the pistol, and as I stooped to grope for it in the grass, fussing and fuming inwardly, but trying to be as quiet as possible, out of the corner of my eye I saw something moving. I challenged, "Flash," straining to hear the countersign, "Thunder." No answer came, and as I knelt, still fumbling in the grass, I recognized in the dim moonlight the bulky outline of a cow. I could have kissed her. The presence of a cow in this field meant that it was not mined.

**Pvt. John E. Fitzgerald, 502nd Parachute Infantry Regiment, 101st Airborne:** If you can picture the cardboard of an egg carton and have someone with a handful of peas and drop them on this carton, the peas would all land in different compartments, in ones and twos and threes, and that's exactly how we landed. Everyone had the feeling they were alone or almost alone.

**Cpl. Francis W. Chapman, 377th Parachute Field Artillery Battalion, 101st Airborne:** I landed in water about five feet deep. Managed to stand up after a bit of swimming. Reached down, got my jump knife from the boot top and slashed my harness, cutting right through my jump jacket in the process. I managed to wade toward shallow water.

**Pvt. James O. Eads, 508th Parachute Infantry Regiment, 82nd Airborne:** As I started to sit up to get out of my chute, I promptly slid flat again. After 2 or 3 more attempts and a sniff of the air, I finally discovered that I was lying in cow manure. I recall that I even snickered at my own predicament.

**Capt. Francis L. Sampson, chaplain, Headquarters Division, 501st Parachute Infantry Regiment, 101st Airborne:** I lay there a few minutes exhausted and as securely pinned down by equipment as if I had been in a strait jacket. None of our men was near. It took about ten minutes to get out of my chute—it seemed an hour, for judging from the fire, I thought that we had landed in the middle of a target range. I crawled back to the edge of the stream near the spot where I landed, and started diving for my Mass equipment. By pure luck, I recovered it after the fifth or sixth dive.

**Sgt. Dan Furlong, 508th Parachute Infantry Regiment, 82nd Airborne:** I landed flat on my back in a cement cow trough. It was full of water. There was a farmhouse back up about 150 yards from where I dropped, so I snuck up to it, and inside I could hear Germans talking. I was going to sneak away and then one came out—maybe he heard me or something. He came round the corner. I was standing flat against the wall, and I killed my first German right there. I hit him on the side of the head with my rifle butt, then gave him the bayonet treatment. Then I took off, ran like hell.

**T/4 Dwayne Burns, radioman, 508th Parachute Infantry Regiment, 82nd Airborne Division:** We went back across the field I had landed in and found some troopers coming up the hedgerow. While we were stopped I thought I'd have a look over the top of the hedgerow to see what was on the other side. I climbed up and slowly looked over, and as I did, a German on the other side raised up and looked over. I couldn't see his features, just a square silhouette of his helmet. We stood there looking at each other, then slowly each one of us went back down. I sat there wondering what to do about him. I could throw a grenade over, but I might kill more troopers than Germans. While I sat there thinking, we started to move again, so I left him sitting on his side of the hedgerow wondering what to do about me.

**Pvt. Clayton E. Storeby, 326th Airborne Engineer Battalion, 101st Airborne:** The hedgerows of Normandy were so confusing and so congested with a few men in this field, a few in that field, Germans on this side of the hedgerow, Americans on the other. Nobody knew which way was up, which way to go.

**Pvt. Len Griffing, 501st Parachute Infantry Regiment, 101st Airborne:** The drop zone was like a scene from a dream. Guys appeared from the darkness and then disappeared back into it.

**Pvt. Donald R. Burgett, 506th Parachute Infantry Regiment, 101st Airborne:** During this time I had no success in finding anyone, friend or foe. To be crawling up and down hedgerows, alone, a whole ocean between yourself and the nearest allies sure makes a man feel about as lonely as a man can get.

**Lt. Col. Nathaniel R. Hoskot, 507th Parachute Infantry Regiment, 101st Airborne:** We had these damn cricket things and you could hear crickets all over the place, but I couldn't tell which were the real crickets and which were these tin things. We finally found seven guys of the thirteen who were on the plane. I don't know what happened to the rest. It was about one-fifteen in the morning, a very clear moonlit night. How did I feel? Well, I'd have liked to sit down and cry. I had absolutely no idea where we were and I was supposed to lead these guys, and they had no idea where we were either. They kept asking, "What are we going to do now colonel?"

**1st Lt. Bill Sefton, 501st Parachute Infantry Regiment, 101st Airborne:** A wild-eyed trooper came charging out of the darkness. No helmet, no weapon. He paused long enough to ask, "Are you okay?" I mumbled an affirmative and he sprinted off again. So far as I know, he is still running somewhere through Europe.

**Pvt. John E. Fitzgerald:** Shortly, I met a captain and a private from the 82nd Airborne Division. We decided to band together for safety in numbers. No sooner had we moved out when another wave of planes appeared overhead. They were some of the last elements of the flight to be dropped. German anti-aircraft guns opened up all around us. We spotted a gun firing nearby and knew we would have to try to knock it out. With all the noise, we were able to crawl to within 25 yards of it. The gun was firing from a raised platform. Surprisingly, it had no protection. The captain gave us a brief plan of attack: "Let's get those bastards!" The private from the 82nd set up his Browning Automatic Rifle and pulled back the bolt. He fired several short bursts and hit the two men on the right of the platform. The captain threw a grenade that exploded directly under the gun. I emptied my M-1 clip at the two Germans on the left. In a moment it was all over.

**Pvt. Donald R. Burgett:** Small private wars erupted to the right and left, near and far, most of them lasting from fifteen minutes to half an hour, with anyone's guess being good as to who the victors were. The heavy hedgerow country muffled the sounds, while the night air magnified them. It was almost impossible to tell how far away the fights were and sometimes even in what direction. The only thing I could be sure of was that a lot of men were dying in this nightmarish labyrinth.

**Pvt. Waylen "Pete" Lamb, Headquarters Division, 501st Parachute Infantry Regiment, 101st Airborne:** There was a little trooper who was dug in with me. I never knew his name, never had seen him before, nor did I know where he got the second M-1 rifle he gave me. All I remember about that lad is that he had a good shooting eye, and every time he squeezed off a round Hitler lost a soldier. He would holler, "Sue-eee!" and smile. He taught me more about shooting in five minutes than I learned all the other times on the rifle range.

*About two hours after the paratrooper landing, they were to be reinforced by glider-borne troops, who would arrive both with additional manpower as well as heavier, mobile supplies, including jeeps and antitank guns. In the American sector, these two waves of CG-4 Waco gliders each consisted of 52 gliders and were known as Operation* CHICAGO, *to support the 101st Airborne, and* DETROIT, *to support the 82nd Airborne.* CHICAGO *was largely successful, with about 90 percent of its gliders landing within two miles of their intended drop zone, whereas* DETROIT *saw only about 60 percent of its gliders land near their targets. Amid the predawn darkness, many of the flimsy plywood gliders crash-landed into hedgerows, trees, and even homes, but most troopers and crew survived. In one* CHICAGO *crash, though, the assistant division commander of the 101st Airborne, Brig. Gen. Don Pratt, was killed.*

**Lt. Robert Butler, glider pilot, 434th Troop Carrier Group, 53rd Troop Carrier Wing:** Nearing our landing zones at Ste. Mère Église, the tow planes kept getting higher and higher, which was our largest worry, and because the higher they went, when we released, we had to circle and circle in order to come back to our proper landing area. A lot of this was caused by mass confusion, and too many planes coming in at pretty much the same time, and an exceptionally large amount of ground fire coming up at us.

**Capt. Charles O. Van Gorder, 326th Airborne Medical Company, 101st Airborne:** Finally, our twelve-hundred-foot landing field came into view, pictured just as we had learned in the briefings. After turning loose from our C-47 tow ship, we made a landing in an area that seemed perfect. It would have been perfect had it not been for the grass being wet with dew. With the brakes on, we slid about a thousand feet into a hedgerow. A tree, approximately one and a half feet in diameter, stopped us suddenly. The glider struck the tree center between the pilot and co-pilot.

**Sgt. Leonard Lebenson, Operations/G-3, Division Headquarters, 82nd Airborne:** We were cut loose. That is a very unusual feeling—flying through the air without a motor. It's noiseless. All you hear is the rushing sound of the air, but basically it's very quiet. Then there was a sudden up movement on the aircraft and it was like a little bit of an elevator uplift you could feel it pancaking. Then we hit something, and then again. We twisted around; it was a series of very rapid, violent movements. We had seatbelts on. There was some movement of various articles of equipment—packs, rifles, etc. throughout the cabin, but basically, the 14 men climbed out of the wreckage. Only one guy was hurt. We had hit a tree, bounced off the corner of a shed, and landed in another tree, not in the air, but against it.

**Pvt. John E. Fitzgorald:** The gliders were coming in rapidly, one after the other, from all different directions. Many overshot the field and landed in the surrounding woods, while others crashed into nearby farmhouses and stone walls. In a moment, the field was complete chaos. Bodies and bundles were thrown all along the length of the field. We immediately tried to aid the injured, but knew we would first have to decide who could be helped and who could not. A makeshift aid station was set up and we began the grim process of separating the living from the dead. I saw one man with his legs and buttocks sticking out of the canvas fuselage of a glider. I tried to pull him out. He would not budge. When I looked inside the wreckage,

I could see his upper torso had been crushed by a jeep. I felt as if I was becoming ill.

**Flight (Warrant) Officer Charles E. "Chuck" Skidmore, Jr., glider pilot, 91st Troop Carrier Squadron, 439th Troop Carrier Wing:** We caught a burst of machine gun fire from the ground which missed my head by about a foot, and then stitched the right wing from end to end. Upon landing, we discovered the source of the ground fire which nearly got me. It turned out to be a bunker containing about a dozen conscripted Polish soldiers with one German in charge. After the glider infantrymen from several gliders, including ours, directed a hail of rifle fire at the bunker, the resistance ceased. There was silence in the bunker, and then a single shot. Then there were shouts and laughter, and the Poles emerged with their hands held high and surrendered. They weren't about to fight the Americans, so they simply shot the Kraut sergeant.

*Through the rest of the twilight-ish June night and the coming dawn, the paratroopers and glider pilots ranged across the Normandy hedgerows, trying to locate each other, fight Germans, and—most of all—figure out where they were.*

**Pvt. Arthur B. "Dutch" Schultz, 505th Parachute Infantry Regiment, 82nd Airborne:** There was a total lack of organization. I found out later, of course, that our Battalion Commander, Major Kellan, had been killed very early in the morning. Our Battalion Executive Officer, Major McGinty, was also killed. Two or three of the Battalion staff officers were also killed. Captain Stef had been seriously wounded, our Company Commander. Tallenday was out of action. All of our Platoon Leaders were wounded except one. Most of our Assistant Platoon Leaders were wounded. I didn't see any officers. I didn't see any Senior NCOs, for that matter. Most of us were in combat for the first time.

**Maj. David E. Thomas, regimental surgeon, 508th Parachute Infantry Regiment, 82nd Airborne:** We scarfed up a few more people here and there and we had eight or ten by dawn. We crossed the Merderet River, which was flooded. They dammed up the thing and the flood plain was covered with water. A lot of troops that landed in there drowned.

**Pvt. Harry L. Reisenleiter, 508th Parachute Regiment, 82nd Airborne:** The fact that we were all scattered made the Germans think that there were about 10 times as many people on the peninsula as there actually were, and I believe this one thing helped us to make our job a success.

**T/5 J. Frank Brumbaugh, 508th Parachute Infantry Regiment, 82nd Airborne:** They were so screwed up by the way the whole peninsula of Normandy was apparently sprinkled with paratroopers and glider men that they really didn't know what to do.

**T/5 George Koskimaki, 101st Signal Company, 101st Airborne:** What turned out to be one of the first enemy encounters occurred as we advanced on another field corner. From the other side of the thick hedgerow came a gruff command in German—"Halte!" Our trio pulled up short and the major quickly responded in French, "I come from visiting my cousin."

**Maj. Lawrence J. Legere, Division Headquarters, 101st Airborne:** When challenged by the Germans, I wanted to stall for time. I figured that, even if the Germans understood no French, they would recognize the language as French and hesitate a little.

**Capt. Tom White:** Legere pretended to be a Frenchman. While talking, he tossed a hand grenade and yelled for us to duck. I rolled into a ditch.

**T/5 George Koskimaki:** It exploded with a loud "whump." Immediately we were on our feet running low and retreating in the direction from which we had come.

**Pvt. Len Griffing:** We cut all the phone lines we came across to sever the German communications. And some guys set up road blocks when ever they came to a cross road.

**Maj. Gen. Matthew Ridgway:** Soon the German commanders had no more contact with their units than we had with ours. When the German commander of the 91st Division found himself cut off from the elements of his command, he did the only thing left to do. He got in a staff car and went out to see for himself what the hell had gone on in this wild night of confused shooting. He never found out.

**Lt. Malcolm Brannen, commander, Headquarters Company, 508th Parachute Infantry Regiment, 82nd Airborne:** We decided to ask directions at [a] large stone farmhouse. We had about 12 enlisted men and two officers in our party now. [Then] I said, "Here comes a car—STOP IT." Lt. Richard moved out of the doorway towards the side of the house and some of the men went to the stone wall at the end of the house. I went to the road and put my hand up and yelled, "STOP"—but the car came on faster. All of us fired at the car at the same time. I fell to the road and watched the car crash into the side of the house. The car was full of bullet holes and the windshield was shattered.

The chauffeur, a German Corporal, was thrown from the front seat of the car. An officer sitting on the front seat of the car was slumped onto the floor with his head and shoulders hanging out the open front door, dead. The other occupant of the car, who had been riding in the back seat was in the middle of the road crawling towards a Luger pistol that had been knocked from his grasp when the car hit. He looked at me as I stood 15 feet to his right, and as he inched closer and closer to his weapon he pleaded to me in German and also saying in English, "Don't kill! Don't kill!" I thought, *I'm not a cold hearted killer, I'm human—but if he gets that Luger, it is either him or me or one or more of my men.* So I shot! Upon examining the personnel that we had encountered we found that we had killed a Major and a Major General.

**Jack Schlegel, 3rd Battalion, 508th Parachute Infantry Regiment, 82nd Airborne:** One of the dead was General Wilhelm Falley, CO of the 91st German Infantry Division.

**2nd Lt. Parker A. Alford, Headquarters Battery, 26th Field Artillery Regiment, 9th Division:** We came to a crossroads where we met several other officers and men of various battalions including some of our own men. We had a head count of one general, one full colonel, three lieutenant colonels, four lieutenants, and several NCO radio operators—also several other NCOs— other paratroopers and in all about 30. It was at this point General Taylor made his classic remark: "Never before in the annals of warfare had so few been commanded by so many." This lessened the tension. We discovered Gen. Taylor was exactly the type of fearless warrior you needed to run an airborne division.

**Pvt. William M. Sawyer, 508th Parachute Infantry Regiment, 82nd Airborne:** We tried to keep the Germans off-balance all day.

**Sgt. Schuyler W. "Sky" Jackson, 502nd Parachute Infantry Regiment, 101st Airborne Division:** There seemed to be snipers everywhere. There were four of us now and we chased two snipers behind a hedgerow. Feeling sure of the odds being with us, we rushed up and sprayed the hedge with bullets. Imagine our consternation when we found there were twenty-eight Germans behind that hedge. Those who survived surrendered to the four most startled American soldiers in France.

**Pvt. John E. Fitzgerald:** Most of us were exhausted. I laid down against a stone wall and immediately fell into a deep sleep. When I awoke a short time later, it was almost dawn. While looking for water to fill my canteen, I spotted a well at the rear of a nearby farmhouse. On my way to the well, the scene I came upon was one that has never left my memory. It was a picture story of the death of one 82nd Airborne trooper. He left a graphic heritage for all to see. He had occupied a German foxhole and made it his personal Alamo. In a half circle around the hole lay the bodies of nine German soldiers. The body closest to the hole was only three feet away, a potato masher [grenade] clutched in its fist. The other distorted forms lay where they fell, testimony to the ferocity of the fight. His ammunition bandoliers were still on his shoulders, empty of M-1 clips. Cartridge cases littered the ground. His rifle stock was broken in two, its splinters adding to the debris. He had fought alone, and like many others that night, he had died alone. I looked at his dog tags. The name read Martin V. Hersh. I wrote the name down in a small prayer book I carried, hoping someday I would meet someone who knew him. I never did.

**Pvt. John W. Richards, 508th Parachute Infantry Regiment, 82nd Airborne:** We traveled several miles, staying close to the hedgerows. We came to a brick wall along the roadway, and on the other side of the road, there was a white farmhouse, so we decided to check it out. One by one we climbed the wall. I was last to get over the wall. There was a squad of German soldiers just at the bend in the road. Right there and then, the war was over for us. They took our weapons and marched us back up the road. Much to our surprise, we were in a German bivouac area. The Germans were washing clothes and cooking in a wooded area, and there was a large building in this area. After we were stripped of our gear, we were taken one by one into a room for interrogation. All they got from us was name, rank, and serial number. That evening, we were turned over to some S.S. guards and started our move towards Paris.

*"Awakened by the bell ringing"*

# Liberation Comes to Sainte-Mère-Église

Two members of the 82nd Airborne Division dine
with the mayor of Sainte-Mère-Église and his family.

*The focal point of much of the first night's fighting in Normandy was the town of Sainte-Mère-Église, a small commune on the Cotentin Peninsula that sits at a vital road juncture and was a key objective for the 82nd Airborne and its 3rd Battalion of the 505th Parachute Infantry Regiment. On the morning of June 6, 1944, Sainte-Mère-Église would be the first town in France liberated by the Allies.*

*For some 900 years, its square has been anchored by the stone Norman church that gave Sainte-Mère-Église its name, and in 1944 it was occupied and defended by a German garrison of about 200 men of the 30th Flak-Regiment, led by Oberst Ernst Hermann. As it turned out, much of the town was already awake that night of June 5 and 6 as a fire consumed a villa near the town square. Many paratroopers, particularly those from 2nd Platoon, F Company, of the 505th, landed in and around the town and found themselves instantly thrust into combat. The night's fighting—and the town's liberation—was, arguably, the only one of the 82nd Airborne's missions that went according to plan.*

**Sgt. Rudi Escher, Grenadier-Regiment 1058, 91 Luftlande Infanterie-Division:** On the night of June 5, about eleven o'clock, it was still fairly light. There were two sentries in the church tower at Ste. Mère-Église and the rest of us had had the evening free. To kill time we cycled around the church square on our bikes until it was time to turn in.

**Jean Flamand, resident, Sainte-Mère-Église (age 16):** We were sleeping soundly when around 11:00 p.m., we were awakened by the bell ringing in the old church. Anguish gripped us all. My parents got up; my father went out, looked out over the town, came back, and declared, "There is a fire in Sainte-Mère." I got up, as did my sister. Behind the church, we could see an enormous red and orange glow shooting up into the sky. It was the house of Mademoiselle Pommier which was on fire. Everyone in the hamlet was outside. We had been standing on the steps to the door for several minutes when we turned our eyes toward the coast. A rumbling sound grew nearer to us; my parents thought that a bombardment was imminent. We went back inside. From the window of the house suddenly appeared a multitude of Dakota planes flying at low altitude and headed straight for Sainte-Mère-Église. They came by the hundreds, covering the sky with their big wings.

**Alexandre Renaud, Mayor, Sainte-Mère-Église:** Suddenly, what looked like huge confetti dropped out of their fuselages and fell quickly to earth.

**Jeannette Pentecôte, resident, Sainte-Mère-Église (age 16):** I saw a transport plane skimming the roofs of the village and passing over my house. The plane was flying so low that I could very clearly distinguish its wide-open door on the side. In its frame stood a paratrooper who was ready to jump into the void, but who seemed surprised by the meager height from which he had to jump. To this day I remember this paratrooper's face as he prepared to jump and was stunned to find himself so low.

**Pvt. Charles "Chuck" Miller, 505th Parachute Infantry Regiment, 82nd Airborne:** I remember going out the door, and I was just awed by the sight. There was Ste. Mère Église down below on fire, and I could see all the people in F Company getting slaughtered as they landed. We could see the tracers coming up at us. Beautiful. The machine gun tracers were beautiful. Everything was gorgeous—of course it was deadly, but you couldn't help but wonder, how could men create something so beautiful as this to kill people? It was just fabulous, it looked like a great big 4th of July celebration. You could just see everything. The whole sky was lit up like a big show. It was fantastic.

**Sgt. Rudi Escher:** We slept in the church tower, and as we were turning in, an airplane went over very low and the sentry on duty saw eight or ten parachutes starting to descend. We thought it was the crew ejecting from a crippled plane. Our orders were to track down and capture any enemy parachutists, so we grabbed our weapons and went off in the direction where we thought they had landed, leaving two sentries in the church tower. It was dark by then and they must have hidden, for we found nothing.

**Jean Flamand:** Each wave of planes unloaded their cargo of large red, white, green, and blue domes into the inferno of crackling machine-gun fire. Anti-artillery gunners fired on the paratroopers, who were unable to defend themselves as they flew down. Many of them fell to the ground, dead or mortally wounded. It was a sight I will never forget! I even saw a paratrooper fall right in the garden in front of our house. He landed in a row of garden peas, breaking the stakes. We watched without saying a word, dumbstruck, astonished, not knowing what was going to happen.

**Alexandre Renaud:** The work at the pump stopped, all eyes were raised, and the flak started firing. By the light of the fire, we clearly saw a man manipulating the cables of his parachute. Another, less skillful, came down in the middle of the flames.

**Pvt. Ken Russell, 505th Parachute Infantry Regiment, 82nd Airborne:** The fire gave life for miles around. We came in and when we saw the fire, we jumped. I knew we were in trouble, and it was so horrifying. Most of our stick were killed.

**Pvt. Arthur De Filippo, 505th Parachute Infantry Regiment, 82nd Airborne:** When my chute opened, it was about 1000 feet up. I could see tracer bullets coming up at us and all I did then was pray to God that he would get me down safely and then I would take care of myself. I did land safely and dropped just behind the church in St. Mère Église.

**Pvt. Ken Russell:** Sgt. Ray came down and he missed the edge of the church, but he hit in front of the church. One of the few red-haired Germans, a Nazi soldier, came around from behind the church, he shot Ray in the stomach. John, being the sergeant, had been armed with a .45 pistol. And while he was dying in agony, he got his .45 out, and he shot the German soldier in the back of the head and killed him. It was an agonizing death that Ray went through.

**Sgt. Tommy Horne, 508th Parachute Infantry Regiment, 82nd Airborne:** The moon was out full, very bright. We jumped when our green light came on. They were shooting everything at us, and I could hear the church bell at Sainte-Mère-Église. I could see the fire in the town. It looked like a wheat field below us, but when we hit, it turned out to be water. The water wasn't that deep—it was flooded land. I got my leg straps off, but I couldn't get my chest straps off, and finally I reached down and got my knife off of my leg, and I rammed it up in there and sawed this chest strap. We finally got out of the water, and we curled up in a briar patch and were exhausted and scared. We didn't have our compasses, and our maps of the area were faded out, so we didn't know where we were, and we really didn't know which way to go.

**Alexandre Renaud:** Soon the anti-aircraft gunners, realizing the significance of the event, ordered us to go inside quickly. I couldn't resist going to the garden, from where I had a view of the entire surrounding area. To the right and left, the parachutists were fanning out, and two of them landed in the garden. A few seconds later, shadows appeared on the garden wall. A third parachute, the last to come out of the plane, was gliding toward me. Suddenly, I saw the paratrooper start to wiggle on the end of his rope a few yards above my head. Then, with a loud thud, he fell into the river. The parachute, stuck in an apple tree, hung across the path. Weighed down by his supplies, his munitions, tangled up in his cables, the poor fellow was drowning without a cry, without a murmur. Thanks to the parachute, I had no trouble pulling him to the bank. He had lost his helmet, was half unconscious, coughing, spitting, trying to clear the water from his eyes. Then he looked at me, and I saw an expression of surprise on his face. "I am French," I said, laughing, "your friend." He must have thought he had been taken prisoner, and now, realizing the truth, he quickly freed himself from the ropes.

**Sgt. Tommy Horne:** We finally came to an old Frenchman and a lady, and we asked them where the Germans were, and they didn't know what we were talking about. So I drew a swastika on the ground with my trench knife, and she said, "Oh, Boche, Boche—they're everywhere." Well, that didn't help, because we didn't have any idea which way to go; we just started out.

**Pvt. Arthur De Filippo:** I could hear the Germans shouting orders from the front of the church and I believe they were the anti-aircraft gunnery people. Several others in my company finally joined with us including my squad leader. We continued to group and clear the area of resistance. We were up all night and into the next day fighting along the hedgerows.

**Pfc. Ray Aebischer, 506th Parachute Infantry Regiment, 101st Airborne:** One man whose chute had gotten caught high in the trees in the church yard, was hanging there lifeless. He had either been shot while descending or upon being trapped in the tree, high above the ground. Another man, who landed in the street proper, never did get up. My only thought all along, was how to defend myself against any enemy soldier without any weapon but this one knife. I kept a firm grip on it, realizing that I would have to be quick to survive.

**Jean Flamand:** Abruptly, the door opened and a man—his face blackened and his head covered with a helmet—entered. It was a sight worthy of Dante, this black man from the sky. I looked at him from head to foot, front and back; I looked at his legs and his arms. His uniform had many pockets, all filled to bursting. Around his waist were grenades and bullets. He stared at us one after the other. I got closer to my father, and my sister stuck close to my mother's skirts. Abruptly, he raised his machine gun on us and made us understand that we were not to make a move. We were overcome with fear. He moved forward, searched the house, opened the furniture, and looked everywhere. Then he once more approached us, but now he began to smile, speaking to us in English. On the fifth of June, 1944, at 11:30 p.m., we were all smoking an Old Gold, our first American cigarette, and also sizing up chewing gum—a kind of candy that was unknown to us, but which this man took out of many of his pockets. Then with a movement of his hand, he said good-bye, then came back once more and said in broken French: "Okay, don't be afraid, it's the landings!" With that he disappeared into the night. My father's first reaction was to say: "Well well, he speaks French!"

**Sgt. Rudi Escher:** Naturally, with Americans landing everywhere we were afraid for our lives, so we assembled on the church square and discussed what we should do. Several of my men had gathered up a few bits of equipment that had either been lost or discarded by the Americans. We got some cigarettes and chocolate and thought we were doing pretty well out of it. We still had a telephone link with our unit, which was dug in two kilometers from the village. A sentry made contact to ask what we should do, and we were told, initially, to stay put. There was by now quite a bit of shooting, and while we were standing by the church wondering what to do, one of our men fell down dead, shot through the heart. After this, we decided to return to our unit. There was only about six of us and there was very little we could do. Leaving our dead comrade behind, we retrieved our bicycles and cycled back to our unit—each frightened of being shot by the Americans.

**Pvt. Ken Russell:** There was gun fire all around the area. The Germans pulled out of town temporarily.

**Sgt. Ronald Snyder, platoon sergeant, 505th Parachute Infantry Regiment, 82nd Airborne:** We moved quickly, filing past the darkened houses that lined the street named rue Chef du Pont in Sainte-Mère-Église. Enemy vehicles were roaring by on the main road ahead, and suddenly one truck braked to a stop, and troops from the back began firing wildly down the street. We sought refuge in doorways, and I ordered my men to withdraw. I feared the truck might drive down the street and shoot us like fish in a barrel. I left two riflemen to fire on the truck, to hold their attention, and with the rest of the men I ran down a connecting street and then up a street paralleling the first, hoping to outflank the enemy. As we approached the main road, many German vehicles were still whizzing by, some with the headlights on, and the truck I was trying to outflank was gone. But through the trees on the town square and illuminated by the dancing light and shadows from a burning house or a barn, I could see enemy soldiers loading several trucks, and against these we directed all of our fire and drove them out of town in a hail of bullets.

**Alexandre Renaud:** Little by little, the night began to dissolve, and a milky dawn began to filter through. As the contours became more precise, we were astonished to see that the town was occupied neither by the Germans nor the British, but by the Americans.

**Maurice Mauger, resident, Sainte-Mère-Église:** At dawn, when we opened the door of our home, we saw that the canopy of a parachute was covering most of the garage roof.

**Alexandre Renaud:** The first thing we recognized were the big round helmets we had seen illustrated in the German magazines. Some of the soldiers were sleeping or smoking under the trees; others, lined up behind the wall and the town building, stood with arms in hand, watching the Church still held by the enemy. Their wild, neglected look reminded us of Hollywood movie gangsters. Their helmets were covered with a khaki colored net, their faces were, for the most part, covered with grime, like those of mystery book heroes.

**Maurice Mauger:** In a corner of the property, a para with a hostile expression was hidden in a bush, holding a machine gun in his hand. The man was groggy and seemed to be in shock from his rough landing. He was moving with difficulty. He pointed to the roof of the farm and made us understand that he had hit it, creating a hole in the slate before falling again heavily to the ground.

**Madame Hamel-Hateau, schoolteacher, Neuville-au-Plain (near Sainte-Mère-Église):** Four or five soldiers with round helmets and guns in hand enter the courtyard. One of them, presumably the commander, knocks hard on the door while shouting, with a strong Yankee accent: "We are American soldiers. . . . Are there any Germans here?" His manner is so imperious and sure, you would think he had already won the war. We greet them with open arms. Their confidence is so contagious that we consider the Liberation to be already accomplished.

**Alexandre Renaud:** A parachutist came and knocked. I opened the door. He introduced himself, "Captain Chouvaloff." He asked my name. "Would you please tell me where I can find the German commander of your town?" I offered to accompany him. "Okay," he said. He offered me some chewing gum and we set off together. The commander, together with his entire anti-aircraft unit, had taken off.

**Oberstleutnant Günther Keil, commander, Grenadier-Regiment 919, 709 Infanterie-Division:** During the night of 5 June 1944, at 24 hours, enemy parachute troops made a jump over my command post at the quarry at Hill 69 north of the Quinéville–Montebourg highway. The parachutists were taken prisoner. From the maps in the possession of the captured parachutists, it was evident that the main locality for the drop would be Ste Mère-Église. At 0200 hours, a special mission staff officer of the Georgian Battalion, located east of Ste Mère-Église, and a messenger from Christ Engineer Company, 790th Engineer Battalion, from Émondeville, arrived at the regimental command post and reported that thousands of parachutists had jumped, and that their units had been surrounded. Previous to this time, I had not made so serious an estimate of the situation, because I had believed that in this hedge-covered terrain the parachutists would have difficulty in orienting themselves and that some would even land in the wrong spots. After receiving the reports, I requested the division to authorize an immediate attack against Ste Mère-Église.

**Pvt. John E. Fitzgerald, 502nd Parachute Infantry Regiment, 101st Airborne:** We were organized into squads and sent north to defend the town against an expected counter attack. Ste. Mère Église was the first large town in Europe liberated by the Americans, and they intended to keep it.

**Ist Lt. Charles E. Sammon, Headquarters Company, 505th Parachute Infantry Regiment, 82nd Airborne:** Col. Vandervoort instructed me to set my platoon up in a defensive position about one mile north and east of Sainte-Mère-Église. I established three machine-gun positions and set up a platoon command post. Just as dawn of June 6 was just breaking, I started out to check the three positions to make sure everything was in order. There was at the time sporadic firing in the distance, but we had not seen or heard anything of the Germans in our area up to that point. As I approached the first position with another man, I called out to the corporal who was in charge, and the answer came back in the form of a long burst from what was unmistakably a German machine gun and one or two machine pistols. The bullets hit the dirt at our feet and the two of us hit the ditch beside the road. The Germans had infiltrated our positions during the night and had either killed or captured the men I had placed in this position.

**Pvt. John E. Fitzgerald:** The Germans held the high ground to our front. They were quickly gaining command of the entire area and were shelling it with artillery and chemical mortars. The mortars would announce themselves with an unholy scream that was spine-chilling. A few seconds later, they would land, spreading shovel-size fragments of shrapnel. The heaviest guns we had were one .50 caliber machine gun and a few 81mm mortars. The Germans soon singled out our machine gun position. They were pouring heavy concentrations of 88mm artillery fire on it.

**Alexandre Renaud:** The shrapnel banged on the roofs like big hailstones.

**Pvt. John E. Fitzgerald:** The tales the Americans would later tell about this 88mm gun would later make it a legend. It could be fired from a great distance to a target, and some said it had the accuracy of a rifle. It was rumored that there were more soldiers converted to Christianity by this 88 than by Peter and Paul combined.

**Madame Hamel-Hateau:** I hear the crackling of bullets. On the road I hazard down, a soldier is crouching behind the hedge. He remains still and bent over, as if on guard. As soon as he sees me, he mysteriously puts a finger to his lips, then points out something to me on the left. As soon as I turn my gaze in that direction, the words I am about to speak are strangled in my throat. At the bend in the road, German soldiers advance in single file with guns in hand, bending down, scraping the hedge. I realize the imminence of the danger and flee toward the house. No sooner do I get in than several rounds from machine guns make the windows shake. The Germans are still here! The joy we felt in the morning has been replaced by a heavy anxiety.

**Oberstleutnant Günther Keil:** Major Förster ordered the battalion to attack Ste Mère-Église at 0230 hours. At 0700, however, I received a message saying that Major Moch and his battalion were still stationed at the southern exit of Montebourg. I then ordered Moch to march at once against Ste Mère-Église. It must accordingly have been 1200 when Moch made his appearance before Ste Mère-Église. This lapse of time had been sufficient to allow the American parachutists to take up firm positions. It was now impossible for Moch's battalion to take Ste Mère-Église.

**Emil Ozouf, resident, Gambosville (near Sainte-Mère-Église) (age 11):** [In the morning, I raced through] the garden and fields receiving the valuable silk chutes—there must have been about eighty. We spent a memorable few days, wandering the countryside, making friends with the Americans, collecting anything we found.

**T/5 J. Frank Brumbaugh, 508th Parachute Infantry Regiment, 82nd Airborne:** On the 6th of June, in daylight, everywhere you looked, there's a parachute hanging. Every tree had a parachute in it, every telephone pole had a parachute hanging on it. They were scattered all over the place.

**Jean Flamand:** The parachutes we recovered were resting on a green and luxuriant meadow between our house and the Vallée de Misère. Eventually, the silk of these parachutes would serve to make corsages, blouses, shirts for us to use as clothing. We weren't rich, and to wear such soft and silky clothes seemed to us to be a luxury we would otherwise never be able to give ourselves.

**T/5 J. Frank Brumbaugh:** On the 7th of June, there wasn't a parachute in sight.

*"A bucket of ships in a bath tub"*

# NEPTUNE Rises

British sailors aboard HMCS *Algonquin* mark
church services en route to France.

*The first ships of the* NEPTUNE *armada actually left port on May 31, long before the commanders had settled on the final invasion schedule—the old, slow-moving ships designated to be sunk as part of the temporary breakwaters known as "Gooseberries" departed Oban, Scotland, for their ten-day sail to the Normandy coast. Then, over the first days of June, the rest of the* NEPTUNE *armada embarked, readied, and steamed from ports across the British Isles. Next to depart were the bombardment fleet coming from Belfast and the Scottish Firth of Clyde, followed by Admiral Moon's Task Force U, bound for Utah, which left from eight ports in western England, carrying the men of VII Corps under Maj. Gen. J. Lawton*

*Collins. It assembled in the evening of June 5 into 12 cross-Channel convoys—*
*their speeds carefully calculated to conform to the slowest vessels. Admiral Hall's*
*Task Force O, carrying the men of V Corps under Maj. Gen. Leonard Gerow,*
*represented another nine convoys, with 16 more bound for Gold Beach, 10 for*
*Juno, and 12 for Sword.*

*Altogether, it was surely the largest fleet ever assembled, just shy of 7,000*
*total ships, although the precise number varies according to what's included in*
*the count: The US Navy later calculated that 2,727 ships crossed the Channel*
*on their own in its main task forces, but since the larger landing ships carried*
*aboard smaller landing crafts, there were on the morning of June 6 5,333 ships,*
*boats, ferries, and craft off of Omaha Beach and Utah Beach, bringing the total*
*slightly higher. Crewing the entire Allied armada required 285,000 sailors, and*
*in the final days of May and early days of June, they dispersed from 171 different*
*ports and anchorages across the United Kingdom.*

*The fleet represented an incredible feat of industry and, particularly, main-*
*tenance. Admiral Kirk reported that 99.3 percent of the US beaching landing*
*craft were available to proceed, and the British figure was equally impressive,*
*97.6 percent, an achievement all the more remarkable given that the assault*
*ships had been in near-constant use in training and exercises right up until the*
*invasion itself.*

*The* NEPTUNE *fleet was overwhelmingly British, about 80 percent of the*
*fleet, a point of pride for the United Kingdom in a campaign that would later be*
*largely credited to the Americans, but a mix of personnel and craft meant that, for*
*the technical designation of "American" beaches and "British" ones, the reality was*
*more integrated—a US flotilla manned by Coast Guard personnel would land*
*Brits on Sword Beach, British personnel and craft would ferry the US Ranger*
*battalions ashore, and of the 15 large troop transports heading to Omaha, eight*
*were British and only seven American. And there were far more than US Navy*
*and Royal Navy personnel offshore during the invasion—the fleet included nine*
*French vessels, three Polish, three Norwegian destroyers, two Greek corvettes, and*
*two sloops from the Netherlands. It was a truly Allied effort.*

**Pvt. Joseph Barrett, 474th Anti Aircraft Battalion:** We arrived at the Mar-
itime City of Plymouth in England's West End. We had come through
picturesque Cornwall and saw no civilian traffic, nary a lorry nor bus let
alone a private car. No civilian traffic was allowed in this ancient town

from which Sir Francis Drake set sail in 1577 in the *Golden Hind*. It was also from here that 40 years later the Pilgrim Fathers set sail across the vast Atlantic to found a new land called America. And now nearly 400 years later their English counterparts gladly gave up their ordinary life style to make room for a million of the Pilgrims' descendants to defend England and the world from a modern day tyrant. What strange turns life sometimes takes.

**2nd Lt. Cyril Rand, platoon commander, Company C, 2nd Battalion, Royal Ulster Rifles:** Laden like Christmas trees, we moved off very early the next day, with the transport that was to take us to the docks. We saw the Canadians moving off on our right flank, and I smiled as I thought how relieved the squirrels would be to see them go.

**Pvt. John Barnes, Company A, 116th Infantry Regiment, 29th Division:** We left the staging area by truck and were driven down to the port of Weymouth for boarding our ship. It was the *Empire Javelin*, a British ship.

**Capt. Douglas Aitken, medical officer, 24th Lancers, 8th Armoured Brigade:** American military police in a jeep led us all the way. I must say I take a deeper than normal interest in these last glimpses of England. The girls look much more attractive when we know we won't see any for a long time to come.

**Violet Bingley, St. John's nurse, Bow, East London (age 18):** As one truck passed, the soldiers inside sang "Two Little Girls Blue" to my sister and me. We were both in our uniforms. Even today, I still get a lump in my throat when I hear that song.

**Pvt. John Barnes:** We marched down to the dock. The commanding general of the division, Gen. [Charles] Gerhardt, was observing the loading. As we passed him, he called out, "Are you men ready now?" Ahead of me was Pvt. Bedford Hoback, one of three sets of brothers from the original Virginia National Guard company from Bedford, VA. "Yes sir, general. We're sure ready!" he responded. I know he really thought so.

**Maj. John Dalgleish, Planning Staff, Royal Army Service Corps:** I hurried to the coast to see the streaming lines of ships and craft pounding steadily along the English Channel. Here on the white cliffs, with the grey-crested waves lapping the shore, I stood and cried, and was not ashamed. The pent-up emotions of months surged through. I cried, with my head in my hands, a spectator of destiny. The planning was ended.

**Lt. Gen. Omar Bradley, commander, First Army:** OVERLORD was underway; The Plan had taken over.

**Pocket Guide to France:** You are about to play a personal part in pushing the Germans out of France. Whatever part you take—rifleman, hospital orderly, mechanic, pilot, clerk, gunner, truck driver—you will be an essential factor in a great effort, which will have two results: first, France will be liberated from the Nazi mob and the Allied armies will be that much nearer Victory, and second, the enemy will be deprived of coal, steel, manpower, machinery, food, bases, seacoast and a long list of other essentials which have enabled him to carry on the war at the expense of the French.

The Allied offensive you are taking part in is based upon a hard-boiled fact. It's this. We democracies aren't just doing favors in fighting for each other when history gets tough. We're all in the same boat. Take a look around you as you move into France and you'll see what the Nazis do to a democracy when they can get it down by itself.

In "Mein Kampf" Hitler stated that his plan was to destroy France first, then get England, after which he would have the United States cornered without a fight. The Allies are going to open up conquered France, re-establish the old Allied liberties and destroy the Nazi regime everywhere. Hitler asked for it.

**Lt. Gen. Omar Bradley:** For the next few tortured hours we could do little but pace our decks and trust in the men to whom The Plan had been given for execution.

**Pvt. Dennis Bowen, 5th Battalion, East Yorkshire Regiment:** I realized that I was going to be part of something that was going to be big. I didn't realize how big, although when you stood on the deck and looked round—you couldn't see anything else but ships, north, south, east, and west.

**Ainsley Hickman, Mechanical Leading Rate, HMS *Hydra* (J275):** The atmosphere had become terribly tense, and we waited impatiently for the Skip to give us the inside information. It was not until the afternoon at 2:30 pm that he did tell us. The QM pipes "All hands muster in the starboard minesweeping mess desk," and we did at the double. No one wanted to miss this. His first words were, "Well lads, this is It." The faces around me were a picture I don't think I could easily forget. Most of the young follows received the news with inward jubilation—see it written on their faces. The elderly, or married fellows, looked more pensive and took the matter more seriously. As for myself, I must admit it made me feel a little queer, but I had to bite my lip to stop myself showing my joy. To think that this was the real thing—that I would be in it—it was great.*

**Capt. Powell Rhea, commander, USS *Nevada* (BB-36):** [The minesweepers] not only swept and buoyed a remarkably clear and geographically accurate channel through the German mine fields, but did so at night, unescorted, in severe cross currents, in mine-infested waters, and in the face of possible enemy attack.

**Percy Wallace, coast guardsman, St. Alban's Head Lookout Post, off the coast of Poole:** During that day those of us at St. Alban's Head witnessed something no man had seen before. Close under the headland I looked down on the landing craft; I could see the troops in battle dress on board. Beyond them, line after line of tank landing craft side by side, escorted by motor launches. Then came the armed trawlers, the oceangoing tugs, and behind them, echelons of minesweepers. Out to sea, destroyers and frigates took up their stations. On the horizon, coming up from the west beyond Portland, the battleships and heavy cruisers waited.

**Lt. Edwin Gale, deputy commander, USS *LCT-853*:** The LCTs in the Dart river started moving out. It was quite a moving spectacle because hundreds and perhaps thousands of people lined the shore and were waving good bye to

---

* Ainsley Hickman was killed in battle shortly after D-Day.

us as we left. I remember very well that my captain turned to me and said, "Edwin you know we may not do anything as worth while as this again in our lives but it is a fine thing to be here."

**Sub Lieutenant William T. Longley, HM LCF I (Landing Craft Flak), Royal Navy, writing to his wife, June 2, 1944:** My darling, Everything here is OK and we are thankful for a little breeze, which makes the heat a little more bearable. It seems a long time since June 1936, but they have been the happiest years of my life and I only hoped that we could be together on our anniversary on the 6th. However, great pending events preclude any such possibility, but my thoughts, darling, will be very much with you on that day. I love you more than ever cherub and long for the time when we resume our life together. Would you as a special favor get a nice bouquet of red roses out of the cheque enclosed as a special reminder of the 6th. I know it is rather unusual but as you know I have no other way of doing it. All my love and thoughts, darling, for the SIXTH. Ever yours, Will.*

**Trooper W. J. Blackwell, co-driver, 3 Troop, B Squadron, Westminster Dragoons:** Soon we were away. As we left the shore, I called to a Black American soldier—there were a few there—to throw me a pebble, which he did. It was a rather sentimental gesture to have a piece of England in my pocket.

**Percy Wallace:** Throughout the day, the ships weighed anchor, and by dusk the sea was empty once again. Then the sound of aircraft in the sky. I said to my wife, "This is it." Later, when we were going to bed, we looked at one another for a moment. I said quietly, "A lot of men are going to die tonight. We should pray for them."

**Capt. A. D. C. Smith, 4 Commando, 1st Special Service Brigade:** I never loved England so truly as at that moment.

**Lt. John Mason Brown, aide to Rear Adm. Alan Kirk, USS *Augusta* (CA-31):** We are on the move and so is history.

---

* Sub Lieutenant William Longley was killed in battle off the Normandy coast on August 17, 1944, age 39.

**Adm. Bertram Ramsay, Naval Commander-in-Chief, Allied Naval Expeditionary Force, Special Order of the Day:** The hopes and prayers of the free world and of the enslaved people of Europe will be with us and we cannot fail them. I count on every man to do his utmost to ensure the success of this great enterprise which is the climax of the European War. Good luck to you all and God Speed.

\*      \*      \*

*As the ships gathered, the hundreds of thousands of men aboard were left with last-minute preparations, inspirational words from their commanders and leaders, and, most of all, their own thoughts about what came next. They played games, read, paced, wrote, dozed, talked, ate hearty, final meals—a decision many would soon come to regret amid the rolling seas—and spoke with a number of war correspondents who had been specially selected to ride along for the landing, including Robert Capa, whose 11 photographs for* Life *magazine from Omaha Beach would be the most visceral window the world ever got into the first hours ashore.*

*The assault fleet contained the famous and someday famous—from writer Ernest Hemingway to the actor Henry Fonda, who had enlisted in 1942 and served aboard the destroyer USS* Satterlee, *to future baseball star Yogi Berra, and future actors Alec Guinness, Obi-Wan Kenobi in* Star Wars, *who piloted a British landing craft, and James Doohan, the Canadian who would play "Scotty" in* Star Trek *and who was bound for Juno Beach, as well as a young aspiring writer named J. D. Salinger and a young medic named Elliot Richardson, who would later be one of just two men in history to hold four separate presidential cabinet appointments.*

**Pvt. Ray Howell, 3466th Ordnance Medium Automotive Maintenance Company, 5th Engineer Special Brigade:** One good thing I remember very clearly was that Ernest Hemingway was aboard the *Dorothea L. Dix* as a correspondent. I got his autograph. I have that.

**Ens. George McKee Elsey, White House Map Room watch officer, attached as an observer to USS *Ancon* (AGC-4) flagship:** Ernest Hemingway was the most conspicuous and about the noisiest. Bandages covered fifty-two stitches on his head. A taxi accident in London? A drunken brawl? His stories varied from day to day.

**Robert Capa, photographer, *Life* magazine:** On my boat, the *U.S.S. Chase*, the population fell into three categories: the planners, the gamblers, and the writers of last letters. The gamblers were to be found on the upper deck, clustering around a pair of tiny dice and putting thousands of dollars on the blanket. The last-letter-writers hid in corners and were putting down beautiful sentences on paper leaving their favorite shotguns to kid brothers and their dough to the family. As for the planners, they were down in the gymnasium in the bottom of the ship, lying on their stomachs around a rubber carpet on which was placed a miniature of every house and tree on the French coast. The platoon leaders picked their way between the rubber villages and looked for protection behind the rubber trees and in the rubber ditches on the mattress.

**Sgt. Hyman Haas, A Battery, 467th Anti Aircraft Artillery Battalion:** I don't remember anybody speaking about what it might possibly be like in combat, yet, of course, it was on our minds—always wondering, "How will I do?" It really scared me. As I recall, what really frightened me was that I wouldn't measure up. I might be too frightened to move.

**S.Sgt. Harry Bare, Company F, 116th Infantry Regiment, 29th Division:** I went to mass and received communion. I needed all the help I could get.

**Seaman Ronald Seaborne, Naval Telegraphist, HMS *Belfast*:** After lunch, "Hands to Church" was piped. Although attendance was entirely voluntary, every soldier on board seemed to be at the service which was held on the upper boat deck.

**Sgt. Hyman Haas:** There were religious services. I can remember being at a mass for the Jewish boys with a Catholic priest holding mass on one side and a Protestant minister holding a service for the Protestant boys on the other. It was really strange—everyone praying in different religions and denominations, each watching the other. If you know anything about Jewish religious services, you know that when a Jew is praying he wraps himself in a prayer shawl and wears phylacteries, especially in the morning. We had a rabbi who was fully equipped, wearing a prayer shawl which completely covered him. I felt very strange, as though somebody was saying a prayer for the dead. This sticks out in my mind.

**Seaman Ronald Seaborne:** In the bows stood an Army chaplain behind a table covered by a table cloth on which stood a small silver cross. As we waited for the service to begin, the wind started to increase in vigor. A sudden gust flipped up the table cloth, the cross slipped to the deck and broke in two. Utter consternation in the congregation. What an omen! For the first time I realized what "fear of God" really was. All around, men were looking absolutely shattered. This event is one of the most vivid memories I have of the whole Normandy campaign.

**Maj. Ralph Ingersoll, Allied planning staff, attached to Task Force Raff, aboard an LCT bound for Utah Beach:** A little lieutenant from Brooklyn, whose platoon of engineers was going overside to take out the underwater obstacles, had a waking fantasy. He used to lean on the rail next to me and say, "You don't suppose there has been an armistice and nobody has told us, do you? Gee, it would be funny if it were all over and we didn't know it, wouldn't it?" Every few hours you would see him kicking this idea around with someone. He liked it and his face lit up when he talked about it and it gave him comfort.

**2nd Lt. John L. Ahearn, commander, Company C, 70th Tank Battalion, 6th Armored Group:** I knew I wouldn't be able to sleep, but I wanted to get as much rest as possible, so I returned to my cot below deck and began reading a book that I had wanted to read for some time, *A Tree Grows in Brooklyn*. I particularly wanted to read it because it was about an area of Brooklyn which I had some familiarity, Williamsburg. I managed to read.

**Pvt. Joseph Barrett, 474th Anti-Aircraft Battalion:** In the hurry up and wait situation which we were in, I always turned to the Armed Services Edition PocketBook, which was 4 by 5 ½ inches and slipped easily into the shirt pocket. They came with the rations and were written by great authors from Herman Melville and Walt Whitman to Dorothy Parker and Robert

Benchley. I found a dry section of deck and just read until I tired of sitting on steel and took another turn around the deck.

**Lt. Frank Beetle, Cannon Company, 16th Infantry Regiment, 1st Division:** I read aboard that ship and I remember what I read. It was a book of a trilogy by John Dos Passos—the *Manhattan Transfer*. It was rather interesting, and I like the way it was done. Also I remember reading some Plato believe it or not, which I think may have been Durant's *Story of Philosophy*.

**Lt. Gen. Omar Bradley:** I shuffled impatiently about my cabin. First I sat down with a copy of *A Bell for Adano*. But I was too restless to read it and exchanged it for the previous day's *Stars and Stripes*. Detroit had won a 16-inning game from New York. I tossed the paper aside and went back up to the bridge.

**Capt. John F. Dulligan, executive officer, 2nd Battalion, 26th Infantry Regiment, 1st Infantry Division, letter to his wife:** I love these men. They sleep all over the ship, on the decks, in, on top, and underneath the vehicles. They smoke, play cards, wrestle around and indulge in general horseplay. They gather around in groups and talk mostly about girls, home and experiences (with and without girls). They are good soldiers, the best in the world. Before the invasion of North Africa, I was nervous and a little scared. During the Sicilian invasion I was so busy that the fear passed while I was working. This time we will hit a beach in France and from there on only God knows the answer. I want you to know that I love you with all my heart. I pray that God will see fit to spare me to you and Ann and Pat.

**Sgt. Alan Anderson, 467th Anti Aircraft Artillery Automatic Weapons Battalion:** I remembered at the time trying to think what this really meant to me. All I could think about was the fact that I was 25 years old, still single and a college graduate, and whether this was to be all of my life and really what for. I was thinking about the meanings of democracy, and that sort of thing, but it doesn't have any meaning to a man in a situation such as that. The only thing that meant anything to me was that as long as I was there and some of my relatives, especially my two brothers, were not, that maybe we could get this mess over with before any more of the family had to be dragged into this situation. Very few men are very patriotic when they're faced with these suicide missions.

**Pvt. John Barnes:** We were handed a printed sheet of paper with Eisenhower's address to the troops: "You are about to embark upon the Great Crusade. Toward which we have striven these many months. The eyes of the world are upon you. . . ." We didn't feel like Crusaders.

**Pvt. Ernest Hilberg, Company H, 18th Infantry Regiment, 1st Division:** I had mixed feelings. Somehow or other, I didn't feel like there was much glory in what I was about to do. I was doing a job that had to be done, that we were going to get rid of the bastard Hitler.

**Pvt. John Hooper, Headquarters Company, 115th Infantry Regiment, 29th Division:** I carefully folded the leaflet and put it into my shirt pocket. I would include it in my next letter home. I still have it.

**Seaman Joseph A. Dolan, radioman, USS *Bayfield* (APA-33):** After midnight, I went up to the open bridge from the radio room to get some air. It was so black due to overcast skies, and of course no light so I couldn't see the individuals who were on the open bridge. A man spoke to me and asked me how I felt going into an invasion. From his voice, I knew he was a lot older than I, and he had a cultured voice. I often wondered if he could have been General Theodore Roosevelt.

**Capt. John A. Moreno, air officer and assistant planner, staff of Admiral Don P. Moon, U.S. Navy:** One of the men we had on board the *Bayfield* was Brigadier General Theodore Roosevelt Jr., son of the former president. In 1944 he was fifty-seven years old and serving as the assistant commander of the 4th Infantry Division. He was a lovable old man—I was then thirty-five—and very much a politician rather than a professional soldier. He had previously been Assistant Secretary of the Navy and Governor of Puerto Rico and the Philippines. We all liked him, because he had a charming personality and was very cultured. He was among the few American general officers ashore during the assault landings on D-Day, and I daresay the oldest man to hit the beach.

**Sgt. Jim McKee, Company K, 12th Infantry Regiment, 4th Division:** Nobody slept well that night; except the Germans.

**Lt. John Mason Brown, aide to Rear Adm. Alan Kirk, USS *Augusta* (CA-31):** The span of a short night separated us from a destination we knew and from a dawn and day we had yet to know.

**Brig. Gen. Theodore Roosevelt, Jr., Supernumerary General Officer, 4th Division, letter to his wife, Eleanor, June 3, 1944:** Well Bunny Dear, We are starting out on the great venture of this war, and by the time you get this letter, for better or for worse, it will be history. We are attacking in daylight the most heavily fortified shore in history, a shore held by excellent troops. We are throwing against it excellent troops, well-armed and backed by superb air and good naval support. We are on transports, buttoned up. Our next stop, Europe.

\*          \*          \*

*As the* NEPTUNE *flotilla assembled and turned south toward France, a fleet of 245 wooden minesweepers and support craft, all but a couple dozen of which were crewed by the Royal Navy and the Royal Canadian Navy, moved ahead of the convoys, clearing designated channels to each beach that were then marked by the Royal Navy with lighted buoys. Overnight they found and detonated a total of 78 mines that would have otherwise lain in the fleet's path.*

*Overhead, the first waves of the similarly massive air armada assembled to support the landings began—first, the planes carrying paratroopers, then later, bombers, and, finally, fighter planes to provide an unprecedented umbrella of protection.*

**Ernest Hemingway, correspondent, *Collier's Weekly*:** I wish I could write the full story of what it means to take a transport across through a mine-swept channel; the mathematical precision of maneuver; the infinite detail and chronometrical accuracy and split-second timing of everything from the time the anchor comes up until the boats are lowered and away into the roaring, sea-churning assembly circle from which they break off into the attack wave. The story of all the teamwork behind that has to be written, but to get all that in would take a book.

**Ens. Doug Birch, USS *Subchaser-1358*:** It is difficult for a layman to realize the complete darkness that prevailed in the English Channel. During those days there were no lights, no beacons and our surface radar only picked up large landmasses at that time.

**Lt. Cdr. John D. Bulkeley, commander, Patrol Torpedo Boat Squadron 102:** The minesweepers went back and forth for hours, detonating mines. The PT boats blew up some with their machine guns. We kept on the alert through-out the night for a possible challenge from the E-boats, but fortunately they remained in Cherbourg. After the minesweepers cleared the lanes, they put down dan buoys to mark them. But it was awfully hard to keep those minesweepers going straight and in line. We did our best.

**Ainsley Hickman:** The Skip, every now and again would warn the look-outs we were approaching a heavily mined area and then there would come the thuds of the mines going up as they surfaced—but some didn't explode—those were the dangerous ones, because they floated under your bows if you weren't careful. Skip had just sung out a warning when the G.I. yelled "What's that, sir, right ahead?" Came the order "Wheel hard a starboard!" and whilst we were waiting for the seemingly inevitable crash the mine slid by not more than a few yards from our stern. Phew! How shaky I felt after that. It happened again not long afterwards, but the first time was the worst. We had expected the area to be more heavily mined than it was, but the task was grim enough, believe me.

**Sub-Lt. Brendan A. Maher, navigator, HM *Motor Launch 137*:** We commenced destruction by shooting at the mines that had come to the surface when the sweep cut their mooring lines. This target shooting was done by our machine gunners and anybody else who was available.

**Lt. Dean L. Rockwell, flotilla commander, USS *LCT-535*:** We proceeded east-ward for the rest of the morning and early afternoon. In the p.m., we met up with the other forces or units, battleships, cruisers, destroyers, on-shore bombardment craft, picket boats, mine sweepers, and finally, cargo vessels carrying the infantry, the soldiers and war material to be landed.

**Capt. James E. Arnold, Naval Officer in Charge (NOIC), Utah Beach:** The speed of the convoy was limited to the top speed of the slowest component—in this case, the wallowing little LCTs laden with their precious burden of modern fighting equipment and carefully trained men. Through the silent night, the LCI skipper and I studied charts, following the plan. The ripple of the bow wave sounded like Niagara Falls in the tense silence. Though we were still so far from the French shore that Hitler's reception committee couldn't possibly have heard the report of a 40-millimeter, everybody on board spoke in whispers.

**Lt. Lambton Burn, RNVR, Navy editor, *Parade* magazine:** In the light of a cloudy afternoon we surf steadily south of the island heading for "Piccadilly Circus," the marshalling terminus from which ten channels are being swept through mined waters towards the Cherbourg peninsula. As daylight flickers and darkness looms ahead we find ourselves entering dan-buoyed and lighted channels which need only traffic policemen to complete their likeness to broad arterial roads.

**Homer Carey, storekeeper second class, USS *LST-505*:** In the soft twilight, two British cruisers raced past us headed south for the coast of France. They looked beautiful as their shapely bows cut the water and passed us as if we were standing still. It was a comfort to know they were on our side. At the sight of them, all I could think of were two greyhounds in a dog race.

**Lt. Stanley C. Bodell, commander, LCT:** We were located in one of the inside columns and spent our entire time trying to keep station. We had the misfortune to have a British craft behind us which had the ability to go ahead twice as fast as the Americans, but lacked the backing power we had. We would pound along, the whole boat bending and buckling; then the one ahead would slow down. We would go full reserve to keep from riding up its stern, then the Britisher would start to climb ours. The vessels of different columns would close to about five feet or less, usually crashing together, then separating.

**Lt. Roy Clark, commander, USS *LCT-770*:** I didn't think I was a heavy smoker, but there was the evidence in my duffle coat pockets: Three empty packs of Capstan Navy-Cut. It must have been about 0130 hours when I saw the bombing of France over the horizon, which was then about forty miles away, to judge from the flashes in the sky.

**Sgt. Alan Anderson, 467th Anti Aircraft Artillery Automatic Weapons Battalion:** We were all very ill. The U.S. sailors on the landing craft had given us paper bags, and we wanted to know what they were for, and they said "You'll find out." And of course, we did, because these flat-bottomed boats were very very rough due to the weather conditions on the channel, where the winds were quite strong, the waves were high, and we all became violently seasick due to the rocking motion of the landing craft. The bags came in very handy.

**Alan Higgins, telegraphist, Royal Navy, HM *LCI(L) III*:** The stench of vomit was terrible.

**Homer Carey:** It was a slow pace all through the night.

**Pvt. Clair R. Galdonik, Company A, 359th Infantry Regiment, 90th Division:** The night was filled with the drone of our aircraft moving across the channel to bomb inland, and the C-47s to drop paratroopers of the 82nd and 101st airborne divisions.

**Cpl. Maurice Chauvet, French Troop, 4 Commando, 1st Special Service Brigade:** There is what sounds like thunder in the sky above us, and I go on deck. It is hundreds of planes flying above us, most of them towing gliders. This is the 6th Airborne Division, which will be dropped inland from where we're going to land in about an hour. If we do not succeed in joining them in the morning, they won't survive.

**Lt. Cdr. John R. Blackburn, Sky Control, USS *Quincy* (CA-71):** After midnight we observed heavy sporadic antiaircraft fire ahead of us and on the starboard bow. Most of it appeared to be machine-gun fire. Often, a yellow ball would start glowing out in the middle of a field of red tracers. This yellow ball would slowly start to fall, forming a tail. Eventually, it would smash into the black loom of land, causing a great sheet of light to flare up against the low clouds.

**Lt. Anthony Drexel Duke, commander, *LST-530*:** You got a feeling of living in a dream, and you had to keep looking around to see if what you thought you were seeing was for real.

**Maj. Ralph Ingersoll:** We could see neither the beginning nor the end of our line of ships and out on the horizon on each side of us. We could barely make out the dots which were other lines of ships, without beginning or end.

**Seaman Ferris Burke, USS *LST-285*:** A highway of ships and barrage balloons going to France.

**Lt. John Mason Brown:** Like clay ducks moving slowly in a shooting gallery.

**Lt. Anthony Drexel Duke:** Ships, ships, ships, everywhere, everywhere you looked.

**Lt. Edward Giller:** Going in every direction, it seems, and every size. Just a massive armada.

**Pvt. Clayton E. Storeby, 326th Airborne Engineer Battalion, 101st Airborne:** Like someone had dumped a bucket of ships in a bath tub.

**W. B. Courtney, correspondent, *Collier's Weekly*:** This was the real beginning of the greatest single adventure in the history of mankind. No one living in our time will see its like again.

**Robert E. Adams, LCVP coxswain, assigned to the USS *Samuel Chase* (APA-26), U.S. Coast Guard:** All I can remember is that while we were sitting around, we'd say, "What will that first Kraut or that first German think when he looks out and he sees all of us, all of these ships? What on earth are they going to think?"

*"Napoleon's hat is in the ring"*

# Confusing the Enemy

While the main convoy steamed toward Normandy,
the Allies continued an elaborate deception operation.

*While the main invasion force steamed south toward Normandy, the Allied intelligence effort played the last few tricks they had up their sleeves. As part of a final pre-invasion deception operation, they sent another army force (the one made up by the* FORTITUDE *planners) east, to make the Germans think that a large invasion force was on the move to a different location and obstruct their radar efforts. Operation* TAXABLE *and Operation* GLIMMER *each involved a flight of British Lancaster and Stirling planes dropping "window," small pieces of aluminum foil (what's now commonly known as "chaff") over the Channel toward Pas-de-Calais in a carefully planned pattern that would simulate the radar returns of a invasion fleet, while on the Channel itself 30 total launches, in two separate columns, towed giant balloons that would to a radar appear to be the size of a 10,000-ton ship. Fake wireless traffic filled the night airwaves. A third operation, known as* BIG DRUM, *involved cloaking the actual invasion force with a special screen of radar-jamming boats.*

*Another particularly successful mission, known as* TITANIC, *involved 12 Halifax bombers dropping dummy paratroopers—three-foot-tall sand-filled contraptions, known as "Ruperts," that exploded upon landing and gave the impression that a gun battle was under way in the night. In four* TITANIC *missions, the Halifax planes dropped hundreds of dummies across drop zones far from where British and American paratroopers would actually land, helping to confuse and confound German forces both about the overall scale of the airdrop as well as the actual targeted location.*

*In the end, though, the most powerful deception weapon for the Allies was the bad weather itself.*

**Lt. Gen. Sir Frederick Morgan, Deputy Chief of Staff, SHAEF:** Just as viciously as on the sea, on the land, and in the air was the war fought out in the ether. The enemy had his radar, as had we, and he was as fairly and squarely defeated in this contest as in all the others.

**Winston Churchill, Prime Minister of the United Kingdom:** From Calais to Guernsey the Germans had no fewer than one hundred and twenty major pieces of radar equipment for finding our convoys and directing the fire of their shore batteries. These were grouped in forty-seven stations. We discovered them all, and attacked them so successfully with rocket-firing aircraft that on the night before D-Day not one in six was working.

**Brig. David Belcham, head of Operations and Planning Staff, British Army:** On the night of D-1/D-Day, between Le Havre and Barfleur—a few miles east of Cherbourg—not one single radar installation remained operative; and of the normal ninety-two stations in the coastal chain, only eighteen were serviceable during this vital period. Most of the latter were jammed by specially equipped Allied aircraft and naval craft circling in the Channel, but a sufficient number located north of the River Seine were purposely left unharmed in order that they should pick up and report the decoy "invasion fleets" code-named GLIMMER and TAXABLE.

**Lt. Gen. Sir Frederick Morgan:** Partly it was done by brute force, by Commando raid, or by aircraft rocket or bomb against radar installations. But, more subtly, it was first arranged that the enemy should receive news over his system that was incorrect in detail and, later, that he should receive evidence that was hardly founded on fact at all.

**Lt. Ludwig, signals intelligence unit, Asnières (outside Paris), Luftwaffe:** Shortly before midnight lively activity of RAF 100th Group commenced obviously for the purpose of neutralizing the German radar sets on the Channel coast. The jamming screen moved slowly from East to West, so that it was immediately assumed that the jamming was screening a large shipping formation. Something special was underway.

**Sgt. Joan A. Jackman, Auxiliary Territorial Service, Anti Aircraft Command:** I was called to the Brigadiers Office, asked to reaffirm my allegiance to the "Secrets Act." It was an "Operation Order" to be expressly despatched to all our Regimental H.Q.s, Battery H.Q.s, Gun Sites, Searchlight Sites and other Radar and Observation Corps installations. The Brigadier dictated, I typed, a staff major duplicated, other staff officers dashed around collating the pages for handing over to the waiting team of dispatch riders, who I am sure were blissfully unaware of the major importance of their midnight mission. It was the final act of Operation FORTITUDE. It gave details of aircraft recognition marks, their flight paths on "missions to nowhere"—a ruse to confuse the enemy. It told of bogus massive army convoys of troops and guns tearing around the Essex country lanes, presumably heading for East Coast seaports—only to turn around and re-run back to nowhere. Another ploy to distract the enemy's attention from the theatre of war where the real action was taking place.

**Squadron Leader Les Munro, No. 617 Squadron, Royal New Zealand Air Force:** I considered this operation to be, in one sense, one of the most important that we carried out. There was absolutely no latitude for deviation from ground speed, compass bearing, rate of turn, and timing.

**Brig. David Belcham:** At sea level, the dummy invasion fleets GLIMMER and TAXABLE were simulated by groups of motor launches in convoy formation, towing balloons carrying radar reflectors and emitting smoke and radar-jamming signals. Finally, a number of fast launches carrying highly specialized equipment were dispatched to jam the radar sets installed in the sighting equipment of the guns of the heavy coastal artillery batteries, and to "feed" distracting readings to the one remaining active radar installation at Cherbourg.

**Sir Arthur Travers Harris, Air Chief Marshal, RAF Bomber Command:** The bundles of "Window" had to be dropped from exactly the right height to give the same reaction as a number of large ships would do, and, what was far more difficult to contrive, the "Window" had to be dropped in such a way as to suggest the steady approach of a convoy at seven knots. This was done by the Lancasters circling with great accuracy in a long series of overlapping orbits for about five hours; in this way, as each orbit came a little closer to the enemy coast, the bundles of metallised paper seemed to be approaching equally slowly. To do this so accurately that the enemy did not suspect that aircraft and not ships were producing the reactions was, of course, a remarkable feat of navigation.

**Gen. Dwight Eisenhower, Supreme Allied Commander, SHAEF:** As events proved, the decision to launch the assault at a time when the weather was so unsettled was largely responsible for the surprise which we achieved. The enemy had concluded that any cross-Channel expedition was impossible while the seas ran so high and, with his radar installations rendered ineffective as a result of our air attacks, his consequent unpreparedness for our arrival more than offset the difficulties which we experienced.

*     *     *

*Beyond confusing the German radars and commanders as to the true invasion target, the Allies also sought help to sow confusion and damage key infrastructure, which would help slow any German response in the opening hours of OVER-LORD. Over months, intelligence officials stayed in careful touch with the French Resistance—colloquially known as the "Maquis" and officially as the "French Forces of the Interior"—to plot out possible targets and tasks that would aid the war effort.*

*A key communication channel was the BBC's Radio Londres broadcast, which regularly carried coded messages and phrases for Resistance cells and fighters. On June 1 the BBC included in the broadcast the first three lines of a poem by Paul Verlaine, "Chanson d'automne," a phrase that meant the invasion was imminent:*

> *Les sanglots longs / When a sighing begins*
> *Des violons / In the violins*
> *De l'automne / Of the autumn-song*

*Then, on June 5, it aired the next three lines, a sign that sabotage campaigns should begin as the invasion would occur in the next 24 hours:*

> *Blessent mon coeur / My heart is drowned*
> *D'une langueur / In the slow sound*
> *Monotone / Languorous and long*

*The words—and other, similar coded phrases broadcast by the BBC in the hours leading up to D-Day ("La chapeau de Napoleon set dans l'arène," Napoleon's hat is in the ring) set off a frenzy of excitement and activity on the occupied continent, as cells of fighters began to mobilize and carry out their intended invasion tasks.*

**Michel Bancilhon, architect and Resistance member, Aubenas (southern France):** The Resistance was very strong in the public services—railways, postal services, and Ponts et Chaussees [Public Works Department]. We knew everything about German movements direct from the post office in Valence. One official in the PTT at Largentière put a telephone line completely at our disposal, cutting out all risk of being overheard. By June 1944 we had 2,400 men in the southern Ardèche structured into companies, equipped with arms, but still mostly living at home. After 6 June they all took to the maquis. The whole organization owed an incredible amount to a Spanish anarchist who had fought in the Spanish Civil War and had become a communist. He gave us all the know-how and ideas.

**Jean-Louis Cremieux-Brilhac, secretary, Free French Propaganda Committee (London):** My job was to draw up the D-Day orders. We knew that the invasion was coming but of course we did not know exactly when. We had to be ready. The main message we sent was to put France in a state of general alert. And then there were specific instructions for particular sectors of the population—like town mayors, police, factory workers, and so on. The policy we decided on was of a gradual, phased insurrection, developing in accordance with the advance of Allied forces. In the end this is exactly what happened.

**André Heintz, student, member of the Resistance in Caen (age 24):** Toward the end of April the wife of my new leader made me learn by heart several messages—six I think—that I was to listen for on my crystal set. For region M (Normandy), the warning message was "L'heure du combat viendra" and it was heard on June 1. The messages for action were "Les des sont sur le ta pis" and "Il fait chaud a Suez," which meant to try and hinder all German lines of communication for the next twelve hours. If I remember right there was also "Les enfants s'ennuient au jardin," which fortunately was never heard because it meant cancellation.

**Jean Dacier, member of the Resistance, southern France:** On the evening of 5 June we were all gathered round our little radio, which we had christened "Biscuit" because of the tin in which it was hidden. The captain had his headphones on and I was almost lying on top of him trying to hear what was being said. Suddenly London announced D-Day was happening. We all jumped around delirious with joy.

**M. La Naves, member of the Resistance:** Jean Renaud Dandi-colle had told me to stay at Bernier's close to the radio because it won't be much longer, and on the evening of June 5, I heard the message: "The call of the plough-man in the misty morning." So, I cycled back to Saint Clair at full speed, through unknown paths.

**"Yvon," member of the Resistance, Saint-Donat:** 1 a.m. Suddenly the village exploded into unusual activity. Despite the black-out, lights suddenly burst on in the windows of apartments and houses in the town. Someone knocked on the door. The order for mobilization had been given. Right under the noses of the Germans, everyone was alerted. In the darkened streets, silhouettes flitted from door to door and shadows moved silently down walls and streets.

**M. La Naves:** Five of us went to Grimbosq to blow up the railroad track. It was not far from the station, and in the long curve right before it, we blew up a length of about five or six carriages. The Germans chased us and fortunately, we managed to stay hidden in the woods of Grimbosq all day and could hear the Germans looking for us.

**Instructions from the Free French Propaganda Committee, released for D-Day:** All French must consider themselves as engaged in the total war against the invader in order to liberate their homeland. It is not a question of choosing to fight or not to fight; or when to fight. They are all soldiers under orders.

# Ashore in Normandy

On D-Day morning, the German army in Normandy
was heavily reliant on horses and bicycles.

*Over the course of June 5, many residents of the Normandy region began to
suspect something serious was unfolding, and as the first fragmentary reports of
Allied movements began to trickle into occupying German defenders, commanders
tried to make sense of what was happening, and where. Notably, though, and
unexpectedly, Rommel himself was absent from Normandy that day—he had
headed back to Berlin for a quick trip to see his wife and, he hoped, to meet with
Adolf Hitler. His absence, paired with the complicated command structure of the
German forces, left defenders flat-footed at the moment it mattered most. Within
a few hours of the first scattered paratrooper reports, everyone across Normandy,
citizen or soldier, could hear the unmistakable sounds that the invasion was
under way.*

**Vice Adm. Friedrich Ruge, naval adviser to Erwin Rommel, Army Group B:**
Nothing indicated on the morning of June 5, 1944, that on the other side
of the Channel the decision for the attack had been made, and that a giant
armada was on its way to storm Fortress Europe. At the headquarters of
Army Group B everybody did his work as on other quiet days.

**Maj. Hans von Luck, commander, Panzer-Grenadier-Regiment 125, 21 Panzer-Division:** The general weather conditions, worked out every day by naval
meteorologists and passed on to us by division, gave the "all clear" for 5 and
6 June. So we did not anticipate any landings, for heavy seas, storms, and
low lying clouds would make large-scale operations at sea and in the air
impossible for our opponents.

**Lt. Gen. Hans Speidel, Chief of Staff to Erwin Rommel:** Again and again Hitler
postponed his declared intention of visiting the Western Front. Rommel
wanted to inform him without fail before the invasion of the military and
political situation and demand certain political concessions. So he consulted
Marshal von Rundstedt, telephoned to Hitler's senior adjutant, Lt.-General
[Rudolf] Schmundt, and arranged for a personal interview with Hitler,
leaving for the Obersalzberg by car on the morning of 5th June. It was
forbidden for senior officers to use aircraft for travel, as it was impossible
to protect them against the Allied air forces.

**Field Marshal Erwin Rommel, diary, June 3, 1944:** Planning a trip to Germany. 5th–8th June 1944. Fears of an invasion during this period were
rendered all the less by the fact that tides were very unfavourable for the
days following, and the fact that no amount of air reconnaissance had
given the slightest indication that a landing was imminent. The most
urgent need was to speak personally to the Fuehrer on the Obersalzberg,
convey to him the extent of the man-power and material inferiority we
would suffer in the event of a landing, and request the dispatch of two
further panzer divisions, an A.A. corps and a Nebelwerfer [artillery]
brigade to Normandy.

**Vice Adm. Friedrich Ruge:** Early, at 0600, Rommel left for Germany.

**Oberstleutnant Friedrich August Freiherr von der Heydte, commander, 6th Fallschirmjäger Regiment:** Although the authorities were frequently at odds in their estimates as to where and how the Allied invasion would take place, it was nevertheless apparent that since the middle of May commanders as well as troops were agreed in assuming that an invasion was to be expected during the first ten days of June. Consequently, the lower headquarters were astonished when all division commanders and one regimental commander from each division, the corps artillery commanders, and the commanders of corps headquarters reserves were ordered to report to Rennes on 6 June 1944 at 0830 in order to spend the entire day in an army group map exercise.

**Lt. Gen. Karl-Wilhelm von Schlieben, commander, 709th Infantry Division:** The division commanders on the Cotentin peninsula and the commander of the Channel Islands division received an order to participate in a wargame, which was to take place at Rennes, together with two subordinate commanders. I, like other division commanders, left for Rennes late in the afternoon of 5 June together with the commander of the 739th Grenadier Regiment and the commander of the Seventh Army assault battalion.

**Oberstleutnant Friedrich August Freiherr von der Heydte:** Consequently, about 50 percent of the division commanders and possibly 25 percent of the regimental commanders were not with their troops during the night of 5 June 1944.

*The first sign of the invasion was the arrival of the British, Canadian, and American paratroopers in the air overhead—but their confusingly widely scattered drop and the widespread small pockets of fighting left German officials paralyzed to respond. Some units had even been engaged that very day in exercises intended to repel an invasion force and, now, in the twilight of a June Normandy night, they found the real thing arriving.*

**Lt. Gen. Josef Reichert, commander, 711 Infanterie-Division:** We were still in the Casino [Officers' Mess] of the divisional staff until about 0030 hours on 6 June, and were just about ready to retire, when an exceedingly loud noise of motors of single planes, flying apparently very low over our quarters at tremendous speed, attracted our attention. The fact of the air activity as such, at that time, was not surprising, because our own and the enemy's busy air routes of incoming and outgoing planes lay directly over us, which were used nearly every night. It struck us as strange, however, that the planes were flying so low; we had the feeling that they might almost touch the roof.

**Obergefreiter Rudolf Theil, 6th Fallschirmjäger-Regiment:** [I] saw all kinds of red flares and glaring white light signals. That could only mean one thing to any experienced soldier: "The enemy is attacking." I reported to Major von der Heydte, who replied, "Sound the alarm!" We took our positions and waited for the unknown monster: Invasion. It was 0011 hours, German time.

**Maj. Hans von Luck:** About midnight, I heard the growing roar of aircraft, which passed over us. I wondered whether the attack was destined once again for traffic routes inland or for Germany herself. The machines appeared to be flying very low—because of the weather? I looked out the window and was wide awake; flares were hanging in the sky. At the same moment, my adjutant was on the telephone, "Major, paratroops are dropping. Gliders are landing in our section. I'm trying to make contact with No. II Battalion. I'll come along to you at once."

**Gren. Josef Horn, signaler, 191st Artillerie-Regiment, 91st Luftlande Division:** Shortly after midnight I heard the sound of low-flying airplanes and saw parachutes coming down. Some were white, others appeared blue, many were camouflaged. Knowing the lie of the land, I was able to evade the Americans, but once in a while I could hear a clicking sound, but I didn't know until much later what it was.

**Lt. Gen. Hans Speidel:** The Chief of Staff of Army Group B received reports in the first hours of the morning of 6th June that enemy parachute troops had been dropped in the vicinity of Caen and the south eastern area of the Cotentin peninsula. It was not at all clear at first whether these were airborne landings in strength or just groups of parachutists dropped to support the French forces of resistance. Between the Seine and Orne, the parachutes were widely strewn.

**Capt. Ernst During, commander, heavy machine gun company, Grenadier-Regiment 914, 352 Infanterie-Division:** When I got to my command post I telephoned battalion headquarters, two miles to the rear, and said, "Paratroops have landed here." The answer came back, "Here, too," then the line went dead.

**Lt. Gen. Josef Reichert:** The first prisoners—two parachutists who had landed in the strongpoint itself—were taken, who, however, could not give exact details as to the purpose of the undertaking, and probably did not want to. I realized that it was a sure sign of the beginning of the invasion.

**Lt. Col. Hubert Meyer, senior general staff officer, 12 SS Panzer-Division Hitlerjugend:** On the night of June 5th my wife was staying with me, on a visit. It was totally illegal, but I hadn't had any leave for ages.

**Irmgard Meyer, wife of Lt. Col. Hubert Meyer:** My husband had a house in a place called Tillières, a pretty house with a garden. It was a beautiful spring, warm, and I can still remember the scent of the jasmine when I arrived.

**Lt. Col. Hubert Meyer:** That night the brigade leader, Major General Witt, came upstairs and knocked on my door and said, "On your feet, Meyer, the invasion has begun!" I got up, dressed quickly, and went downstairs and telephoned division headquarters. They said, "No, it's not the invasion. They aren't paratroops, they're just straw dummies." So I thought, well, I'll go back to bed.

**Irmgard Meyer:** Then, later in the night we were waked up by a knock on the door and a voice saying, "Wake up, the invasion's started."

**Lt. Col. Hubert Meyer:** We immediately put the division on standby. But no orders came through. No alert, nothing.

**Lt. Gen. Hans Speidel:** The Army Group ordered all units to battle stations. The reports of parachute landings became more numerous between 3 and 4 a.m. Then there was bombing of coastal defences and strong Allied air forces were detected approaching. The Panzer divisions in reserve were ordered to be ready to move.

**Irmgard Meyer:** At 5:00 A.M., my husband came and told me, "They have landed. You have got to get out of here as quickly as possible. Get up immediately and pack. You are going in a car with two other women, Frau Wuensche and Frau Witt." Another young woman whose husband was an SS lieutenant was crying, crying bitterly, since she, too, was saying goodbye to her husband. But I will never forget how bitterly this young woman wept. Ten days later, her husband was dead. She must somehow have sensed it.

**Maj. Hans von Luck:** The hours passed. We had set up a defensive front where we had been condemned to inactivity. The rest of the division, with the panzer regiment and Panzer Grenadier Regiment 192, was equally immobilized, though in the highest state of alert. My adjutant telephoned once more to division. Major Forster came to the phone. He too was unable to alter the established orders. Hitler, who used to work far into the night, was still asleep that early morning. At the command post, I paced up and down and clenched my fists at the indecision of the Supreme Command in the face of the obvious facts. If Rommel had been with us instead of in Germany, he would have disregarded all orders and taken action—of that we were convinced.

*As dawn arrived, civilians and personnel along the coast finally saw for themselves what had been planned for months: a looming invasion armada, an unambiguous sign that the long-awaited landing was under way. Then the naval bombardment removed any remaining doubts. Today, the shells said, would be different. Within moments, German soldiers and military leaders were awakened with the news.*

**Gren. Franz Gockel, 3 Kompanie, Grenadier-Regiment 726, 716 Infanterie-Division, Wehrmacht, posted to Widerstandsnest 62 at Colleville-sur-Mer (Omaha Beach):** Out of a deep sleep we were ripped by the call of "Alarm!" A Kamerad stood in the bunker entrance and roared out "Highest Alarm Status and you'd better damn hurry!" The man was still in the entrance when our Unteroffizier yelled from behind him "Boys, it's for real!" In a short time we had our rifles and the MG [machine gun] crews were in place, all the tiredness had gone away. The cook came and gave us hot red wine, the "spirit of life."

**Obergrenadier Karl Wegner, 3 Kompanie, Grenadier Regiment 914, 352 Infanterie-Division:** Violently my arm was shaken by Willi. I sat straight up and looked at him, his face was pale. I asked him what was wrong. He just pointed towards the sea. I looked out and saw ships as far as one could see. I'm not ashamed to say that I was never so scared in my life. But the sight was so impressive that no one could help but just stare in amazement. Just then Obergefreiter Lang burst into the bunker. The look on his face was serious, no more games. This was real, some of us will not be here when the sun sets today.

**Pvt. Franz Rachmann, 352 Infanterie-Division:** My sergeant came running and said, "There are a thousand different ships coming in the English Channel."

**Obergrenadier Karl Wegner:** That's when we heard the planes again.

**Gren. Franz Gockel:** The bombers were suddenly over us and it was too late to spring into the prepared dugout for cover. I dove under the gun as bombs screamed and hissed into the sand and earth. Two heavy bombs fell on our position, and we held our breath as more explosions fell into the hinterland. Debris and clouds of smoke enveloped us; the earth shook; eyes and nose were filled with dirt, and sand ground between teeth.

**Gefreiter Obergrenadier Peter Simeth, Grenadier Regiment 916, 352 Infanterie-Division:** We crawled from our tents and saw the fire show. Bombs of all types were hitting the ground. All sorts of bombers filled the sky; a couple were on fire. We got dressed and fumbled with getting our gear on. The Feldwebel yelled for us to dig one-man holes for cover as fast as we could.

**Gren. Franz Gockel:** But that [the air bombardment] was not enough.

**Lt. Gen. Hans Speidel:** At 5.30 a.m. hundreds of ships' guns at sea roared out at once as the naval bombardment of the Calvados coast began.

**Pierre Pipre, proprietor of Hotel Casino in Vierville-sur-Mer (near Omaha Beach):** Hell broke loose. There was not a single glass left on the windows in Vierville, and suddenly we could believe that we were in the middle of night, due to the smoke of explosions and the artificial fog through which we could see red flashes, which were probably shells. Everybody was scared and the inhabitants on their thresholds were discussing what to do: *Stay home or go away—but to where?*

**Irène Othon-Meillat, resident, Dozulé, east of Caen:** It was hell, a veritable deluge of fire. We all took refuge under a table at the farm. We pressed against one another and prayed. We were convinced that we were going to die.

**Major Werner Pluskat, Artillerie-Regiment 352, 352 Infanterie-Division:** One of the first shells hit the base of our bunker and literally shook it. I was thrown to the ground and my binoculars were smashed.

**Fernand Broekx, resident, Colleville-sur-Mer (directly south of Omaha Beach):** I had the feeling that the house was going to collapse on us. The walls were damaged and the floor-boards lifting up. You could hear the tiles falling, one after the other, as well as the crash of breaking glass. The volleys of naval cannon and the bombs released by planes made a deafening racket. The coast was nothing more than a gush of flames. A strong odor of powder caught at our throats. Soon afterward, an exploding bomb broke the kitchen window and struck the wall at an angle. My wife was hit by a small fragment.

**Obergrenadier Karl Wegner:** We saw the landing craft, it seemed like hundreds of them. They rocked back and forth in the wake of the larger ships. Suddenly they all turned and began to come straight in towards the beach. My stomach was in knots.

**Private Werner Beibst, infantry, 15th Army:** The sight of the ships was almost inconceivable, they just covered the water.

**Gren. Franz Gockel:** The sea had come alive.

*"A huge, fire-rimmed boiling cauldron"*

# In the Air Over the Beaches

The skies over the invasion beaches were filled with
the distinctively marked Allied fighters and bombers.

*The fighters, bombers, and transports of the Allied air forces flew 25,275 missions
in the 48 hours surrounding D-Day, a Herculean effort that saw many crews fly
two or even three missions a day. Altogether Air Marshal Trafford Leigh–Mallory
had some 11,322 airplanes available, including 3,266 fighters split about 65/35
between the US air forces and the Royal Air Force. Beginning in the evening of
June 5 and across the day of the 6th, waves of transports, gliders, bombers, and
fighters were a near-constant presence in the English and French skies, stretching
from large loops made by C-47 Dakotas to the west to drop paratroopers over*

*the Cotentin Peninsula to P-47 fighters protecting the approach to the invasion
fleet to the east. To help distinguish and identify the Allied planes, ground crews
painted participating aircraft with a special recognition pattern.*

*According to the OVERLORD plan, two waves of bombers would strike the
beaches. Beginning early in the morning, 1,136 Royal Air Force bombers would
blast German defenses up and down, dropping 5,853 tons of bombs, and then, an
hour before the invasion fleet hit the beaches at H-Hour, another wave of 1,083
American bombers would drop another 7,348 tons of explosives. Unfortunately,
though, that closely timed schedule meant that the final wave of American bombers
from the 8th Air Force were encouraged to wait an extra second or two before
dropping their bombs, to avoid hitting the incoming landing craft. That pause
rendered most of the last-minute bombing ineffective. Not a single bomb fell on
Omaha Beach that morning.*

**Flying Officer Douglas Gordon, Hawker-Typhoon pilot, No. 440 (City of Ottawa)
Squadron, Royal Canadian Air Force:** We knew something was about to be
screwed up when we saw the "erks" [ground crew] painting black-and-white
stripes on our kites [planes]. They looked like prison stripes.

**Lt. Charles Mohrle, P-47 pilot, 510th Squadron, 405th Fighter-Bomber Group:**
These broad stripes, alternating black and white, were intended to identify
us as friendly aircraft to the allied ground we were to fly over.

**Col. Joseph Harkiewicz, commander, 29th Troop Carrier Squadron, 313th Troop
Carrier Group:** It was pouring down rain, and we were directed to paint black
and white stripes on the wings and around the fuselage of the gooneys
[C-47s] and the gliders. Can you imagine that—in the rain? Like from
out of nowhere, cans and cans of paint, masking tape, and brushes were
pushed at us.

**Lt. Charles Mohrle:** The wake-up call came early on the morning of June
6th—about 3:45 a.m. Overhead, as we walked to headquarters for the mission
briefing, we could hear the steady drone of transport aircraft—lots of them.
And then a formation of DC-3's flew very low over our base and, through
the gloom, we could see that each was towing three gliders.

**Lt. Al Corry, bombardier, B-26 Marauder, 387th Bomb Group:** Everybody was real quiet that morning.

**Lt. Charles Mohrle:** A hard knot in the pit of my stomach accompanied the realization that this was the beginning of the invasion. I said a prayer for the guys in those gliders.

**1st Lt. James M. DeLong, pilot, B-26 Marauder, 387th Bomb Group:** By this date, I had participated in fifty-five missions over Europe, and with enough harrowing experiences to last me a lifetime, with the enemy flak and fighters, and about as bad at times, the weather. I was only 24.

**1st Lt. William J. Moriarty, B-26 Marauder, 556th Squadron, 387th Bomb Group, Chipping Onger, England:** We had been told in briefing that traffic would be one way and to continue across the Cherbourg peninsula, then turn right, fly around the tip of the peninsula and up to England. Under no circumstances were we to turn around. Otherwise, gunners on the ships below had orders to shoot us down. If you had mechanical trouble and could not keep up, drop out of the formation but continue to follow the traffic. As we left the target and flew inland across the peninsula, we could see the parachutes and the paratroops dotting the countryside.

**Sgt. Walter Peters, *Yank* magazine correspondent, with the 9th Air Force, aboard a Douglas A-20 Havoc:** For miles, you could see ships, like spots of pepper in a light soup.

**Group Captain Desmond Scott, Commander, No. 123 Wing, Royal New Zealand Air Force:** All along the fringe of the bay, as far as visibility would permit, I could see smoke, fire, and explosions. Inland some areas were completely smudged out by evil clouds of smoke. Underneath it, great flashes of fire would erupt and burst, like bolts of orange lightning. Normandy was like a huge, fire-rimmed boiling cauldron.

**Lt. Al Corry:** As we kept going further and further, I looked through my bomb sight and checked it and the map again, and there we were coming closer to a cloud layer. I told our pilot that the cloud layer was covering all the target area. I couldn't see a thing below that. "We're going to have to go down lower," I said. "I can't see the target! I can't bomb. I can't identify that bomb line on the ground! The cloud's too low." We finally agreed that we'd all go down. The other flights followed us.

**Sgt. Roger Lovelace, radio operator, B-26 Marauder, 553rd Bomb Squadron, 386th Bomb Group:** We broke up into flights of 6 and then we dropped closer and closer down towards our scheduled bombing altitude. Then we went into trails, which means one aircraft behind the other, and we're on our own. As we approached the beachhead, all of the action came into view again. One of the best views anyone could get of the invasion of Normandy had to be the one we were looking at. Eisenhower himself had no position to stand where he could see the view that I was privy to see. You could see people, tanks, and trucks running every which way on the ground. By now the first wave was just a couple hundred yards offshore, zig-zagging towards the beach.

**2nd Lt. J. K. Havener, copilot, B-26 Marauder, 497th Bomb Squadron, 344th Bomb Group:** Our mission was not to knock out the gun positions, but to stun the German gunners and infantry keeping them holed up and to create a network of ready-made foxholes which our troops could use once they gained a foothold on what was to become known as Utah Beach.

**Sgt. Roger Lovelace:** The bombardier shouted on the intercom, "Bombs away!" We turned off the shore line, gained altitude again, and flew over part of the invasion fleet. We even drew a few rounds of friendly fire from someone down there who couldn't identify us. They missed.

**Capt. Charles E. Harris, B-17 pilot, 418th Squadron, 100th Bomb Group:** The target for our C group was Ouistreham, a town near Caen. Our group was the last to drop at 0649 hours, just one minute before troops hit the beaches. The last item in briefings was always a time hack in which everyone synchronized their watches. A mission of the magnitude and complexity of these flown in England during World War II required split-second precision and timing.

**1st Lt. James M. DeLong:** Out over the French countryside, scattered everywhere, were parachutes and patches of huge crashed gliders. I don't believe I saw an undamaged one in the lot. We had a sickening feeling that things were not going well and it's just started.

**Lt. Gen. Omar Bradley, commander, First Army:** Not until later did we learn that most of the 13,000 bombs dropped by these heavies had cascaded harmlessly into the hedgerows three miles behind the coast. In bombing through the overcast, air had deliberately delayed its drop to lessen the danger of spillover on craft approaching the shore. This margin for safety had undermined the effectiveness of the heavy air mission. To the seasick infantry, bailing their craft as they wallowed through the surf, this failure in air bombing was to mean many more casualties upon Omaha Beach.

**2nd Lt. J. K. Havener:** As we left the scene of battle and headed back to base, I realized that in the space of a few short minutes, I had seen almost every type of modern warfare and had lived through it to come back to a second breakfast at 0800. We were lucky.

**Lt. Al Corry:** Everybody—all the ground crews, etc. were standing along the runways and hard stands, waiting for planes to come down. We taxied back to the hard stands, turned around, shot the engines off, and jumped out of the plane. The Red Cross gals were waiting with hot coffee and doughnuts. It felt good just to get back on the ground.

**Sgt. Michael N. Ingrisano, 37th Troop Carrier Squadron, 316th Troop Carrier Group:** I recall little about the flight home. At the debriefing by our intelligence officers, all I remember was the shot of scotch each of us was given to "calm our nerves." When I got back to my barracks which were across the street from the mess hall, I sat on my bed, pulled Eisenhower's message out of my flight suit, unfolded it and read it. On the front, upper right hand corner, I wrote: "June 6, 1944."

*         *         *

*With the bombing runs complete, the skies belonged to the fighters, who were tasked with protecting the invading forces both from the Luftwaffe in the sky and surprise attacks from the Kriegsmarine's E-boats or U-boats down below. Even as hundreds of planes marshaled in the sky, at all altitudes, they soon found themselves bored, just aerial spectators to the drama below. Months of punishing assaults had finally broken the German air force, and the Luftwaffe managed no organized resistance to the landings. The German air force launched only about a hundred sorties on D-Day, most little more than nuisance attacks; while several German fighters managed to surprise the Allies and strafe the beaches, incredibly, not a single bomb hit any of the five invasion beaches. Similarly, the also-battered German navy ended up presenting no meaningful threat.*

**Lt. Edward Giller, leader, 55th Fighter Group, 8th Air Force:** Because the whole 8th Air Force was going to be in this one area, it had to be organized. Therefore, with this in mind, it was decided that the P-38's, because of their distinctive shape, would be recognizable by the ground gunners, friendly ones, and presumably would not be fired upon. The P-47's and 51's, which looked somewhat like German aircraft, were therefore scheduled to stay away from the local beachhead, and the P-38's essentially had a high altitude foxhole, around 20,000 feet over the beaches.

**Lt. Charles Mohrle:** I can't remember a more disappointing assignment. All three squadrons of the 405th Group were to fly "area patrol." Each 4-ship flight was given a specific, rectangular-shaped area, about 60 miles long, to be patrolled from before dawn until after sundown. With these assigned patterns adjoining, our Group covered about 180 miles of coastline. We cruised at 12,000 feet, ten miles north of the shore of France, in constant contact with British radar.

Flying back and forth over the same stretch of water for four hours, watching for an enemy that never appeared, was tedious to say the least. But there was a compensating feature to our job on D-Day and the following 48 hours: We had a box-seat view of the greatest amphibious operation ever carried out.

**Lt. William Eldridge Satterwhite, P-38 pilot, 392nd Fighter Squadron, 367th Fighter Group:** The entire spectacle was awesome. Perhaps the greatest display of gunfire history has recorded was in progress throughout the early morning hours of D-Day.

**Lt. Jack Barensfeld, P-47 pilot, 377th Squadron, 362nd Fighter Group:** Back on the ground, our crew chiefs' faces I'll never forget, as they saw the tape over the muzzles of our guns were still in place. Our guns had never been fired. They were as surprised as we were. *Can this be the big show? What is going on?* This was our feeling. We couldn't have had such a placid sight-seeing mission as we'd had.

**Lt. Pierre Clostermann, Free French Forces, No. 602 Squadron:** Everybody was worn out. 602 carried out a sortie at 0355 hours, another at 9 o'clock, one at 12 o'clock, one at 1730 hours, and finally one at 2035. I took part in the last two. The Channel was angry and choppy and the smaller craft seemed to be making heavy weather of it. There were fires all along the coast.

**Gen. Dwight Eisenhower, Supreme Allied Commander, SHAEF:** During the 24 hours of 6 June, the Strategic Air Forces flew 5,309 sorties to drop 10,395 tons of bombs, while aircraft of the tactical forces flew a further 5,276 sorties.

**Lt. Charles Mohrle:** I specifically remember thinking that Hitler must have been mad to think that Germany could defeat a nation capable of filling the sea and sky with so much ordnance and man it.

# Heading Ashore at Utah

US troops head to shore during the early stage of the invasion at Utah.

*The* NEPTUNE *armada was in position, officially, at 2:29 a.m., when the USS* Bayfield *command ship lowered its anchor off Utah Beach in what was known as the "Transport Area." From there, over the horizon from the beach themselves, troops transferred to the craft that would carry them to shore. As dawn came to Normandy, they gathered into their designated boat teams and were lowered into landing craft—many recall climbing down rope ladders into small boats bucking in the rough seas as one of the more hazardous moments of the day. The loading process unfolded quickly, roughly an hour per troopship to fill its landing crafts, and the sea grew crowded with 233 large LSTs and 208 LCIs, as well as 768*

*smaller LCTs, and countless more British LCAs and American LCVPs—the*
*small, flimsy craft known as Higgins Boats. Many troops, loaded in landing craft*
*as far as 11 miles off the French coast, would spend two to four hours in the choppy*
*seas before hitting the beach. It was a long, slow, wet ride, with the beach barely*
*visible until the trip's halfway point.*

*The procedure at each beach was roughly the same: After minesweepers desig-*
*nated the area to be safe and destroyers, cruisers, and battleships from each beach's*
*"bombardment force" took up positions on either side of the beach, the invasion*
*force would move through designated boat lanes toward shore, guided by two*
*lead 173-foot patrol craft, supported by two LCCs—Landing Craft Control—*
*equipped specially with then-innovative radar to ensure their exact positioning.*
*There wasn't a moment to spare in the day's tight timetable: At Utah and Omaha,*
*a total of 26 assault waves were scheduled to land before noon. H-Hour differed*
*slightly from beach to beach, spread from 0630 on the US side to 0755 on the*
*British sector to address local tidal conditions.*

*Utah Beach, the second, westernmost beach added to the invasion plans by*
*Eisenhower in January, was strategically vital for the Americans, providing*
*ready access to the Cherbourg Peninsula and the possibility of seizing ports.*
*Fires along the shore started by Allied bombers and naval shelling obscured the*
*expected beach landmarks, which coupled with an unexpectedly strong tidal*
*current and Utah's lack of distinct geography—it was a long sandy stretch*
*backed by low grassy dunes—meant that the initial craft arriving at the beach*
*were thousands of yards from where they were originally supposed to be. (That*
*mistake, though, fortuitously delivered them to a relatively peaceful and easy*
*landing.)*

*The beach's three landing zones were known as Tare Green, Uncle Red, and*
*Victor. From there, the military's mission was to cross the few exit causeways—*
*the agricultural fields rear of the beach had been mostly flooded by the German*
*military—and link up with the paratroopers dropped earlier in the night. All*
*told, some 23,000 of mostly US forces from the VII Corps, composed of three*
*regiments from the 4th Infantry Division—the 8th Infantry, 12th Infantry, and*
*22nd Infantry—as well as the 359th Regimental Combat Team, from the 90th*
*Infantry Division, as well as other smaller units, were involved.*

**Top Secret "Bigot-Neptune" analysis, April 21, 1944:** "Utah" Beach, 9655 yards
long. Low lying and without distinctive terrain features, is composed of

compact gray sand between high and low water marks. . . . The beach is backed for its entire length by a masonry seawall, with the exception of a stretch of piling 210 yards in length. Behind the wall, from approximately the center of the beach and extending southward, sand dunes approximately 10 to 25 feet high extend inland nearly 150 yards. Inland of the entire beach area are inundated lowlands. Numerous exits in the form of ramps exist off the beach for its entire length. However, as these exits lead through gaps in the seawall, all of them have been blocked. Normally a good network of roads leading into the interior exists, but because of the inundated area, the interior can be reached only by three roads at present.

**Pvt. Clair R. Galdonik, Company A, 359th Infantry Regiment, 90th Division:** "Unique" was the code name for our 359th Infantry Regiment. The first password sign for D-Day was "thirsty victory," and an alternate one was "wagon wheel" because the Germans could not pronounce a "W."

**Seaman Joseph A. Dolan, radioman, USS *Bayfield* (APA-33):** The plan of D-Day was issued by the executive officer to all hands, and read as follows: "U.S.S. Bayfield. Plan of D-Day. 6 June 1944, Tuesday. 2400. Commissary Officer will send coffee and sandwiches to men at general quarters stations. 0030. Breakfast for both crews and troops on mess deck. Men must not go on deck. Use passage through compartments. 0030. Breakfast for troop officers in ward room. 0200 approximately. Anchor in transport area. Set condition one able. Lower all boats. Boats carry out orders. 1. Damage control in repair one and two, will see that no unauthorized persons go on deck and that complete darkened ship conditions prevailed throughout. When troops are ordered on deck, watch openings closely. 2. All hands will wear impregnated clothing and carry all equipment. 3. As soon as boats are lowered, prepare to debark troops and equipment promptly as LCM's and LCVP's come alongside. 4. Prepare to receive casualties. 5. As soon as boat teams have debarked, lower starboard and port accommodation ladders. 6. Food will be delivered at general quarters stations. 7. Prepare to execute all emergency orders promptly, calmly, and quietly." Signed by, G.A. Littlefield, Commander, U.S. Coast Guard, Executive Officer and distributed to Commanding Officer, Executive Officer, and all hands.

**Ens. Hans E. Bergner, assistant gunnery officer, USS *LST-282*:** At 2:42 A.M. on D-Day we anchored off Utah Beach. We had something brand new on board for this operation—an amazing aid to navigation known as LORAN. It gave us precise bearings and ranges on two different transmitting stations, so we could accurately fix the position of the transport area.

After we followed the minesweepers in and anchored, then the transports anchored in relation to the *LST-282*. We also carried demolition teams to destroy beach obstacles; they shoved off for the beach in our LCVPs at 2:46. Two of our six boats were swamped on the beach, but the officers and crews were recovered.

**Pfc. Ralph Della-Volpe, Company A, 87th Chemical Mortar Battalion, 4th Division:** From the rear, coming from England, we saw a row of airplanes and then another row of bombers and then another row of bombers and then another. They came and they covered the whole sky in perfect formation. They seemed to blot out the sky; you couldn't see the sky, it just seemed that way and the gray day combined with these massive bombers and the drone, made it a very, very dramatic sight to see.

**Lt. Cyrus C. Aydlett, U.S. Coast Guard, USS *Bayfield* (APA-33), from diary:** At times it looked as if a solid sheet of flame covers the entire area, especially when the bombers were making their run.

**Sgt. Jim McKee, Company K, 12th Infantry Regiment, 4th Division:** Our side was putting a lot more fire on that beach than the Germans were returning.

**Petty Officer Morton Block, signalman, *LCG-6*:** I was given sea duty aboard the gunfire support craft LCG-6, this amphibious ship built by the British on loan to the United States Navy was armed with two 5-inch guns, plus several 40-millimeter and 20-millimeter anti-aircraft. The ship was able to stay close to the beach.

**Maj. Ralph Ingersoll, Allied planning staff, attached to Task Force Raff, aboard an LCT bound for Utah Beach:** The trick about landing on UTAH was that the beach itself was hardly more than a long narrow spit of sand beyond which the surface of the ground dropped a few feet. In normal times, the sand spit kept the sea away and there were fields beyond in which cattle grazed; now, these fields glittered bright with water in the aerial photographs. The Germans had flooded them, and they made a shallow lake two miles wide. On Utah the first assault waves were to take the concrete pillboxes that were set in the dunes along the sea beach and then the amphibian tanks and the infantry—waist deep—were to cross this lake and fan out up the slopes beyond.

**Capt. James E. Arnold, Naval Officer in Charge (NOIC), Utah Beach:** German shore batteries recovering from the shock of surprise were returning the slugging salvos of the naval fire-support ships, raising great gouts of water as they plumbed for the correct range. They got it on the little *PC-1261*, the control vessel of Green Beach. She was standing broad on our starboard bow about three cable lengths when she took it.

**Lt. Cdr. Rency F. Sewell, Jr., commander, USS *PC-1261*:** The coastal batteries opened fire upon us; one shell seemed to hit about 30 yards off the starboard quarter. I knew immediately the next one would probably hit us, which it did. It hit us right in the starboard side, aft of midships. The ship immediately took a 20-degree list to starboard. We felt that we might be able to save it. However, two minutes later the ship took a 90-degree roll and order was given to abandon ship. All hands walked over the side as one would walk over a treadmill. There was very little confusion as we walked over the side of the ship and tried to get to their life rafts.

**Ens. Sam Grundfast, commander, *LCT-707*:** I didn't hear the explosion, but when I opened my eyes, the next thing I knew, I was underwater.

**Capt. James E. Arnold:** She had hit a mine, turning her completely over.

**Ens. Sam Grundfast:** I opened my eyes, I looked up, and I saw the surface of the water somewhere above my head, and I can only vividly remember paddling as fast as I could to reach the surface, which I obviously did. Were it not for the Mae West life jackets that I had everybody wear and tie up tight, I don't think I would be here today.

**Lt. Cdr. Rency F. Sewell, Jr.:** The water was very cold; in fact, I think that most of the men that were lost were lost by the coldness of the water. I, myself, was stiff from my shoulders down.

**Lt. Sims Gauthier, *LCC-60*:** These four LCTs with the DD tanks were going in all directions. They were only four boats, but they were trying to avoid running over men that were in the water. They wound up with no leader—it was just like geese flying in the flock when the leader is killed. We went to regroup and reorganize the LCTs, and brought them back into formation. Lt. Ricker decided that to make up time, if the DD tanks were to be of any use to the first wave going in, that instead of dispersing the tanks into the water at five thousand yards as planned, we would disperse them at three thousand yards. I went around with the loud-hailer to all the commanders of the DD tanks and gave them instructions.

**Brig. Gen. Theodore Roosevelt, Jr., Supernumerary General Officer, 4th Division, Letter to his wife, Eleanor, June 11, 1944:** We passed a capsized craft, some men clinging to it, others bobbing in the waves. As we peered over the gunwale the shore seemed nearer, but veiled as it was in the smoke and dust of the bombardment it was hard to make it out. Suddenly the beach appeared before us—a long stretch of sand studded with wire and obstacles.

**Capt. John P. McGirr, 65th Armored Field Artillery:** The noise was terrific as we neared the beach; but the scene changed quickly from an orderly line of boats knifing through the surf to—well, carnage. Anyone who tells you that Utah was a cakewalk is mistaken. One Higgins boat ahead of us completely disintegrated when hit by something from the shore. There were no survivors.

**Pvt. Clair R. Galdonik:** The ramp went down. Then something dreadful happened. A boy in my squad started crying and yelling that he could not leave the boat and begged to be left on the craft. I had to make a quick decision for the beach area was no place to hang around. I inflated my life jacket and grabbed his arm and pulled him into the water with me. I needed help so another soldier came to my aid and grabbed his other arm. We inflated his life jacket and got him going. The crying had not stopped, I felt so sorry for him, but it did make me forget my own fear as we headed for the beach.

**Pvt. Harper Colman, Company H, 8th Infantry Regiment, 4th Division:** The history books claim this was one of the easier landings. It did not seem good at the time. We went into the water more than waist-deep. Our first casualty was just behind me with a serious wound to the stomach. A second man, in front of me, stepped on a land mine. Our squad of six was down to four very early.

**Petty Officer Morton Block:** The waters began to get filled with wounded and dead. We spent hours picking up people in the water, and we kept them on the ship for as long as we could, then we proceeded to a hospital ship that was out further off the coast.

**Pfc. Joseph S. Blaylock, Sr., Baker Battery, 20th Field Artillery, 4th Division:** We'd got to I'd say about three or four hundred yards from the beach when the ramp went down and Lt. Fitzpatrick asked me to get off to see if I could feel any mines. I had learned to tread water in Black and Red Creek in Mississippi, so I got off and treaded water and told them no, there wasn't anything, no mines or anything, so to come on off. So twenty-five assault troops from the 101st Airborne Division came off, then next came the jeeps. The first one that went off went right down to the bottom; then the other two came off and proceeded on in toward shore. In the meantime I had lost my carbine, and I wondered what I was going to do for a gun when I got in. Anyway, I hung on to the back of the jeeps, kind of paddling and pushing the jeeps on in toward the shore. There were some 88s and some ack-ack and some mortar shells coming in, and as we got into the shore, the jeep proceeded on ahead toward the causeway. I ran up against a sand dune while we caught our breath a little bit.

**Pfc. Robert Gangewere, Headquarters Company, 90th Infantry Division:** The ramp went down in front and we got out. There were around 40 of us. We had to hold our stuff up in the air, and we were almost up to our necks in the water. I had to hold the bazooka over my head; I couldn't get salt water in it. I carried a rifle as well, over one shoulder.

**Pvt. Bruce Bradley, radio operator, B Battery, 29th Field Artillery Battalion:**
We had to keep our heads down. I had been tired from all the tension, but I was not tired anymore. The noise of the shelling and counterfire was much louder, then there was a deafening blast and we were thrown down or knocked sideways. We had been hit by a shell. The coxswain was gone, the ramp was down, the boat was sinking. I dog-paddled toward shore until my feet hit sand.

**Pfc. Robert Gangewere:** It took maybe 20 minutes to get to the beach, with all the stuff you had to carry and of course you had to watch for the bodies. You couldn't make a straight run for it. You had to wade your way in. And the Germans had a lot of obstacles in the water. When I got in, I laid down on the dry sand. I had to have a little break.

**Capt. George Mabry, operations officer, 2nd Battalion, 8th Infantry Regiment, 4th Division:** We'd been trained that once you hit the beach, you run. Ahead of me was a man carrying ammunition, which he was to drop at the seawall for Company H's mortars. A round came in and hit the top of his head; his rounds detonated also, and this man's body completely disappeared. I felt something hit me on my thigh; it was his thumb. It was the only discernible part of a human being you could see.

**Sgt. J. D. "Jerry" Salinger, Counter Intelligence Corps, 4th Infantry Division:** You never really get the smell of burned flesh out of your nose entirely, no matter how long you live.*

**2nd Lt. John L. Ahearn, commander, Company C, 70th Tank Battalion, 6th Armored Group:** My tanks did not have flotation gear, but we had been weatherized, and we were able to get into five or six feet of water. The boats brought us in on the beach, and we got off in 5 or 6 feet of water, as I recall.

---

* As he landed on Utah Beach in the second wave, Salinger had in his backpack six short stories about a family known as the Caulfields, the pieces of which would grow into the manuscript known as *Catcher in the Rye*. Later that month, amid 26 straight days in combat during the Normandy campaign—a bloody toll that would reduce his regiment from 3,080 men to just 1,130—he sent a postcard to his mentor saying he was "too busy to go on with the book right now."

Owen Gavigan, because his tank was in front, was the first tank to land on Utah Beach, and mine was the second.

**Brig. Gen. Theodore Roosevelt, Jr., letter to his wife, Eleanor, June 11, 1944:** With a crunch we grounded, the ramp was lowered, and we jumped into water waist-deep and started for the shore. We splashed and floundered through some hundred yards of water while German salvos fell. Men dropped, some silent, some screaming. Up the 400 yards of beach we ran—Grandfather puffed a bit—then we reached the seawall. The company CO with whom I was, [Capt. Howard] Lees [of Company E], a great tower of a man, led his troops splendidly. He with his men started into the dunes to attack the German strongpoints.

**Message from Rear Adm. Don Moon, commander, Task Force O, sent at 8 a.m.:** NAVSITREP1: To Naval Commander Western Task Force. Force U arrived transport area without incident. Complete surprise achieved. No enemy attack. First wave despatched to beach as scheduled.

*Upon arriving onshore, confused—and often soaking wet—troops tried to figure out where they were and what they should do next as the beach, parts of which were still under fire from German positions, filled up around them with new units and vehicles. As it turned out, many units were far away from where they were supposed to land. The error would save lives.*

**Lt. Edwin Gale, deputy commander, _LCT-853_:** The skipper kept asking me if we were headed into the right part of the beach, and I was totally unable to see anything because of the smoke, but in any event if I could have seen it would have been very confusing because as it turned out we landed well to the left of where we were intended to land. We did not know even when we landed that morning that we were not in the correct place.

**2nd Lt. John L. Ahearn:** I saw General Teddy Roosevelt on the beach, and got out of my tank and reported to him, and told him who I was and what my mission was. He told me to go ahead, the lateral parts of the beach, both north and south, and to take care and to get inland as fast as we could. I directed my second in command and told him to take half of the tanks and proceed up to the north, and I would proceed to the south.

**Brig. Gen. Theodore Roosevelt, Jr., letter to his wife, Eleanor, June 11, 1944:** There was a house by the seawall where none should have been were we in the right place. It was imperative that I should find out where we were in order to set the maneuver. I scrambled up on the dunes and was lucky in finding a windmill which I recognized. We'd been put ashore a mile too far to the south.

**Petty Officer Dennis Shryock, frogman, Naval Combat Demolitions Unit:** We moved from obstacle to obstacle, lacing each with sixty pounds of explosives, working off data supplied by the French Resistance and aerial photos. We were lucky—on Utah our demolition teams suffered only six dead and eleven injured, but nearly all on Omaha became casualties. That's where thirty-one of my buddies died and sixty were injured.

**Col. Eugene Caffey, deputy commander, 1st Engineer Special Brigade:** I undertook to get word to the Navy that we were completely out of position and induce them to continue the landing at the place where we were instead of trying to conform to the original plan.

**Lt. Edwin Gale:** It wasn't till much later that we realized that no one on Utah Beach had landed in the correct place—and that it was a good thing that we didn't. There was considerable German gunfire from the right, or westward, part of the beach and if we would have been closer to the Germans it would have been worse than it was.

**Pfc. Joseph S. Blaylock, Sr.:** General Roosevelt said, "Men, you've landed about two thousand yards south of where you were supposed to have landed. We will start the war from here."

*"So that's what it's like to be hit"*

# Naval Forces at Utah

Coast Guard cutters and rescue ships pulled
hundreds of soldiers and sailors from the Channel.

*The naval bombardment was one of the most dramatic moments of the day at Utah Beach, as dozens of giant guns aboard battleships, cruisers, destroyers, and gunboats opened fire, while specially designed landing craft converted to carry arsenals of thousands of rockets let loose their own fire toward the beach. The rate of fire that morning of the destroyers, cruisers, battleships, and other naval craft was all but unequaled, a feat of coordination and detailed planning, one that required every element to exceed expectations, and that surprised participants and observers alike. Later, many involved would remember the pluck of the agile destroyers—many of which came in close to shore and made combat with the German defenders personal with their five-inch guns. Not all of the destroyers, though, would survive the day.*

**Grant G. Gullickson, chief machinist's mate, USS *Corry* (DD-463):** On June 6 we were assigned to lead the first wave of boats into Utah Beach. I had been promoted to chief machinist's mate and was in charge of the forward engine room on the USS *Corry*.

**Matt Jayich, boatswain's mate, USS *Corry*:** Very early on the morning of June 6, 1944, as I looked out of Number 4 gun, which was my battle station, as a shellman, I saw the most beautiful sight I ever was to see in my life. There in the sky were, I guess, thousands of airplanes of all kinds, flying to France to drop their bombs to stop that madman Hitler and his armies. I was never in my life prouder than at that moment, to be an American, to be a sailor on an American man-o-war in the greatest task force in the world with the feeling that we were the best and we would win this war.

**Lt. Cdr. George Dewey Hoffman, commander, USS *Corry*:** We began to pound our assigned targets, which were German pillboxes and machine gun positions. We eliminated a couple of them, and then another battery opened fire on us. The visibility was improving, which meant that we would have a better chance to get him, and that he would have a better chance to get us. We increased our rate of fire. Empty powder tanks came pouring out of turrets.

**Matt Jayich:** When we began firing, I threw those shells in as fast as I could. Later I found out that our gun put out 155 shells. I don't know how or who counted them but that was the word I got.

**Chief Petty Officer Francis "Mac" McKernon, radio technician, USS *Corry*:** The Nazis had taken over a Utah Beach hotel for use as one of their observation posts. The *Corry*'s guns homed in on the hotel and blew it to smithereens—an observation post no more.

**Ens. Jake Henson, USS *Corry*:** As most of the B-25s flew past we noticed there were two B-26 bombers that broke off and flew out to sea about 1000 yards, at which point they made a sharp left turn and started laying a smoke screen. They screened all the hundreds of ships except the *Corry* and perhaps one or two others.

**Lt. Paul N. Garay, USS *Corry*:** It looked just like a regular curtain, but it was all smoke. The only trouble was, they didn't go to where the *Corry* was. The smoke went behind her. We were sitting out in front, fully exposed. One of the planes that had been spreading the smoke went into the water. Another was blown out of the air.

**Chief Petty Officer Francis "Mac" McKernon:** As the action increased, and big ones from the many shore batteries began exploding all around us, erupting towering plumes of water taller than the *Corry*'s mast, to say that we felt "scared" was to put things mildly.

**Lt. Cdr. John R. Blackburn, Sky Control, USS *Quincy* (CA-71):** The *Corry* was having a duel with a shore battery to the northwest of our target. I saw the splashes falling around the little destroyer and saw her blazing back with grim determination. Suddenly, her stern hit a moored enemy mine.

**Dr. Howard Andersen, medical officer, USS *Corry*:** We had been hit by a few shells with no serious damage when, at 0633, there was a tremendous explosion beneath me. I was in the process of helping a sailor who had a large gash in his left shoulder from shrapnel. I was thrown across the wardroom to the opposite side, but was not significantly hurt.

**Capt. Robert Beeman, USS *Corry*:** Suddenly I was in midair, flying some ten or fifteen feet down the deck. I had a brief struggle to regain my balance, at the same time trying to dodge a shower of miscellaneous debris coming down from the flying bridge. I had several instantaneous impressions. My first was, *So that's what it's like to be hit.* At the same time, I saw that my phones and helmet had been blown off my head and thrown aft.

**Grant G. Gullickson:** The floor plates came loose, the lights went out, and steam filled the space. It was total darkness, with severely hot and choking steam everywhere.

**Lt. Paul N. Garay:** Destroyers are not very strong ships, they're fairly light. When we ran into this mine it broke the back of the ship.

**Bill Beat, radio technician, 2nd class, USS *Corry*:** I, my chair, the desk, file cabinets and everything in the room were thrown up into the air. After a few blank minutes, B.J. Petersen stuck his head in the door and said, "Are you alright?" I was too dazed to know.

**Lt. Paul N. Garay:** I was on damage control. A couple of the sailors brought what is called a handybilly, a little gasoline powered pump. They dropped the suction pipe down into the crack in the ship and started trying to pump it out. But as fast as they were pumping the water out, it was coming in through the rest of the crack.

**Elmer Maurer, machinist's mate, 1st class, USS *Corry*:** As I tried to turn the hatch wheel, it would not turn. The blast had jammed it. It was askew with about an inch opening on the one side. I stuck my fingers through the opening and yelled at the top of my voice. Fortunately I was heard. Men on deck secured a pry bar and forced the hatch open.

**Chief Petty Officer Francis "Mac" McKernon:** With the *Corry* starting to jack-knife into a "V," I ran back to the manual steering hatch at the stern and yelled to the men below, "Pass the word! Prepare to abandon ship! Prepare to abandon ship! Everybody out!"

**Bill Beat:** There was orderly confusion, but no panic. Everyone on deck seemed to be busy getting injured people into lifeboats and helping ship-mates that needed help.

**Dr. Howard Andersen:** I was the physician on board and my two corps-men joined me amid ship where we splinted major fractures and carried men who had been badly burned by super-heated steam from boilers and burning oil. We put all of them into a life boat—all within about ten minutes before the ship sank. I was wading in water up to my knees before leaving.

**Lt. Paul N. Garay:** As the ship was going down, with water coming up over the main deck, there was a lot to take care of. The captain was right next to me. He was getting ready to go over the side. I looked at him and said, "Captain, you'd better take your shoes off, you'll be able to swim better." So he did.

**Lt. Cdr. George Dewey Hoffman:** We got all the men over and, then, I stepped off into the water from the main deck and all this time the ship was being rather heavily shelled; in fact, probably the majority of the casualties occurred in the water, for as late as an hour and a half after the ship had been sunk the batteries continued to shell the men in the water.

**Ens. Mort Rubin, combat information center officer, USS *Corry*:** The step overboard was a leap over a cliff, though the water was only inches below. The icy water woke me up in a hurry.

**Elmer Maurer:** Once in the water I and the others took off swimming away from the ship, trying to make it out to the ships on the outer firing line. The going was very difficult. Headway was out of the question due to the tide and roughness of the Channel. It was a most difficult time—with the cold sea, the firing of shells at us in the water and men being wounded—a very, very bad experience.

**Everett Dale Howard, quartermaster, 1st class, USS *Corry* (DD-463):** I guess I was the last one to see Lt. Bensman alive since he was hit with a piece of shrapnel right before my eyes. I was hanging onto a float and he swam up to me and said, "How are you doing, Howard?" and about that time a piece of shrapnel took the top of his head off. He just rolled back into the water. Of the 19 officers and 244 men on board, 24 were killed or trapped in the vessel and many more wounded, but survived.

**Elmer Maurer:** The first ship that came into the area was the *USS Fitch (DD-462)*. It dropped its whale boat and gig. What a welcome sight.

**Grant G. Gullickson:** The *Fitch* people reached over the side and some literally came down and dragged us out of the water and brought us aboard. Later we were transferred to the *USS Barnett*, a troop transport that was loaded with the bodies of sailors, soldiers, airmen, and the wounded, plus survivors of sunken ships. On this ship was Chief Rouinsky, "Big Chief," of the forward fire room. He had steam burns over 99 percent of his body. We tended to him and he could talk a little, but the burns were too much. He passed away the next day. We were off loaded in England and, in time, were transferred back to the States.

*Among the massive 865-ship armada off Utah, there were battleships, cruisers, destroyers, and troopships off the assault beaches—even a lone Dutch naval gunboat—and a fleet of hundreds of smaller craft, including kitchen ships specially designed to feed personnel whose own craft didn't have galley facilities, rescue boats, and small PT boats, fast torpedo motorboats like the German E-boats, primarily used for quick strikes, that on D-Day were tasked with rescue missions. Their presence, while not focused on direct combat, was invaluable; 10 Coast Guard rescue cutters and 13 PTs were responsible for saving more than 400 soldiers and sailors who ended up in the water. Over the course of the day, another of those 83-foot cutters, CGC-16, known as "Homing Pigeon," was responsible alone for saving 126 personnel.*

**Carter Barber, USCG combat correspondent, aboard USCG *Rescue Cutter 16*:** The cutter had just made a round trip to a transport standing out in the harbor mouth, to discharge some ninety casualties picked up earlier this morning when she saw a stricken LCT which was slowly capsizing as it sank, and dashed to the aid of the stranded personnel. On the decks of the LCT over thirty men were trapped, including a wounded man with nearly severed legs, dangling only by pieces of flesh, who was unable to leave his ship. When the rescue cutter was skillfully maneuvered under the slowly lowering side of the LCT, all the other men were safely brought aboard the smaller craft, except for the wounded sailor. When the sailor's plight became apparent, Arthur Burkhard, Jr., a member of the cutter's crew, jumped over the side of the rescue cutter, rushed to the wounded man's side, and helped to secure a line around him.

**Arthur Burkhard, Jr., coxswain, USCG *Rescue Cutter 16*:** The man helped me get the line around him. He was the bravest man that we picked up. He was unable to talk because of weakness, but he managed to keep a grin on his face. Even when we were cutting his clothes off him to administer morphine when we saw that his two legs were severed above the knees, he kept himself under control, and even winked at us.

**Carter Barber:** Once the wounded sailor had the line secured about him, Burkhard unsuccessfully tried to lower him from the settling LCT to the smaller rescue cutter. The LCT's starboard side was dropping lower and lower as the whole ship began to capsize, and it was impossible for the skipper to keep his craft under the LCT. The only alternative was for Burkhard to throw the wounded man off the LCT deck into the water, where he could be pulled aboard the rescue craft.

**Arthur Burkhard, Jr.:** I never saw anyone so game as that man. I hated to throw such a badly wounded man into the water, but that was the only way I could get him to safety. But he helped himself, and pulled himself hand-over-hand up the side of our boat when our fellows had towed him to the boat's side.

**Carter Barber:** Once his charge was aboard, Burkhard himself had to plunge into the water and make his way back to his ship. Although he couldn't swim himself, he was dragged aboard by his mates.

**Arthur Burkhard, Jr.:** I've got a brother in the Navy myself, and figured that he might be the man aboard the sinking LCT. So the fact that I couldn't swim didn't stop me.

**Carter Barber:** No more than two minutes after Burkhard and the casualties were taken aboard the rescue cutter and the boat had left the LCT, the burning ship completely turned turtle and disappeared from sight.

*Burkhard, the cutter's commander Lt. (jg) R. V. McPhail, and the rest of the 15-man cutter crew all received the Navy and Marine Corps Medal for their "gallant action" and heroism that morning.*

*"Just weapons and ammo. Leave everything else here."*

# The Second Wave at Utah

The 8th Infantry Regiment move over the seawall
and crest of the hill at Utah Beach.

*By 9:45 a.m., some fifteen different assault waves had landed on the sandy shores of Normandy; by midday, major troopships offshore, like HMS* Empire Gauntlet, USS Dickman, *and USS* Barnett, *had emptied and begun their return trip to England. Simultaneously, the arriving and advancing infantry and tanks had met up with units of the paratroopers and secured a meaningful beachhead. By day's end, Utah would receive 21,328 troops, 1,742 vehicles, and 1,742 tons of weapons and supplies.*

*One of the most dramatic and consequential actions for Utah Beach came inland just as the landing force started to move off the beach and up the causeways. Easy Company, 2nd Battalion, 506th Parachute Infantry—the unit that would be immortalized in Stephen Ambrose's* Band of Brothers *and the later TV series and which had landed overnight in the hedgerows behind the beach and already spent the night fighting and ambushing German positions—was charged with silencing a four-gun German battery of 105mm artillery, firing down what the Allied forces called Causeway #20. Their commander, 1st Lt. Richard "Dick" Winters, was able to round up just 13 men for the mission, including Sgt. Bill Guarnere, who had just learned on June 5 that his brother had been killed in action fighting in Italy.*

**S.Sgt. C. Carwood Lipton, platoon sergeant, Company E, 506th Parachute Infantry Regiment, 101st Airborne:** By this time in E Company, we had two officers and 11 men, a total of 13. By about 8:00, which was H hour when the assault on the beaches and the beach landings from the channel began, we were close to Sainte-Marie-du-Mont. The column stopped at a small village, that we learned later was called Le Grand Chemin, and Lt. Winters was called to the Headquarters Group. He returned in a few minutes to tell us there was a German Battery of four 105 mm guns in positions off the road to the right, and E Company, all 13 of us, was to capture the guns and knock them out.

**Pvt. Don Malarkey, Company E, 506th Parachute Infantry Regiment, 101st Airborne:** The German guns were about two hundred yards up ahead, positioned opposite a large French farmhouse that, we'd later learn, was called Brécourt Manor, about five miles inland. The farm wasn't a nice rectangular block; instead it had half-a-dozen angles to it, flanked by hedgerows.

**1st Lt. Richard "Dick" Winters, Company E, 506th Parachute Infantry Regiment, 101st Airborne:** I crawled out there and got close enough to see where this position was. I noticed, *That's a trench up there—that's a connecting trench.* When you run into a position like that, if you've studied your lesson, the way to attack it is from the flank. Don't take the whole thing on at once. Get in the trench on one of the flanks and then you can take them on one at a time. That's exactly what we did.

**S.Sgt. C. Carwood Lipton:** He outlined his attack plan to us. Two of our men had machine guns. They and two riflemen were to form a base of fire into the gun positions from positions to the right of the road. One of the other E Company men, Mike Ranney, and I were to move quickly out along a tree line to the right of the gun positions and put flanking fire into them. Lt. Compton and two men were to attack into the positions from the left front. The other men, with Lt. Winters, would make a frontal assault into the enemy positions.

**Pvt. Don Malarkey:** "Just weapons and ammo," he said. "Leave everything else here."

**2nd Lt. Lynn "Buck" Compton, Company E, 506th Parachute Infantry Regiment, 101st Airborne:** We put this thing together by ear. With our machine gunners laying down fire over my head, I worked my way across the field on my belly. I never knew how many German guns we were supposed to take out—I couldn't tell you if there were one or four or twenty.

**S.Sgt. C. Carwood Lipton:** When Ranney and I got out to our position to the right along that tree line, we found that heavy brush and ground cover prevented us from seeing into the gun positions, so I decided to climb into the trees. It gave me a ringside seat, looking right down into the German positions that were only about 75 yards away and I could see about 15 of the Germans, some in prepared positions and some prone in the open, all of them firing towards the frontal attack.

**Pvt. Don Malarkey:** I could see two Germans down the trench, firing a machine gun. I pulled a grenade and threw it, but meanwhile, someone—Compton, Winters, maybe both—had opened fire and the soldiers went down.

**S.Sgt. C. Carwood Lipton:** I continued firing as fast as I could shift my position from my shaky perch in the branches. It was easy to pick off the men in prone positions in the open, but I couldn't be sure how many hits I got on the men in the trenches and foxholes. Then I saw Bill Guarnere and Lt. Compton running into the German positions throwing grenades as they went.

**Sgt. Bill Guarnere, Company E, 506th Parachute Infantry Regiment, 101st Airborne:** The Germans ran like hell down the trench in the other direction. Winters and the other guys were right behind us, and all of us started lobbing grenades and shooting everything we had. Tossing grenades and attacking—it was stupid, but we did it so quick, so fast, they thought an entire company was attacking. We caught them with their pants down.

**Pvt. Don Malarkey:** I eyed the first big gun, scrambled out of the trench and headed toward it, spraying the area with automatic-weapons fire. I tucked up under the gun, firing and being fired upon.

**2nd Lt. Lynn "Buck" Compton:** A big tall kid [Pfc. John Hall] came down the trench and ran by me. He had served as a waiter in the officers' mess, where I knew him, but he wasn't in my platoon and I didn't know his name. From the trench, I saw him spin around and sprint back toward me. He took a bullet in the back and collapsed in front of me, dead.

**Pvt. Don Malarkey:** I spotted a dead German soldier out in the open. I could see he had a case on his hip, which I figured was probably holding a nice German Luger. I needed a souvenir. Now seemed to be my chance. It made no sense, of course, but I bolted for the dead German soldier. "Malarkey you idiot," I heard Winters yell from the trench. I slid in, confirmed he was dead, and reached for what I thought was a Luger. Instead, it was some gun-sighting device. *Damn!*

**1st Lt. Richard "Dick" Winters:** Leaving three men at the first gun to maintain supporting fire, we then charged the next position with grenades and lots of yelling and firing.

**S.Sgt. C. Carwood Lipton:** The Germans who hadn't been hit pulled out and moved back towards a far tree line on the other side of the clearing. About that time, they saw me and apparently Germans already in the far tree line saw me, and they all opened up on me. Bullets were cracking and clipping branches all around me, but I scrambled down without a scratch.

**Pvt. Don Malarkey:** Those machine guns opened fire like a late-spring hailstorm back in Oregon. A German machine gun sounds terrifying.

Ours went *put-put-put*. Theirs sounded like tearing of a piece of paper. *Riiiiiiiiiiiip.*

**1st Lt. Richard "Dick" Winters:** We took the [third] gun position, capturing six prisoners in the process. As the German soldiers advanced toward us down the connecting trench with their hands over their heads, they called, "No make me dead!" I sent all six back to headquarters and asked for additional ammunition and men. Finally I spotted Captain Hester coming forward. Hester informed me Lt. Ronald C. Speirs of D Company was bringing five men forward.

**Pvt. Don Malarkey:** Winters wanted me on the machine gun between the first and second German guns. I fired that gun for almost an hour, shooting at German positions on the farm road along Brécourt Manor. As we left, I threw a fragmentation grenade down the barrel of the first gun to put it out of commission.

**1st Lt. Richard "Dick" Winters:** Speirs came forward and led the assault on the [final, fourth] battery. Guarnere fought like a man possessed.

**Sgt. Bill Guarnere:** I killed every German I could.

**1st Lt. Richard "Dick" Winters:** In all, we had suffered four dead, six wounded, and we had inflicted fifteen dead and twelve captured on the enemy. About three hours had passed since I had first received the order to dispose of the battery.

**S. Sgt. C. Carwood Lipton:** The fortune of war was with us, I would say, on this action. We attacked those guns just as the beach landings were getting under way.

*Winters would receive the Distinguished Service Cross for his assault that morning, and of the rest of the 13-person team, four received Silver Stars, including Compton and Guarnere, and eight, including Lipton and Malarkey, the Bronze Star.*

\*           \*           \*

*With light resistance in the unintended landing zone on Utah Beach, supplies and follow-on waves continued to arrive at the shoreline, and infantry and tanks were quickly able to move forward and off the beach. There, along the dunes and hedgerows inland—and still under fire from German artillery—they confronted the minefields that served as the second line of defense for the Germans. Ultimately, it would take days to seize or destroy the in-shore German batteries shelling the beach.*

**Sgt. Jim McKee, Company K, 12th Infantry Regiment, 4th Division:** We landed on Utah about 10:30 in the morning, walked down the twin gangplanks at the bow, hardly got our boots wet. The beach had already been swept of mines and obstacles. The Germans had been driven from the beach, and the seawall had been breached to let vehicles reach the causeway exits from the beach. German artillery was firing on Utah from inland batteries, and our ships were answering this fire. Battleship shells flew overhead like freight trains, and I actually saw the shells.

**Pvt. Herschel W. Peterson, 286th Joint Assault Signal Company, 531st Engineer Shore Regiment:** We made a dash to cover—artillery shells were falling all around us. Many of them were duds. One fell right beside me and didn't explode. I was face down in the sand and nothing happened. I jumped up and ran again.

**Pvt. Clair R. Galdonik, Company A, 359th Infantry Regiment, 90th Division:** The beach area had taken its toll from enemy shelling. Tanks and trucks were gutted and burning but only a few dead Americans were there. It shook me up. Just a short while ago, they were among the living. I moved away from the beach area just as fast as my legs would move.

**Col. Eugene Caffey, deputy commander, 1st Engineer Special Brigade:** One thing that had my attention all of D-Day while Utah Beach was under double enfilade artillery fire, which kept the air fairly full of scrap iron, was the way in which the bulldozer drivers went about their work with complete nonchalance. All during that long day they drove back and forth along the beach assisting in dragging out drowned artillery and vehicles, in shoving off landing craft, and in grading out rough roads and trails. They were remarkable people.

**2nd Lt. John L. Ahearn, commander, Company C, 70th Tank Battalion, 6th Armored Group:** At this time I was leading seven tanks. We proceeded southward, trying to find an opening off the beach. When we got inside the seawall, we proceeded laterally between the seawall and the road, where we saw a number of infantrymen from the 2nd Battalion of the 8th Division who were at this time proceeding northward. As we looked, it became evident to us that there was another strongpoint of the Germans. I had our tanks fire some shells into it. A number of—as it turned out to be, impressed—soldiers, who were not really of German nationality, came out with their hands in the air and began running towards us. I dismounted the tank to take them as prisoners, and we delivered these thirty or so odd prisoners to the infantry. After doing this, we again proceeded southward, to where we came across a country road leading to the town of Pouppeville.

At this juncture, I told Lt. Tighe, who was one of my junior officers and who was commanding the platoon with which I had associated myself, for him to proceed inward, and that I would, along with a couple of other tanks, continue to proceed down this rather narrow road, across the dunes and across the hedgerows to see if there was any further strongpoints that we might assault.

**Maj. Ralph Ingersoll, Allied planning staff, attached to Task Force Raff:** Somewhere back in those hills there were the American airborne troops who, if they had not been lost in the drop, would need our tanks intact.

**2nd Lt. John L. Ahearn:** Shortly after this, as my tank proceeded down this small lane, the tank hit a land mine, and the front left bogie of the tank was blown, and we, of course, were immobilized. I proceeded on foot to cross over to go down the land, crossing over several hedgerows, to see if there was anything I could view that we might take a look at.

**Seaman First Class Martin Fred Gutekunst, signalman, 2nd Beach Battalion, Naval Construction Battalions (SeaBees):** We could see many German gun emplacements protected by their concrete walls and roofs. These were placed for miles along the seawall. Inside the bunkers, they had scenery painted along the walls that appeared to represent the area that you would look at if you were outside. They had narrow slots through which they could look and do their shooting.

**2nd Lt. John L. Ahearn:** I heard cries for help, and looking toward the beach, I saw three figures who I surmised were paratroopers and had been injured. I returned to the tank and got the rather large first aid kit that we carried, and came back. When I saw a break in the hedgerow, I was going to try to get as close to them as I possibly could. While I was standing there contemplating my next move, a personnel mine went off under me. The mine explosion threw me into the bank of the hedgerows, and I was unconscious for a while.

**T/4 Anthony Zampiello, Company C, 70th Tank Battalion, 6th Armored Group:** Lt. Ahearn was seriously wounded by mines to the extent of losing one of his feet and possibly the other. When we saw what had happened, we ran to Lt. Ahearn's assistance, but he ordered us not to venture near him, asking instead for a rope with which to pull him to safety.

**2nd Lt. John L. Ahearn:** Two of my crew, Sergeant Zampiello and Corporal Beard, came out to take a look. It was hard to find me, because I had rolled up against the embankment, but when they did, I cautioned them not to come over, because of the presence of mines. Anyway, they went back to the tank and got a long rope, and threw the rope to me, and then dragged me out from over the hedgerow.

**Lt. Elliot L. Richardson, medical platoon commander, 12th Regimental Combat Team, 4th Infantry Division:** The first hard thing I had to do after my unit landed on D-Day—a soldier [John Ahearn] with his foot blown off by an antipersonnel mine was lying in a patch of barbed wire just back of the dune line. He was in agonizing pain. Someone had to get to him. I stepped carefully across the barbed wire, picked up the wounded soldier, and retraced my steps. All I could do was put down one foot after another, hoping each time that nothing would go off.

**T/4 Anthony Zampiello:** When he was rescued, [Ahearn] encouraged us by saying, "We must get in there and take chances, otherwise we'll never get anywhere."*

*Given how the few narrow causeways limited egress from the beaches, many arriving troops and units were forced to wade across the adjacent fields that had been flooded by the German military—a slow, wet crossing of a mile of man-made marsh that took many more than an hour to cross. From there, they journeyed up to the neighboring towns like Sainte-Mère-Église, Sainte-Marie-du-Mont, and Saint-Germain-de-Varreville.*

**Sgt. Jim McKee:** After climbing the seawall and crossing the mined dunes behind it, we waded knee-deep or waist-deep or neck-deep across a good mile of marshland or pasture that Rommel had ordered to be flooded. Buddies with toggle ropes paired up.

**Col. Russell "Red" Reeder, Commander, 12th Infantry Regiment, 4th Division:** I gave an arm signal and 3,000 heavily burdened infantrymen walked into the manmade lake. When I saw non-swimmers near me in the lake struggling to go forward, hanging on to their weapons and equipment, I knew that we would win the war.

**Maj. Gerden Johnson, executive officer, 1st Battalion, 12th Infantry Regiment, 4th Division:** Every man followed, the first sergeant directly behind querying in a low voice, "What about mines?" Every field was surrounded by fences on which were hung white signs with red letters: "Achtung! Minen!" And for no reason at all except my own fear I said, "There aren't any mines here."

**Sgt. Jim McKee:** One buddy would hold the toggle while the other wrapped the noose around his chest. If either stepped into an underwater ditch his

---

* The U.S. Army awarded Ahearn the Distinguished Service Cross; Zampiello and gunner Pvt. Felix Beard were awarded Silver Stars. It was Beard's second Silver Star. Richardson, who would go on to be Richard Nixon's attorney general, later said that this minefield rescue was the only moment of his life that compared to the stress of the Saturday Night Massacre in October 1973.

flotation gear would keep him afloat while his buddy pulled him to the next patch of higher ground. Other men roped themselves together like mountain climbers.

**Sgt. Clifford Sorenson:** I was so angry. The Navy had tried to drown me at the beach, and now the Army was trying to drown me in the flooded area. I was more mad at our side than I was at the Germans, because the Germans hadn't done anything to me yet.

*One of the morning's first missions was to link up the paratroopers inland and the arriving infantry flowing off the beach.*

**2nd Lt. Eugene Bierre, 50Ist Parachute Infantry Regiment, 10Ist Airborne Headquarters:** After taking the village [of Pouppeville], General Taylor ordered me to take a patrol and go and make contact with the soldiers coming from the beach. Some Germans had been reported seen on the road heading towards the beach. I took eight men and went along a hedgerow about 50 yards to the east of the road. We got to a place where there was no more cover and started to head back to the road, which seemed to be clear.

**Capt. George Mabry, operations officer, 2nd Battalion, 8th Infantry Regiment, 4th Division:** I pulled out my square of orange cloth and hoisted it on a stick over my head. I spotted a reply: an orange flag waved back and forth from a spot on the other side of the bridge. It had to be the paratroopers. [Moments later,] I heard a noise in front of me and looked up. An airborne soldier jumped over a hedgerow with his rifle at the ready. The soldier was a member of the 101st Airborne.

**2nd Lt. Eugene Bierre:** The firing stopped, and we could see the troops starting to come up the road. When they got to a bridge, about six Germans came out with their hands up and surrendered. I went to the road and met a Captain Mabry.

**Capt. George Mabry:** He told me that Gen. Maxwell Taylor, commanding general of the 101st, was [nearby] and would surely be glad to see me.

**2nd Lt. Eugene Bierre:** I recorded on my watch the time that I met him. I think that it was 11:10 or 11:12 A.M. I brought Captain Mabry to General Taylor who made a notation in his records of the time that we arrived at his headquarters.

**Capt. George Mabry:** I saluted and we shook hands.*

---

* Mabry, ultimately, would receive the Distinguished Service Cross, the nation's second-highest award for extraordinary heroism, for his actions on D-Day. Later, for his combat in the Hürtgen Forest in November 1944, he would receive the Medal of Honor, the highest honor.

*"The most fantastic thing that happened in the war"*

# The Rangers at Pointe du Hoc

The Rangers at Pointe du Hoc faced a quick,
steep climb to reach the German gun emplacements.

*Between Utah and Omaha Beaches lay a narrow promontory that had long stood
as one of the main redoubts of Germany's Atlantic Wall. In fact, when work began
at the point—known as Pointe du Hoc—by the German engineering group,
Organization Todt, in November 1942, it was the first and only such fortified
strongpoint along the entire Bay of the Seine between Cherbourg and Le Havre.*

*The point's name derives from the French word for "jib," the triangular sail at the bow of a ship, and referred to the unforgettable knife-shaped stone formation that rose from the ocean at the shoreline.*

*Gradually the fortifications there had been expanded and designated as Stütz-punkt (Stongpoint) Pointe du Hoc. As invasion planners mapped out the assault along the coast, Allied intelligence believed the Germans had located a battery of some of the largest artillery on the Normandy coast, giant old French guns known as K418, atop the 100-foot-tall rust-colored cliffs. The guns belonged to the 2nd Battery of Coastal Artillery Battalion 1260—known as 2./HKAA 1260.*

*Capturing and destroying the guns atop Pointe du Hoc fell to the Rangers, a new combat unit that had debuted in World War II, modeled on the British commando units, and which—long before the creation of the Navy SEALs or the Delta Force—stood as one of the first elite "special forces" units in the US military.*

**Pfc. Morris Prince, Company A, 2nd Ranger Battalion:** The Pointe was a massive fortress. Hitler himself had boasted of the impunity of this position and of the foolishness of the Allies to ever think, less try, to break through.

**Lt. Gen. Omar Bradley, commander, First Army:** Lt. Col. James E. Rudder, a rancher from Brady, Texas, was to take a force of 200 men, land on a shingled shelf under the face of a 100-foot cliff, scale the cliff, and there destroy an enemy battery of coastal guns.

**Lt. James W. Eikner, Headquarters Company, 2nd Ranger Battalion:** Hardly anyone would conceive that the cliff side of the fortress would be assaulted from the sea—how could you do it? Back towards the land there was the usual defenses set up, machine guns, anti-aircraft weapons, mine fields, barb wire, large underground bunkers of reinforced concrete connected by underground tunnels. It was a formidable position to attack from land. The closest beach suitable for landing was at Omaha Beach some five miles away—to try and land a unit there with the specific mission of taking the Pointe Du Hoc set up would have been fighting through five miles of enemy territory and that would have given the big guns there the opportunity to bring destruction down on Omaha Beach.

**Col. Lucian Truscott, Commander, VI Corps:** I had discussed with General Eisenhower the organization of American units along Commando lines.

In one of our discussions General Eisenhower had said, "I hope you will find some other name than 'Commando' for the glamour of that name will always remain—and properly so—British." Accordingly, when the designation of such a unit was decided upon, I selected "Rangers" because few words have a more glamorous connotation in American military history. In colonial days, men so designated had mastered the art of Indian warfare and were guardians of the frontier.

**Lt. James W. Eikner:** The plan that was presented to General Bradley, and accepted, [was that] there would be three companies from 2nd battalion—D, E, and F companies—that would be especially equipped and trained to assault directly the cliff from the sea. Col. Rudder would command that assault force, against the advice of General Bradley and his staff—they thought he should remain in a HQ somewhere—but Col. Rudder insisted that he would have to be there to make sure that the attack came off. If the assault were not successful within the time frame, a floating reserve would land at Omaha Beach. This floating reserve was made up of the entire 5th Battalion and two companies of the second battalion. They would then fight their way up to Pointe Du Hoc about five miles away. We expected that they would arrive there by noon on D-Day, but if things did go well, we all hoped of course, then the reserve force moved in at Pointe Du Hoc and fighting together we would quickly clean up the Pointe and then move west.

Sometimes we were called a suicide group—but not at all. We were simply spirited young people who took the view that if you were going to be a combat soldier you may as well be the very best.

**Pvt. Salva P. Maimone, Company E, 2nd Ranger Battalion:** We trained close to six months on various cliffs in England, which was pretty hard to do.

**1st Lt. Elmer H. "Dutch" Vermeer, Headquarters Company, 2nd Ranger Battalion:** This was a British Navy mission also, since they had acquired a great deal of experience in the Mediterranean and other areas in raids which required cliff climbing. We trained with British LCAs, which have very wide gunwales. On the gunwale we placed rockets with grapnel hooks on the end and trailed them with ropes, rope ladders, and toggle ropes so that we could fire them over the cliff and then climb them after the grapnels took hold.

**Lt. George Kerchner, Company D, 2nd Ranger Battalion:** The projectors would be fired electrically, and the rocket would carry the head on a high arc. The head had a large grappling iron affixed to the end of it, and it would go into the air three or four hundred feet and over the edge of the cliff. We would get out of the craft, go to the base of the cliff, and pull down on the ropes, digging the grapnels into the sod above, and then we would start climbing. A good climber could get up in under a minute.

**1st Lt. Elmer H. "Dutch" Vermeer:** Another British innovation was to mount fire ladders, which were taken from the London Fire Department, on American DUKWs. These are vehicles that will travel both in water and on land.

**Sgt. Donald L. Scribner, Company C, 2nd Ranger Battalion:** However, all the plans drawn up that we were to do—none came true.

*The attack on Pointe du Hoc on June 6 began from the air, with an attack shortly after 5 a.m. by 108 Royal Air Force Lancaster bombers that dropped 635 tons of bombs on the site. The raid was the fourth major air assault in the weeks leading up to D-Day; aerial planners had deliberately hit the 40-acre area with bomber raids since mid-April, but, as with many of the OVERLORD targets, had avoided singling it out, for fear of drawing attention to it as a specific target. By the time the Lancaster bombers arrived for the big show, Allied planes had already dropped nearly 1,000 tons of bombs—about 25 tons of explosives per acre—across just six weeks. There was only so much more German defenses could withstand. When the smoke cleared, all that was left to see was landing craft on the water.*

*Soon thereafter, the USS* Texas *and USS* Arkansas *opened fire. (Eight decades later, the landscape of Pointe du Hoc still is pockmarked by giant craters.) When the Allied fleet ceased fire around 6:30 a.m., it was time for the 225 Rangers, known Assault Force O-4, to make their move.*

**Sgt. Gene E. Elder, platoon sergeant, Company F, 2nd Ranger Battalion:** Being farm-oriented, along with another sergeant from Indiana, we prepared and braided all the ropes for launching from the rockets which were mounted on the LCAs. At 0400, we loaded into our craft in a very rough sea and headed for Pointe du Hoc.

**1st Lt. Sidney A. Salomon, commander, 2nd platoon, Company C, 2nd Ranger Battalion:** [Aboard the *Prince Charles*] the Ranger Battalion commander stood at the railing of the boat deck, wishing every man good luck, and shaking the hands of the two platoon leaders and company commander.

**Lt. Gaylord K. Hodenfield, correspondent, *Stars and Stripes*:** "All aboard for the Hoboken ferry! Leaving in five minutes!" one Ranger called into the darkness, and there was nothing forced about the laughter that followed. I had joined the Rangers only three days earlier, as a correspondent, and I was not looking forward to the next few hours with such anticipation as these men.

**Sgt. Frank E. South, medic, Headquarters Company, 2nd Ranger Battalion:** I had read in one of the Army medical journals about problems with hair, etc., entering head wounds and I figured that this would be a good time for me to shave my head. If I took a head wound, I might keep it as clean as possible. I was all prepared for D-Day with a shaved head and a newly-grown mustache.

**Lt. Gaylord K. Hodenfield:** It was a matter of but a few minutes before our craft was lowered into the inky-black English Channel. "We're off boys," cried the sergeant in front of my craft, "and this time it's really the forty-nine-cent tour!"

**Lt. James W. Eikner:** We put it into the water and of course it was pitch black and nothing could be seen, the waves were rough and we hadn't been underway very long and water began to leak in through the front ramp.

**Pvt. Sigurd Sundby, Company D, 2nd Ranger Battalion:** I took my liner out of my helmet and used my helmet and started bailing, and I don't think I stopped bailing.

**Lt. James W. Eikner:** Before too long we lost one entire boat—and this was about 26 to 27 people plus one of the most gung-ho captains of the Rangers. Most of these men were picked up later and taken back to England. We also lost a supply craft that went down and all six hands on board were lost. A second supply craft had to throw off about half of its load to stay afloat.

**Sgt. Frank E. South:** The British Combined Operations boat that was to pilot us in wandered off course. Apparently he had not properly adjusted for set and drift and we were, instead of going towards Pointe du Hoc, headed in towards Omaha Beach.

**Ist Lt. Elmer H. "Dutch" Vermeer:** Following the coast in, we were fired on by a machine gun, which was about a half-mile east of the Pointe. We could hear the bullets rattle against the boats as we went by.

**Sgt. Frank E. South:** The situation was picked up by Col. "Big Jim" Rudder and by Ist Sgt. Len Lomell and the proper course change was made. This meant that we had to come in more or less parallel to the cliffs and started picking up fire from the German positions along the top of the cliffs. On our boat, one of the British sailors returned fire with a Lewis machine gun, to little or no effect, of course.

**Ist Lt. Elmer H. "Dutch" Vermeer:** The error in judgment of bringing us in caused a delay of about a half-hour to 45 minutes. The artillery was lifted at H-Hour, and so the Germans did have a chance to get out of their fortifications and over to the edge of the cliff. The destroyer *Satterlee* and, I think, one other destroyer kept blasting away because they could see that we had not yet landed.

*The navigation error that delivered Rudder's Rangers to the base of Pointe du Hoc roughly forty minutes late fatefully meant that the backup elements of the 5th Ranger Battalion, which had waited at sea for a sign that the cliff operation had succeeded, were dispatched instead to Omaha Beach, where they would end up in the midst of some of the day's bloodiest fighting.*

**Capt. John Raaen, commander, Headquarters Company, 5th Ranger Battalion, Ranger Force C:** Ranger Force C lay off Pointe du Hoc and Pointe de la Percée for better than 45 minutes. We circled and circled, praying for the message from Force A that they had landed successfully. The message never came.

Our radio was at my feet in the forward part of an LCA. We did hear two messages. One was a beachmaster on Dog White saying the troops were landing without resistance. Another one had the word "Charlie" in it, but we couldn't make it out. We were supposed to wait until 0700. If we did not receive the success signal by that hour, we must land on Dog Green behind the 116th. Schneider waited until 0710 before ordering us to divert.

*Despite the confusion, the Rangers at Pointe du Hoc actually managed to scale the cliffs quickly (albeit not quite easily), and were atop the cliffs by around 7:10 a.m., only to discover that the guns atop the cliff were missing.*

**Lt. George Kerchner:** As we approached the beach, I gave the order to fire our rockets, and they fired in sequence, two at a time. Out of our six ropes, five of them cleared the cliff, which was a good percentage, because some of the landing craft had a great deal of trouble. Some fired too soon and the ropes were wet and they didn't get up the cliffs.

**Lt. Gaylord K. Hodenfield, correspondent, *Stars and Stripes*:** The grapnels were to bite into the bomb-blasted earth on Pointe du Hoc, and when the slack was taken up, the ladders would be ready to climb. Those rope ladders were the secret weapon of this expedition.

**Lt. George Kerchner:** The idea and the hope and desire of all of us was that we were going to run right up on the beach and make a dry landing. I hollered "Okay, let's go" and ran off the ramp, first one out, and immediately sank in eight feet of water. It was a large bomb crater. Everyone else filed around the crater and instead of being the first one ashore, I was one of the last after I paddled in there with all the weight.

**Sgt. Frank E. South:** As soon as my LCA landed, the ramp dropped and the Rangers waded ashore the best they could, I followed. Instead of finding knee or hip deep water, my pack and I found a bomb crater, and the world turned completely to water—green water.

**Lt. George Kerchner:** I was angry because I was soaking wet, and I turned around and wanted to find somebody to help me cuss out the British navy for dumping me, but everybody was busily engrossed in their own duties, so I didn't get much sympathy.

**Sgt. Frank E. South:** I clawed my way out, my pack still on my back, and got up onto the beach. Then, instantly, I was being shot at! Before I could take a good breath, the first cry of "Medic!" went out and I shrugged off the pack, grabbed my aid kit, and ran to the wounded man.

**Ist Lt. Elmer H. "Dutch" Vermeer:** Just to the right of where our boat landed, at the base of the cliff, there was an overhang. Doc Block soon had a first aid station set up there to take care of the men who'd been hit by the machine gun, by German hand grenades and rifle fire. I did help carry one of the men who had been hit on the beach by the machine gun to the safety of the aid station. Doc Block helped quite a number of wounded there.

One of the big problems on the little, short beach was that the machine gun which had fired on us in the boats was now firing on everybody as they crossed the beach on their way up the cliff.

**Unteroffizier Rudolf Karl, artilleryman, 2nd Battery, Heeres-Küsten-Artillerie 1260, Wehrmacht:** From the Pointe, we started throwing grenades until we couldn't see them anymore. For the Americans down on the beach, the effect would have been devastating. They had no protection there at all.

**Ist Sgt. Leonard G. Lomell, platoon leader, Company D, 2nd Ranger Battalion:** We just rushed to the base of that cliff and grabbed any rope we could get, and up the cliff we went just as fast as we could go.

**Sgt. Frank E. South:** I felt a blast over to my left. The other F Company boat was unable to get its rockets into position to fire them properly. So, Tech Sergeant Cripps had taken the rockets off, I think two of them as I remember, put them on the beach itself, and hand-fired them while standing only three feet off. In the process of firing the first one, he was partially blinded, with carbon particles embedded deeply in his face. Nevertheless, he went on, and again, in almost direct line of fire from the machine gun, was able to get the second one in position, fired it, again taking a terrible blast. It took extraordinary courage, determination and self control. I still feel this act of bravery was never properly recognized or rewarded.

**Pvt. Bill Hoffman, Company D, 2nd Ranger Battalion:** I was assigned a specific rope to a specific gun. I supposed to do some specific damage. I had a big stick of C-2 in my pocket. I just grabbed a rope and somebody yelled, "Hey, hey—that's mine!" They were firing down the cliff and throwing down potato masher grenades, and they also cut some ropes. I don't really know how we got up that cliff.

**Sgt. Frank E. South:** First one, and then another, and then a few more, made it to the top, all within a period of maybe five minutes, ten minutes, fifteen minutes. Time was fluid and passed in erratic leaps.

**Lt. George Kerchner:** Climbing the cliff was very easy. The shelling from the warships and the bombing had caused dirt and a large amount of clay and shale to fall down, so that you could almost walk up the first twenty-five feet. I went up a smooth rope and had no trouble.

**Lt. Gaylord K. Hodenfield:** My own trip up the ladder was interrupted only by numerous stops to catch my breath. We were able to hear the firing of small arms and loud roars from the top of the cliff, but we had no way of telling what was going on. Finally I tumbled over the top of the cliff into a shell hole.

**lst Lt. Elmer H. "Dutch" Vermeer:** There was still an awful lot of machine gun fire, and the Germans were also shelling the area from the Maisey batteries near Grandcamp. Col. Rudder was already topside, and he set up a CP in a bomb crater that was right next to an anti-aircraft site.

**Lt. James W. Eikner:** I sent the [radio] message, "Praise the Lord," this was a code phrase which meant all the men were up the cliff. I can tell you in less than five minutes the first men got up the cliff and in less than 30 minutes all the essential people were up there.

**Sgt. Frank E. South:** The battle for Pointe du Hoc began in earnest.

**Lt. George Kerchner:** I went over the top of the cliff and the ground didn't look anything at all like what I thought it was going to look like.

**Lt. Gaylord K. Hodenfield:** Straight ahead of me for a mile was nothing but shell holes.

**Lt. George Kerchner:** I headed toward the portion of the Pointe where the guns were, and every now and then came across other Rangers from one shell crater to the next. I picked up men as I went across the terrain toward the casemated guns and at one time was in a hole with three or four others, and we saw a 40-millimeter antiaircraft gun firing direct fire at the Rangers. This was our first live German, and we all wanted to shoot at him, but he turned the gun in our direction and we all took off from our little hole.

**1st Sgt. Leonard G. Lomell:** We didn't stop; we played it just like a football game, charging hard and low. We went into the shell craters for protection— because there were snipers around and machine guns firing at us—and we'd wait for a moment, and if the fire lifted, we were out of that crater and into the next one. We ran as fast as we could over to the gun positions, to the one that we were assigned to. There were no guns in the positions!

**Lt. Gaylord K. Hodenfield:** Our men fanned out to destroy the guns, and then, learning that four of them had been removed, two companies formed a big patrol and set out to find them. While this patrol was out searching for our target, other Rangers were fighting snipers and seeking out German machine-gun nests.

**1st Lt. Elmer H. "Dutch" Vermeer:** One of the major problems was the machine gun over to our left, just a little over a quarter of a mile from the CP. This gun could cover the beach area, and it was almost impossible for men to cross that beach and get ammunition and supplies up the cliff. Lt. James Eikner, the signal officer, bought a small lamp with shutters in England for his own personal collection. He did bring it ashore on D-Day, and it proved to be the only communication we had with the Navy for quite a period of time. He was able, with his signal lamp, to relay our problem to the Navy, and one of the destroyers was visually able to see the machine gun and did blow it off of the cliff with its guns.

**Sgt. Frank E. South:** In about an hour or two, I went up to the top of the cliff where I was now more needed. Since we were taking heavy casualties, Rudder had set up his CP just seaward of an antiaircraft bunker and shelter—a concrete emplacement with two rooms. We turned the structure into our aid station and since it was pitch black in there, at first we worked using only flashlights. Later, someone was able to get some gasoline lanterns. Nevertheless we had one or two gasoline lanterns, as I remember, to work with during those first days while we were on the cliff.

**lst Lt. Elmer H. "Dutch" Vermeer:** The Germans were mounting a very heavy attack with riflemen, machine guns, and mortars. Masny and his men stayed cool and killed a great number of German soldiers, truly displaying the Ranger spirit and training. Captain Masny was an excellent leader. One of his men was operating a mortar by placing it against his knee. He could see where the Germans were, and, without using a bi-pod or any instruments, he was firing the mortar just by sight. He almost dropped every shell right where he wanted it. Later reconnaissance let us know how effective he had been. An orchard, just beyond where the Germans had attacked was literally covered with dead Germans who had been killed during that raid.

**Sgt. Frank E. South:** The wounded were coming in at a rapid rate, and we could only keep them in rows on a few litters we had or on the floor in blankets. The dead we took into the adjoining room.

**lst Lt. Elmer H. "Dutch" Vermeer:** We found out that Jake Hill had been killed. Lt. Hill was an F-company officer who was one of the first men on top of the cliff. The story goes that on reaching the top he called back to those below, "Those crazy S.O.B.'s are using live ammunition." This even brought a smile to some of their faces while they were being shot at. Hill was killed after throwing a grenade, turned out to be a dud, into an enemy position.

*      *      *

**1st Sgt. Leonard Lomell:** The road was our next objective. We were supposed to get into the coastal road and set up a roadblock, which we did. Sergeant Koenig destroyed the communications along the coastal road by blowing up the telephone poles, and then Jack Kuhn and I went down this sunken road not knowing where the hell it was going, but it was going inland. We came upon this vale or little draw with camouflage all over it, and lo and behold, we peeked over this hedgerow, and there were the guns.

**Lt. James W. Eikner:** One patrol led by Sergeant Lomell from D Company ran up on the big guns about a mile inland. The enemy had moved them up there for better protection.

**1st Sgt. Leonard G. Lomell:** It was pure luck. They were all sitting in proper firing condition, with ammunition piled up neatly, everything at the ready, but they were pointed at Utah Beach, not Omaha. There was nobody at the emplacement. We looked around cautiously, and over about a hundred yards away in a corner of a field was a vehicle with what looked like an officer talking to his men. We decided that nobody was here, so let's take a chance.

**Lt. George Kerchner:** Lo and behold, they came on five 155-millimeter rifles sitting alongside the road, all ready to fire, but with not a single German around them. This was the most fantastic thing that happened in the war, as far as I was concerned.

**Lt. James W. Eikner:** While a buddy of his was standing guard, the sergeant sneaked into where the guns were camouflaged and put thermite grenades in the beach blocks to make them inoperable. There was a large enemy force within eyeball distance across the fields from there.

**1st Sgt. Leonard Lomell:** I put the thermite grenades in the traversing mechanism, and that knocked out two of them because that melted their gears in a moment. And then I broke their sights, and we ran back to the road, which was a hundred or so yards back, and got all the other thermites from the remainder of my guys manning the roadblock, and rushed back and put the grenades in traversing mechanisms, elevation mechanisms, and banged the sights.

And suddenly the whole place blew up. We thought it was a short round from the *Texas*. What it was, was another patrol from Company E, led by Sergeant Rupinski, had come around to the left of us, and came upon the ammo depot of this gun emplacement, and blew it up. We went flying, and dust and everything was settling on us, and we got up and ran like two scared rabbits as fast as we could back to our men at the roadblock.

**Pvt. Salva P. Maimone:** I'd say within an hour, we had everything destroyed.

**Lt. James W. Eikner:** By nine o'clock on D-Day morning the big guns had been put out of commission.

**1st Lt. Elmer H. "Dutch" Vermeer:** Col. Rudder came back into the CP having been shot through the leg. It was a flesh wound and Doc Block ran a swab through it and put a little iodine on it. Col. Rudder refused to stay in the CP and soon went out again with Captain Harwood and Lt. Norton in one of the gun emplacements. One of the shells from the *Texas* battleship hit the gun emplacement the three were in. The direct hit turned the men completely yellow. It was as though they had been stricken with jaundice. It wasn't only their faces and hands, but the skin beneath their clothes and the clothes which were yellow from the smoke of that 14-inch shell fired from the battleship. It was probably a colored marker shell. It wasn't long before Captain Harwood died, and his body was left on a stretcher placed just outside the CP. We could see his body until the third day, when we were relieved.

**Sgt. Frank E. South:** We started counting heads. Of the 250 men who had landed on the Pointe, there were less than 95 who could still bear arms.

**Lt. George Kerchner:** I felt awfully lonesome realizing how few men we had there and that all three company commanders had become casualties, and lieutenants like myself had taken command in each case. We decided to establish a perimeter around the road and try to defend ourselves and wait for the invading force from Omaha to come up. We figured that we only had a few hours to hold, and with sixty rangers, D, E, and F Companies took up positions on the right, center, and left flanks.

**Gen. Dwight Eisenhower, Supreme Allied Commander, SHAEF:** The Rangers were to be cut off for two days while reinforcements struggled overland from Omaha to relieve them.

**Ist Lt. Elmer H. "Dutch" Vermeer:** Seeing Col. Rudder controlling the operation, it still makes me cringe to recall the pain he must have endured trying to operate with a wound through the leg and the concussive force he must have felt from the close hit by the yellow-colored shell. He was a strength of the whole operation through the next day and a half in spite of his wounds, and he was in command all of the time.

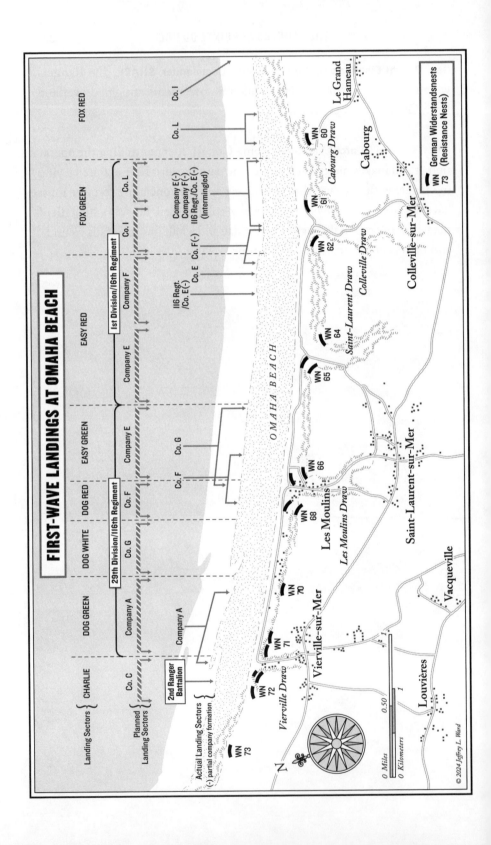

# FIRST-WAVE LANDINGS AT OMAHA BEACH

Landing Sectors { CHARLIE }
Planned Landing Sectors {

| CHARLIE | DOG GREEN | DOG WHITE | DOG RED | EASY GREEN | EASY RED | FOX GREEN | FOX RED |

29th Division/116th Regiment

1st Division/16th Regiment

Co. C | Company A | Co. G | Co. F | Company E | Company F | Co. L | Co. I

Actual Landing Sectors
(−) partial company formation.

2nd Ranger Battalion

Company A

Co. F
Co. G

116 Regt.
/Co. E(−)

Co. E  Co. F(−)

Company E(−)
Company F(−)
116 Regt./Co. E(−)
(Intermingled)

Co. I

Co. L

Co. I

OMAHA BEACH

Vierville Draw
Les Moulins Draw
Saint-Laurent Draw
Colleville Draw
Cabourg Draw

Vierville-sur-Mer
Les Moulins
Saint-Laurent-sur-Mer
Colleville-sur-Mer
Cabourg
Le Grand Hameau
Vacqueville
Louvières

WN 73
WN 72
WN 71
WN 70
WN 68
WN 66
WN 65
WN 64
WN 62
WN 61
WN 60

German Widerstandsnests
(Resistance Nests)
WN 73

N

0 Miles   0.50   1
0 Kilometers   1

© 2024 Jeffrey L. Ward

*"There goes our holes on the beach"*

# Omaha Beach

The first, fateful wave of landing craft make their way toward Omaha Beach.

*By the end of June 6, Omaha Beach would enter the pantheon of America's greatest, costliest battles—standing in history alongside honored, sacred names like Antietam, Gettysburg, Shiloh, the Argonne Forest, Tarawa, Iwo Jima, Chosin Reservoir, and Hué. Although they didn't necessarily realize it at the time, the troops destined for the shores of Omaha had many factors aligned against them that morning—the sea, the beach, the defenses, and even the defenders themselves.*

*Concerned about the reach of the large German guns at Pointe du Hoc, Allied planners had located the transport anchorage at Omaha farther offshore than at the other beaches, and while the ocean before Utah Beach was comparatively sheltered by the Cotentin Peninsula from the worst weather, the Omaha anchorage faced the brunt of the huge post-storm Channel swells that morning—meaning troops both spent longer in their small invasion craft and in worse seas and were more tired and more seasick when they reached shore.*

*The beach itself also had a foreboding geography. Almost exactly in between Utah and Gold Beaches—just about fifteen miles away from each—the crescent-shaped beach stretched nearly a half-mile wide at low tide, and was defined ashore at either end by tall cliffs, ideal for defenders. Inland along the backside of the beach ran a high grassy bluff. There was precious little concealment or protection available on the beach for invading forces, although an artificial seawall ran about half the length of the beachfront, and a high mound of small rocks, called "shingle" or "popplerocks," provided an additional layer of possible concealment for the assaulting forces if they survived to the high-water mark.*

*Omaha Beach had long been a vacation destination and so was dotted by fancy villas and, at its westernmost edge, by a road and villa that had been transformed into a German command post. That exit to the nearby village of Vierville was one of just five "draws" off the beach, which were closely guarded and defended by fourteen interlocking "resistance nests." (Utah, by comparison, had only three.)*

*Those facts were all known heading into the morning, but what the Allies didn't know was just as crucial: The 352nd Infantry Division, commanded by Lt. Gen. Dietrich Kraiss and composed of veterans from the Eastern Front, had moved into the beach positions in the weeks preceding the invasion, replacing the small force of poorly trained conscripts Allied intelligence had anticipated as defenders. While the 352nd wasn't the top-of-the-line unit some historians have made it out to be in dramatic retellings since, its presence increased both the quantity and quality of the beach defenders.*

*The hope on D-Day was to land 34,000 men on the beach in the morning, with 3,000 vehicles, but from almost the first moments, the plans went awry: Offshore, after loading into their landing craft for the long journey to the beach, the first waves of infantry watched the impressive naval bombardment and then, with rising dread, watched how both of the morning's grand spectacles—thousands of rockets fired from special boats, and the day's aerial bombing run, intended to blast the German defenses and create ready-made foxholes across the beach—missed the shoreline entirely.*

**Pfc. Max D. Coleman, Company C, 5th Ranger Battalion:** I have witnessed many sunrises in my thirty-four years, but this one stayed in my mind. The first rays of the sun turned the few clouds to crimson. It would have captured the imagination of any artist or poet.

**Lt. Arthur Newmyer, speaking over the public address system of Rear Adm. Hall's flagship USS *Ancon* (AGC-4):** In a few minutes, coinciding with the first break of dawn on this historic day, the most tremendous naval bombardment ever to blast out against the European Continent will start. Our big ships are in very close to bombard in this assault. The *Texas* is going to fire at 12,000 yards. The *Arkansas* is going to fire at a range of only 6,000 yards. At those ranges those fourteen-inch guns mean business. Battleships, cruisers, destroyers, and monitors are going to blast at Hitler's Normandy defenses with rapid fire—concentrated fire, pinpoint fire—for forty minutes before the first troops hit the beach. We know where Hitler's guns are. They are banked in concrete. And they will be hard to knock out. But we are going to give them an awful wallop.

In addition to the warship firepower I spoke about before, we have some more items to dish out. Our LCTs carry medium tanks, and these tanks will be cutting loose on the way in. They are scheduled to hit the beach at exactly H-hour—0630. Just before the tanks hit the beach, our rocket ships, carrying many banks of rockets apiece, will open up. The naval bombardment is about to begin. H-hour is fast approaching. The Liberation of Europe is on the way!

**William N. Solkin, pharmacist's mate, 2nd class, *LCTR-450* (Landing Craft Tank Rocket):** Our intrepid little flotilla of floating barges lined up, nine abreast, with geysers of water spouting up all around us, and with the bombardment a continuous din of noise, moved out of the transport area, heading toward the beach.

**Martin Waarvick, motor machinist, USS *LCT-589*:** It sure was noisy. I think if I put all the thunderstorms together in my lifetime, it would never amount to anything like that.

**Seaman 1st Class Lawrence "Yogi" Berra, crewman, LCSS (Landing Craft Support Small):** Being a young guy, I thought it was like the Fourth of July, to tell you the truth. I was looking out and my officer said, "You better get your head down in here, if you want it on."

**Ernest Hemingway, correspondent, *Collier's Weekly*:** Those of our troops who were not wax-gray with seasickness, fighting it off, trying to hold onto themselves before they had to grab for the steel side of the boat, were watching the *Texas* with looks of surprise and happiness. Under the steel helmets they looked like pikemen of the Middle Ages to whose aid in battle had suddenly come some strange and unbelievable monster.

**Martin Sommers, foreign editor, *Saturday Evening Post*, aboard USS *McCook* (DD-496):** Our five-inch guns speak as one, and to us they are louder and truer than any we've ever heard. By 6:15 all our assigned targets that we can reach have been knocked out. We have fired 200 rounds in twenty-five minutes.

**William N. Solkin:** We, the crew were huddled aft in the mess deck. Each of us was armed—with a fire extinguisher. Our skipper was in the conning tower with his finger on a button. We held our breath, hanging on to anything that was stationary. Then we fired our rockets. I can't describe the sound of a thousand rockets being released in less than a minute. I remember a ship mate describing it as the rush of a hurricane. The ship, which was drifting when we fired, shuddered and momentarily lost steerage. I have no recollection of being frightened. Our moment of activity happened so fast and was over so soon that there wasn't time for fear, if such a thing were possible.

**Sgt. Warner "Buster" Hamlett, Company F, 116th Infantry Regiment, 29th Division:** It looked like geese flying through the sky in quick succession.

**Sub-Lt. Jimmy Green, Royal Navy, HMS *Empire Javelin*:** The rockets went up in the air and then down in the sea about a mile off the shore, nowhere near the coast. They killed a few fish but that was about it. I was furious. They'd come all that way just to misfire. *Doing, doing, doing! Bang, bang, bang!* It woke those Germans up who didn't know we were already coming, but that was it.

**Sgt. Gilbert Gray Murdoch, Company A, 116th Infantry Regiment, 29th Division:** One guy yelled, "Well there goes our holes on the beach!"

**William N. Solkin:** My final recollection was the sight of the small boats, loaded with infantry men, going in.

*A key part of the Omaha invasion plan called for the deployment of 32 swimming DD tanks offshore, but the combination of the high waves and the long swim in meant almost all of those launched were swamped and sank. It was quickly apparent that rather than landing and advancing under the cover of armored tanks with high-powered guns, the first waves of infantry ashore would be all but alone.*

**Lt. (jg) J. G. Barry, USS *LCT-549*:** It was obvious even before launching that the sea at that distance was too choppy for the tanks.

**S.Sgt. Paul Ragan, Company D, 741st Tank Battalion, aboard *LCT-600*:** I saw the yellow flags go up, which meant to start launching. The ramp went down, and the first tank went off. I watched it clear the ramp and turned my head to start giving instructions to the other ones, and at that time there was a big explosion near our craft, and all the tanks were pushed against each other and tore the screens. [I saw] that the only tank that went off the LCT had sunk. The water was very rough. I went to the skipper and said that we must pick the men up. We picked them up, and I also noticed a lot of other [tank crews] who were in life rafts.

**Ens. Richard Crook, executive officer, USS *PC-553*:** We really felt sorry for the poor soldiers in the duplex-drive tanks. They weren't seaworthy enough for the rough conditions that day; they just went down to the bottom like rocks. Some men were able to jump out in time, but not all.

**Ens. R. L. Harkey, commander, USS *LCT-602*, carrying four DD tanks of 741st Tank Battalion:** [The tank] bobbed for a moment, then suddenly sank. The soldiers in it promptly inflated a rubber life raft. The third and fourth tanks were launched and when both were in the water, one sank. I am not proud of the fact, nor will I ever cease regretting, that I did not take the tanks all the way to the beach.

**Lt. Dean L. Rockwell, flotilla commander, USS *LCT-535*:** I was in communication by low power tank radio with a Captain [Ned] Elder, of the 743rd tank battalion. We made the joint decision that it would be insane to launch any more tanks and the signal was given by tank radio to all craft to cease the launch.

**Ens. Richard Crook:** We picked up perhaps twenty-five to thirty men from those tanks, and more of them were corpses than survivors. They were all around us. The *PC-552* picked up even more than we did. After our crew pulled the bodies out of the water, they were laid out on deck. The live ones were given such medical attention as we could. Then we sent the soldiers—both living and dead—back out to the transports in landing craft.

**Lt. Dean L. Rockwell:** I believe that our wave was the only wave of units making the invasion to land on time. And the *LCT 535*, from which I commanded these landing craft, touched the beach at H-hour minus 30 seconds.

**Martin Waarvick:** When our LCT hit the beach, I dropped the ramp. The tankers had lowered their flotation skirts that were up around the tank. They started out down the tank deck, clanking and grinding. They sure made a racket on that steel deck. They went down the deck and down the ramp and I was waving at every one of them.

**Lt. Dean L. Rockwell:** As soon as we landed our tanks, we pulled that famous naval maneuver, known through naval history as "getting the hell out of there." But not before some of the tanks we landed were already in trouble from a German 88, which was in a pillbox on the extreme right flank of our landing area, protected by heavy overhead concrete shields. It was firing through a slit in the pillbox down the beach. Initially it concentrated on our landing craft, two of which were hit by the 88, one of which had three sailors killed and three wounded, but as soon as the tanks were landed on the beach, the German 88 turned its attention to the tanks, and today in my mind's eye, I can see some of the tanks burning from the direct hits of the German 88.*

**Martin Waarvick:** Edward Bacalia—"Bugs" was his nickname—was [our] coxswain, from Michigan. Bugs later said that he and the skipper were

---

* Later, in his seminal book, *D-Day, June 6, 1944*, author Stephen Ambrose—who spent more than a decade studying and collecting the stories of D-Day from veterans—concluded, "By using his courage and common sense, Lt. Dean Rockwell made the single most important command decision of any junior officer on D-Day by ordering his landing craft flotilla to keep their ramps up and dive on to Omaha Beach to deposit their battle tanks." For his leadership that morning, Rockwell received the Navy Cross.

damned scared up there. Bugs, he turned that LCT around pretty fast and headed out to the Channel, and he started to set a zig-zag course. I guess a German gun emplacement must have gotten zeroed in on us because we started getting shelled. Every time Bugs would go to the port, why, a big shell would land right where we were at on the starboard just moments before. And this happened four more times. The last shell exploding right on our stern. We finally got out of range. We owed our skins to Bugs' seamanship, too, that day. The following September, Bugs would have been 18—how about that: 17 years old and piloting a landing craft onto Omaha Beach on D-Day? Not just once, but twice.

# Into the Devil's Garden

Soldiers of the 1st Division disembark a Coast Guard landing craft,
with the smoke-shrouded bluffs of Omaha Beach beyond.

*Planners had divided the five-mile-long Omaha Beach into eight sectors from
west to east: Charlie, Dog Green, Dog White, Dog Red, Easy Green, Easy Red,
Fox Green, and Fox Red. After Omar Bradley's initial concern about the inexpe-
rience of the 29th Division and Utah's 8th Division, the 1st Division, which had
extensive combat experience in North Africa and Sicily, was added to the mix.
Moving forward, the 29th Division's 116th Regimental Combat Team would be
set to land on the western sectors, and the 1st Division—known as the "Big Red
One" for its distinctive patch—would land on the eastern sectors with its 16th
Infantry Regiment and the 18th Infantry Regiment.*

*The men of the 29th Division had waited eagerly and sometimes impatiently for years to enter combat. The first major unit dispatched to England way back in 1942, it was primarily made up of federalized National Guard units, including the 115th Infantry Regiment, largely recruited from Maryland, and the 116th Infantry Regiment, largely recruited from Virginia. The 116th traced its history to the original Virginia militias and, later, had been led in the Confederate Army by Thomas J. "Stonewall" Jackson himself. Together, the 29th was known as the "Blue and Gray," its patch a yin-yang of blending the uniform colors of the armies from both sides of the Mason-Dixon line. Much of the 116th's Company A, commanded by 29-year-old Capt. Taylor Fellers, had come from Bedford, Virginia, a town that would bear a uniquely tragic D-Day toll.*

*Among those troops of the 116th, Companies A, E, F, and G were all set to be in the first wave of the assault on Omaha Beach, with Company B set to follow Company A about 30 minutes later. Their section, Dog Green, was at the base of the so-called Vierville Draw on the western edge of the beach—a particularly well-defended corner of the beach that included a giant antitank wall blocking the road up from the beach. The Germans called it "der Garten des Teufels," the Devil's Garden. Of the 230 members of Company A who departed the* Empire Javelin *that morning offshore, just 18 would survive the day unscathed. Company B, meanwhile, would be reduced to just 28 men by nightfall.*

**Pvt. Harold "Hal" Baumgarten, Company B, 116th Infantry Regiment, 29th Division:** Capt. Taylor N. Fellers (Bedford, Virginia), commanding officer of Company A, 116th Infantry, had a sore throat and high fever the night before the landing but was not going to allow his men to land without him.

**Forrest Pogue, combat historian, V Corps:** They were tired of waiting, these men of the 29th Division. They had trained in Ireland for North African service and then had been left behind to aid in the defense of the United Kingdom. "The bulk of England's defense command," they liked to boast. For what seemed an endless time, they had marched up and down England, participated in exercises, and drilled in assault training centers, until it seemed that they would never do anything but practice war. Here at last their time had come. Just do this job and they could start back to Pennsylvania, Maryland, and Virginia, where many of them came from. So, without worry about the fact that the first day of battle might be their final day of life, they hailed the announcement of the invasion with great joy.

**Sub-Lt. Jimmy Green, Royal Navy, HMS** *Empire Javelin*: We referred to ourselves as the suicide wave, and to be honest we were all quite proud of the label. It was Fellers's first action.

**Capt. Taylor Fellers, commander, Company A, II6th Infantry Regiment, 29th Division, letter to his mother, 1943:** I am beginning to think it is hard to beat a Bedford boy for a soldier. I am truly proud to be commanding my old hometown outfit, and just hope I can carry them right on through and bring all of them home.

**Maj. Sidney Bingham, commander, 2nd Battalion, II6th Infantry Regiment, 29th Division:** They were proud that the 116th was a direct descendant of the "Stonewall Brigade," which had been Stonewall Jackson's first command during the Civil War. They were magnificently trained, superbly equipped, had confidence in one another and their leaders, and were equally confident of their ability to do the job assigned to them.

**Sub-Lt. Jimmy Green:** [Fellers] told me his troops were National Guard, and he was worried how they would react under fire. He asked if I could put them ashore as quickly as possible when we got near the beach, and then fire over their heads to give them some encouragement. He said they'd need all the help they could get to get them moving forward.

**Sgt. Gilbert Gray Murdoch, Company A, II6th Infantry Regiment, 29th Division:** All of the fellows went around shaking their friends' hands for we all knew that this would be it and it would be rough. Our first sergeant back in the staging area had jokingly told the fellows that as soon as we had taken the beach we would all receive Bronze Star medals. So we all kidded each other about this.

**Sgt. Roy Stevens, Company A, II6th Infantry Regiment, 29th Division:** [My twin brother] Ray said he wasn't afraid, but I was. We made a point that we would meet each other at the Vierville crossroads when we landed. He put out his hand to shake mine and I said, "I'll shake your hand at the crossroads." I've regretted not shaking his hand because that was the last time I saw him.

**Pvt. John Barnes, Company A, 116th Infantry Regiment, 29th Division:** Dawn lightened, and we could see more and more ships and more planes in the sky. We were entranced at this huge scene. Someone shouted, "Take a good look! This is something you will tell your grandchildren!" At this point, we were excited, and not frightened.

**Sub-Lt. Jimmy Green:** [The coast looked] menacing, dark. You knew the Germans were there. It was creepy, especially because of the silence. We'd been expecting the Germans to open up as soon as we arrived. But they didn't. It was the calm before the storm.

**Pvt. John Barnes:** Suddenly, a swirl of water wrapped around my ankles, and the front of the craft dipped down.

**Sgt. Roy Stevens:** I never saw water that bad. [The seas] were just rolling and rolling, and there were white caps way out where we were. It was really, really rough.

**Pvt. John Barnes:** The water quickly reached my knees. We shouted to the other boats at our side. They waved in return but continued on. I was in the rear of the craft. I had heard no noise nor felt any impact. Quickly, the boat fell away below me, and I squeezed the CO tubes in my life belt. Just as I did, it popped away. The buckle had broken. I was going under. I turned and grabbed the back of the man behind me. I climbed on his back and pulled myself up in a panic. Our heads bobbed up above the surface of the water. We could still see some other boats moving on to the shore. It was with a strange feeling when, in a short time, I heard gunfire in the distance. The battle had started and I wasn't there. I felt relieved of a great weight.

**1st Lt. Ray Nance, Company A, 116th Infantry Regiment, 29th Division:** Of our six assault boat sections, we lost #5 at sea. Another one, #2, with Captain Bellegin on it, there were thirty-two men on—not one single person is known to have survived. It could have exploded with all the demolitions on board, too. We lost the #5 and #2 boats out of the six boats of Company A [before we even reached the beach].

**Pvt. George Roach, Company A, 116th Infantry Regiment, 29th Division:** When the boat finally hit what sounded like the sand, or the shore, the ramp was down. Lt. Anderson was the first off the boat with the riflemen, one of which was Alexander Dominguez, and I remember in the next few seconds or so in my getting off the boat, I saw Alexander Dominguez had been shot and was laying in the water and sand.

**Sgt. Gilbert Gray Murdoch:** At the same time that Dominguez jumped, I jumped from the port side of the ramp and found myself in about nine feet of water. The landing craft had not landed on the beach, it had landed on a runnel, or a sandbar. As I came back up, I punched my $CO_2$ tubes for buoyancy, helped by my gas-mask casing, which also was buoyant.

**Pvt. George Roach:** Everybody did supposedly what they had to do. The riflemen were fanning out, but the casualty rate was very bad.

**Sgt. Thomas Valance, Company A, the 116th Infantry Regiment, 29th Division:** We attempted to do what we had practiced doing for so many months in England, except that it was all to no avail. There was a rather wide expanse of beach, and the Germans were not to be seen at all. They were firing at us, rapidly, with a great deal of small-arms fire.

**Pvt. George Roach:** We didn't know whether the firing was coming from there or whether it was coming from the top of the hill, or where it was coming from. I can remember just dropping myself into the sand, taking my rifle and firing it at this house up there. Sergeant Wilkes said to me, "What are you firing at?" I said, "I don't know. I don't know what I'm firing at."

**Sgt. Thomas Valance:** I saw some tracers coming from a concrete emplacement which to me, looked mammoth. I never anticipated any gun emplacements being that big. I attempted to fire back at that. The water kept coming in so rapidly and the fellows I was with were being hit and put out of order so quickly that it became a struggle to stay on one's feet.

**Sgt. Gilbert Gray Murdoch:** As soon as I could get myself oriented and get the strength to get up, I realized I could hardly see because I was wearing glasses and my glasses were coated with salt water and were spotted. I saw a mortar team in front of the craft on the port side about twenty yards away, and the men were lying down next to the mortar, not firing. I called up to them and asked what happened, and they said they were hit and they just couldn't fire it even though it was set up. So the sergeant in charge asked me to fire it. I fired two or three rounds and they flew out of the tube, but they didn't explode. The sergeant yelled, "Murdoch, you dumb bastard, you're not pulling the firing pins!" So for the remainder of the rounds, which I'd never fired before, I pulled the firing pin, and we knew we got some mortar fire on the beach, but with the smoke and my fogged glasses, I couldn't tell what we hit.

**Sgt. Thomas Valance:** It became evident rather quickly that we weren't going to accomplish very much. I remember floundering in the water with my hand up in the air—trying to get my balance—when I was first shot. I was shot through the left hand and suffered from a broken knuckle. And I was shot through the palm of the hand. I remember feeling nothing but a little sting at the time, but I was aware that I was shot. Next to me in the water, a fellow named Hank Witt—Private Henry G. Witt—was rolling over towards me. I remember him very clearly saying, "Sergeant, they're leaving us here to die like rats. Just to die like rats." I remember that statement so clearly. I made my way forward as best I could. My rifle jammed. I remember picking up a carbine. I got off a couple of rounds. There was no way I was going to knock out a German concrete emplacement with a .30 caliber rifle. I was hit several other times, once in the left thigh, which broke a hip bone—I didn't know it at the time—and several other bits that were not injurious. I remember being hit in the pack a couple of times, feeling a tug and my chin strap on my helmet which was not around my chin and was severed by a bullet. I worked my way up onto the beach and staggered up against a wall, and collapsed there.

**Col. S. L. A. Marshall, Historical Section, War Department:** Within 7–10 minutes after the ramps had dropped, "A" had become inert, leaderless and almost incapable of action. The company was entirely bereft of officers. Lt. Edward

N. Garing was back where the first boat had foundered. All of the others were dead except Lt. Elijah Nance who had been hit in the heel as he left the boat, and then in the body as he reached the sands. German machine gunners along the cliff directly ahead were now firing straight down into the party.

**Company A, 116th Infantry Regiment, 29th Division Group Critique Notes ("After Action Report"):** Within 20 minutes of striking the beach, Company A ceased to be an assault unit.

*Company B soon followed Company A into Dog Green. Their fate would be the same. Among the troops aboard the British landing craft, only one man, Pfc. Robert Sales, made it through the day unscathed.*

**Pfc. Robert Sales, Company B, 116th Infantry Regiment, 29th Division:** I was on the command boat with Captain Zappacosta as his radio operator, and I landed right at the Vierville draw where I was supposed to be.

I crawled up to look over the side of the ship. We were not too far from the beach, and I could not see anyone. Company A was supposed to be on that beach, and I couldn't see an A Company man. All I could see was machine-gun tracers. The ramp went down and Captain Zappacosta was the first man off, and they just riddled him. It didn't kill him instantly, but he was hollering at me. Everybody who went off, they just cut them down. We got caught in a cross fire. The only thing that saved me, I stumbled and went off the side of that ramp.

**Pvt. Harold "Hal" Baumgarten:** The lowering of the ramp was like a signal for every German machine gun to open up on the exit from our boat. Lt. Donaldson and some of the guys around him were gunned down in our LCA. Clarius Riggs was shot dead on the ramp and fell facedown into the water. I dove in behind him, and only my helmet was creased by a bullet. There I was, standing in neck-deep, bloody red water, with my rifle above my head.

**Pfc. Robert Sales:** There was nobody in the water around me when I started to make my way in. In a little while, a mortar shell hit real close to me and really knocked me groggy; it almost put me under, but I grabbed hold to a log that was floating. Somebody in that water, I don't know who it was, helped me get that assault jacket off. I pushed that log in front of me real close and made my way to the beach. It took me a long time. When I got to the beach, Dick Wright, who was the communications sergeant, who was the second man off, had been washed ashore and was still alive, and when he saw me, he tried to raise up on his arms and elbows and was trying to tell me something. When he moved to pull himself up, a sniper in the rocks hit him right in the head. He dropped his face right back in the sand.

**Pvt. Harold "Hal" Baumgarten:** I hit the sand behind one of the hedgehog obstacles, whose steel rails didn't afford much cover. To my right Pvt. Robert Dittmar had been hit in the chest. He was yelling, "I'm hit, ma—Mother!" and then he was silent. Six feet to my right lay a gravely wounded Nicholas Kafkalas. I knew Nick from Company A. About thirty yards to my left front were Bedford Hoback and Sgt. Elmere Wright, both of Company A. Sergeant Wright, who had had a future as a pitcher with the St. Louis Browns of the American League, was already dead. Bedford was wounded. On my left was Sgt. Clarence "Pilgrim" Roberson, from my boat team. He staggered by me in the now three inches of water. Pilgrim was helmetless, with a gaping hole in his left forehead. His blond hair was streaked with blood. I yelled for him to get down, but the noise on the beach was horrendous. I am certain he couldn't hear me. Reeling to my left, he knelt down facing the seawall and started praying with his rosary beads. The machine gun in the trench on the bluff literally cut him in half. With tears in my eyes, I drew a bead on the shine coming from a German helmet on the bluff. A miracle! My rifle fired, but failed to eject the spent cartridge shell. However, the machine gun fire from that area was silent after my shot. My being an expert rifleman paid off.

**Pfc. Robert Sales:** If you moved, you were dead.

**Pvt. Harold "Hal" Baumgarten:** I was weaponless, surrounded by dead buddies, and the pillbox on the right was shooting up the sand around me. I rarely curse, but I lifted my head and swore at the pillbox on the right flank. At that moment, an 88 mm shell went off in front of me. A fragment of it hit me in my left cheek. It felt like being hit with a baseball bat, but the results were much worse. My left cheek was ripped away, the left upper jaw was gone, and teeth and gums were lying on my tongue. I washed my face in this water and luckily did not lose consciousness.

**Pfc. Robert Sales:** I just crawled a few inches at a time along that beach and whenever possible I crawled around bodies. I never knew who they were. The first man I saw from B Company after Dick Wright was a boy from one of the other boats that had an eye laying out. He'd been hit in the face, and he had made it to some rocks and kind of a wall there, and when I got over there I bandaged his eye up and we stayed behind that wall for a good while. A Company and B Company landing in the same spot were annihilated.

**Pvt. Harold "Hal" Baumgarten:** Gazing in front of me, I saw that Bedford Hoback had been hit in the face with another fragment of the same shell. He died immediately. I thought to myself, *When will I die?*

**Pfc. Robert Sales:** I heard later that Captain Fellers and Captain Zappacosta—couple of great buddies—were washed up on the beach within thirty feet of each other.

**Radio message from *PC-552* to USS *Samuel Chase*, 0641 hours:** Entire first wave foundered.

\*　　　　\*　　　　\*

*The 2nd Ranger Battalion's C Company landed just yards to the west of where the 116th Infantry's Company A and Company B arrived. These Rangers had been supposed to follow the 116th Infantry right through the German defenses, up the hill, and on to their own goal—neutralizing another German gun position at Pointe de la Percée, in between the western end of Omaha Beach and Pointe du Hoc, five miles away, where the other Rangers of the 2nd Battalion had landed. However, after seeing the carnage of the 116th, the Rangers had to switch to a backup plan: Climbing the cliffs at the end of the beach and trekking west to Pointe de la Percée.*

**1st Lt. Sidney A. Salomon, commander, 2nd Platoon, Company C, 2nd Ranger Battalion:** Of the six line companies comprising the 2nd U.S. Ranger Infantry

Battalion, the mission of C Company had been deemed to be the most hazardous.

**Lt. James W. Eikner, Headquarters Company, 2nd Ranger Battalion:** They were to neutralize the large enemy defensive setup there [at Pointe de la Percée] that would be raining fire down on Omaha Beach then after that they would fight on another two miles down Omaha to Pointe Du Hoc.

**Sgt. Donald L. Scribner, Company C, 2nd Ranger Battalion:** We almost got to the beach when all hell broke loose. We were hit by artillery fire, mortars, machine guns, you name it. The LCA I was on was hit three times. The first shell hit the very front and tore the ramp completely off. The young man that was sitting in the front never knew what hit him. I know the LCA started filling up with lots of blood. It was just as red as anything could be. Then it was hit again, on the port side. I started to go over the rear starboard side. When I looked back, I noticed a 6omm mortar was lying on the bottom. The young man that was to carry that ashore was dead. Just as I reached down to get it, a shell took out the rear starboard side that I was going to go over.

**1st Lt. Sidney A. Salomon:** The Rangers waded to the shoreline, and started across the sand, striving to reach the cover of the base of the cliff. Machine gun, small arms fire, and mortars cut down some of the men as they attempted to run across the sand.

**Capt. Ralph Goranson, commander, Company C, 2nd Ranger Battalion:** I told the men to get from the water's edge under the overhang of the cliffs as fast as they could because that's where safety will be. Right after we landed we took at least three or four rounds of 88s. The first was wide, but number two took the landing ramp off. Number three hit in the rear, and number four amidships.

**Pfc. Nelson Noyes, Company C, 2nd Ranger Battalion:** All of us ran across the beach as fast as we could. I ran about 100 feet before hitting the ground when we ran into enemy cross fire from the right and in front.

**Capt. Ralph Goranson:** We lost a third of our company that morning going across that beach. Another third were already wounded. But we all gathered at the foot of the cliffs. The one thing that has always stuck in my mind—one of the first things that I was cognizant of when I got across the beach—I looked up and there was one of the youngest men in my company, and he had his Psalm book out, and he was reading "Yea, though I walk through the shadow of death, I will fear no evil." And I said, "Stanley, put that away. Come."

**Ist Lt. Sidney A. Salomon:** Several did make it to the base of the cliff, which afforded them some cover from the deadly machine gun fire, but now hand grenades were being tossed down at them by the Germans on top of the cliff.

**Sgt. Donald L. Scribner:** The only alternative we had left was to climb the cliffs to the right of the beach head.

**Capt. Ralph Goranson:** I signaled to Bill Smith to effect plan two—put up two fingers and pointed straight up.

**Ist Lt. Sidney A. Salomon:** Quickly, the men gathered at the base of the cliff, and they proceeded to return some of the small arms fire to the Germans. Two of the huddled group started up the cliffs with ropes. Inching up hand hold and foot hold, slipping a little here, then flattening themselves against the cliff, as they dug into it with their fingers for a hand hold, progress was slowly made.

**Capt. Ralph Goranson:** Within about 5 minutes, [Smith] and two of his leading NCOs were topside and called down, "Just come on over." And we started going up.

**Ist Lt. Sidney A. Salomon:** Ultimately, I made it to the top, and spotted a series of trenches some twenty-five yards distant. I pointed [and] indicated all should run to the trench.

**Capt. Ralph Goranson:** We got topside and we got into labyrinths of foxholes, trenches; it looked just like a big beehive, but dug into the ground.

**Ist Lt. Sidney A. Salomon:** I looked around to see who was still with me. Nine men remained from the thirty-nine that had been jammed in the landing craft.

**Sgt. Donald L. Scribner:** We had a lot of sniper fire that day—an awful lot of it. I remember Lt. Moody, he and some of his men started toward a fortified house on top of the cliffs back a few yards held by the Germans. They were firing their machine guns from there and directing artillery fire. They took that fortified house, and in doing so, Lt. Moody lost his life.

**1st Lt. Sidney A. Salomon:** Taking two men, I worked my way through the trenches and approached the entrance to a dugout. I tossed a white phosphorous grenade into the dugout, we waited several seconds, then blasted away with Tommy guns and rifles. Okay, that dugout was cleared. Further down the trench, and around a curve, we came upon a German mortar crew in a fixed gun position. Some more grenades, more rifle and Tommy gun fire, as the three of us continued through the trenches. Now, I returned to the beginning of the trench for the rest of the platoon.

**Capt. Ralph Goranson:** I went with a patrol towards Pointe de la Percée, and thanks to the United States Navy that had been taken care of pretty good. It was no longer effective.

*             *             *

*As the clock marched steadily past H–Hour and Omaha Beach began to fill with subsequent waves of assault troops, the few survivors on the beach and in the water of the 116th Infantry Regiment's Company A and Company B began to assess their situations and seek aid.*

**Pvt. George Roach:** I didn't see anybody except Gil Murdoch, who was laying next to me, and the water was coming in rather rapidly, and I said to him, "Gil, how do you feel?" He said, "I can't see—I lost my glasses." And I said, "Well, can you swim?" He said, "No, I can't swim too well." I said, "Well, look, we can stay here—there's nobody around here that seems to have any idea of what to do." I said, "Let's go back in the water and come in with the tide."

**Sgt. Gilbert Gray Murdoch:** George Roach said, "Let me swim you out to that knocked-out tank in the water out there." When we got there, we hung onto the port side of the tank. We could see three men from the tank crew with their faces all powder burnt. The tank commander, a buck sergeant, was sitting behind the turret with his left leg off at the knee and the bone floating in the water. He asked us to get him a shot of morphine. I crawled inside the turret, and on the right-hand side where they had their aid packet, I grabbed it, pulled it out, and gave him a shot. After fifteen minutes the sergeant said he wanted to get on the beach, he thought it would be safer. George Roach and I said no—the beach was not safer, but he wanted to go.

**Pvt. George Roach:** I realized I couldn't stay there indefinitely, but Gil was in no position at that time to move. I felt that I did all that I could for him at the time, and I said, "Look, there's a patrol boat that's supposedly in the area that will pick up survivors. Can you stay here, and will you be OK?" He seemed to indicate that he would.

**Sgt. Gilbert Gray Murdoch:** I was finally rescued by an army control craft and survived to also be in the first group to cross the Rhine River the following year.

**Pvt. George Roach:** I started to swim into towards shore, and made it almost to shore when I was picked up by a boat—this had to be probably around 10:30 in the morning. And I promptly fell asleep.

**Pvt. Harold "Hal" Baumgarten:** I reached a corner where the wall angled inward (south). This afforded me safety from the pillbox on the right flank, but not the snipers, nor the exploding mortar shells. When I reached the area adjacent to [the] D-1 [draw], the seawall towered twenty-five feet above me. At the base of the wall, lying face down in the shallow, bloody red water, was Robert Garbett, Jr. My best buddy. I started to cry, and my tears ran down red from my bloody face. This was one of the saddest moments in my life.

**Sgt. Thomas Valance:** I've wondered over the years about one thing: Why we, in A Company of the 1st Battalion, 116th Infantry, 29th Division, were chosen to be the American equivalent of storm troopers? Was it because we were so highly trained? Was it because we had such potential? We had no combat duty, and the other troops that were around and with us in the invasion, such as the 1st Division, were highly trained. Or was it simply because we were considered expendable? I just have never come across the answer to that.

*"Come a long way to die"*

# Ashore at Omaha

Bodies from the 16th Infantry Regiment line the shoreline
after the landing of the initial waves.

*The good news—if there was any—for many of the other units bound to the east of the Vierville Draw in the initial waves for Omaha Beach was that almost all of them landed in the wrong places. Smoke from shore obscured the navigation landmarks and with the strong ocean current many found themselves further east than planned, navigating unfamiliar portions of the beach upon arrival; in fact, none of the units bound for the Dog White sector managed to arrive there at all.*

*The experience of those initial waves varied greatly depending on where, exactly, the craft and men put ashore—some, including Company G, which ended up at Dog Red, found themselves nearly untouched, while others, like*

*Company F and Company K, found themselves unexpectedly directly in the line of fire of German defenses. Up and the down the beach, though, chaos reigned during the first hour of the invasion as units, briefed back in England with ambitious goals of charging inland, found themselves broken in men and spirit. Landing craft with follow-on waves, meanwhile, faced terrible choices as they confronted an overcrowded beach under withering fire—some struggled for hours for an open landing spot. Four LCTs, which were supposed to arrive at 8:30 with badly needed reinforcements, instead circled for much of the day, awaiting an opening. They arrived between eight and eleven hours late on the beach.*

**Robert E. Adams, LCVP coxswain, assigned to the USS *Samuel Chase* (APA-26), U.S. Coast Guard:** At the time of the Normandy invasion I was twenty-five years old, assigned to the Coast Guard, aboard the USS *Samuel Chase*. Prior to Normandy, our boat division had participated in landings in Sicily, so we were a fairly experienced group. Our [LCVP] was destined for Omaha Beach, and we had men of the 1st Infantry Division—the Big Red One—on board. We had taken them ashore during several invasions in the previous year, so we had a lot of respect for them.

**Pfc. Duwaine Raatz, 16th Infantry Regiment, 1st Division:** I had made two invasions before this, North Africa and Sicily, so I thought I knew a little bit of what it might be like, but in the morning of June 6, 1944, when I saw the beaches of Normandy, France, my spirits dropped. There were stakes, ramps, obstacles, curved rails sticking out of the water. That's when I started to pray and think about what I was going to do.

**Sgt. Clayton Eugene, forward observation party, B Battery, 32nd Field Artillery, attached to 18th Infantry Regiment, 1st Division:** I've always wanted to be a soldier from the time I was about three years old. The *Boston Sunday Post* ran some pictures of WWI and the Kaiser. As I looked at the pictures, I said to mother, "I wish I could be a war soldier someday." My mother said, "Don't ever say that again." Still, nothing changed my desire to become a soldier. As soon as I was able I enlisted as a volunteer in the regular army. A few seconds before landing, all this flashed through my mind. I volunteered. I asked for this or whatever was to come.

**Pvt. Steve Kellman, Company L, 16th Infantry Regiment, 1st Division:** As we made our run to the beach, we passed several life rafts filled with airmen who had been shot down. As we went by they gave us the thumbs up gesture, indicating that everything was all right. Looking towards the beach, we couldn't believe that anybody would be left alive after the tremendous bombardment.

**Pfc. John Robertson, Company F, 116th Infantry Regiment, 29th Division:** Most of my boat team was seasick. I remember heaving over the side, and someone aid, "Get your head down! You'll get killed!" I said: "I'm dying anyway!" So here we are, all seasick, ahead of everyone else, no bomb craters to get in, and heading straight into machine gun fire. That was my definition of Hell.

**Capt. Richard P. Fahey, Clearing Company, 60th Medical Battalion:** While waiting our turn, our craft came upon a bunch of American soldiers floating around helplessly in the water. They had been blown out of their craft. We fished them out of the water and, since they had nothing but the clothes on their back, we told them that we would transfer them onto some craft that were traveling back to the main ships and they would be taken back to England. To a man, they protested and insisted on going in. They had nothing, no guns, nothing! We each had a supply of six boxes of K rations, which was to last us for the first two days, so we each shared two boxes of our K rations with them, and these men came into the beach with us.

**Seaman William T. O'Neill, USS *LCT-544*:** An LCVP came running in on close to our starboard side. It dropped its ramp, and the load of troops came running off. They were still some distance from the shore, and they were met with machine gun fire, and a number of the soldiers appeared to be hit. The enemy unseen gunner next went to work on the LCVP itself, and you could see chips just flying all over the place from the plywood hull.

**Pfc. John Sweeney, Company L, 16th Infantry Regiment, 1st Division:** All of a sudden the British coxswain said we were going into the beach. We landed on the sand and started running out, Lt. [Jimmie] Monteith leading the way. I and others got out of the landing craft and started running toward the cliff. I must have run 20 or 30 yards. All of a sudden I got hit by machine gun fire coming from the left-front. I was turned completely around, the bazooka that I had been carrying was full of holes, the life belt I had been wearing was taken right off me. I laid there on the sand, but I thought to myself: I can't lay here on the beach. People were falling all around me so I got up and started running toward the cliff. Somehow I made it. I didn't realize that I was hit in the arm and leg until later. The carnage and destruction were unbelievable—bodies in the water, destroyed landing craft, confusion.

*       *       *

*While larger artillery onshore focused on attacking the landing craft and ships at sea, the German infantry troops and so-called static division defenders arrayed up on the bluffs and in their trenches and fortifications along Omaha Beach watched the landing craft near, waiting carefully until the arriving troops were within range and at their most vulnerable before opening fire. Few positions on Omaha Beach were more formidable than Widerstandsnest 62, in the center of the beach by the beach exit known as the Colleville or E-3 Draw. There, troops like Franz Gockel and Hein Severloh watched through their gunsights as the boats carrying Company E and Company F from the Big Red One's 16th Infantry—as well as Robert Capa, the famed photographer who would be the only civilian photographer on the beach that day—churned toward shore to land in front of them.*

**Gren. Franz Gockel, 3 Kompanie, Grenadier-Regiment 726, 716 Infanterie-Division, Widerstandsnest 62:** Assault boats and landing craft rapidly approached the beach and the first closely packed landing troops sprang from their boats, some in knee-deep water, others up to their chests. There was a race over the open beach toward the low stone wall running parallel to the waterline, which offered the only protection.

**Obergrenadier Karl Wegner, 3 Kompanie, Grenadier Regiment 914, 352 Infanterie-Division:** I tucked the butt of my MG into my shoulder, resting my cheek on it. I braced myself for the recoil. I checked the view down my sights but, somehow, I just couldn't watch what was happening. I closed my eyes and waited for the order to fire.

**Gren. Franz Gockel:** Now we sprang into action. It had been futile to attempt to defend against air and sea bombardment, and until now we could only attempt to save our own lives. Now we heard the first machine-gun bursts, and within seconds the first assault wave troops collapsed after making only a few meters headway.

**Obergrenadier Karl Wegner:** I was frozen, I saw all those men in olive brown uniforms splashing through the water towards the sand. They looked so unprotected in the wide open space of the beach. Lang took the butt of his pistol and crashed it down on the top of my helmet. The metallic clang brought me to life and I pulled the trigger up tight. The MG roared, sending hot lead into the men running along the beach. I saw some go down, I knew I hit them. Others dived for whatever cover was out there. The bullets ripped up and down the sand. This 19-year-old lad from Hanover had just cut down several men. My mind rationalised it; this was war. Even so it left a sour taste in my mouth. Now was not the time to think of right or wrong, only of survival.

**Gefreiter Hein Severloh, 321st Artillerie-Regiment, 352 Infanterie-Division, assigned to Widerstandsnest 62 (overlooking Easy Red and Fox Green at Omaha):** I could see the water spouts where my machine-gun bursts were hitting, and when the little fountains got close to the GIs, they threw themselves down. Oberleutnant Ferking appeared next to me and observed the Americans. "Poor swine," he said softly to himself and picked up the handset of the field telephone to send the coordinates and firing orders for our artillery.

**Pvt. Franz Rachmann, 352 Infanterie-Division:** This is the first time I shoot on living men, and I go to the machine gun and I shoot, I shoot, I shoot! For each American I see fall, there came ten hundred other ones!

**Lt. Col. Fritz Ziegelmann, Chief of Staff, 352 Infanterie-Division:** I succeeded in establishing telephone communication with the troops in Pillbox "76" (Pointe et Raz de la Percée). The commander, whom I knew personally, described the situation in detail.

**Report to Ziegelmann from unknown German troop:** At the water's edge at low tide near St Laurent and Vierville the enemy is in search of cover behind the coastal zone obstacles. A great many motor vehicles—and among these ten tanks—stand burning at the beach. The obstacle demolition squads have given up their activity. Debarkation from the landing boats has ceased; the boats keep farther seawards. The fire of our battle positions and artillery was well placed and has inflicted considerable casualties upon the enemy. A great many wounded and dead lie on the beach. Some of our battle positions have ceased firing; they do not answer any longer when rung up on the telephone. Hard east of this pillbox, one group of enemy commandos [the 2nd Ranger Battalion] has set foot on land and attacked Pillbox "76" from the south.

**Gren. Franz Gockel:** The battle raged back and forth for some hours. The beach became strewn with dead, wounded, and soldiers seeking shelter. The tide crept forward, and anything that could move on the beach sought shelter. We began to notice our own losses. The lightly wounded were bandaged and sent to the rear. The seriously wounded were carried to a sheltered area. Dead comrades were left lying where they fell; there was no time to look after them.

**Obergrenadier Karl Wegner:** After the first few moments had passed my mind became automated. I would fire as I had been trained to do, in short bursts 15 to 20 cms above the ground. When I pulled back the bolt for what seemed to be the thousandth time, I paused for a good look down the beach. I saw Amis [German slang for American troops] lying everywhere. Some were dead and others quite alive. Landing boats were backing away from the beach. Some of them were burning, hit by our PAK guns or they had struck mines. I saw one of the boats hit a mine while it backed away from us, sending shrapnel into the sea and a group of men who had just landed from it. What I saw convinced me that, for the moment, it was worse there than where we were, although we had taken—and still were getting—a pounding.

\*          \*          \*

**S.Sgt. Harry Bare, Company F, 116th Infantry Regiment, 29th Division:** The well made plans made back in England just didn't exist when we hit the beach.

**Robert Capa, photographer, *Life* magazine:** My beautiful France looked sordid and uninviting, and a German machine gun, spitting bullets around the barge, fully spoiled my return. The men from my barge waded in the water. I paused for a moment on the gangplank to take my first real picture of the invasion. The boatswain, who was in an understandable hurry to get the hell out of there, mistook my picture-taking attitude for hesitation, and helped me make up my mind with a well-aimed kick in the rear. The water was cold, and the beach still more than a hundred yards away. The bullets tore holes in the water around me, and I made for the nearest steel obstacle. A soldier got there at the same time, and for a few minutes we shared its cover. He took the waterproofing off his rifle and began to shoot without much aiming at the smoke-hidden beach. The sound of his rifle gave him enough courage to move forward and he left the obstacle to me. It was a foot larger now, and I felt safe enough to take pictures of the other guys hiding just like I was.

**2nd Lt. John Spalding, leader, Ist Section, Company E, I6th Infantry Regiment, Ist Division:** When we got about two hundred yards offshore the boat halted and a member of the crew yelled for us to drop the ramp. Because we were carrying so much equipment and because I was afraid that we were being landed in deep water, I told the men not to jump out until I had tested the water. I jumped out of the boat slightly to the left of the ramp into water about waist deep. The men began to follow me. We headed toward shore and the small arms fire became noticeable.

**Robert E. Adams:** When our LCVP's ramp opened, our brave group from Big Red One bounded out onto Omaha Beach. I recall that I looked to my left and two soldiers were holding up another one in between them and yelling words of encouragement to him. Fortunately for my crew and me, I was able to back off the beach without mishap. Even so, I have a memory that will stick with me the rest of my life. My boat grazed one of the Germans' telephone-pole beach obstacles. On top, so close I could almost touch it, was a teller mine. It could have blown us all to bits. So our first landing was successful—but just barely.

**Pfc. John Robertson:** Our skipper told us he was unloading us and he was getting the hell out of there. He lowered the ramp and our guys started jumping out in water up to their necks.

**Pvt. Buddy Mazzara, Company C, 16th Infantry Regiment, 1st Division:** It was either swim or drown.

**Capt. Robert E. Walker, 1st Battalion, 116th Infantry Regiment, 29th Division:** We began to have casualties from small arms fire on the front deck. As I backed away from the flames on the port side, I heard a blast and saw that a man wearing a flame thrower had been hit and his fuel tank was on fire. Several men standing near by had burns. I noticed one man had a water blister on his face that seemed to be six inches across. The man with the flame thrower was screaming in agony. He went over to the starboard side and dived into the sea. I could see that even the soles of his boots were on fire. Just then the captain of the ship came running to the front deck, waving his arms and yelling, "Everybody over the side." I climbed over the port rail and dropped into the sea, my hob-nailed combat boots scratching on the side of the boat.

**Pvt. Albert Mominee, Company I, 16th Infantry Regiment, 1st Division:** About 400 yards from shore, the craft gave a sudden lurch as it hit an obstacle and in an instant an explosion erupted followed by a blinding flash of fire. The LCI was enveloped in flames. Flames raced around and over us. Before I knew it I was in the water. I inflated the life preserver around my waist and moved away from the craft towards the shore. About 50 yards from shore the water was shallow enough for me to wade. I was exhausted and in shock.

**Capt. Richard Merrill, commander, Company E, 2nd Ranger Battalion:** I was the first one off the craft. Capt. Frank Corder, from Texas, was the next man off. And I remember Frank's exact words: "This is no place for Mrs. Corder's little boy Frank." Of the first seven off the boat—if I was the first one out, the seventh man was the next one to get across the beach without being hit. All the ones in between were hit. Two were killed, three were injured. One of the men from my boat, we saw him get hit and tumble and get up and we were hollering, "Keep going, Rusty! Keep going!" He got across the beach, was evacuated and sent home. I saw Frank Corder, too, but he was tough to recognize because he'd lost an eye and teeth. Someone had gotten to him and put a big bandage over part of his face. I put him up on an amphibious tank so they could carry him down to a more quiet area of the beach, where they were collecting people to evacuate them. He survived.

COSSAC Planner Lt. Gen. Sir Frederick Morgan

Allied naval commander
Adm. Sir Bertram Ramsay

US Army Chief of Staff
Gen. George Marshall (*left*)
talks to British military
chief Lord Alan Brooke.

From left: Lt. Gen. Omar
Bradley, Maj. Gen. Leonard
Gerow, Rear Adm. John Hall,
and Lt. Gen. Clarence
Heubner (*back to camera*)
during an invasion exercise.

5

The war effort in Britain relied heavily on women, like these radar operators.

US troops, embarked in England, await the launch of OVERLORD.

6

Ike spent the evening of June 5 talking with the paratroopers of the 101st Airborne.

Brig. Gen. James M. Gavin, assistant division commander of the 82nd Airborne, readies for a jump.

The paratroopers were heavily loaded for their jump into Normandy.

The Churchill AVRE (*left*) and the DD Sherman tanks (*right*), with shroud inflated, were specially built for the invasion.

A flaming landing craft makes its way to Omaha Beach.

The presence in the Normandy bunkers of Mongolian troops, pressed into service by the Germans guarding the Atlantic Wall, surprised many US troops.

The wounded at Omaha Beach often huddled for hours under the cliffs until they could be evacuated on landing craft.

17

The 320th Barrage Balloon Battalion was the sole all-Black unit to land on D-Day and immediately went to work setting up their air defenses.

18

Stanley Hollis, of the Green Howards, was the one British soldier to receive the Victoria Cross for his actions on D-Day.

19

Waverly Woodson, Jr.'s, bravery on Omaha Beach never received the honor it should.

Canadian soldiers advance on Juno Beach.

Royal Marine Commandos make their way inland from Sword Beach.

22

The sight of the afternoon gliders filling the skies was one few invasion troops would forget.

23

24

Today, the churches of Normandy mark the invasion with unique stained glass windows honoring US paratroopers.

**Pvt. Kenneth L. Romanski, Company I, 3rd Battalion, 1st Division:** I got on the beach and it was just nothing but confusion. There was already men there. There was wreckage. There were men there, some dead, some wounded. So there was just complete confusion. Didn't know what to do, so I picked a rifle from a dead man. And luck would have it, it had a grenade launcher on the end of it. So I fired my six grenades over the cliff. Of course, I don't know where they went but I do know that they went up on enemy territory.

**1st Lt. Edward McNabb, Company H, 116th Infantry Regiment, 29th Division:** I ran into a burst of machine gun fire at about the center of the beach and was hit in a couple of places in the left shoulder. Lt. Tomasi, our battalion surgeon, was close by and ran over and cut off my equipment under fire and sent me back to the water's edge if I could make it. I didn't make it, but the tide came up, and I washed ashore in front of the three-story house on Easy Green.

**Capt. John Raaen, commander, Headquarters Company, 5th Ranger Battalion, Ranger Force C:** Our Ranger chaplain, Father Lacy [was] old, probably in his late thirties or early forties. Short, he couldn't have been over 5′6″. Fat, at least 30 pounds overweight. Thick glasses. He was assigned to my boat, so I checked him and his equipment out a dozen times as we went through our boat drills. The next time I saw him, I was kneeling on Omaha Beach right next to the seawall, looking back at my LCA, as my men still poured out of it and began running toward me and the safety of the wall. There was Father Lacy, the last man out. He was no more than ten feet clear of the boat when a German shell hit the fantail of the LCA. I looked away and did not see Father Lacy again until much later. Others saw him, and like minstrels sang his praises. Lacy didn't cross the beach like we did. He stayed down there at the water's edge pulling the wounded forward ahead of the advancing tide. He comforted the dying; calmly said prayers for the dead. Father Lacy stayed behind at the water's edge, doing the work for which God had chosen him.

**S.Sgt. Harry Bare:** As ranking non-com, I tried to get my men off the boat, and make it somehow to get under the cliff. God, it was awful. It was absolutely terrible.

**2nd Lt. John Spalding:** I noticed a number of my men on the beach, all standing up and moving across the sand. They were too waterlogged to run, but they went as fast as they could. It looked as if they were walking in the face of a real strong wind.

**Pvt. John Hooper, Headquarters Company, 115th Infantry Regiment, 29th Division:** As I got to the beach I flopped down, not on the sand as I expected, but on round, smooth rocks—everywhere! I crawled forward between two tanks at the water's edge about fifty or so yards apart. The one to my left appeared to be on fire, but both were firing their seventy-five millimeter guns. Wounded and dead seemed to be scattered everywhere. I was crawling over rocks slippery with blood.

**Leroy Jennings, 20th Combat Engineers:** Everywhere you looked was sinking boats and dead GI's.

**Pfc. John Robertson:** I got to the bank and tried to survive. Our company was 50 percent casualties, and I didn't know exactly what I was supposed to do. I joined several others along the bank for the next couple of hours.

**S.Sgt. Harry Bare:** While under the cliff, I tried to get the men organized. There were only six out of my boat alive.

**Pfc. Felix Branham, Company K, 116th Infantry Regiment, 29th Division:** They were firing at us with everything.

**Pvt. John Hooper:** I felt the whole German army was firing at me.

**Pvt. John H. MacPhee, Company E, 16th Infantry Regiment, 1st Division:** At one point, I found myself trying to take cover behind one of those fence post type obstacles. It must have looked like an ostrich hiding. But believe me, at that time it looked like a wall.

**Sgt. Victor H. Fast, Company E, 5th Ranger Battalion:** When I crawled up the beach to the sea wall, I had an M-1 rifle, two bandoliers of Ammo, and several grenades. No helmet, no gas mask, no pack because I had peeled all these off so I could swim. I crawled around to find a helmet from a dead buddy, only to find it half full of a head. I quickly found another and wore it as well as a .45 automatic [I found on the beach], throughout the rest of the war.

**1st Lt. Francis W. Dawson, platoon leader, Company D, 5th Ranger Battalion:** We all ended up behind the seawall. It was crowded, the men from the 29th division were there, and you just had to push in for space. The wall was probably four feet high, made of wood. Being six foot four, I had to keep my head down.

**Capt. Robert E. Walker:** Here I was on Omaha beach. Instead of being a fierce, well trained, fighting, infantry warrior, I was an exhausted, almost helpless, unarmed survivor of a ship wreck.

**Maj. Sidney Bingham, commander, 2nd Battalion, 116th Infantry Regiment, 29th Division:** An impression that overcame me at this juncture was one of complete futility. Here I was, the battalion commander, unable for the most part to influence the situation or do what I knew had to be done. Another impression that I had, as I am sure others did as well, was the profound shock of seeing dead and wounded comrades in substantial numbers and being unable to help in any way.

**Capt. Richard P. Fahey, Clearing Company, 60th Medical Battalion:** Sergeant Braasch came running to me at one point and told me that Col. Bernard E. Bullock, our commanding officer, had been wounded. He was a rugged Texan we all liked. I never saw him again. He was shot through the helmet and died. Another one of our officers was lying dead on the beach, and one of my fellow soldiers induced me to place my hand into the gash in his back. A shell fragment had shattered his spine. He was a regular army officer and had been in Pearl Harbor at the time of the Japanese attack. He had come a long way to die.

**Cpl. Walter Eckert, Headquarters Company, 3rd Battalion, 115th Infantry Regiment, 29th Division:** I would have qualified for the most scared guy on that beach.

**Capt. Henry Seitzler, Army Air Forces, 6th Engineer Special Beach Brigade:**
I can still see those men—our men—rolling in the surf, like water-soaked logs. Nobody paid any attention to them. They didn't pull them out of the water at the time. There was nothing we could do for them. They were dead, and they couldn't help us, we couldn't help them, and there were so many other things going on. It would have been foolish for men to risk their lives pulling dead men out of the water.

**Capt. Edgar Arnold, commander, Company B, 2nd Ranger Battalion, Ranger Force C:** I began to get visions of being pushed back into the sea.

**Lt. Cdr. Lindsay Henry, commander, Landing Craft Infantry Group 34, letter to his wife, June 7, 1944:** We were in the center of the attack, and it was a shambles.

*"If you stay on, you're dead or about to die!"*

# Getting Off Omaha Beach

By midmorning, the tide begins to turn. As subsequent waves arrive, troops in the distance can already be seen mounting the bluffs.

*The original* NEPTUNE *plans called for the first waves at Omaha to break through the German defenses, storm the heights, and open the beach for follow-on landings within about an hour. But as follow-on waves arrived, the new troops found themselves still under devastating artillery and gunfire. They greeted onshore shell-shocked and traumatized soldiers, many wounded, huddled at the seawall and behind the low rise of shingle rocks. "All along Omaha there was a disunited, confused, and partly leaderless body of infantry, without cohesion, with no artillery support," wrote historian Samuel Eliot Morison in his official naval history of the invasion. "There were two long stretches of beach where no one had landed. Only two companies of eight were on the beaches where they were supposed to be."*

*Step by step, though, progress began to materialize as the morning progressed thanks to the training and experience of the 1st Division veterans and the individual actions of junior officers, NCOs, and even a few senior officers—including, notably, Brig. Gen. Norman "Dutch" Cota, the second in command of the 29th Division and the highest-ranking officer in the initial assault waves, and Col. George Taylor, the commander of the 16th Infantry Regiment. One by one on the beach, they began to rally troops, inspire confidence, and lead and direct an advance on the German positions.*

*Training began to kick in, and select unit leaders began to shine into a forward-moving assault over the course of the 7 a.m. and 8 a.m. hours. In the end, as fierce as the German resistance had been, the US invasion was saved, in ways, by the Germans' poor strategy; despite routing the initial landing, they had no units ready to capitalize on the traumatized men on the beach and destroy the landing at the shoreline. And, as the US forces finally organized and advanced, they found the German defense line miles wide but only yards deep. There were few second-line positions and few units past the initial ridgeline, and it turned out to be easy—relatively speaking—to capture German positions from the rear and sides.*

**S.Sgt. John B. Ellery, Company B, 16th Infantry Regiment, 1st Division:** When you talk about combat leadership under fire, on the beach at Normandy, I don't see how the credit can go to anyone other than the company grade officers and senior NCO's who led the way. It is good to be reminded that there are such men, that there always have been and that there always will be. We sometimes forget, I think, that you can manufacture weapons, and you can purchase ammunition, but you can't buy valor, and you can't pull heroes off an assembly line.

**Pvt. Warren Rulien, Intelligence and Reconnaissance ("I&R") Platoon, 16th Infantry Regiment, 1st Division:** On the shore, there were officers sitting there, stunned. Nobody was taking command. Landing crafts were continuing to bring waves of soldiers in and they were bunching up on the beach. Finally, out on the water, coming towards the shore, walking straight up with a staff of officers with him, I recognized Col. Taylor, Regimental Commander. He stepped across the sandbar and bullets began hitting the water around him.

He laid down on his stomach and started crawling towards shore, his staff officers doing the same. I kind of chuckled to myself, thinking: "Crawl on your stomach, like I did."

**Capt. William Friedman, Headquarters Company, 16th Infantry Regiment, 1st Division:** Col. Taylor, then commanding officer of the 16th, looked around and in a great stentorian voice screamed, "Get the hell off the beach! If you stay on, you're dead or about to die!" It worked, and people got themselves organized in small groups.

**Pvt. Harold "Hal" Baumgarten, Company B, 116th Infantry Regiment, 29th Division:** Brig. Gen. Norman D. Cota, with a pistol in his hand, came running up our beach from the west. He was accompanied by a major I didn't recognize. I couldn't talk, due to my face wound, but some of the guys called to him to get down. It was reassuring to us to see this brave man on the beach, disregarding the snipers. We were advised that the only ones who were going to remain on the beach "were the dead, and those who were going to die." The call was "Twenty-nine, let's go," and we went.

**Pfc. Arden Earll, mortarman, Company H, 116th Infantry Regiment, 29th Division:** He said, "If you stay here, you're gonna get killed. If you go inland, you may get killed. But let's go inland and get killed. Not stay on this Damn beach. The tide was coming in. Don't stop. Get the hell out of here, and get em." If it hadn't have been for a few people like him, D-Day could have very well been turned into what the British went through at Dieppe.

*After getting waved off from landing at Pointe du Hoc and seeing the devastation of Company A and B of the 116th Infantry Regiment, the units of the 5th Ranger Battalion had abandoned plans to land at the far western edge of the beach at the bloody Dog Green sector. Instead, they had redirected to the east, to Dog White and Dog Red sectors, and arrived all but unmolested onshore and made their way to the seawall atop the beach. It was there, about 0830, two hours after H-Hour, that Cota found them and urged the highly trained unit onward.*

**Capt. John Raaen, commander, Headquarters Company, 5th Ranger Battalion:** I had been on the beach no more than ten minutes, checking the men for firearms, ammunition and other equipment while awaiting orders from battalion. Several of my men called my attention to a man about 100 yards to my right moving along the edge of the beach. He was chewing on a cigar, yelling and waving at the men in the dunes and at the seawall.

**S.Sgt. Richard N. Hathaway, Jr., Company A, 5th Ranger Battalion:** It was Brigadier General Norman Cota, the Assistant Division Commander of the 29th Infantry Division. I couldn't help but wonder what in hell was he doing on this beach.

**Capt. John Raaen:** As he approached, I rose to meet him. I reported to him with a hand salute. "Sir, Captain Raaen, 5th Ranger Battalion." "What's the situation here?" "Sir, the 5th Ranger Battalion has landed intact, here and over a 250 yard front. The battalion commander has just ordered the companies to proceed by platoon infiltration to our rallying points." "Where is your battalion commander?" "I'll take you to him, Sir," pointing out the location of Lt. Col. Schneider. "No. You remain here with your men." As General Cota started away, he stopped and looked around saying, "You men are Rangers. I know you won't let me down." And with that, he was off to see Schneider.

**Brig. Gen. Norman "Dutch" Cota, letter to J. C. Raaen (Capt. John Raaen's father), March 24, 1949:** I was glad to see them at that particular time, for they were badly needed. The 5th Rangers were a wonderful outfit. It was lads like [Raaen] who our nation can thank for the beachhead it won on D-Day in Normandy. Believe me, they were the only reason that enabled an old crock like myself to shake fear loose and "roll on."

**T/5 Tom Herring, Company C, 5th Ranger Battalion:** Before Cota reached Schneider, a flurry of artillery fire caused him [Cota] to hit the dirt. I was lying to the left of Pfc. William Stump, also C Company. Stump asked me for a match, saying his were wet. "Mine too," I said. Stump reached across my back and punched a soldier next to me and asked, "Hey, Buddy, you got a light?" As the soldier rolled onto his left side, the star on his jacket epaulet was visible to both Stump and me. Stump said, "Sorry, sir!" Cota reached into his jacket, pulled out a Zippo, flicked it, held it for Stump to light up and said, "That's OK, son, we're all here for the same reason."

**T.Sgt. Herb Epstein, Intelligence NCO, Headquarters Company, 5th Ranger Battalion:** I was lying on the sand next to Col. Schneider as Cota walked up and called for him. Schneider stood up and the two were standing there while all this firing was going on and General Cota said to him, "Col. we are counting on the Rangers to lead the way!" Schneider said, "yes sir!" and Cota walked back east. And as Schneider dropped down to the ground near me I said to him "What the hell were you doing?" And he said to me, "Well he was standing and I wasn't going to be laying down here."

**Capt. John Raaen:** After Cota finished speaking with Col. Schneider, he turned toward the men nearby and said, "Rangers! Lead the way!"

**S.Sgt. Donald L. Chance, Company C, 5th Ranger Battalion:** This was the spark needed.

**T.Sgt. Herb Epstein:** Using Bangalore torpedoes, they blew the holes in the wire and we pushed forward.

**1st Lt. Francis W. Dawson, platoon leader, Company D, 5th Ranger Battalion:** I can still smell that powder smell as I traveled through the trail that the explosives had made.

**Pfc. Randall Ching, Company B, 5th Ranger Battalion:** Company D's Captain led his men through the wire and then we [Company B] followed. Then some of the 29th infantry boys followed in with us up the hill.

*Across the beach, small groups—and sometimes even individual soldiers—began to find holes in the German defenses and make their way up to the bluffs behind. At multiple locations, they blew holes through the barbed wire fences using Bangalore torpedoes—extensions of pipe packed with explosives that could be slid under the wires to destroy them—and then, sometimes at great personal risk, they began to chart paths through the minefields beyond.*

**Capt. Joe Dawson, commander, Company G, 16th Infantry Regiment, 1st Division:** Bullets were dropping around us like rain, but the good Lord seemed to be with us. The first wave was totally disorganized by their tremendous number of casualties. [They were] pinned down mentally, if not physically. There was no coordinated fire from the Americans ashore. They were bunched shoulder to shoulder and were huddling on patches of ground, which gave them partial cover from the enemy's fire.

**John B. Burkhalter, chaplain, 1st Division:** I don't think [the Germans] expected anyone to get off the beach, because once we'd started moving up the hill and clearing their positions, it just became a matter of time. The [defensive] positions really did not have any depth to them.

**2nd Lt. John Spalding, leader, 1st Section, Company E, 16th Infantry Regiment, 1st Division:** We decided to rush [a] machine gun about fifteen yards away. As we rushed it, the lone German operating it threw up his hands and yelled, "Kamarad!" We would have killed him, but we needed prisoners for interrogation. He was Polish.

**Capt. Joe Dawson:** I was fortunate enough to realize that there wasn't any point in me standing there and, frankly, I felt the only way I could move was forward, and to go up and see if I could get off the beach. I felt the obligation to lead my men off, because I felt the only way they were going to get off was to follow me. They wouldn't get off by themselves.

**2nd Lt. John Spalding:** We were on top of the hill by 0900. We advanced cautiously. We were the first platoon of the 16th [Infantry Regiment] to hit the top. We now had twenty-one or twenty-two men in the section.

**1st Lt. Francis W. Dawson:** I could see the enemy positions ahead of me, but so far, they had not seen me. I continued my climb up to the crest of the hill. There I found myself among Germans. The ones I did dispose of quickly caused the others to decide to surrender.

**2nd Lt. John Spalding:** I spied a piece of stovepipe about seventy yards away sticking out of the ground. Sergeant Streczyk and I now went forward to investigate. We discovered an underground dugout. There was an 81mm mortar, a position for a 75 [mm gun], and construction for a pillbox. All this overlooked E-1 draw. We started to drop a grenade in the ventilator, but Streczyk said "hold on a minute" and fired three shots down the steps into the dugout. He then yelled in Polish and German for them to come out. Four men emerged. They brought out two or three wounded.

**Pvt. Donald Nelson, Company E, 5th Ranger Battalion:** We moved up north a ways. We ran into the doggonest bunch of Germans you ever did see. We got pinned down and we really couldn't move. Col. Max Schneider, our commanding officer came up behind us and wanted to know what the trouble was. We told him it was snipers, and we couldn't go any further. He said "Can't you attack them?" We said "No, we can't even see them." Everytime you raised up, they'd shoot at you. So, he showed us a little trick. He took his helmet off, got a stick, put his helmet on the stick and eased it up. The moment that helmet got up above the hedgerow, the snipers started shooting at it. He said "O.K., you guys, you find the snipers and I'll draw their attention." That's the way we got a few of the snipers.

**2nd Lt. John Spalding:** I started down the line of [German] communications trenches [atop the ridge]. They led to the cliff over the beach. We were now behind the Germans, so we routed four out of a hole and got thirteen in the trenches. After losing my carbine in the water, I had picked up a German rifle, but found I didn't know how to use it too well. When I went to check on the trenches I traded the German rifle to a soldier for a carbine, but I failed to check it. In a minute I ran into a Kraut and I pulled the trigger, but the safety was on. I reached for the safety catch and hit the clip release, so the clip hit the ground. I ran about fifty yards in nothing flat.

**Cpl. Gale Beccue, Company B, 5th Ranger Battalion:** When we reached the outskirts of Vierville we dropped our packs and extra equipment and went through the town house by house. There was some small arms fire, but not a lot. Most of the Germans had left their village by then. I was still wet from the soaking I had had on the beach, so when I found some German officers' clothing in a billet, I changed into German socks, underwear, and a heavy turtleneck sweater under my own uniform clothing. Most of the rest of the day, we spent rooting out snipers or looking for artillery observers.

**Pvt. Jack Keating, Company A, 2nd Ranger Battalion:** It was quite a day for medals.

**Maj. Carl Plitt, operations officer, 16th Infantry Regiment, 1st Division:** Summing it all up, the plan for Operation NEPTUNE was a good one, but it didn't work. It was the individual courage and heroism of the American soldier that won the beaches Easy Red and Fox Green on 6 June 1944.

*By around 1000, units of the Rangers and the 116th Infantry—including, amazingly, a surviving boat team of Company B—had taken control of the village of Vierville. On the eastern end of the beach, at what was known as the Cabourg or F-1 Draw, a 26-year-old first lieutenant named Jimmie W. Monteith, Jr., from Company L of the 16th Infantry Regiment, had led the way fighting up the beach exit by Widerstandsnest 60. At its top, Monteith—already a veteran of fighting in Algeria and Sicily—faced off against multiple machine guns firing across the hedgerows.*

**1st Lt. Jimmie W. Monteith, Jr., platoon commander, Company L, 16th Infantry Regiment, 1st Division, letter to his mother, early 1944:** I would not change if I were given the chance—even to have some easy job in the rear area. Of course I can't say that should I ever be lucky enough to have a son that I would want him to go through something like this. But if events forced him I would want him to prove himself. As for the 1st Division, every time I look at the shoulder insignia (the red one) I get a thrill—there is no better fighting unit in the world. When the Germans were confident of victory on several occasions and all circumstances were against the 1st, the men rose to the occasion and hurled them back in great confusion and disorder. There is a great feeling of satisfaction that one gets within oneself. I would not change.

**S.Sgt. Aaron B. Jones, Company L, 16th Infantry Regiment, 1st Division:** Lt. Monteith brought his men together and faced the first obstacle, layers of heavy barbed wire. After selecting a place where it could be blown open, he led men with a Bangalore torpedo in blasting the wire open. Beyond this were two mine fields and he led the way through these. The field was traversed by machine gun fire from the two enemy emplacements and from a pillbox, and when the men took cover, he stood studying the situation and then ran back to the beach.

On the beach were two tanks, buttoned up and blind because of heavy machinegun fire that was directed on them. He walked through all that fire to bang on the sides of the tanks and instruct the men inside to follow him. Walking in front, he led the tanks to the pillbox, where they put it out of action. He then led his men against two machine gun positions and knocked them out and then set up a defensive position to hold until more units could be brought from the beach.

In that sector the enemy was not fighting from fixed positions, but was moving around in the hedgerows and setting up automatic weapons. A fairly large group started an attack on the position and set up machineguns on the flanks and rear. The Germans yelled to us to surrender because we were surrounded. Lt. Monteith did not answer, but moved toward the sound of voices and launched a rifle grenade at them.

**Sgt. Hugh Martin, Company L, 16th Infantry Regiment, 1st Division:** When [Lt. Monteith] knocked out the machine gun with the rifle grenade, he stood in full view at 40 yards, and the first shot fell short. The full fire of the gun was turned on him, but he held his position and fired the second grenade to knock out the position.

**S.Sgt. Aaron B. Jones:** Even with a larger force the Germans couldn't break through our positions, so they set up two machineguns and started spraying the hedgerow. Lt. Monteith got a squad of riflemen to open up on the machinegun on the right flank. Under cover of the fire he sneaked up on the gun and threw hand grenades, which knocked out the position.

He then came back and crossed a 200-yard stretch of open field under fire to launch rifle grenades at the other machinegun position. He either killed the crew or forced them to abandon the weapon. Back on the other flank enemy riflemen opened up on us again, and Lt. Monteith started across the open field to help us fight them off, but was killed by the fire of a light machinegun that had been brought to our rear.

*Monteith's bravery that day—which helped secure the F-1 Draw and the eastern flank of the landing long enough for reinforcements from the beach to arrive and then push forward toward Cabourg—posthumously earned him the Medal of Honor, one of just two given to members of the 16th Infantry Regiment on D-Day*

*and one of just ten given to US soldiers across the opening days of Operation OVER-*
*LORD. Eisenhower, in approving of the award, wrote, simply, "This man was good."*

*    *    *

*The medics on Omaha Beach quickly became overwhelmed at the scale of the*
*catastrophe there. For hours, under fire, they triaged the horrific wounds of the*
*initial assault waves, comforted the dying, and loaded casualties back onto landing*
*craft for treatment at offshore, makeshift hospital facilities aboard the invasion*
*fleet. While many soldiers have tales of the specific breed of heroism by the medics*
*on the beach, no medical personnel equaled the heroism and pure stamina of S. Sgt.*
*Waverly B. Woodson, Jr., of the 320th Barrage Balloon Battalion, the only unit*
*of Black troops to land on the D–Day beaches.*

**S.Sgt. Waverly B. Woodson, Jr., combat medic, 320th Barrage Balloon Battalion:**
There was a lot of debris and men were drowning all around me. I swam
to the shore and crawled on the beach to a cliff out of the range of the
machine guns and snipers. I was far from where I was supposed to be, but
there wasn't any other medic around here on Omaha Beach. It was just about
ninety minutes after the start of D-Day. I had pulled a tent roll out of the
water and so I set up a first-aid station. It was the only one on the beach.

**Capt. Henry Seitzler, Army Air Forces, 6th Engineer Special Beach Brigade:**
I think the medics were the bravest men in the war. Sometimes, Jerry [a
pejorative term for German soldiers] would deliberately shoot the medics
so they couldn't help others. I think that the hottest place in hell is reserved
for the man that would do that.

**S.Sgt. Waverly B. Woodson, Jr.:** The men that got hit, we treated those. A
lot of them that we treated weren't worth it—they were dying—but you
got to help. They were scared as hell. They were shouting. They were mad
as hell. And some were praying. They were like most men—they loved life.

**Capt. Oscar Rich, artillery liaison pilot, 5th Field Artillery Battalion, 1st Division:**
You'd see the medics going up and down the beach, working on people
who had been hit. The casualties, the ones who were dead, were gathered

in one or two central places, were covered up with blankets or raincoats or something, and their weapons were stacked separately. When an LCT was there ready to go back at the beach, the medics would load him down with the injured, and they'd take them back out to the hospital ships.

**S.Sgt. Bernard Friedenberg, medic, Headquarters Company, 1st Battalion, 16th Infantry Regiment, 1st Division:** On the beach, I raced from one wounded soldier to the next, administrating morphine, sulphur power, and talking to them. I lied; I'd say anything to put them at ease, keep their blood pressure down. I would claim their wound was not so bad even if it was.

I'm still haunted by this one kid who had a sucking hole in his chest and as he breathed, air would come out the hole. I tried to seal it with adhesive tape, but there was so much blood the tape wouldn't stick. Looked like a high school kid. Died under my hands. I never got over that.

**S.Sgt. Waverly B. Woodson, Jr.:** We'd put the bodies up by the rocks on the beach, under the cliffs. That way the waves couldn't wash them back out to sea. The quartermasters who collected the bodies, they were all Black.

**Capt. Hank Hangsterfer, commander, Headquarters Company, 1st Battalion, 16th Infantry Regiment, 1st Division:** There were so many troops on the beach it was difficult to find a space to take cover from the enemy small arms fire. On the beach, I saw Bob Capa, the combat photographer, taking pictures of the carnage.

**Robert Capa, photographer, *Life* magazine:** The camera trembled in my hands. It was a new kind of fear shaking my body from toe to hair, and twisting my face. The men around me lay motionless. Only the dead on the waterline rolled with the waves. An LCI braved the fire and medics with red crosses painted on their helmets poured from it. I just stood up and ran toward the boat. The water reached to my neck. I held my cameras high above my head. Suddenly I knew that I was running away. I couldn't face the beach and told myself, "I am just going to dry my hands on that boat." I reached the boat. The last medics were just getting out. I climbed aboard. As I reached the deck I felt a shock, and suddenly was all covered with feathers. I thought, "What is this? Is somebody killing chickens?" Then I saw that the superstructure had been shot away and that the feathers were the stuffing from the kapok jackets of the men that had been blown up. The skipper was crying. His assistant had been blown up all over him and he was a mess. The barge brought us to the USS *Chase*, the very boat I had left only six hours before. On the *Chase*, the last wave of the 16th Infantry was just being lowered, but the decks were already full with returning wounded and dead.

**S.Sgt. Waverly B. Woodson, Jr.:** All day, we medics continued to dress many, many wounded and consoled the frightened. This went on until around 3 o'clock in the afternoon. With all of this going on I didn't have time to see how bad I was wounded—I only wanted to help the survivors. After about 8 hours, one of the medics redressed my wounds and I continued, as I didn't have a place to lie down.

**Lt. Col. Charles Horner, commander, 3rd Battalion, 16th Infantry Regiment, 1st Division:** The casualty ratio normally is about one [killed] to seven [wounded]. [On D-Day,] it was one-to-one. The reason was that when people were hit getting out of the boat or coming across the beach, [medics] couldn't get to them. And as a result they died when they might have been able to survive. One of my company commanders laid there for nearly 24 hours, and as a result he lost his foot. If we could have gotten him up to good medical facilities, we may have been able to save that foot.

**S.Sgt. Waverly B. Woodson, Jr.:** This was a horrible day for everyone. This D-Day, Army prejudices took a backseat, as far as the soldiers helping one another was concerned. Afterwards, it was an altogether different story. Even to this day, the Black soldiers were never given credit for their outstanding services beyond the call of duty. *

---

* Woodson would be recommended for the Medal of Honor by his commander, but received the lesser recognition of the Bronze Star, the fourth-highest award for valor. The nation's oldest Black newspaper, *The Philadelphia Tribune*, concluded, "the feeling is prevalent among negroes that had Woodson been of another race the highest military honor would have been granted him." In fact, Black soldiers received none of the 433 Medals of Honor awarded during World War II. A push during the Clinton administration to address that previous era's pervasive racism resulted in nine Black World War II veterans—only one still living—receiving the nation's highest honor, but Woodson, again, was not among them. He died in 2005. In recent years, members of Congress have introduced legislation to award Woodson the Medal of Honor—a position supported by senior military leaders—but none of the bills has passed.

*"Destroyers came thundering toward the shore"*

# Afloat Off Omaha Beach

Landing craft offshore pass the cruiser USS *Augusta* (CA-31)
headed toward Omaha Beach.

*With the situation ashore on Omaha critical and tenuous, the naval armada moved to provide as much covering fire and artillery support as it could. In particular, the brave maneuvers and close-in support of the naval destroyer fleet helped silence many German guns and clear the way for troops to advance. While the battleships and cruisers with longer ranges concentrated on targets farther onshore, nine US destroyers and three British ships, HMS* Melbreak, Talybont, *and* Tanatside, *closed to almost point-blank range to fire salvos of five-inch guns at cliffs—some journeyed so close that they were struck by bullets from machine guns ashore. Their collective efforts—especially around what was known as the Colleville or E-3 Draw in the middle of the beach and the E-1 Draw, where Company A of the 116th had landed—unleashed a phenomenal*

375

*cascade of artillery fire at close range: The USS* McCook *shot 975 rounds, and the USS* Carmick *1,127. The naval armada off Omaha also included the battleship USS* Nevada, *which was the only ship present at both Pearl Harbor on December 7, 1941, and at D–Day on June 6, as well as a number of Free French naval ships.*

**Capt. Lorenzo S. Sabin, commander, Assault Convoy, Force O, US Navy:** Shortly before six o'clock the eerie silence was shattered by a deafening roar. The big guns of the heavy bombardment group had opened up. We wondered how the Frenchmen in the light cruisers *Georges Leygues* and *Montcalm* felt as they hurled bullets on their homeland. For the rest of us it was an inspiring spectacle, and for this spectator, personally, it was a scene filled with emotion and pride.

**Rear Adm. Robert Jaujard, Free French Forces:** You may well imagine what emotion was aroused when we were ordered to bombard our homeland, but it was part of the price we had to pay for defeat in 1940.

**James Jones, gunner's mate, 3rd class, USS *Harding* (DD-625):** At H-plus-4 hours [10 a.m.], we opened up on enemy trenches in the same area left of Saint-Laurent to blast out machine-gun nests, with the other ships in that district firing on targets of opportunity. At this time our men were still on the beaches and had advanced only in the valley that we had shelled elsewhere. They were pinned down, and a gun from the Vierville draw was knocking out landing barges right and left, and dozens of them were burning on the beach.

**Cpl. William T. O'Neill, USS *LCT-544*, US Marines:** Suddenly, like the cavalry in an old western movie, several US Navy destroyers came thundering toward the shore. As near as they probably dared to go, they started to pound the hills and casements.

**Sgt. Barnett Hoffner, 6th Engineer Special Brigade:** It was them more than anything else—more so than the battleships—that knocked out the pillboxes, since they could come right up, almost a thousand yards offshore.

**Sp.(x)1c Tom Bernard, Navy correspondent, *Yank* magazine:** From the *Doyle's* decks, I could see the shells strike with the naked eye.

**Rear Adm. Carleton F. Bryant, commander, Center Support Group, Western Naval Task Force, aboard the USS *Texas*, message to destroyers:** Get on them, men! Get on them! They are raising hell with the men on the beach, and we can't have any more of that! We must stop it!

**Ens. Richard Crook, executive officer, USS *PC-553*:** Destroyer Squadron 18, under its commodore, Captain Harry Sanders, really did a magnificent job. The *Frankford*, commanded by James Semmes, was the flagship, and she went into shallow water, less than a thousand yards off the beach, to engage the German batteries. The others that contributed were the *McCook*, *Carmick*, *Doyle*, *Emmons*, *Thompson*, *Satterlee*, and *Barton*. They all did a lot of firing—very close in.

**Edward T. Duffy, fire controlman, 2nd Class, USS *Shubrick* (DD-639):** During a lull in our assignments, the rangefinder operator in the gun director above the bridge spotted a German officer walking along the beach to the right of the channel by which we entered the mined area, and which now was the graveyard for the *Corry* and *Forester*. Both ships had received direct hits along their water lines and settled in about 25/30 feet of water. Our officers suspected that the German was scouting and spotting for the shore guns in this area. We trained our main battery and director out in his direction, took a range on his location and sent him a four-gun salute. Another direct hit and the tension was relieved because we had gotten one of the bastards ourselves.

**Sp.(x)1c Tom Bernard:** While searching for targets with the *Emmons* and the *Harding*, the *Doyle* moved east of the beachhead. One of the others opened up on what appeared to be a pillbox when suddenly, from an undetermined position, 88mm shells started bursting astern of her. The *Doyle* hastened in to assist. Her five-inch batteries were turned on other concealed pillboxes. At this point, the enemy battery turned its attention to us. Its first salvo fell astern but it soon obtained more accurate range. For a frightening two minutes it pumped shell after shell within bare yards of us. Two screamed between the *Doyle*'s stacks. Others whistled overhead in a nerve-wracking whine. Our guns continued to fire. The three destroyers worked slowly along the shore, plastering every grove of trees, every battered emplacement, every visible gulley and hole in the cliffside—everything that might conceivably hide enemy guns.

**Col. Benjamin Talley, Deputy Chief of Staff, V Corps, letter to U.S. Army Historian G. Harrison, February 18, 1948:** It is suggested that the official history give credit to fire from destroyers in breaking the stalemate in front of E-1, inasmuch as I observed destroyers keeping up a heavy fire at point blank range on the trenches on the military crest immediately west of the exit and on the emplacements until they were silenced.

**Pvt. Bill Ryan, Company I, 16th Infantry Regiment, 1st Division:** I firmly believe that the firepower of these small ships turned certain defeat on Omaha Beach into a victory.

*        *        *

*To the Allied commanders in the fleet offshore, the fragmentary reports coming back from Omaha Beach were ominous. Communication with the landing forces was poor—by one estimate three-quarters of the 116th Infantry Regiment's radios ashore were sunk, destroyed, or inoperable—but from what the commanders could determine, casualties appeared heavy. Numerous landing craft were being knocked out by German fire, stuck on the beach, or disabled by collisions with obstacles, threatening the ability of follow-on waves to deliver reinforcements; of the 33 Higgins Boats launched by the troop ship USS Samuel Chase, only nine returned. These numbers were true across much of the fleet: The USS Thurston (AP-77) launched 25 Higgins boats in the first wave of the attack, and just three survived undamaged enough to return to the ship and deliver troops in subsequent waves. The commanders realized that success hung in the balance and pondered what defeat on Omaha might mean.*

**Ens. George McKee Elsey, White House Map Room watch officer, attached as an observer to *USS Ancon* (AGC-4) flagship:** The first reports to us on *Ancon* after H-hour about conditions on the several sectors of Omaha were alarming.

**Rear Adm. Carleton F. Bryant, commander, Gunfire Support Group, Assault Force 0-4:** From our distance offshore we could see men, tanks, guns, and landing craft on the beach. Nothing was moving. We knew instinctively that something was wrong. The beach was a most alarming sight.

**Ens. George McKee Elsey:** I asked Commander Munson for his estimate. "It's in the balance now. You can't tell which way it's going. The Germans will probably try to hold the beaches until nightfall and then come after us. It doesn't look good. The obstacles are bad, and there are lots of mines." This assessment from a veteran of amphibious landings was not what I had hoped to hear. By 8:30, the navy beach masters had signaled for all landing attempts to stop.

**Lt. Gen. Omar Bradley, commander, First Army:** As the morning lengthened, my worries deepened over the alarming and fragmentary reports we picked up on the navy net. From these messages we could piece together only an incoherent account of sinkings, swampings, heavy enemy fire, and chaos on the beaches. It was almost 10:00 before the first report came in from Gerow. His message was laconic, neither conclusive nor reassuring: "Obstacles mined, progress slow. . . . DD tanks for Fox Green swamped."

**Capt. Lorenzo S. Sabin:** The wave-control officers notified the force commander, Admiral Hall, that they were stopping the advance of follow-up waves.

**Lt. Gen. Omar Bradley:** When V Corps reported at noon that the situation was "still critical" on all four beach exits, I reluctantly contemplated the diversion of Omaha follow-up forces to Utah and the British beaches. Scanty reports from both those sectors indicated the landings there had gone according to plan.

**Rear Adm. Alan G. Kirk, commander, Western Naval Task Force:** The delay in the movement at Omaha meant that all the follow-up forces coming in from across the Channel—the next division, the tanks, the merchant ships full of ammunition and stores—were piling up.

*     *     *

*While the commanders offshore of Omaha were worried about the specific beach before them, the larger picture of OVERLORD that emerged by early and mid-morning appeared encouraging. Omaha's carnage was the exception, rather than the rule, across the beaches. The initial reports from the airborne units, Utah, Omaha, and the other beaches filtered back to the Allied leadership waiting anxiously for news in England. Overall, it appeared the invasion was proceeding far better than the Allied leadership had feared.*

**Capt. Harry C. Butcher, naval aide to Dwight Eisenhower, SHAEF:** At H-Hour, by coincidence, I was awake, that being 6:40, and was contemplating the underside of the drab tent roof, wondering how come such a quiet night in contrast with other D-Nights, when this was supposed to be the biggest and most superduper of all, when suddenly there came the call. It was Leigh-Mallory, himself. Wanted to speak to the boss. He was filled with information, good information. Surprisingly, said the Air Marshal, only twenty-one of the American C-47s out of the 850 were missing. Only four gliders were unaccounted for. *Grand*, said I, *grand, I'll tell the boss as soon as he wakes up.* So I tiptoed down the cinder path to Ike's circus wagon to see if he was asleep and saw him silhouetted in bed behind a Western. Ike grinned as he lit a cigarette.

**Gen. Dwight Eisenhower, Supreme Allied Commander, SHAEF:** The first report came from the airborne units I had visited only a few hours earlier and was most encouraging in tone. As the morning wore on it became apparent that the landing was going fairly well. Montgomery took off in a destroyer to visit the beaches and to find a place in which to set up his own advanced headquarters. I promised to visit him on the following day.

**Field Marshal Lord Alan Brooke, writing in his diary, June 6:** By 7:30 I began to receive first news of the invasion. The airborne landings had been successful, the first waves were reported as going in, opposition not too serious, batteries firing from flanks, etc. Throughout the day information has gone on coming in. On the British front the landing has gone well and the whole of 3 divisions are ashore. On the American front the western landing was a success, but the Eastern Corps (V) has failed practically along its whole front!

**Capt. Harry C. Butcher:** A GI came grinding along with the morning papers from Portsmouth, with headlines of the fall of Rome and the Fifth Army's crashing victory, with personal statement by [Gen. Mark] Wayne Clark. Ike said, "Good morning, good morning," to the GI, most cheerfully indeed.

*     *     *

*Eisenhower's Order of the Day message was printed in mass quantities and handed out on leaflets to every far-flung participant in the invasion, but few knew that the Supreme Commander had penned a second message, apparently sometime either on the 5th or 6th, that he hoped no one would ever read: A press statement to use in the event the landings went poorly and the Allied forces had to withdraw. The handwritten message is dated in his scrawl "July 5th," a confused and obviously wrong day that has left historians guessing whether he actually wrote it on the 5th, ahead of time, or on the morning of the 6th, as the first garbled news of the invasion would have arrived and there were genuine concerns about the success of the landing. Elsewhere, in a note to his son John Eisenhower, he also confused the 5th and 6th, not adjusting in his own mind for the fact that the invasion had been postponed a day.*

*That second message survived only because an aide later found it and saved it for posterity.*

**Gen. Dwight Eisenhower, Supreme Allied Commander, SHAEF:** Our landings in the Cherbourg-Havre area have failed to gain a satisfactory foothold and I have withdrawn the troops. My decision to attack at this time and place was based upon the best information available. The troops, the air and the Navy did all that Bravery and devotion to duty could do. If any blame or fault attaches to the attempt it is mine alone.

*"Never seen men so resolute"*

# Jig Sector, Gold Beach

Bicycle-carrying troops of the 50th Infantry Division land at Gold Beach.

*The audacity of the Allied mission on D-Day was nowhere more evident than in the goal of the British 50th Northumbrian Division: Capture of the thousand-year-old Norman town of Bayeux, most famous for its 11th-century 230-foot-long tapestry depicting the cross-Channel invasion and Battle of Hastings led by William, Duke of Normandy, 878 years earlier—the last time any invader had successfully crossed the English Channel. Amazingly, Bayeux had been largely spared from Allied bombing, so its giant cathedral, consecrated in 1077, and small stone Norman buildings remained. Much as at Omaha, this entire stretch was a vacation zone, known as the Pearl Coast, dotted with villas, tourist hotels, and even a narrow-gauge railway for visiting cosmopolitan Parisians. The 1st Hampshire and 1st Dorset Regiments, along with supporting units like the 47 Royal Marine Commando, Sherwood Ranger tanks, and 2nd Devonshire, were to land at the Jig Sector. The 6th Battalion of the Green Howards and 5th East Yorkshire, along with tanks from the 4th and 7th Dragoon Guards and the 7th Battalion of the Green Howards, were meant to arrive at King Sector. A two-mile marsh between them meant that each landing would have to stand on its own, fight inland, and link up only inshore.*

*At first, the well-organized landing on the ten-mile-long stretch designated as Gold Beach met little resistance from the German 716th Division, a unit built only for beach defense that included a large number of conscripts from Poland and Ukraine. The specially built flail-tanks of the Westminster Dragoons, part of the Hobart's Funnies, accompanied both Allied groups and helped clear paths through minefields. Meanwhile, the 81st and 82nd Assault Squadrons, made up of other Hobart's Funnies tanks and armored bulldozers helped silence German strongpoints and clear paths for follow-on vehicles.*

*Not all the forces bound for the beach, though, found it easy. The western side of the beach, at Le Hamel, was protected by Widerstandsnest 39 and Widerstandsnest 37, while the far eastern side of King Sector, at La Rivière, was guarded by Widerstandsnest 33. What's more, the British strategy called for two hours of naval bombardment—double the time afforded to the US beaches—before landing 18,381 men. From there, they would link up to the American Omaha Beach westward and the Canadian Juno Beach to the east and capture Bayeux. The division was a mix of new conscripts and volunteers, as well as grizzled veterans who had fought at every stage of the war, including some from 5th East Yorkshires, who had been pulled off the beach at Dunkirk and later fought at El Alamein and been part of the invasion of Sicily.*

**Sub Lt. Peter Miles, RNVR:** It was stressed to us that our job was to keep the men under our command alive and afloat; expect exhaustion as you have not known before. We were also given Benzedrine to keep us awake.

**Trooper W. J. Blackwell, co-driver, 3 Troop, B Squadron, Westminster Dragoons:** Somebody shouted out that the French coast was in view, and suddenly my seasickness was forgotten.

**Lance Cpl. C. Morris, No. 3 Troop, 6 Commando:** Everyone was now sitting very quiet and kept looking at each other and making efforts to smile; but it was all very forced and tense, though we knew that we should be all right once we started to land and had something to occupy our minds.

**Lt. D. C. Potter, troop leader, B Squadron, Westminster Dragoons:** My memory of landing is particularly vivid. It was 7:30 in the morning, cool and dry, the sky part blue and part clouded. There was this enormous beach scattered with obstacles looking like metal gates. Behind the beach was flat land. To the right, further away than I had expected, was the village of Asnelles, with a large building, said to be a sanatorium, direct on the beach at Le Hamel. No sign of any Germans, not that we expected them to be visible.

**Sgt. W. E. Wills, 2nd Battalion, Devonshire Regiment:** A sneaky little thought crept into my mind, which was "How's this for a wedding anniversary?" June 6, 1944, was the sixth anniversary of my marriage, and I felt I had more fireworks for its celebration than any other living person. Rocket ships, assault ships, battleships, cruisers, frigates, and destroyers were all thumping away at the shore, and fighter and fighter-bomber aircraft were passing overhead.

**Lt. D. C. Potter:** My tank was going at, I suppose, eight or ten miles an hour, when, to my horrified surprise, we slithered to a halt. We had bogged down on a patch of clay. I waved furiously to Corporal Adams who was following me in the second flail, yelling that he should give me a wide berth lest he also be stuck, and go on ahead. He went on, reached the minefield, flailed a path through it to the road, flailed and widened the path, opening the route for tanks and vehicles to get off the beach and on to the road.

**Sgt. W. E. Wills:** When about three hundred yards from the shore our LCM stopped and the front ramp was lowered for us to disembark. Both our jeeps were able to drive off together, and into the sea we went—the CO and the rest followed. Unfortunately the sea was deeper than anticipated and after only a few yards both jeeps drowned as water poured into the extended exhaust pipes and also shorted out all our electrics.

**Trooper Joe Minogue, gunner, B Squadron, Westminster Dragoons:** When the ramp of our landing craft went down, the two Churchills left first, followed by two flails, Captain Stanyon's straight Sherman and the armoured bulldozer. We slid into about four feet of water and headed for the beach. It was exactly 07.25 and we seemed to be a little early, for there was a little delay before the Hampshires landed. But we were on the Jig Green and beginning our run up the beach, where we were not to start flailing until just short of the high water mark.

**David Jeffries, visual signalman, *LCT-2442*:** Our skipper, a young New Zealander, maneuvered our craft with skill and purpose until we were able to beach safely. The first two tanks were hit as soon as they touched the beach, but the third roared on guns blazing until we lost sight of it. Just as the last troops left, we were hit forward. With the ramp damaged and counting our blessings, we went full astern. Our craft was the lone survivor of a flotilla of eight.

**Major Richard Gosling, forward observation officer, 147th Field Regiment (Essex Yeomanry), Royal Artillery:** Our driver reckoned he was close enough; pleading that he had to return for another load of passengers, he let down the ramp and we plunged into the sea to an uncomfortable height. We were holding hands in case of unexpected deep holes, and sure enough, almost at once, I found only a hand behind me protruding from the water and Sergeant Cecil Hall was temporarily submerged.

**Lt. D. C. Potter:** I instinctively felt I should get out of my tank. Thus it was that I can justly claim to have been the first soldier with 50 Division to set foot on the coast of France on D-Day. I did not have long to wait. A few hundred yards behind me boats were coming ashore and soon a line of soldiers, single file, came up the beach, passing close to my tank.

**Trooper Joe Minogue:** I will never forget the view through the periscope, seeing the infantry coming ashore, some being hit by guns firing across the beach on fixed lines. As men fell, their mates dragged them from the water and then ran on, not a frantic running motion but a sustained slow trot.

**Capt. Eric Hooper, 9th Battalion, Durham Light Infantry:** I gasped as the freezing surf swirled around. It was the hardest ten yards I ever had to do, but we all got ashore. I think we were all mightily thankful to be off *LCI-501* and her terrible motion, though one poor chap was crushed to death, falling between the gangplank and the rocking side of the vessel. One thing was immediately apparent—the water had brought me around like a footballer's magic sponge: my seasickness evaporated immediately.

**Pvt. James Donaldson, 2nd Battalion, Devonshire Regiment:** One thing I remember—very outstanding—was 47 Royal Marine Commando, who were part of our brigade for this individual landing, coming past us, soaked to the skin. A lot of their landing craft had turned over, but I've never seen men so resolute as these commandos.

**Lt. Cdr. Brian T. Whinney, principal beach master (Gold):** The beach defenses were not as numerous as I had been led to believe, and I was able to calm the LCA, whose coxswain, a royal marine, did extremely well and avoided everything. We beached at about 0745 with about a hundred to a hundred and fifty yards to run to the top of the beach.

**Brig. Sir Alexander Stanier, commanding officer, 231st Infantry Brigade:** 47 Royal Marine Commando had a terribly rough landing. The seas got rougher as the tide came in and they lost seventy men before they actually reached the beach. Then, when they got on to the beach, they found none of their wirelesses would work. How their commanding officer collected them, I don't know. They were very independent, if I may say so. They knew what to do and they were quite happy to get on with it.

**Sgt. Maj. Jack Vilander Brown, 147th Essex Yeomanry:** Some commandos landed just after us. Their boats had been completely tipped up and so they swam ashore. They had lost most of their small arms, so we gave them some of ours, ammunition, and whatnot. Their CO was a brave bloke; I remember seeing him standing on the top of the seawall, waving his stick to direct the blokes where to go.

**Maj. David Warren, 1st Battalion, Royal Hampshire Regiment, 231st Infantry Brigade:** This position, at Le Hamel, where we landed, was going to cause us a great deal of trouble. It had excellent fields of fire and the Germans in fact did not show much signs of giving up.

**Lance Cpl. Norman Travett, 2nd Battalion, Devonshire Regiment, 231st Infantry Brigade:** There was a wall at the top of the beach. It seemed to take a long, long time just to get from the boat to the wall. We got what cover we could underneath the wall, because there was still considerable enemy firepower from pillboxes. There were lots of soldiers with me.

**Maj. David Warren:** I realised that we should have to "gap" our way ourselves—cut our way through the wire, and started to do that. Meanwhile the casualties were piling up because the fire was very strong and it was raking along the top of the beach where people were trying to get. This particular beach was enfiladed: that is, there was a German position at the end of it and they could rake the whole beach with fire. Also there was a gun, which appeared to be some sort of anti-tank gun, and that of course was in concrete and steel.

**Sgt. W. E. Wills:** There were already one or two amphibious tanks moving up the beach from the sea and towards the sand dunes about thirty yards from the water. The LCTs were off-loading more tanks, and shells and mortar bombs were falling, but not in any concentrated manner, fortunately.

**Trooper Joe Minogue:** We started to flail, throwing up gobs of wet sand at first, then creating a fine dust cloud as we hit the dunes and began to blow landmines. We were into the serious business now and our speed at the maximum 1 ½ miles an hour when flailing made us an easy target. But seeing a flail in action for the first time, as the German defenders were doing, is puzzling and confusing and we got through the minefield among the low sand dunes safely. Some of our companions had not been so successful. Major

Elphinstone was killed as soon as he landed, while Captain Stanyon's tank was hit and set on fire and some of his crew wounded.

**Signaler I. G. Holley, 1st Battalion, Royal Hampshire Regiment, 231st Infantry Brigade:** We were in the sea to the tops of our thighs, floundering ashore with other assault platoons to the left and right of us. Mortar bombs and shells were erupting in the sand, and I could hear the burp-burp of Spandau light machine guns through the din. There were no shouts, only the occasional cry as men were hit and went down. To my right I spotted my friend Laffy, another signaler, crawling on his hands and knees, with the radio floating in the water behind him, attached to him by the long lead from the microphones still on his head. I thought he had been hit and only learned later that he had had a relapse of malaria—a legacy quite a few of us had from the Middle East—and had no idea what he was doing.

**Sgt. W. E. Wills:** As I walked along the beach trying to locate the track up which it had been intended the vehicles should drive to the de-waterproofing area, I heard a voice say, "Hello, Will. Get me a blanket if you can." There was a bedraggled figure half sitting, half lying against the sand dunes. He had a Devon Regiment shoulder badge and a major's crown. I looked hard at his badly smashed face and was eventually able to recognize Major Howard, who commanded C Company of our battalion.

Looking around the beach the only blankets to be seen were draped, regimentally, around the haversacks on the backs of the military policemen who were sign-posting the various beach areas. As I walked by one he dropped suddenly and lay very still, except for twitching in his hands. A bullet, maybe from a sniper, because I could not hear automatic fire, had gone straight through his tin hat from front to back and taken some of his brains with it. There was nothing I could do for him, so I removed his neatly folded blanket and took it back to Major Howard. It was then that I learned he had been in the LCA which had capsized and that several of his company had been drowned.

At this stage I felt no fear, only discomfort and disgust at losing my kit, my gun, and the jeep.

**Signaler I. G. Holley:** The beach was filled with half-bent running figures, and we knew from experience that the safest place was to get as near to Jerry as we could. A near one blasted sand over me. A sweet rancid smell, never forgotten, was everywhere; it was the smell of burned explosives, torn flesh, and ruptured earth. We got to the seawall, where a Spandau from a pillbox to our left flattened us until it was silenced a few minutes later. We got on the road, running as fast as our equipment would allow. A Sherman tank had collapsed in a great hole, its commander sticking his head out of the turret going mad with rage. Past this we turned off the road through a wire fence with a sign on it saying "Achtung Minen." There were six of us left.

**Lt. Cdr. Brian T. Whinney:** From then on, for most of the day, we were unable to beach any more craft. They all had to be diverted to the beaches to the east.

**Lance Cpl. Norman Travett:** No way could we possibly advance until this troublesome pillbox had been destroyed. We laid there in our wet trousers and water oozing out of our boots for what seemed ages.

**Trooper W. J. Blackwell:** We reached our road but before we got very far a shell exploded beside the tank and we slid sideways into a deep ditch. Don Fullerlove tried everything to get out, but we stuck fast. It was hopeless, so we did what all highly trained and disciplined British soldiers do: We had a brew up. As we sat there drinking tea and chewing a biscuit, a line of infantry men came through the smoke. None stopped for tea.

*The fire from WN37, the German gun bunker at Le Hamel, was intense enough that the Jig beachmaster suspended landings and redirected approaching craft to King. The German pillbox complex would not fall until the afternoon, when Le Hamel finally fell to a combined arms assault of armor and infantry. For much of the time until the beach and its exits were opened, the already landed forces tried to take care of their wounded or push further inland with lonely initiative.*

*Across the British and Canadian beaches, the Royal Engineers deployed the Hobart's Funnies, new specially modified British tanks, including not just the "Crab" flail tanks for clearing minefields, with their giant rotating drum of chains to slap the ground ahead of the lumbering vehicle and explode mines harmlessly, but also the flamethrowing "Crocodiles" and the AVRE—Armoured Vehicle Royal Engineer—which was armed with a "Petard" gun that fired a devastating 40-pound mortar-style round nicknamed the "flying dustbin." There was also the "Bobbin," which unrolled a long soft mat as a makeshift road to make it easier for heavy vehicles to cross loose sand, and bridging tanks that could deploy "fascines," rolls of sticks that could fill in antitank vehicles, or giant, top-heavy tanks that carried bridges that could be dropped into place. These military engineering innovations would prove decisive in multiple encounters up and down the beaches, defeating minefields, pillboxes, and defenses that the Germans hoped would slow up or halt an Allied advance.*

**Sgt. Herbert "Bert" Matthew Scaife, AVRE commander, 82nd Assault Squadron, Royal Engineers:** Our task was to clear the beach and clear a path. We got off the beach and went straight into a minefield. Then we went to aid a regiment which had got stuck.

**Maj. David Warren:** I met a tank—an AVRE, a Royal Engineers assault tank—specially equipped. This particular one had a mortar-like gun on it, called a Petard, which fired a large bomb. I spoke to the commander of the tank, I told him I wanted him to support this attack on Le Hamel, and the tank came forward and it fired the bomb into the buildings.

**Sgt. Herbert "Bert" Matthew Scaife:** We had a special type of gun. It was short-range and fired a big missile which was designed to crack concrete. The only thing was you had to get fairly close up with it. I put one or two shots into the sanatorium and smashed it up.

**Maj. David Warren:** When [Scaife] did that we assaulted it and went inside and it was silenced. And that was a great relief to all concerned because there was a lot of landing craft having difficulties on our beach. They could now come ashore; the beach masters could get things organised rather better.

**Lance Cpl. Norman Travett:** Eventually [Le Hamel] was silenced. That was where I saw my first dead Germans, up there in that pillbox. Gruesome. I thought those chaps had probably been called up for service like myself and had no wish to be where they were. They didn't stand a chance, really. Not there. What could they do?

**Trooper Charles Wilson, regimental survey party, 147th Essex Yeomanry:** Eventually a way was cleared off the beach and the battery half-track moved inland. I walked along behind it with the rest of the command post staff, as it crawled along a narrow lane which the engineers were sweeping for mines. Then we came to fields and hedges, two poor stone cottages, and our first Frenchmen, two gray-stubbled old men who kissed us on both cheeks and jabbered away in the Normandy dialect. The road was crowded with vehicles and infantry moving inland.

**Lt. Cdr. Brian T. Whinney:** Things quieted down during the afternoon, and at about 1700, I accompanied the commanding officer of the beach crew, Col. Philips, on a recce along the beach, and up into Arromanches and Le Hamel. All was quiet, but an eerie feeling remained, and not a soul in sight. We were about to return to the beach, when we heard a noise in a cottage. The colonel rapped on the door, and to our astonishment, an old lady appeared, and seemed quite unconcerned. She had apparently been there all day, carrying out her household chores as usual—although the house was backed onto the pillbox that had caused us so much trouble all day.

**Lt. M.J. Eedy, acting adjutant, Westminster Dragoons:** The local villagers appeared very soon, interested only in getting to us wreak mayhem on the occupying Germans who, of course, had gone. I well remember the superb old woman described the local German commander walking around with a great black dog, terrorizing the locals—she said, with great understandable venom, he was a swine, a devil, and she spat.

*"Personally dedicated to winning the war"*

# The Green Howards Take King Sector

British armor and the Green Howards begin their push inland.

*Down the beach from Jig Sector, units arriving in the King Sector found them-*
*selves facing stiff opposition from the defenses of the German bunker and guns*
*at La Rivière. There, Westminster Dragoons tanks moved up the beach for battle*
*against the German bunkers securing the waterfront.*

**Lt. B. M. S. Hoban, troop leader, Troop I, C Squadron, Westminster Dragoons:** The
familiar juddering thud as the LCT ran aground at La Rivière, the familiar

rattle of chains, as the ramp was lowered. From then on things seemed to happen fast. We were soon down in the water, appreciating the fact that our waterproofing seemed to have been efficient.

**Trooper C. T. Smith, driver, Troop I, C Squadron, Westminster Dragoons:** The Germans had expected that the landings would be made at high water and had placed their "Hedgehogs" or anti-tank obstacles further up the beach. These consisted of short lengths of railway line welded together with a mine on top. Fortunately, they were placed far enough apart to allow us to pass between them.

**Lt. B. M. S. Hoban:** Two AVREs from our LCT charged ahead up the beach until in quick succession they simply exploded.

**Trooper C. T. Smith:** I saw the flash as the leading one was hit. Immediately after, the second AVRE began to burn and then there was an enormous cloud of black smoke and the two Churchills disappeared. We heard later that they had been carrying "Wade" charges for blowing up the beach defences. Their crews did not have a chance. An 88mm anti-tank gun in a massive pill box untouched by the bombing and bombardment was enfilading the beach.

**Lt. B. M. S. Hoban:** Everything stopped of a sudden; then got going again in response to the resolute Canadian tones on the wireless of Major Tim Thompstone RE, our breaching-squadron commander, saying "Get on up that bloody beach, all of you!"

**Trooper H. W. J. Smith, gunner, C Squadron, Westminster Dragoons:** Capt. Bell ordered our driver to halt and came over the intercom for our assessment of the situation. Capt. Bell at first suggested that we might run the gauntlet and try to outrun the Germans, but this was voted out because we would not be able to gather enough speed to have any sort of chance and we convinced him to let me try to disable it.

**Trooper C. T. Smith:** [That 88mm gun] could have turned the assault into a disaster but for the action of Capt. Roger Bell, commanding the assault team nearest to the pill-box, who brought his tank within one hundred yards of the gun. Trooper H. W. J. Smith, his gunner, fired several rounds.

**Trooper H. W. J. Smith:** I asked to be loaded with HE, aimed and fired. The round exploded close to the gun apron with very little effect. The second round was the same. I asked to be loaded with Armour Piercing to try and penetrate the gun mantle. As I sighted on the target he fired off another round at something on the beach and at this moment I decided to try and hit the barrel of their gun while they were reloading. I aimed and fired, the AP hit their gun barrel, deflected, and found its way between the mantle and the concrete, entering the emplacement and spinning around inside, killing all the crew.

**Lt. B. M. S. Hoban:** After his fifth round, the gun fell silent.

*Captain Bell later received the Military Cross, the UK's third-highest award for gallantry, for his tank's actions that morning.*

\*        \*        \*

*While the tanks silenced the main pillboxes, arriving infantry at King Sector from the Green Howards moved to rout defenders hidden in trench complexes. The Green Howards were a particularly experienced regiment, with veterans—like Sgt. Stanley Hollis, the command sergeant major of Company D, who had fought at Dunkirk and in North Africa before readying for* OVERLORD.

**CSM (Company Sgt. Maj.) Stanley E. Hollis, Company D, 6th Battalion, Green Howards:** As we were coming in, I lifted a Lewis gun off the floor of the landing craft and belted [fired] this thing with a full pan of ammunition. It was then that I received the most painful wound I had in the whole war. I lifted the stripped Lewis gun off the gunwale of the landing craft and it was white-hot and I got a bloody great blister across my hand, as thick as my finger!

**Lt. Col. Robin W. S. Hastings, commander, 6th Battalion, Green Howards:** There was no danger of being trampled in the rush [off the landing craft]. No one moved; all stared at the sea which came right up into the craft. The only thing was for me to test the depth of the water for all to see. Very gradually I sat down, like a Brighton paddler, and dangled my feet over the edge. The water came up to my knees. Confidently, I rose to my feet and set off up the beach.

**Henry Lovegrove, chaplain, 6th Battalion, Green Howards:** One's first impression upon landing was the narrowness of the beach. We had to lay flat whilst in front of us the engineers were busy clearing the barbed wire and beach obstacles. These impeded our movements. A Company on the left of Gold Beach were pinned down under the seawall, while on that right, D Company was faced with a pillbox at the end of a trench within twenty yards of the point where they had advanced and were immediately under fire. At which point, company sergeant major Stan Hollis rushed forward, climbed on top of the pillbox and managed to deal with it single-handed.

**CSM Stanley E. Hollis:** We charged about waist-deep in the water and the man in front of me, Sergeant Hill, who had been a very good soldier all throughout the war—a real fighting man—dropped into a shell hole under the water. He couldn't come up with all the stuff he was carrying and the landing craft went over him and the propellers cut him to bits. On reaching the high-water mark, we lost one of our very important officers. We lost the beach master. He was the man who was supposed to say, "Right you go this way and you go that way!" So he was out of action. By this time, shells and mortar bombs were dropping, but we were getting no small arms casualties.

**Lt. Col. Robin W. S. Hastings:** They got across [the beach] but met a certain amount of machine-gun fire sweeping the beach from one pillbox and also found some mortar bombs landing among them. They got up under the sea wall, and huddled as men will under fire in the comparative safety of its shelter. It was the sort of moment when an operation can so easily bog down however careful the planning. However, there they were, under the wall, and it was they who broke the deadlock. They threw grenades over the sea wall and rushed after them themselves, turning their Tommy guns on the defenders. After that, the battle went better and A Company soon had their objective in safekeeping.

**Pvt. Dennis Bowen, 5th Battalion, East Yorkshire Regiment:** I seem to remember just a continual roar of sound; there was no individual sound of *bang-bang-bang*, it was a roar. Whether it was us firing at Jerry or Jerry firing at us, I don't know.

**Pvt. Francis Williams, 6th Battalion, Green Howards:** On our left a flail tank went forward and blew up, whether from a shell or a mine I don't know. One of its wheels rolled right along the beach and just missed one of our sergeants, who was lying on the sand with a wound in his leg and half his jaw blown away.

**Pvt. A. Baker, wireless operator, 4th/7th Dragoon Guards:** The beach was black with men and machines and LCTs discharging their cargoes. The sea was still rough and obviously making things very difficult. I saw several lorries overturn in the breakers. My memories of the beach are very confused. I remember noticing a number of DD tanks still there, but I couldn't see whose they were. Dabby, our commander, seemed to know where he was going fairly well, and in quite a short time we were off the beach altogether and going up a track with a procession of other vehicles.

**CSM Stanley E. Hollis:** We ran up to the top of the beach and along a ridge. There were heaps of rolled wire. An Irishman was alongside me and believe it or not there were two or three birds sat on this wire. This Irishman, Mullally, said to me, "No bloody wonder they are there, Sergeant Major, there's no room in the air for them!" Up to now, things had gone pretty well and we had expected far heavier casualties than we had had. The minefield extended in depth quite a lot from the beaches to the bottom hedge. The platoons of D Company were led through by the assault pioneers of the battalion—they went ahead with their Hoover things [mine detectors] and laid the white tapes behind them, and we trod on the tape.

**Pvt. Francis Williams:** One of our platoons was moving up the road which was to have been our left boundary, but we had landed well to the left of it. I jumped up and ran at the machine-gun post, firing short bursts from the hip. I was on them before they knew what was happening. I shot two of the occupants and shouting "Hände hoch!" the other six gave themselves up. I ran them towards the track with their hands on their heads, and when we reached it, there in the ditch was about six or so of 18 Platoon, all of whom had been hit in the legs. I ran the six Germans down to the beach and left them as there was a lot of people ashore now. Before I left them I noticed one of them had a sort of band around the bottom of his sleeve and on it were the words "Afrika Korps." I had a few words with him. As far as I can remember I said to him, "You Rommel's man?" He said, "Ja." Pointing to my Africa Star, I said, "Me Eighth Army." It was a bit like Tarzan and Jane. I shook his hand and went back to what was left of 17 Platoon.

**Lt. Col. C. MacDonald Hull, second in command, 6th Battalion, Green Howards:** We waited for the codeword from the battalion to come through on our set. Suddenly the codeword! The battalion had got its first objective—it was through the beach defences and had captured the enemy coastal battery. It was fantastic in that short space of time. It was H hour +47. So that in the space of some 40 minutes, 6th Battalion and The Green Howards had burst through the coastal defenses that Hitler's army had been four years preparing. I passed the message to the naval signallers, who flashed it all over the armada and back to London. Never had I before, or have I since, been so proud of being a Green Howard.

**CSM Stanley E. Hollis:** When we got to where the crossroads are, the fire was a lot closer—we were getting more casualties—and so we got down and crawled up this hill. Major Lofthouse and I came forward to see what we could see and we saw where the firing was coming from. Major Lofthouse said to me, "There's a pillbox there Sergeant Major." Well, when he said that I saw it—it was very well camouflaged. I saw these guns moving round in the slits and I got my Sten gun and I rushed at it, spraying it hosepipe fashion. They fired back at me, and they missed. I don't know whether they were more panic-stricken than me, but they must have been. I got on top of it and threw a grenade through the slit.

**Lt. Col. Robin W. S. Hastings:** Without hesitation, he simply charged it, and shot the inhabitants. How he survived is hard to imagine, as one bullet had grazed his eyebrow and taken a clip out of his ear.

**CSM Stanley E. Hollis:** I went round the back and went inside and there were two dead and quite a lot of prisoners. They were quite willing to forget all about the war. I could never understand how I got so many prisoners—I got about eighteen or twenty prisoners—but we found out later that this was the command post for the Mont Fleury gun battery, which was just over the brow of the hill. We didn't bother with escorts for the prisoners, we just pointed the way back down to the beach and they were quite happy to go by themselves.

**Maj. Henry "Jo" Gullet, Australian Army, 6th Battalion, Green Howards:** The pillboxes had fallen and our leading companies were mustering up the prisoners, a motley collection, mostly Russians. Some were big and blond, but there were many Mongol types also, nasty-looking men. We found out afterward they had no idea where they were, but had been conned and bullied by the Germans into manning Hitler's West Wall.

**CSM Stanley E. Hollis:** Then we came over this field to advance to the Mont Fleury gun positions, and it was at the top of that field that I looked back. I had been firmly convinced that The Green Howards were the only people fighting this bloody war, but when I looked back I couldn't see any water at all—it was covered from horizon to horizon with thousands of ships—and it was then that I realised that somebody else was helping us, and it gave us a great feeling of confidence.

*Later that morning, as the Green Howards advanced, Hollis found himself in charge of 16 Platoon after its commander was killed. Many of the units coming off Gold Beach headed inland, passing through the village of Crépon, about three miles from the beach. There, when clearing and securing farmhouses one by one, Hollis's unit found itself under fire from a German gun position. After an attack by the Green Howards faltered, Hollis retreated, only to discover that two of his men remained stuck at the nearby farmhouse.*

**Trooper H. W. J. Smith, gunner, C Squadron:** Although we were a specialized unit with the flail, because the bad weather was still holding up the landing of extra reinforcements we had to carry out the role of the armored fighting unit. The hedgerows alongside the fields and the lanes well below the level of the land on either side made it an ideal area for ambush and for the Germans to use their anti-tank weapons to good effect. All thoughts of what had happened on the beach were now put behind us and what might lie ahead was now taking over.

**CSM Stanley E. Hollis:** We heard a terrific racket coming from the farm, and somebody told me that the two Bren gunners that I had brought in were still in the rhubarb. They were pinned down and couldn't get out! I said to Major Lofthouse, "Well I took them in, I'll go and try and get them out." I waited behind a wall until there was a lull in the firing, and I ran straight out across the farmyard and sprayed the hedge with the Bren gun. It quietened [the Germans] down and I was able to shout to the lads to get out and come back and join me, which they were able to do.

*Hollis's actions that day made him the only British soldier on D-Day to be awarded the Victoria Cross, Britain's highest award for gallantry. Across the entire war, he sustained wounds a total of six times in combat.*

**Citation for Stanley Hollis's Victoria Cross, August 15, 1944:** Wherever fighting was heaviest, C. S. M. Hollis appeared and in the course of a magnificent day's work, he displayed the utmost gallantry and on two separate occasions his courage and initiative prevented the enemy from holding up the advance at critical stages. It was largely through his heroism and resource that the Company's objectives were gained and casualties were not heavier, and by his own bravery he saved the lives of many of his men.

**Lt. Col. Robin W. S. Hastings:** He was absolutely personally dedicated to winning the war, one of the few men I ever met who felt like that.

**CSM Stanley E. Hollis:** All these fellers were my mates. There wasn't only me doing these things—there were other people doing things as well. The things that I did, if I hadn't done them, somebody else would have.

# Ashore at Juno

The Canadian troops at Juno Beach soon found the rising tide
left them with little beach to maneuver.

*While D-Day was fraught and emotional for every one of its million-plus
participants, there was a specifically poignant feeling for the Canadians involved,
as Canada had borne the brunt of the disastrous 1942 raid on Dieppe, and its
shadow hung over every aspect of the commonwealth's planning and contribution
to the new Allied invasion. D-Day, for the Canadians, was a chance to avenge
the losses and embarrassment of Dieppe.*

*The beach designated for the Canadian troop landing, code-named Juno, was
located by the mouth of the Seulles River.*

*Manned by the 736th Grenadier-Regiment, Juno Beach was home to the
strongest German defense structure other than those at Omaha Beach, guarded
by Stützpunkte-Courseulles, an interlinked series of three Widerstandsnester, two*

*of them at the mouth of the river, Nos. 29 and 31, and a third, WN30, inland. The land directly off the beach was urban—within steps of the seawall, there were houses, hotels, apartments, and shops, and many of the buildings had been fortified to provide cover for machine guns and snipers.*

*Capturing Juno was the primary mission assigned to Maj. Gen. Rod Keller, leading the 3rd Canadian Infantry Division. Under his command, the 7th and 8th Canadian Brigades would land at two sectors. The leading wave of the 7th Brigade was to include the Royal Winnipeg Rifles, the Regina Rifles, and the 1st Battalion of the Canadian Scottish, which would all land adjacent to the small towns of Courseulles-sur-Mer and Graye-sur-Mer—sectors known as Mike Green, Mike Red, and Nan Green—while 8th Brigade's Queen's Own Rifles of Canada and Régiment de la Chaudière, would land adjacent to Bernières-sur-Mer at Nan White. At Nan Red's eastern end of the beach, the North Shore (New Brunswick) Regiment would lead the way. Follow-on units would include the North Nova Scotia Highlanders, the Highland Light Infantry of Canada, the Cameron Highlanders of Ottawa, and the Stormont, Dundas, and Glengarry Highlanders. Tanks from the 1st Hussars and Fort Garry Horse as well as flail tanks from the 22nd Dragoons would back up the infantry. As with the other British beaches, H-Hour was set about an hour later than the US beaches, at 0735 for the 7th Canadian Brigade and 0745 for the 8th Brigade.*

**Pvt. Robert Rogge, Stormont, Dundas and Glengarry Highlanders, 9th Infantry Brigade, 3rd Canadian Division:** I can remember standing there by the railing of that ship and thinking that we were going back to the same beaches that William the Conqueror had used when he invaded England in 1066.

**Matthew Halton, CBC correspondent:** It was absolutely astonishing to stand on deck in the early morning before H-Hour, the moment when the battle was to start. It was bewildering. There was this enormous armada anchoring right off the coast of France in broad daylight and nothing was happening. Not a thing. Not a gun. Not a bomb. It was fantastic. We stared at the villages and the tall church spires of Normandy and there was not a sound.

**Bernard Martin, resident, Courseulles-sur-Mer (age 17):** From the window of our bathroom, we saw the first ships about 7 or 7:15. My dad was swearing at the time. There was a warship—I later learned it was the [French destroyer] *La*

*Combattante*—which was very close to the coast. My dad said, "Stupid—he's going to wreck on the beach!" We tell ourselves maybe we are seeing Dieppe, where the Canadians had been thrown back into the water with many dead.

**Cdr. Peter MacRitchie, *LC-250*:** It looked like the dawn that marked the opening of the season's regatta rather than the dawn of freedom. We pirouetted around that bay almost endlessly, and suddenly you forgot about the regatta atmosphere for *Nelson* and *Warspite* and *Ramillies* were firing. We were driving around in line ahead when all of a sudden the flotilla leader's lamp flashed and in a second we were line abreast and striking for the beach at Bernières-sur-Mer at full speed.

**Sgt. Wes Alkenbrack, gun commander, Troop D, 14th Field Artillery, Royal Canadian Artillery:** And then the beach itself became visible, with a few figures scattered across it, some running, some standing, and some lying motionless on the sand.

**Lt. Bill Little, commander, 5th Troop (Sherman DD tanks), C Squadron, Fort Garry Horse, 3rd Canadian Division:** The landing probably was the most exciting and most invigorating period of my life. It was like going out deer-shooting for the first time—the emotion of that first shot. It wasn't necessarily revenge, but we were there to eliminate the German army one way or another.

**Sgt. Leo Gariepy, Sherman DD tank commander, B Squadron, 1st Hussars:** The minesweepers leading us in slowed down and began making a semicircle. The flotilla of LCTs began manoeuvring for launching our DD tanks. Our LCT was having great difficulty trying to maintain its position for launching. Finally the launching officer called us together and said that High Command had vetoed launching in such a rough sea. Suddenly, at 7,000 yards, our squadron commander, Major Duncan, asked us if we would prefer to risk it. Cheers went up, we were all for it and we prepared to launch. The LCT once again took its launching position in the wind, the ramp was lowered and we each, in turn, rolled off.

**Lt. Bill Little:** My tank went into the water about a thousand meters from the beach, and our DD tank swam to shore.

**Sgt. Leo Gariepy:** At about 3,000 yards, I looked around and saw Maj. [J. S.] Duncan about 30 yards to my starboard and the rest of the DDs behind us. The port aft strut broke and the crew had to wedge a fire extinguisher between the screen and the hull. We had been showered with small arms fire, but suddenly I saw two pillars to the right near Maj. Duncan's tank, and the first shell fire we had received on the way in. I looked ahead again and when I turned around once more the major's tank had disappeared.

**Pvt. J. H. Hamilton, Royal Winnipeg Rifles, 7th Infantry Brigade, 3rd Canadian Division:** We were being swamped by heavy waves. Because the waves were so high, they were washing over our landing craft, and our first casualty was Rifleman Andrew G. Munch, who was, as we all were, very, very seasick. He was lying on the gunwale, and as we came in to about two miles offshore, a large wave washed him off, and he went down. We never saw him again.

**Sgt. Leo Gariepy:** A midget submarine [X20] appeared just a few yards in front of me. His duty was to lead me to my primary target on the beach, a blockhouse sheltering a naval gun. High wind was forcing me to drift and the man in the submarine was trying to wave me back into line. It was impossible; the wind was too strong. As the water became shallower, the submarine stopped, its occupant [Lt. Hudspeth] stood up and wished me luck with his hands clasped over his mouth. I was a few yards off my target, but not too bad, and at exactly 0745, I touched the sand and drove out of the water.

*Despite the losses at sea, Leo Gariepy's unit was one of the few Sherman DD units of the invasion to succeed—whereas so many of the Sherman DD tanks had sunk at the American beaches or been held up at sea, 14 of the 19 tanks of the 1st Hussars at Juno made it to shore roughly on time, providing vital covering fire for the first waves of infantry. Ashore, the first waves of the Canadian infantry faced a challenge different than those at Omaha and Utah: Juno had too little beach. The quickly rising tide meant that there were only yards between the invaders and the defenders' guns.*

**Pvt. Gerald Marley Henry, unit mechanic, Royal Winnipeg Rifles, 7th Infantry Brigade, 3rd Canadian Division:** Somewhere about 7:30 or 7:45, the first of our battalion stormed the beaches. All the softening up did was alert the enemy of the landing and gave them the chance to be settled in for our guys to run into. With the seas being so heavy, their landing was most difficult. They were being dumped off in water four, five and six feet deep. Consequently, this gave all the advantage to the Germans. It took a great deal of heroics and casualties to silence the concrete emplacements and the machine gun nests.

**Pvt. Heinrich Siebel, 6 Kompanie, Panzerjägerkompanie, 716 Infanterie-Division:** We shot and shot, especially at the strange tanks that came up the beach. It was hard for us to see much because of the smoke but I believe we destroyed two tanks before our gun received a direct hit. There was a flash and a great bang and I was blown backwards onto the concrete floor and knew nothing else for a time. When I woke up I found two of our men dead and more wounded. Our gun was destroyed.

**Lionel Shapiro, correspondent, *Maclean's* magazine:** On both flanks of Bernières were situated the main German defences, from which the Germans could pour devastating fire onto the Bernières beach. On those flanking positions, Canadians won their greatest glory. Here, there was only a 10-yard depth of sand beach, then a 15-yard depth of barbed wire and behind this the most modern German steel and concrete defences. Under the covering fire of tanks, some still in their landing craft 50 yards at sea, the Canadians swarmed against the flank positions. The first wave of troops were caught by machine-gun fire and died on the barbed wire. Other troops leaped over the bodies of their comrades, and into the very mouths of the cannon, to fling grenades through the small ranging apertures.

**CSM (Company Sgt. Maj.) Charlie Martin, Company A, Queen's Own Rifles, 8th Infantry Brigade, 3rd Canadian Division:** The moment the ramp came down, heavy machine-gun fire broke out from somewhere back of the seawall. Mortars were dropping over the beach. The men rose, starboard line turning right, port turning left. I said to Jack, across from me, and to everyone: "Move! Fast! Don't stop for anything. Go! Go! Go!" We raced down the ramp. None of us really grasped at that point—spread across such a large beach front—just how thin on the ground we were. Each of the ten boatloads had become an independent fighting unit. Bert Shepard, Bill Bettridge, and I were running at top speed and firing from the hip.

**Cpl. Wilfred Bennet, Royal Winnipeg Rifles, 7th Brigade, 3rd Canadian Division:** We hit the water waist deep, and men were falling in the water, and then they fell on the beach—the machine gun fire was so devastating. My buddy, Kelly McTier, who was on my right, was shot in the face and the neck. We were told not to stop and help any of our buddies as we too might be hit, and we were to carry on as best we could to get across the beach.

**Pvt. J. H. Hamilton:** I got off the landing craft and crossed the narrow sandy beach to the edge of the beach sand dune. I got some protection, but still, I suffered a piece of shrapnel lodged in my right nostril. I was unconscious for some time, and being one of the early waves on the beach, there was no first-aid station. When I came to, I tried to put one of our field dressings on, but it's pretty hard to dress your own face wound, so I just continued to let it bleed.

**Cpl. Fred Barnard, Company B, Queen's Own Rifles, 8th Infantry Brigade, 3rd Canadian Division:** My brother Don was on the boat with me. You could claim your brother to your regiment—get them to transfer him to your regiment—and I claimed him in 1944. As we were going down the ramp, I yelled to my brother, "Don, give 'em Hell!" And the next thing I know I'm in water maybe four feet of deep. When I went up the beach, I passed one of the guys in my platoon—just a kid, about 19—he had been ripped right down, crying for his mother. The next thing I know, there was Don, lying on his back, a bullet right there in the heart. There was just a black hole in his uniform right in the middle of his chest. No blood. It was as if he was asleep.

**Capt. L. N. "Nobby" Clarke, Number I Movement Control Unit:** Those last few moments were pretty awful. We were coming under intense small-arms fire and every-one was down as much as possible. Many of the lads on our LCA never got ashore: a *Spandau* opened up just when the water was full of men struggling to get ashore. The beach was littered with those who had been a jump ahead of us and a captured blockhouse being used as a dressing station was literally surrounded by piles of bodies.

**Jack Heath, *LCT-522*, 20th Flotilla:** All this time there were shells and mortars and small arms fire all around, a proper hellhole. We were just coming free of the beach and the winch party had just come from the winch housing, when there was an almighty bang and the bows went up in the air. We had hit a mine and the boat settled on the sand. We [were] marooned on the beach for five weeks.

**Lt. Cdr. Kenneth Edwards (Ret.), Royal Navy historian:** The Landing Craft Obstacle Clearance Unit did magnificent work, but the speed of the assault was such that they had insufficient time to neutralize or demolish many of the obstacles. On the whole, however, the majority of the obstacles were cleared by the simple method of the larger and heavier types of landing craft charging the beaches and crashing their way through the obstacles.

**Rifleman John McLean:** [There were] rolls of concertina wire. It was about twenty to thirty feet across this wire and it was about two feet high. Just beyond the wire were the sand dunes and at least temporary safety. However, our Bangalore torpedo man never made it out of the water so we had to make our way through the wire as best we could. One of the pioneers section attached to us [B Company] threw himself on the barbed wire so the men could walk over his back and reach the safety of the dunes.

**Lt. Reg Weeks, intelligence officer, 3rd Canadian Division:** The thing I remember is that the people who had not been killed—the people who had gone ashore ahead of me—there was a look in their eye which I have never seen repeated under any circumstances. Unless you have been under those conditions, you will not see that look in anyone's eye. A combination of fear, uncertainty, disbelief, all there in one heap.

*          *          *

**Pvt. J. H. Hamilton:** Finally, there were five or six walking wounded, and we formed up a section and moved off the beach to follow the route of our company inland, and I went to the village of Sainte-Croix, which our battalion had taken. There were a number of dead Germans lying in the streets. When we came off the narrow sandy beach, I saw a number of Canadian-Scottish that had been killed. They were laying about and the red poppies were in bloom then. It struck me then of a poem that we learned in school by Col. McCrae: *In Flanders fields the poppies blow / Between the crosses, row on row.* That certainly struck me, seeing the Canadian-Scottish laying dead amongst the red poppies blooming in the wind.

**Russ Munro, war correspondent, Canadian Press:** From dune to dune, along the German trench systems and through the tunnels, these Manitoba troops fought every yard of the way. They broke into the big casemates, ferreted out the gun crews with machine guns, grenades, bayonets and knives. The Canadians ran into crossfire. They were shelled and mortared mercilessly even in the German positions but kept slugging away at the enemy. The 1st Hussar's tanks churned through the dunes in close support and after a struggle which was as bitter and savage as any the Winnipegs broke through into the open country behind the beach.

**Sgt. Leo Gariepy:** We then started to head into the town of Courseulles. Fearing a mine pattern on the unused street leading away from the beach, I ploughed through the back gardens of the houses. A frantic Frenchman appeared in front of my tank, gesticulating wildly. I stuck my head out of the turret and asked him what he wanted and he shouted "Boche, Boche" in an excited voice and pointed up the street. When he tried to explain in extremely bad English, I cut him short in French and asked him what was the matter. He was flabbergasted that I could speak French but I finally cooled him long enough for him to tell me that there was a group of enemy hidden inside a large park behind an eight-foot-high wall. I took a position directly in front of the wall, butted through it with my tank and fired a smoke shell into a large enclosure, following it up with machine-gun fire. Then we fired two HE shells into a sentry box in the far corner of the area. This had the desired effect and some thirty-two German prisoners gave themselves up. I believe this was the first large group of the enemy taken on the beach area.

*             *             *

*The main beach positions were quickly cleared out, but mortar fire and longer-range artillery continued to dog the landing beaches for hours. As the Canadian units and their vehicles edged into the urban areas inland, the beach quickly became*

*congested—an untimely and unfortunate situation for hundreds of trapped vehicles*
*soon swamped by the rising waters.*

**Trooper Hubert Thistle, wireless operator, Sherman tank, C Squadron, Sher-
brooke Fusiliers:** By the time we came in, it was just a matter of driving
onto the beach. We got in about ten miles or so and we were ordered off
the road and to dig in for the night.

**Cpl. John McDonald, Stormont, Dundas, and Glenngarry Highlanders, 9th Infantry
Brigade, 3rd Canadian Division:** We landed about 11 a.m. They hadn't been able
to clear all the guys off that part of the beach. When I saw a half-a-dozen
bodies—you could see a half-dozen Winnipegs with blankets on them—it
struck me that things are going to happen here.

**Sgt. Stanley Dudka, Company C, North Nova Scotia Highlanders:** There was
tremendous congestion all along the beaches to your left and to your right
where troops were landing at the same time and vehicles coming. The roads
were very narrow and very limited, and when we got ashore at Bény sur
Mer, we were held up there for approximately three hours.

**Rifleman Bull Ross:** There was heavy congestion of equipment. Some vehicles
were directed to go left into an apple orchard. On the right of the road tanks
and self propelled guns moved into a hayfield. Several tanks had taken hits.

**Lance Cpl. Stuart Stear, 619 Independent Field Park Company, 103 Beach Group,
Royal Engineers:** Behind the seawall, the German defences seemed to be
freshly built and the ground floors of the houses had been filled with concrete to make camouflaged bunkers. They had been badly shelled and were
badly pitted but it was mainly superficial damage. Lying all about were
khaki and field grey bodies. More field grey than khaki but it didn't mean
anything to me, as I was numb and overwhelmed by all that was going on.
Beyond the sea front, there was less damage than I had expected.

**Pvt. Robert Rogge:** The 7th Brigade had cleared the town and now the 8th and
9th Brigades were all jammed up in there because there was some trouble
on the road up through Bernières sur Mer. There was a couple of 88s up

there that had knocked down some of the Shermans and boys from the 7th Brigade were taking out the gun crews before any of us could go any further.

**Lt. Bill Little:** We were a western regiment, and a lot of country boys. As we broke through this hedgerow, this line of [German] troops were marching out of this village. I said, "Troops, 500 yards, high-explosive, load, fire, give them hell!" We caught a whole company. We must have killed most of them and the recce troops of the North Shores came up and got the rest and made them prisoners. The excitement was just fantastic, and I called my other tank and pointed out the target and said, "let them have it!" It was a real bird-shoot. We caught them in the open, with all the guns. The exhilaration after all the years of training, the tremendous feeling of lift, excitement, exhilaration, of doing this!

**Pvt. Robert Rogge:** We were issued bicycles. Yes, bicycles. We were supposed to cycle from the beaches to our D-Day objective.

**Cpl. John McDonald:** Those damn bicycles. They were just slowing us down. We dumped them in an orchard. That's the last we ever saw of them.

**Pvt. Robert Rogge:** We moved out toward Bény-Sur-Mer which is about a mile or so inland. When we got to Bennie we were told to dig in and we started digging our trenches underneath the exits. We didn't know any better and while we were digging in the orchard next to the church at Bennie, a mortar shell hit in the hedges and Bert Bocks was killed. Bert was our first casualty and there were a bunch of men wounded by splinters—not by shrapnel, by splinters. We buried Bert in the churchyard and had a couple of Jerry P.O.W.'s dig his grave.

**Pvt. Roland Johnston, driver, MI0 Tank Destroyer, 52nd Battery, 3rd Anti-Tank Regiment:** We came into a corner and we met the British commandos. We were about the first troops that they had run into and one of their officers said, in his British accent, "You have to turn left heah!" I looked and saw there were bodies lying on the road and I said, "Oh my God, not for a minute." I said, "We're gonna have to move some of those bodies, because I am not going to run over any more of my own bodies today." The bodies were still warm—I know because we moved them. There were lots; I guess a machine gun nest or something caught them.

**Pvt. Gerald Marley Henry:** We passed through small villages on our way to regain contact with the regiment. I was very surprised to hear how many French people could speak English. They were very thankful for the invasion and were trying to give us wine and food; however, we had been warned not to accept anything, not even water, for fear that it would be poisoned. My, it was tempting.

**Lance Cpl. Stuart Stear:** During the afternoon, I saw German prisoners passing us being marched back to the beach. They seemed very young and as frightened as we were. Later, others came back on their own, unescorted, happy to be on their way to England and out of the war. The German prisoners helped with carrying stretchers onto the empty landing craft and were put to work burying their dead.

**Capt. Vassar Hall, Mike Red beachmaster, Regina Rifles:** I just hung around the beach. There was lots to see, people to help. We started to collect casualties. German prisoners of war started to come on to the beach in fair numbers. Later in the day, when the tide went out, we saw a lot of the casualties that had been drowned, so I got a party of prisoners to start picking up bodies, including the body of the company commander who had followed me in but didn't make it. We brought them in and part of my job was also gathering the effects of those killed in action, turning money over to the paymaster and anything else belonging to them to the Padre. I made notes on how they were killed—shell wound, drowning and so on.

**Lance Cpl. Stuart Stear:** By late afternoon, the seeming chaos of the morning had been replaced by order, with signs and military police everywhere and by early evening even the sporadic artillery fire had stopped.

**Capt. L. N. "Nobby" Clarke:** The afternoon and evening was devoted to "de-lousing" the houses behind the beach of snipers and quite a job it was. We were a bit clumsy at first and lost quite a few because of it, but it soon became more or less a drill. I had a small group of two sergeants and six

Sappers with plenty of guts. Some of the houses just refused to be de-loused and so we burnt them down. We set one on fire which had caused us a lot of grief and when it really started to brew a young Jerry made an effort to escape through a window. He got partly out when a gunner on an LCT saw him and hit him with a streak of about fifty Oerlikon rounds.

**Lt. Garth Webb, commander, 105mm Self Propelled Gun, C Troop, 14th Field Regiment, Royal Canadian Artillery:** Everybody knew some of us would be killed. Then the 88 blew up three of our guns and two of the guns—the crews—were all killed.

**Sgt. Wes Alkenbrack:** Clear above the sound of our laboring engines came the grinding screech of an armor-piercing shell. Smoke and dust billowed up from the stricken vehicle. With incredible swiftness the second gun was struck. It was obvious our deployment was rapidly falling apart.

As Dog 4 [our gun] cleared the corner and moved forward, the field gun in front of us erupted in a massive and hideous sheet of red flame. The concussion of the explosion leapt from it in a shock wave of paralyzing force. The next moment revealed the stark and utter disintegration of what had been thirty tons of moving steel, now strewn on the ground like scattered garbage—the gun barrel and bits and pieces of steel plate and the remnants of tracks and heavy castings blown here and there, and not the slightest evidence that six men had stood on the deck when sudden destruction came. Before the [88mm gun] had a chance to correct his aim, the Chaudières closed in on the gun and killed the gun crew. But for those of us on Dog 4, it was as close as that.

**Lt. Garth Webb:** A lot of us wondered, "What the hell are we going to do?"

**Sgt. Stanley Dudka:** We got inland that night to about eight miles, and then the orders came that we should dig in for the night, that we should not advance any further; however, we should put out continuous patrols and expect a counter-attack.

**Pvt. Gerald Marley Henry:** That evening when we dug in for the night was a welcome stop. Seasickness forgotten, there was still no need for food yet.

We had been issued a quantity of hard candy, which was excellent to curb hunger and yet full of energy. We also had cans of cocoa, at least it was called cocoa, and it might have been. These cans had a wick and an igniter so when you pulled the top off, it ignited and within a very short time, you had a warm drink. Not good—but warm.

**Lionel Shapiro, correspondent, *Maclean's* magazine, dispatch from Juno Beach, June 6, 1944:** History is standing astride these rolling Norman fields and resolving its own direction for perhaps a thousand years to come. We mortals who sit below can only be awed by its mighty presence.

*"For us it was the liberation of France"*

# Sword Beach

Piper Bill Millin awaits his turn at Sword Beach as commandos of
1st Special Service Brigade led by Brigadier Lord Lovat (*in the water,
to the right of his men*) land on Queen Red beach around 8:40 a.m.
Sherman DD tanks of 13th/18th Royal Hussars can be seen on the beach beyond.

*The easternmost beach of D-Day, Sword, belonged to the British 3rd Infantry
Division, who would storm ashore near the mouth of the Orne River and Caen
Canal, a few miles down from where Maj. John Howard's glider forces had cap-
tured Pegasus Bridge and other key crossings hours earlier. There, across a five-mile*

*front divided into four sectors, Queen Green, Queen White, Red, and Roger, regiments landed to secure the east flank and back up the nervous and outgunned airborne forces before the Germans could organize a counterassault. Responding units included the 1st South Lancashires, 2nd East Yorkshires, and the 1st Special Service Bridge, the British special commandos led by the colorful Lord Lovat. The ambitious hope of British generals Bernard L. Montgomery and Miles Dempsey was that these troops would be able to push quickly inland and south eight miles and surround, perhaps even seize, the major regional hub of Caen on D-Day itself.*

*Similar to the neighboring Juno, Sword backed up against urban areas and a long line of villas loomed over the beach, which—again like Juno—would narrow quickly as the tide rose. While much as at the other British sector landings, the beach quickly grew congested and the streets nearby jammed with vehicles, the day's fiercest fighting around Sword came not on the sand but as forces pushed inland and confronted unexpected German strongpoints.*

*As it was, Sword Beach would be the only one of the five beaches where the Germans managed to launch counterattacks via air, land, and sea. In fact, it was the only place where the German navy showed its face at all during the day of the landings. (Later, eight Ju-88 bombers made the only organized—and mostly harmless—air raid on any of the beaches.) Indeed, the morning began inauspiciously, at 0537, with the first—and only—attack by the German navy, as three Kriegsmarine torpedo boats, from Korvettenkapitän Heinrich Hoffmann's 5th Torpedoboot-Floittille, journeyed out of the Le Havre harbor and struck the eastern edge of the Allied invasion armada. These speedy ships, larger than the E-boats that bedeviled Exercise* TIGER, *carried crews of 120 and were dispatched at 0445 after the night's confusing radar reports of possible ships in the Channel. Arriving amid the invasion force—and stunned by the sheer mass of shipping arrayed before them—they launched 17 torpedoes and then retreated. Amazingly, the torpedoes passed through the entire naval armada harmlessly and then, on the far western edge, hit only a single target—the HNoMS* Svenner *(G03), a Royal Norwegian destroyer, but her sinking and wreckage off the beach would be one of the defining memories for many of the early waves at Sword, who wondered if the attack portended ill ahead.*

**Seaman Edward Wightman, HMS *Ramillies*:** Enemy destroyers attacked with torpedoes, three came perilously close, no more than fifty yards away; one fired at us hit the destroyer *Svenner*, a Norwegian escort of ours.

**Seaman Lars Aursland, gun crew, HNoMS *Svenner*:** I saw the first torpedo coming towards us, but we probably slid into a position that allowed it to pass without coming into contact at all. Then I saw another incoming and said, "Now it's just bang." There was an unbelievable explosion that I have never seen the likes of and I flew up out of the turret.

**Stan Hough, HMS *Princess Astrid*:** One great column of smoke goes up and she breaks in two.

**Lt. Stephen Brown, HMS *Scourge*:** As she went down, her bow and stern stuck up like a defiant "V" for victory.

**Lt. Philip Webber, 1st South Lancashires:** Soon twinkling lights appeared from the lifejackets of the crew as they dived overboard.

**David Cottrell, able seaman gunner, HMS *Swift*:** We went in and dropped scrambling nets, and our men got down on the scrambling nets, so they could pull the people in. People on the upper deck gave them a hand to pull them aboard. When it was time to go to take up our position [in the invasion], we had no alternative but to go. What's stuck in my memory all these years is a Norwegian man—he wasn't more than ten feet away—and he had his hand out. We had to leave him. I hope he survived.

**Lt. Stephen Brown:** She was a sister ship of ours, and in the same 23rd Destroyer Flotilla. We had no time to grieve, but afterwards it hit us—with only eleven officers, a fleet destroyer is like a family.

**Seaman Ralph Woolnough, gun crew, HMS *Kelvin*:** She had the unfortunate distinction of being the only ship to be sunk by German naval action on D-Day. It could have been us on the *Kelvin*: we were next in line and close enough.

**Thomas Nutter, HMS *Belfast*:** Then the invasion started, X turret on *H.M.S. Belfast* fired one gun—a signal, and all hell was let loose. Behind us and firing over us was a monitor *H.M.S. Roberts* flinging over its fifteen-inch shells. Capital ships were also firing, aircraft of the R.A.F. were above and swooping down on the coastline defences, bombers high above bombing German emplacements and hundreds and hundreds of landing craft, crammed with troops and equipment driving forward to the coast. It was a wonderful sight.

**Rear Adm. Arthur George Talbot, commander, Naval Task Force S, Royal Navy:** The enemy was obviously stunned by the sheer weight of [gunfire] support we were meting out.

\*          \*          \*

*On the Queen White end of the beach, arriving regiments found themselves pinned down by the German Widerstandsnest 20 bunker. The facility, known by its Allied fish-themed code name, "Cod," would not end up falling for more than two hours, knocking the already ambitious arrival schedules and follow-on waves hopelessly behind.*

**2nd Lt. Cyril Rand, platoon commander, Company C, 2nd Battalion, Royal Ulster Rifles:** As we closed in on the beach, ready for our run-in, the whole coast line, as far as the eye could see, was ablaze and belching thick black smoke, making it extremely difficult to pin point our exact position. At this stage it all seemed to be quite unreal—rather like watching an epic film being projected on to a circular screen; only 48 hours ago we were in the heart of the peaceful English countryside, and now we were about to set foot on the shores of occupied France, welcomed by a frightening barrage of shell and mortar fire.

**Lt. Anthony Drexel Duke, commander, *LST-530*:** We were creeping now towards the beachhead and we could smell the cordite from bursting shells and see all the shock waves from high explosives bursting all over the place and you could feel it right through the steel deck plates of the ship. It was a very pronounced and strong feeling that you were in war now.

**Maj. A. R. Rouse, South Lancashire Regiment, 8th Infantry Brigade, 3rd British Division:** We had studied [the obstacles] on air photographs and knew exactly what to expect but somehow we had never realised the vertical height of them, and as we weaved in between iron rails and ramps and pickets with Teller mines on top like gigantic mushrooms we seemed to be groping through a grotesque petrified forest.

**Edwin Webb, landing craft bowman, 538 LCA Flotilla, Royal Marines:** We circled round for about a quarter of an hour, maybe longer, until everybody was lowered away, and then away we went. We were due to go on the extreme left of Sword Beach, and we got through the obstacles all right and got our chaps off. They hardly got their feet wet. There was sniping and bits and pieces going on, but we had too much to think about to worry. As we swung around, we caught an obstacle and it ripped through the bottom of the craft. It went down like a stone and we had to swim for it.

**Derek Pratt, landing craft bowman, LCA, assigned to SS *Empire Broadsword*:** Out of the nine landing craft in the first wave, all got back safely. But in the second wave, only two made it back.

**Lt. W. S. Hall, troop leader, 4 Troop, A Squadron, Westminster Dragoons:** The bow of a very large LST loomed up to our left, its hooter giving six blast signals, just before it struck us a few feet away. Beard said "it meant out of control" and added, "Bloody Hell, we're not even going to make it to the shore!" As it hit alongside us it appeared to bounce off and vanish astern. It left a huge dent in the catwalk, and we carried on our way much relieved.

**2nd Lt. Cyril Rand:** Damaged craft from the first wave were floating around out of control, some containing dead and wounded men who had never even set foot on shore. The pillboxes on the beach wall had been dealt with, but fighting was still going on in some of the ruined houses; a certain amount of small-arms fire was still being directed on to the beach by those members of the enemy who had chosen to make a vain but heroic last stand. I rushed down the ramp at the head of my platoon in what I considered to be an extremely war-like manner, only to spoil it all by disappearing in five feet of water, which occasionally rose to six feet at the whim of the swell and the rising tide. Later a fellow Platoon Commander described my platoon's landing as thirty-six men being led ashore by a mushroom floating on the surface!

**Rev. Cyril Patrick Crean, chaplain, 29th Armoured Brigade, 11th Armoured Division:** I landed on D-Day in water waist deep and waded ashore in the midst of the most incredible sight in history. The fleet of ships was terrific and my first sight of France was a church steeple with a hole clean through the side of it—a German plane appeared, and as if by magic six of ours were on his tail and down he came.

**Capt. Robert Neave, second in command, B Squadron, 13th/18th Royal Hussars:** I made my way straight up the beach. Having ascended a line of dunes, which weren't very big, I got out of the tank to tell the other people what I was doing. I remember feeling the wind of a bullet going under my nose and then going between my two fingers. It just broke the skin; it really was remarkable, feeling the wind and the sting of the bullet.

**Cpl. Patrick Hennessy, Sherman tank commander, 13th/18th Royal Hussars:** We'd landed at low tide, so the longer we stood still and waited for the mines to be cleared on the beach, the deeper the water became. It wasn't long before the driver started complaining bitterly that, because we'd dropped our screen and the water was getting deeper, it was now coming in over the top of his hatch and he was sitting in a pool of water. He said, "For God's sake, let's move on up the beach!" This was a failure on my part: I should've used my initiative and said, "Go for it!" but I didn't. And as we sat there, wondering what to do, the problem was solved for us because a particularly large wave hit the stem of the tank and swamped the engine compartment and the engine spluttered to a halt and was drowned. Well, now we had a thirty-two ton tank and no power so we couldn't move even if we'd wanted to. So we sat there and fired and continued firing until such time as the tank became swamped.

**Pvt. Lionel Roebuck, 2nd Battalion, East Yorkshire Regiment:** The sand seemed to drag on your feet. It just seemed you couldn't get going, what with the weight of your equipment and things like that.

**Capt. Albert Cooke, 101st Amphibious Company, Royal Army Service Corps:** I was to be in the recce party and my job was to mark the beach exits so that the DUKWs coming ashore later would land at the right place. This meant I would be among the first to land. The four of us in the recce party were supposed to crawl along the beach so we didn't make too conspicuous a target, and we were doing this when we came to a main beach exit, where there was a military policeman standing directing the traffic, which was as busy as Piccadilly Circus. When I saw him, I stood up and started walking with the others following behind. There were bullets shooting into the sand quite near—so there were obviously snipers about—and as I was going past this MP, he said, "Get down sir, it's dangerous." So I got down and he continued to stand there directing the traffic.

**Pvt. William Edward Lloyd, 2nd Battalion, East Yorkshire Regiment:** Bullets just came at you like raindrops.

**Lt. W. S. Hall:** Our superb Navy was as good as their word and landed us almost dry, well up the beach as the tide was well in by now. The skipper came ashore to wish me luck, which was impressive so I dismounted, glad to be on firm ground at last, thanked him and he departed back to his ship. My Beachmaster was only a few yards away and indicated our exit route. The noise was utterly indescribable and things seemed to be rather chaotic. Amongst many casualties, the horrific sight of one poor dead man mangled and blown apart—the unreal vivid red of his remains—are to this day etched in my mind.

**Cpl. Bill Bowdidge, Company D, 2nd Battalion, Royal Warwickshire Regiment:** Caen was our objective on the first evening. The original idea was D Company should cycle like mad behind the Sherman tanks into Caen.

**Rifleman John Shanahan, 2nd Battalion, Royal Ulster Rifles, 9th Infantry Brigade, 3rd British Division:** Lots of us were given these fold-up bikes; personally I couldn't see the point of them. Perhaps it was some sort of trick by the brass—to make us believe we could just stroll on up the beach and bike over to Caen, as though it were a Sunday afternoon. Coming down the gangplank from the landing craft, I stumbled and my bike tried to drown me. Once we got away from the beach, I couldn't wait to get rid of it. We just dumped them in a great pile. Such a waste, but it was obvious we wouldn't be cycling anywhere. I believe they disappeared in the night, and presumably the French thought they were a gift!

**2nd Lt. Cyril Rand:** On reaching the beach we crossed it just as fast as we could. The battalion's casualties were surprisingly light, due no doubt to the speed with which all companies dis-embarked and made for the comparative safety of the sea wall. I was delighted to find that the only casualties sustained by my platoon were three cycles which were lost in the water, and one man with a wound on his leg, but not serious enough to put him out of action.

**Lt. Cdr. Edward Gueritz, Beachmaster, Fox Beach Landing Group, Royal Naval Commandos:** We had considerable difficulty in clearing the vehicles off the beach, partly because of mining by the Germans and partly because we were victims of our own success in getting so much ashore and the exits were ill-suited to the volume of traffic. We had to close our beach for a period because of the difficulty of dispersing the vehicles away from the beach area to their respective tasks.

**2nd Lt. Cyril Rand:** The Beachmaster and his team were doing a remarkable job in getting vehicles and troops moving, working the whole time under intense fire. I witnessed an altercation between one of his team and a fat German officer who, with half a dozen of his men, had been taken prisoner and were now crouching under the sea wall. The officer, in reasonably good English, was demanding that he and his men should be taken to a place of safety and not left to the mercy of what were, of course, his own guns. The Sergeant did not waste words; throwing a spade at him he shouted "Well, dig yourself a f****** hole, then," and continued with his work.

**Lt. Eric Ashcroft, lst Battalion, South Lancashire Regiment, 8th Infantry Brigade, 3rd British Division:** I remember, when we were in the sand dunes, I was looking down and saw a procession of ants and thought, "Goodness me, they're not affected by the war." These silly thoughts you get.

**2nd Lt. Cyril Rand:** There was an exchange of fire from my left hand section, who shortly afterwards brought in a wounded German soldier. They laid him, unconscious, by the roadside and after a brief examination I realised that he had no chance of survival; sure enough, within minutes he was dead. He was, I thought, in his early twenties, but did not belong to an SS

Regiment. As I looked down at him I experienced a feeling bordering on compassion; he had probably been quite happy at home with his family and friends, but suddenly, like the majority of the British Army, he was put into uniform, taught how to kill, and sent into battle. I imagined his mother at home, thinking of him as she prepared tea for the family, or maybe a young wife, who at this very moment was putting the children to bed, telling them to ask God to Bless daddy and send him home safely. Since dawn I had witnessed men suffering and dying, and found myself asking "Why?" I wondered cynically how God made his decisions; Christian families from both sides would be praying to him to spare their loved ones—but only one family would get their prayers answered. I quickly stood up, banished the thoughts and feelings I had just experienced, told myself that sentiment could play no part in this war, and once more became a fighting soldier.

\*       \*       \*

*With the initial waves of troops at Sword feeling bogged down by German fire, it fell to units in the follow-on wave to seize the initiative. Nearly everyone who arrived on Sword that morning remembers the inspiring example of the beach's detachment of British commandos, led by the Lord Lovat, whose bagpiper Bill Millin was always close at hand. Much as the US relied on paratroopers and Rangers for discrete specialized missions on D-Day, the British strategy for its beaches included a heavy reliance on seven of its elite commando units—each about 500 to 600 men—who were tasked with missions like linking up with adjacent beachheads. At Sword Beach, the commandos—which included 177 Free French Forces, known as the Kieffer Commandos, as well as Troop X, made up of Jewish refugees from German-occupied Europe—were meant to get inland as fast as possible and reinforce the British 6th Airborne paratroopers holding Pegasus Bridge and other key crossings. When they landed, the commandos' esprit de corps presented an inspiring presence and helped to motivate forward other units already on the beach.*

**Cdr. L. R. Curtis, captain, *LCI-519*:** The beaches were obscured by smoke and haze until we were quite close in. When, at last, we were able to discern the silhouettes of the houses, our lookout picked up the chateau-like building at the eastern end of Queen Red; by the grace of God, it seemed to me, we were spot-on. I gave the order for the troops to land, the ramps were man-handled over the bows, and the commandos began to land in about three feet of water as calmly as though on exercise. We bade goodbye to Lord Lovat and wished him good luck, and I carry in my mind a mental picture of him wading ashore with his men. As the commandos crossed the fireswept sands, the skirl of Bill Millin's pipes gave heart and encouragement to all.

**Brig. The Lord Lovat, commander, 1st Special Service Brigade:** The run-in took forty minutes. At the lowering position we changed formation. The flotilla divided into equal flights, landing ten minutes apart. I did not want the whole brigade boiling on the beach at the same time.

**Leon Gautier, Free French Forces, Kieffer Commando:** For us it was special. We were happy to come home. We were at the head of the landing. The British let us go a few meters in front, "Your move, the French," "After you." Most of us had left France in 1940, four years earlier, so for us it was the liberation of France, the return into the family.

**Pvt. Patrick "Paddy" Gillen, 6 Commando, 1st Special Service Brigade:** We began to pour out of the landing craft in single file, with weapons kept above our heads to keep them dry. We were moving as fast as our pack-laden bodies would carry us and I saw many bodies floating in the sea and lying on the beach. We didn't find out until later that night who was dead, wounded or missing from our unit. Some tanks were hit but it was a welcome sight to see how many got ashore and it lifted our morale no end.

**Brig. Lord Lovat:** The water was knee-deep when Piper Millin struck up "Blue Bonnets," keeping the pipes going as he played the commandos up the beach.

**Cpl. Peter Masters, No. 3 Troop, 10 Commando, 1st Special Service Brigade:** A vast assortment of flags should have awaited us on the beach, and everyone was supposed to know exactly what they all stood for. "Mines cleared along here" was one. Another: "Mines being detonated here. Keep down for 30 seconds and then proceed." And yet another: "Guide to the assembly point here." And so on. However, everything can't possibly work during an operation of this scale, and there was a remarkable absence of flag-waving.

I did not see a one, but someone told me afterwards that they had seen the flag that meant "Intelligence guides here" floating in the shallow water.

**Brig. Lord Lovat:** Five launches out of twenty-two were knocked out, but the water was not deep and commandos got ashore wading; a few took a swim in the shell craters.

**Lt. Lambton Burn, RNVR, Navy editor, *Parade* magazine:** Over to starboard we see a great triangular-shaped crowd of infantry advancing doggedly over the wet sand. They are the Free-French and British 4 Commando of Lord Lovat's Brigade. They stride forward with shoulders hunched like boxers ready for in-fighting. Shells explode among them. Their leader falls, but they shoulder him upright and surge on. Never can any nation have given birth to finer men than these.

**Pvt. Patrick "Paddy" Gillen:** The whole thing was to move fast, not to be an object for the snipers. They used to say, if you want to see your grandchildren then get off the landing craft faster than Jesse Owens [Olympic sprinter]. Seemingly I was fast.

**Midshipman Rene Le Roy, Landing Craft Obstacle Clearance Unit:** 4 Commando came in, in five LCIs, with Bergen rucksacks which were all full of equipment, and they realised more than anybody as they were approaching the beach that the beach hadn't been taken and they thought, "We attack." So they came in and they passed through a wave of men on the beach, ditching their rucksacks and immediately firing their way forward. They came up in lines, straight up, passing us, passing through, attacking the pillboxes, attacking any buildings and within a period of ten minutes they'd disappeared and the beach organisation started to get up and move. It was quite incredible. Their role wasn't to capture the beach but that role had been greatly assisted by the commando advance.

**Pvt. Reginald Barnes, 4 Commando, 1st Special Service Brigade:** We made an immediate move to clear the beach and not to dig in or stay there. The first obstacle we came across was a sign saying "Minen" and a whole lot of barbed wire, etc. There was suddenly a halt and Lovat shouted out, "Come on, boys, what's keeping you? What's the matter? Move!" And a friend of mine, who had been specially trained for this type of thing, he ran forward. He knew he shouldn't cut those wires in case they were mined and would blow up so what he did, he threw a jacket on, threw himself on and let the boys jump over. And once two or three got through we knew it was clear, we broke away and we all filed through.

**Cpl. Peter Masters:** I had begun to wonder about the assault infantry that had landed just ahead of us, because they seemed to be sitting around here and there, not doing anything in particular, but I changed my mind when I heard a signaller next to me crouching in a ditch decoding a message for an officer. "No. 2 Platoon, 6 men left, Sir," he reported.

**Archibald "Doon" Campbell, war correspondent, Reuters:** We hit the beach, the ramps went down, and the commandos, many of them with collapsible bicycles and their faces smeared black, went down the ramp. When it was my turn I fell off, up to my chest in the Channel, and with the pack on my back I would never have made it, but for a lunge forward accelerated by a push from a huge commando behind me. I staggered up the beach, dripping wet, crossed a mined road into a field, and stumbled into a ditch some two hundred yards from the beach. The commandos were racing on ahead through a lot of mortar fire and small-arms fire.

**Pvt. Andrew Brown, 6 Commando, 1st Special Service Brigade:** Running up the beach I heard a "moaning minnie" scream and one or two shells falling about so I dived into this shell hole and there was a bloke out of the East Yorks with a Bren gun there. I asked him what he was doing, and he said he'd lost his mates and was digging in. I said, "Well, if you dig in there you're going to die. Come along with me because if you stop on the beach you're going to die. You've got to get off the beach." So he came along with me and he stayed with me to the end of D-Day, when he just told me he'd better get back and look for his mates. They took a plastering, they did.

**Cpl. Peter Masters:** Our Brigadier General, Lord Lovat, was walking about in the forming-up area urging on people. He seemed to be a man perfectly at ease, and shots and the noise in general didn't seem to bother him at all. "Good show, the Piper," he said as Piper Millin came dashing up, the bagpiper who they say, had piped us ashore. I hadn't heard him. He was panting and catching his breath dragging the bagpipes as well as all his other equipment.

**Pvt. Bill Millin, bagpiper, Brigade Headquarters, 1st Special Service Brigade:** Lovat looked round and seen me standing and said, "Aw, give us a tune." The whole idea was ridiculous, cause people were shell-firing and all kinds of things were going on at the time. It was mad enough the three of us standing there; we shouldn't have been standing, really, we should've been lying down. The whole thing was ridiculous and I thought I might as well be ridiculous as well. I said, "What tune would you like, sir?" and he said, "Well, play *The Road to the Isles.*" I said, "Would you like me to march up and down?" and he said, "Yes, yes, march up and down. That'll be lovely." The whole thing was ridiculous, in that the bodies lying in the water were going back and forward with the tide and I started off piping and going a few paces along.

**Cpl. Peter Masters:** I saw Lovat walking around in the forming-up area, urging everybody on, saying, "Come on, get a move on, this is no different than an exercise." He was very calm. He carried no weapon other than his Colt .45 in his holster. Instead, he had a walking stick, a slim long stick forked at the top.

**Brig. Lord Lovat:** The landing was a soldier's battle—total confusion, which favours spirited assault—and it was soon over. Soon a trickle of grey uniforms appeared: bewildered men in shock, their hands clasped behind bare heads. The captured Germans seemed pleased to throw their hats away.

**Cpl. Peter Masters:** There were a couple of prisoners at the forming-up point, and I immediately started to interrogate them. Lovat noticed that and said, "Oh, you are the chap with the languages. Ask them where their howitzers are." I did and got absolutely no reaction. There were two of them. One was a very big burly balding fellow. The reaction was so nonexistent on the part of the Germans that I suddenly realized, looking at their paybook, that they were not German at all but Russian and Polish. It occurred to me that some Poles learned French in school, and so I tried my high school French. His face lit up and he started to talk immediately.

**Archibald "Doon" Campbell:** In the ditch the wounded were being treated, and one literally clawed at the earth to try and get deeper because of the withering fire coming from woods some two or three hundred yards ahead of us and into which the commandos had disappeared. I got the pack off my back and undid it, took out my portable typewriter, and put some paper in. I had landed at six minutes past nine on the morning of D-Day, and l have been told since that it was the most incongruous spectacle in that sector of the beach—Campbell of Reuters trying to beat out a message on his portable typewriter with all hell breaking loose around him.

Anyway; it was no good. A mortar hit the lip of the ditch in which we were lying and threw earth all over the typewriter, clogging the keys. So I put it away and on a notebook with a dateline "In a ditch, 200 yards away from the beach" described in two hundred or three hundred words just what was happening—that we had landed, that we were two hundred yards inland, we had seen the first prisoners being taken, and more tanks, guns, and men were landing. Having written it, I put it in an envelope addressed to Reuters, London, and then, in one of the occasional pauses in heavy fire, sort of wriggled and crawled and stumbled back to the beach, where one could see little boats coming in, dropping supplies and men, then beating back to the UK. I gave the envelope to one of these men, with five pounds, and said, "Try and get it to Reuters." That was the first dispatch from Sword Beach.

\*　　　　\*　　　　\*

*At the top of Sword Beach, flail tanks cleared the way through the surrounding minefields for the following infantry and commandos, and then advanced inland themselves. The tanks of the Dragoons' 2 Troop were knocked out quickly, but had, in one sense, already achieved their goal for the day by opening up the path behind them for advancing soldiers and punching an important hole through the Atlantic Wall.*

**Lt. R. H. W. Bullock, 2 Troop Leader, A Squadron, Westminster Dragoons:** We drove through the village of Hermanville, a little way inland, without event. Most of the local people were so shaken by the bombardment that only a few ventured out to wave a welcome. We rendezvoused with the rest of the half-squadron on a broad plain sloping gently up to a crest. I noticed a tank a couple of hundred yards away burst into flames. Another vehicle came up to help and it too burst into flames; when a third tank went up, I belatedly realized that someone was shooting at the great array of vehicles spread over the plain.

**Trooper N. T. "Tom" Kelly, co-driver, 2 Troop, A Squadron, Westminster Dragoons:** The first [shot] I saw was an "over" but the second and third shots each hit tanks ahead of us—at this stage I remember thinking that the next one could hit us. It did.

**Lt. R. H. W. Bullock:** I ordered my crews to mount and my gunner to traverse the turret while I vainly search for any sign of where the shooting was coming from. A few seconds later, I saw a nearby tank of my troop hit—it was hit fair and square.

**Trooper W. H. Jennings, loader, 2 Troop, A Squadron, Westminster Dragoons:** Then came an enormous *CLANG* with a great shower of sparks and flame and I knew that we had been hit. The turret floor was obscured by flame and smoke.

**Trooper George H. W. Woodhouse, driver, 2 Troop, A Squadron, Westminster Dragoons:** Next thing I was aware of was that the tank was on fire. On looking towards my co-driver I could not see him. I shouted out to the rest of the crew but got no answer. When I tried to reach up to the hatch I then found I had no use in my legs. It was at that moment I prayed to God for a miracle to happen.

**Trooper N. T. "Tom" Kelly:** I opened the hatch and bailed out into long grass or corn, then found I was unable to stand or walk.

**Trooper W. H. Jennings:** I had no option but to wriggle my way over the recoil guard, with some difficulty, to make my escape. Outside, I found Tom Kelly, our co-driver, lying wounded by the side of the tank. He told me that our driver, George Woodhouse, was still inside, being severely wounded in the legs and unable to move. I climbed up on the tank and somehow found the strength to lift George out by his epaulettes just as the ammunition was starting to "cook off."

**Trooper George H. W. Woodhouse:** How long I sat in that time bomb I do not know but it must have only been minutes. The hatch above my head was opened up and I remember the beautiful blue sky that I had thought I would never see again above me. After pulling me up from my seat and outside, they lowered me to the ground—I was smouldering—not realizing that both my legs were smashed.

**Trooper W. H. Jennings:** Two Germans appeared from the corn with their hands up. Geoff Stedall volunteered to escort them back to Military Police in Hermanville.

**Lt. R. H. W. Bullock:** I heard later that two men in German uniforms had surrendered—an anti-tank gun had got left behind in the German retreat, and its crew decided to fire off their remaining ammunition before surrendering.

**Trooper N. T. "Tom" Kelly:** Very little coherent thoughts from now on—can remember being given morphia and being taken on a Jeep and being in a tented hospital with the continual sound of planes overhead all night.

**Trooper George H. W. Woodhouse:** The rest of Tuesday and Tuesday night I spent in a little Field Hospital tent with people being brought in, dying and being taken out again.

**Trooper W. H. Jennings:** The three of us [on the disabled tank crew] remained, watching the traffic. A battalion of [commandos] on bicycles rode past on their way to receive the airborne troops holding the bridges on the left flank of the bridgehead.

**Brig. Lord Lovat:** We were almost through the Atlantic Wall.

**Pvt. Bill Millin:** The local French people were delighted that there were French commandos with the British and they gave us help by pointing out the strongpoints which enabled the commandos to eliminate them.

**Cpl. Peter Masters:** The villagers stood in their doorways often leading to now crumbling houses and gazed and gazed and waved at us, heedless or beyond caring about the danger of shells and shrapnel. One young man in a light blue smock and the dark blue beret, as the farmers in Normandy are wont to dress, pasted up posters on a doorway. Passing, I was quite impressed at last. There were Germans in the vicinity and shooting going on, and here these people just stood and stared. On the posters it said "Invasion," and carried instructions on what to do when the time came. They had obviously been waiting for the day, and as we went by, they said things like, "Vive les Tommies," or "Vive la France!"

*"Good morning, this is D-Day"*

# The News Spreads

News of D-Day attracted attention across the US,
including from crowds like this in Times Square.

*While everyone had long anticipated the coming invasion, the enormous efforts
to protect the secrecy of the exact timing of Operation* OVERLORD *worked, and
the world was taken by complete surprise in the early-morning hours of June 6
as the first news of the invasion began to spread. As monumental as the recent
days' news of the fall of Rome had been, D-Day was instantly set to dwarf it
and be the biggest story in the world. Reporters and radio executives had been
working for months to be ready for the invasion, knowing it would soon come.
Then, that day, minute by minute and hour by hour, as word of the invasion
broke and spread, news alerts flashed around the globe. Nearly everyone first*

*heard the arrival of D-Day over the radio, and many tuned in hungrily for updates throughout the day. Correspondents juggled breaking news live on-air as they worked to convey the sheer scale and expanse of the operation, and military planners released a carefully scheduled series of recorded statements from key Allied leaders. Not surprisingly, that morning saw record radio listenership; CBS later calculated that from the hours of 8 a.m. to noon on the US East Coast, more than double the normal number of radios were tuned in. NBC ran commercial-free for twenty-hour hours, and CBS carefully thanked the 17 sponsored programs that day—from Procter & Gamble to General Foods—who gave up their time to concentrate on the unfolding news.*

**Paul White, news director, CBS News, memo, February 1944, on how to cover an invasion:** Keep an informative, unexcited demeanor at the microphone. . . . Give sources. . . . Don't risk accuracy for the sake of a beat. . . . Use care in your choice of words. . . . Don't say "German defenses were pulverized." Say "German defenses were hard hit." . . . When you don't know, say so. Locutions like "Allied troops were believed to be progressing, etc." are out. Rather say "Nothing has been released during the past 24 hours, etc." . . . Exaggeration and immoderate language breed dangerous optimism. . . . Respect the listener's trust. Remember that winning the war is a hell of a lot more important than reporting it.

*The first news reports of D-Day came in Berlin, from Germany's Trans-Ocean News Service, which announced that a possible invasion appeared under way at 6:33 a.m.—just 43 minutes after the first bombardments had begun. Four minutes later, the Associated Press followed with an international news bulletin:*

12:37 A.M. WASHINGTON, D.C. / 6:37 A.M. LONDON

**Bulletin London Tuesday June 6 (AP):** THE GERMAN NEWS AGENCY TRANSOCEAN SAID TODAY IN A BROADCAST THAT THE ALLIED INVASION HAS BEGUN.

12:48 A.M. WASHINGTON, D.C. / 6:48 A.M. LONDON

**Jim Sirmons, CBS News:** We are interrupting this program to bring you a special bulletin. A bulletin has just been received from the London office of the Associated Press which quotes the German Transocean News Agency as asserting that the invasion of Western Europe has begun.

This report—and we stress it is of enemy origin with absolutely no confirmation from Allied sources—says that American landings were made this morning on the shores of northwestern France. There is as yet no reason to believe that this report is anything more than a German propaganda move or a fishing expedition for information. You will recall that Prime Minister Churchill warned us not long ago that the actual invasion would be preceded by feints and diversions. Nevertheless, until confirmation or denial of this German report is forthcoming, the CBS World News staff is standing by and will bring you developments as reported.

*Beginning at 3:32 a.m. in Washington, 9:32 a.m. in London, the Allies officially confirmed the landings and issued a series of messages from key leaders of occupied nations—a series, again, carefully calculated to sow doubt and confusion among the Germans about whether the Normandy landings represented an initial stage or the entirety of the landings. It began with a message from the Norwegian king meant to suggest a landing might soon be imminent there too. Then, correspondents from various news organizations who had participated in the early stages of the aerial invasion and bombing campaigns began to file their firsthand accounts.*

**Martha Gellhorn, correspondent, *Collier's Weekly*:** In a great guarded room in the Ministry of Information, a good percentage of the world's press sat and waited, watching the clock. An English officer rose and said, "In five seconds the first communique will be given to the world. You may leave. Go!" The press rushed out as if fleeing a fire, to get the story on the air and on the cables. But there is always a small quiet and humble side to everything. When I rushed out with the others and told the driver of my hired car that the invasion had started, he said firmly, "You're kidding! I'm a volunteer. I'm on twenty-four-hour duty when the invasion starts. They'd have told me if it was starting. They wouldn't start it without calling me." He refused to change his mind until his friend, the doorman at the Dorchester, said that he, for one, believed the invasion really had started, and he, for one, planned to drink a bottle of champagne in France next week.

3:32 A.M. WASHINGTON, D.C. / 9:32 A.M. LONDON

**Col. R. Ernest Dupuy, senior public relations officer, SHAEF:** Under the command of General Eisenhower, allied naval forces, supported by strong air forces, began landing allied armies this morning on the northern coast of France.

3:47 A.M. WASHINGTON, D.C. / 9:47 A.M. LONDON

**Message from Dwight Eisenhower, Commander-in-Chief of the Allied Forces, speaking to the captive people of Western Europe:** People of Western Europe, the hour of your liberation is approaching. Follow the instructions you have received. Continue your passive resistance, but do not needlessly endanger your lives until I give you the signal to rise and strike the enemy. A premature uprising of all Frenchmen may prevent you from being of maximum help to your country in the critical hour. Be patient. Prepare. Those who have common cause with the enemy and so betrayed their country will be removed. As France is liberated from her oppressors, you yourselves will choose your representatives and the government under which you wish to live.

In the course of this campaign for the final defeat of the enemy you may sustain further loss and damage. Tragic though they may be, they are part of the price of victory. I assure you I shall do all in my power to mitigate your hardships. I know that I can count on your steadfastness now, no less than in the past. This landing is but the opening phase of the campaign in Western Europe. Great battles lie ahead. I call upon all who love freedom to stand with us. Keep your faith staunch. Our arms are resolute. Together we shall achieve victory.

3:5I A.M. WASHINGTON, D.C. / 9:5I A.M. LONDON

**King Haakon of Norway:** From now on, hinder and impede the enemy by every subtle and covert means that does not expose yourself or others. This order does not apply to organized resistance groups, who are in touch with the Allied military authorities. They have been given their special orders with the knowledge that, if they are in need of a hiding place or food or any other help, they will always find it. Stand firm.

We salute the forces which have now gone into battle. We know that they will not fail us, and we promise not to fail them. Fellow countrymen, keep together and be prepared. Long live the cause of freedom!

**Pieter Sjoerds Gerbrandy, Prime Minister of the Netherlands:** Now that the Allied sledgehammer blows are falling on Hitler's Atlantic wall we are filled with emotion. Our men of the Army, Navy, the Air Force and the Merchant Marine must fulfill the tasks allotted to them by the military commander-in-chief. In the hearts of all of us rises the urgent prayer to the Almighty for help and assistance in what is for us the righteous fight.

Dutchmen, go with us for victory. Long live the fatherland.

**Hubert Pierlot, Prime Minister of Belgium:** The hour is near. Operations for the liberation of Europe have begun. This first assault is the certain signal for your deliverance. You are going to undergo trying days in anxious waiting. This is the time to show once again those fine qualities of discipline and self-control which for four years you have so often displayed. . . .

The Allies are grateful to you for the magnificent resistance which you have shown in the German oppression, and the government is convinced that you will do everything possible to contribute to the overthrow of the German war machine. The watchwords are courage, discipline, unity and confidence.

4:15 A.M. WASHINGTON, D.C. / 10:15 A.M. LONDON

**Robert Trout, CBS News:** The story is now moving very swiftly and even as we are talking the bulletins are coming in thick and fast. In a few moments we'll go to London again. I don't know just exactly what we'll have. Oh, yes, we are going to hear from Wright Bryan, representing the Combined American networks in London.

**Wright Bryan, reporter, WSB (Atlanta, Georgia), broadcasting across all four radio networks:** I rode with the first group of planes from a troop-carrier command to take our fighting men into Europe. I watch from the rear door of our plane, named "Snooty," as 17 American paratroopers led by a Lt. Colonel, jumped with their arms, ammunition, and equipment into German-occupied France.

They blinked as the pilot threw his switch and before I could look up they began jumping. I wanted to know how long it would take the eighteen men to jump. I tried to estimate the number of seconds. Before seconds, it may have been eleven or twelve passengers had left us, all but one of them. One man among the last half-dozen hit the rear of the door so heavily that he was thrown into the back of the cabin and dazed. The men behind shoved him aside and went on jumping. Before the unhappy soldier could get to his feet our plane was well past the drop zone and in a matter of minutes it was back over the water and setting a course for home.

## 4:40 A.M. WASHINGTON, D.C. / 10:40 A.M. LONDON

**John Vandercook, NBC News, reporting from London:** The announcement has just been made that the invasion of western Europe has begun. The feints and diversions promised by Winston Churchill are now relegated to the limbo of dead words. Be sure of it—we're moving with the weight of mountains. The skies are a hum with the ceaseless passage of great planes that shuffle smoothly back and forth from the countless airports of England.

## 4:48 A.M. WASHINGTON, D.C. / 10:48 A.M. LONDON

**James Wellard, NBC Blue Network correspondent, reporting from London:** This is James Wellard, speaking from SHAEF. I have just seen the first American troops preparing to storm ashore on the continent of Europe. At 6:23 the Marauder bomber in which I was riding dropped the last load of bombs on the coastal target just before H-Hour. I could see no evidences of the landings beyond the small number of parachutes lying on the ground. With the exception of German tanks moving up the beachheads or hiding in hedges, we saw no signs of enemy resistance. At this point I'd like to report that Sgt. Paul Stopp of Cedartown, Ga., the waist-gunner with whom I was riding, promptly turned his machine guns on one German tank by a crossroads and claims to have set it on fire. I saw the tank burning. You will have to forgive the superlatives, but they are an accurate description of the facts in this case. The air and sea armadas I saw this morning were the biggest that nations at war have ever launched at one time. At briefing, our pilots were told to stay at a level below 6,000 feet over England. The air was filled with

other planes—Fortresses, Liberators, Thunderbolts, Spitfires—hundreds of
them crossing and criss-crossing above and below us.

Our flight was as peaceful as a skyride between New York and Chicago.

**5:15 A.M. WASHINGTON, D.C. / 11:15 A.M. LONDON**

**Dave Anderson, NBC:** There is no doubt in my mind that Hitler was literally
caught with his pants down by the Allied landing on the north coast of
France. I was able to gain substantiation for this opinion while working
together with a wing of an RAF Tactical Air Force, somewhere in England,
up to a few hours ago. For some time after H-Hour, there was practically
no sign of German Army transport on any of the roads in the whole of the
invasion area.

*      *      *

*The first official public comment on the invasion came in Parliament in London,
where Winston Churchill used a prescheduled speech to confirm the landings.*

**Winston Churchill, Prime Minister of the United Kingdom:** At noon on June 6 I
asked the House of Commons to "take formal cognisance of the liberation
of Rome by the Allied Armies under the command of General Alexander,"
the news of which had been released the night before. There was intense
excitement about the landings in France, which everyone knew were in
progress at the moment. Nevertheless I devoted ten minutes to the campaign in Italy and in paying my tribute to the Allied Armies there. After
thus keeping them on tenterhooks for a little I said:

> I have also to announce to the House that during the night and the early
> hours of this morning the first of the series of landings in force upon the
> European Continent has taken place. In this case the liberating assault fell
> upon the coast of France. An immense armada of upwards of 4,000 ships,
> together with several thousand smaller craft, crossed the Channel. Massed
> airborne landings have been successfully effected behind the enemy lines,
> and landings on the beaches are proceeding at various points at the present
> time. The fire of the shore batteries has been largely quelled. The obstacles

that were constructed in the sea have not proved so difficult as was appre-
hended. The Anglo-American Allies are sustained by about 11,000 firstline
aircraft, which can be drawn upon as may be needed for the purposes of
the battle. I cannot, of course, commit myself to any particular details.
Reports are coming in in rapid succession. So far the Commanders who
are engaged report that everything is proceeding according to plan. And
what a plan! This vast operation is undoubtedly the most complicated and
difficult that has ever taken place. It involves tides, wind, waves, visibility,
both from the air and the sea standpoint, and the combined employment
of land, air and sea forces in the highest degree of intimacy and in contact
with conditions which could not and cannot be fully foreseen. There are
already hopes that actual tactical surprise has been attained, and we hope
to furnish the enemy with a succession of surprises during the course of
the fighting.

\*       \*       \*

6:24 A.M. WASHINGTON, D.C. / 12:24 P.M. LONDON

**Charles Shaw, CBS News, reporting from London:** For an hour after the
broadcast of communique No. 1, I played town-crier to a London generally
unaware that France had been invaded. I rode and walked thru the Strand,
Fleet Street, past St. Paul's along the Thames Embankment to the Houses
of Parliament and Westminster Abbey, up to Piccadilly Circus and other
parts of so-called downtown London, asking people here and there what
they thought of the news. In most cases, I found out that I had to report
the news before getting any comment. It looked like London any morning,
between 9:30 and 10:30 . . . the streets comparatively deserted, soldiers of all
nations ambling about, street cleaners running their brushes along the curbs.

I asked a taxidriver to take me around the city, because I wanted to see
how people were reacting to the news. "Incidentally," I asked him, "have you
heard the news?" "I heard something about it," he said, "but I don't know
whether it's official." I assured him it was, because I had just returned from
the studio where the communique was broadcast. Waiting for a traffic light,
we drew alongside a car driven by a girl, wearing the uniform of France. I
leaned out and said: "What do you think of the news?"

"What news?" she asked. "The Allies have landed in France." All she said was: "Thank God!"

Fleet Street, headquarters of the press in London, was normal.

A couple of men who might have been reporters were seen dashing into buildings. And up to St. Paul's Cathedral . . . to see whether there were worshippers inside. The only person in the vast auditorium was a black-robed guide to the crypt, who hadn't heard the news. His comment, after being informed, was: "That's good!"

## II:30 A.M. WASHINGTON, D.C. / 5:30 P.M. LONDON

**Brig. Gen. Charles de Gaulle, chairman, French National Committee:** The supreme battle is at last under way, after great sorrow and long suffering; here at last is the decisive clash for which we have waited so long. Yes, this is the Battle of France, and this is France's battle. Help has gone out to us, in the vast machinery of war which is now beginning to flow from the shores of old England. This same England, not so long ago Western Europe's outermost bastion of defense, before which the tide of German oppression was stopped, today has become the base for the launching of our liberation. And France, submerged for four years, but not destroyed nor vanquished, is rising again today to take her own part in this fight for freedom.

## NOON WASHINGTON, D.C. / 6 P.M. LONDON

**Kate Smith, host, *The Kate Smith Hour*, CBS:** Today is a day that no living American can ever forget. Invasion Day, forged into our consciousness in letters of fire. It marks the pinnacle of weeks and months and years of anguished preparation. We must concentrate our thoughts on victory, turn our earnest, united thought into devout, unceasing prayer to God. Wherever you are at this moment, whatever you're doing, join your prayers with mine—a prayer for Victory. Pray that our crusaders may be strong, that success will crown their every effort. Pray that they may speedily accomplish their mission and bring their adversaries to unconditional surrender. Pray to our Father in Heaven to look down with compassion upon this sick and sorrowing world and guide the forces of right against the forces of evil and insanity. If millions of us—every man, woman and child in America—will lift our fervent prayers to God, those prayers will be answered!

*　　　　*　　　　*

*Public reaction to the surprise news of D-Day varied widely; many people— particularly those touched by the ongoing conflict, involved in the war effort themselves, or with family members serving in the armed forces and now in harm's way—pondered how the next stage of the war would unfold and tried to balance the mental disconnect between their regular daily life on a June Tuesday and the fighting now under way in France.*

*In some US cities, where the news broke in the middle of the night, fire alarms, air raid sirens, and clanging church bells awoke sleeping residents; in Amarillo, Texas, as in many other communities, churches and synagogues opened for special nighttime prayer sessions. In one Oakland, California, hotel, the operator delivered wake-up calls with "Good morning, this is D-Day. The Allies have invaded France." Over the course of the day, crowds gathered to pick up fresh newspaper editions and extras. In New York the financial markets on Wall Street marked a two-minute moment of silence before the trading day started, Broadway shows were canceled, and that evening Mayor Fiorello La Guardia hosted 50,000 in Madison Square Park for a prayer service.*

*And, in Philadelphia, during a solemn but celebratory radio broadcast, the mayor of Philadelphia rang the Liberty Bell for the first time since 1835. For many—including those like Martha Gellhorn and Mollie Panter-Downes, who had been covering the war for years—the day brought a sense of hope that the end of almost a decade of conflict was beginning, hope that extended even to a young girl hiding in Amsterdam.*

**Bernard Samuel, Mayor of Philadelphia, after ringing the Liberty Bell seven times:** Let it proclaim liberty throughout the land, and the return of liberty throughout the world.

**Martha Gellhorn, correspondent, *Collier's Weekly*:** June 6th was a gray, cold day. People moved quickly through the streets, and you would never have known that this day was different from any other, though it had been awaited for four and a half years. Only at noon, the regular editions of the noonday papers were quickly sold out.

**Mollie Panter-Downes, London correspondent,** *The New Yorker:* D-Day sneaked up on people so quietly that half the crowds flocking to business on Tuesday morning didn't know it was anything but Tuesday, and then it fooled them by going right on being Tuesday. The principal impression one got on the streets was that no one was smiling. Everybody seemed to be existing wholly in a preoccupied silence of his own.

**Nora Knox, coding specialist, WRENs, Roysth, Scotland:** D-Day, for me, was really an N-Day. On June 6th—silence. It seemed that every east coast ship had gone off the air. I remember wondering if the entire navy had gone off to sea. There was an uncanny feeling that something big was happening—and a somewhat sad feeling that we were not part of it. For me, at any rate, it was a nothing-day.

**Martha Gellhorn:** In Westminster Abbey on that historic morning, a man was cleaning the carpet of the altar with a vacuum cleaner, and there were three groups of American soldiers on a sightseeing tour of the church. They had heard of the invasion, it developed, at the Red Cross where they met to go on this tour, but, as one of them said, "When you've given up your wife and your children and your house, anything else that happens is just so much dust. We'll start cheering when we get home."

**Capt. James O'Neill, correspondent,** *Yank* **magazine, Rome:** A dogface in Rome on June 6 was a befuddled gent. He hadn't the time to get over the Fifth Army's historic and raucous entry into Rome when the biggest news of World War II, the opening of the second front, dropped like a bombshell on the local hysterical scene. We went out into the streets after the astounding news came over the BBC radio. Pvt. Robert J. Kitchen, an artillery-man with the 85th Division, from Vero Beach, Fla, said, "I'm damned glad it finally came. For a long while, especially when we were at Anzio, we thought they'd never start it."

**Molly Harris, staffer, Air Ministry, Kensington:** I had looked forward to this day for as long as I could remember. A 21st birthday conjured up so much for a young girl, and I was no exception. At last my day had arrived and there I was recovering from chicken pox! I awoke to the strains of "I'm 21 today" being played on our portable gramophone, presents, cards, and gold and silver keys on my bed. But the greatest thrill of all was the news of the allied landings! Oh, what a wonderful 21st birthday after all!

**Peggy Cornish, UK:** I was working in a government ministry, in the typing pool, with about 30 other girls. In the same room was a teleprinter. When the news came through, the girl operating the machine screamed with excitement. This upset the rhythm of the clacking typewriters, and the head and shoulders of the supervisor—an absolute dragon of a woman—rose above her frosted glass screen to see what all the noise was about. When she heard the reason for the uproar, her fury abated and she allowed a 20-minute break. Cigarettes were lit and we all left our desk to exchange conversation.

*Time* **magazine, June 12, 1944:** In Moscow the people literally danced in the streets. There the populace, from Stalin down to the lowest party member, had waited for two and a half years for the Second Front. This was the happiest capital. The Russian radio called it "The Victory Front." In the lobby of the Metropole Hotel, an ecstatic Muscovite threw her arms around an American correspondent, exclaimed, "We love you, we love you, love you. You are our real friends."

**Eva Crawford, resident, West Worthing:** On June 6th, I received the notice to say my husband had died in a Japanese camp after three years of captivity. I shall never forget the crowds dancing and singing around me in the city square in Nottingham. I realize a joyous day for all, but sad indeed for me.

**Helen Davidson, resident, Glasgow:** News of the liberating assault bounded into the butcher's shop as I waited in the queue. The pompous butcher stood beaming and towering above us all, and I'm sure he felt something of what it means to be God when he announced that coupons only were required that day—no cash. So my particular recollection of D-Day is bangers and steak on the one plate.

**Barbara Desmond, resident, Manchester:** My "special experience" on D-Day was the birth of our eldest daughter. After a long and tedious birth on 6th

June, my mother told me of the Normandy landing, and I thought whilst I was giving birth, these heroes were fighting to make England a safe place for us.

**M. J. Colman, schoolteacher, Oxford:** June 6th is my birthday. My husband and I were teachers and decided to go after-school to a cafe in the nearby town of Swindon for a "celebration tea." As we began to eat our birthday tea of baked beans on toast, we became aware of the excitement in the air, and soon learned our forces had crossed the Channel and invaded Europe. Our baked beans tasted like ambrosia.

**Mrs. M. Kaye, resident, Liverpool:** In one of the still unblitzed halls, our dramatic society were giving Noel Coward's "Blithe Spirit," but the audience didn't pay it much attention—they decided to celebrate D-Day instead. In the middle of the first act, the whole audience stood on their seats and roared out "Land of Hope & Glory" till the ceilings echoed and we on stage joined in. Every single person was singing with tears running down their cheeks. We sang every hymn and war song until we were hoarse, then all went into the street arm in arm and created a traffic jam.

***Time* magazine, June 12, 1944:** The US people had wondered for weeks how they would behave on D-Day. When it came, they went about their regular business. Race tracks called off programs for the day; many stores closed at noon. The citizens stuck to their radios, read newspaper extras as they rolled off the presses, sat, and thought, stood and drank, knelt and prayed.

**Ivylyn Schenk, wife of Sgt. John Schenk, Company A, 116th Infantry Regiment, 29th Division, Bedford, Virginia:** Mama brought me what she thought I would enjoy eating, and she sat there with me most of the day as we listened to all the reports. I knew that John would be involved in the invasion. He had not told me anything directly but in a round-about way I knew.

**C. A. Norred, pastor, Central Church of Christ, Amarillo, Texas:** I have a feeling we are going to lose a lot of men, but at the same time we probably will save many also. As bad as it is, it is bringing on what we are hoping for, the end of the war.

**Vernon O'Reilly, correspondent, *San Francisco Examiner*, June 6, 1944:** Most San Franciscans awakened this morning to learn that they'd slept through some of the most momentous hours of history. "So it's finally started," was the most frequent comment. There was little elation. Behind it was anxiety as taut as an E-string. For almost every home and business in San Francisco has a living stake in the success of the operations for the liberation of the Old World. Maps were in prime demand as armchair strategists fingered points along the invasion coast.

**F. J. Hutchin, Kohat District Signals, British Army:** I was an Army signalman on the northwest frontier of India. We were taking down high-speed Morse code from Reuters, for practice, when we realized this was the announcement our troops had landed in Normandy. Our fellow signalman would not believe us until the news came on All India Radio.

**Gordon "Bert" Hemmings, flight engineer, Stirling bomber, 196 Squadron:** On D-Day I was a Prisoner of War in Stalag Luft 1 at Barth on the Baltic coast. I had crashed in France whilst on an S.O.E. arms drop to the French Resistance. We had a radio in the camp which obviously was concealed from the Germans, and the news which was received from British Stations was circulated daily very discreetly. However on D-Day the news was much too important to be written out and passed around. It was relayed verbally to the first group of people and they simply exploded into a demonstration of joy which was repeated and repeated and went round the camp like a shock wave. Within minutes of the reception of the BBC morning news a "parade" of prisoners had been created and it started to move round the inner perimeter of the camp in a skipping, jumping, waving crocodile which lengthened continually as the news flashed from hut to hut. The men were banging cooking pots, tin plates, Red Cross boxes—anything that would make a noise!

Not unnaturally the German guards were quite astonished by this wild demonstration because the invasion had not been reported on German Radio. It was of course asking too much to expect the prisoners to keep their mouths shut and so with great glee they announced to the guards the news that the landings had taken place. This was at first treated with some scepticism by the guards, but as the demonstrations continued they came to accept that it was in fact genuine. Much later in the day German Radio did broadcast the news and confirmed what we had been saying for some hours! The result was that the Germans at last had actual proof of what they had long suspected—that we were in contact with Britain by radio. But who cared!

**Edward J. Anderson, chief mechanician, HMS *Exeter*, prisoner of war, Nagasaki, Japan, diary entry, June 6, 1944:** Almost certain we've landed in France. A Jap kept drawing ships and soldiers on a boiler and kept saying "Franso, Franso." Flogged before a crowd of Jap workers, male and female; didn't collapse, denied the bastards the climax of their entertainment, but can't sit as a result. Four men were killed today, one of these a young English soldier; Nippon's daily sacrifice to her war machine. Rat hunt after our meal; caught six this time, best haul yet.

**Anne Frank, diary entry, June 6, 1944:** "This is D Day," the BBC announced at twelve. "This is the day." The invasion has begun. Is this really the beginning of the long-awaited liberation? The liberation we've all talked so much about, which still seems too good, too much of a fairy tale ever to come true? Will this year, 1944, bring us victory? We don't know yet. But where there's hope, there's life. It fills us with fresh courage and makes us strong again.

*       *       *

9:51 A.M. WASHINGTON, D.C. / 3:51 P.M. LONDON

**Herbert Marshall, BBC News, reporting from the UK:** I've just come back from the beaches, and as I've been in the sea twice, I'm sitting in my soaked-thru clothes, with no notes at all. My notes are sodden and they're at the bottom of the sea. I was in a barge which was due to pick up the Brigadier of an assault group and we were going in with the first assault wave. So we circled round with the various types of vessels opening fire on the beach, which we could see quite plainly in the dim morning light in their own manners and at the appointed time. First of all the cruisers started with a rather loud bang and soon the air grew heavy with the smell of cordite and loud with the sound of explosions and, looking along the beach, we could see the explosions of our artillery creating a great cloud and fog of smoke. We could see, as we went in, that particular portion of the beach wasn't altogether healthy and, as we drove towards it with our planes overhead, giving us the sort of cover we've been hoping for and which we'd been expecting—as we drove in we could see shell bursts in the water, along the beach and just behind the beach, and we could see France with a certain amount of difficulty because the wind was driving the sea in with long rollers.

IO P.M. WASHINGTON, D.C., JUNE 6, 1944 / 4 A.M. LONDON, JUNE 7, 1944

**Franklin D. Roosevelt, President of the United States:** My fellow Americans: Last night, when I spoke with you about the fall of Rome, I knew at that moment that troops of the United States and our allies were crossing the Channel in another and greater operation. It has come to pass with success thus far. And so, in this poignant hour, I ask you to join with me in prayer:

Almighty God: Our sons, pride of our Nation, this day have set upon a mighty endeavor, a struggle to preserve our Republic, our religion, and our civilization, and to set free a suffering humanity.

Lead them straight and true; give strength to their arms, stoutness to their hearts, steadfastness in their faith.

They will need Thy blessings. Their road will be long and hard. For the enemy is strong. He may hurl back our forces. Success may not come with rushing speed, but we shall return again and again; and we know that by Thy grace, and by the righteousness of our cause, our sons will triumph.

They will be sore tried, by night and by day, without rest—until the victory is won. The darkness will be rent by noise and flame. Men's souls will be shaken with the violences of war.

For these men are lately drawn from the ways of peace. They fight not for the lust of conquest. They fight to end conquest. They fight to liberate. They fight to let justice arise, and tolerance and good will among all Thy people. They yearn but for the end of battle, for their return to the haven of home.

Some will never return. Embrace these, Father, and receive them, Thy heroic servants, into Thy kingdom.

And for us at home—fathers, mothers, children, wives, sisters, and brothers of brave men overseas—whose thoughts and prayers are ever with them—help us, Almighty God, to rededicate ourselves in renewed faith in Thee in this hour of great sacrifice.

With Thy blessing, we shall prevail over the unholy forces of our enemy. Help us to conquer the apostles of greed and racial arrogancies. Lead us to the saving of our country, and with our sister Nations into a world unity that will spell a sure peace, a peace invulnerable to the schemings of unworthy men. And a peace that will let all of men live in freedom, reaping the just rewards of their honest toil.

*On NBC, President Roosevelt's comments were immediately followed by a regularly scheduled program hosted by entertainer Bob Hope, who spoke at the top of his show for six minutes about the day's news before continuing with his regular show, featuring servicemen at a P-38 airfield near Van Nuys, California.*

**Bob Hope:** What's happened during these last few hours, not one of us will ever forget. How could you forget? You sat up all night by the radio and heard the bulletins, the flashes, the voices coming across from England, the commentators, the pilots returning from the greatest of all missions, newsboys yelling in the street. And it seemed that one world was ending. And a new world beginning. That history was closing one book and opening a new world. And somehow we knew it had to be a better one.

# PART III

# THE END OF D-DAY

# Holding the Eastern Flank

Beyond Sword Beach, British forces found
themselves quickly engaged in urban fighting.

*In the hours after the landing, the fight in the British sector quickly moved inland,
with troops racing to reinforce the eastern flank and link up with the British
6th Airborne Division while other units tried to reach the Normandy hub city
of Caen and its Carpiquet airfield, the overly ambitious objectives the British
had set for D-Day. For their part, after the British 6th Airborne captured the
key bridges along the eastern flank of the invasion, behind Sword Beach, in the
literal first minutes of D-Day, Maj. John Howard and the other paratroopers of
the 6th Airborne had settled in for the hours-long wait for reinforcements. They
spent much of D-Day fighting off counterattacks as the Germans, still hesitant
and unsure of the Allied forces, tested their strength.*

449

**Maj. John Howard, commander, Company D, 2nd Battalion, Oxfordshire and Buckinghamshire Light Infantry, 6th Airborne Division:** I thought the first enemy action would come from the west, where all those German troops were billeted in villages and were ready to jump into lorries and tanks and God knows what, and to counterattack the canal bridge. I was therefore a bit surprised when the first enemy activity took place on the river bridge.

**Lt. Tod Sweeney, platoon commander, Company D, 2nd Battalion, Oxfordshire and Buckinghamshire Light Infantry, 6th Airborne Division:** A patrol came up from the direction of Caen, and they were challenged by the section on that side of the road, and they shouted something back that sounded like German so the section opened fire and killed them all. We found them there the next morning.

**Maj. John Howard:** I heard tracked vehicles moving up, and we all became extremely apprehensive. Two of these vehicles started to move down from the road junction down toward the bridge. We could see them moving very, very slowly about twenty-five yards apart, obviously not knowing what to expect when they got down to the bridges.

**Sgt. Martin "Wagger" Thornton, Company D, 2nd Battalion, Oxfordshire and Buckinghamshire Light Infantry, 6th Airborne Division:** The tanks were making their way down probably to recapture the bridge, and I suddenly found myself entrusted with the PIAT [bazooka]. I took a chap with me, to be a number two, and off we went. I lay down with this other guy about thirty yards from the T-junction of the road. I was shaking like a bloody leaf. In about three minutes this bloody thing appears, the old wheels were rattling away, and I could more hear it than see it. I took an aim, and bang—off it went. The thing exploded right bang in the middle.

**Maj. John Howard:** Putting that tank out of action stopped any enemy counterattack upon the bridges before the paras arrived. The other tank turned around and ran away.

*As the men of the Oxs and Bucks settled in to wait, they were baffled to find life going on around them normally in the French village.*

**Maj. John Howard:** Two miserable little men were brought to me in civilian clothes, very scantily dressed, looking very, very hungry, and none of us could understand them. At first we thought they were speaking French, but it wasn't, and we eventually found out it was Italian, and after long questioning, it turned out that they were members of the German Todt Organization, which was a construction organization working under the direct control of Rommel, strengthening the front all around the Continent. These chaps had been given orders to erect poles on the landing zones. We gave them a couple of hard biscuits to eat and then let them loose. They, to our great amusement, immediately went off toward the canal bridge landing zone, where they proceeded to put up the poles. You can just imagine the laughter that was caused all the way around the bridges to see these silly buggers putting up the poles. In their estimation the Germans would be back within a day or so, and if they hadn't done the job, they'd be for the bloody high jump.

*Finally, around midday, still under fire from various German fighters in nearby buildings, the troops at the canal bridge heard their much-awaited reinforcements coming.*

**Pvt. William Gray, Company D, 2nd Battalion, Oxfordshire and Buckinghamshire Light Infantry, 6th Airborne Division:** We heard the sound of bagpipes, and the firing all stopped. It had been noisy, what with us firing at Jerry and Jerry firing at us, and then you could hear the bagpipes.

**Pvt. Bill Millin, bagpiper, Brigade Headquarters, 1st Special Service Brigade:** I was up front playing the bagpipes, Lord Lovat behind, the rest of the troop stretched out behind, and all along the side was these tall poplar trees and piping away there I could see a sniper in a tree on the righthand side of the road. Then there was a flash and the sound of a shot and I looked round and Lovat was on his knee so I stopped playing. Next thing, about half a dozen commandos rushed past me firing at this character, he was struggling down the tree by this time, and then he disappeared into the cornfield. I could see his head bobbing up and down. Lovat was shooting, his rifle was blazing away. Lovat sent some commandos into the field to drag the body out and we dumped him at the side of the road. Lovat said, "Well, start playing your pipes again, piper." He wanted the Paras to know that we were coming.

**Cpl. Wilfred Robert Howard, Company D, 2nd Battalion, Oxfordshire and Buckinghamshire Light Infantry, 6th Airborne Division:** Lo and behold, probably five minutes later, chaps with green berets came streaming along the road who happened to be Lord Lovat's commandos. Walking along with Lord Lovat was his piper, Bill Millin, blowing the bagpipes, and we just sat there and watched in amazement as these green-bereted commandos came along. There seemed to be an endless stream of them. There must have been six or seven hundred of them moving through.

**Pvt. Bill Millin:** I stopped immediately across the road from the cafe and there was a right battle going on and huge columns of black smoke. Even where I was standing I could hear the shrapnel or the bullets hitting the metal side of the bridge. The wounded were being carried up from along the canal banks and into the cafe. It was a real hot spot. Lovat went forward to speak to John Howard and he said, "John, today we are making history."

**Brig. The Lord Lovat, commander, 1st Special Service Brigade:** So far, so good. We retained the initiative and events had clicked into place.

*The commando reinforcements arrived just in time, as counterattacks continued, and heavy combat took place across the afternoon around the captured village of Ranville.*

**Lt. Leonard Wrigley, 6th Airborne Division:** There was chaos that day. Every unit that was fighting was a conglomerate of what fell together. I was with the Airborne troops and we did not all come down in a neat pattern. Because [the paratroopers in] the other Dakota landed down somewhere else, I was in fact responsible for the men. I was, in fact, the battle commander. So I had to hold this ground, a little hamlet just outside Ranville, to stop any tanks coming through; that was all.

**Capt. David Tibbs, regimental medical officer, 13th Parachute Battalion, 6th Airborne Division:** Fierce fighting was going around while the Germans tried to recapture the bridges over the canal and the river. The Germans were only a few hundred yards away from Le Bas de Ranville and attacking it fiercely all the time, just as Ranville itself was under counter-attack from the Germans who were beginning to send in elements of the 21st Panzer Division.

**Lt. Leonard Wrigley:** The [German] infantry were no problem to us; we could cut them to ribbons with our machine guns. However, we only had a few anti-tank guns. At about two in the afternoon we heard the rumble of tanks so I gave a simple order. It was the first tank that was to be knocked out. Every anti-tank gun, every bazooka [PIAT] we had was to knock out that first tank. Then the second tank would come up and we knocked that out. The third tank came up and we knocked that out. And then the [German tank column] commander, who was about twelve tanks back [must have] said, thank God for us, "to hell with this, we're getting away from here," which is what I wanted.

**Capt. David Tibbs:** The scene around the Field Ambulance, which was occupying a chateau in Le Bas de Ranville, was extraordinary. A large number, perhaps a hundred or two wounded, had been brought in and were filling the main building and outlying buildings including a barn, many of them desperately wounded. The surgeons were doing their best to cope with some of the worst wounded who would benefit most; for example, those with hemorrhage or thoracic wounds.

**Cpl. Peter Masters, No. 3 Troop, 10 Commando, 1st Special Service Brigade:** Towards evening, the teams came back from their demolition tasks having accomplished them as best they could, and somebody brewed up some food. It was either porridge or some dehydrated soup, the difference was hard to tell. It was pretty bad, but we were pretty hungry, having eaten at the most maybe bites of our emergency ration chocolate during the day. As soon as night was upon us, the Germans kept prodding around in the neighborhood, firing machine guns and mortars and shelling us. We had some captured German Maxim-machine guns, with drum magazines. They looked prehistoric, but to preserve our own ammunition, we started to fire back, probably much too soon, being fairly green troops, instead of holding our fire. The Germans responded and started to hit our positions. It had become quite obvious that the people who were supposed to have made it as far inland as we had, to our right and left, had either not made it or failed to make contact with us up to this point.

*About three miles from the 6th Airborne's flank, the British and Canadian troops coming off Gold, Juno, and Sword met with strong resistance, too, from German batteries and bunkers inland—sometimes even finding the fight inland more deadly and violent than what those units had faced at the beach. The main afternoon combat focused on a German command post code-named Hillman by the Allies and known to the Germans as Widerstandsnest 17, a sprawling 60-acre bunker complex atop a hill behind Sword and Juno—a fortress, as it turned out, that Allied planners had badly underestimated. It took seven hours and two assaults by the 1st Suffolk Regiment, finally backed up by tanks from the 13/18 Hussars, to capture Hillman, by which point any hope of reaching Caen or its airport had slipped away.*

**Cpl. Edwin Byatt, Company B, 1st Suffolk Regiment:** The Hillman position was a mass of concrete emplacements and armoured gun cupolas removed from old French tanks, which were virtually impervious even to anti-tank gunfire.

**Sgt. George Rayson, Company A, Suffolk Regiment, 8th Infantry Brigade, 3rd British Division:** We were the first platoon supposed to be in this Hillman attack. It must've been the size of a bloody football pitch, really, with several guns on the top, which we couldn't see. It looked as though they'd piled up dirt and then built this place in the middle. There was an underground barracks, electric light, a hospital; everything was done there. I think there was about twenty gun emplacements on the top, machine guns, and round it triple Dannet [wire] and a thirty-foot minefield. We'd trained for this so we knew exactly what to expect. We had an engineer officer and two men and they cleared the mines from the first lot of wire, about six foot wide, and put some white tape out.

**Pvt. Eric Rowland, Company A, Suffolk Regiment, 8th Infantry Brigade, 3rd British Division:** A breaching party crawled through standing corn and managed to blow the first belt of wire with Bangalore torpedoes. A mine-clearing section of Royal Engineers then cleared a path through the mines and the second belt of wire was blown, but an attempt to rush the gap resulted in several casualties.

**Sgt. George Rayson:** Two blokes got killed to start with. Right opposite was a machine gun in a turret. We all got down quick, otherwise he'd have had the lot of us. We laid there quite a long time and suddenly everything went quiet.

**Pvt. Eric Rowland:** Eventually, word was passed back that we were to dash, one at a time, through the gap and into a small crater just inside the wire, and from there get into a trench. I managed to get into the trench unharmed and joined the small party gathered there.

**Sgt. George Rayson:** I found myself in a deep trench. I couldn't see over the top, but following the trench to the left, then to the right, and so on, I eventually caught up with the others—although there weren't many of us left.

**Pvt. Leslie Perry, 1st Battalion, Suffolk Regiment, 8th Infantry Brigade, 3rd British Division:** One of our chaps, Jim Hunter, he was in a sunken road very close. This German kept firing this machine gun and it kept spattering him with earth and he said to his mate, "I've bloody well had enough of this," only his language was a little bit stronger than that as British soldiers sometimes use. He picked up his Bren and advanced on this German position firing.

**Lance Cpl. Jim "Tich" Hunter, Company A, 1st Battalion, Suffolk Regiment, 8th Infantry Brigade, 3rd British Division:** There was bullets spattering all around me but I was so annoyed I just didn't care.

**Pvt. Leslie Perry:** This German saw him coming but he ducked down and he dropped a couple of grenades in the emplacement, then he jumped down into the zigzag trench and as he turned one corner of the trench a German came round the other. They both fired together and Jim is only about five foot two and the German's bullet went right through his helmet and out the other side and creased across the top of his head. He got the German in the chest and killed him and he carried on and got one or two others and cleared the position. He was awarded the DCM for what he did.

**Sgt. George Rayson:** As we were wondering what to do next, a runner came round the corner and told us to get out as quickly as we could. We didn't need encouraging. A flail tank then appeared from somewhere and made a large track through the minefield, then up came three Sherman tanks, and in we went again.

**Pvt. Eric Rowland:** This time we got in to the position with little trouble and proceeded to mop up. We took several prisoners, but we could not clear the objective properly because so much of it was underground. However, we neutralized it and withdrew to dig in for the night. I decided to make a cup of cocoa using a Tommy cooker and my enamel mug, and proceeded to burn my fingers. Considering what we had been through that day, I got off lightly!

**Sgt. George Rayson:** We couldn't get down into the position owing to some steel doors which we couldn't open, but to wake them up we put several grenades down the ventilation shafts, plus a few smoke ones. After this we dug in around the place. Things got quieter, so we opened the 48-hr ration packs and brewed up some tea in our tin mugs. The tea, sugar, and milk, looked like a cube, but at least it tasted like tea.

**Pvt. Eric Rowland:** The next day the remainder of the German garrison surrendered, and that was the end of "Hillman."

# The Walking Wounded

By the afternoon, US assault troops at Omaha had begun
to commandeer the German fortifications as their own.

*The relentless and seemingly endless waves of landing crafts and arriving troops
had firmly broken the initial stalemate on Omaha Beach by midmorning, as leaders
like Gen. Dutch Cota and Col. George Taylor, as well as countless more junior
lieutenants and sergeants, rallied small groups of men forward, up off the beach,
through minefields, and onto the ridge beyond. Infantry troops pushed steadily
inland, but, exhausted and often wounded from the morning battle, they didn't
get far, and the day's most ambitious goal of establishing a large beachhead fell
short. Being ashore was, in the end, enough.*

457

**Pvt. Harold "Hal" Baumgarten, Company B, 116th Infantry Regiment, 29th Division:** I call our group the "walking wounded," all of them already had been wounded. I didn't know any of these soldiers, but most of them were probably Company B men.

**T.Sgt. William Boleslaw Otlowski, Cannon Company, 16th Infantry Regiment, 1st Division:** We went up the road up to St. Lô. A young soldier came walking up and he's got a big roll of wire on his back, communication wire. And the lieutenant says, "Oh, boy, do we need that. Sit down right here. Give me that wire." He says, "I can't, lieutenant. What will I do with this?" And in the other hand he was carrying his arm. He had his arm blown off and he ran up the road with the arm in his hand. Believe it or not, they took the wire off his back, and put a tourniquet around the part of the arm that was still there, laid him down, and yelled for the medics. You see what shock can do to people.

**Pvt. Harold "Hal" Baumgarten:** Probably due to my adrenaline, I was feeling remarkably strong for someone who had been wounded twice and hadn't had any food since the evening before. I had only fired one shot since 7:00 A.M., but a German soldier looked up from behind the wall, and I picked him off.

**Sgt. Barnett Hoffner, 6th Engineer Special Brigade:** We came to the top of the beach and proceeded along and up there was a machine gun nest in front of us.

**Pvt. Harold "Hal" Baumgarten:** The objective of the 116th was to head west towards Pointe du Hoc. Soon we came under automatic gunfire from a nest of five German soldiers. One of our fighters got hit in the neck and died quickly. After about one hour, the skirmish was over and we had prevailed. I know I nailed one of the enemy. I was surprised to see how young these German soldiers were.

**Sgt. Barnett Hoffner:** We came to a machine gun nest and there were three bodies in it. The men had long blond mustaches, blond hair, and had probably been hit by a grenade. The lieutenant said go and check them out and see what outfit they are from. Since I could speak German, I was acting the German interpreter for the outfit. I started to go through their pockets and I couldn't read the writing. In short, it was Cyrillic writing, handwriting. And he said, "You're supposed to be able to read German." And I said, "This is not German." We called one of our men who had been one of our cooks, named Panishuck, a Ukrainian. Sure enough, he read the letters and it turned out they were men from a Ukrainian Brigade which was holding this section of the front.

**Pvt. John Hooper, Headquarters Company, 115th Infantry Regiment, 29th Division:** The trenchworks we were encountering were producing prisoners, but obviously not Germans. They resembled orientals, and might possibly be Japs. They were held in little groups on the slope of the hill, and we told them to go head toward the beach.

**Capt. Robert E. Walker, 1st Battalion, 116th Infantry Regiment, 29th Division:** I heard the sound of someone groaning nearby and calling for help. It was about 15 or 20 feet away. Cautiously I went over to investigate and saw it was a German soldier, gravely wounded in the area in his groin. He had already been treated by a medical aid man. He had a bandage loosely fixed over the wound and it had been sprinkled with sulfa powder. He was gasping, "Wasser, wasser," German for water. I assumed he had been given a sulfa pill which causes great thirst. In German I told the man I had no water with me and didn't know where to get any. He then said there was a spring, he called it "ein born," about 50 feet away. I didn't believe him but I made my way over to the area he indicated. Incredibly, there actually was a spring, a sort of water hole with apparently clear water in it. I filled my helmet with water and brought it to him. After drinking thirstily, he thanked me profusely. I left him some water in his canteen cup.

**Capt. Henry Seitzler, Army Air Forces, 6th Engineer Special Beach Brigade:** We were freezing to death. That water had been like taking a bath in ice, and we had no way to dry off or anything, so we just stayed wet and went ahead and did the best we could.

**S.Sgt. John B. Ellery, Company B, 16th Infantry Regiment, 1st Division:** I didn't think about eating until afternoon, when I decided that one of my apples would taste good. I quickly discovered that my apples had become apple sauce. So, I settled for a K ration, and enjoyed it. I enjoyed it so much, that I decided to have another. It seemed to me that I wasn't likely to outlast my supply of rations, so there was no point in going hungry.

**Pvt. John Hooper:** It was now mid-afternoon. Creeping forward, ever-so-cautiously, I tripped a Bouncing Betty mine. It popped into the air and I hit the ground expecting to be blown to bits. It fell back to earth with a thump—a dud, probably failing to explode after several years in position.

**Pvt. Harold "Hal" Baumgarten:** I was crawling up to a low hedgerow when I felt a stinging in my left foot. It felt like a rock had hit the sole of my left shoe and a larger one had exited through the top. My canvas legging had a hole in the material that covered my shoe. It was now about 5:00 P.M. and I had just received my third wound on D-Day. Apparently, I had tripped some kind of "castrator" mine with my left foot. We had heard about them. It had fired a bullet through my left foot, instead of between my thighs. Leaning with my back against the hedgerow, I removed my left shoe. When I turned the shoe over, blood poured out like water from a pitcher. Utilizing my first-aid kit, I powdered the clean hole through my foot with sulfa. I proceeded to put on a good pressure bandage; however, just as I finished putting on a great dressing, we came under shell fire. I ripped off the dressing, pulled my shoe back over my bare, bleeding foot, and dove behind the hedgerow. My adrenaline was pumping, and I felt little pain. The seven of us remained there for a long time.

**Pvt. John Hooper:** Greatly fatigued, I just lay there wondering if the war would last much longer.

*Behind the advancing infantry, the beaches themselves remained as busy as ever—filled both with the carnage of the morning—including many wounded still waiting for treatment, like Thomas Valance, who had survived the massacre of the 116th's Company A in the morning's opening minutes—as well as the mounting numbers of men, supplies, and vehicles being raced ashore. In the afternoon, landing craft that had survived the morning and slogged for hours back to their transport ships now returned for a second and sometimes third trip to the beach; their crews, who had last glimpsed the beach at H-Hour, found themselves horrified by its transformation and wreckage in the interim. A top priority as the afternoon progressed was the push to open the beach exits—the five draws—for vehicles to get them inland and support the infantry. The largest and most important route—the Vierville Draw, near where Company A had been slaughtered in the morning—was still blocked by a large antitank barrier.*

**Sgt. Thomas Valance, Company A, 116th Infantry Regiment, 29th Division:** Sometime that afternoon, there was a caterpillar tractor going down the beach, parallel to the water line, and the driver stopped it when he saw me; he saw me alive. He came running up to me and handed me three comic books, which I guess he thought was the right thing to do, and the humanitarian thing to do. Needless to say, I was not in the mood for reading comics or anything else. Sometime after he went on his way, another fellow came up and bandaged my hand and later on that day another fellow came up and gave me a can of soup. It was the type that had a built-in sterno device so that you could heat the soup in the can itself. That I appreciated. I was lying amongst all of my dead comrades and I was getting uncomfortable.

**Lt. Dean L. Rockwell, flotilla commander, *LCT-535*:** We were scheduled to go back in the afternoon around 2:00. The *LCT-535* on which I rode cruised along the beach parallel for hundreds of yards, looking for an opening through.

**Charles R. Sullivan, 111th Naval Construction Battalion (SeaBees):** We manned pontoon barges—rhinos—that off-loaded LSTs of men, tanks, trucks, artillery, jeeps a mile or more off shore and brought them into the beach. Each "Rhino" could take the full load of an LST. We trained for months along the English and Welsh coast till we could hook up to and unload a LST in less than 30 minutes. We had, I believe 18 Rhinos, and each unloaded 3 or 4 LST's on D-Day at Omaha Beach. For most of D-Day we were under fire from German gun emplacements and machine guns, and we did hit and explode a few mines, but our casualties were light considering all that was happening.

**Lt. Dean L. Rockwell:** We did try to nose our way in, only to make contact with one of the beach obstacles holding a mine which exploded and blew a hole in our landing gear. This meant that we could not let our ramp down, and as a result, we kept the jeep and trailers aboard. We were able, however, to put the poor soldiers ashore, and let me say that I have never seen anybody more reluctant to execute orders. The beach was literally covered with military personnel, backed up, held down by enemy fire from the overlooking bluffs. We put the poor soldiers ashore, and we felt very, very sorry for them, but thanking God that we had decided to join the Navy instead of the Army.

**Charles R. Sullivan:** We continued to operate on Omaha Beach in the same manner till the Port of Cherbourg became operational.

**Capt. Henry Seitzler:** D-Day for me was rather a hodge-podge of events. Busy going from here to there, trying to help out one place or another. One group would need some help pushing a car or maybe move a tank, and you'd lend your shoulder to that. Always you were on the move because Jerry was pouring in fire at an awfully fast rate, and the 88's kept coming in, 20 millimeters, and .50 caliber machine guns.

**1st Lt. John MacAllister, administration officer (S-1), 121st Engineer Combat Battalion, 29th Division:** I proceeded into Vierville to the intersection with the road up from the beach exit. I remember just how lonely I felt. Some time later Gen. Cota and an infantry rifleman came up. He said, "Where's the rest of the invading army?" He then noticed the castle on my collar [the U.S. Army Engineer symbol], and his next question was, "Why has the beach exit not been opened?" When I replied that I didn't know, he said, "Well suppose you go find out." I started down the road to the beach, and he called out, "Wait, we'll go with you." By that time Maj. [Allan] Olson, our battalion's executive officer, had joined the group, and we all started back to the beach.

**1st Lt. Jack Shea, aide-de-camp to Brig. Gen. Cota, 29th Division:** There were a few scattered rounds of small arms fired at the patrol, but a dozen rounds of carbine and pistol fire sufficed to bring five Germans down from the caverns in the east wall of the draw. They were stripped of their weapons as they reached the road and herded before the patrol as it proceeded to the mouth of the draw. At the mouth of the exit, the patrol found that the anti-tank wall still stood. A concrete, covered emplacement, housing an antitank gun had been partially demolished near the western edge of the threshold.

**Lt. Col. Robert Ploger, commander, 121st Engineer Combat Battalion, 29th Division:** Word reached me that a C Company bulldozer was on the beach with its 1,000 pounds of TNT, and we scrambled to get it to the wall. I don't remember who the driver was. In general, dozer operators were of a remarkably tough breed, and I've always marveled at the guts of that operator in driving onto a beach under fire with a load of enough TNT to blow the dozer into a hole in the ground.

**Sgt. Noël Dubé, Company C, 121st Engineer Combat Battalion, 29th Division:** My mission as the 9th Squad leader, 3rd Platoon was to go up the D-1 draw after the anti-tank wall was blown by someone else who was given that mission. It took me from around 0715 when we landed to get to the wall around 1630. When we arrived, the wall was still standing, and many vehicles were still stuck on the beach. I arrived with my entire squad of 15 men intact. The B Company major was standing and hoping for some engineers to turn up. When he saw he asked "are you with the 121st Engineers?" I said "yes Sir." He said to me "take a couple of men with you and go and reconnoitre beyond the wall and prepare to blow it."

I started to move up to the wall, and to my surprise it was a double wall with about 3 foot between them. This allowed the people from the village who wanted to go to the beach to pass between the two halves of the wall to the beach. The Demolition man in my squad was John Obnack from Scranton, Pennsylvania. I brought him up to the wall to take a closer look. We had two bulldozers sitting on the beach and each had ten cases of TNT on them. Obnack said to have some men bring up the cases, we then put 4 across the bottom and three on each end thus making a big U.

I had Obnack turn the handle on the detonator and a ball of fire went over our heads about another 60 feet out to sea. We clung as close to the sea wall as we could as we did not want to be hit by falling debris. When everything stopped falling we looked up and saw that we could see through both walls. Now all the bulldozer drivers had to do was to fill in the ditch the explosion had made in front of the wall. Then they widened the edges of the holes in the wall and by 1730 vehicles that had been stranded on the beach started to move up the draw and catch up with the infantry who had passed through much earlier and continue onwards.

# The Battle of La Fière Bridge

These German tanks were knocked out by
paratrooper bazookas on the La Fière Causeway.

*While Normandy experienced battles big and small across the entire sixty miles
of the invasion zone on June 6, there was one still-little-known fight that stands
out for its ferocity, fought by paratroopers of the 82nd Airborne—primarily from
A Company and the 1st Battalion of the 505th Parachute Infantry Regiment
under the command of 1st Lt. John "Red Dog" Dolan. Less well known than the
British 6th Airborne's raid on Pegasus Bridge or the 101st Airborne's assault on
Brécourt Manor, the Battle of La Fière Bridge ranks as one of the most important
turning points of June 6 and the initial stages of what would turn into a 77-day
battle for Normandy.*

*The old arched, stone bridge at La Fière is hardly impressive—barely a few
dozen yards long, it appears still today exactly as it was when originally built, a*

464

*rural low-traffic crossing of a relatively minor stream. And yet its humbleness belies its importance on D-Day: It was one of just two passages across the Merderet River in the invasion zone. Holding it meant both preventing German reinforcements from the Cotentin Peninsula from storming across to attack the Utah beachhead and, also, speeding American forces along to their own attack toward Cherbourg.*

*US Army historian S. L. A. Marshall, who would write more than 30 books on US military history and was present himself in the Normandy invasion, later declared that the fight for the causeway was not just "the fiercest battle in the European war," but "probably the bloodiest small unit struggle in the experience of American arms." It was, too, an opportunity for true bravery; participants of the four-day battle would earn 18 Distinguished Service Crosses and two Medals of Honor.*

**Sgt. Robert M. Murphy, pathfinder, Company A, 1st Battalion, 505th Parachute Infantry Regiment, 82nd Airborne:** La Fière and nearby Chef-du-Pont were the two essential bridges and causeways that permitted the Allies to move inland from the beaches and cut off the Cotentin Peninsula.

**1st Lt. John J. Dolan, Company A, 505th Parachute Infantry Regiment, 82nd Airborne:** The specific mission of Company A was to seize and defend the bridge crossing the Merderet River on the road that ran east to west from Ste. Mère-Église, with the purpose of preventing the movement of German troops down to the beachhead.

**Lt. Donald C. O'Rourke, platoon leader, Company I, 507th Parachute Infantry Regiment, 82nd Airborne:** From our study of aerial photos of the Merderet River, it appeared to be a narrow stream running clearly through a well-defined trench, and the meadows on both sides being reasonably dry and flat. Actually, however, this area had been underwater for nearly a year, was as deep as a man's chest, and at La Fière, which was the river crossing, it was approximately six hundred fifty yards from shore to shore. Detailed study of the most recent air photographs of this terrain, taken a few days prior to the invasion, failed to reveal the marsh.

**Pvt. Marcus Heim, Company A, 505th Parachute Infantry Regiment, 82nd Airborne:** We were to hold the bridge until the soldiers who landed on the beach arrived later that day, but it was three days before they reached our position.

**Sgt. Robert M. Murphy:** Dolan and A Company had the best assembly of Operation NEPTUNE, with about 90 percent of the men accounted for. The officers gathered around Dolan while the A Company men put their weapons together and secured the para-bundles containing our 60mm mortars, bazookas and ammunition boxes for the .30-caliber light machine guns.

**Lt. Donald C. O'Rourke:** The buildings around the eastern end of the La Fière causeway, known as the Manoir de La Fière, were already under attack by a group of approximately 45 men.

**Brig. Gen. James M. Gavin, assistant division commander, 82nd Airborne:** About a half mile from La Fiére I came across the 1st Battalion of the 505th Parachute Infantry, organized, under control, and already launching an attack on the La Fière bridge.

**Sgt. Robert M. Murphy:** By 0800 hours the action around the Manoir was getting intense, initiating the full-fledged beginning of the vicious, continuous four-day battle that was likely the worst killing ground in the airborne battle zones of Normandy.

**1st Lt. John J. Dolan:** We had traveled about two-thirds of the way up the hedgerow, they opened up on us with rifle fire, and at least two machine-pistols. I returned the fire with my Thompson submachine gun at a point where I could see leaves in the hedgerow fluttering. Major McGinity was killed instantly. As luck would have it, there was a German foxhole to my left, which I jumped into and from where I continued to fire. I could only guess where to shoot, but I had to, as part of the 3rd Platoon was exposed to their fire. Lt. McLaughlin, the assistant platoon leader, was wounded and died later that day. His radio operator was also killed. The platoon by now was under fire from two directions, from the point where I was pinned down, and also from the direction of the bridge.

**Sgt. Robert M. Murphy:** The Germans, holed up in the massive stone Manoir homestead and farm buildings, practically had a built-in fortress with small battlement-type rear windows. This enabled them to control a field of fire with little possibility of successful retaliation from our small arms fire. The foot-thick sidewalls could not be penetrated. The large, long retaining wall just off the south side by the bridge, as well as the thick trees were natural spots for the German defense. They used it well, but we knew it could be taken.

**1st Lt. John J. Dolan:** I can't estimate how long we were pinned down in this fashion, but it was at least an hour. I made several attempts to move, but drew their fire. On my last attempt I drew no fire. They obviously had pulled out.

**Sgt. Robert M. Murphy:** The moment that Dolan and others describe—when all the shooting stopped—occurred when an A Company bazooka man put a rocket through the front first floor window. The Manoir battle now was over as far as we in A Company were concerned; it was only a matter of capturing any Germans who remained trapped inside.

**1st Lt. John J. Dolan:** I thought that all of the Germans had retreated; but unknown to us there were about ten or 12 Germans holed up on the second floor of a stucco-type farmhouse.

**Sgt. Robert M. Murphy:** Then suddenly shooting started in the backyard. Some ten or 12 Germans started firing out of the second floor windows of the [neighboring] Leroux homestead. Everyone in the 508 patrol and the 505 and 507 men returned fire. A final surrender took effect, ending the battle for the Manoir. The bazooka round into the Manoir had helped speed that decision.

**Madame Louis Leroux, French civilian, witnessed the Battle of La Fière:** The Germans placed some white bed linen at the window to say they were surrendering. Then the American troopers entered the house and drove the German soldiers downstairs with their hands raised above their heads. They lined them along a wall and searched them. Then they took the prisoners to the rear. Afterwards, we got a good bottle of Calvados for the Americans; they asked us to drink some first, which we did. Then they all drank some Calva, and left us to go back to the fight. For them, the war was just beginning.

**Sgt. Robert M. Murphy:** Now 1st Sgt. Ralph Thomas spoke to farmer Leroux, who had been holed up in the wine cellar during the entire battle along with his wife and three children. The family left the Manoir that day, going to the home of another farmer friend; this was indeed fortunate, because a battle royal that would rage non-stop for three more days and nights would soon begin. Farmer Leroux would not recognize his homestead when he returned: nearly half of the front of the rugged stone family home would be blown away in the ensuing battle.

**Lt. Donald C. O'Rourke:** The eastern end of the causeway came under American control.

**Pvt. Marcus Heim:** There was a broken down German truck by the Manor House, which we pushed and dragged across the bridge and placed it across the causeway.

**1st Lt. John J. Dolan:** We dug in with the disposition of my company as follows: 1st Platoon on the north side of the road, the 3rd on the south and the 2d in reserve, about 400 yards back, so that it could also protect the rear.

**Sgt. Robert M. Murphy:** We in A Company were on both the left and right sides, with two bazookas on each side of the bridge. All available land mines were put on the west side end of the bridge.

**Pvt. Marcus Heim:** The four bazooka men included: Lenold Peterson, and myself, John Bolderson and Gordon Pryne. Peterson and I took up positions on the Manor House side facing Cauquigny, below the driveway. There was a concrete telephone pole just in front of us and we dug in behind it.

**Brig. Gen. James M. Gavin:** As soon as the 505th drove the Germans across the bridge, a group of the 508th Parachute Infantry crossed to the other side. Their drop zones had been planned for the west side of the river, and many troopers were known to be cut off over there. However, they had hardly reached the far side when they were attacked by a German force, and they withdrew into the position held by the 505th.

**1st Lt. John J. Dolan:** At least a company of the 508 passed through our position and moved over the causeway to their objective. They were gone at least an hour when we saw several of them retreating back across the marsh. I remember that we helped several of them out of the river, which was quite shallow.

**Brig. Gen. James M. Gavin:** From then on the German forces attacked aggressively and increased in strength. It was the reinforced 1057th regiment.

**Sgt. William D. Owens, 1st Squad, Company A, 505th Parachute Infantry Regiment, 82nd Airborne:** We placed our antitank mines right on the top of the road where the Germans could see them, but could not miss them with their tanks. We placed our bazooka teams where they had a good field of fire. There were two men to a team.

**1st Lt. John J. Dolan:** On the bridge I had three bazooka teams. Two of them were from Company A and the third was either from B or C Company. The two Company A bazookas were dug in to the left and right of the bridge. They were dug in below the level of the road, so that in order to fire, they had to get out of their foxholes. The third bazooka was over more to the south where better cover was available.

**Pvt. Marcus Heim:** We knew that when the Germans started the attack with their tanks, we would have to get out of our foxhole and reveal our position to get a better view of the tanks. Bolderson and Pryne were on the right side of the road just below the pathway. I do not remember how many paratroopers were around us—all I saw was a machine gun set up in the Manor House yard. On the right side down the pathway a few riflemen took up positions.

**Sgt. Robert M. Murphy:** Several God-sent gifts like the small 57mm artillery cannon were hauled out and put to excellent use. The 57mm cannon is like an oversized rifle. It is very accurate and can be fired from a short or medium distance, but the trouble with firing a 57mm is that once you have the enemy in sight, the enemy too has a line of sight on you. Generally the guns did not long stay hidden behind the hedgerows, but were instead situated out front, where the crew (or any soldier) could get a direct shot at a tank or opposing cannon.

**Pvt. Marcus Heim:** All that afternoon the Germans kept shelling our position.

**Sgt. Robert M. Murphy:** After their extremely heavy artillery bombardment, the Germans became very aggressive: at 1600 hours, three tanks moved very slowly forward in an easterly direction along the causeway, heading for us at the bridge. The panzers were followed by approximately 200 infantrymen, many of whom were intermingled with and between their supporting armor.

**1st Lt. John J. Dolan:** The machine gun fire from the Germans was very heavy by now. We didn't return their fire as there were no visible targets and our ammunition supply was limited. They attacked with three tanks. The tanks were firing on us.

The first two tanks were within 15 or 20 yards of each other, the third was back about 50 yards. When the lead tank was about 40 or 50 yards away from the bridge, the two Company A bazooka teams got up just like clockwork to the edge of the road. They were under the heaviest small arms fire from the other side of the causeway, and from the cannon and machine gun fire from the tanks.

**Sgt. William D. Owens:** When the lead tank got approximately forty feet from the mines, the tank stopped.

**1st Lt. John J. Dolan:** The tank hatch opened, and the commander stood up for a quick look. That was the last look he ever took.

**Pvt. Marcus Heim:** The machine gun let loose a burst and killed the commander. At the same time, the bazookas, 57 millimeter, and everything else we had were firing at the Germans. They in turn were shooting at us with cannons, mortars, machine guns, and rifle fire.

**Sgt. William D. Owens:** Our bazooka teams let loose and both got direct hits, disabling the first tank—they were old French Renault tanks with comparatively thin armor.

**Pvt. Marcus Heim:** Lenold Peterson and I—the [bazooka] loader—in the forward position got out of the foxhole and stood behind the telephone pole so we could get a better shot at the tanks. We had to hold our fire until the last minute because some of the tree branches along the causeway were blocking our view. The first tank was hit and started to turn sideways, and at the same time was swinging the turret around and firing at us. We had just moved forward around the cement telephone pole when a German shell hit it and we had to jump out of the way to avoid being hit as it was falling.

**Sgt. Robert M. Murphy:** Peterson then ran 20 feet to get an unobstructed shot at the tanks, with Heim beside him carrying a bag of extra rockets.

**Pvt. Marcus Heim:** I was hoping that Bolderson and Pryne were also firing at the tanks for with all that was happening in front of us there was not time to look around to see what others were doing. We kept firing at the first tank until it was put out of action and on fire. The second tank came up and pushed the first tank out of the way.

**1st Lt. John J. Dolan:** To this day, I'll never be able to explain why all four of them were not killed. They fired and reloaded with the precision of well-oiled machinery. Watching them made it hard to believe that this was nothing but a routine drill. I don't think that either crew wasted a shot.

**Pvt. Marcus Heim:** We moved forward toward the second tank and fired at it as fast as I could load the rockets in the bazooka. We kept firing at the second tank, and we hit it in the turret where it connected to the body, also in the track, and, with another hit, it also went up in flames.

**1st Lt. John J. Dolan:** They fired every rocket that they had and then jumped into their foxholes.

**Pvt. Marcus Heim:** Peterson and I were almost out of rockets, and the third tank was still moving. Peterson asked me to go back across the road and see if Bolderson had any extra rockets. I ran across the road. With all the crossfire I still find it hard to believe I made it to the other side in one piece. When I got to the other side I found one dead soldier and Bolderson and Pryne were gone. Their bazooka was lying on the ground and it was damaged by what I thought were bullet holes. Not finding Bolderson or Pryne I presumed that either one or both were injured. I found the rockets they left and then had to return across the road to where I left Peterson. The Germans were still firing at us and I was lucky again, I return without being hit. Peterson and I put the new found rockets to use on the third tank.

**Ist Lt. John J. Dolan:** The 57mm during this time was firing and eventually knocked out the last tank. The gun crew did an excellent job.

**Pvt. Marcus Heim:** After that one was put out of action the Germans pulled back to Cauquigy and continued shelling us. They also tried two other counter attacks on our position.

**Ist Lt. John J. Dolan:** My two bazooka crews called for more ammunition. Major Kellam ran up toward the bridge with a bag of rockets followed by Captain Roysdon. When they were within 15 or 20 yards of the bridge, the Germans opened up with mortar fire on the bridge. Major Kellam was killed and Captain Roysdon was rendered unconscious from the concussion. He died later that day. Both of the bazookas were destroyed by the mortar fire. Lt. Weir (Regimental Headquarters Company) and I carried Captain Roysdon back. I then took over command of the battalion, being the senior officer present.

**Sgt. William D. Owens:** The Germans pulled back on the other side, and in about a half hour or so, they began throwing 88s and 120 mm. mortars at us. They really clobbered us. All our communications were knocked out. And the fellow, Private Ross, with our walkie-talkie, took a direct hit with an 88, so from then on, as far as we were concerned, we were a lost platoon. Then they sent the infantry again, and again we drove them back. Our platoon leader, Lt. Oakley, was badly wounded (he died a few hours later).

I began crawling around, getting all the ammunition and grenades from the dead and wounded, for I knew we would need every round we could get our hands on. I took stock of what weapons we had, and it turned out to be a good thing, for right after that the Germans hit us again. They must have received reinforcements, for the artillery shells and mortars were coming in like machine gun fire. I don't know how it was possible to live through it. Then the infantry came again and we gave them everything we had. The machine gun I had was so hot it quit firing. I took Private McClatchy's BAR—he had been wounded earlier—and I fired it until I ran out of ammunition. I then took a machine gun that belonged to a couple of men who took a very near hit. They were killed. The gun had no tripod, so I rested it across a pile of dirt and used it. With this and one other machine gun and a 60 mm. mortar, we stopped them, but they had gotten to within twenty-five yards of us. I really thought we'd had it, but then they threw up a Red Cross flag and stopped firing. I quickly stood up and stopped my men. I sent a man back to see if he could find some help for us. I moved to where I could get a good view of the causeway. I estimated that I could see at least two hundred dead or wounded Germans scattered about. I don't know how many were in the river. It took them about two hours to get their wounded out, then they started shelling us again but not a bad as before.

**Sgt. Robert M. Murphy:** The infantry did not attempt to force the La Fière bridge crossing again during the evening or the night of D-Day.

**Sgt. William D. Owens:** They never tried to get the infantry across again after they raised the Red Cross flag.

**Pvt. Marcus Heim:** Why we were not injured or killed only the good Lord knows.

*Heim, Peterson, Bolderson, and Pryne all received the Distinguished Service Cross for their defense of the causeway; Owens received the Silver Star.*

# Afternoon for the Germans

German machine guns put up a fierce resistance throughout D-Day,
and Allied troops would come to fear their distinct sound.

*The clear picture that we now have of the Allied assault—the five separate beaches
and designated landing sectors, the distinct efforts by the US airborne on the
western flank and the British airborne on the eastern flank—of course did not
exist to the German leadership at all on June 6. All they had were scattered
reports of paratroop landings across the Calvados region and assault craft landings
that stretched across sixty miles of beaches from Ouistreham to Saint-Martin-
de-Varreville. They also remained confused by the TITANIC drops of exploding
dummy paratroopers across an even wider geography. From prisoners, they began
to learn the armies and individual units—and even nationalities—involved,
but, as with any unfolding event, their information remained fragmentary, even*

*contradictory, for hours. (The disorganization of their command structure, the one that had often frustrated Rommel, did not help matters.)*

*In a final attempt to seize the initiative, the Germans launched their only meaningful counterattack of the entire day in the late afternoon, sending tanks and units from the 21st Panzer Division down the open fields toward Sword and Juno Beaches. The counterattack came close to succeeding—and could have very well been devastating to the Allied landing if it had—but the commander, uncertain about the strength of the Allies and worried that his forces might by cut off by the late-afternoon glider-borne troops landing behind him, ultimately ordered a withdrawal.*

**Gefreiter Georg Seidl, Grenadier-Regiment 916, 352 Infanterie-Division:** I was a member of the *Aufklärungszug* [reconnaissance battalion]. This was not as glamorous as it appears. One might think we had armoured scout cars or motorcycles, but we were 27 men who rode around on bicycles looking for the enemy.

**Gren. Wilhelm Gerstner, 352 Infanterie-Division:** It was terrifying; we were always scanning the skies for Jabos [Allied Jagdbombers—fighter-bombers]. We were on and off our saddles all morning cowering in ditches while they flew past. It was uncomfortable. I had no water; my bicycle had no brakes—there was a lack of rubber. In the night some partisans had spread tacks across the roads and there were many punctures—but I was fine because I rode on tires full of stuffing because there were no inner tubes available. Several of us whose bicycles buckled or twisted in these manoeuvres got a lift on the French *camions* carrying our heavy guns and ammunition. Then you would ride clinging to the front right mudguard—facing rearwards and shout a warning to the driver if you saw anything in the sky. We had to travel slowly because a higher speed meant dust, which we soon learned would attract aircraft like flies.

**Gefreiter Georg Seidl:** We had three *Gruppen* [squads], each of nine men. The strength of the Gruppe was one MG42, one *Schiessbecher* [rifle with grenade launcher], one MP40, which was carried by the Gruppe leader, one semi-auto rifle and the rest with K98s [bolt-action Mauser rifles]. I carried the semi-auto. On the morning of 6 June, our Zug was with the Stabszug at the regimental Headquarters. Hauptmann Steneck then ordered each of our Gruppen on different missions. My Gruppe, Nr 3, was detailed to stand guard at the command bunkers. We were lucky; we didn't have to pedal anywhere. Nr 2 Gruppe was sent to secure the telegraph and phone offices in Tréviers. Nr 1 Gruppe was sent to the front as battle reserves. So the first part of the invasion day I spent standing guard at the bunker entrance, listening to the sounds of heavy fighting coming from the beach.

**Lt. Hans Heinze, a Stalingrad survivor, Grenadier Regiment 916, 352nd Infantry Division:** We had launched our attack to retake WN62b [on Omaha Beach] at about 1300 hrs. I split the company into three groups. One stayed in the wood line as reserves, and I led the other two in the attack. Moving like rabbits, hopping from one bush to another, we retook the position, and with it some prisoners from the US 1st and 29th Divisions. They looked depressed and tired; this gave us hope. Soon the Americans bombarded us with all they had. After a long time I knew we couldn't hold out any longer. I ordered the men to try to get out.

**Maj. Hans von Luck, commander, Panzer-Grenadier-Regiment 125, 21 Panzer-Division:** My II Battalion was engaged in heavy defensive fighting against the paratroops that had landed, who were obviously trying to extend their as yet very small bridge-head. I could free only limited elements of the battalion for the attack. In the late afternoon, almost at the same time as the armored group west of the Orne, we set off. Our goal: to push through via Escoville–Hérouvillette to Ranville and the two Orne bridges. The reconnaissance battalion went straight into the attack from its march and, supported by the panzer company, penetrated to Escoville against their surprised opponents.

Then all hell broke loose. The heaviest naval guns, up to 38cm in caliber, artillery, and fighter-bombers plastered us without pause. Radio contacts were lost, wounded came back, and the men of the reconnaissance battalion were forced to take cover. I had gone up with the attack and saw the disaster. I managed to run forward to the commander of the battalion and gave him fresh orders. "To avoid further heavy losses, break off the attack at once and take up defensive positions on the southern edge of Escoville. Set up a line of defense there and prevent any further enemy advance."

**Lt. Gen. Hans Speidel, Chief of Staff to Erwin Rommel:** The I S.S. Panzer Corps was at last released on 6th June about 3 p.m., but it could not have been moved by daylight. If the Panzer Corps had been thrown in immediately, the three Panzer divisions might have had an important local success at the most critical moment of the enemy landing.

**Maj. Hans von Luck:** I concealed my anger and remained calm and matter-of-fact. The tragedy took its course. After only a few hours, the brave fighting units in the coastal fortifications could no longer withstand the enemy pressure, or else they were smashed by the Allied naval guns; while a German panzer division, ready to engage, lay motionless behind the front and powerful Allied bomber formations, thanks to complete air superiority, covered the coastal divisions and Caen with concentrated attacks. We continued to wait for clearance for a counterattack.

**Oberstleutnant Friedrich von Criegern, staff, LXXIV Corps:** At 1620 the counterattack began.

**Lt. W. S. Hall, 4 Troop leader, A Squadron, Westminster Dragoons:** During the late afternoon some enemy Mk IV tanks appeared to our right flank and were soon engaged by the Staffordshire Yeomanry and beaten off.

**Lt. R. H. W. Bullock, 2 Troop Leader, A Squadron, Westminster Dragoons:** Later we saw some way ahead a tank battle with a counter-attacking force from 21st Panzer Division. About 5 pm—by which time the sun was shining brightly—we saw the second airborne force of the invasion passing almost overhead to land east of the River Orne; dozens of Lancasters and Halifaxes discharged their loads of paratroopers, and Stirlings released the gliders they were towing. It was a splendid and heart-warming sight. Little did I know at the time that the arrival of this force was what persuaded the German commander that he would not be able to achieve his objective of breaking through to the sea between the British and Canadian armies, and to call off the counter-attack—which, if successful, could have fundamentally changed the course of events in the British sector of the landing.

**Oberstleutnant Friedrich von Criegern:** The counterattack near Ryes by the 915th Grenadier Regiment of the 352nd Infantry Division also failed. In the evening, the enemy reached the Bayeux–Caen road east of Bayeux.

Counterattacks against the beachhead east of Ste Mère-Église from the north and west were ineffective. The attacking troops were delayed, weakened and partly jumbled on the approach by battles with airlanded enemy forces.

**Maj. Hans von Luck:** Feuchtinger sent word that the armored group had reached the coast through the gap between the landed elements of the British 3rd Infantry Division and the 3rd Canadian Infantry Division. Heavy fire from the navy, relays of attacks by fighter-bombers and, in the rear of the armored group, newly landed paratroops had forced them to withdraw, to avoid being encircled. My sister regiment, 192, had taken up a defensive position at about the same level as us. Now the very thing Rommel had feared had happened: the enemy had not been attacked by our whole division and thrown back into the sea in the first hours of the landing.

**Oberstleutnant Friedrich von Criegern:** The result of the first day of the invasion was not very hopeful. We did not succeed in taking full advantage of the favorable situation, caused by the temporary weakness of the enemy, immediately after the landing.

**Gefreiter Georg Seidl:** I was ordered to bring back a prisoner to the command bunker where the aid station was. He was a wounded sergeant of the famous Rangers. He had a bandage on his head and was very tall. I sat him on the handlebars of my bicycle and pedaled off down the dark road. His feet almost dragged on the ground and because he had a head wound, he lost balance many times, wobbling back and forth. It was dark and I couldn't see very well with him sitting in front of me. We almost went into the ditch a couple of times. I eventually had to hold onto him with one hand and steer with the other. As we made our way along the road, I thought to myself that this was the end of his last day of fighting, but only the first for me.

**Maj. Hans von Luck:** The "second front" had been established. Even the bravest and most experienced troops could no longer win this war.

# End of D-Day

By the end of the D-Day, the beaches were packed with landing craft,
equipment, supplies, and the detritus of the day's fighting.

*Afternoon turned to evening while Allied supplies and men continued to land on
the beaches amid sporadic German artillery, mortar, and sniper fire. Across the five
beaches and the airborne sectors, Allied troops had lost more than 10,000 casualties;
modern research by the National D-Day Memorial in Bedford, Virginia, has
uncovered at least 4,414 Allied deaths on D-Day, including 2,499 Americans
and 1,915 British, Canadian, Norwegian, and people from other Allied nations.
Some units were particularly hard hit: The British 9th Parachute Battalion saw
423 casualties out of a force of just 650. But, overall, losses were actually lighter*

*than the* OVERLORD *planners had feared or anticipated, and some 167,000 troops landed across Normandy that day. German resistance would continue along the beaches for multiple days, until the final strongpoints were defeated and the final batteries inland were captured.*

*The June twilight settled across Normandy around 11 p.m., bringing to a close a day that had forever altered not just the landscape of the countryside but the arc of the world beyond. Norman residents and soldiers from more than a dozen nations—American, Canadian, British, German, Polish, French, and more— settled back temporarily into the thousands of small and large encampments, foxholes, aid stations, and vehicles that marked the Allies' new sixty-mile-wide hole in the Atlantic Wall. D-Day, while bloody, had succeeded.*

**Edward T. Duffy, fire controlman, 2nd Class, USS *Shubrick* (DD-639):** About 1600 hours, an inventory of our ammunition indicated that we expended all of our five inch projectiles to a very low level. The Task Group Commander instructed the *Shubrick* to withdraw and return to England for more ammunition. We eased off our position back into the channel and turned north to Plymouth. Our D-Day participation was over. We survived.

**Sgt. Jim McKee, Company K, 12th Infantry Regiment, 4th Division:** We spent the late afternoon of D-Day digging foxholes in the hedgerows outside a hamlet named Beuzeville-au-Plain five miles from Utah. We heard small arms fire that night, saw some tracers. But we lay low, did not smoke, barely talked, hoped not to draw sniper fire. It sounds odd, yet nobody in my squad fired his weapon on D-Day or saw a German soldier, though snipers took potshots at us.

**Pfc. William J. Hollis, Company B, 50th Signal Battalion:** This was D-Day for me. I did not fire either of my weapons. I did not see an actual German soldier.

**Sgt. Alan Anderson, 467th Anti Aircraft Artillery Automatic Weapons Battalion:** We went up the hill up off of Omaha Beach towards the village of Vierville Sur Mer which was the village just above us. I saw four or five soldiers there—these were Rangers—I said to them, "Where is the front line?" He said, "This is the front line. There are Germans over on the other side over there and across south of there on the other corner, and they've got machine guns and there's a lot of fire, so stay down because there's heavy fire at times from those weapons."

**Pfc. Kenneth Moore, medic, 2nd Battalion, 501st Parachute Infantry Regiment, 101st Airborne:** Private Robert Wright and I were the only medics to assemble with the 2nd Battalion at Angoville-au-Plain and Les Droueries. During the day we assembled 75 casualties in a church. We collected the men in light two-wheeled farm carts. In the church little was said. The men had been hit and kept some of their weapons, and I was afraid one of our people would kill the Germans and then we would have been cooked. At dusk on D-Day, we were told our troops could not hold the church. We both stayed with the wounded and shortly after that, the Germans came into the church. An officer asked if we would care for their wounded also till we could be evacuated. We agreed and the German officer left.

**Homer Carey, storekeeper, 2nd Class, USS *LST-505*:** *LST-505* dropped its stern anchor in 10 fathoms of water at 7:27 pm. All six small boats were lowered, and the bow doors opened at 7:45 p.m. Condition 2 was set at 8:30 p.m. Ensign Perry and four boats left for Omaha Beach. The small boats, LCVP, were carrying Army personnel to the beach. Boat No. 1, 2, and 3 returned, but No. 4 hit a mine and sunk.

**Frederick G. Harris, signalman, 2nd Class, Army Tug *ST-761*:** We arrived off Omaha Beach in the last couple hours of D-Day, just after dark. We were just off shore and you could still hear the gunfire of artillery and the flashes in the sky. At that time on D-Day the beachhead was barely a mile deep, so you could still hear the action going on.

**Pvt. Gerald Marley Henry, unit mechanic, Royal Winnipeg Rifles, 7th Infantry Brigade, 3rd Canadian Division:** After sunset, there was the largest fireworks display one could ever witness. The German Air Force came at the beaches by the dozens and the only protection for the Allies were the anti-aircraft guns which were lined up by the beach and waiting for them. The tracer shells made a red ball of display for us on our higher ground vantage point, likely four or five miles away.

**Homer Carey:** The LCVPs return[ed] carrying disturbing news. Upon approaching the beach they found the beach covered with bodies of men who had been caught in the enemy gunfire. There were so many dead that the LCVPs cruised along the beach looking for a place where they could come in without having to lay the ramp onto dead men. They could not find such a spot and did what they had to do—lowered the ramp and the soldiers walked out over the dead.

**S.Sgt. C. Carwood Lipton, platoon sergeant, Company E, 506th Parachute Infantry Regiment, 101st Airborne:** We reach Culoville about dusk and after making sure the area was clear, we set up a perimeter defense and settled down to get some rest for the first time in two days and a night. We hadn't had any rest to speak of and certainly no sleep since the night of June 4th and this was the night of June 6. Lying there getting some rest, I reflected with satisfaction on the day because I felt that my unit and I had conducted ourselves quite well in our first taste of combat.

**Pfc. Felix Branham, Company K, 116th Infantry Regiment, 29th Division:** That night, as we started the digging in, I would dig a little while and my buddy, Jim Macy—he died later from wounds—he would dig a while. I began crying. I cried like a baby. He looked at me and said, "Felix, why are you crying?" I said, "I've been thinking about how close to death [we've come]—and the things that I've seen today." I don't know how we made it through all this. He'd say, "Felix, I know exactly how you feel."

**Homer Carey:** In my eight to twelve midnight watch, a plane flew over and dropped his bombs. The first one hit 400 yards off our portside. The next one was 300 yards away. The third was only 200 yards off. Then, too close for comfort, was one just 100 yards away. We could hear each successive explosion increasing in volume. We just knew the next one would be marked for us so what to do. Hold your ears? Jump overboard? Duck? However, the next one didn't hit us because the one that had missed by 100 yards was apparently the last bomb on that stick. Call it luck, divine providence, call it what you please, but here I am. They missed me.

**Robert Giguere, 5th Engineers Special Brigade:** When I came to, I was in the 40th General hospital in Cirencester, England. It was my eighteenth birthday, June 10th.

**Robert Capa, photographer, _Life_ magazine:** I woke up in a bunk. My naked body was covered with a rough blanket. On my neck, a piece of paper read: "Exhaustion case. No dog tags." My camera bag was on the table, and I remembered who I was. In the second bunk was another naked young man, his eyes staring at the ceiling. The tag around his neck said only: "Exhaustion case." He said: "I am a coward." He was the only survivor from the ten amphibious tanks that had preceded the first waves of infantry. All these tanks had sunk in the heavy seas. He said he should have stayed back on the beach. I told him that I should have stayed on the beach myself. The engines were humming; our boat was on its way back to England. During the night the man from the tank and I both beat our breasts, each insisting that the other was blameless, that the only coward was himself.

**Sgt. Alan Anderson:** About this time, I was absolutely overtaken by fatigue. You have to remember I had not slept for two nights and all of the day. I was utterly fatigued. My clothes were still wet, and that chemical-impregnated material used against the possibility of being gassed smelled to high heaven. I remember I had a chocolate bar from my C-rations, and I managed to eat a bite or two of that. I had picked up a canteen, so I had a little water, and I managed to take a drink. My lips were parched, and I could hardly close my mouth because it was full of sand and other debris from the artillery pounding we had taken on the beach.

Finally, one of the Rangers said, "Well, Sergeant, why don't you catch a little nap here? I'll stay awake for a couple hours and then I'll wake you and then maybe I can get a little sleep." I laid down and there was a burst of machine gun fire—it was coming at kind of an angle and it was pretty close to my head—so I just moved over a little bit and thought, _Well, he can't get me here._ And I fell sound asleep. I was absolutely totally exhausted. The Ranger woke me at about 1:00 in the morning on the 7th of June, and then he laid down and I took over.

**Maj. Gen. Matthew Ridgway, commander, 82nd Airborne:** I was in fine physical shape, but never in all my life have I been so weary as I was at the end of that first day in Normandy. Just before midnight, tottering on my feet as was many another soldier who had fought there on that day, I rolled up in a cargo chute and lay down for the first sleep I'd had in forty-eight hours. The town of St. Mère Église was only a short distance away, and all that night German airplanes were overhead, dropping five hundred-pounders, and German artillery was shelling the city heavily.

**Pfc. John Robertson, Company F, 116th Infantry Regiment, 29th Division:** Somehow, nighttime came but there was still plenty of activity. German fighters came over our area very low, heading out toward the ships and they drew so many tracer bullets from the ships that the sky was lit up with white streaks.

**Flight (Warrant) Officer Charles E. "Chuck" Skidmore, Jr., glider pilot, 91st Troop Carrier Squadron, 439th Troop Carrier Wing:** We took refuge in a thatched roof farmhouse nearby to get ourselves organized and were surprised to find an American paratrooper in bed. He had jumped and had fallen through the thatched roof. He broke his leg.

We left him there after awhile, but at the time, he was being aided by a young French lady and didn't seem to care whether the war continued or not. I hope he made it back home. By nightfall, we were looking for somewhere safe to, maybe, catch a few winks.

**Pvt. Gerald Marley Henry:** No one was allowed to sleep until after 2300 hours, 11:00. As we dug in, with two men in each slit trench, one guy had to be awake at all times. I don't think anyone, not one of us, could have slept anyway.

**1st Lt. Richard "Dick" Winters, Company E, 506th Parachute Infantry Regiment, 101st Airborne:** I remember going out on a patrol, and I was by myself, and it was dark. I heard some troops coming the other way. I listened, I stopped. I got in a ditch and I listened. I could hear those hobnails—*CLUMP, CLUMP, CLUMP, CLUMP*—uh-oh. Germans. I dove into the ditch and was hiding, and as the Germans came by and walked by, it was my first time being exposed to how strong German tobacco was, because I could smell the German tobacco. I knew that was German; I could smell them.

**Pvt. Gerald Marley Henry:** Some time during our two-hour watch, I heard someone approaching on the roadway, a very stealthy movement. I stood perfectly still next to the bankway and waited. Finally, I saw a shadow approaching, perhaps 30 or 40 feet away, so I very carefully leaned over against the wall of the embankment. I guess he saw my movement because he did the same thing and melted into the shadows of the embankment. I waited but nothing happened. He must have retreated. No trace, never for me to know if friend or foe.

**Flight (Warrant) Officer Charles E. "Chuck" Skidmore, Jr.:** We came upon several Americans busily digging holes in one small field, so figuring out that misery loves company, several of us sunk our shovels at the edge of the field. "Hey, you guys can't dig in here." "Why?" we asked. "Because we're starting a temporary American cemetery here." That did it. We went elsewhere.

**Pvt. Harold "Hal" Baumgarten, Company B, 116th Infantry Regiment, 29th Division:** Around midnight, shells started landing in front of us. We crossed to the north side of the road by 12:30 A.M. We were ambushed by an MG42 from the left. All of us were hit. Since I was limping and bent over, I was shot through my left lip. Wound number one on June 7 was not a minor one. It took away part of my right upper jaw, teeth, and gums. Moving forward, I tripped over and fell on top of two of my buddies, but they could no longer complain. The others were moaning. One of the guys yelled, "Help me, Jesus." I expected the Germans to come down the road and finish us off, but they never came. I was all alone now. All my comrades were silent.

At about 3:00 A.M., while I was saying my last prayers, I saw an army ambulance approaching along the road from the west. I couldn't yell at it, due to my mouth injury. Aiming above the ambulance, I fired a burst. It was really there, because two frightened GIs came out with their hands raised momentarily. I could not talk to them. Placing my arms over a shoulder of each, I limped to the back of the ambulance. I was taken down the beach, east of Vierville, near St. Laurent-sur-Mer. They laid me out on the sand in a stretcher with about eleven others. The army medics gave us water, blankets for warmth, and morphine for pain. After four hours on the beach awaiting evacuation, I was carried by four U.S. Navy men, one of them a combat underwater demolition man, to a waiting LCVP assault boat. I was ferried out to *LST-291* and hoisted up to the top deck by means of ropes.

**Pvt. James O. Eads, 508th Parachute Infantry Regiment, 82nd Airborne:** An officer from the 82nd came up and told me my group were assembled at Hill 30 and I was to join them. He had another mission scheduled for that evening. I joined what was left of my people at the edge of Hill 30, and after one hell of a battle, we captured it. This lasted until the wee hours of the morning. After the hill was secure, we set up a perimeter defense, and by morning light, June 7, had beat off 4 counter attacks. We had started with 30 men for this particular mission; 6 were left. I said a silent prayer and slept for 2 hours.

**Pvt. Herbert Zafft, 115th Infantry Regiment, 29th Division:** We had come this far and I haven't seen any Germans except dead ones and captured ones. I have not even fired one shell yet through my rifle. I made the landings, I made it up the hill, I made it all the way to where the Germans had stopped us for the first night. I guess I made it up the hill of manhood. I was only 20 years old. One of the proudest things of my life I think that I ever accomplished was making it through the landings of Normandy.

**Trooper Joe Minogue, Gunner, B Squadron, Westminster Dragoons:** In some ways we were lucky not to know just what a small area of Normandy we were actually holding at this stage. Had the Germans been given the right order by Hitler on D-Day plus One, as it was known, they could have wiped the bloody floor with us.

**S.Sgt. John A. Beck, Sr., Company A, 87th Chemical Mortar Battalion, 4th Division:** This was the end of the first day of combat. With 338 more days to fall out, including the Battle of the Bulge and the link-up with the Russians.

**Capt. John Semken, Sherman tank commander, Sherwood Rangers, 8th Armoured Brigade:** The terrible thing was that there we were ashore. It bore in upon us that we hadn't really given any thought to what happened next. For five months our sleeping and waking thoughts had been preoccupied with how the hell we were going to get ashore and what the hell was going to happen if we couldn't? Now it was all over, and we hadn't really thought about what happened next.

**S.Sgt. John B. Ellery, Company B, 16th Infantry Regiment, 1st Division:** The first night in France I spent in a ditch beside a hedgerow wrapped in a damp shelter-half and thoroughly tired. But I felt elated. It had been the greatest experience of my life, the greatest adventure. I was 10 feet tall. No matter what happened, I had made it off the beach, and reached the high ground. I was king of the hill, at least in my own mind, for a moment. My contribution to the heroic tradition of the United States Army might have been the smallest achievement in the history of courage, but at least, for a time, I had walked in the company of very brave men.

*"They got the lot of us in the end"*

# Epilogue

French civilian workers began to place crosses on graves on
a temporary American cemetery at Omaha Beach.

*In one sense, D-Day marked an end to years of planning and anticipation, but for*
*all its historic significance, bravery, and sacrifice, June 6, 1944, mostly represented*
*a beginning, the start of a hard, violent ten-month fight through occupied Europe*
*to defeat the Third Reich. The Rangers at Pointe du Hoc would have to survive*
*for three days before US forces finally reached them, and after the initial success*
*of the landings, it took 77 days—and thousands more lives—just for the Allies to*
*break out of Normandy. The ongoing combat would devastate large swaths of the*
*Norman countryside. Some 19,000 French civilians were killed and hundreds of*
*thousands more lost their homes; by the time Caen—just a few miles inland, a*

*city so close the British hoped to reach it on the first day—was finally liberated in mid-July just a quarter of the city survived.*

*Surviving the Normandy campaign itself would be a rare badge of honor for those who fought in it. Many units were so ravaged by the landing and subsequent fighting that the veterans who survived could be counted by name.*

*As the fighting advanced through the Normandy hedgerows, the Allies unloaded a staggering amount of war matériel into Europe over the course of the rest of June, including 570 Liberty ships, 372 LCIs, 905 LSTs, and 1,442 LCTs. As Samuel Eliot Morison wrote, "Admiral Ramsay estimated that in supplies alone, the daily tonnage handled in France during this period was one-third of the normal import capacity of the United Kingdom." The one millionth Allied soldier arrived in France on July 4. Along the way, the Mulberry floating harbors more than proved their worth, even though the American Mulberry at Omaha Beach was destroyed by a massive storm in late June. The Gold Beach Mulberry, though, continued operating for months. As much as a quarter of all the Allied supplies for the European invasion were flowing through the Gold Beach Mulberry in October.*

*For all of those who survived D-Day, the morning of June 7 marked the start of the rest of their lives—lives forever altered by the events of June 6.*

**Pvt. John E. Fitzgerald, 502nd Parachute Infantry Regiment, 101st Airborne:** At about 3:00 a.m., a sergeant woke me and said we would be moving out soon. I had to stop for a minute to remember where I was. My whole body felt as if I had just returned from a three-day binge.

**Andy Rooney, correspondent, *Stars and Stripes*:** The war didn't end on D-Day. When we got out into the French countryside, it was only beginning.

**Alexandre Renaud, Mayor, Sainte-Mère-Église:** The battle began again in earnest at dawn on Wednesday.

*German counterattacks on June 7 came from all sides. At the western side, a new force of tanks and 200 infantry began to advance across the La Fière Causeway.*

**Sgt. Robert M. Murphy, pathfinder, Company A, 505th Parachute Infantry Regiment, 82nd Airborne:** At 1000 on D+1, the enemy attack began. More

Germans were attacking than our meager stockpile of ammunition could conceivably handle. Our platoon strength was dwindling rapidly. The machine gun ammunition supply in the frontline was now down to one box per gun. Sergeant Owens, standing in the key position, had lost all but 15 men. He sent me, the 1st Platoon runner, over to tell Lt. Dolan that we were out of ammunition, could not stand another tank and infantry attack, and needed to move back. What should we do? I got out of my hole and ran back to the incline and across the road where Dolan was looking down at the bridge with a few wounded men nearby. I told him what Owens had said. "Stay where you are," Dolan said. He took a piece of paper from a little notepad, wrote something on it, and told me, "Here—give this to Sergeant Owens." Ducking incoming shells and bullets, I ran back to Owens and gave him the note. Owens opened it, looked at it, and said, "We stay." I said, "What's it say?" and he said, "There's no better place to die."

**1st Lt. John J. Dolan, Company A, 505th Parachute Infantry Regiment, 82nd Airborne:** We held the bridge until relieved. In Company A alone, in those three [days] in all, we had 17 known dead and about three times that number wounded. The rest of the battalion also had heavy casualties.

*Sixty miles away on the eastern, British end of the beachhead, Canadian troops advanced inland through the village of Authie, and ran into a particularly fierce— and bloody—fight as their tank columns, moving fast and overextended from artillery support, ran into the first major counterattack by the 12th SS Panzer Division, populated by many fresh teenaged Hitlerjugend who would demonstrate in the following Normandy campaign a uniquely savage brand of warfare. In the ensuing battle, the Canadian infantry and tanks destroyed 34 top-of-the-line German Mark IV tanks, while suffering more than 300 casualties—the North Nova Scotia Highlanders, known as the "North Novies," lost 84 dead alone. Some 120 Canadians, meanwhile, were taken prisoner.*

**Trooper Hubert Thistle, wireless operator, Sherman tank, C Squadron, Sherbrooke Fusiliers:** The next day, the 7th, was the day we were actually engaged in a heavy battle. It's getting on in the afternoon, we were in the lead tank, and the next thing I knew the other three tanks had high-tailed it back. That's the last we saw of those three tanks. We got hits on three of their tanks—we had a gunner, Freddie, a crack shot. The next hit was ours—an 88 hit right under my foot in the turret. Lt. McLean gave the order to bail out. We jumped where there was some high grass, and we had to crawl on our belly. We looked through the bush—it's the Jerry's. The 12th SS. That was the end of the road as a fighting man.

These were young SS—they took out our watches, anything we had. They took us to Abbaye d'Ardenne. Eighteen Canadians got killed [there] in cold blood. We saw them, right in front of this barn. They took us in this barn—five of us, and lined us up. We are next. Had a sniper all ready to go, when in came some high-ranking officer and stopped him. Just a split second, another five would have been amongst the eighteen.

*          *          *

**Lt. Anthony Drexel Duke, commander, *LST-530*:** We went on with the business of the war which was to load up more troops and more tanks and so forth and turn around and go back to France. We did that 42 times over the next several months. We carried, I don't know, 20 to 25,000 men, untold tonnage of weaponry.

**Don Whitehead, correspondent, Associated Press:** "With the American Troops in France, June 9": Four days after landing amid bitter fighting on the beach the American troops in this sector have launched an attack to push their beachhead deeper into Normandy. This was accomplished as a result of the unprecedented speed with which troops, guns and supplies were landed once the crust of the enemy's opposition was broken.

**Gen. Dwight Eisenhower, Supreme Allied Commander, SHAEF:** A captured enemy document, written by a division commander, perhaps pays as great a tribute to all the forces responsible for supply of the front-line troops as could be found. He wrote: "I cannot understand these Americans. Each night we know that we have cut them to pieces, inflicted heavy casualties, mowed down their transport. We know, in some cases, we have almost decimated entire battalions. But—in the morning, we are suddenly faced with fresh battalions, with complete replacements of men, machines, food, tools, and weapons. This happens day after day. If I did not see it with my own eyes, I would say it is impossible to give this kind of support to front-line troops so far from their bases."

**Trooper H. W. J. Smith, gunner, C Squadron, Westminster Dragoons:** The advance pressed on. Place names were seen that meant little to us at the time, but in later years are written in the history books. Some events stay with you as though they happened yesterday, like the day we were pulled back, put on to lorries and taken to Bayeux to get a hot shower in the town's public bathhouse; or the day we came across the remnants of a Canadian armoured division that had been destroyed at a French chateau. A fierce battle had taken place and numbers of German dead were all around, the acrid smell of death stays with you forever.

**Capt. Joe Dawson, letter to his sister, June 12, 1944:** Just a line to say I'm OK and have managed to get along this far. The news has covered the situation pretty well, though words can never describe the hell that was created on the beach that I stormed. God was with me, and I survived to get the job done, but it was terrible. Am returning to the front after having a little medical attention to a couple of items that I received on D-Day. Am fit as a fiddle, and I'll be paying my respects to Jerry again soon. Well, darling, just keep your fingers crossed, and know that everything goes well over here. We're on the final road now, and it shouldn't be too long before we manage to finish the job.

**Peggy M. Hart, Voluntary Aid Detachment, Cambridge Military Hospital, Aldershot:** When the casualties from Normandy started to arrive it suddenly became "all hands to the pumps." Even the "up patients" were allocated tasks to assist, such as cleaning and washing up. Everyone had a job to do and had to make sure it was done. But they all joined in cheerfully, even the officers. "Off duty" was virtually non-existent. From D-Day the 6th June I did not have one day off until the end of August, by which time I, and everyone else because we were all in the same situation, was suffering from exhaustion.

**Maj. Gen. Matthew Ridgway, commander, 82nd Airborne:** For thirty-three days the division was in continuous action in the peninsula. From time to time we thought we'd have a chance to rest and lick our wounds—"lie down to bleed a while, then rise to fight again," in Mr. Shakespeare's phrase—but these hours of inaction were brief. When we were finally withdrawn, forty-six out of every hundred infantrymen had been killed or so severely wounded they had to be evacuated to England. Many others had suffered minor wounds which they ignored to keep on fighting. One thousand two hundred eighty-two men were dead, and 2,373 had suffered serious wounds. We had gone into battle with four regimental and twelve battalion commanders. In the course of the fight, fifteen of these infantry leaders had been killed, wounded or captured. I doubt very much that any major unit during the war suffered heavier casualties and kept on fighting.

**Pvt. Harry L. Reisenleiter, 508th Parachute Regiment, 82nd Airborne:** The regiment and the division continued on in the war and we made the drops in Holland. By the way, the casualties in Normandy were right at 80 percent, and the casualties in Holland were approximately the same, and after we were pulled out of Holland, we were also sent then to the Battle of the Bulge to try to stop the German offensive which turned out to be the last big offensive of the war. We were attached again to the British 2nd Army on the northern end of the Bulge, and we were successful of stopping the enemy short of Liège. And from the Battle of the Bulge we were moved from the Ardennes Forest down in to the Hürtgen Forest and the campaign down there.

**S.Sgt. Harry Bare, Company F, 116th Infantry Regiment, 29th Division:** I fought with my outfit until war's end. Suffered—I would say—a minor wound in February of 1945. After getting out of the hospital, I again rejoined my outfit, and at war's end, arrived back home in January of 1946. I was discharged about January 13th as a 2nd Lt. with seven American medals, one French, including the Combat Rifleman's Badge and the Presidential Unit Citation.

**Pfc. Jacob N. Cutler, military policeman, 1st Army:** Then, we crossed into Germany, we just marched across Germany. Crossing into the Rhineland—the Rhine River—was the big thrill. Of course, it was not a very impressive river. I think the Hudson River is bigger or nicer, but it's a famous river. Now we were in the heart of Germany, now we went through and we saw the destructions that our planes did, all the bombed-out facilities and whatnot.

We went across Germany. I entered the Buchenwald concentration camp. I was a bodyguard for the Jewish chaplain, I was Jewish like him. It was only a few days after it had been freed. We saw many of these victims. It's a bad memory. These people were being fed by the soldiers. They couldn't feed themselves. The dead bodies were stacked like cordwood because the Germans had been routed and couldn't clear the area. We saw the gas chambers. Made me happy when I saw the destruction in Germany. We had no use for any Germans.

*While the fighting continued, the military compiled lists of the dead and wounded and started to make the sad notifications back home. It was almost a month before Bedford, Virginia, began to understand the unprecedented loss it had experienced on June 6. On just one July day, nine telegrams arrived from the War Department in Bedford, saying the town's sons had died in Company A on the beach at D-Day. Indeed, across the rest of the country and other Allied nations, it often took months to sort through the notifications of who was dead, wounded, or missing.*

**Elizabeth Teass, clerk, Western Union Office, Bedford, Virginia:** I had a job to do and a responsibility. I don't remember crying, but it was shocking to get so many messages and keep them confidential and find someone to take them out to the families. It was one quiet, still little town. Everybody's heart was broken. With a lot of the boys, if you didn't know them, then you knew members of their family. It was a very sad time. Fine young men had gotten killed.

**Telegram to the parents of Cpl. Clayton H. Dermer, Headquarters Company, 2nd Battalion, 50Ist Parachute Infantry Regiment, IOIst Airborne, in Willard, Ohio:** NSBG88 42 GOVT=WASHINGTON DC 5 914 A / MR GUY B DERMER = / WILLARD VILLAGE = /THE SECRETARY OF WAR DESIRES ME TO EXPRESS HIS DEEP REGRET THAT YOUR SON CORPORAL CLAYTON H DERMER HAS BEEN REPORTED KILLED IN ACTION ON EIGHT JUNE IN FRANCE LETTER FOLLOWS = / ULIO THE ADJUTANT GENERAL.*

---

* This telegram was, unfortunately, the second such announcement to arrive at the Dermer household: The Dermers previously lost their other son, Sgt. Wayne E. Dermer, who was killed in 1943 in the Pacific campaign in New Georgia.

**Lt. Col. W. B. K. Gordon, Commanding Regiment, letter, October 23, 1944, to the parents of Hubert Thistle:** Dear Mr. Thistle, I have your letter of October 1st in regard to your son. I quite realize the strain under which you and your wife have been laboring not having any definite news of him. He was the wireless operator in Lt. Ian McLean's tank. The tank was hit on D plus 1, June 7th. The driver of the crew, Trooper Redman, got back. We believe the remainder were taken prisoner. Lt. McLean has recently been announced as a prisoner of war. I feel therefore that there is every chance that your boy is a prisoner of war, but it may be well over two months before you have any definite word.

*For those who survived the battles and the rest of the war, the experiences of D-Day and combat changed them forever.*

**Pfc. Robert Sales, Company B, 116th Infantry Regiment, 29th Division:** You never got used to combat. Every damn morning, you got up wondering if you were going to live through the day. You didn't sleep too damn much—the Germans would send out patrols, and they wouldn't shoot you because that would alarm everybody. They'd cut your throat. That's why most of the time we slept two to a hole. Neither of you were ever really sound asleep.

**James Bentham, 3rd British Division:** By the time we arrived at Bremen in Germany, my battalion had been reinforced four times and there were only three of us remaining from the original complement of men who landed on D-Day. All the others had either been killed or wounded.

**T/5 Bayer Noen Ross, combat medic, 3rd Battalion, 16th Infantry Regiment, 1st Division, writing in his diary, September 1, 1944:** I'm not the same fellow who went in the Army two years ago. I never thought one person could see this much horror in a lifetime! I feel like I'm 76 instead of 26.

**George Nicolson, Company D, 7th Battalion, Green Howards:** I survived until 13 August, when I was wounded in the head by shrapnel. By then I was the last surviving member of the platoon that came ashore on D-Day. The officer and two men were killed on D-Day, and the rest were wounded. They got the lot of us in the end.

**Howard Melvin, Company I, 505th Parachute Infantry Regiment, 82nd Airborne:**
We had 146 guys including eight officers in Company I go out the gates of
the camp in England, and we had forty-seven who came back.

**T/4 Dwayne Burns, radioman, 508th Parachute Infantry Regiment, 82nd Airborne
Division:** Maybe I led a charmed life. I fought through the invasion, jumped
into Holland on September 17, fought in the Battle of the Bulge and on
into Germany. As far as I know, I'm the only one in F company who didn't
get the purple heart.

*After the formal surrender of Germany was signed, General Eisenhower's chief of
staff, Lt. Gen. Walter Bedell "Beetle" Smith, recalled: "The staff prepared various
drafts of a victory message appropriate to the historic event. I tried one myself and,
like all my associates, groped for resounding phrases as fitting accolades to the Great
Crusade and indicative of our dedication to the great task just completed. General
Eisenhower rejected them all, with thanks but without other comment, and wrote
his own. It read: 'The mission of this Allied force was fulfilled at 0241 local time,
May 7, 1945.'" Then, after the fall of Japan, it was time for the fighters to come home.*

**Frank R. Feduik, pharmacist's mate, 2nd Class:** We left from Belfast, Ireland,
after VE Day was proclaimed. I remember them telling us that we would
be one of the first ships to be ordered back to the United States and they
kept their word. We loaded up with supplies to come home.

**Pvt. J. Robert Patterson, 474th Antiaircraft Artillery Automatic Weapons Bat-
talion:** We returned home on an American ship. Of course, the war was
over. We came back to a place called Camp Patrick Henry. Interestingly
enough, we hadn't had any ice cream or any milk products and we were
crazy for ice cream.

**Frank R. Feduik:** Our convoy took approximately 23 days through the North
Atlantic. It was a very rough journey and it seems that some days we just went
backwards. I remember it seemed being up near 50 feet, coming down and
the ship just vibrating, bowing, we could see the front end of the ship actually
bend. We had to tie ourselves into our bunks in order to sleep. We arrived
in Norfolk, VA and were given a nice reception by the ships in the harbor.

**Pvt. J. Robert Patterson:** When I left the Army, they gave me a spec number and they gave me a piece of paper. The spec number was to help me get a job. My trade in the Army was a combat machine gunner. When I got out of the Army, the fellow gave me a paper and he said, "Here's a number. This is what they taught you in the service. I think you're going to have a little difficulty getting a job at this trade." And he was right: 50 years later, I still have never found an advertisement for anybody that wanted a combat machine gunner.

**Pvt. Maynard Marquis, Company H, 115th Infantry Regiment, 29th Division:** About 2:00 a.m. on Saturday, February 2nd, 1946, I hit the door of the house I left 32 months before. Free at last! What did I have to show for those 32 months of blood, sweat and tears? I was much smarter. I had nightmares that would last for years. I had a purple heart in a fancy little box.

**Pvt. J. Robert Patterson:** One night we went down to the PX and we had ice cream and we had milk-shakes and sundaes and everything else. We were going back to sleep and we were coming up a wooden pathway that they built so you wouldn't be in the mud and there was a Black soldier coming down the street and there were three of us. He looked at us and we looked at him and he said, "Get out of the way, white man. I'm never gonna step aside for a white person again." I think that was perhaps the first time we got the message that there was a new world ahead of us. And perhaps the world of 1940 was gone.

**1st. Lt. Richard "Dick" Winters, Company E, 506th Parachute Infantry Regiment, 101st Airborne:** I married Ethel Estoppey in 1948. We have two children. I returned to Pennsylvania, to farm and to sell animal health products. In 1951 I bought a farm along the foothills of Blue Mountain—seven miles east of Indiantown Gap. That's where I find the peace and quiet that I promised myself on D-Day.

*          *          *

**Pfc. Felix Branham, Company K, 116th Infantry Regiment, 29th Division:** There is not a day that D-Day does not cross my mind.

**Capt. Jack Dulaney, Ranger:** I dream about D-Day all the time. In it I'm going back, but this time I don't get shot. But it's always the most frustrating dream. I'm in civilian clothes; I don't have a gun; I don't have my helmet; I can't find my ammunition. I'm trying to borrow a gun from somebody. Yet here I am with all these Germans around me.

**Pvt. Waylen "Pete" Lamb, Headquarters Division, 501st Parachute Infantry Regiment, 101st Airborne:** I don't remember names too well, but sometimes when I'm alone with my memories, I can still see the faces of those wonderful guys, and get a lump in my throat remembering how I was a part of their team.

**Pfc. Henry Basey:** I feel like I've come a long way in these years, but there's some things that just never leave you. The scent of the dead is like nothing else. Sometimes I can still smell it. Sometimes I can't stay in the house by myself because I feel like I did then.

**James Bentham, 3rd British Division:** Some of their names I have forgotten, but their deeds that morning and their faces as they lay on that beach, I shall never forget.

**Pvt. Maynard Marquis:** It's too bad we have to have wars, but I think we always will. People never change. Only the weapons change.

**Gen. Dwight Eisenhower:** These people gave us a chance and they bought time for us so that we can do better than we have before. Every time I come back to these beaches—or any day when I think about that day—I say, once more, we must find some way to work to peace, and to gain an eternal peace for this world.

**Pvt. Buddy Mazzara, Company C, 16th Infantry Regiment, 1st Division:** I still think the principles a lot of men died for that day are still important and we should preserve them.

**S.Sgt. Waverly B. Woodson, Jr., combat medic, 320th Barrage Balloon Battalion:** We raised our family. I got two girls and a boy. We got lots of land here in Clarksburg, Maryland, and we're happy. I did get a Purple Heart and a

Bronze Star. Joann, my wife, made a display case for it, and we hung it up near the door. On the fiftieth anniversary of D-Day the French government recognized me. It sent three of us on a weeklong, all-expenses-paid trip to France, where they gave me a medal during a ceremony on Omaha Beach. I don't know why they chose me, but it was a wonderful thing. I was the only Black man of the three. I think it was the French's way of saying, "Thanks."

**Seaman Richard A. Freed, Sr., US Coast Guard:** I have been back to Normandy probably three or four times. I have gone back, and I have taken my children back, and when you stand up over the beach there's a cemetery—when you look how peaceful it looks now, all those crosses, you can't help but think, what a terrible, terrible waste. I also visited the German cemeteries there on Normandy, and you see they were 18- and 19-year-olds, on average. We were all children up until that moment.

**Pvt. Frank Palys, Regimental S-2 Section, 506th Parachute Regiment, 101st Airborne:** I was just a young kid, like the rest of them, trying to free the world from the Nazis. We did that, but we still haven't learned a damn thing.

**Pvt. Don Malarkey, Company E, 506th Parachute Infantry Regiment, 101st Airborne:** There is not a day that has passed since that I do not thank Adolf Hitler for allowing me to be associated with the most talented and inspiring group of men that I have ever known.

**Holbrook "Hobie" Bradley, correspondent, *Baltimore Sun*:** I've been through quite a bit in my lifetime, both as a journalist and later as a foreign service officer for the United States. I was with the United States Information Agency, first with the State Department and then with the USIA. I ended up in Korea, and then Vietnam. But, in looking back on this whole period, the landing on D-Day was the high point of my life.

**Charles R. Sullivan, 111th Naval Construction Battalion (SeaBees):** Normandy and D-Day remain vivid, as if it only happened yesterday. What we did was important and worthwhile. How many ever get to say that about a day in their lives?

# Sources, Methods, and Acknowledgments

It's often hard to know as a writer when you begin to write a book; they often gestate for years, churning over in the mind during quiet moments of washing dishes, reading, or walking, and the emotional commitment and intellectual interest necessary to research and write an entire book usually come long before an official book deal is inked. For this book, for me, there were three pivotal moments in the life of this book.

In some ways, I've probably been working toward this book ever since June 6, 1993. That Sunday morning, a month shy of my twelfth birthday, I opened the comics in the local *Burlington Free Press* on the floor of my parents' living room in Montpelier, Vermont, and was instantly caught by the day's edition of *Peanuts*. It was perhaps the most startling edition of Charles Schulz's cartoon he ever drew—a dramatic departure from his normal fare. That Sunday, a year before the grand celebrations of the fiftieth anniversary, Schulz depicted the D-Day invasion across three stark panels. It began with a view of the German coastal bunkers, then re-created the famous scene of soldiers heading ashore in a Higgins Boat, and lastly, in an oversized panel that filled maybe a quarter of a newspaper page, he showed Snoopy, dressed as a GI, scared, huddled in the tide among metal beach obstacles. The only words that appeared in the entire comic were a simple caption: "June 6, 1944, To Remember." I was at age 11 already on the track of being a history nerd and the bleak cartoon began my lifelong interest in the day. I tore it from the paper and it hung on the wall of my childhood bedroom for years. Today, still, now framed, it's in my office.

Fast-forward a few decades, and, soon after agreeing to write this book, I was on vacation in Wells, Maine, and walked into a used bookstore there that specialized in military history. Inside the chaotic, overcrowded barn— shelves and floor overflowing with piles of books, maps, and pamphlets—I spoke out loud for the first time, "I'm writing a book on D-Day," and the proprietor, George Arrington, launched into what turned into an after- noon-long master class on the historiography of D-Day, as he—knowing where every book in the cavernous barn was located—climbed among his store's piles, handing me volume after volume. I walked out with two full cartons of books and a lifetime's worth of downloaded knowledge.

The best part of this book, though, was meeting and spending time with Paul "Woody" Woodadge, the self-proclaimed "Limey" historian in Bayeux who has dedicated three decades to understanding the fight for Normandy, from D-Day through the campaign's conclusion 77 days later at the Falaise Gap. Woody was my narrator across those Normandy sites during my weeklong research trip, which began by traveling across the English Channel from Portsmouth to Ouistreham's Sword Beach. I have never met anyone anywhere who knew as much about a single subject as he does about the invasion and battle of Normandy. ("Every footstep here is a life lost," he said, as we paced 110 steps up Juno Beach, where the Queen's Own Rifles came ashore.) We hiked in hedgerows, down one beach draw and up another, crouched in German Tobruks and bunkers, and journeyed to the old mill site near the Chateau de Bernaville where General Wilhelm Falley was killed after his staff car came under attack by paratroopers, the marks of the crash still visible 79 years later on the mill wall. We walked Omaha Beach at low tide, seeing it just as the assault waves would have as they landed, and imagined—looking up at the vast sand reaches of the beach—what it must have been like to see how far away safety was that morning. Joined for the trip by my friend Jon Murad, we stood in the town square of Sainte-Mère-Église as the church bells tolled noon, imagining how their incessant bonging would have resonated among the fire of that June evening so long ago, and we walked the churchyard of L'église Notre-Dame de Ranville, where uneven rows of tombstones mark where the first D-Day graves were dug even before dawn on the morning of June 6, 1944. He shared with us, too, the story he excavated personally of the medics at the church in Angoville-au-Plain who treated

Germans and Americans alike that day, which he published in his own book *Angels of Mercy*.

After I had spent months studying D-Day from afar—focused often on the big decisions of the Ikes and Montys of the day—Woody taught me to see the fight as individual soldiers did, to understand D-Day less as one big fight or even as five separate beaches, but as 167,000 individual experiences and battles, to look at the land where Jimmie Monteith bravely held a vital draw off Omaha Beach, to see the trees where paratroopers hung up and died at the hands of German tormentors, to see the view from the resistance nests where German machine-gunners looked out, surprised, at the giant invasion fleet, to marvel at the skill of Jim Wallwork to land his glider in the tiny space astride Pegasus Bridge, and to stare at the small, unassuming stone bridge at La Fière where so many died. (My most unexpected new life skill from the trip is it taught me to identify at a glance the difference between German concrete poured in 1942 and that poured in 1944.) Then and in the months following, Woody provided dozens of references and tips, and he mined his own lifetime of archives for stories, reports, and details—including Noël Dubé's unpublished account of blowing the antitank wall at the Vierville Draw and his great-uncle Cyril Rand's memoir of coming ashore at Sword Beach—fielded questions from me on dozens of subjects, read an early draft, and pointed out areas for improvement.

It's through Woody's influence—although, to be fair to him, not his explicit recommendation if he doesn't care for my approach—that I chose to zoom in and highlight specific mini-stories, like the battles for Brécourt Manor and the La Fière causeway, the sinking of the USS *Corry*, Stanley Hollis's day on Gold Beach, and even Exercise TIGER, which typically gets only passing mentions in comprehensive D-Day histories. Regardless, I'm deeply indebted to him for helping to shape this story and for all of his work to keep the story of Normandy alive—and as true as possible—and I'm forever appreciative, too, to my friend Jon for accompanying me on the research trip and his beloved family—Vonnie, Cady, and Mac—for letting him take the time to join me.

Along the way of researching and assembling this book, I've been pleasantly surprised to be universally warmly welcomed to the subject by so many other scholars and historians who have graciously shared their own research, files, and interviews, including Linda Hervieux, whose groundbreaking work *Forgotten* excavated the story of the Black soldiers of D-Day, and who then generously shared with me Waverly Woodson's first-person account, and Stephen Rabe, who wrote an important book, *The Lost Paratroopers of Normandy*, about a unit who ended up far off-track that night in Graignes.

Canadian journalist and historian Ted Barris, who didn't know me from Adam, cheerfully—and almost instantaneously—excavated decades-old transcripts of interviews with Canadian D-Day veterans that made up the research for his own book, *Juno: Canadians at D-Day, June 6, 1944*. The Canadian side of D-Day is woefully understudied by history, and Barris's transcripts—and the other first-person accounts he gathered—stand as one of the best collections anywhere and are, at this point, literally impossible to re-create.

British writer Mike Morgan generously allowed me permission to publish excerpts from his book, *D-Day Hero: CSM Stanley Hollis VC*, which—amazingly—is the only real biography of the Green Howards' incredible hero and, as such, has authoritatively assembled some of the only tellings of Hollis's day and military career. Military historian Tim Saunders shared permission to draw upon his incredible research and interviews for his book *Juno Beach*, including his fantastic interview with his uncle-in-law Stuart Stear. Similarly, Kevin Shannon and Stephen Wright warmly granted me permission to republish portions of their classic *One Night in June*, about the glider pilots of D-Day, which luckily preserved their valuable accounts before the pilots' memories were lost to history. Many others pointed the way to me for a single story here or a memoir there, including *Washington Post* editor David Shipley, who turned me to Gardner Botsford, and others fielded single, one-off questions like Anthony Buccino at the Nutley, New Jersey, historical society, or helped gather up far-flung research materials, like Gail Ham at the Dartmouth History Research Group in the UK, which I appreciate. Archivists and historians are some of my favorite people in the world. I'm also thankful to the regimental units and associations who helped me dig into their experiences, including Steve Erskine and the Green Howards Museum Trust, as well as the Westminster Dragoons Association for making available to me the collected accounts of their unit on D-Day.

Peter Caddick-Adams' book *Sand & Steel* served as my bible every day I was writing this book—an immensely valuable narrative and deeply researched collection of facts, names, titles, and anecdotes. His book, which was published for the 75th anniversary of the invasion, will likely stand forever now as the definitive narrative history of that day. It was ultimately, though, one of more than a hundred volumes I mined for this project—many of which were patiently delivered in a seemingly endless daily stream of packages and envelopes by our friendly neighborhood mailman Joel—and these piles of old used books I collected hinted, too, at the day's huge shadow; one was inscribed by a veteran of *LST-56* and others had mementoes of remembrances and memorials tucked inside.

Other uniquely valuable resources I relied upon include two official histories, Samuel Eliot Morison's *Invasion of France and Germany* and Gordon Harrison's *Cross-Channel Attack*, as well as three of Joseph Balkoski's excellent books on D-Day, his classic *Beyond the Beachhead*, about the 29th Division, and then his two volumes, *Omaha Beach* and *Utah Beach*. Craig Symonds's *Neptune* masterfully laid out the years and months of strategic choices and questions that led the Allied commanders to the Normandy beaches on that particular June Tuesday. John McManus's *The Dead and Those About to Die: D-Day: The Big Red One at Omaha Beach* was invaluable in untangling the confusion that abounded in the first hours on Omaha. Alex Kershaw's *The Bedford Boys* was one of the first efforts to trace the contribution of Company A and that Virginia community to D-Day. Nigel West's *Exercise Tiger* is the standout best of the handful of books that have examined that tragic night in the Channel. Robert Murphy is almost single-handedly responsible for resurrecting from history the battle of La Fière, and his own memoir and history, *No Better Place To Die*, is the definitive collection of stories from that bloody fight. I owe all of these works gratitude above and beyond the specific footnotes, quotes, and citations where they appear.

Most of all, though, this book stands on the shoulders of a half-dozen historians who conducted or originally gathered many of these interviews and testimonials personally: Stephen Ambrose, Ronald Drez, George Koskimaki, Cornelius Ryan, Roderick Bailey, and Russell Miller, whose 1993 oral history, *Nothing Less Than Victory*, was perhaps the last great "new" trove of veteran interviews.

Ryan, of course, all but founded the field of D-Day history with his seminal book *The Longest Day*, later to be made into one of the biggest war movies of all time. Koskimaki gathered an unreplaceable treasury of stories from his fellow members of the 101st Airborne in the 1970s with his book

*D-Day with the Screaming Eagles.* Roderick Bailey's *Forgotten Voices of D-Day* is an invaluable gathering of the archives of the Imperial War Museum.

And then there are Ambrose and Drez, the widely respected deans of D-Day scholarship. In 1983, they began, through the Eisenhower Center, what turned into a massive effort to gather the stories of D-Day veterans before they were lost. As Drez recalled, "We wrote letters to newspapers and magazines, asking veterans of D-Day to contact us. When they did, slowly at first, we sent them a brief set of instructions on making an oral history on tape. We asked them to tell us about their birth, education, when they got into the army or navy, where they trained, when they arrived in the United Kingdom, their relations with the British people, their training, and so forth—and then to walk us, minute by minute, from midnight to midnight on June 6, 1944. As the tapes began to come in, it was quickly obvious that we had a big success. The stories we were hearing were stories of courage, of slaughter, of pathos, of breakdown. There were funny stories. There was a high emotional content. And there were wonderfully revealing anecdotes." Those thousands of interviews, and others he did at great length, formed the backbone of Ambrose's own trio of books on D-Day, including *Pegasus Bridge*, *Band of Brothers*, and his seminal *D-Day: June 6, 1944*, published for the 50th anniversary, as well as Drez's own *Voices of D-Day* book, all of which guided me through the day hour by hour.

Today, those interviews—a national treasure—are housed at the National WWII Museum in New Orleans, open for historians and scholars, and there I am deeply grateful to Director of Collections Management Toni M. Kiser, who happily provided nearly 200 transcripts for my research that form the backbone of this book.

Across the pond, I'm grateful to the curatorial staff at the Imperial War Museum in London—an international and unrivaled treasure of archival history and scholarship about World War II and more—and to Andrew Whitmarsh, the curator of military history at the D-Day Story museum in Portsmouth, as well as the reading room staff of the Portsmouth Public Library, who helped me access the museum's materials during my visit. When writing history, there's nothing that compares to the experience of holding history. In its own way, paging through those archives—including hundreds of handwritten postcards and letters of first-person accounts of D-Day at the Imperial War Museum—and reading contemporaneous letters in the Portsmouth collection, tightly clipped by wartime censors, and in some cases—like the letters of Ainsley Hickman—whose writers were soon to die in the Normandy fight ahead, brought the day uniquely alive.

This was the second book I did with my fabulous researcher, Will DiGravio, who helped assemble the thousands of accounts we gathered and did yeoman's duty organizing them, researching units and speaker names, and tracking down ever more obscure memoirs, histories, and books online and in the bowels of the New York Public Library. At times, it felt like writing about D-Day was almost as detail-heavy as organizing D-Day in the first place. With Will's help, I have done my best to accurately denote ranks and units of the speakers in this book with a reasonable degree of specificity, without needlessly burying the reader in military hierarchies. Doing so took us days and weeks laboring over award citations, unit morning reports, pay records, news coverage, obituaries, and gravesite details to best discern the most accurate labels, and we often found ourselves making imperfect choices, working with incomplete or sometimes contradictory information that left us trying to balance including a "best guess" versus leaving only a partial ID. Despite that effort, I'm sure mistakes remain, and I apologize in advance to anyone who I've misidentified. Similarly, I'm sorry for all the stories, big and small, that I didn't and couldn't include here. Scholars of D-Day, both serious and casual, will surely spot "seminal" stories of Operation OVERLORD that I skip right past. I know of dozens more that I wish I'd included. There were simply too many. I'm sure someone who started with the same pile of primary sources I did could carve out of it a fascinating book that didn't repeat a single one of the quotes I used.

At Avid Reader Press, this is the fifth book I've written with the incredible duo of Jofie Ferrari-Adler and Julianna Haubner. I am forever grateful for Julianna's careful editing and the myriad times in a draft she zeroes in on the worst tangles and reorders a story in just the most blindingly-obvious-in-hindsight way. Reading her edits is always a master class in the mind of a literary genius at work.

Behind and beyond Jofie and Julianna is the excellent team at Avid Reader and Simon & Schuster, including Associate Director of Copyediting Jonathan Evans and copyeditor Fred Chase—simply the best in the business and a man whom I desperately owe a cold beverage for helping to sort out the IDs of this book's 700-plus speakers—and art director Alison

Forner and designer Kyle Kabel, both of whom helped transform the words on these pages into a work of art. I'm grateful, too, as always, to publicist David Kass, marketing leader Meredith Vilarello, and Avid's other team members, including Caroline McGregor, Carolyn Kelly, and many more. (For the full list, see the box at the back of this book, which underscores how many people touch a project like this and how many different "publishing" careers there can be!) Jon Karp remains a great champion for my work, and I'm proud to be in his S&S stable. My literary agent, Howard Yoon, now at WME, has been a fantastic sounding board for me for nearly a decade now, backed by Gail Ross, Dara Kaye, Jennifer Manguera, and the rest of the Ross Yoon team. In the UK, I'm thankful for the help and guidance, too, of my editors and publishers there, Jake Lingwood and Mala Sanghera-Warren, at Monoray Books, whose advice early on greatly shaped my approach to the British side of this book.

At the Aspen Institute, I'd also like to thank Vivian Schiller, the world's greatest boss,™ for giving me the freedom to tackle "hobbies" like books, and my colleagues at Aspen Digital, especially Beth Semel, Jeff Green, Chris Krebs, and Ryan Merkley, as well as my wider web of professional colleagues, including Andrew Couts, John Gravois, and Maria Streshinsky at *Wired* and John Patrick Pullen at Long Lead, who all let me pursue such fascinating stories. More broadly, I'd like to thank my core of friends who feign interest in my latest book projects, including Mary Sprayregan, Dave Schilling, Katie and Rich Van Haste, Dan Reilly, Tam Veith, Meg Little Reilly, Libby Franklin, Elizabeth Ralph, Nicco Mele, J.P. Fielder, Erin Delmore, and Shane Harris. Here I deeply miss Savilla Pitt and Blake Hounshell too. Jenny Pachucki, who was the heart of my previous 9/11 oral history, *The Only Plane in the Sky*, has taught me an incredible amount about the art and science of oral history over the years and, in addition to being a great friend, was a particularly valuable resource in the early stages of this book as Will and I tried to make sense of the thousands upon thousands of stories we'd gathered.

In every one of my books, I thank an ever-growing list of people who have touched my life and been critical to me being who and where I am today, not the least of whom are the history teachers this book is dedicated to. Among those who shaped my life path: Charlotte Stocek, Mary Creeden, Mike Baginski, Rome Aja, Kerrin McCadden, and Charlie Phillips; John

Rosenberg, Peter J. Gomes, Richard Mederos, Brian Delay, Stephen Shoemaker, and Jennifer Axsom; Kit Seeyle, Pat Leahy, David Bradley, Rusty Greiff, Tim Seldes, Jesseca Salky, Paul Elie, Tom Friedman, Jack Limpert, Geoff Shandler, Susan Glasser, John Harris, and, not least of all, Cousin Connie, to whom I owe a debt that I strive to repay each day. My parents, Chris and Nancy Price Graff, have encouraged me to write since an early age, instilling in me a love of history and research and an intellectual curiosity that benefits me daily, and my marine biologist sister, Lindsay, has always been my biggest fan—and I hers—although she now takes her "aunt" duties even more seriously.

At home, our nanny Renèe Hallowell has given me the time and space to write for more than four years now, and I'm forever grateful for her calm and caring presence in my family's crazy and chaotic life, as I am for the extra help we get from Katey McMaster and Lexie George, who together help us balance, as best we can, that never-quite-right line of parenting and work. Along those lines, reading my friend Mary Louise Kelly's book last summer, *It. Goes. So. Fast.*, changed my whole mental approach to parenting, and the highlight of every day of writing this book was walking my daughter home from school. Similarly, I am enormously grateful to my wonderful in-laws Donna and Paul Birrow, a daily presence in our lives—and, more important, their grandchildrens'—and my wife, Katherine, who is a constant source of encouragement even when my work and travel stretch our family. Thank you, KB. I promise that I'm going to take some time off now that this project is complete.

—Garrett M. Graff
Burlington, Vermont
February 13, 2024

# Source Listings

The bulk of the 700 or so voices in this book are pulled from large-scale oral history projects, primarily conducted by the Eisenhower Center, now housed at the National World War II Museum in New Orleans, and the Imperial War Museum in the United Kingdom, as well as from first-person participant memoirs and autobiographies published across the eight decades since D-Day.

Primary sources for these quotations are listed below, arranged alphabetically by archival repository or publication. Some collections are available online, in which case the web address is noted. Other, more limited or atypical sources—including books, magazines, and videos—are noted in specific endnotes that follow. In some cases, like Gen. Dwight Eisenhower, quotations have been drawn from multiple locations. In those situations, the primary source responsible for the majority of that individual's quotations is listed below and exceptions, gleaned from other interviews with journalists or historians over the years, are noted specifically in the endnotes that follow.

## EISENHOWER CENTER / National World War II Museum Collection
*Interviews and memories collected by Stephen Ambrose, Ronald C. Drez, et al.*

| | | |
|---|---|---|
| Ray Aebischer | Jack Bailey | Gale Beccue |
| John Ahearn | Leland Baker | John Beck |
| Parker Alford | Harry Bare | Frank Beetle |
| Alan Anderson | Jack Barensfeld | Wilfred Bennett |
| Cyrus Aydlett | John Barnes | Sidney Bingham |
| William Garwood Bacon | Joseph Barrett | Doug Birch |

Joseph S. Blaylock Sr.

Oliver Boland

Bill Bowdidge

Holdbrook Bradley

Felix Branham

Eugene Brierre

Joseph Frank Brumbaugh

Ferris Burke

Dwayne Burns

Robert Butler

C.D. Butte

Carl Carden

Homer Carey

Gordon Carson

William A. Carter

Carl Cartledge

A.H. Corry

Roy Creek

Francis Dawson

Arthur Defilippo

Vincent Del Guidice

Ralph Della-Volpe

James DeLong

Joseph A. Dolan

Joseph Dragotto

Stanley Dudka

Edward T. Duffy

Anthony Duke

James Eads

James Eikner

John Ellery

Victor Fast

Frank Feduik

John Fitzgerald

Dennis Fox

Richard Freed

J.C. Friedman

James Fudge

Clair Galdonik

Edwin Gale

Robert Giguere

Edward Giller

Franz Gockel

Len Griffing

Samuel Grundfast

Martin Gutekunst

Fred Hall

J.H. Hamilton

Warner Hamlett

Clayton E. Hanks

Charles E. Harris

J.K. Havener

Robert Healey

Gerald Henry

Ernest A. Hillberg

Barnett Hoffner

John Hooper

Tommy Horne

John Howard

Ray Howell

Donald Irwin

Jack Issacs

Leroy Jennings

Edward Jeziorski

Lagrande Johnson

David Jones

Jack Keating

Steve Kellman

Edward Kelly

John Kemp

George Kerchner

Leonard Lebenson

John Lewis Jr.

R.J. Lindo

Carwood Lipton

Leonard Lomell

Roger Lovelace

John MacPhee

Salva Maimone

M.C. Marquis

Peter Masters

John Mather

Buddy Mazzara

Sidney McCallum

Benjamin McKinney

John McLean

Allen McMath

Howard Melvin

John Meyer

Charles Middleton

Charles Miller

Robert Miller

Charles Mohrle

Albert Mominee

William Moriarty

Gilbert Gray Murdoch

Ray Nance

Donald Nelson

William O'Neill

William Otlowski

Francis Palys

Harry Parley

Robert Patterson

Debs Peters

Robert Piauge

Harold Pickersgill

Exum Pike

Malvin Pike

| Nigel Poett | Sidney Salomon | Sigurd Sundby |
| Donald Porter | William Satterwhite | James Taylor |
| Duwaine Raatz | William Sawyer | John Taylor |
| Harry Reisenleiter | Arthur Schultz | David Thomas |
| John Reville | Donald Scribner | Wagger Thornton |
| John W. Richards | Ronald Seaborne | Sidney Ulan |
| Oscar Rich | Henry Seitzler | Thomas Valance |
| George Roach | Walter Sidlowski | Elmer Vermeer |
| John Robertson | Charles Skidmore | Martin Waarvick |
| Dean Rockwell | Joe Smith | Robert Walker |
| Robert Rogge | Sandy Smith | Jim Wallwork |
| Kenneth Romanski | Ronald Snyder | Harry Welsh |
| John Rosevere | William Solkin | B.T. Whinney |
| Warren Rulien | Frank South | Robert Wilkins |
| Ken Russell | Allen Stephens | Richard Winters |
| George Ryan | Clayton Storeby | Richard Wright |
| Robert Sales | Charles Sullivan | Herbert Zafft |

## FIRST-PERSON MEMOIRS, AUTOBIOGRAPHIES, ESSAYS, AND HISTORIES

John Barnes, *From Omaha Beach to the Elbe River: Fragments of My Life With Company A, 116th Infantry*. Holland Patent, NY: JAM Publications, 2000.

Harold Baumgarten, *D-Day Survivor: An Autobiography*. Gretna, LA: Pelican Pub, 2006.

David Belchem, *Victory in Normandy*. London: Chatto & Windus, 1981.

Gardner Botsford, *A Life of Privilege, Mostly*. New York: St. Martin's Press, 2003.

Grace Bradbeer, *The Land Changed Its Face: The Evacuation of Devon's South Hams, 1943–1944*. Newton Abbot, Devon: David and Charles, 1973.

Omar Bradley, *A Soldier's Story*. New York: Holt, 1951.

Alan Brooke, *War Diaries, 1939–1945: Field Marshal Lord Alanbrooke*, eds. Alex Dancheve and Daniel Todman. Berkeley: University of California Press, 2001.

John Mason Brown, *Many a Watchful Night*. New York: Whittlesey House, McGraw-Hill, 1944.

Lambton Burn, *"Down Ramps!" Saga of the Eighth Armada*. London: Carroll & Nicholson, 1947.

Harry Butcher, *My Three Years with Eisenhower: The Personal Diary of Captain Harry C. Butcher, USNR, Naval Aide to General Eisenhower, 1942 to 1945*. New York: Simon & Schuster, 1946.

Robert Capa, *Slightly Out of Focus*. New York: Modern Library, 1999.

Winston S. Churchill, *The Second World War*, six volumes:

- *The Gathering Storm*. Cambridge: Houghton Mifflin, 1948.
- *Their Finest Hour*. Cambridge: Houghton Mifflin, 1949.
- *The Grand Alliance*. Cambridge: Houghton Mifflin, 1950.
- *The Hinge of Fate*. Cambridge: Houghton Mifflin, 1950.
- *Closing the Ring*. Cambridge: Houghton Mifflin, 1951.
- *Triumph and Tragedy*. Cambridge: Houghton Mifflin, 1953.

Lynn Compton, with Marcus Brotherton, *Call of Duty: My Life Before, During and After the Band of Brothers*. New York: Berkley Caliber, 2008.

John Dalgleish, *We Planned the Second Front: The Inside History of How the Second Front Was Planned*. London: V. Gollancz., 1945.

Charles de Gaulle, Charles, *The War Memoirs of Charles de Gaulle: Unity, 1942–1944*. New York: Simon & Schuster, 1959.

Francis de Guingand, *Operation Victory*. London: Hodder and Stoughton, 1960.

Dwight Eisenhower, *Crusade in Europe*. Garden City, NY: Doubleday, 1948.

George McKee Elsey, *An Unplanned Life: A Memoir*. Columbia: University of Missouri Press, 2015.

Simon Fraser, *March Past: A Memoir*. London: Weidenfeld and Nicolson, 1978.

James Gavin, *On to Berlin: Battles of an Airborne Commander, 1943–1946*. New York: Viking Press, 1978.

Richard Gale, *With the 6th Airborne Division in Normandy*. London: Sampson Low, Marston & Co., 1948.

Arthur Travers Harris, *Bomber Offensive*. Mechanicsburg, PA: Greenhill Books, 1998.

Roger Hesketh, *Fortitude: The D-Day Deception Campaign*. New York: Overlook Press, 2000.

Ralph Ingersoll, *Top Secret*. New York: Somerset Books, 1946.

Hastings Ismay, *The Memoirs of General Lord Ismay*. New York: Viking Press, 1960.

Ernest Joseph King and Walter Muir Whitehill, *Fleet Admiral King: A Naval Record.* New York: W. W. Norton, 1952.

William Leahy, *I Was There.* New York: Whittlesey House, 1950.

Brendan Maher, *A Passage to Sword Beach: Minesweeping in the Royal Navy.* Annapolis, MD: Naval Institute Press, 1996.

Don Malarkey, with Bob Welch, *Easy Company Soldier: The Legendary Battles of a Sergeant from World War II's "Band of Brothers."* New York: St. Martin's Press, 2008.

Bernard L. Montgomery, *The Memoirs of Field Marshal the Viscount Montgomery of Alamein, K.G.* New York: Da Capo, 1958.

Alan Moorehead, *Eclipse.* New York: Harper & Row, 1968.

Frederick Morgan, *Overture to Overlord.* Garden City, NY: Doubleday, 1950.

Marie-Louise Osmont, *The Normandy Diary of Marie-Louise Osmont: 1940–1944.* New York: Random House/The Discovery Channel Press, 1994.

Mollie Panter-Downes, *London War Notes, 1939–1945.* New York: Farrar, Straus and Giroux: 1971.

Sverre Petterssen, *Weathering the Storm: Sverre Petterssen, the D-Day Forecast, and the Rise of Modern Meteorology*, ed. James Rodger Fleming. Boston: American Meteorological Society, 2001.

Forrest Pogue, *Pogue's War: Diaries of a WWII Combat Historian.* Lexington: University Press of Kentucky, 2001.

Ernie Pyle, *Ernie's War: The Best of Ernie Pyle's World War II Dispatches*, ed. David Nichols. New York: Random House, 1986.

Bertram Ramsay, *The Year of D-Day: The 1944 Diary of Admiral Sir Bertram Ramsay*, ed. Robert W. Love Jr. and John Major. Hull: University of Hull Press, 1994.

Alexandre Renaud, *Sainte-Mèr-Eglise: First American Bridgehead in France, June 6, 1944.* Paris: Julliard, 1986.

Elliot L. Richardson, *The Creative Balance: Government, Politics, and the Individual in America's Third Century.* New York: Holt, Rinehart and Winston, 1976.

Matthew Ridgway and Harold H. Martin, *Soldier: The Memoirs of Matthew B. Ridgway, As Told to Harold H. Martin.* New York: Harper, 1956.

Andrew Rooney, *My War.* New York: PublicAffairs, 2002.

Friedrich Ruge, *Rommel in Normandy: Reminiscences.* San Rafael, CA: Presidio Press, 1979.

Alister Satchell, *Running the Gauntlet: How Three Giant Liners Carried a Million Men to War, 1942–1945.* Annapolis, MD: Naval Institute, 2001.

George Sefton, *It Was My War: I'll Remember It the Way I Want To!* Manhattan, KS: Sunflower University Press, 1994.

Walter Bedell Smith, *Eisenhower's Six Great Decisions: Europe, 1944–1945.* New York: Longmans Green, 1956.

Hans Speidel, *We Defended Normandy,* trans. Ian Colvin. London: Herbert Jenkins, 1951.

James Martin Stagg, *Forecast for Overlord: June 6, 1944.* New York: W. W. Norton, 1972.

Kay Summersby, *Eisenhower Was My Boss.* New York: Prentice-Hall, 1948.

Hans von Luck, *Panzer Commander: The Memoirs of Colonel Hans von Luck.* New York: Dell, 1991.

Don Whitehead, *Beachhead Don: Reporting the War from the European Theater, 1942–1945,* ed. John Beals Romeiser. New York: Fordham University Press, 2004.

Chester Wilmot, *The Struggle for Europe.* New York: Harper, 1952.

Dick Winters, with Cole Kingseed, *Beyond Band of Brothers: The War Memoirs of Major Dick Winters.* Waterville, ME: Large Print Press, 2008.

## THIRD-PARTY HISTORIES, ORIGINAL INTERVIEWS, AND COLLECTED FIRST-PERSON MEMORIES

Russell Miller, *Nothing Less Than Victory: The Oral History of D-Day* (New York: William Morrow, 1993)

| | | |
|---|---|---|
| Douglas Aitken | Lewis H. Brereton | Patrick Devlin |
| George Alex | Jack Vilander Brown | Ernst During |
| Celia Andrews | Archibald "Doon" Campbell | Rudi Escher |
| A. Baker | | Curt Fromm |
| Werner Beibst | John Chalk | Heinrich Fuerst |
| Violet Bingley | Maurice Chauvet | Dan Furlong |
| Dennis Bowen | L.N. "Nobby" Clarke | Wilhelm Gerstner |
| Bruce Bradley | Albert Cooke | Frank Gillard |
| Felix Branham | Aloysius Damski | Hyman Haas |

Jack Harries
Andre Heintz
I.G. Holley
Nathaniel R. Hoskot
Werner Kortenhaus
George Lane
John Madden
Hubert Meyer
Irmgard Meyer

Joe Minogue
C. Morris
Robert Neave
Werner Pluskat
Derek Pratt
Rosie Rosevere
John R. Slaughter
William C. Smith
N. Travett

Gerd von Rundstedt
Percy Wallace
A.E.M. Walter
Edwin Webb
Charles Wilson
John Wilson
Alan Winstanley
Fritz Ziegelmann

Roderick Bailey, *Forgotten Voices of D-Day: A Powerful New History of the Normandy Landings in the Words of Those Who Were There.*
(London: Ebury Press, published in association with the Imperial War Museum)

Eric Ashcroft
Reginald Barnes
Francis Bourlet
Andrew Brown
James Donaldson
William Gray
Edward Gueritz
Patrick Hennessy
John Howard

Robert Howard
Jim "Tich" Hunter
Rene Le Roy
William Edward Lloyd
Henry Lovegrove
Bill Millin
Leslie Perry
George Rayson
Goronwy Rees

Lionel Roebuck
John Semken
Alexander Stanier
David Tibbs
Norman Travett
David Warren
Bruce White

*Assault on Normandy: First-Person Accounts from the Sea Services*
(Edited by Paul Stillwell, Annapolis, MD: Naval Institute Press, 1994)

Robert E. Adams
James E. Arnold
John R. Blackburn
John D. Bulkeley
Carleton F. Bryant

Barbara Clare (Fauks.
Richard Crook
Eugene E. Eckstam
George M. Elsey
Paul S. Fauks

Alan G. Kirk
John A. Moreno
Lorenzo S. Sabin
Walter Trombold

USS *CORRY* (*DD-463*). Survivors' Firsthand Accounts of D-Day
(Available online at www.uss-corry-dd463.com)

| | | |
|---|---|---|
| Howard Andersen | Jake Henson | Francis "Mac" McKernon |
| Bill Beat | Dewey Hoffman | Mort Rubin |
| Robert Beeman | Everett Dale Howard | Emil Vestuti |
| Paul N. Garay | Matt Jayich | |
| Grant G. Gullickson | Elmer Maurer | |

Personal Recollections of Members of the Westminster Dragoons Who
Landed in Normandy on D-Day
Westminster Dragoons Association, 1997
(Held at the Imperial War Museum, Item # Documents.6530.)

| | | |
|---|---|---|
| W.J. Blackwell | B.M.S. Hoban | D. C. Potter |
| R. H. W. Bullock | W. H. Jennings | C. T. Smith |
| M.J. Eedy | N.T. "Tom" Kelly | H. W. J. Smith |
| W. S. Hall | Joe Minogue | George H. W. Woodhouse |

"D-Day Eye Witness Accounts," *Sunday Express* Collection for the 30th
anniversary, 1974
(Held at the Imperial War Museum, Item # Documents.10491.)

| | | |
|---|---|---|
| Edward J. Anderson | Eva Crawford | F.J. Hutchin |
| James Bentham | Helen Davidson | David Jeffries |
| M.J. Colman | Barbara Desmond | M. Kaye |
| Peggy Cornish | Molly Harris | Nora Knox |

*Fighting the Invasion: The German Army at D-Day*
(Edited by David C. Isby, Mechanicsburg, PA: Stackpole Books, 2000)

| | | |
|---|---|---|
| Günther Blumentritt | Josef Reichert | Karl Wilhelm |
| Günther Keil | Friedrich von Criegern | von Schlieben |
| Max Pemsel | Walter Warlimont | Fritz Ziegelmann |

Mary Louise Roberts, *D-Day Through French Eyes*
(Chicago: University of Chicago Press, 2022)

| | | |
|---|---|---|
| Fernand Broek | Maurice Mauger | Pierre Pipre |
| Jean Flamand | Irène Othon-Meillat | |
| Madame Hamel-Hateau | Jeannette Pentecôte | |

Bruce Connor and Vince Milano, *Normandiefront: D-Day to Saint-Lô Through German Eyes*
(Stroud, Gloucestershire: The History Press, 2011)

| | | |
|---|---|---|
| Josef Brass | Georg Seidl | Karl Wegner |
| Heinz Fuehr | Peter Simeth | |

Robin Neillands and Roderick de Norman, *D-Day, 1994: Voices from Normandy*
(Osceola, WI: Motorbooks International Publishers, 1994)

| | | |
|---|---|---|
| Edwin Byatt | George Nicolson | Eric Rowland |
| Ron Colledge | George Rayson | |

Laurent Lefebvre, *They Were on Utah Beach: The story of D-Day, told by veterans*
(Self-Published, 2004)

| | | |
|---|---|---|
| William A. Bostick | Michael N. Ingrisano | Herschel W. Peterson |
| William J. Hollis | Jim McKee | |

Robert Murphy, *No Better Place to Die: The Battle for La Fière Bridge*
(Havertown, PA: Casemate, 2009)

| | | |
|---|---|---|
| John Dolan | Louis Leroux | Robert M. Murphy |

# Source Notes

## Foreword

xxii *This battle was the beginning:* Interview in *Newsweek*, June 11, 1994, p. 20.

xxv *A grandson asked:* Stephen Ambrose, *Band of Brothers* (New York: Simon & Schuster, 1992), 316.

## War Begins

4 *World War II began at 5:20 a.m.:* Olivia B. Waxman, "The Invasion of Poland Wasn't Hitler's First Aggression. Here's Why That Move Marked the Beginning of WWII," *Time*, August 30, 2019, https://time.com/5659728/poland-1939.

4 *I was twelve and Peter, my brother:* Pauline Tookey née Edmondson, "A Girl in Falconwood," WW2 People's War: An Archive of World War Two Memories— Written by the Public, Gathered by the BBC, February 08, 2004, https://www.bbc.co.uk/history/ww2peopleswar/stories/16/a2275616.shtml.

6 *We all gathered round the wireless:* Ibid.

6 *I am speaking to you from the Cabinet Room at 10 Downing Street:* Neville Chamberlain, "Radio Address by Neville Chamberlain, Prime Minister, September 3, 1939," Lillian Goldman Law Library, Yale Law School, accessed January 17, 2024, https://avalon.law.yale.edu/wwii/gb3.asp.

6 *The world war is on:* William L. Shirer, *This Is Berlin: A Narrative History: 1938–1940* (London: Hutchinson, 1999), 75.

6 *Now that there is a war, the English:* Mollie Panter-Downes, *London War Notes, 1939–1945* (New York: Farrar, Straus & Giroux, 1971), 3.

9 *London was as quiet as a village:* "London," ibid., 69.

11 *The skill and audacity of the RAF youngsters:* "The skill," ibid., 79.

12 *My mum and dad and everyone else who lived:* Tookey née Edmondson, "A Girl in Falconwood."

13 *My mother, sister and I tried to get home:* Ronald Allen, "Memories of the Blitz: Your Stories," BBC, September 7, 2010, https://www.bbc.com/news/world-south-asia-11222260.

13 *Night after night, just as darkness was falling:* Peter Caddick-Adams, *Sand & Steel: The D-Day Invasions and the Liberation of France* (New York: Oxford University Press, 2019), 51.

13 *As we all looked skywards we watched as wave after wave:* Susan Stefiuk, "Memories of the Battle of Britain," WW2 People's War: An Archive of World War Two Memories—Written by the Public, Gathered by the BBC, November 28, 2004, https://www.bbc.co.uk/history/ww2peopleswar/stories/44/a3339344.shtml.

15 *I deem it of paramount importance:* W. Averell Harriman and Elie Abel, *Special Envoy to Churchill and Stalin, 1941–1946* (New York: Random House, 1975), 77.

15 *The overriding motivation of President Roosevelt:* Ibid., 74.

16 *The city of Honolulu has also been attacked:* NBC News, "Listen to a Historic Broadcast from the Attack on Pearl Harbor," NBC News, uploaded December 7, 2018, YouTube video, https://www.youtube.com/watch?v=6muWK4VMbEI.

16 *I was going out in the hall to say goodbye to our cousins:* Eleanor Roosevelt, "Eleanor Roosevelt's 'My Day,' 12/8/1941: Response to Pear Harbor," White House Historical Association, accessed January 17, 2024, https://www.whitehouse history.org/eleanor-roosevelts-my-day-12-8-1941.

17 *The Battle of Britain was over:* Pamela Harriman, "When Churchill Heard the News . . . ," *Washington Post*, December 7, 1991, https://www.washingtonpost .com/archive/opinions/1991/12/07/when-churchill-heard-the-news/e6e33a3b -9509-4c55-b1f4-4f4387bb55c6.

18 *It was a little while before I was free to go:* Eleanor Roosevelt, "Eleanor Roosevelt 1950s Interview Discussing FDR on December 7, 1941," FDR Library, uploaded November 7, 2016, YouTube video, https://www.youtube.com/watch?v=r-Vm 7JuZehM.

## War Comes to America

20 *Altogether, about 10 million of the 16 million:* David Reynolds, *Rich Relations: The American Occupation of Britain, 1942–1945* (New York: Random House, 1995), 71.

20 *Everybody was very worried:* Alex Kershaw, *The Bedford Boys: One American Town's Ultimate D-Day Sacrifice* (Cambridge, MA: Da Capo, 2003), 21.

20 *We kept our feelings to ourselves:* Ibid., 22.

20 *As preparations began stateside to activate:* Reynolds, *Rich Relations*, 29.

## 1943

33 *Prior to leaving my Headquarters in North Africa:* Dwight D. Eisenhower, *Report by the Supreme Commander to the Combined Chiefs of Staff on the Operations in Europe of the Allied Expeditionary Force 6 June 1944 to 8 May 1945* (Washington, D.C.: Government Printing Office, 1946).

### The Start of SHAEF

36  *General Eisenhower had placed me:* Bernard Law Montgomery, *The Memoirs of Field Marshal Montgomery* (New York: Da Capo, 1958), 201.

37  *The more I examined the proposed tactical plan:* Ibid., 197.

40  *My planners had advised me that:* Dwight D. Eisenhower, *Report by the Supreme Commander to the Combined Chiefs of Staff on the Operations in Europe of the Allied Expeditionary Force 6 June 1944 to 8 May 1945* (Washington, D.C.: Government Printing Office, 1946).

### Crossing the Pond

44  *The* Queen Mary *was carrying about 15,000 American troops:* Alfred Johnson, "HMS Curacoa Tragedy," "Memories of the Battle of Britain," WW2 People's War: An Archive of World War Two Memories—Written by the Public, Gathered by the BBC, June 11, 2004, https://www.bbc.co.uk/history/ww2peopleswar /stories/13/a2733013.shtml.

44  *We were berthed close to the privates:* Alex Kershaw, *The Bedford Boys: One American Town's Ultimate D-Day Sacrifice* (Cambridge, MA: Da Capo, 2003), 46.

46  *I said to my mate:* Johnson, "HMS Curacoa Tragedy."

46  *Her huge white bow wave seemed:* Daniel Allen Butler, *Warrior Queens: The Queen Mary and Queen Elizabeth in World War II* (Mechanicsburg, PA: Stackpole Books, 2002), 114.

46  *The* Queen Mary *sliced the cruiser:* Johnson "HMS Curacoa Tragedy."

46  *The boat jarred:* Kershaw, *The Bedford Boys*, 50.

46  *I was in the office on the main deck:* Daniel Allen Butler, *Warrior Queens*, 115.

47  *The* Mary *simply continued:* Ibid.

47  *My first thought was that we had been torpedoed:* Kershaw, *The Bedford Boys*, 48.

47  *I was sick at what we had done:* Butler, *Warrior Queens*, 116.

48  *These craft, built to support:* For more on the landing craft production, construction, and crewing, read the fascinating chapter on LSTs in Craig Symonds, *Neptune: The Allied Invasion of Europe and the D-Day Landings* (New York: Oxford University Press, 2014), 147–70.

49  *Most of the crew had never seen a ship:* Nigel Lewis, *Exercise Tiger: The Dramatic True Story of a Hidden Tragedy of World War II* (New York: Prentice Hall, 1990), 27.

### The American Invasion

50  *In the spring of 1944, roughly 10 percent:* Peter Caddick-Adams, *Sand & Steel: The D-Day Invasions and the Liberation of France* (New York: Oxford University

Press, 2019), xxxix; see also Craig Symonds, *Neptune: The Allied Invasion of Europe and the D-Day Landings* (New York: Oxford University Press, 2014), 129–39.

52 *It is hard for anyone who did not experience the total darkness:* Norman Longmate, *How We Lived Then: A History of Everyday Life During the Second World War* (London: Pimlico, 2002), 45.

52 *It seemed to me the first few months in England:* Kershaw, *The Bedford Boys: One American Town's Ultimate D-Day Sacrifice* (Cambridge, MA: Da Capo, 2003), 55.

52 *You couldn't stay dry:* Ibid., 58.

56 *Our Wrenney was on a hill overlooking:* Caddick-Adams, *Sand & Steel*, 57.

58 *"Black soldiers had been largely purged":* Linda Hervieux, *Forgotten: The Untold Story of D-Day's Black Heroes, at Home and at War* (New York: HarperCollins, 2015), 27.

58 *Because the people had never seen:* https://www.loc.gov/collections/veterans -history-project-collection/serving-our-voices/diverse-experiences-in-service /veteran-changemakers/item/afc2001001.10648/.

58 *The English people show our lads every possible:* Hervieux, *Forgotten*, 157.

58 *I had the opportunity to hear all the Black choirs:* Caddick-Adams, *Sand & Steel*, 65.

59 *We were told by the chaplain:* David Reynolds, *Rich Relations: The American Occu- pation of Britain, 1942–1945* (New York: Random House, 1995), 230.

59 *The small-town British girl would:* Norman Longmate, *The G.I.'s: The Americans in Britain, 1942–1945* (New York: Charles Scribner's Sons, 1975), 118.

59 *It is not the policy of His Majesty's Government:* Ibid., 120.

60 *Whites would come into a pub:* Hervieux, *Forgotten*, 182.

60 *The negro problem has been very poorly:* Reynolds, *Rich Relations*, 313.

60 *The Americans have exported:* Longmate, *The G.I.'s*, 122.

60 *I am an American Negro:* Reynolds, *Rich Relations*, 315.

### Building the Atlantic Wall

62 *By 1944, the German army looked:* Peter Caddick-Adams, *Sand & Steel: The D-Day Invasions and the Liberation of France* (New York: Oxford University Press, 2019), 19.

62 *Much of the military's vehicle fleet:* Ibid., 39.

63 *In the East, the vastness of the space will:* "Directive No. 51," Fuehrer Headquarters, November 3, 1943, accessed January 18, 2024, https://history.army.mil/books /wwii/7-4/7-4_d.htm.

63 *Arrived safely yesterday:* Erwin Rommel, *The Rommel Papers*, ed. B. H. Liddell- Hart (New York: Da Capo, 1982), 461.

64 *The West is the place that matters:* Ibid., 453.

64 *The Seventh Army, Rommel wrote:* Caddick-Adams, *Sand & Steel*, 23.

65 *We have fortified the coast of Europe:* Dan Harvey, *A Bloody Dawn: The Irish at D-Day* (Newbridge, Ireland: Merrion Press, 2019), 100.

65 *It used to make me angry to read the stories:* Russell Miller, *Nothing Less Than Victory* (New York: William Morrow, 1993), 104.

65 *I had over 3,000 miles of coastline:* Joseph Balkoski, *Omaha Beach: D-Day, June 6, 1944* (Mechanicsburg, PA: Stackpole Books, 2004), 37.

66 *We had considerable shortages of minefield equipment:* Caddick-Adams, *Sand & Steel,* 506.

69 *In February, 1944, during his inspection of the defenses:* Ronald J. Drez, *Voices of D-Day: The Story of the Allied Invasion Told by Those Who Were There* (Baton Rouge: Louisiana State University Press, 1994), 49.

70 *Rommel's authority was not enough:* Caddick-Adams, *Sand & Steel,* 506.

71 *The important thing is to ensure that all territory which:* Rommel, *The Rommel Papers,* 460.

71 *The obstacles which Rommel planned consisted of stakes:* Ibid., 460.

73 *If the enemy should ever set foot on land:* Ibid., 458.

74 *From day-to-day, week-to-week:* Balkoski, *Omaha Beach,* 37.

### Keeping Secrets

76 *I don't have to tell you what a big show this is:* Max Hastings, *Overlord: D-Day, June 6, 1944* (New York: Simon & Schuster, 1984), 55.

76 *The possibility of Hitler's gaining a victory:* Ibid., 60.

### Operation FORTITUDE

84 *In wartime, truth is so precious:* Anthony Cave Brown, *Bodyguard of Lies* (New York: Bantam, 1976), 389.

### The Mulberry Plan

90 *The success of our amphibious operations in North Africa:* Ernest J. King, *U.S. Navy at War, 1941–1945: Official Reports to the Secretary of the Navy* (Washington, D.C.: US Navy Department, 1946), 135.

### At Slapton Sands

96 *We drove through a maze of narrow lanes:* Nigel Lewis, *Exercise Tiger: The Dramatic True Story of a Hidden Tragedy of World War II* (New York: Prentice Hall, 1990), 11.

96 *A parish meeting was arranged:* Ibid.

97  *We just took things as they came then:* Ibid., 12.

97  *They were so brave and cheerful:* Ibid., 13.

97  *We were one of the last to leave:* Ibid.

97  *It is hard enough to be hunted:* Ibid., 15.

99  *We learned how to handle ourselves:* Roderick Bailey, *Forgotten Voices of D-Day: A New History of the Normandy Landings* (London: Ebury Press, 2009), 94.

100  *Boy, was it cold:* Peter Caddick-Adams, *Sand & Steel: The D-Day Invasions and the Liberation of France* (New York: Oxford University Press, 2019), 200.

101  *We'd pull out into the bay:* Ibid.

102  *This little barge turned and headed towards us:* Tim Saunders, *Juno Beach: Canadian 3rd Infantry Division—July 1944 (Battleground Europe)* (Havertown, PA: Pen & Sword Books, 1990), 31, Kindle Edition.

102  *They were one of the best-kept secrets:* Caddick-Adams, *Sand & Steel*, 218.

102  *My brother Pete and I were members:* Ibid., 216.

103  *We built a replica of the Atlantic Wall:* Saunders, *Juno Beach*, 33–34.

103  *We were known as the "Funnies":* Interview in *Newsweek*, June 11, 1994, 24.

104  *We were taught how to fit extensions to exhausts:* Saunders, *Juno Beach*.

104  *We were checking them over:* Matthew A. Rozell, *The Things Our Fathers Saw: The Untold Stories of the World War II Generation from Hometown, USA, Vol. V: D-Day and Beyond* (Hartford and New York: Woodchuck Hollow Press, 2019), 57.

## Exercise TIGER

107  *On April 25 the ship loaded army troops:* This and subsequent Eckstam quotes are from Eugene E. Eckstam, "The Tragedy of Exercise Tiger," *Navy Medicine* 85, No. 3 (May–June 1994), 5–7.

107  *On the morning of April 27, 1944:* This and subsequent Harlander quotes are from Douglas Harlander, "Douglas Harlander Survivor Story—LST 531," Exercise Tiger Memorial, accessed January 17, 2024, https://exercisetigermemorial.co.uk /douglas-harlander-survivor-story-lst-531.

108  *First heard were the [E-boat] motors:* Joseph Balkoski, *Utah Beach: The Amphibious Landing and Airborne* (Mechanicsburg, PA: Stackpole Books, 2006), 62.

108  *I was asleep in my sack:* This and subsequent Sadlon quotes are from Steve Sadlon, "Steve Sadlon Survivor Story—LST 507," Exercise Tiger Memorial, accessed January 17, 2024, https://exercisetigermemorial.co.uk/steve-sadlon-survivor-story -lst-507.

108  *I was a little nervous:* Nigel Lewis, *Exercise Tiger: The Dramatic True Story of a Hidden Tragedy of World War II* (New York: Prentice Hall, 1990), 83.

109  *I was lifted from my feet and hurled back:* Ibid., 84.

109  *All of the army vehicles naturally were loaded:* Ibid., 87.

110  *Fred jumped first, and caught a board:* Ibid., 90.

110  *There were about fifty:* Ibid., 91.

110  *A gigantic orange ball explosion:* Ibid., 92.

110  *I was in my bunk asleep when it blew:* Report from the *Kansas City Star,* May 31, 1994, "Veldon Downing Survivor Story—LST 531," Exercise Tiger Memorial, accessed January 17, 2024, https://exercisetigermemorial.co.uk/veldon-downing -survivor-story-lst-531.

111  *I jumped overboard and went down until I stopped:* Lewis, *Exercise Tiger,* 94.

111  *The chill of the water was almost paralyzing:* Ibid., 93.

111  *Cries, screams, and moans filled the night:* Ibid., 91.

111  *When I arrived on deck:* Nathan Resnick, "Nathan Resnick Story—LST 511," Exercise Tiger Memorial, accessed January 17, 2024, https://exercisetigermemorial .co.uk/nathan-resnick-story-lst-511.

112  *The convoy was given orders to scatter:* Paul Gerolstein, "Paul Gerolstein Story— LST 515," Exercise Tiger Memorial, accessed January 17, 2024, https://exercise tigermemorial.co.uk/paul-gerolstein-story-lst-515.

112  *I had become almost unbearably cold:* Lewis, *Exercise Tiger,* 99.

112  *I was beginning to get drowsy:* Ibid., 98.

112  *I remember the cold, the wet:* Ibid., 101.

113  *It was as if I were looking down from the sky:* Ibid., 102.

113  *It is a very distinct possibility that many lives:* Ibid., 114.

113  *As we neared the disaster area:* Ibid., 105.

114  *My boat crew stayed busy:* Ibid., 109.

114  *A lot of men died that night and piled up on us:* Ibid.

114  *By now the sun was coming up very bright:* Ibid.

115  *We arrived in the area at daybreak:* Ibid., 111.

116  *This was a costly egg in our omelet:* Ibid., 127.

116  *[We were told] in less than an hour:* Peter Caddick-Adams, *Sand & Steel: The D-Day Invasions and the Liberation of France* (New York: Oxford University Press, 2019), 239.

116  *They put the clamp on us:* Ibid.

116  *A stream of ambulances and trucks were pouring:* Ibid.

116  *The next day we were taken to an army base:* Lewis, *Exercise Tiger,* 121.

116  *Like all men who live through something like that:* Ibid., 149.

### The Transportation Plan

121  *The fate of a continent depended upon the ability:* Dwight D. Eisenhower, *Report by the Supreme Commander to the Combined Chiefs of Staff on the Operations in Europe of the Allied Expeditionary Force 6 June 1944 to 8 May 1945* (Washington, D.C.: Government Printing Office, 1946).

123 *Sometimes it was one mission a day:* Peter Caddick-Adams, *Sand & Steel: The D-Day Invasions and the Liberation of France* (New York: Oxford University Press, 2019), 150, quoting Bill Youngkin, "Carlos B. Pegues, WWII Veteran," *The Eagle*, May 9, 2016, https://web.archive.org/web/20240208214913/https://theeagle.com/veterans/carlos-b-pegues-wwii-veteran/article_8db307c4-16c7-11e6-80d9-1bb7dda858ae.html.

124 *In serving a returning mission:* Ibid., 154.

125 *All told, the execution of the spring:* Ibid., 286–87.

### Picking the Date

127 *London to me was a magic carpet:* Stephen Ambrose, *Band of Brothers* (New York: Simon & Schuster, 1992), 47.

127 *Living on this little island just now uncomfortably:* Mollie Panter-Downes, *London War Notes, 1939–1945* (New York: Farrar, Straus & Giroux, 1971), 322.

128 *[In] July 1943, some 750,000 tons of supplies:* Dwight D. Eisenhower, *Report by the Supreme Commander to the Combined Chiefs of Staff on the Operations in Europe of the Allied Expeditionary Force 6 June 1944 to 8 May 1945* (Washington, D.C.: Government Printing Office, 1946).

130 *The night before D-Day had to be reasonably light:* Peter Caddick-Adams, *Sand & Steel: The D-Day Invasions and the Liberation of France* (New York: Oxford University Press, 2019), 347.

132 *Meteorologically, D-Day was bound to be a gamble:* Ibid.

133 *On Monday, May 15th, the commanders and leaders assembled:* Ibid., 247–48.

135 *On 17 May, I set 5 June as the "final" date:* Eisenhower, *Report by the Supreme Commander.*

### Into the Sausages

139 *Everywhere through London it was the same greeting:* Peter Caddick-Adams, *Sand & Steel: The D-Day Invasions and the Liberation of France* (New York: Oxford University Press, 2019), 262.

140 *I was very conscious of the fact that there:* Courtesy of the Green Howards Museum Trust.

142 *We ate the best food:* Alex Kershaw, *The Bedford Boys: One American Town's Ultimate D-Day Sacrifice* (Cambridge, MA: Da Capo, 2003), 101.

### Keep Calm and Carry On

147 *I used to tell them we were all one great army:* Bernard Law Montgomery, *The Memoirs of Field Marshal Montgomery* (New York: Da Capo, 1958), 202.

### Learning the Details

155  *The verbal challenge for all airborne was:* Donald R. Burgett, *Currahee!* (Cambridge, MA: Riverside Press, 1967), 68.

157  *Well, of course, the Prime Minister didn't want:* Dwight Eisenhower, interview by Walter Cronkite, *CBS Reports*, CBS, June 5, 1964, https://www.youtube.com /watch?v=vNaxTXfjfXk&ab_channel=CBSNews.


### Spring in Normandy with the Germans

160  *Knowing that every day mattered, Rommel continued:* Peter Caddick-Adams, *Sand & Steel: The D-Day Invasions and the Liberation of France* (New York: Oxford University Press, 2019), 34.

160  *The middle of May already and still nothing doing:* Erwin Rommel, *The Rommel Papers*, ed. B. H. Liddell-Hart (New York: Da Capo, 1982), 464.

161  *I had a long talk with Rommel at La Roche Guyon:* Ibid., 468.

162  *It is true that the hour of invasion draws nearer:* Russell Miller, *Nothing Less Than Victory* (New York: William Morrow, 1993), 125.

164  *It wasn't in our interests:* Max Hastings, *Overlord: D-Day, June 6, 1944* (New York: Simon & Schuster, 1984), 65.

164  *The war will be won or lost on the beaches:* Erwin Rommel, quoted in Cornelius Ryan, *The Longest Day: June 6, 1944* (New York: Simon & Schuster, 1959), 27.


### The D-Day Weather Forecast

166  *We came down here hoping and praying:* Dwight Eisenhower, interview by Walter Cronkite, *CBS Reports*, CBS, June 5, 1964, https://www.youtube.com/watch?v=v NaxTXfjfXk.

168  *We used data garnered from special weather recce:* Peter Caddick-Adams, *Sand & Steel: The D-Day Invasions and the Liberation of France* (New York: Oxford University Press, 2019), 343.

169  *We six never agreed about anything:* Ibid., 340.

169  *None of us were operating with any of the technology:* Ibid., 343.

170  *All we knew was there were several storms blowing across:* Ibid.

173  *On June 4, a plane came wheeling into the Air Base:* George E. Koskimaki, *D-Day with the Screaming Eagles* (New York: Vantage Press, 1970), 44.

174  *Our reports were the first to show:* Teresa Mannion, "Mayo's D-Day Heroine Receives Special US Honour," *RTÉ*, June 20, 2021, https://www.rte.ie /news/2021/0619/1229119-maureen-sweeney; "Irish Woman Whose Forecast Saved D-Day Dies at 100," BBC, December 18, 2023, https://www.bbc.com /news/articles/czkjr34r2zzo.

174 *There were probably four or five reconnaissances:* Ted Barris, *Juno: Canadians at D-Day, June 6, 1944* (Toronto: Thomas Allen, 2004), 13–19.

177 *It certainly increased my confidence in Captain Stagg:* Dwight Eisenhower, interview by Walter Cronkite.

177 *I was scared—I think we all were:* Caddick-Adams, *Sand & Steel*, 349.

178 *The forecast for the following day contained a gleam of hope:* Dwight Eisenhower, interview by Walter Cronkite.

### Paratroopers Take Off

190 *With the weather turned and the invasion force finally at sea:* Peter Caddick-Adams, *Sand & Steel: The D-Day Invasions and the Liberation of France* (New York: Oxford University Press, 2019), 433.

193 *In dramatic conclusion, he whipped out his throwing knife:* G. William Sefton, *It Was My War: I'll Remember It the Way I Want To* (Lawrence, Kan.: Sunflower University Press, 1994), 48.

194 *Ike stuck his head in the door of our plane:* George E. Koskimaki, *D-Day with The Screaming Eagles* (New York: Vantage Press, 1970), 439.

194 *Just before the take-off General [Anthony] McAuliffe had each man:* Ibid., 37.

195 *General Eisenhower stepped back:* Ibid., 38–39.

195 *As our plane was taking off I could look back down:* Sefton, *It Was My War*, 49.

### Operation COUP DE MAIN

200 *It was difficult to imagine that by dawn:* John Buckley, *Monty's Men: The British Army and the Liberation of Europe, 1944–1945* (New Haven, CT: Yale University Press, 2013), 55.

201 *The noise ceased and was replaced with an ominous:* Kevin Shannon and Stephen Wright, *One Night in June: The Story of Operation Tonga, the Initial Phase of the Invasion of Normandy, 1944* (Shrewsbury, England: Airlife, 1994), 45.

202 *The pilots had done a fantastic job:* Ibid.

202 *As I hit the ground I glanced quickly around:* Ibid.

203 *This is where the training comes in:* Stephen Ambrose, *Pegasus Bridge: D-Day: The Daring British Airborne Raid* (London: Simon & Schuster, 1985), 93.

204 *The poor buggers in the bunkers didn't have much:* Ibid.

204 *They even frightened me:* Ibid., 95–96.

204 *Having cleared the dugouts:* Ibid., 101–2; Roderick Bailey, *Forgotten Voices of D-Day: A New History of the Normandy Landings* (London: Ebury Press, 2009), 104.

205 *I first saw the bridge at 800 feet and was able to land:* Shannon and Wright, *One Night in June*, 48.

### The 6th Airborne Arrives in Normandy

210 *My own glider carried a full complement:* Kevin Shannon and Stephen Wright, *One Night in June: The Story of Operation Tonga, the Initial Phase of the Invasion of Normandy, 1944* (Shrewsbury, England: Airlife, 1994), 118–19.

210 *Turning in from the coast, the visibility became very poor:* Ibid.

211 *In the last few yards one post:* Ibid.

211 *Soon after landing I found that Chester Wilmot's recorder:* Ibid.

211 *Just as we made our way to the woods:* Ibid., 50–52.

212 *The plane took violent evasive action:* Hillborn and following Metcalf quotes are both courtesy of Ted Barris.

213 *Out of 120 of our company:* Ibid.

213 *I picked up three others of my stick:* Ibid.

216 *[My copilot] Stan and I moved:* Shannon and Wright, *One Night in June*, 123–26.

217 *Meanwhile, just one of the eight gliders designated:* Peter Caddick-Adams, *Sand & Steel: The D-Day Invasions and the Liberation of France* (New York: Oxford University Press, 2019), 468.

218 *Nobody had moved about very much:* Alan Jefferson, *Assault on the Guns of Merville: D-Day and After* (London: John Murray, 1987), 98–99.

219 *When I reached the [rendezvous point] beside a clump of trees:* Ibid., 105.

220 *The CO [Otway] decided that I must lead the assault:* James Maule Parry, "Major Allen James Maule Parry," Pegasus Archive, accessed January 17, 2024, https://www.pegasusarchive.org/normandy/allen_parry.htm.

221 *I was conscious of something striking my left thigh:* Ibid.

221 *Inside the battery terrific hand-to-hand fighting developed:* "Parachutists Take a Battery Feat in Normandy Landings," *The Times* (London), June 24, 1944, p. 3.

221 *There were quite a few soldiers still in there:* Parry, "Major Allen James Maule Parry."

222 *I wasn't pleased, I was bloody angry:* Terence Otway, "The Battle of Merville Gun Battery: Lieutenant-Colonel Terence Otway DSO," *Warriors in Their Own Words*, November 30, 2023, https://evergreenpodcasts.com/warriors-in-their-own-words/the-battle-of-merville-gun-battery-lieutenant-colonel-terence-otway-dso.

### The Paratrooper Skytrain

224 *Our mission was to use radar and lights:* George E. Koskimaki, *D-Day with the Screaming Eagles* (New York: Vantage Press, 1970), 49.

224 *Serials of aircraft, made up almost entirely:* Peter Caddick-Adams, *Sand & Steel: The D-Day Invasions and the Liberation of France* (New York: Oxford University Press, 2019), 436.

225 *While the planes were droning on:* Koskimaki, *D-Day with the Screaming Eagles*, 61.

225 *The moon was shining real bright:* Ibid.

225 *The night air was filled with thousands of strings of fiery tracers:* Ibid., 83.

226 *The order to "Stand up" and "Hook up" saved my life:* Ibid., 69, 70.

226 *As we approached our drop zone:* Ibid., 77.

226 *We were lined up in the first positions in the doorway:* Ibid., 76.


### Night in the Hedgerows

230 *I landed in water about five feet deep:* George E. Koskimaki, *D-Day with the Screaming Eagles* (New York: Vantage Press, 1970), 256.

231 *I lay there a few minutes exhausted:* Ibid., 344.

232 *During this time I had no success in finding anyone:* Ibid., 87.

232 *A wild-eyed trooper came charging out of the darkness:* G. William Sefton, *It Was My War: I'll Remember It the Way I Want To* (Lawrence, KS: Sunflower University Press, 1994), 55.

233 *There was a little trooper who was dug in with me:* George E. Koskimaki, *D-Day with the Screaming Eagles* (New York: Vantage Press, 1970), 133.

234 *Finally, our twelve-hundred-foot landing field:* Ibid., 325.

236 *What turned out to be one of the first enemy encounters:* Ibid., 112.

236 *When challenged by the Germans:* Ibid.

236 *Legere pretended to be a Frenchman:* Ibid.

237 *The chauffeur, a German Corporal:* Malcolm D. Brannen, "Malcolm D. Brannen," D-Day: Etat Des Lieux, accessed January 17, 2024, http://www.6juin1944.com /veterans/brannen.php.

238 *There seemed to be snipers everywhere:* Koskimaki, *D-Day with the Screaming Eagles*, 193.


### NEPTUNE Rises

251 *Altogether, it was surely the largest fleet:* Samuel Eliot Morison, *The Invasion of France and Germany, 1944–1945: History of United States Naval Operations in World War II, Vol. 11* (Annapolis, MD: Naval Institute Press, 2011), 77; see also the sailing schedule and embarkation details in Craig Symonds, *Neptune: The Allied Invasion of Europe and the D-Day Landings* (New York: Oxford University Press, 2014), 224–36.

251 *Crewing the entire Allied armada:* Peter Caddick-Adams, *Sand & Steel: The D-Day Invasion and the Liberation of France* (New York: Oxford University Press, 2019), 232.

251 *The* NEPTUNE *fleet was overwhelmingly British:* Ibid., 399.

251 *And there were far more:* Ibid., 247.

254 *The atmosphere had become terribly tense:* This and later quotation from Ainsley Hickman taken from letter to his parents, dated June 12, 1944, held in the archives collection of the the D-Day Story museum, Portsmouth, UK.

254 *[The minesweepers] not only swept:* Craig Symonds, *Neptune*, 245.

255 *My darling, Everything here is OK:* Letter from William T. Longley, held in the archives collection of the the D-Day Story museum, Portsmouth, UK.

255 *I never loved England:* Hilary St. George Saunders, *The Green Beret: The Story of the Commandos* (London: Michael Joseph, 1949), 267.

259 *I love these men:* Cornelius Ryan, *The Longest Day: June 6, 1944* (New York: Simon & Schuster, 1959), 68.

261 *Well Bunny Dear:* Joseph Balkoski, *Utah Beach: The Amphibious Landings and Airborne Operations on D-Day, June 6, 1944* (Mechanicsburg, PA: Stackpole Books, 2005), 70.

261 *As the* NEPTUNE *flotilla assembled:* Morison, *The Invasion of France and Germany, 1944–1945, Vol. 11*, 77–79; Caddick-Adams, *Sand & Steel*, cites the number as 255, p. 363.

261 *Overnight they found and detonated:* Caddick-Adams, *Sand & Steel*, 364.

263 *We were located in one:* Ibid., 405.

263 *I didn't think I was a heavy smoker:* Ibid.

264 *The stench of vomit was terrible:* Ibid.

265 *This was the real beginning:* W. B. Courtney, "The Victory Tide," *Collier's Weekly*, July 29, 1944.

265 *All I can remember:* Michael Green and James D. Brown, *War Stories of D-Day: Operation Overlord: June 6, 1944* (Minneapolis: Zenith Press, 2009), 123.

### Confusing the Enemy

267 *In four* TITANIC *missions:* Peter Caddick-Adams, *Sand & Steel: The D-Day Invasion and the Liberation of France* (New York: Oxford University Press, 2019), 417–23.

268 *Shortly before midnight lively activity:* Ibid., 419.

268 *I was called to the Brigadiers Office:* Frank and Joan Shaw, *We Remember D-Day* (Hinckley, England: Echo Press, 1994), 29.

268 *I considered this operation:* Caddick-Adams, *Sand & Steel*, 418.

269 *As events proved, the decision to launch:* Dwight D. Eisenhower, *Report by the Supreme Commander to the Combined Chiefs of Staff on the Operations in Europe of the Allied Expeditionary Force 6 June 1944 to 8 May 1945* (Washington, D.C.: Government Printing Office, 1946).

270 *The Resistance was very strong:* H. R. Kedward, *In Search of the Maquis: Rural Resistance in Southern France, 1942–1944* (Oxford: Clarendon Press, 1993), 249.

270 *My job was to draw up the D-Day orders:* Hugh Schofield, "The Man Who Prepared France for D-Day," BBC News, June 4, 2014, https://www.bbc.com/news/magazine-27682001.

271 *On the evening of 5 June:* Caddick-Adams, *Sand & Steel*, 312.

271 *1 a.m. Suddenly the village exploded:* Paddy Ashdown, *The Cruel Victory: The French Resistance, D-Day and the Battle for the Vercors, 1944* (Glasgow: William Collins, 2014), 162.

272 *All French must consider themselves:* Schofield, "The Man Who Prepared France for D-Day."

## Ashore in Normandy

274 *Planning a trip to Germany:* Erwin Rommel, *The Rommel Papers*, ed. B. H. Liddell-Hart (New York: Da Capo, 1982), 470.

276 *[I] saw all kinds of red flares:* Peter Caddick-Adams, *Sand & Steel: The D-Day Invasion and the Liberation of France* (New York: Oxford University Press, 2019), 441.

276 *Shortly after midnight I heard the sound:* Ibid.

279 *The bombers were suddenly over us:* Ronald Drez, *Voices of D-Day: The Story of the Allied Invasion Told by Those Who Were There* (Baton Rouge: Louisiana State University Press, 1994), 169–70.

280 *The sea had come alive:* Ibid., 235.

## In the Air Over the Beaches

281 *The fighters, bombers, and transports:* Peter Caddick-Adams, *Sand & Steel: The D-Day Invasion and the Liberation of France* (New York: Oxford University Press, 2019), 154.

282 *Beginning early in the morning:* Ibid., 358.

282 *We knew something was about to be screwed up:* Ibid., 424.

286 *The German air force launched only:* Ibid., 358.

287 *Everybody was worn out:* Pierre Closterman, *The Big Show: Some Experiences of a French Fighter Pilot in the R.A.F.*, trans. Oliver Berthoud (London: Corgi Books, 1951), 119.

287 *During the 24 hours of 6 June:* Dwight D. Eisenhower, *Report by the Supreme Commander to the Combined Chiefs of Staff on the Operations in Europe of the Allied Expeditionary Force 6 June 1944 to 8 May 1945* (Washington, D.C.: Government Printing Office, 1946).

### Heading Ashore at Utah

289 *H-Hour differed slightly from beach to beach:* Samuel Eliot Morison, *The Invasion of France and Germany, 1944–1945: History of United States Naval Operations in World War II, Vol. 11* (Annapolis, MD: Naval Institute Press, 2011), 33.

289 *"Utah" Beach, 9655 yards long:* Joseph Balkoski, *Utah Beach: The Amphibious Landings and Airborne Operations on D-Day, June 6, 1944* (Mechanicsburg, PA: Stackpole Books, 2005), 58.

293 *The water was very cold:* Cmdr. Walter Karig, *Battle Report: The Atlantic War, Vol. II* (New York: Farrar & Rinehart, 1946), 332.

293 *The noise was terrific:* Peter Caddick-Adams, *Sand & Steel: The D-Day Invasion and the Liberation of France* (New York: Oxford University Press, 2019), 502.

294 *The history books claim:* Ibid., 510.

295 *We'd been trained that once you hit the beach:* Ibid., 505.

295 *You never really get the smell:* https://www.americanheritage.com/catcher-rye-d-day; https://www.vanityfair.com/culture/2011/02/salinger-201102.

296 *With a crunch we grounded:* Balkoski, *Utah Beach,* 190–91.

296 *NAVSITREP1: To Naval Commander Western Task Force:* Caddick-Adams, *Sand & Steel,* 482.

297 *There was a house by the seawall:* Balkoski, *Utah Beach,* 192.

297 *We moved from obstacle to obstacle:* Caddick-Adams, *Sand & Steel,* 503.

### Naval Forces at Utah

302 *We got all the men over:* Cmdr. Walter Karig, *Battle Report: The Atlantic War, Vol. II* (New York: Farrar & Rinehart, 1946), 335.

302 *The* Fitch *people reached over the side:* Michael Green and James D. Brown, *War Stories of D-Day: Operation Overlord: June 6, 1944* (Minneapolis: Zenith Press, 2009), 257–61.

303 *The cutter had just made a round trip:* All of this section, both Burkhardt and Barber, are from Karig, *Battle Report,* 338.

### The Second Wave at Utah

305 *By day's end, Utah would receive:* Peter Caddick-Adams, *Sand & Steel: The D-Day Invasion and the Liberation of France* (New York: Oxford University Press, 2019), 536.

306 *I crawled out there and got close enough:* https://www.history.com/videos/dick-winters-on-brecourt-manor-assault.

308 *The Germans ran like hell:* https://warfarehistorynetwork.com/article/screaming-eagles-at-brecourt-manor/.

309 *I killed every German I could:* https://www.latimes.com/local/obituaries/la-xpm
-2014-mar-10-la-me-william-guarnere-20140311-story.html.

310 *One thing that had my attention:* Joseph Balkoski, *Utah Beach: The Amphibious
Landings and Airborne Operations on D-Day, June 6, 1944* (Mechanicsburg, PA:
Stackpole Books, 2005), 238.

313 *When he was rescued:* Ibid., 241.

313 *I gave an arm signal:* Ibid., 236.

314 *I was so angry. The Navy had tried:* Stephen Ambrose, *D-Day: June 6, 1944* (New
York: Simon & Schuster, 1994), 287.

314 *I pulled out my square of orange cloth:* Balkoski, *Utah Beach*, 243–44.

### The Rangers at Pointe du Hoc

317 *The Pointe was a massive fortress:* https://warfarehistorynetwork.com/the-pointe
-du-hoc-rangers-a-madmans-d-day-mission/.

317 *I had discussed with General Eisenhower:* Lucian K. Truscott, *Command Missions:
A Personal Story* (Mount Pleasant, SC: Arcadia Press, 2019), 40.

320 *It was a matter of but a few minutes:* This quote and Hodenfield's other comments
in this section are all from Gaylord K. Hodenfield, "I Climbed the Cliffs with
the Rangers," *Saturday Evening Post*, August 19, 1944.

321 *Ranger Force C lay off Pointe du Hoc:* Joseph Balkoski, *Omaha Beach: D-Day,
June 6, 1944* (Mechanicsburg, PA: Stackpole Books, 2004), 172.

323 *From the Pointe, we started throwing grenades:* This quote is from a collection of
German and French accounts of Pointe du Hoc gathered, translated, and generously shared with me by D-Day historian and general mensch Paul Woodadge.

324 *I was assigned a specific rope:* Patrick K. O'Donnell, *Dog Company: The Boys of
Pointe du Hoc* (Cambridge, MA: Da Capo, 2012), 71.

### Omaha Beach

332 *That exit to the nearby village:* Peter Caddick-Adams, *Sand & Steel: The D-Day
Invasion and the Liberation of France* (New York: Oxford University Press, 2019),
559.

332 *I have witnessed many sunrises:* Noel F. Mehlo, Jr., *D-Day General: How Dutch
Cota Saved Omaha Beach on June 6, 1944* (Mechanicsburg, PA: Stackpole Books,
2021), 179.

333 *In a few minutes, coinciding:* Cmdr. Walter Karig, *Battle Report: The Atlantic War,
Vol. II* (New York: Farrar & Rinehart, 1946), 320–21.

333 *Being a young guy, I thought it:* https://www.nbcnews.com/id/wbna5210564.

334 *The rockets went up in the air:* Alex Kershaw, *The Bedford Boys: One American
Town's Ultimate D-Day Sacrifice* (Cambridge, MA: Da Capo, 2003), 125.

334 *One guy yelled:* Joseph H. Ewing, *29 Let's Go!: A History of the 29th Division in World War II* (Washington, D.C.: Infantry Journal Press, 1948), 39.

335 *It was obvious even before launching:* Joseph Balkoski, *Omaha Beach: D-Day, June 6, 1944* (Mechanicsburg, PA: Stackpole Books, 2004), 102.

335 *[The tank] bobbed for a moment:* John C. McManus, *The Dead and Those About to Die: D-Day: The Big Red One at Omaha Beach* (New York: Penguin, 2014), 69.

### Into the Devil's Garden

339 *The Germans called it:* Peter Caddick-Adams, *Sand & Steel: The D-Day Invasion and the Liberation of France* (New York: Oxford University Press, 2019), 572.

340 *I am beginning to think:* Joseph Balkoski, *Omaha Beach: D-Day, June 6, 1944* (Mechanicsburg, PA: Stackpole Books, 2004), 119.

340 *They were proud that the 116th:* Ibid., 29.

340 *[Fellers] told me his troops were National Guard:* Alex Kershaw, *The Bedford Boys: One American Town's Ultimate D-Day Sacrifice* (Cambridge, MA: Da Capo, 2003), 111.

340 *[My twin brother] Ray said:* Balkoski, *Omaha Beach,* 70

341 *[The coast looked] menacing, dark:* Kershaw, *The Bedford Boys,* 128.

341 *I never saw water that bad:* Ibid., 120.

344 *Among the troops aboard the British landing craft:* Caddick-Adams, *Sand & Steel,* 573.

346 *I heard later that Captain Fellers:* Kershaw, *The Bedford Boys,* 143.

346 *Entire first wave foundered:* Caddick-Adams, *Sand & Steel,* 666.

347 *I told the men to get from the water's edge:* Balkoski, *Omaha Beach,* 114.

347 *All of us ran across the beach:* Ibid., 116.

347 *We lost a third of our company:* Eisenhower Center, "Conversations with Veterans of D-Day," June 5, 2000, https://www.c-span.org/video/?157508-1/conversations-veterans-day.

348 *I signaled to Bill Smith:* Ibid.

348 *Within about 5 minutes:* Ibid.

348 *We got topside and we got into labyrinths:* Ibid.

349 *I went with a patrol towards:* Ibid.

### Ashore at Omaha

352 *Four LCTs, which were supposed to arrive at 8:30:* Peter Caddick-Adams, *Sand & Steel: The D-Day Invasion and the Liberation of France* (New York: Oxford University Press, 2019), 584.

353 *Most of my boat team was seasick:* Joseph Balkoski, *Omaha Beach: D-Day, June 6, 1944* (Mechanicsburg, PA: Stackpole Books, 2004), 124.

353 *While waiting our turn:* Michael Green and James D. Brown, *War Stories of D-Day: Operation Overlord: June 6, 1944* (Minneapolis: Zenith Press, 2009), 212–13.

354 *All of a sudden the British coxswain:* Balkoski, *Omaha Beach*, 133.

355 *Now we sprang into action:* Ronald Drez, *Voices of D-Day: The Story of the Allied Invasion Told by Those Who Were There* (Baton Rouge: Louisiana State University Press, 1994), 235–37.

355 *I could see the water spouts:* Caddick-Adams, *Sand & Steel*, 641.

357 *When we got about two hundred yards offshore:* This and other Spalding quotes are from Forrest Pogue's remarkable contemporaneous interview with Spalding just after D-Day, in Pogue, *Pogue's War: Diaries of a WWII Combat Historian* (Lexington: University Press of Kentucky, 2001), 62–75.

358 *I was the first one off the craft:* Interview in *Newsweek*, June 11, 1994, p. 24.

359 *I ran into a burst of machine gun fire:* Balkoski, *Omaha Beach*, 161–62.

359 *Our Ranger chaplain, Father Lacy:* Ibid., 176.

361 *An impression that overcame me:* Ibid., 230.

361 *Sergeant Braasch came running:* Green and Brown, *War Stories of D-Day*, 214.

362 *I began to get visions:* Balkoski, *Omaha Beach*, 173.

362 *We were in the center of the attack:* Ibid., 261.

### Getting Off Omaha Beach

364 *"There were two long stretches of beach":* Samuel Eliot Morison, *The Invasion of France and Germany, 1944–1945: History of United States Naval Operations in World War II, Vol. 11* (Annapolis, MD: Naval Institute Press, 2011), 138.

365 *Col. Taylor, then commanding officer of the 16th:* Joseph Balkoski, *Omaha Beach: D-Day, June 6, 1944* (Mechanicsburg, PA: Stackpole Books, 2004), 198.

365 *He said, "If you stay here":* Noel F. Mehlo, Jr., *D-Day General: How Dutch Cota Saved Omaha Beach on June 6, 1944* (Mechanicsburg, PA: Stackpole Books, 2021), 194–95.

366 *As he approached:* Ibid., 183–86; Major General John C. Raaen, Jr., USA (Ret.), *Witness Statement to Congress for Cota Medal of Honor Upgrade,* June 6, 2018.

366 *I was glad to see them:* Balkoski, *Omaha Beach*, 197.

366 *Before Cota reached Schneider:* Mehlo, Jr., *D-Day General*, 188.

367 *After Cota finished speaking:* Balkoski, *Omaha Beach*, 197.

367 *This was the spark needed:* Mehlo, Jr., *D-Day General*, 190.

367 *Using Bangalore Torpedoes, they blew:* Ibid., 189.

367 *Bullets were dropping around us:* Cole Kingseed, *From Omaha Beach to Dawson's Ridge: The Combat Journal of Captain Joe Dawson* (Annapolis, MD: Naval Institute Press), 149; https://www.sonsoflibertymuseum.org/library/army/1st-infantry-division-wwii/1id-dday-v2.pdf.

368  *I don't think [the Germans] expected:* Peter Caddick-Adams, *Sand & Steel: The D-Day Invasion and the Liberation of France* (New York: Oxford University Press, 2019), 657.

370  *Summing it all up:* John C. McManus, *The Dead and Those About to Die: D-Day: The Big Red One at Omaha Beach* (New York: Penguin, 2014), 302.

370  *I would not change if I were given the chance:* Clara B. Cox, "Jimmie Monteith: An American Hero," *Virginia Tech Magazine*, Summer 2009, https://www.archive.vtmag.vt.edu/sum09/retrospect.html.

370  *Lt. Monteith brought his men together:* This and following Jones quotation are from "Richmonder Gets Nation's Highest Award," *The (Danville, Va.) Bee*, March 22, 1945, p. 5, at https://www.newspapers.com/article/the-bee/5540967/.

371  *When [Lt. Monteith] knocked out the machine gun:* Balkoski, *Omaha Beach*, 293.

372  *The men that got hit, we treated those:* https://www.baltimoresun.com/news/bs-xpm-1994-06-05-1994156028-story.html.

373  *On the beach, I raced:* Caddick-Adams, *Sand & Steel*, 649.

373  *We'd put the bodies up by the rocks:* Terril Jones, Associated Press, "D-Day's Black Combat Unit Honored in Paris," *Potomac News*, Woodbridge, VA, June 9, 1994.

373  *There were so many troops:* Caddick-Adams, *Sand & Steel*, 677.

374  *The casualty ratio normally:* Balkoski, *Omaha Beach*, 331.

### Afloat Off Omaha Beach

376  *The USS* McCook *shot 975 rounds:* Samuel Eliot Morison, *The Invasion of France and Germany, 1944–1945: History of United States Naval Operations in World War II, Vol. 11* (Annapolis, MD: Naval Institute Press, 2011), 144.

376  *You may well imagine what emotion:* Ibid., 119.

376  *Suddenly, like the cavalry:* Peter Caddick-Adams, *Sand & Steel: The D-Day Invasion and the Liberation of France* (New York: Oxford University Press, 2019), 627.

377  *Get on them, men:* Craig Symonds, *Neptune: The Allied Invasion of Europe and the D-Day Landings* (New York: Oxford University Press, 2014), 290; Morison, *The Invasion of France and Germany*, 143.

378  *It is suggested that the official history:* Joseph Balkoski, *Omaha Beach: D-Day, June 6, 1944* (Mechanicsburg, PA: Stackpole Books, 2004), 255.

378  *I firmly believe that the firepower:* Caddick-Adams, *Sand & Steel*, 628.

378  *Communication with the landing forces:* Ibid., 600.

378  *Numerous landing craft were being knocked out:* Ibid., 649; Craig Symonds, *Neptune: The Allied Invasion of Europe and the D-Day Landings* (New York: Oxford University Press, 2014), 275.

### Jig Sector, Gold Beach

383 *The division was a mix:* Peter Caddick-Adams, *Sand & Steel: The D-Day Invasion and the Liberation of France* (New York: Oxford University Press, 2019), 707.

383 *It was stressed to us that our job:* Ibid., 186.

384 *Everyone was now sitting very quiet:* Hilary St. George Saunders, *The Green Beret: The Story of the Commandos* (London: Michael Joseph, 1949), 268.

386 *I gasped as the freezing surf:* Caddick-Adams, *Sand & Steel*, 411.

390 *We had a special type of gun:* https://www.yorkpress.co.uk/news/7886016.going-for-gold.

### The Green Howards Take King Sector

394 *As we were coming in:* This quote and other Stanley Hollis quotes are used with permission from Mike Morgan, from his remarkable and thorough *D-Day Hero: CSM Stanley Hollis VC* (London: The History Press, 2014), 93–107.

394 *There was no danger of being trampled:* Peter Caddick-Adams, *Sand & Steel: The D-Day Invasion and the Liberation of France* (New York: Oxford University Press, 2019), 727.

395 *One's first impression upon landing:* https://www.iwm.org.uk/collections/item/object/80033422.

395 *We charged about waist-deep:* Morgan, *D-Day Hero*, 93–107.

395 *They got across [the beach]:* Ibid., 117–19.

397 *We waited for the codeword:* Ibid., 119–22.

397 *Without hesitation, he simply charged:* Ibid., 117–19.

398 *The pillboxes had fallen:* Henry Gullett, *Not as a Duty Only: An Infantryman's War* (Melbourne: Melbourne University Press, 1976), 137.

399 *Wherever fighting was heaviest:* *The London Gazette*, August 15, 1944, https://www.thegazette.co.uk/London/issue/36658/supplement/3807.

399 *All these fellers were my mates:* Morgan, *D-Day Hero*, 93–107.

### Ashore at Juno

400 *Manned by the 736th Grenadier-Regiment:* Peter Caddick-Adams, *Sand & Steel: The D-Day Invasion and the Liberation of France* (New York: Oxford University Press, 2019), 742.

401 *The land directly off the beach:* Ibid., 744.

401 *It was absolutely astonishing:* Ted Barris, *Juno: Canadians at D-Day, June 6, 1944* (Toronto: Thomas Allen, 2004), 99.

401 *From the window of our bathroom:* Original interview by Ted Barris, courtesy of Ted Barris.

402 *It looked like the dawn: Canada at War*, ed. Michael Benedict (Toronto: Viking, 1997), 165.

402 *And then the beach itself became visible:* Barris, *Juno*, 123.

402 *The landing probably was the most exciting:* Original interview by Ted Barris.

402 *The minesweepers leading us in slowed down:* Tim Saunders, *Juno Beach: Canadian 3rd Infantry Division–July 1944* (Battleground Europe Series) (London: Pen & Sword Books, 1990), 133.

402 *My tank went into the water:* Barris, *Juno*, 131.

403 *At about 3,000 yards, I looked around:* Ibid., 149.

403 *Despite the losses at sea:* Caddick-Adams, *Sand & Steel*, 757.

404 *We shot and shot:* Saunders, *Juno Beach*, 138.

404 *On both flanks of Bernières:* "Assault on Normandy," *Canada at War*, 175.

404 *The moment the ramp came down:* Caddick-Adams, *Sand & Steel*, 761.

405 *My brother Don was on the boat:* Original interview by Ted Barris.

405 *All this time there were shells:* https://www.bbc.co.uk/history/ww2peopleswar /stories/59/a4371059.shtml.

406 *The Landing Craft Obstacle Clearance Unit: Operation Neptune*, quoted in Saunders, *Juno Beach*, 168.

406 *[There were] rolls of concertina wire:* Ibid., 153.

406 *The thing I remember:* Original interview by Ted Barris.

407 *From dune to dune, along the German trench systems:* Saunders, *Juno Beach*, 156.

407 *We then started to head:* Ibid., 147.

408 *We landed about 11 a.m.:* Original interview by Ted Barris.

408 *Behind the seawall, the German defences:* Saunders, *Juno Beach*, 183.

409 *We were a western regiment:* Original interview by Ted Barris.

409 *Those damn bicycles:* Barris, *Juno*, 166.

410 *During the afternoon, I saw German prisoners:* Saunders, *Juno Beach*, 186.

410 *I just hung around the beach:* Ibid., 188.

410 *By late afternoon, the seeming chaos:* Ibid., 186.

411 *Clear above the sound of our laboring engines:* Original interview by Ted Barris.

411 *A lot of us wondered:* Barris, *Juno*, 183.

412 *History is standing astride these rolling:* Shapiro in *Canada at War*, 170.

### Sword Beach

414 *Enemy destroyers attacked with torpedoes:* Peter Caddick-Adams, *Sand & Steel: The D-Day Invasion and the Liberation of France* (New York: Oxford University Press, 2019), 379.

415 *I saw the first torpedo coming towards us:* https://www.oceansandseas.com/lars-the-old-sailor-part-iv/.

415 *Soon twinkling lights appeared:* Caddick-Adams, *Sand & Steel*, 379.

415 *We went in and dropped scrambling nets:* https://www.facebook.com/watch /?v=1005829042807535.

415 *She was a sister ship of ours:* Caddick-Adams, *Sand & Steel*, 378.

415 *She had the unfortunate distinction:* https://www.burnleyexpress.net/news/people /ralph-never-forgot-the-sinking-of-the-svenner-967314.

415 *Then the invasion started:* https://www.bbc.co.uk/history/ww2peopleswar/stories /41/a4024441.shtml.

416 *The enemy was obviously stunned:* Craig Symonds, *Neptune: The Allied Invasion of Europe and the D-Day Landings* (New York: Oxford University Press, 2014), 264.

416 *We had studied:* John Buckley, *Monty's Men: The British Army and the Liberation of Europe* (New Haven, CT: Yale University Press, 2013), 60.

418 *I landed on D-Day in water waist deep:* Dan Harvey, *A Bloody Dawn: The Irish at D-Day* (Newbridge, Ireland: Merrion Press, 2019).

419 *Lots of us were given these fold-up bikes:* Caddick-Adams, *Sand & Steel*, 706.

422 *For us it was special:* https://apnews.com/article/0de61e2fdf0e416c9d24f0370a f00667.

422 *We began to pour out of the landing craft:* Harvey, *A Bloody Dawn*, 119.

423 *The whole thing was to move fast:* Ibid.

### The News Spreads

442 *Mama brought me what she thought:* Alex Kershaw, *The Bedford Boys: One American Town's Ultimate D-Day Sacrifice* (Cambridge, Mass.: Da Capo, 2003), 166.

442 *I have a feeling we are going:* Vince Leibowitz, *A Solemn Hour for Texans Everywhere: The Story of How News of D-Day Came to Texas* (self-published, 2019), 16.

443 *On D-Day I was a Prisoner of War:* Frank and Joan Shaw, *We Remember D-Day* (Hinckley, England: Echo Press, 1994), 7.

### Holding the Eastern Flank

453 *The [German] infantry were no problem:* Dan Harvey, *A Bloody Dawn: The Irish at D-Day* (Newbridge, Ireland: Merrion Press, 2019), 59.

### The Walking Wounded

462 *I proceeded into Vierville:* Joseph Balkoski, *Omaha Beach: D-Day, June 6, 1944* (Mechanicsburg, PA: Stackpole Books, 2004), 276.

462 *There were a few scattered rounds:* Ibid., 278.

463 *Word reached me that a C Company bulldozer:* Ibid., 311.

### The Battle of La Fière Bridge

465 *From our study of aerial photos:* Donald C. O'Rourke, "The Operations of the 1st Platoon, Company I, 507th Parachute Infantry at the Forcing of the Merderet River Causeway at Lafiere, France, 9 June 1944. Personal Experiences of a Platoon Leader." Paper for Advanced Infantry Officers Course No. 2., Fort Benning, GA., undated, circa 1947–1948, https://mcoecbamcoepwprdo1.blob .core.usgovcloudapi.net/library/DonovanPapers/wwii/STUP2/M-R/ORourke DonaldC%201LT.pdf.

467 *The Germans placed some white bed linen:* Robert Murphy, *No Better Place to Die* (Havertown, PA: Casemate, 2009), 202.

468 *The eastern end of the causeway:* O'Rourke, "The Operations of the 1st Platoon, Company I, 507th Parachute Infantry."

### Afternoon for the Germans

475 *It was terrifying; we were always scanning:* Peter Caddick-Adams, *Sand & Steel: The D-Day Invasion and the Liberation of France* (New York: Oxford University Press, 2019), 655.

### End of D-Day

481 *We arrived off Omaha Beach:* Matthew Rozell, *D-Day and Beyond: The Things Our Fathers Saw—The Untold Stories of the World War II Generation, Vol. V* (self-published, 2019), 210.

### Epilogue

489 *The ongoing combat would devastate:* Mary Louise Roberts, *D-Day Through French Eyes* (Chicago: University of Chicago Press, 2014), 69, 82.

490 *The one millionth Allied soldier:* Samuel Eliot Morison, *The Invasion of France and Germany, 1944–1945: History of United States Naval Operations in World War II, Vol. 11* (Annapolis, MD: Naval Institute Press, 2011), 163.

490 *The Gold Beach Mulberry:* Peter Caddick-Adams, *Sand & Steel: The D-Day Invasion and the Liberation of France* (New York: Oxford University Press, 2019), 737.

491 *The next day, the 7th, was the day:* Original interview by Ted Barris, courtesy of Ted Barris.

492 *A captured enemy document:* Dwight D. Eisenhower, *Report by the Supreme Commander to the Combined Chiefs of Staff on the Operations in Europe of the Allied Expeditionary Force 6 June 1944 to 8 May 1945* (Washington, D.C.: Government Printing Office, 1946).

493  *Just a line to say I'm OK:* Cole Kingseed, *From Omaha Beach to Dawson's Ridge: The Combat Journal of Captain Joe Dawson* (Annapolis, MD: Naval Institute Press), 154.

493  *When the casualties from Normandy started:* Frank and Joan Shaw, *We Remember D-Day* (Hinckley, England: Echo Press, 1994), 25.

494  *Then, we crossed into Germany:* Matthew Rozell, *D-Day and Beyond: The Things Our Fathers Saw—The Untold Stories of the World War II Generation, Vol. V* (self-published, 2019), 314–15.

495  *I had a job to do and a responsibility:* Alex Kershaw, *The Bedford Boys: One American Town's Ultimate D-Day Sacrifice* (Cambridge, MA: Da Capo, 2003), 201.

496  *Dear Mr. Thistle, I have your letter:* Original interview by Ted Barris.

496  *You never got used to combat:* Kershaw, *The Bedford Boys,* 181.

498  *I married Ethel Estoppey in 1948:* Stephen Ambrose, *Band of Brothers* (New York: Simon & Schuster, 1992), 315.

499  *I dream about D-Day all the time:* Interview in *Newsweek,* June 11, 1994, 24.

499  *I feel like I've come a long way:* Ibid.

500  *There is not a day that has passed:* Ambrose, *Band of Brothers,* 20.

500  *Normandy and D-Day remain vivid:* Stephen Ambrose, *D-Day: June 6, 1944* (New York: Simon & Schuster, 1994), 367.

# Index

Page numbers in *italics* refer to photo captions.

Abbaye d'Ardenne, 492
Adams, Mr. and Mrs. Frederick, 16
Adams, Robert E., 265, 352, 357
Adriatic Sea, 65, 67
Aebischer, Ray, 226, 244
Africa
    North Africa, *see* North Africa
    South Africa, 6
*Afro-American*, 58
Ahearn, John L., xix, 258, 295–96, 311–13
Ainsworth, John, 200–201
air raid shelters, 12–14, 56
Aitken, Douglas, 252
Alex, George, 225
Alexander, Harold, 7, 23, 436
Alford, Parker A., 193, 237–38
Algeria, 370
Algiers, 87, 88
*Algonquin*, HMCS, 250
Alkenbrack, Wes, 402, 411
Allen, Ronald, 12, 13
aluminum foil "window" (chaff),
    266–67, 269
Amarillo, TX, 439, 442
Ambrose, Stephen, xvii, 306, 336n
*Ancon*, HMS, 76, 378
Andersen, Howard, 300, 301

Anderson, Alan, 148, 152–53, 259–60,
    264, 480–81, 483
Anderson, Dave, 436
Anderson, Edward J., 444
Andrews, Celia, 99
Angoville-au-Plain, 481
Anzio, 35, 440
*Aquitania*, RMS, 43
Arbib, Robert, Jr., 51
Arctic Sea, 65
Ardennes Forest, 494
*Arkansas*, USS, 319, 333
Armed Services Editions, 258–59
Arnold, Edgar, 362
Arnold, James E., 263, 292
Arromanches, 391
Ashbrook, William, 225
Ashcroft, Eric, 420
Asnelles, 384
Associated Press, 431–32, 492
Atlantic, Battle of, 43
Atlantic Charter, 15
Atlantic Wall, xvi, 28, 61–74, 84, 135, *158*,
    160, *182*, 214, 434, 480
    Pointe du Hoc, 316–29, *316*, 331, 346,
        347, 365, 458, 489
    replica of, 103

Atlantic Wall (*cont.*)
  Rommel and, *61*, 63–64, 67–74
  Sword Beach and, 426, 428
*Augusta*, USS, *375*
Aursland, Lars, 415
Australia, 6
Austria, 79–80
Authie, 491
automobile industry, 19
AVRE (Armoured Vehicle Royal
    Engineer), 389, 390, 393
Aydlett, Cyrus C., 291

Bacalia, Edward, 336–37
Bacon, W. Garwood, Jr., 102, 139, 151
Bailey, Jack, 203
Baker, A., 396
balloons, 267, 269
*Baltimore Sun*, 500
Bancilhon, Michel, 270
*Band of Brothers* (Ambrose), 306
Bangalore torpedoes, 367, 370, 406, 454
Barber, Carter, 303, 304
Bare, Harry, 20, 100, 152, 257, 356, 359,
    360, 494
Barensfeld, Jack, 123, 287
Barfleur, 267
Barnard, Don, 405
Barnard, Fred, 405
Barnes, John, 3, 44–45, 60, 98–99, 151,
    152, 252, 260, 341
Barnes, Reginald, 423–24
*Barnett*, USS, 302–3, 305
Barrett, Joseph, 251–52, 258–59
Barry, J. G., 335
Bartholomay, Raymond, 110, 112
*Barton*, USS, 377
Basey, Henry, 499
Baumgarten, Harold "Hal," 100–101,
    140, 339, 344–46, 350, 365, 458,
    460, 485–86

Bayerlein, Fritz, 71, 161–62
Bayeux, 382–83, 477, 493
Bayeux Fire Brigade, 72
*Bayfield*, USS, 260, 288, 290, 291
Bay of Biscay, 65
BBC, xvi–xvii, 8, 270, 440, 443, 444
Beard, Felix, 313n
Beat, Bill, 301
Beattie, Fred, 109–10, 112
Beccue, Gale, 369
Beck, John A., Sr., 53, 486
Bedford, VA, 339, 340, 495
Beeman, Robert, 300
beer, 52, 54
Beetle, Frank, 259
Beibst, Werner, 72, 82, 280
Belcham, David, 84–88, 147
    in final run-through meeting on
        D-Day, 133
    on information given to
        commanders, 151
    Mulberry harbors and, 91–93
    on radar and deception operations,
        267–69
Belfast, 155, 250, 497
*Belfast*, HMS, 156, 415
Belgium, 6, 7, 10, 27, 28, 434
Bell, Roger, 393–94
*Bell for Adano, A* (Hersey), 259
Bennet, Wilfred, 405
Bentham, James, 496, 499
Bény-sur-Mer, 408, 409
Bergner, Hans E., 291
Bernard, Tom, 377–78
Bernières-sur-Mer, 401, 402, 404, 408
Berra, Yogi, 256, 333
Bettridge, Bill, 404
Beuzeville-au-Plain, 480
Bevin, Ernest, 170, 171
bicycles, 62, 66, 245, *273*, 409, 419, 420,
    424, 475

Biddle, Tony, 138–39

Bierre, Eugene, 314, 315

BIGOT classification, 75–77, 106, 151

Big Three Allies, xiv, 29

Bingham, Sidney, 340, 361

Bingley, Violet, 252

Birch, Doug, 262

Bird-Wilson, Harold, 11

Biscay, 28

Black, Timuel D., 58, 59, 60

Blackburn, John R., 264, 300

blackouts, 51–52

Black Sea, 65

Blacksod Lighthouse, 174

Black soldiers, xv, 50, 51, 57–60, 372–74, 498, 500

    Medal of Honor and, xvn, 374n

Blackwell, W. J., 255, 384, 389

Blaylock, Joseph S., Sr., 139, 150, 294, 297

Block, Doc, 323, 328

Block, Morton, 291, 294

blood supplies, 126

Blumentritt, Günther, 65–67, 69, 70, 159

"Bobbin," 389–90

Bocks, Bert, 409

Bodell, Stanley C., 263

Boland, Oliver, 200, 202

Bolderson, John, 468, 469, 471–73

bomb shelters, 12–14, 56

Bordeaux, 28

Bostick, William A., 80, 82

*Boston Sunday Post*, 352

Botsford, Gardner, *xxi*, xxiii

Bourlet, Francis, 203

Bowdidge, Bill, 419

Bowen, Dennis, 141, 143, 253–54, 396

Bracken, Brendan, 60

Bradbeer, Grace, 5, 14, 95–98

Bradley, Bruce, 295

Bradley, Holbrook "Hobie," 500

Bradley, Omar, xix, 22, 23, *34*, 84, 135n, 138, 146, 155, 253, 259, 285

    beginning of war and, 7, 8, 10

    on D-Day scheduling, 131

    on equipment, 129

    Omaha Beach and, 338, 379

    in OVERLORD planning, 27–29, 31–33, 35–39, 81–82

    Pointe du Hoc and, 317, 318

Branham, Felix, xxv, 44, 52, 100, 360, 482, 498

Brannen, Malcolm, 237

Brass, Josef, 62

Brécourt Manor, 306, 309, 464

Bremen, 496

Brereton, Lewis H., 138

Brest, 28, 45

*Bridge Too Far, A* (Ryan), xvii

Britain, *see* Great Britain

British Army Bureau of Current Affairs Bulletin, 54

Brittany, 27, 28, 45, 159

Brixham Harbor, 107

Broekx, Fernand, 280

Bronze Star, 309n, 340, 374n, 500

Brooke, Alan, 31, 40n, 76, 136, 380

    on Churchill, 40n

    Eisenhower as viewed by, 40n, 134n

    in final run-through meeting on D-Day, 134n

    Montgomery and, 134n, 135n

Brotheridge, Den, 203–5

Brown, Andrew, 424

Brown, Ivan, 110

Brown, Jack Vilander, 386–87

Brown, John Mason, 54, 96–97, 100, 125, 255, 261, 265

Brown, Stephen, 415

Brumbaugh, Frank, 227–28, 236, 249

Bryan, Wright, 434–35

Bryant, Carleton F., 377, 379
Buchenwald concentration camp, 495
Buhl, Howard, 49
Bulge, Battle of the, 486, 494, 497
Bulkeley, John D., 147–48, 262
Bull, Harold, 168, 171, 177
bulldozers, 463
Bullock, Bernard E., 361
Bullock, R. H. W., 426–28, 477
Bures, 214
Burgett, Donald R., 155–56, 225–26, 232, 233
Burke, Ferris, 265
Burkhalter, John B., 368
Burkhard, Arthur, Jr., 303–4
Burn, Lambton, 53, 92, 263, 423
Burn, Laurie, 102
Burns, Dwayne, 56, 142, 192, 231, 497
Butcher, Harry C., 93, 119, 134, 194, 196, 380, 381
    and Churchill's desire to accompany invasion, 157
    on Exercise TIGER, 115
    on Norway deception, 85
    on paratroopers, 192
    on Transportation Plan, 121
    weather and visibility conditions and, 130, 132, 135, 168–69
    on wording of communique for OVERLORD, 129
Butkovich, Stan, 226
Butler, Robert, 233–34
Byatt, Edwin, 454

Cabourg, 371
Caddell-Adams, Patrick, xv
Caen, 28, 39, 79, 130, 214, 276, 284, 414, 419, 449, 450, 454, 477, 489–90
Caen Canal, 198, 199, 413
Caesar, Julius, 22
Caffey, Eugene, 297, 310–11

Calvados, 279, 474
Campbell, Archibald "Doon," 153–54, 424, 426
camps, military
    Kilmer, 43, 44
    Patrick Henry, 497
    "sausage," 137–44, 137, 145
    Shanks, 43
Canada, 6
Canadian forces, 21, 144, 383, 400–412, 400, 491–93
    see also Juno Beach
Capa, Robert, xvii, xxv, 127, 256, 257, 354, 356–57, 373–74, 483
Capelluto, Harold A., 227
Carey, Homer, 263, 264, 481–83
Carmick, USS, 376
Carney, Eugene, 114, 116
Carpiquet Airport, 449, 454
Carson, Gordon, 127
Cartledge, Carl Howard, Jr., 77, 156, 195, 227
Casablanca Conference, 24, 25
Cassino, 35
Catcher in the Rye, The (Salinger), 295n
Cauquigny, 468, 472
CBC, 401
CBS, 6, 11, 431, 432, 434, 437, 438
cemeteries, 489, 500
censorship, 78, 140
chaff (window), 266–67, 269
Chalk, John, 54, 128
Chamberlain, Neville, 4, 6, 7
Chance, Donald L., 367
Channel Islands, 63, 275
"Chanson d'automne" (Verlaine), 270
Chapman, Francis W., 230
Chase, USS, 257, 374
Chateau La Roche Guyon, 161
Chauvet, Maurice, 264
Chef-du-Pont, 465

Cherbourg, 28–29, 38–40, 89, 90, 93, 262, 263, 267, 269, 283, 289, 316, 381, 462, 465
Chief Constables, letter from UK Home Office to, 59
Ching, Randall, 367
Churchill, Pamela, 17
Churchill, Winston, xviii, xix, 7, 11, 22, 30, 31, 35, 43, 78, 127, 129, 170, 171, 173, 432, 435
    address to the nation, 84
    Allied bombing campaign and, 120, 121
    Atlantic Charter and, 15
    beginning of war and, 7–11, 16–18
    Brooke on, 40n
    at Casablanca conference, 24
    code words and, 25n, 26, 27
    on date for D-Day, 131, 133
    D-Day landing confirmation speech of, 436–37
    deception operations and, 84, 87
    desire to accompany invasion, 156, 157
    in final run-through meeting on D-Day, 133, 134
    House of Commons speeches of, 8–10
    memoirs of, xvi
    Mulberry harbors and, 90–91, 93
    in OVERLORD planning, 24, 27–29, 31, 35, 79
    on radar operations, 267
    Roosevelt and, 15, 25n
    and secrecy around OVERLORD plans, 76, 78, 79
    on Stalin, 40n
    on training of troops, 95
    troops visited by, 146–48
church services, 153–54, 250, 257–58
cigarettes, 227–28
Cinque Ports, 87

Civil War, 339, 340
Clare, Barbara, 5, 54, 56, 57
Clark, Jim, 116
Clark, Mark Wayne, 381
Clark, Roy, 263–64
Clark, Tom, 107–11, 113, 116–17
Clarke, L. N. "Nobby," 405, 410–11
Clements, John, 98
Clinton, Bill, xvn, 374
Clogstoun-Willmott, Nigel, 80–81
Clostermann, Pierre, 287
clothing, 143–44, 483
Coast Guard, 251, 290, *298*, 303, *338*, 352
Coleman, Max D., 332
Colleville-sur-Mer, xxv, 69
*Collier's Weekly*, xxi, xxii, 53, 124, 261, 265, 333, 432, 439
Collins, J. Lawton, 250–51
Colman, Harper, 294
Colman, M. J., 442
*Combattante, La*, 401–2
commandos, 9, 79–80, 82, 198, *413*, 451–52
    Rangers modeled after, 317–18
    on Sword Beach, 421–24, 428
Compton, Lynn "Buck," 307–9
condoms, 143
Confederate Army, 339, 340
Cooke, Albert, 418–19
Corder, Frank, 358
Cornish, Peggy, 441
Corry, Al, 283–85
*Corry*, USS, 299–302, 377
COSSAC (Chief of Staff to the Supreme Allied Commander), 25–27, 36, 38, 39, 42, 184
Cota, Norman "Dutch," 364–67, 457, 462
Cotentin Peninsula, 28, 37–40, 275, 276, 282, 331, 465
    Sainte-Mère-Église, xvii, 233, 240–49, *240*, 313, 465, 478, 484, 490

Cottrell, David, 415

Coughlan, Bill, 58–59

Courseulles, 401, 407

Courtney, W. B., xxii, 265

Crawford, Eva, 441

Crean, Cyril Patrick, 418

Cremieux-Brilhac, Jean-Louis, 270–71

Crépon, 398

cricket clickers, xvii, 155, 232

Criegern, Friedrich von, 477–78

Crimea, 136

Crocker, John Tredinnick, 197

Crocodile tanks, 389

Crook, Richard, 335, 336, 377

Culoville, 482

Cunard Line, 43, 48

Cunningham, Andrew B., 26

*Curacoa*, HMS, 45–47

currency, 143, 194

Curtis, L. R., 421–22

Cutler, Jacob N., 494–95

Czechoslovakia, 80


Dacier, Jean, 271

*Daily Express*, 146

Dale, Robert, 174

Dalgleish, John, 9, 20, 26, 29, 38, 76, 104,
      105, 138, 141, 166, 253

Dalmatia, 65

Damski, Aloysius, 62, 66

Dandi-colle, Jean Renaud, 271

Danzig, 4

Davidson, Helen, 441

Dawson, Francis W., 361, 367, 368

Dawson, Joe, 367–68, 493

D-Day (Normandy landings;
      Operation NEPTUNE), xiii–xix,
      21, 183, 363, 370, 457–63
   airborne landings in, 183, 190–96,
      *190*, 197–208, *197*
   air campaigns in, 281–87, *281*, 319

beaches in, 184–85, 224; *see also* Gold
      Beach; Juno Beach; Omaha
      Beach; Sword Beach; Utah
      Beach
beginning of, *xxi*, 190–96, *190*, 449
bombing runs in, 282–85, 287, 319
books on, xiv, xvi
British airborne missions in,
      197–208, *197*, 209–22, *209*, 223
British commandos in, *see*
      commandos
British fleet in, 251
casualties in, 479–80, 489, 494
casualty estimates for, 152–53, 155, 191,
      479–80
church services and, 153–54, *250*,
      257–58
date for, 27, 35, 41, 126–36, 159, 160,
      172–79, 188
deception operations in, 83–88, *83*,
      266–72, *266*, 474
eastern flank of, 449–56
Eisenhower's decision to launch,
      177–79, 269
Eisenhower's Order of the Day
      message on, 187–89, 260, 285
end of, 479–87, *479*
Exercise TIGER rehearsal for,
      106–17, *106*, 414
films and television series about,
      xiv, xv
final preparations for, 143–44
final run-through meeting on, 133–35
first Allied soldier killed by enemy
      in, 205
first mission of, 197–208, *197*
French Resistance and, 269–72, 297
German awareness of invasion,
      273–80
German speculation on invasion,
      158–64, 274, 275

glider forces in, *see* gliders

Gold Beach on, *see* Gold Beach

H-Hours in, 3, 152, 183, 194, 282, 289, 333, 349, 365, 380, 401, 435, 436, 461

international nature of, xv–xvi, 126, 127, 251

Juno Beach on, *see* Juno Beach

La Fière Bridge battle in, 183, 464–73, *464*, 490

landing craft in, *see* landing craft

leaders' visits to troops prior to, 145–48, *145*

light and visibility conditions and, 130–32, 135

main invasion fleet in, 250–65, *250*, 266, *266*, 282

medics in, 372–74, 481, 485–86

Mulberry floating harbors in, 89–93, *89*, 490

myths about, xv, xvi

news of, 430–46, *430*

notifications to families of soldiers lost in, 495–96

Omaha Beach on, *see* Omaha Beach

Operation COUP DE MAIN in, 197–208, *197*

paratroopers in, *see* paratroopers

Pointe du Hoc in, 316–29, *316*, 331, 346, 347, 365, 458, 489

postponement of, 172–77, 188

railroads destroyed in preparation for, *118*, 119–23, 158–60

Rangers in, *see* Rangers

rescue ships in, *298*, 303–4

Sainte-Mère-Église in, xvii, 233, 240–49, *240*, 313, 465, 478, 484, 490

sand table models for, 77

ship sunk by Germans on, 415

6th Airborne's arrival in, 209–22, *209*

stripes painted on aircraft in, *281*, 282

Sword Beach on, *see* Sword Beach

tides and, 131, 132, 135, 166, 289, 302, *400*, 403, 418

training at Slapton Sands for, 94–105, *94*, 152

troop briefings on details of, 149–57, *149*

troops and supplies in Britain for, 50–60, *50*, 61, 67, 126–29

use of term, xiii

Utah Beach on, *see* Utah Beach

waterproofing of vehicles for, 103–5, 393

weather conditions and, 41, 130–33, 135, 159, 162, 165–79, *165*, 190, 264, 267, 269, 274

wording of communique for, 129

*see also* Operation OVERLORD

*D-Day, June 6, 1944* (Ambrose), 336n

*D-Day with the Screaming Eagles* (Koskimaki), xvi

DD (Dual-Drive) tanks, 101–3, 293, 335–36, 379, 396, 402, 403, *413*

deception operations, 83–88, *83*, 266–72, *266*, 474

De Filippo, Arthur, 243, 244

de Gaulle, Charles, 8, 23, 438

de Guingand, Francis "Freddie," 38, 40, 41, 105, 134, 172–73, 175, 176, 178

Della-Volpe, Ralph, 291

DeLong, James M., 283, 285

Dempsey, Miles, 35, 36, 414

Denmark, 7, 28, 65, 66

Dermer, Clayton H., 495

Dermer, Wayne E., 495n

Desmond, Barbara, 441–42

Devlin, Patrick, 143

de Vries, Jan, 212, 213

*Dickman*, USS, 305

Dieppe, 21, 37, 65, 365, 400, 402

diplomats, 78

Distinguished Conduct Medal, 455

Distinguished Service Cross, 309n, 313n, 315n, 465, 473

Dittmar, Robert, 345

Dives River, 198, 214

Dolan, John J., 464–72, 491

Dolan, Joseph A., 260, 290

Dominguez, Alexander, 342

Donaldson, James, 386

Doohan, James, 256

*Dorothea L. Dix*, USS, 256

Dos Passos, John, 259

double agents, 77–78, 87

Douglas, Sholto, 135n

Dover, 28

Dowling, Mike, 220

Downing, Veldon, 110, 117

*Doyle*, USS, 377–78

Drake, Francis, 252

Drez, Ronald, xvii

Dual-Drive (DD) tanks, 101–3, 293, 335–36, 379, 396, 402, 403, *413*

Dubé, Noël, 463

Dudka, Stanley, 408, 411

Duffy, Edward T., 51–53, 377, 480

Duke, Anthony Drexel, 49, 138–39, 265, 416, 492

DUKWs, 319, 418

Dulaney, Jack, 499

Dulligan, John F., 259

Duncan, J. S., 402, 403

Dunkirk, *3*, 7, 9, 21, 23, 30, 66, 383, 394

Dunn, Vincent, 108

Dupuy, R. Ernest, 433

Durant, Will, 259

During, Ernst, 276–77

Dutch East Indies, 17

Dyer, Ian, 219

Eads, James O., 155, 230, 486

Earll, Arden, 365

E-boats, 108–17, 262, 414–15

Eckert, Walter, 361

Eckstam, Eugene E., 107, 109, 112, 114, 117

Edmondson, Pauline, 4–6, 12

Edwards, Denis, 201, 202

Edwards, Kenneth, 406

Eedy, M. J., 391

Egypt, 10

Eikner, James W., 317, 318, 320–21, 324–28, 347

Eisenhower, Dwight, xix, xxii, 30, 32, 33, *34*, 69, 78, 84, 85, 93, 115, 119, 127, 129, 146, 155, 157, 167, 168, 170, 172, *187*, 193, 284, 380, 433, 497, 499

   airborne landings and, 191–96

   Allied bombing campaign and, 119, 121, 122

   Biddle and, 139

   on Black soldiers in England, 58, 59

   Brooke's view of, 40n, 134n

   on captured enemy document, 492–93

   on Cherbourg-Havre landings, 381

   and Churchill's desire to accompany invasion, 156, 157

   date and timing of invasion set by, 127, 129, 131–33, 135–36

   on D-Day air missions, 287

   D-Day message to the people of Europe, 433

   Duke and, 139

   in final run-through meeting on D-Day, 133–35

   invasion launch decision of, 177–79, 269

   Monteith and, 372

on movement of units, 138

Mulberry harbors and, 90

Omaha Beach reports and, 380

Order of the Day message of, 187–89, 260, 285

in OVERLORD planning, 36–41, 77, 165, 289

Rangers and, 317–18, 329

and secrecy around OVERLORD plans, 78

selected as Supreme Commander of OVERLORD, 32, 33, 34

Smith and, 32–33

on supplies, 128

troops visited by, 146

victory message of, 497

weather conditions and, 130, 133, 165–68, *165*, 171, 172, 176–79, 269

in wording of communique for OVERLORD, 129

Eisenhower, John, 188

Eisenhower Center, xvii

El Alamein, 383

Elbe River, 3

Elder, Gene E., 319

Elder, Ned, 335

Ellery, John B., xxiii, 364, 459–60, 487

Elsey, George McKee, 4, 15, 21, 76, 256–57, 378, 379

*Emmons*, USS, 377

*Empire Gauntlet*, HMS, 305

*Empire Javelin*, HMS, 101, 252, 334, 340

England, *see* Great Britain

English Channel, xvii, 65, 107, 166–69, 176, 191, 223, 225, 251, 253, 262, 287, 302, 331, 383

first plans for cross-Channel invasion, 21–23, 24–26

radar jamming and deception over, 266–69

rescue ships in, *298*, 303–4

*see also* Pas de Calais

Enigma, 43

Epstein, Herb, 367

Escher, Rudi, 241, 242, 245

Escoville, 476

Estoppey, Ethel, 498

Eugene, Clayton, 352

Evans, James L., 194

Exercise TIGER, 106–17, *106*, 414

Fahey, Richard P., 353, 361

Falley, Wilhelm, 237

fascines, 390

Fast, Victor H., 360–61

Fauks, Barbara, 5, 54, 56, 57

Fauks, Paul S., 56, 57

Feduik, Frank R., 497

Fellers, Taylor N., 339, 340, 346

Ferrari, Gino, 100

FFI (French Forces of the Interior; French Resistance; maquis), 8, 62, 123, 269–72, 297

Finland, 65

fire ladders, 319

*Fitch*, USS, 302

Fitzgerald, John E., 225, 226, 230, 232–35, 238, 247, 248, 490

Flamand, Jean, 241, 242, 244–45, 249

Florida, 49

"flying dustbin," 389

foil "window" (chaff), 266–67, 269

Folsom, Daniel, 116

Fonda, Henry, 256

Fontainebleau, 63

food, 52–53, 55, 142, 143, 290, 410–12, 453, 459–61

rationing of, 14, 53, 55

*Forester*, USS, 377

*Forgotten* (Hervieux), xv

Fox, Dennis, 205–6

France, 6, 500
   Allied destruction of railway system
      of, *118*, 119–23, 158–60
   civilian casualties in, 489
   declaration of war against Germany,
      4, 6
   German occupation of, 7, 8, 10, 61,
      62, 76, 253
   liberation of, xiii–xv, 240–49, 253,
      272, 422, 433, 438, 490
Frank, Anne, 444
*Frankford*, USS, 377
Freed, Richard A., Sr., 500
Free French Forces, 121, 376, 421, 423
Free French Propaganda Committee,
      270, 272
French Forces of the Interior (French
      Resistance; maquis), 8, 62, 123,
      269–72, 297
French money, 143, 194
Friedenberg, Bernard, 373
Friedman, William, 365
Fromm, Curt, 72
Fudge, James T., 48, 49, 108, 150
Fuehr, Heinz, 163
Fuerst, Heinrich, 164
Fuller, Ted, 226
Fullerlove, Don, 389
Furlong, Dan, 231

Galdonik, Clair R., 264, 290, 293–94,
      310
Gale, Edwin, 254–55, 296, 297
Gale, Humfrey, 135n
Gale, Richard "Windy," 198–200, 207,
      212, 213, 215–18
Gangewere, Robert, 294, 295
Garay, Paul N., 300–302
Garbett, Robert, Jr., 350
Gariepy, Leo, 402, 403, 407
Garing, Edward N., 343–44

Gauthier, Sims, 293
Gautier, Leon, 422
Gavigan, Owen, 296
Gavin, James M., 20, 21, 37, 72–73, 85,
      142, 154, 194, 466, 468, 469
Gellhorn, Martha, xv, 53, 124, 432,
      439–40
Genoa, 67
George VI, King, 76, 133, 134, 135n,
      147–48
   and Churchill's desire to accompany
      invasion, 157
*Georges Leygues*, 376
Gerbrandy, Pieter Sjoerds, 434
Gerhardt, Charles, 252
Germany, Nazi, xiv, 15, 60, 79–80, 188,
      253, 435, 436, 458–59, 462, 489,
      494–97, 500
   Allied air campaign against, 35,
      118–25, *118*, 158–60
   Allied invasion awareness in, 273–80
   Allied invasion speculation in,
      158–64, 274, 275
   Atlantic Wall of, *see* Atlantic Wall
   in Battle of the Bulge, 486, 494, 497
   Britain bombed by, 9–14, 30, 51, 54,
      56, 57, 84
   British invasion plans of, 7–11, 61, 65
   Buchenwald camp in, 495
   combined-arms strategy of, 14
   counterattacks by, 474–78, *474*, 480,
      490–92
   D-Day news reports in, 431–32,
      443–44
   declarations of war against, 4, 6
   eastern flank forces of, 449–56
   empire of, 21
   and end of D-Day, 479–86
   Enigma code system of, 43
   France liberated from, xiii–xv,
      240–49, 253, 272, 422, 433, 438, 490

France occupied by, 7, 8, 10, 61, 62, 76, 253

Gold Beach forces of, 383, 384, 387–91, 392, 393, 396–99

Juno Beach forces of, 400–401, 403–4, 407–9, 411, 475

Kriegsmarine of, *see* Kriegsmarine

in La Fière Bridge battle, *464*, 465–73, 490

Low Countries invaded by, 6, 7, 62

Luftwaffe of, 10, 11, 13, 69, 70, 285–86

Normandy occupation of, 61, 68, 71, 72, 231–33, 235–39, 240–41, 243–49, 273–80, *273*

Omaha Beach forces of, 332, 334, 336, 337, 341–50, 352, 354–57, 359, 360, 363, 364, 367–72, 375–79, 400, *457*, 476

paratroopers of, 154

Pointe du Hoc forces of, 316, *316*, 317, 321, 323–27, 331

Poland invaded by, 4, 6

prisoner of war camps in, 443–44

prisoners from, xxiii, 368–69, 397, 398, 409, 410, 420, 425–26, 428, 456, 467

ship sunk by, 415

shortages in, 158, 160, 253

Soviet nonaggression pact with, 6, 14

Soviet war with, 14–15, 17, 29–30, 62, 67, 136

spies of, 77–78

surrender of, 497

Sword Beach forces of, 414–21, 425, 427–29, 475

Utah Beach forces of, 289, 291, 292, 295–97, 298, 299, 306–15

Wehrmacht of, 10, 62, 160

Gerolstein, Paul, 112

Gerow, Leonard, 251, 379

Gerstner, Wilhelm, 475

Geyr von Schweppenburg, Leo Freiherr, 69–70

Gibraltar, 75, 87

Giguere, Robert, 483

Gillard, Frank, 128

Gillen, Patrick "Paddy," 422, 423

Giller, Edward, 122, 265, 286

gliders, 99, *190*, 209–13, *209*, 216–18, 220, 223, 233–36, 282, 283, 285, 380, 413, 475, 477

in Operation COUP DE MAIN, *197*, 198–203, 205, 206

Rommel's "asparagus" defense against, 71–73, 75, 79, 211, 451

Gockel, Franz, 62, 69, 72, 162, 163, 278–80, 354–56

Goebbels, Joseph, 65

Gold Beach, xiv, 184, 251, *382*, 395, 398, 453, 490

German forces on, 383, 384, 387–91, 392, 393, 396–99

Jig sector of, 382–91, 392

King sector of, 383, 389, 392–99

*Golden Hind*, 252

Gondrée Cafe, 203, 204, 207

Goranson, Ralph, 347–49

Gordon, Douglas, 282

Gordon, W. B. K., 496

Gosling, Richard, 385

Grattidge, Harry, 47

Gray, William, 451

Graye-sur-Mer, 401

Great Britain, xiv, 6

airborne missions of, 197–208, *197*, 209–22, *209*, 223

Battle of Britain, 10, 17

commando forces of, *see* commandos

declaration of war against Germany, 4, 6

Great Britain (*cont.*)

evacuations of villagers for troops' training in, 94–98, *94*

German bombing of, 9–14, 30, 51, 54, 56, 57, 84

German invasion threat to, 7–11, 61, 65

German spies and, 77–78

Harrogate program in, 10

Royal Air Force, 10, 11, 119, 125, 131, 281, 282, 319

Royal Navy, 251, 261

Soviet alliance with, 14

Sword Beach forces of, *see* Sword Beach

troops and supplies in, 50–60, *50*, 61, 67, 126–29

U.S. alliance with, 15, 17–18, 20, 21

U.S. soldiers in, 50–60, *50*, 61, 67, 126–28

U.S. soldiers transported to, 30, 42–49, *42*, *50*

Greatest Generation, xv

Greece, 65, 67

Green, Jimmy, 334, 340, 341

Greene, Ralph C., 116

Green Howards, 383, 392–99, *392*

Greenock, 45

Grey, Edward, 18

Griffing, Len, 140, 152, 155, 156, 232, 236

Grimbosq, 272

Grundfast, Sam, 292

Guarnere, Bill, 306–9

Gueritz, Edward, 420

Guernsey, 63

Guinness, Alec, 256

Gullet, Henry "Jo," 398

Gullickson, Grant G., 299, 300, 302–3

Gunther, John, 7

Gustav Line, 135–36

Gutekunst, Martin Fred, 51, 59, 311–12

Haakon VII, King, 432–34

Haas, Hyman, 257–58

Hall, Cecil, 385

Hall, John (private), 308

Hall, John L., Jr. (admiral), 251, 379

Hall, Vassar, 410

Hall, W. S., 417, 419, 477

Halton, Matthew, 401

Hamel-Hateau, Madame, 247–49

Hamilton, George Robert, 99

Hamilton, J. H., 403, 405–7

Hamlett, Warner "Buster," 44, 334

Hammerton, Ian, 102–3

Hangsterfer, Hank, 373

Harbott, Mrs. M., 196

*Harding*, USS, 376, 377

Hare, Nancy, 96–98

Harkey, R. L., 335

Harkiewicz, Joseph, 224–25, 282

Harlander, Douglas, 107, 110, 111

Harries, Jack, 210

Harriman, Averell, 14–17

Harris, Arthur Travers, 119–23, 269

Harris, Burt, 134n

Harris, Charles E., 284

Harris, Frederick G., 481

Harris, Molly, 440–41

Harrison, G., 378

Hart, Peggy M., 493

Harwood, Captain, 328

Hastings, Battle of, 148, 382–83

Hastings, Robin W. S., 394–95, 397, 399

Hathaway, Richard N., Jr., 366

Havener, J. K., 284, 285

Healey, Robert, 139, 140, 150–51

Heath, Jack, 405–6

"Hedgehogs," 393

hedgerows, 229–39, 285, 398–99, 490

Heim, Marcus, xix, 465, 468–73

Heintz, André, 79, 271

Heinze, Hans, 476

Hel Peninsula, 4

Hemingway, Ernest, xiv, xv, xxi, xxii, 256–57, 261, 333–34

Hemmings, Gordon "Bert," 443–44

Hennessy, Patrick, 418

Henry, Gerald Marley, 403–4, 410–12, 481–82, 484, 485

Henry, Lindsay, 362

Henson, Jake, 299

Hermann, Ernst, 241

Hermanville, 426–28

Hérouvillette, 476

Herring, Tom, 366

Hersh, Martin V., 238

Hervieux, Linda, xv, 58

Hesketh, Roger, 78, 90
    deception operations and, 84–87

Heydte, Friedrich August Freiherr von der, 275, 276

H-Hour, xiii
    in D-Day, 3, 152, 183, 194, 282, 289, 333, 349, 365, 380, 401, 435, 436, 461

Hickey, Raymond, 13

Hickman, Ainsley, 254, 262

Hickman, Heinrich Heinz, 204

Hicks, Floyd, 113–14

Higgins, Alan, 264

Higgins, Gerald, 225

Higgins Boats (LCVPs), *xxi*, 113, 184, 289–91, 293, 352, 353, 357, 378, 481, 482, 486

Hilberg, Ernest, 260

Hilborn, Richard, 212–14

Hill, Jake, 326

Hill, James, 214, 218

Hillman, Paul F., 104–5

Hillman position, 454–56

Hitler, Adolf, xiv, 6–11, 14, 15, 18, 22, 60, 69, 70, 76, 160, 162, 260, 274, 287, 299, 436, 486, 500
    Allied invasion and, 274, 278

Allied invasion speculation of, 158, 159

Atlantic Wall and, 63, 64, 67, 68

Chamberlain and, 4

generals and, 67–68

*Mein Kampf,* 253

Pas de Calais viewed as prospective target by, 28–29

Pointe du Hoc and, 317

Rommel and, 67, 70, 273, 274

Stalin's nonaggression pact with, 6, 14

war plan of, 253

Hitlerjugend, 491

Hoback, Bedford, 252, 345, 346

Hoback, Lucille, 20

Hoban, B. M. S., 392–94

Hobart, Percy, 102–3

Hobart's Funnies, 101, 103, 383, 389

Hodenfield, Gaylord K., 320, 322, 324, 325

Hoffman, Bill, 324

Hoffman, George Dewey, 299, 302

Hoffmann, Heinrich, 414

Hoffner, Barnett, 115, 376, 458–59

Hogben, Lawrence, 132, 168–70, 177

Holland, 10, 27, 28, 494, 497

Holland, William, 111

Holley, I. G., 388–89

Hollis, Stanley E., xix, 394–99

Hollis, William J., 480

Holmes, Patrick, 45, 46

Hooper, Eric, 386

Hooper, John, xxiv, 260, 360, 459, 460

Hope, Bob, 446

Horn, Josef, 276

Horne, Tommy, 243, 244

Horner, Charles, 374

Horsa Bridge, 198

Hoskot, Nathaniel R., 232

Hough, Stan, 415

Howard, Everett Dale, 302

Howard, John, xix, 198, 199, 201–3, 205–8, 209, 216, 413, 449–52

Howard, Roy, 205

Howard, Wilfred Robert, 452

Howell, Ray, 104, 105, 144, 150, 256

Huddleston, Allen, 52

Huebner, Clarence, 115

Hughes-Hallett, John, 90

Hull, C. MacDonald, 397

Hungary, 80

Hunter, Jim "Tich," 455

Hürtgen Forest, 315n, 494

Hutchin, F. J., 443

Île-de-France, 161

Imperial War Museum, xvii

India, 30, 443

"In Flanders Fields" (McCrae), 406–7

Ingersoll, Ralph, 10–11, 26, 27, 30, 120, 129, 258, 265, 311
    on American soldiers in England, 55
    on Dieppe mission, 21
    on Exercise TIGER, 117
    on "sausage" camps, 140
    on Utah Beach landing, 291–92

Ingrisano, Michael N., 285

Ireland, 78, 84, 92, 154, 155, 174, 250, 339, 497

Irving, Bill, 214, 215

Isaacs, Jack R., 155

Ismay, Hastings, 30–32, 35, 37, 40, 78, 129, 170–71
    Allied bombing campaign and, 119–21
    and Churchill's desire to accompany invasion, 156, 157
    on D-Day timing, 131
    deception operations and, 86, 87
    Mulberry harbors and, 90–91
    weather and, 173

Italy, xiv, 10, 64, 65, 67, 69, 90, 99, 120, 135–36, 154, 155, 160, 436
    Rome, 135–36, 430, 436, 440, 445

Ivy Bridge, 60

Jackman, Joan A., 268

Jackson, Schuyler W. "Sky," xxii, xxiv, 225, 238

Jackson, Thomas J. "Stonewall," 339, 340

James, Clifton, 87–88

Japan, xiv, 15, 17, 18, 21, 30, 497
    Pearl Harbor attacked by, 15–17, 19, 19, 20, 361, 376
    prisoner of war camps in, 441, 444

Jaujard, Robert, 376

Jayich, Matt, 299

Jefferson, Alan, 218–21

Jeffries, David, 385

Jennings, Leroy, 360

Jennings, W. H., 427–28

Jersey, 63

Jewish people, xxv, 79, 257–58, 421, 495

Jeziorski, Edward J., 16, 144

Johnson, Alfred, 44–46

Johnson, Gerden, 313

Johnson, Legrand "Legs," 155

Johnston, Roland, 409–10

Jones, Aaron B., 370–71

Jones, James, 376

Juno Beach, xiv, 184, 251, 256, 383, 400–412, 400, 414, 453, 454
    German forces on, 400–401, 403–4, 407–9, 411, 475
    sectors of, 185, 401

Jutland, Battle of, 148, 157

Kafkalas, Nicholas, 345

Karl, Rudolf, 323

Kaye, Mrs. M., 442

Keating, Jack, 370

Keil, Günther, 247, 249

Kellam, Major, 472
Keller, Rod, 401
Kellman, Steve, 353
Kelly, Edward J., 55
Kelly, N. T. "Tom," 427, 428
*Kelvin*, HMS, 415
Kent, 86, 87
Kerchner, George, 319, 322–25, 327, 328
Kesselring, Albert, 136
Key, Hazel, 196
Kieffer Commandos, 421
Kindersley, Hugh, 210
King, Ernest, 90
Kirk, Alan G., 35, 37–38, 54, 76, 96, 130, 147, 251, 379
Kitchen, Robert J., 440
Knox, Nora, 440
Koenig, Marie-Pierre, 121
Korean War, 500
Kortenhaus, Werner, 164
Koskimaki, George, xvi, 191, 192, 194, 195, 236
Kraiss, Dietrich, 332
Kriegsmarine, 70
   E-boats of, 108–17, 262, 414–15
   U-boats of, 15, 30, 43, 45, 286
Kuhn, Jack, 327

Lack, Norman, 105
Lacy, Father, 359
La Fière Bridge, Battle of, 183, 464–73, *464*, 490
La Guardia, Fiorello, 439
Lamb, Waylen "Pete," 226, 233, 499
La Naves, M., 271, 272
landing craft, 126, *126*, 151, 183–84, 264, 364, *375*, 378, 394–95, 422
   Landing Craft Assault (LCA), 184, 289, 318, 319, 322, 344, 347, 359, 386, 405
   Landing Craft Control (LCC), 289

Landing Craft Infantry (LCI), 184, 288, 358, 373, 423, 490
Landing Craft Mechanized (LCM), 290
Landing Craft Tank (LCT), 184, 254, 263, 289, 293, 303, 304, 333, 335–37, 352, 373, 387, 392, 393, 396, 402, 411, 490
Landing Craft Vehicle/Personnel (LCVP; Higgins Boat), *xxi*, 113, 184, 289–91, 293, 352, 353, 357, 378, 481, 482, 486
Landing Ship Tank (LST), 48, 49, *106*, 107–17, 184, 288, 291, 417, 461, 490
   obstacle clearance units for, 406
   in operation plan, *185*
   production of, 38, 48
Lane, George, 79, 80
La Roche Guyon, 161
*Last Battle, The* (Ryan), xvii
Latta, Kermit R., 193
leadership, xix, 364
Leahy, William D., 21, 22, 31, 32
Lebenson, Leonard, 234
Lees, Howard, 296
Legere, Lawrence J., 236
Le Grand Chemin, 306
Le Hamel, 384, 387, 389–91
Le Havre, 28, 39, 212, 267, 316, 381, 414
Leigh-Mallory, Trafford, 34, *34*, 37, 39, 119, 155, 176, 194, 281, 380
Le Moulin, 151
Lend-Lease program, 15, 20
Leningrad, 65
Leroux family, 467, 468
Le Roy, Rene, 423
Les Droueries, 481
Leslie, Charles A., 59
letters, 140–41
Levin, Philip, 46, 47

Liberty Bell, 439

Library of Congress, xvi

Libya, 17

Liège, 494

*Life*, xxv, 127, 192, 256, 257, 356, 373, 483

Lindo, R. J., 4

Lipton, C. Carwood, 306–9, 482

Little, Bill, 102, 402, 409

Littlefield, G. A., 290

Lloyd, William Edward, 419

Lofthouse, Ronald, 397, 399

Lomell, Leonard G., xix, xxii, 321, 323, 325, 327–28

London, 5, 9, 53, 56, 78, 125, 127
   Blitz in, 11–13
   D-Day news in, 434, 437–38

London Fire Department, 319

*Longest Day, The* (Ryan), xvii

Longley, William T., 255

Longmate, Norman, 52

LORAN, 291

Lovat, Simon Fraser, Lord, 99, 153, 154, 198, 451–52
   on Sword Beach, *413*, 414, 421–24, 428

Lovegrove, Henry, 395

Lovelace, Roger, 284

Low Countries, 62, 119
   Belgium, 6, 7, 10, 27, 28, 434
   Luxembourg, 7
   Netherlands, 6, 7, 434

LSTs (Landing Ship Tanks), 48, 49, *106*, 107–17, 184, 288, 291, 417, 461, 490

Luck, Hans von, 71, 161, 162, 274, 276, 278, 476–78

Ludwig, Lt., 268

Luftwaffe, 10, 11, 13, 69, 70, 285–86

Luxembourg, 7


Mabry, George, 295, 314, 315

MacAllister, John, 462

MacArthur, Douglas, 30

machine guns, 308–9, 375, 453, *474*

*Maclean's*, 404, 412

MacPhee, John H., 100, 360

MacRitchie, Peter, 402

Macy, Jim, 482

Madden, John, 213

Maher, Brendan A., 262

Maimone, Salva P., 318, 328

Malarkey, Don, 306–9, 500

Malley, Charles, 173–74

Malta, 10

*Manhattan Transfer* (Dos Passos), 259

Manoir de la Fière, 466–69

maquis (French Forces of the Interior; French Resistance), 8, 62, 123, 269–72, 297

Marcks, Erich, 162

Markum, Arkie, 148

Marquis, Maynard, 52, 60, 498, 499

Marshall, George C., xix, 31–32, 120

Marshall, Herbert, 444–45

Marshall, S. L. A., 343–44, 465

Martin, Allin, 46

Martin, Bernard, 401–2

Martin, Charlie, 404

Martin, Hugh, 371

Masson, A. W., 47

Masters, Peter, 55, 79–80, 422–26, 429, 453

Mather, John, 143

Mauger, Maurice, 246

Maurer, Elmer, 301, 302

Mazzara, Buddy, xxiii, 358, 499

McAuliffe, Anthony, 194

McCallum, Sidney L. "Mickey," 193

McCann, Joseph "Eddie," 114

*McCook*, USS, 376

McDonald, John, 408, 409

McGirr, John P., 293

McKee, Jim, 261, 291, 310, 313–14, 480

McKernon, Francis "Mac," 299–301

McLean, Ian, 496

McLean, John, 123, 406

McMath, Allen, 101, 142

McNabb, Edward, 359

McPhail, R. V., 304

McTier, Kelly, 405

Medal of Honor, xvn, 315n, 371–72, 374n, 465

medics, 372–74, 481, 485–86

Mediterranean, 10, 22, 48, 65, 155

Meehan, Thomas, 227

*Meet the Americans*, 54

*Mein Kampf* (Hitler), 253

*Melbreak*, HMS, 375

Melvin, Howard, 497

Merderet River, 235, 465

Merrill, Richard, 358

Merville Battery, 183, 191, 198, 214, 216–22

Metcalf, Graeme, 212

Metropole Hotel, 441

Meyer, Hubert, 277–78

Meyer, Irmgard, 277–78

Miele, Valentine M., 100, 101

Miles, Peter, 383

Military Cross, 394

Miller, C. H., 95

Miller, Charles "Chuck," 242

Miller, Russell, xvi

Millin, Bill, *415*, 421, 422, 425, 428, 451, 452

mines, 66, 71, 73, 79, 101, 103, 230, 254, 261, 262, 454, 460, 469

   on Gold Beach, 383, 389, 390, 393, 396

   on Juno Beach, 402

   on Omaha Beach, 356, 357

   on Sword Beach, 417, 418, 420, 422–24, 426

   on Utah Beach, 289, 292, 310–13

Minogue, Joe, xxiii, 102, 103, 385–88, 486

Modeste, Charles E., 115

Mohrle, Charles, 20, 123, 282, 283, 286, 287

Mominee, Albert, 128, 142, 358

*Montcalm*, 376

Monteith, Jimmie W., Jr., 353, 370–72

Mont Fleury, 398

Montgomery, Bernard L., xviii, xix, *34*, 38, 69, 134, 171, 174, 176–78, 380

   beginning of war and, 4

   Brooke and, 134n, 135n

   deception operation and, 87–88

   in final run-through meeting on D-Day, 133, 134, 134n

   in OVERLORD planning, 33, 34–37, 39, 40n

   Sword Beach and, 414

   troops visited by, *145*, 146–48

   workers visited by, 147

Moody, Lt., 349

Moon, Don P., 106, 116, 250, 260, 296

Moore, Kenneth, 481

Moorehead, Alan, 146–47

Moreno, John A., 260

Morgan, Frederick, xviii, 22, 88, 170, 267, 268

   Mulberry harbors and, 90–92

   in OVERLORD planning, 25–31, 33, 36–38, 84

   on waterproofing vehicles, 104, 105

Moriarty, William J., 123, 283

Morison, Samuel Eliot, 363–64, 490

*Morning Call*, xvi

Morris, C., 141, 384

motor torpedo boats (MTBs), 80, 81

Mountbatten, Louis, 21, 79, 91

Movement Control, 138

Mulberry harbors, 89–93, *89*, 490

Munch, Andrew G., 403

Munro, Les, 268

Munro, Russ, 407

Munson, Curtis, 379

Murdoch, Gilbert Gray, 334, 340, 342, 343, 349–50
Murdoch, James F., 109
Murphy, Robert M., 465–71, 473, 490–91
Murray, Iain, 210, 211
Murrow, Edward R., 11–14
music, 58–59, *187*
Mussolini, Benito, 18, 30

Nance, Ray, 20, 341–42, 344
Naples, 155
Napoleon, 22
National D-Day Memorial, 479
National Guard, 339, 340
National World War II Museum, xvii
Navy Cross, 336n
Nazi Germany, *see* Germany, Nazi
NBC, 7, 15–16, 431, 435, 436, 446
Neave, Robert, 418
Nelson, Donald, 369
*Nelson*, HMS, 402
Netherlands, 6, 7, 434
*Nevada*, USS, *19*, 376
Nevins, Arthur S., 168–69
New Georgia, 495n
New Jersey, 43, 44
Newmyer, Arthur, 333
New Orleans, LA, 49
*Newsweek*, xvi
New York (state), 43
New York, NY, 439
    Times Square, *430*
*New Yorker*, 6, 127, 440
New Zealand, 6
Nicolson, George, 496
Nixon, Richard, 313n
Norfolk, VA, 497
Norfolk House, 25, 90
Normandy, 29, 143, 230, 489–90, 500
    cemeteries in, 500
    farms in, 143

German occupation of, 61, 68, 71, 72, 231–33, 235–39, 240–41, 243–49, 273–80, *273*
    hedgerows in, 229–39, 285, 398–99, 490
    Rommel's "asparagus" in, 71–73, 75, 79, 211, 451
Normandy landings, *see* D-Day
Norred, C. A., 442
North Africa, 10, 22, 32, 33, 90, 99, 114n, 224, 259, 338, 339, 352, 394
    Rommel in, 30, 64, 161–62
    "TO GIB" designation and, 75
North Sea, 28, 65, 66
Norway, 7, 27, 65, 66, 67n, 432–34
    Allied deception plan and, 83–85
*Nothing Less than Victory* (Miller), xvi
Noyes, Nelson, 347
Nutter, Thomas, 415–16

Oakland, CA, 439
Oakley, Lt., 472
Obnack, John, 463
Ockenden, Frank, 211
Ogden-Smith, Bruce, 81
Ohio University, xvii
Olson, Allan, 462
Omaha Beach, xiv–xvi, *xxi*, xxv, 183, 184, 251, 256, 289, 297, 383, 403, 457, *457*, 462, 480, 481, 490, 500
    advance from, 363–74, *363*
    air bombing and, 282, 285
    cemetery on, *489*
    Charlie sector of, 184, 338
    creation of chart/maps of, 82
    Dog Green sector of, 3, 150, 185, 322, 338, 344, 365
    Dog Red sector of, 338, 351, 365
    Dog sector of, 184
    Dog White sector of, 322, 338, 351, 365

Easy Green sector of, xxiv, 338, 359
Easy Red sector of, xxiii, 338, 370
Easy sector of, 184
1st Infantry Division (Big Red One) at, 338, 352, 254, 257, 364
first wave of landings on, 331–37, *331*, 338–50, *338*, 351–62, *351*
first wave of landings on, diagram of, 330
Fox Green sector of, xiv, xxi, 338, 370, 379
Fox Red sector of, 338
Fox sector of, 184
geography of, 332
German forces on, 332, 334, 336, 337, 341–50, 352, 354–57, 359, 360, 363, 364, 367–72, 375–79, 400, *457*, 476
medics on, 372–74
naval forces at, 375–81, *375*
Pointe du Hoc and, 316–18, 321, 327–29, 331, 365
Rangers on, 346–49, 356, 365–67, 370
reports to Allied commanders from, 378–80
subsoil of, 81–82
troop briefings for invasion of, 150
villas on, 332
O'Neill, Bill (corporal), 376
O'Neill, James, 440
O'Neill, William T. (seaman), 100, 353
Operation ALBANY, 224
Operation BIG DRUM, 267
Operation BOSTON, 224
Operation CHICAGO, 233
Operation COUP DE MAIN, 197–208, *197*
Operation DEADSTICK, 198, 199, 209
Operation DETROIT, 233
Operation FORTITUDE, 83–88, *83*, 266, 268
Operation GLIMMER, 266–69

Operation MALLARD, 198
Operation OVERLORD, xiii–xv, xix, 25, 319
bombing of transportation lines in, 118–25, 158–60
deception operations in, 83–88, *83*, 266–72, *266*
Eisenhower selected as Supreme Commander of, 32, 33, 34
first plans for cross-Channel invasion of Europe, 21–23, 24–26
information-gathering about targets in, *75*, 78–82
landing craft shortage and, 38
launch of, *see* D-Day
leadership team formed for, 34–35
location chosen for, 27–29
naming of, 26, 27
planning of, xix, 24–33, *24*, 34–41, 61, 138, 165, 282, 289, 489
scope of, xiii–xiv, 29, 89, 134, 153, 165
secrecy surrounding, 75–82, 83, 167, 430
selection of commander for, 24–25, 27, 31–32, 34
shipping issues and, 30–31, 38
target date for, 27, 35, 41
transport of U.S. soldiers to Britain for, 30, 42–49, *42*, 50
U.S. soldiers in Britain for, 50–60, *50*, 61, 67
wording of communique for, 129
*see also* D-Day
Operation TAXABLE, 266–69
Operation TITANIC, 267, 474
Operation TONGA, 198, 218–19
Operation TORCH, 22, 30
O'Reilly, Vernon, 443
Orne River, 37–38, 198, 199, 205, 209, 276, 413, 476, 477
O'Rourke, Donald C., 465, 466, 468

Othon-Meillat, Irène, 280

Otlowski, William Boleslaw, 458

Otway, Terence, 216–22

Ouistreham, 38, 39, 284

Owens, William D., 469, 470, 472–73, 491

Oxfordshire and Buckinghamshire Light Infantry (Oxs and Bucks), 198, 205, 216, 450

Ozouf, Emil, 249

Pacific theater, 15, 48, 495n

Paget, Bernard, 171

Palys, Frank, 500

Panter-Downes, Mollie, 6, 9–11, 127, 439, 440

Panzers, 151, 277, 278, 452, 470, 475–77, 491

*Parade*, 53, 92, 423

paratroopers, 154–55, 163, 183, 190–96, 197–98, 200, 207, 209, 210, 223–28, *223*, 229–39, *229*, 261, 281–83, 289, 314, 421, 434–35, 449, 451, *464*, 474, 477, 478

drowning of, 229, 235

dummy, 267, 277, 474

faces blackened by, 192, 225

Germans' awareness of, 273, 275–77

hedgerows and, 229–39

Rommel's "asparagus" defense against, 71–73, 75, 79, 211, 451

in Sainte-Mère-Église, 240–47, 249

Paris, 29, 239

Parr, Wally, 203, 204

Parry, Allen, 220–22

Pas de Calais, 27–29, 63, 89, 267

Allied deception plan and, 83, *83*, 85–86

Passover, xxv

pathfinders, 224

Patterson, J. Robert, xxiv, 4, 497, 498

Patton, George, 86, 87

Peacock, Ascy, 101

Pearl Coast, 383

Pearl Harbor, attack on, 15–17, 19, *19*, 20, 361, 376

Pegasus Bridge, 183, *197*, 198, 205, 216, 413, 421, 464

Pegues, Carlos, 123

Pemsel, Max-Josef, 63, 64, 66, 68, 69, 73, 159–60

Pentecôte, Jeannette, 241–42

Perkin, Julian, 115

Perry, Leslie, 455

Petard gun, 389, 390

Peters, Debs H., 148

Peters, Walter, 283

Petersen, B. J., 301

Peterson, Herschel W., 310

Peterson, Lenold, 468, 471–73

Petterssen, Sverre, 130–32, 168–70, 175

Pflocksch, Gustav, xxii

Philadelphia, PA, 439

*Philadelphia Tribune*, 374

Pierlot, Hubert, 434

Pike, Exum, xxiii

Pilgrims, 252

pillboxes, 99, 101, 203, 217

on Gold Beach, 387, 389–91, 394, 395, 397, 398

on Omaha Beach, 336, 345, 355, 356, 376, 377

on Sword Beach, 417, 423

on Utah Beach, 292, 299

Pine, Winnifred, 56

Pipre, Pierre, 279–80

Plato, 259

Plitt, Carl, 370

Ploger, Robert, 463

Pluskat, Werner, 280

Plymouth, 107, 251–52

Pocket Guide to France, 143, 253

Poett, Nigel, 208, 213

Pogue, Forrest, 56–57, 76, 129, 339–40

Pointe de la Percée, 321, 346, 347, 349

Pointe du Hoc, 316–29, *316*, 331, 346, 347, 365, 458, 489

poison gas, 143, 483

Poland, 4, 6

Pompadour, Madame de, 64

pontoon barges, 461

Portsmouth, 128, 135, 166, 168, 170, 176

Portsmouth D-Day Story Museum, xvi

Port Staging Areas, 43

Portugal, 67

Potter, D. C., 384, 385

Pouppeville, 311, 314

Pratt, Derek, 417

Pratt, Don, 233

Prince, Morris, 317

*Prince Charles*, HMS, 320

Pryne, Gordon, 468, 469, 471–73

Puck, 4

Purple Heart, 497–99

Pyle, Ernie, 125

Q Planning Branch, 26

*Queen Elizabeth*, RMS, 43, 44

*Queen Mary*, RMS, 43–47

Raaen, J. C., 366

Raaen, John, 321–22, 359, 365–67

Raatz, Duwaine, 352

Rabe, Gunther, 107, 108

Rachmann, Franz, 279, 355

racial prejudice, 57–60, 126, 498
    *see also* Black soldiers

radar, 10, 43, 224, 262, 267, 269, 286, 289, 414
    jamming and deception operations, 266–69

Rader, Robert "Rook," 226

Ragan, Paul, 335

railroads, bombing of, *118*, 119–23, 158–60

*Ramillies*, HMS, 402

Ramsay, Bertram H., xix, 34, *34*, 37, 134n, 156, 166, 171, 176, 256, 490

Rand, Cyril, 140, 144, 153, 252, 46, 417, 420–21

Rangers, xxii, 251, 421, 478, 481
    creation of, 317–18
    on Omaha Beach, 346–49, 356, 365–67, 370
    at Pointe du Hoc, 316–29, *316*, 489

Ranney, Myron "Mike," xxv, 307

Ranville, 208, 209, 216, 452, 453, 476

Rayner, Ralph, 97–98

Rayson, George, 454–56

Reagan, Ronald, xxii

Red Cross, 124, 142, 191, 227, 285, 440, 473

Reeder, Russell "Red," 313

Rees, Goronwy, 25

refugees, xvi, 80, 421

Reichert, Josef, 275–77

Reisenleiter, Harry L., 236, 494

Renaud, Alexandre, 72, 163, 241–44, 246–48, 490

Rennes, 275

rescue ships, *298*, 303–4

Resnick, Nathan, 111–12

Reuters, 153, 424, 426, 443

Reville, John J., xxiv

Rhea, Powell, 254

Rhine River, 350, 494

"rhinos" (pontoon barges), 461

Rich, Oscar, 372–73

Richards, Albert, 221

Richards, John W., 194, 195, 225, 227, 238–39

Richardson, Alvin, 110

Richardson, Elliot L., 256, 312, 313n

Richmond Shipyards, 48

Ridgway, Matthew, 154, 155, 194, 224, 230, 236–37, 484, 493–94

Riggs, Clarius, 344

Ritchie, Gerald, 200

Roach, George, 342, 349–50

Roberson, Clarence "Pilgrim," 345

Roberts, Hazel, 13

*Roberts*, HMS, 415

Robertson, John, 353, 357, 360, 484

Rockwell, Dean L., 173, 262, 335, 336, 461–62

Roebuck, Lionel, 418

Rogge, Robert, 401, 408–9

Romanski, Kenneth L., 359

Rome, 135–36, 430, 436, 440, 445

Rommel, Erwin, 22, 79, 158–61, 164, 274, 313, 397, 451, 475, 476, 478
  in Africa, 30, 64, 161–62
  Allied invasion and, 273, 274, 278
  "asparagus" defenses of, 71–73, 75, 79, 211, 451
  Atlantic Wall and, *61*, 63–64, 67–74
  Bayerlein and, 161–62
  Hitler and, 67, 70, 273, 274
  letters to his wife, 63–64, 160

Rooney, Andy, xxi–xxv, 490

Roosevelt, Eleanor, 16, 18

Roosevelt, Franklin Delano, 6, 31
  Atlantic Charter and, 15
  and beginning of World War II, 6, 14–16
  at Casablanca conference, 24
  Churchill and, 15, 25n
  code words and, 25n
  D-Day prayer of, 445–46
  in OVERLORD planning, 24, 29, 31
  and U.S. entry into World War II, 16, 20
  war strategy of, 20–21
  World War I and, 14

Roosevelt, Theodore, Jr., 260, 261, 293, 296, 297

Rosevere, John "Rosie," 214–15

Ross, Bayer Noen, 496

Ross, Bull, 408

Rouen, 143

Rouinsky, Chief, 303

Rouse, A. R., 416–17

Rowland, Eric, 454–56

Royal Air Force, 10, 11, 119, 125, 131, 281, 282, 319

Royal Navy, 251, 261

Roysdon, Captain, 472

Rubin, Emanuel "Manny," 110

Rubin, Mort, 302

Rudder, James E., 317, 318, 321, 324, 326, 328, 329

Ruge, Friedrich, 63, 65, 68, 71, 73–74, 159, 161, 274

Rulien, Warren, 364–65

Rundstedt, Gerd von, 61–62, *61*, 64, 65, 69, 70, 162, 274

"Ruperts," 267

Russell, Ken, 243, 245

Ryan, Bill, 378

Ryan, Cornelius, xvii

Ryes, 477

Sabin, Lorenzo S., 376, 379

Sadlon, Steve, 108–10

St. Alban's Head, 254

Sainte-Croix, 406

Sainte-Marie-du-Mont, 306, 313

Sainte-Mère-Église, xvii, 233, 240–49, *240*, 313, 465, 478, 484, 490

Saint-Germain-de-Varreville, 313

Saint-Laurent-Sur-Mer, 151, 355, 376, 485

Saint-Lô, 458

St. Paul's School, military planning session at, 133–35

*Saladin*, HMS, 113

Salerno, 38, 69

Sales, Robert, 344–46, 496

Salinger, J. D., 256, 295

Salomon, Sidney A., 320, 346–49

Sammon, Charles E., 248

Sampson, Francis L., 231

Samuel, Bernard, 439

*Samuel Chase*, USS, 346, 352, 378

Sanders, Harry, 377

sand tables, 77

*San Francisco Examiner*, 443

Sark, 63

Satchell, Alister, 43

*Satterlee*, USS, 256, 321, 377

Satterwhite, William Eldridge, 286

*Saturday Evening Post*, 334

Saturday Night Massacre, 313n

"sausages" (camps), 137–44, *137*, 145

Sawyer, William M., 191, 238

Scaife, Herbert "Bert" Matthew, 390

Scandinavia, 83, 85

   Denmark, 7, 28, 65, 66

   Norway, *see* Norway

   Sweden, 67n

Schenk, Ivylyn, 442

Schenk, John, 442

Schlegel, Jack, 237

*Schleswig-Holstein*, SMS, 4

Schlieben, Karl-Wilhelm von, 69, 70, 275

Schmidt, Birdie, 124

Schmundt, Rudolf, 274

Schneider, Max, 322, 366, 367, 369

Schultz, Arthur B. "Dutch," 235

Scotland, 84–85, 250

Scott, Desmond, 283

Scott, Kenneth, 113

Scott-Bowden, Logan, 80, 81

Scribner, Donald L., xxiv, 319, 347–49

Seaborne, Ronald, 257, 258

seasickness, 130, 264, 285, 332–34, 353, 386, 403, 411

Sefton, Bill, 193, 195, 232

Seidl, Georg, 475–76, 478

Seine, 28, 37, 85, 123, 143, 161, 267, 276

Seitzler, Henry, xxi, 362, 372, 459, 462

Semken, John, 486–87

Semmes, James, 377

Seulles River, 400

Severloh, Hein, 354, 355

Sewell, Rency F., Jr., 292, 293

SHAEF (Supreme Headquarters, Allied Expeditionary Force), 33, 34–41, *34*, 42, 94, 123, 435

Shakespeare, William, 494

Shanahan, John, 419

Shannon, Bill, 199, 200

Shapiro, Lionel, 404, 412

Shaw, Charles, 437–38

Shea, Jack, 462

Shepard, Bert, 404

Shiloh, Battle of, xxi

Shirer, William, 6

*Short Guide to Great Britain, A*, 51

short snorters, 194

Shryock, Dennis, 297

*Shubrick*, USS, 480

Sicily, 30, 36, 90, 114n, 154, 155, 259, 338, 352, 370, 383

Sidlowski, Walter, 143

Siebel, Heinrich, 404

Siegfried Line, 29, 170

Silver Star, 309n, 313n, 473

Simeth, Peter, 279

Sirmons, Jim, 431–32

Skidmore, Charles E. "Chuck," Jr., 152, 235, 484, 485

Slapton Sands, 94–105, *94*, 152

   Exercise TIGER at, 106–17, *106*, 414

Slaughter, John Robert "Bob," 47, 52, 142, 150

Smith, A. D. C., 255
Smith, Bill, 348
Smith, C. T., 393–94
Smith, H. W. J., 393, 394, 398–99, 493
Smith, Kate, 438–39
Smith, Sandy, 202–4
Smith, Walter Bedell "Beetle," *34*, 115,
    128, 135, 155, 166–67, 170
  Allied bombing campaign and,
    120–22
  D-Day timing and, 130–32
  deception operations and, 86–88
  Eisenhower and, 32–33
  on invasion launch decision, 177–79
  Mulberry harbors and, 91–93
  in OVERLORD planning, 25, 32, 33,
    36–39, 79
  victory message and, 497
Smith, William C., 101
Snyder, Ronald, 245–46
Solkin, William N., 333, 334
Somaliland, 10
Sommers, Martin, 334
Sorenson, Clifford, 314
South, Frank E., 320–24, 326, 328
South Africa, 6
Southampton, 67
South Hams, 94–98
Southwick House, 166, 172, 176, 177
Soviet Union, xiv, 441, 486
  British alliance with, 14
  German nonaggression pact with,
    6, 14
  German war with, 14–15, 17, 29–30,
    62, 67, 136
  Poland invaded by, 4, 6
  U.S. alliance with, 14, 15
Spaatz, Carl "Tooey," 37, 67n, 119–20,
    134n, 146
Spain, 66, 87–88
Spalding, John, 357, 360, 368–69

Spanish Civil War, 270
Speidel, Hans, 63, 66, 68–71, 73, 158–61,
    274, 276, 277, 279, 476–77
Speirs, Ronald C., 309
spies, 77–78
Stagg, J. M., 130–33, 135, *165*, 166, 168–72,
    174–79
Stalin, Joseph, 29, 441
  at Casablanca conference, 24
  Churchill on, 40n
  Hitler's nonaggression pact with,
    6, 14
Stanier, Alexander, 386
*Stars and Stripes*, xvi, xxi, 259, 320, 322,
    490
State Department, 500
Stear, Stuart, 103, 104, 408, 410
Stedall, Geoff, 428
Stevens, Roy, 44, 46, 340–41
Stewart, Ollie, 58
Stocker, Ernie, 216
Stopp, Paul, 435
Storeby, Clayton E., 192, 231, 265
*Story of Philosophy, The* (Durant), 259
Strait of Dover, *see* Pas de Calais
Stump, William, 366
Sullivan, Charles R., 461, 462, 500
Summersby, Kay, 78, 127, 146, 167, 172,
    177, 178, 193, 195–96
*Sunday Express*, xvii
Sundby, Sigurd, 320
Supreme Allied Commander, 24–25
  Chief of Staff to (COSSAC), 25–27,
    36, 38, 39, 42, 184
  Eisenhower selected as, 32, 33, 34
Supreme Headquarters, Allied
    Expeditionary Force (SHAEF),
    33, 34–41, *34*, 42, 94, 123, 435
Sussex, 87
*Svenner*, HNoMS, 414–15
Swann, Frank, 212, 213

Sweden, 67n

Sweeney, John, 353–54

Sweeney, Maureen Flavin, 174

Sweeney, Tod, 205, 206, 450

*Swift*, HMS, 415

Sword Beach, xiv, 184, 198, 209, 251,
    413–29, *413*, 449, *449*, 453, 454

  commandos on, 421–24, 428

  first dispatch from, 426

  German forces on, 414–21, 425,
    427–29, 475

  sectors of, 184, 414, 416, 421

  villas on, 414


Talbot, Arthur George, 416

Talley, Benjamin, 378

*Talybont*, HMS, 375

*Tanatside*, HMS, 375

tanks, 163, 311, 333, 394, 419, 426–28, 450,
    453, 455, *464*, 469–71, 483, 491–92

  AVRE, 389, 390, 393

  Crocodile, 389

  Dual-Drive, 101–3, 293, 335–36, 379,
    396, 402, 403, *413*

  German defenses against, 393, 399

  Hobart's Funnies, 101, 103, 383, 389

  Panzers, 151, 277, 278, 452, 470, 475–77,
    491

Task Force U, 106

Tateson, Tom, 140–41

Taylor, George, 364–65, 457

Taylor, John, 226

Taylor, Maxwell D., 174, 192–94, 224,
    237–38, 314, 315

Taylor, Ray, 226

Teass, Elizabeth, 495

Tedder, Arthur W., 34, *34*, 37, 77, 119,
    146, 172

*Texas*, USS, xvii, 319, 328, 333, 334, 377

Thames, 92

Theil, Rudolf, 276

Thistle, Hubert, 408, 491–92, 496

Thomas, David E., 235

Thomas, Ginger, 26

Thomas, Ralph, 468

*Thompson*, USS, 377

Thompstone, Tim, 393

Thornton, Martin "Wagger," 450

*Thurston*, USS, 378

Tibbs, David, 452, 453

tides, 131, 132, 135, 166, 289, 302, *400*, 403,
    418

TIGER Exercise, 106–17, *106*, 414

*Time*, xvi, 4, 441, 442

TNT, 463

Todt Organisation, 63, 70, 316, 451

Tomasi, Lt., 359

torpedo boats

  British motor torpedo boats, 80, 81

  German E-boats, 108–17, 262, 414–15

torpedoes, Bangalore, 367, 370, 406,
    454

tow planes, *190*, 233

Transportation Plan bombing
    campaign, 118–25, 158–60

Trappes, 122

Travett, Norman, 387, 389, 390

*Tree Grows in Brooklyn, A* (Smith), 258

Troarn, 214, 215

Trombold, Walter, 48

Troop X, 421

Trout, Robert, 434

Truscott, Lucian, 317–18

Tunisia, 36

Turk, Walter M., 194

Turkey, 67

Twenty Committee, 77–78


U-boats, 15, 30, 43, 45, 286

Ulan, Sidney M., 227

uniforms, 143–44, 483

United Kingdom, *see* Great Britain

United States
  British alliance with, 15, 17–18, 20, 21
  isolationism in, 6
  Lend-Lease program of, 15, 20
  soldiers from, in Britain, 50–60, 50,
    61, 67, 126–28
  soldiers transported to Britain from,
    30, 42–49, 42, 50
  Soviet alliance with, 14
  World War II entry of, 6, 14–15,
    19–20
United States Information Agency
  (USIA), 500
USO, 59
Utah Beach, xiv, xxiii, 39, 130, 183, 184,
    190, 195, 250, 251, 284, 331, 332, 379,
    380, 403, 465, 480
  Bigot-Neptune analysis of, 289–90
  casualties on, 117n
  Company E, 506th Parachute
    Infantry on, 306–9
  creation of chart/maps of, 82
  Exercise TIGER rehearsal for
    landing at, 106–17, 106, 414
  geography of, 289–92
  German forces on, 289, 291, 292,
    295–97, 298, 299, 306–14
  landing on, 288–97, 288
  naval forces at, 298–304, 298
  paratroopers on, 154
  Pointe du Hoc and, 316, 327
  second wave at, 305–15, 305
  strategic importance of, 289
  Tare sector of, 184, 289
  Transport Area on, 288
  troop briefings for invasion of, 152
  Uncle sector of, 184, 289
  Victor sector of, 289

Valance, Thomas, 342, 343, 350, 460, 461
Vandercook, John, 435

Van Gorder, Charles O., 234
Varaville, 214
Varreville, 39
Vaughn, John Jacob, 205
VE Day, 497
Verlaine, Paul, 270
Vermeer, Elmer H. "Dutch," 318, 319,
    321, 323–26, 328, 329
Vestuti, Emil "Moe," xxiv
Veterans History Project, xvi
Vian, Philip, 35
Victor, Arthur, 107, 109, 110, 112, 113,
    116
Victoria Cross, 399
Vierville, 69, 150, 151, 279, 332, 340, 344,
    351, 355, 369, 370, 376, 461, 462,
    480, 485
Vietnam War, 500

Waarvick, Martin, 333, 336–37
Wagemann, Eberhard, 164
Wales, 159
Walker, Robert E., 358, 361, 459
Wallace, Percy, 254, 255
Wallwork, Jim, 200–201
Walsh, Tom, 192
Walter, A. E. M., 92–93
Warlimont, Walter, 159
Warren, David, 387, 390
Warspite, HMS, 402
water, drinking, 129, 410, 459
waterproofing, 103–5, 393
weather, 41, 130–33, 135, 159, 162, 165–79,
    165, 190, 264, 267, 269, 274
  forecasting technology and, 169
  meteorological teams and, 167–68
Webb, Edwin, 417
Webb, Garth, 411
Webber, Philip, 415
Weeks, Reg, 406
Wegner, Karl, 278–80, 354–56

Wehrmacht, 10, 62, 160
Weir, Lt., 472
Wellard, James, 435–36
Westerplatte, 4
Westminster Abbey, 440
Weygand, Maxime, 10
Weymouth, 252
Whalen, Father, 152
Whinney, Brian T., 386, 389, 391
White, Bruce, 91
White, Paul, 431
White, Tom, 236
Whitehead, Don, 492
Wightman, Edward, 414
Wilhelm, Fred, 224
Wilkins, Robert A., 55
Will, Godfrey, 97
Williams, Francis, 396–97
Williams, Paul, 223
Williamson, Harvey "Willie," 102
William the Conqueror, 22, 129, 382–83,
    401
Wills, W. E., 141–42, 384–85, 387, 388
Wilmot, Chester, 200, 210–11, 214–16
Wilson, Charles, 390–91
Wilson, J. B., 113
Wilson, John, 211–12
Winant, John Gilbert, 16
"window" (chaff), 266–67, 269
Winstanley, Alan, 141
Winters, Richard "Dick," xix, 228,
    306–9, 484–85, 498
wireless transmissions, 86, 87
Witt, Henry G., 343
women
    housewives, 53
    in workforce, 20, 48

Women's Auxiliary Air Force
    (WAAF), 119, 124
Women's Land Army, 14
Women's Royal Naval Service
    (WRNS; Wrens), 26
Women's Voluntary Service (WVS),
    96–97
Wood, David, 202–4, 206, 207
Woodhouse, George H. W., 427–28
Woodson, Waverly B., Jr., xv, xix, 59, 60,
    372–74, 499–500
Woollcombe, Robert, 139
Woolnough, Ralph, 415
World War I, 6, 14, 19, 32, 58, 66, 143, 352
World War II
    Atlantic Charter and, 15
    Battle of the Bulge in, 486, 494, 497
    beginning of, 3–18, 3
    end of, 497
    Pearl Harbor attack in, 15–17, 19, 19,
        20, 361, 376
    U.S. entry into, 6, 14–15, 19–20
Wright, Dick (communications
    sergeant), 345, 346
Wright, Elmere, 345
Wright, Richard (pathfinder), 224
Wright, Robert, 481
Wrigley, Leonard, 452, 453

Yank, xvi, 192, 377, 440
Young, Charles H., 224
"Yvon," 271

Zafft, Herbert, 139, 150, 486
Zampiello, Anthony, 312, 313
Zappacosta, Captain, 344, 346
Ziegelmann, Fritz, 70, 160, 355–56

# Image Credits

## Chapter Openers

*Author's Note*: US National Archives #205578609, Official Coast Guard Photograph

*Foreword / A Day Like None Other*: US National Archives #176888694, U.S. Army Signal Corps Photograph

*War Begins*: Imperial War Museum #MH 2397, German official photographer

*War Comes To America*: US National Archives #12009029, Department of the Navy

*1943*: © Imperial War Museum #A18751, Lt. J.A. Hampton/Royal Navy

*Start of SHAEF*: © Imperial War Museum #TR 1631, British official photographer/ Ministry of Information Second World War Colour Transparency Collection

*Crossing the Pond*: US National Archives #205577842, Official Coast Guard Photograph

*American Invasion*: US National Archives #178140808, Department of the Army

*Building the Atlantic Wall*: German Federal Archives (Bundesarchiv) Bild 101I-718-0149-12A, Photograph by Jesse/Bundesarchiv

*Keeping Secrets*: U.S. Marines Corps Photograph, from the Robert O. Bare Collection (COLL/150) at the Marine Corps Archives and Special Collections

*Operation Fortitude*: Photograph by Kemp/Popperfoto/Getty Images

*Mulberry Plan*: © Imperial War Museum #A25798, Lt. Ernest Ellen Allen/Royal Navy

*At Slapton Sands*: US National Archives, Catalog # 80-G-59388

*Exercise Tiger*: US National Archives, Catalog # 80-G-283502

*The Transportation Plan*: US National Archives #204894431, Department of the Air Force

*Picking the Date*: US National Archives #219775714, Department of the Army

*Into the Sausages*: © Imperial War Museum #EA25409, US official photographer

*Keep Calm and Carry On*: © Imperial War Museum #H36436, Sgt. Morris/ War Office Official Photographer

*Learning the Details*: © Imperial War Museum #H 39089, Cpt. Edward George Madeline/ War Office Official Photographer

*Spring with the Germans*: German Federal Archives (Bundesarchiv), Bild 101I-263-1580-05, Photograph by Wette/Bundesarchiv

*Weather Forecast*: US National Archives #148728520, Department of the Navy

*Author's Note*: German Federal Archives (Bundesarchiv), Bild 101I-674-7773-0, Photograph by Helmut Grosse/Bundesarchiv

*Eisenhower Order of the Day*: US National Archives #205578570, Official Coast Guard Photograph; Author collection

*Paratroopers Take Off*: US National Archives #204879614, Department of the Air Force

*Operation Coup de Main*: © Imperial War Museum, #B 5288, Sgt. Christie/No. 5 Army Film and Photo Section, Army Film and Photographic Unit

*6th Airborne Arrives in Normandy*: © Imperial War Museum #CL 59, Royal Air Force official photographer/Air Ministry Second World War Official Collection

*Paratrooper Skytrain*: US National Archives #12003986, Department of the Air Force

*Night in the Hedgerows*: US National Archives #204891572, Photograph by U.S. Army 9th Air Force

*Liberation Comes to Sainte Mere Eglise*: US National Archives #176888640, U.S. Army Signal Corps Photograph

*Neptune Rises*: US National Archives #176887798, U.S. Army Signal Corps Photograph

*Confusing the Enemy*: US National Archives #205578459, Coast Guard Combat Photographer S. Scott Wigle/Official Coast Guard Photograph

*Ashore in Normandy*: German Federal Archives (Bundesarchiv), Bild 101I-586-2224-02, Photograph by Slickers/Bundesarchiv

*In the Air Over the Beaches*: US National Archives #12003988, Department of the Air Force

*Heading Ashore at Utah*: US National Archives #176887852, Kaye/U.S. Army Signal Corps Photograph

*Naval Forces at Utah*: US National Archives #205578532, Official Coast Guard Photograph

*Second Wave at Utah*: US National Archives #176887808, Shelton/U.S. Army Signal Corps Photograph

*Rangers at Pointe du Hoc*: US National Archives #148728680, Department of the Navy

*Omaha Beach*: US National Archives #176887792, Wall/U.S. Army Signal Corps Photograph

*Into the Devil's Garden*: US National Archives #513173, Robert F. Sargent, chief photographer's mate/United States Coast Guard

*Ashore at Omaha*: US National Archives #12003934, Department of the Army

*Getting Off Omaha Beach*: US National Archives #176887738, U.S. Army Signal Corps Photograph

*Afloat Off Omaha Beach*: US National Archives, Catalog #80-G-45720

*Jig Sector Gold Beach*: © Imperial War Museum #B 5261, No. 5 Army Film and Photo Section, Army Film and Photographic Unit

*Green Howards at King Sector*: Courtesy of The Green Howards Museum Trust

*Ashore at Juno*: Canadian National Archives #GM-2176, Gilbert Alexander Milne/ Canada. Dept. of National Defence/Library and Archives Canada/PA-122765

*Sword Beach*: © Imperial War Museum #B 5103, Cpt. J.L. Evans/No. 5 Army Film and Photo Section, Army Film and Photographic Unit

*The News Spreads*: US Library of Congress #2017645530, F. Palumbo/*New York World-Telegram*: https://www.loc.gov/item/2017645530/

*Holding the Eastern Flank*: UK War Office Photograph, MH 2012, Sgt. G. Laws/ Army Film and Photographic Unit

*With the Walking Wounded at Omaha*: US National Archives #176887890, Todd/U.S. Army Signal Corps Photograph

*The Battle of La Fière*: Still from US Signal Corps video

*Afternoon for the Germans*: © Imperial War Museum #MH 12789

*End of D-Day*: US National Archives #176888002, Steck/U.S. Army Signal Corps Photograph

*Epilogue*: US National Archives #176888362, Weintraub/U.S. Army Signal Corps Photograph

*Rear Endpaper*: Author photo

### Photo Insert

1  © Imperial War Museum #EA 33078, American (US) Embassy Second World War Photograph Library
2  © Imperial War Museum #A 23443, Lt. C.J. War/Royal Navy
3  US National Archives #350486907, U.S. Army Signal Corps Photograph
4  US National Archives #219775928, Department of the Navy
5  © Imperial War Museum, #C 1868, Air Ministry Second World War Official Collection
6  US National Archives #12008276, Department of the Army
7  US National Archives #778813, Department of the Army
8  US National Archives #221951747, U.S. Army Signal Corps Photograph
9  Courtesy of the National World War II Museum
10  Author photo
11  UK War Office Photograph
12  US National Archives #205578422, Official Coast Guard Photograph
13  US National Archives #205578600, Official Coast Guard Photograph
14  US National Archives #176887742, Taylor/U.S. Army Signal Corps Photograph
15  US National Archives #176887740, Taylor/U.S. Army Signal Corps Photograph
16  US National Archives #205578594, Official Coast Guard Photograph
17  US National Archives #148727150, Gedicks/U.S. Army Signal Corps Photograph
18  Courtesy of The Green Howards Museum Trust
19  Official U.S. Army portrait of Waverly B. Woodson Jr.

20  Canadian National Archives ZK-1083-1, Department of National Defence / Library and Archives Canada
21  UK War Office Photograph, Cpt. J.L. Evans/No. 5 Army Film and Photo Section, Army Film and Photographic Unit
22  National Museum of the U.S. Air Force, #050606-F-1234P-034, U.S. Air Force Photo
23  Author photo
24  Author photo

# About the Author

Garrett M. Graff has spent nearly two decades covering politics, technology, and national security. The former editor of *Politico Magazine* and longtime *Wired* contributor, he's written for publications from *Esquire* to *Rolling Stone* to *Vanity Fair*. Today, he serves as director of cyber initiatives at the Aspen Institute and writes a regular column for the *Washington Post* on leadership and history. Graff is the author of multiple books, including the FBI history *The Threat Matrix*; *Raven Rock*, about the government's Cold War Doomsday plans; *UFO*, the inside story of the search for extraterrestrial intelligent life; and the *New York Times* bestsellers *The Only Plane in the Sky* and *Watergate*, which was a finalist for the Pulitzer Prize in History.